MODERN ENGLISH PAINTERS

MODERN
ENGLISH PAINTERS

SICKERT TO MOORE

by

John Rothenstein
DIRECTOR OF
THE TATE GALLERY

with
sixty-four
plates

London 1957
READERS UNION
EYRE & SPOTTISWOODE

This RU edition was produced
in 1957 for sale to its members only by Readers Union Ltd at
38 William IV Street, Charing Cross, London, W.C.2, and at
Letchworth Garden City, Hertfordshire. Full details of membership may be obtained from our London address. The book is set
in 11 pt Bembo type leaded and has been reprinted with the
photogravure illustrations and bound by Jarrold and Sons Ltd of
Norwich. The book was first published by Eyre & Spottiswoode
Ltd in two volumes: the first in 1952 and the second in 1956.

CONTENTS

Preface to this Edition–xi

VOLUME ONE

Preface–14

Introduction–17

CONTENTS

VOLUME TWO

LIST OF PLATES

VOLUME ONE

VOLUME TWO

PREFACE
TO THE READERS UNION EDITION
1957

THE present is a one-volume edition of the two volumes of my *Modern English Painters: Sickert to Smith* (1952) and *Lewis to Moore* (1956).

Preparation of the two volumes extended over some ten years, and I have accordingly left the respective Prefaces as they were originally published.

The first volume is photographically reproduced and no corrections are possible. With regard to the second, I have for this edition made some few corrections of fact to which correspondents have kindly drawn my attention since publication. There are, however, two substantial changes from the first edition. A paragraph in my chapter on Wyndham Lewis has been rewritten. In this paragraph I had characterized some of the activities of some members of the Bloomsbury circle in terms that now seem to me to be in one respect misleading, and in another too categorical in view of the nature of the evidence. Misleading, because in a book in which there were few if any moral judgments such judgments in connection with one set of people took on an obtrusive emphasis, and misleadingly suggested that this group was uniquely or quite especially wicked. Too categorical, in that the evidence for the view that I then set down is essentially not documentary, but what painters have themselves described to me as being the effect that Bloomsbury activities had on their lives; the evidence, then, is what men have said who seriously and consistently believed that their careers were adversely affected by these activities; it is convergent but, of course, its reliability turns on the credibility of the witnesses. Since, however, many of these witnesses were reluctant to be quoted or named, it has seemed to me to be more equitable to confine myself to the recording of what these painters were seriously convinced was the case, without any categorical comment of my own about whether it was or was not the case. Secondly, in the chapter on William Roberts, I have taken account of the version of the facts published by the artist in a pamphlet (1957) entitled 'A Reply to my Biographer Sir John Rothenstein'.

JOHN ROTHENSTEIN

Newington,
    Oxon.

VOLUME ONE

SICKERT to SMITH

★

FOR JASPER RIDLEY
a too late token of gratitude

PREFACE

THE seventeen painters who are the subjects of chapters in this book are introduced strictly in the order of their appearance in the world. To insist upon an artist's identity with a group is to compromise his individuality. Groups have a way of dissolving under scrutiny, of proving to be more fortuitous in their composition and more ephemeral than they at first appeared. Unlike the individuals who compose them, they have no hard core. In earlier, less disintegrated periods, there was some meaning in the classification of artists according to the tradition to which they belonged, but in our time the general enfeeblement and even collapse of traditions has made the classification of original artists almost impossible: they exist by virtue of their individual selves alone. The chronological arrangement of the chapters that follow is intended to emphasize the individuality of their subjects by cutting them off from all fortuitous and ephemeral groupings.

My treatment of my various subjects has been deliberately varied. In the cases of painters such as Steer, Tonks, Pryde, Augustus John and my father, who are the subjects of adequate biographies either already available or in preparation, it has been mainly critical, or else directed towards the elucidation of some lesser-known or neglected aspects of their art and personalities. But when my subjects have been artists whose lives and personalities are in danger of being altogether forgotten, such, for example, as Ethel Walker, Gwen John or Gore, I have tried to reconstruct their personalities and to put down the principal landmarks of their lives. How necessary this is in the case of these neglected and vanishing figures may be inferred from the fact that the birth-date even of Augustus John, so far as I am aware, has never been precisely recorded.

I would emphasize, however, that not only, in some cases, do I omit biographical details or even landmarks, and do not always, in my criticism or appreciation of an artist's work, consider it from its beginning to its end. In the chapters on Sickert and on Steer, for example, I have been concerned to discuss their painting rather at those points at which, as it appears to me, it changed direction, and to concentrate my attention on the turnings that it took, and on other features of it that, as it seems to me, have been unduly neglected. The volume of critical and other writing on these two painters is already considerable. My own accounts of them – unlike the other chapters in this book – are in the nature of supplements, or, it may be, of correctives.

I have described them as English rather than British painters because (with the exception of Gwen John) England was their home and it was by the climate of England, intellectual, emotional, physical and social, that they were, all I believe, (with the exception of Pissarro) predominantly formed. Several of them were not English-born, and I have in fact dwelt at some length upon the effects of their place of birth and early environment – French in the case of Pissarro, Irish in that of Orpen and Scottish in that of Pryde. I have often been made aware that Scots at least are apt to draw a firm distinction between Scottish artists who have remained in the country of their birth and those who have settled in England. Only this week came a batch of Press cuttings from Scottish newspapers reporting that the chairman of an Edinburgh art society had stated publicly that the Tate had not on view a single example of work by a Scottish artist.

In writing of living artists, even when referring to their writings, I have taken the liberty of omitting any prefix. It seems to be arbitrary to reserve the honorific suppression of prefix to the illustrious dead.

For information, for permission to reproduce pictures and to quote from letters, for assistance in collecting the necessary photographs, and for help of many kinds, I am so deeply in debt that no full list of my obligations is possible. By gracious permission of Her Majesty Queen Elizabeth the Queen Mother, I have been able to reproduce Steer's *Chepstow Castle*. To the custodians of public collections and to private owners who have allowed me to include reproductions of their pictures I am indebted for their ready and invariable helpfulness. For exceptional help I am indebted to Mrs. Lucien Pissarro, Mme. Fourmaintraux-Winslow, Miss Olivia Walker, Mrs. Gilman, Mr. E. M. O'R. Dickey, Mr. H. L. Wellington, Mr. and Mrs. Augustus John, Mr. Edwin John, Mrs. Spencer Gore, Mr. Frederick Gore, Mrs. Alan Bazell, Mr. and Mrs. Matthew

Smith, Father Vincent Turner, Miss Grace English, Mrs. Silvia Hay, Mr. Norman Reid, Mr. Derek Hudson, Mr. Eric Westbrook, the Matthiesen and Mayor Galleries and Messrs. Arthur Tooth.

Finally, I must record my thanks to Mrs. Geoffrey Pooley, Miss Perdita Craig, Miss Jennifer Howard-Langton, Miss Jane Ryder and Miss Doreen Plunkett-Ernle-Erle-Drax for secretarial assistance of various kinds given in what would otherwise have been their leisure hours.

JOHN ROTHENSTEIN.

Newington.
June 1951.

INTRODUCTION

IT is unlikely, it is hardly indeed imaginable, that the twentieth century will be accounted one of the great periods of painting. Yet painting in our time shows certain characteristics of surpassing interest. The waning of traditional authorities has encouraged an unequalled diversity in all the arts – a diversity which has been stimulated by the accessibility of a variety of examples of the arts of every time and place inconceivable in any previous age.

An artist working to-day has to accommodate himself to circumstances unlike any which have previously existed. A few prints after paintings by Michelangelo were sufficient to produce an intense and lasting impression upon the imagination of Blake; and I remember hearing someone describe the delighted agitation of Morris and Burne-Jones when, as undergraduates at Oxford, they happened to see a small coloured reproduction of a painting by Botticelli. How almost infinitely greater are the opportunities of the artist of to-day for acquiring knowledge! With what little effort can a provincial art student gather an impression of the sculpture of, say, the Etruscans or the Minoans, or of the present wall painting of the Mexicans! I am far from being persuaded that the advantage of easy access to the art of other ages and peoples – it can give to the student an unprecedented breadth of critical experience and to the lonely original artist precisely the examples he needs to justify and enrich his own vision – outweighs its disadvantages. Reproductions which in time past would have germinated new movements are now apt to be accepted as a matter of course and regarded with listless eyes. Even the most sensitive cannot respond to more than a relatively few reproductions any more than the most compassionate to more than a relatively few of the atrocious crimes against humanity of the prevalence of which we are aware. Indeed the vast multiplicity of the art forms by which the painter of to-day can hardly avoid being aware disinclines him from the intensive and therefore fruitful exploitation of the possibilities of a limited range of art forms, and tends to overwhelm his imagination and to prevent his opinions from becoming dynamic convictions.

The manner, nevertheless, in which gifted and resourceful painters have responded to a complex of circumstances that is in this and in certain other respects unique in the history of art, and, perhaps, uniquely unpropitious to the creation of great works, provides a subject which one would suppose to be of absorbing interest. In England, at all events, this has not proved to be the case. When we consider the serious character of more than a few of the English painters of our time, the numbers of perceptive writers interested in painting, and the avid and increasing interest of the public in the fine arts, the paucity of substantial writings devoted to the work of these painters is astonishing. Not long ago in one of the consistently intelligent London weekly journals there appeared a review by one of the best-known British art critics of a collection of reproductions of paintings and drawings by Augustus John prefaced by a longish essay by myself. The review ended with the observation that the various points I had made had been more extensively developed in previous books on the same artist. In preparation for writing my own essay I must have read most of what had been written about Augustus John, and was in a position to know that not only had no book upon this artist ever appeared, but how surprisingly little had been written about him. Two or three brief prefaces to slight volumes of reproductions, a handful of articles, none of them exhaustive, scattered references in books of memoirs, an informative entry in a foreign dictionary of artists, these represent approximately the extent – apart of course from innumerable reviews of exhibitions – of the critical writings on Augustus John.

The relative critical neglect of the most celebrated of living English artists – a painter whose work carries a strong popular appeal, who is also an eloquent writer and a dramatic personality – gives some measure of the neglect suffered by lesser-known painters, indeed by English painting in general. Of recent years there have been signs of awakening literary interest in this subject. Biographies as readable as they are authoritative have been published on Steer, Sickert and Tonks, and the Penguin Modern Painters are making widely known a number of our most gifted contemporaries.

Year by year, however, I have been expectantly awaiting some treatment of British painting of somewhat wider scope – some work in which the principal figures would be placed in relation to one another, their works compared and subjected to critical investigation. I have waited, so far, in vain, and in the meanwhile the notion of making some slight attempt at something of this kind gradually took hold of me, but it was a notion to which I yielded with reluctance, for I am very conscious of my manifold disqualifications. I lack, first of all, a clear-cut view of the subject. The view of Post-Impressionism adumbrated by Sickert and belligerently developed by Dr. Thomas Bodkin is not one which I find credible. 'The modern cult of Post-Impressionism', Sickert wrote, 'is localized mainly in the pockets of one or two dealers holding large remainders of incompetent work. They have conceived the genial idea that if the values of criticism could only be reversed – if efficiency could only be considered a fault, and incompetence alone sublime – a roaring and easy trade could be driven. Sweating would certainly become easier with a Post-Impressionist personnel than with competent hands, since efficient artists are limited in number, whereas Picassos and Matisses would be painted by all the coachmen that the rise of motor traffic has thrown out of employment.'[1]

However effective the machinations of dealers and other interested persons – if they have succeeded, that is to say, in suborning this or that influential critic, in securing the acceptance, or indeed the apotheosis, of this or that spurious artist – there still remains, in the Post-Impressionist movement and in its more recent derivatives, a consistency of vision and a logical coherence of doctrine which, even were I unimpressed by the painting and sculpture in which they are actually made manifest, would preclude my regarding them as other than spontaneous, even, perhaps, as historically inevitable developments.

Nor, on the other hand, can I fully accept the contrary view implicit in the critical works of Mr. Herbert Read. This writer, more interested, perhaps, in the philosophical ideas which may be supposed to underlie works of art than in the aesthetic or representational content of works of art themselves, has treated the principal revolutionary artistic movements of our time with a serious objectivity. But Mr. Read's pages, judicious though they are,

[1] 'The Old Ladies of Etchingneedle Street,' *The English Review*, January 1912.

unmistakably convey the impression that there is an inherent superiority in revolutionary art and that representational art is a curious survival, condemned by its very nature to sterility and hardly worthy therefore of the attention of the critic. For me, a canon of criticism according to which, say, Hans Arp is accounted a figure of greater significance than, say, Stanley Spencer, is one which takes inadequate account of the evidence of one's eyes.

For Sickert the more 'advanced' schools of art were 'the biggest racket of the century', for Mr. Read they are the whole of art now. For me, as for Sickert, the ramp is a reality: I have seen it in action at close quarters, but it does not seem to me nearly so influential as it did to him. For me, as for Mr. Read, the advanced movements are the chief focus of interest, and they have in general resulted from the activities of the most vigorous and original personalities; but the wind bloweth where it listeth, and genius shows itself in representational as well as abstract form.

I cannot therefore envisage the twentieth century either as a period of retrogression or of progress, still less of stability. I am mainly conscious of a complex interplay of innumerable personalities; of the action upon these personalities of numerous and various forces – economic necessity, fashion, the momentum of traditional aesthetic movements, social change, patronage, psychological and archaeological discovery and so forth – forces which neutralize each other often and are, for the time being, incalculable in their effects. With the passage of time much of what presents itself to our eyes as confused will insensibly assume a settled pattern; then there will be written a history of this period accurate in perspective and secure in its critical judgements. But I am not at all certain that the historian of that distant time who looks back with justified condescension upon ours may not perhaps envy a little the historian, however ludicrous his errors, to whom the artists who are the common objects of their study were familiar figures, known either directly or through their friends. Therefore it seems to me that there is an obligation upon those to whom has fallen the privilege of knowing artists, to place on record something about their personalities and their opinions. (Even if, at certain points, the portraits, like those in 'Modern Painters', as Ruskin noted in the margin of his own copy, are 'drawn mild because . . . men are living'.) For the memory of these fades away with a pathetic swiftness. Some months ago an acquaintance told me she was engaged upon a study of Innes. This painter died only thirty-eight years ago, yet with what labour will the materials for her study be assembled!

But of what use is the study of an artist's personality? There are many critics who answer this question with an emphatic 'None whatever. The work of art transcends the artist; all that need be known of him can be learnt from the study of his work.'

It is a truism that we can be deeply moved by a work of art of whose creator we are entirely ignorant, as also indeed by works of art produced by societies that have vanished without other trace. But are we not moved yet more deeply by the works of art which we are able to see in relation to the personalities of the artists who made them, or against the background of the society from which they came? It is my conviction that we are, and that the more we know about both the artist and his subject the fuller is likely to be our comprehension of the work of art. It is difficult to think of any fact about an artist, any circumstance of his life, that may not have its effect upon his work. The idea that a painting or any other work of art can in fact transcend its creator is one which is tenable only on the assumption that the creative capacity of the artist is enhanced by a form of 'inspiration' derived from some source outside himself. Until we have some knowledge of the nature of such extraneous assistance it is reasonable to assume that the artist possesses within himself the power of giving visible form to his conceptions. If this assumption is well founded, in what sense can a work of art, which is the expression of a part of a human personality, be said to transcend the whole? For me, therefore, the artist is, in a sense, more not less important than anything he creates, which is not to say that the work of art may not be more comprehensible and more attractive than the man. (I remember, years ago, someone saying to my father, after meeting A. E. Housman, 'so far from writing "A Shropshire Lad" I shouldn't have thought him capable of reading it'.) Nor do I overlook the possibility of an artist's having an imaginative comprehension of certain qualities, magnanimity, for example, or singleness of purpose, which may enable him to realize them in his art but not in his conduct; yet

comprehension forms, nevertheless, an element in his own personality. In any case, the greater our knowledge of a personality, the
better able we are to understand how apparently inconsistent and
even irreconcilable elements form parts of a whole which can,
roughly speaking, be considered one whole. And so it comes about
that, with my doubts upon fundamental aesthetic problems unresolved (doubting, even, whether aesthetics, in the sense of a
comprehensive system by which the value of a work of art may be
judged, has any validity) and my ignorance of many important and
relevant matters, I am decided to try to give some impression of
certain of the painters who have been at work in England during my
lifetime. It has come suddenly upon me, with a sense of shock, that
Time's Winged Chariot is indeed hurrying near. That I am forty-
seven years old; and that is to be full of years. Ten years ago I had
occasion to reply to a girl who said that she believed I knew her
parents, that this was the case, and that I knew her great-grandmother. This great-grandmother was Lady Burne-Jones, but my
artistic memories extend – tenuously it is true – still farther back than
this, for I can remember, as a child, spending an afternoon with
an original member of the Pre-Raphaelite Brotherhood, William
Michael Rossetti. I still plainly see the darkened room, with blinds
half-drawn, and, reclining upon a couch, an old man with a long
grey beard and a sallow complexion, wearing a black alpaca cap,
whose owl-like eyes, with dark pouches beneath, looked momentarily startled at our entrance. And I still see his relatives grouped
solicitously about him and I hear my mother's voice saying: 'Dear
Mr. Rossetti, pray don't get up.' The couch, which was large and of
uncommon design, made an impression on me which I was unaware
of having received. One morning during the flying-bomb attack on
London, Mrs. William Michael Rossetti's daughter telephoned to
me at the Tate to tell me that the Rossetti's house had been badly
damaged and the family possessions, including Pre-Raphaelite
pictures, were exposed to looters and the elements, and to ask
whether I would take charge of them. 'And I'd be so grateful', she
added, 'if you would take into your care also the couch on which
Shelley's body was placed when it was taken from the sea.' Within
a few hours the precious pictures arrived; also the couch. I instantly
recognized it as that upon which, nearly forty years before, I had

seen Dante Gabriel Rossetti's brother reclining. And I have had opportunities of coming in contact with a number of English painters who have been active during my lifetime, or of hearing first-hand accounts of their characters and ideas and aspects of their lives.

The exceptional complexity, if not the confusion, of the painting of our age, as it offers itself to my contemplation, will be, in one respect at least, radically simplified in the pages which follow. There are in Great Britain to-day practitioners of the fine arts to the number of about twenty thousand. Of these the merest handful will be noticed at length. It is relevant, perhaps, to say a few words about the principle upon which the choice will be made. There exist critics who claim to base their judgements upon consciously held critical canons. They may, for all I know, in fact so form their judgements, but I myself can hardly conceive of a mental process of such a nature. Indeed there is only one way in which I can conceive of judging a work of art, and that is the same as that which the greater part of mankind employs in judging their fellow-men: namely, instinct refined and sharpened and deepened not by personal experience alone but by those standards, created for us by experience through successive generations, which guide us even when we are hardly conscious of our inevitable appeal to their authority. We respond spontaneously to a fine work of art in the same way as we respond to a fine character, and it is only afterwards that we begin the process of analysis in order to try to account for our response. (Equally, of course, we are liable to be deceived by spurious work, as we are by a plausible but meretricious person.) And by the same means – although the process is inevitably more complex and protracted – do we judge the totality of an artist's work, that is to say, the artist himself.

The artists noticed in the chapters which follow have been chosen on account of a series of just such intuitive preferences – preferences founded, that is to say, chiefly upon personal response tempered by inherited canons of judgement. These painters, however, who appear to me to have distilled to its finest essence the response of our times to the world which the eye sees – by which I include both the outward and the inward eye – have few pronounced characteristics in common. A critic with a conservative bias might well object that they were almost all associated, at one time or another, with some innovating movement. That is true, for there does seem to exist some correspondence between inspired art and revolutionary art. Indeed the assumption that there is some such correspondence underlies so much current discussion about painting that it might well be suspect. But so far as Post-Renaissance art is concerned, it appears to be well founded. All the modern masters to a more or less marked degree were innovators, and all of them suffered a measure of contumely and neglect on that account. From Delacroix to Cézanne every great painter made his contribution to a revolutionary process, and the more closely we study the period the more completely is the assumption justified, and the more intimately are important painters, formerly regarded as conservative or even reactionary, understood to be implicated with change. The Surrealists, for example, have directed attention to the revolutionary elements in the early work of the Pre-Raphaelites, and Picasso to those in that of David and Ingres. In our own age, indeed, it is an unconscious assumption that the great artist is a man who innovates, who is original. Originality has become a part of the meaning that we assign to the word 'greatness'. It has not always been so. The outlook of Aristotle, for example, was rather that by 'experience' men discover the right proportion, say, or the 'right' way of doing something, or form and harmony that satisfy; and when it is discovered, it is there once and for all. An artist will be himself, no doubt, but only in abiding by 'the laws'. Is not this the assumption behind the practice, too, of classical Greek art – as it is also of, say, Sienese Quattrocento painting? In Post-Renaissance times, however, if not earlier, there has occurred a radical change in this respect. So that now it is a sign of an inferior gift if a man continues to do, however well, what has been done before. That there should seem to be some correspondence between greatness and innovation among the painters of modern Europe – in which change as radical as it is continuous has come to be accepted as an inexorable law of existence – is hardly surprising. The possessor of superior gifts is likely, in our change-loving age, to be indifferent towards continuing, with whatever distinction or success, procedures already current: his powers will predispose him to attempt what has not been attempted before. But this correspondence arises, I believe, from an impulse deeper than this. The great artist demands of his art that it should express the whole man. Therefore, more sensitive than his contemporaries, he is aware of the particular bias to which the art of his own time is subject, which incites him to a discontent – although sometimes a deeply respectful discontent – with the prevailing modes of seeing and which impels him to a conscious and radical reorientation.

Consider, for example, the origin of the discontent which brought about the new and unforeseen changes which may conveniently be taken as the beginnings of the chief contemporary movements, at the very moment when Impressionism appeared to have imposed itself as a great central tradition of Western painting, and to have established a kind of 'norm' of vision. The doctrines which crystallized around Impressionism were at least as lucid and compelling as those associated with Neo-classical art, which had dominated the academies of Europe since the Renaissance. The aims which it proposed were aims which represented the culmination of centuries of sustained effort on the part of a broad succession of European painters to represent the material world in the closest accord with the facts of vision; its exponents could hardly have been a more brilliant company, indeed they included the most considerable painters of their age.

These considerations were such as to attract any young painter into the Impressionist movement, which did in fact attract a mass following, and it ultimately became the acknowledged academic tradition. It was challenged only by a few of the most sensitive and independent painters of a younger generation, who, although they looked upon the great Impressionists with reverence and affection, were intuitively conscious of a certain incompleteness in their enchanted vision of the world.

The major aim of the Impressionists may be said to have been the representation, on the spot, and with the utmost truth, of a casually selected fragment of visible reality. Impressionist truth was different from that older conception of truth which expressed itself in the accumulation of meticulously rendered detail; it was on the contrary broad and comprehensive. Impressionist painters were not at all concerned with what Sickert used to call 'the august site'. Almost any fragment of the visible world, was, they held, a worthy subject for a picture, but such fragments, arbitrarily come upon, are inevitably without the elaborate balance of subjects either carefully selected or deliberately composed. The Impressionists, therefore, imposed upon their subjects a comprehensive unity of *tone* in the same way as Nature herself invariably binds together in a harmonious envelope of atmosphere any group of objects, however incongruous they may be or however awkwardly disposed. It was through truth of tone that they were able to achieve a new kind of accuracy. The power which they derived from their extraordinary command of tone, of giving unity to any stretch of landscape, to any group of persons, had the effect of inducing painters to visualize the world in terms of its surface and to be forgetful of the rock and bone beneath, to see, that is to say, in terms of colour rather than of form.

In order to set upon their pictures the final stamp of truth, it was logical that these should have the appearance of having been begun and completed at a sitting, under precisely the conditions of weather and light represented in the picture. In northern Europe these notoriously change from hour to hour, and as it is evident that large and elaborately 'finished' pictures could not be painted in such conditions, Impressionist paintings, in order to carry conviction, inevitably have something of the character of sketches.

Preoccupation with colour as distinct from form, and with verisimilitude of so exacting an order, inevitably excluded from Impressionist art many qualities, notably the reflective and monumental qualities which characterized most of the great art of the past. It was the absence of certain of these from the art even of the masters of Impressionism that provoked in the most sensitive and independent among those who were always proud to proclaim themselves their disciples an uneasy awareness of the qualities it lacked. Cézanne's often quoted remark that they must recreate Impressionism according to the art of the museums was an expression, not of a desire to return to a tradition but of a consciousness of how small a part of the whole man was expressed by Impressionist art, of how great a sacrifice had been made to its coruscating perfection. The masters of Cézanne's generation each tried to restore to painting one of the qualities sacrificed : Gauguin an exotic poetry ; van Gogh a passionate humanity ; Seurat monumental and elaborate

formal harmony, and Cézanne himself the rocky or bony framework
of things. The great Impressionists were themselves aware that, in
their intoxicatingly new approach to the actual appearance of
things, in their close pursuit of a beauty miraculous because it was
not an imagination or a dream but the tangible beauty of all created
things, their art lacked a certain massive reflectiveness. There came
a time when the bathers of Renoir became sculptural in themselves
and monumental in their composition, while Pissarro with a sublime
humbleness made experiments under the guidance of Seurat, one of
his own disciples, in directions clearly repugnant to his own innate
genius, and declared that Impressionism 'should be nothing more
than a theory of observation, without entailing the loss of fantasy,
freedom, grandeur, all that makes for great art'.[1]

Now that more than half a century separates us from the decade
when the principal painters of an oncoming generation were
manifesting their awareness of the failure of the art of their great
Impressionist teachers to express the whole man, it is not
difficult to understand the nature of the readjustment which was
taking place. But from that decade onwards how increasingly
difficult it becomes to perceive any 'norm' of vision or any central
traditions. From decade to decade confusion grows, and what
remains of the central traditions of Cézanne, of Gauguin and of van
Gogh becomes more and more dissolved into individual idiosyn-
crasy.

The heaviest emphasis has been laid by art historians on the
effect of monumental qualities in the painting of Cézanne upon his
followers, the Cubists in particular. We are given to understand
that upon the basis of the most austerely structural elements in his
painting and of his precepts a great 'Classical' art has come into
being. A return to Classicism is how the Post-Cézanne movement is frequently described.

'The idea behind the modern movement in the arts is a return
to the architectural or classical idea'[2] are the first words of Mr.
R. H. Wilenski's closely reasoned introduction to contemporary
art, and his whole book may be considered as an amplification of

[1] Camille Pissarro, 'Letters to his Son Lucien', edited by John Rewald, 1943,
p. 23.

[2] 'The Modern Movement in Art', R. H. Wilenski, 1927, p. ix.

them. This may well have been the Cubists' programme, but it is not easy to gather from the innumerable written accounts how far it was from being realized or how quickly it was abandoned. That certain of the early Cubist paintings had a severely structural character is obvious enough. They sacrificed in a passion of dour joy the shimmering surfaces of things in which Manet and Renoir had delighted, and which Cézanne, for all his preoccupation with structure, had striven so strenuously and sometimes, especially in his water-colours, with such breathtaking success to represent, and they created a new order of form, stark and subtle and, after the first brief 'analytic' phase, bearing scarcely more than a remotely allusive relation to the natural order. Among the best of these highly original and momentous works are a number by Picasso. In the light of this artist's subsequent development and the character of the intoxicating but disintegrating influence he has wielded, the fact is significant. But what have been, in fact, the effects of this group of Cubist paintings; the creations of the apostles of solid construction, of dignified, self-sufficient form? It can hardly be denied that they have been, in the main, disintegrating; that in their shadow has grown up an art as remote as any that could be conceived from the ideal of Cézanne 'to make out of Impressionism something as solid and enduring as the art of the museums'. The contrast between the spate of talk and writing about the rebirth of an architectural painting and of the classical ideal, and the overwhelmingly idiosyncratic character of the painting that was actually produced corresponds to the discrepancy, in the political sphere, between the proclamations, which grew thunderous upon the conclusion of both the World Wars, of international solidarity, and the persistent growth of aggressive nationalism. But whereas, in the larger sphere, the discrepancy between the ideal and the actuality is widely recognized and lamented, in the sphere of the fine arts a discrepancy not less startling is virtually denied, and the continuing chatter about 'architecture' and 'classicism' would lead a student who read about works of art instead of looking at them (a practice almost universal among students) to form radically different conclusions about the character of contemporary painting from those of anybody accustomed to use his eyes. Certain ideas about form implicit in the work of Cézanne and expressed in his rare sayings have gained the widest acceptance

throughout the western world, but from the two other commanding figures of the Post-Impressionist movement, Gauguin and van
Gogh, also derive ideas, to a certain degree complementary, which
exercise a decisive influence. Upon the art of Germany and Scandinavia the influence of these two has been even more pervasive
than that of Cézanne. Between the ideas of van Gogh and of Gauguin
there are sharp distinctions, but their influence has been somewhat
similar in its effects. Both painters were acutely aware of the exclusion from Impressionism of poetry and of the deeper human
emotions; both, too, made the discovery that the tonal technique
of the Impressionists, perfectly adapted though it was to the creation
of harmonies in colour and light, was too vaporous to lend itself
readily to the lucid expression of the poetic and dramatic emotions
of their own passionate natures. Gradually both therefore abandoned
the realism of the Impressionists and each evolved an art that was
predominantly symbolic.

From the Impressionists they had learnt to dispense with the older
type of formal, closely integrated composition; they early discarded
the tonal system upon which the Impressionists relied to give
cohesion to their pictures. The highly original poetry of Gauguin
and van Gogh was expressed in terms which proved as fascinating
to these artists' younger contemporaries as they were audacious and
novel.

In this expressionistic art the functions of form and colour were
to convey, symbolically yet forcefully, the emotion of the artist.
Expressionism and Cubism, and its later and highly logical development, Abstraction, have played, as already noted, complementary
parts in the history of contemporary painting; the one, essentially
subjective, with its emphasis upon the artist's emotion, the other,
rather more objective, with its emphasis upon the created form.
The one may be said to correspond to the Romantic as the other to
the Classical motive in the earlier art of Europe; certainly Expressionism took most vigorous roots in Scandinavia and the Germanic
countries, where the Romantic tradition had been persistent, and
Abstraction in France and the Latin countries, where the rational
values had always found a wider acceptance.

But just as the Abstract artists failed to fulfil the achievement of
certain of the early Cubists to build upon the foundation of Cézanne

an art of pure form, nobly defined and exact, so did the Expressionists prove unable to express anything beyond a narrow and, it would
seem, a continuously narrowing range of human emotions; with
the greater part of the human drama and of the poetry of life
Expressionist painters were unable or else unwilling to deal. The
Norwegian Edvard Munch showed himself, in a group of early
paintings, pre-eminent among the rare exceptions. There would
seem, in fact, to have occurred early in the period of which I am
writing a catastrophic change which has profoundly affected the
fine arts. The word 'catastrophic' has been applied to this change
both by those who regard it as the rejection of values which have
been long regarded as constituting the foundation of European
culture, and by those for whom such values represent, at the best,
a series of intrinsically undesirable but historically necessary expedients, at the worst, conventions which served no purpose but
that of confining the creative spirit in the interests of tyranny,
political, religious or academic.

The more closely we read history the more aware do we become
of the strength and intimacy of the relationships by which the fabric
of human society is bound together; the relationship between our
age and another of apparently opposite character, between two
factions, which at first seem irreconcilably opposed. We see, for
instance, how powerfully the forces which produced the Protestant
explosion in the sixteenth century were also active within the Catholic Church; we see how difficult it would be to define with exactitude the issues which divided the North from the South in the War
between the American States. We may therefore take it that the
revolution in the arts which may be said to have begun with Post-
Impressionism in the last decade of the nineteenth century and has
gathered momentum progressively since, may present to the future
art historian an aspect perhaps less radical than it does to us. The
origins of phenomena which appear, even to learned and boldly
speculative art historians, entirely novel, will reveal themselves in
the course of time. '. . . Where, in the immediate ancestry of modern
art', asks Mr. Herbert Read, 'shall we find the forbears of Picasso,
Paul Klee, Max Ernst . . . ?' I suspect that the future art historian will
marvel at our want of perception and at the complacency which
allows us to attribute to our own art an unexampled uniqueness.

It is, however, difficult for someone writing to-day not to share, to a considerable extent, the impression that the characteristic art of our time is, in fact, the product of a catastrophic change. The European tradition of painting owes its cohesion largely to the persistence of two impulses; to represent, as exactly as possible, the visible world, and to evolve the perfect forms of persons and things. These impulses crystallized in what are frequently termed the Realistic and the Classical ideals. Both have asserted themselves throughout the whole history of European art; from the Renaissance to the decline of Impressionism, the development and the intimate interaction of these ideals have been continuous. But towards the end of the last century both began to lose their compelling power for numbers of the most reflective and highly gifted artists. They persisted with reduced vitality, but those who followed them travelled, more and more, along sequestered byways rather than along the high roads. The ultimate causes for the rejection of ideals which had been accepted for so many centuries lie deep in the history of religion, of philosophy, of politics and of several fields of scientific discovery, but certain of the immediate causes are obvious. Their achievement in representing brilliant light gave to the painting of the Impressionists the character of extremity and climax. It seemed that in this, the centuries-long ambition of European artists to represent in something of its fulness the world to which their senses bore witness had been fulfilled; the old excitement in the gradual approach to reality could hardly be experienced so intensely again. But the visible world exercised a diminished attraction over the artists of the Post-Impressionist era on account not solely of their predecessors' close approach to the limits of the possible, but of the doubts which they shared with their fellow-men about the ultimate reality of the world perceptible to the senses. Science has conjured up a world which the senses cannot apprehend, a world in which the stars themselves – to artists and poets for thousands of years the embodiments of an eternal and changeless beauty – have no longer any substantial existence, but are instead hypothetical entities, light rays curving back to the points where once shone suns for millions of years extinct. And the very substances of which the material world is made – even the simplest and most solid among them – are now assumed not to be the stable entities they seem, but on the contrary to be assemblies of whirling particles. But when a man of education rejects the time-honoured 'commonsense' view that things are more or less what they appear to be, it is hardly any longer possible for him to believe that the profoundest truths about the world can be expressed by the representation, however searching, of its deceptive surface. The dissolution of the artist's confidence in the reality of what his eye sees is destructive of both Realist and Classical ideals: for it is equally foolish to represent or to idealize a mirage.

In another age general revulsion against the close representation of the world which the eye sees might have had less 'catastrophic' consequences than it has to-day. (I speak tentatively because the whole history of art records no previous revulsion against realism either so widespread or so deeply felt.) The imaginative treatment of subjects from religion, mythology, or simply from the inward vision might have withdrawn painting beyond the understanding of all but a perceptive few, while preserving a degree of continuity; but the scepticism which has weakened the confidence of modern man in the reality of the world to which his senses bear witness has yet more radically transformed his outlook: it has made him doubtful of its validity. In contemplating the art of past ages we are conscious of how much of it testified to an irrepressible delight in the multitudinous aspects of the world and human society, in its Creator, in the beauty of nature and of man, in the exciting spectacle of the surrounding stream of life, so various and so dramatic as it flowed by. Even the most savage satire was inspired by the sense that mankind was sufficiently precious to be castigated for its own redemption. There would seem to prevail to-day, among artists, little of the sense of majesty of the world and the excitement of the human adventure. What has taken the place of the medieval artist's exalted conception of a God-centred universe in which every man and woman, and every created thing, had its value and its function? Or the Renaissance artist's intoxicating confidence that man, by the intense cultivation of his understanding, his inventiveness, his daring and all his faculties, might himself become godlike? Nothing, except an intense preoccupation with his separate and individual self. This individualism, historically, may be regarded as the culmination of the worship of the spirit of liberty. But now, in Western

Europe and America, there are no more Bastilles to storm. For the artist there is now but one criterion: his own satisfaction.

The history of modern art is constantly depicted in terms of a perpetual struggle against 'convention'. It is true that in the arts as in other spheres of man's activity there is a continuous tendency for the disciples of an audacious innovator to reduce his practice to a system of rules more or less tightly formulated, and in so doing to obscure the true significance of his achievement. Thus they distort something which was a heightening of human perception into a complex of rules which at best alienates those perceptive and independent natures by whom the audacious innovator would have most desired to be understood. The activities of the academic mind, by transforming that which was thrilling and elusive into that which is dull and docketed, is a continual source of misunderstanding. So much is plain; but of recent years it has been habitual to exaggerate the importance of the mischief which pedants have done to painting. Among the forces which form the natures of great artists and bring about the flowering or the decline of traditions these pedants have a minor place.

Time and again we see the man of genius in conflict with the academician, but the activities of the framer of conventions are not for this reason devoid of positive value. If his effect is frequently to provoke the man of genius by repressing him, he plays a necessary part in the education of less gifted men: he makes available to them, in a readily assimilable form, not only the accumulated technical experience of his predecessors but even something of their vision. In those rare ages when many masters are at work they themselves will diffuse directly their fertilizing influence, but in those far commoner ages when there are few or none, the function of the academician in preserving, systematizing and handing on the heritage of the past – even if in a desiccated form – is a useful one. Even though the academician's gaze is directed towards the past and his bias towards the form and away from the spirit, what, without him, would be the plight of the secondary artist, whose nature does not demand that he should have that immediate contact, intuitive or intellectual, with first causes which is one of the distinguishing necessities of genius? A distinctive, closely-knit tradition is the most favourable seed-bed of the secondary artist, just as a profusion of these would seem to create the most favourable conditions for the emergence of genius. Thus the academician, invaluable to the secondary artist, makes his contribution, however pedestrian, however indirect, to the formation of the master also.

According to the contemporary history of art, 'convention' is the great positive evil against which all good artists have had to contend – a kind of artistic fascism – and new movements are explained by the necessity for 'breaking away from' or 'reacting against' such and such a 'convention'. As though the prime motive of those dedicated to one of the most exalted and most exacting of man's vocations was a bicker with obsolescent. regulations! The fundamental causes for the new directions which the arts are forever taking under the hands of the masters are outside the scope of this book (although I have touched upon what I think is the most important of these, namely, the masters' preternatural sensibility to the respects in which the art of their times fails to express the whole man), but if there is one factor which plays no part in the formation of contemporary art it is the 'convention'. For 'convention', comparable to the older, clearly formulated, passionately upheld complexes of rules, can hardly be said to exist any longer. Some contemporary painters and a larger number of their advocates continue to behave as though there were still reactionary and, above all, realistic formulas against which they were under an obligation to struggle. But what restrictions are there upon the absolute liberty of the artist to please himself? The 'Old Bolsheviks' of the Cubist Revolution and their younger followers decline to recognize that they are tilting at a mirage, and aggressively asserting rights which for years nobody has dreamed of challenging. They do not tell us against what they are remaining in this state of perpetual belligerence. The truth is that the revolutionary impulse has largely expended itself, and for the very reason that there are no longer any objects for revolutions; all doors are open. What remains to be seen is whether art can, in fact, flourish without laws. 'Art', declared Ozenfant, 'is structure, and every construction has its laws.' The question is whether the abolition of every law but the satisfaction of the artist is not vitiating those deeper impulses necessary to the creation of great works of art. Modern painters have easy access to the knowledge of all traditions but the powerful support of none.

I say 'powerful support' because many, indeed perhaps all traditions, in attenuated forms, still persist. The present situation in this regard is thus concisely described by Mr. Read:

> . . . we have in some way telescoped our past development and the human spirit, which in the past has expressed itself, or some pre-dominant aspect of itself, diversely at different times, now expresses the same diversity, without any stress on any particular aspect, at one and the same time. I might refer, as a modest illustration of my mean-ing, to those metal cups made of a series of what mathematicians presumably call conic segments which when pressed together, collapse into concentric rings – what was once continuous and spread over several sections of space becomes discontinuous within one section of space.[1]

Mr. Read sensibly disclaims the implication that the human spirit is more diverse to-day than at any other time, but it is true that the very absence of authoritative traditions and of imposed discipline of any kind allows for a more untrammelled expression by the artist of his own personality than at any previous time. Prior to the nineteenth century most art served a religious or a social purpose which demanded some subordination of the artist's personality; whereas for the artist of to-day the expression of himself has become his sole, or at all events his overriding preoccupation. And this preoccupation was shared no less by the Cubists and other Abstract artists, whose work at first glance has an objective look, than by the Expressionists, whose work is frankly personal. 'Cubism differs from the old schools of painting', said Guillaume Apollinaire, 'in that it aims not at an art of imitation, but at an art of conception, which tends to rise to the height of creation.' But in what sense can the concepts and the creations of Cubists be said to be less exclusively the products of the artist's mind than the 'literary' concepts of Expressionists? Both are manifestations of the forthright and un-inhibited expression of personality which is the distinguishing characteristic of the art of our time. In the past artists have been inspired by exalted subjects, most of all by religious subjects, and their talents tempered and directed by tradition, but the artists of our own day rely upon neither of these external sources of strength: they are at once their own subjects and their own teachers. Their art

---

[1] 'Art Now', revised edn., 1936, p. 60.

therefore, in comparison with that of certain periods of the past, conspicuously lacks the sustained dynamic power which can result from the combination of an intrinsically inspiring subject and a comprehensive discipline; it resembles a river which has overflowed its banks. Paradoxically the perfect liberty of which so many artists have dreamed, now achieved, makes it the more difficult to realize the great work of art. But if in our own time the great work of art, rare in the most propitious circumstances, is exceptionally rare, that does not mean that our own highly personal and, in consequence, infinitely various art has not qualities which are precious and unique. We have become so accustomed to regard art as primarily the expression of personality and as being practised for the satisfaction of the artist himself, that we are apt to forget how recently in the history of the world such an art came into existence. Almost all medieval art exhibits an anonymous and collective character; only with the early Renaissance did the artist begin to emerge as a highly differentiated individual, and it was not until the middle of the nineteenth century that the conception of personal and self-sufficient art lately so widely accepted began to prevail. And we have no assurance that it is certain, or even likely, to continue to prevail even in Western Europe and the Americas. Within the last thirty years it ceased to be accepted by the rulers of three great States, Russia, Germany and Italy, and in their dependencies. In all these the arts were transformed overnight into instruments of political propaganda and education and could no longer be the unforced expression of the individual human spirit, and their criterion became, therefore, social utility instead of intrinsic worth. And the time may come sooner than we expect when the kind of art which, to one living in Western Europe or the Americas, is now taken for granted, may have come to an end. There have been in the past many tyrannies and many states where the rulers have employed artists for purposes which allowed only the narrowest scope for the expression of their personalities, yet art as an expression of human personality has always survived and generally flourished. Those who argue from the example of the past that this kind of art can still be pursued in the totalitarian state of the twentieth century fail to distinguish the radical difference between these and the older authoritarian states in which even subversive art was sometimes tolerated, and the consequences of this difference for the artist. This difference arises from the fact that modern totalitarian states have come into existence at a time when democracy has already established itself over large areas of the world and become – in spite of the effeteness of many democratically elected governments – an active and formidable principle. The governments of such states, which by their very nature cannot allow their authority to be challenged, even implicitly, are therefore compelled to control with unexampled vigilance and severity the popular opinion which they have displaced as the most powerful element in politics. There is no manifestation of opinion, however insignificant, which is hostile, or even indifferent, to these régimes which they can safely tolerate. Art, with its unique power over the mind, must be subject to the most rigorous control, or rather, to the most precise direction. To the modern absolutism personal art is at the best an irrelevant display of personal egotism, at the worst the germ of an alternative attitude towards life, and as such a subversive activity.

Let us therefore remember in considering the art of our own day that it is the most extreme expression of the Humanist tradition, which has always set a high value upon personality. Let us remember, too, that it may prove to be its last expression. Of recent years in particular there has been a tendency – an anticipation, perhaps, of what would seem to be the collectivist epochs ahead of us – to deplore Humanism's rejection of the anonymity that marked, during the Middle Ages, so many of man's activities. We may live to see the subordination of the individual to a totalitarian state and his merging in the anonymous mass.

At the beginning of this chapter I voiced my doubt whether the present would ever be counted among the great ages of painting, but its extreme expression of one aspect of Humanism, its astonishing variety and the unprecedented conditions with which its artists have had to come to terms give it, nevertheless, an extraordinary character. In this general interest in the art of our time many share, but very few indeed would seem to attach serious importance to the contribution of our own country. As I write I have before me a number of notices on the Tate Gallery exhibition of the last fifty years of British Painting which was shown at Millbank in 1946 after a tour of the principal capital cities of Europe. The Press, I think without exception, praised the representative character of the selection; but certain of the most responsible papers referred in cool or else frankly disparaging terms to the school of painting it represented. 'What are its characteristics?' asked 'The New Statesman and Nation'[1] and thus answered the question. 'Rarely original, even more rarely powerful, it is usually sensitive especially in colour.' The impression received by 'The Spectator'[2] was one of 'respectable talent, a general level of sensibility without authority. . . . For eyes other than British it is not an impressive period, for we spent most of it in the backwaters of streams already grown stagnant at their source.' Such quotations would seem to be typical not of ignorant but of informed and responsive elements of British public opinion. While nobody would be likely to maintain that during the period with which this book is concerned English painting could compare with French in richness, in perfection or in inventiveness, it must be remembered that the latter derives much of its vitality from forming a part of one of the most inspired movements in all the history of European art. At the beginning of the present century the great Impressionists were alive: with the death of Bonnard in 1946 the last of their disciples departed. And who remains active in France to-day? In my view two figures tower above the crowd, Rouault, the sombre suffering-haunted groping giant, and Picasso (who is not a Frenchman), the prodigiously accomplished and prolific master of all styles and all media; the one a blundering but God-guided sleepwalker, the other very much 'all there', the resourceful master of every situation. To Matisse, gifted though he is with a singing sense of colour, as a designer and as a pure yet engagingly informal draughtsman, and with the nature which so limpidly reflects the temperate gaiety of the French character, I doubt whether posterity will accord so pre-eminent a place as he occupies to-day. There is a flimsiness in the central principle which informs the art of Matisse, which will, I think, grow more apparent in the coming years. These three apart there seem to me to be no painters with serious claim to the title of master. Braque is a grave and beautiful artist whose work projects with a rare and serene distinction a pre-existing vision, but he lacks, quite simply, the magnitude of a master, the magnitude which is not, of course, dependent upon the scale on which an artist

[1] 10 May 1947.   [2] 16 May 1947.

works, and which is, for example, as manifest in a drawing by Rubens or an etching by Goya as in their largest paintings.

Is this commonplace of criticism – hardly less widely accepted here than abroad – that an immeasurable gulf still separates the painting of England from that of France in fact justified? Or is it an inevitable consequence of the dazzling ascendancy of France right up to the immediate past? And of the debt which every English artist of our age – with a single exception to be noticed later – owes to French inspiration in his formative years? I am conscious of the national prejudice, the parochialism, the personal affections that may have gone to the formation of my opinion, but I am conscious also of the obligation to place on record my conviction that no such gulf in fact exists, and that the English school shows no less excellence than the French and considerably more interest. It counts among its members a wide range of mature and highly individual personalities, and, although it cannot, of course, compare in inventiveness with the French School, it has shown a power, not conspicuous elsewhere, of applying the basic discoveries of the most original painters of Continental Europe to the representation of many of the traditional subjects of European art. Wyndham Lewis voiced the permanent disposition of many of his English contemporaries when he wrote, of his own attitude after the First World War:

The geometrics which had interested me so exclusively before, I now felt were bleak and empty. *They wanted filling.* They were still as much present to my mind as ever, but submerged in the coloured vegetation, the flesh and blood, that is life. . . .

1. WALTER RICHARD SICKERT. *Statue of Duquesne, Dieppe* (*c.* 1900).
Oil, 51½ × 39¾ in. The City Art Gallery, Manchester.

2. WALTER RICHARD SICKERT.
The New Bedford (1906–7).
Oil, 36×14 in.
Coll. Dr. Robert Emmons.

WALTER RICHARD SICKERT
1860–1942

S OME months before the beginning of the year 1900, which I
have arbitrarily selected as my point of departure, Walter
Richard Sickert left England, and did not return until five
years later. Apart from being the senior among the subjects of these
studies, Sickert was the most consistently and effectively articulate
painter of his generation, who spoke with insight and authority and
not on his own behalf alone. By taking him as my first subject (in
spite of his initial absence from the main theatre of operations) I shall
be enabled the more readily to refer without delay to ideas about
painting current among artists. He himself has warned us 'to judge
an artist by his works, not by his patter', but if patter is not to be
accepted at its face value it is equally not to be ignored. Sickert's
own placing of himself was very simple:

> I am [he said] a pupil of Whistler – that is to say, at one remove, of
> Courbet, and, at two removes, of Corot. About six or seven years ago,
> under the influence in France of Pissarro, himself a pupil of Corot,
> aided in England by Lucien Pissarro and by Gore (the latter a pupil
> of Steer, who in turn learned much from Monet), I have tried to recast
> my painting entirely and to observe colour in the shadows.[1]

This placing gives an indication of one of the causes of Sickert's
authority among English artists: his familiarity with French painting. Since the early days of Impressionism the more independent
artists in England had been increasingly aware of the momentous
character of French painting and of the stature of Millet, Courbet,
Manet, Pissarro, Degas, Renoir and Monet, but only to very few of
them was the work or the personalities of these masters familiar.
Of those few Sickert was one of the best informed. He went to
France in 1883, in order to take Whistler's *Portrait of his Mother* for
exhibition at the Salon. 'I have a clear recollection', he has told us,
'of the vision of the little deal case swinging from a crane against the
star-lit night and the sleeping houses of the Pollet de Dieppe.'

[1] 'The New Age', 26 May 1910.

Although he was only twenty-three years old he was already well prepared to make the most of all he saw and heard in Paris. Oswald Adelbert Sickert, his father (1828–85), was a capable painter and draughtsman, who studied in Paris with Couture – and his father, Johann Jurgen Sickert (1803–64) was also a painter and head of a firm of decorators employed in the Royal Palace of Denmark. (The family was originally Danish, but Sickert's father acquired German nationality as a result of Germany's seizure of Schleswig-Holstein but was subsequently naturalized in England, where he settled in 1868 with his English wife.) Sickert himself was born in Munich on 31 May 1860. The family was harmonious and united, and Sickert therefore eagerly assimilated, instead of reacting against, as might otherwise have been the case, the sober, professional attitude towards the arts of his father and his grandfather. Of his father Sickert declared that he never forgot anything he told him.

At King's College, London, he must have laid the foundations of an excellent education, especially in the classics, for he read Latin and Greek with pleasure throughout his life. After going down he wished to become a painter, but his father warned him against the uncertainties of an artist's career; so he fell back upon his second choice, the stage. For three years he acted, on occasions in Irving's company, but although he took only minor parts his experience in the theatre was not an irrelevant interlude. It confirmed a love of the stage that lasted as long as his life, and, it is reasonable to assume, the histrionic elements in his own temperament. There was a sense in which, for Sickert, the world was always a stage, and he the player of many parts, but I think that Sir Osbert Sitwell is justified in his opinion that none of these was without a genuine foundation in his own character. In 1881 he became a student of the Slade School, under Alphonse Legros, but a chance meeting with Whistler caused him to leave the well-trodden path. 'You've wasted your money, Walter', he jibed; 'there's no use wasting your time too,' and Sickert went off to help Whistler print his etchings. By forsaking Gower Street for Tite Street, Sickert entered a new world, for in the studio of Whistler he found himself remote from the Slade and near to the mainstream of European painting. The at first almost daily association with Whistler was one of the two most important relationships of Sickert's life. For a time even his sceptical spirit was captivated by the Master, the capricious, scintillating dandy who held sway over courtiers whose subservience was as unexceptionable, if not, perhaps, as demonstrative, as that of the courtiers of Xerxes. Sickert once wished to introduce D. S. MacColl to him, and identified him as the author of an article in 'The Saturday Review' entitled 'Hail, Master!' 'That's all very well, "Hail, Master!" But he writes about Other People, *Other People*, Walter!' 'Of course', Sickert added, 'with Whistler there was always a twinkle.' In time the friendship waned. In 1897 Whistler, giving evidence against him in a lawsuit, described him as 'an insignificant and irresponsible person'. For a man of Sickert's independence, friendship on the terms which Whistler demanded could not have been of long duration, but there existed a still more active cause of disruption: Sickert's admiration for the Master became more and more tempered with criticism, until at last Whistler's art came pre-eminently to stand for some of the weaknesses which Sickert most abhorred. In 1882, he has told us, he began a campaign in the Press on the Master's behalf which he did not wind up until ten years later. Subsequent references to Whistler contain searching criticism; at last there appeared an article entitled 'Abjuro'[1] which was, in his own words, 'an explicit repudiation of Whistler and his teaching'. It is not, however, in 'Abjuro' that Sickert gives most explicitly his reasons for his repudiation. When the Pennells' 'The Life of J. McN. Whistler' appeared, Sickert reviewed it at length.[2] Here he gave his most considered estimate of his master. Insisting that Whistler's art is dominated by his taste he developed the theme that 'Taste is the death of a painter'. 'An artist', he contended, 'has all his work cut out for him, observing and recording. His poetry is in the interpretation of ready-made life. He has no business to have time for preferences.' In a later article[3] he indicted Whistler of a yet more radical defect. After a tribute to 'the exquisite oneness that gives his work such a rare and beautiful distinction' which he obtained by covering the whole picture at one 'wet', he proceeds to show how heavy a price Whistler had to pay for this quality. 'The thinness of the paint resulted in a fatal lowering of tone . . . and necessitated

[1] 'The Art News', 3 February 1910.
[2] 'The Fortnightly Review', December 1908.
[3] 'Where Paul and I Differ', *The Art News*, 10 February 1910.

an excessive simplification of both subject and background.' Sickert
then clinched his argument with an observation of the rarest insight.
'*Mastery*' (he had denied that in the proper sense Whistler was a
master), '*Mastery, on the contrary, is avid of complications*, and shows
itself in subordinating, in arranging, in digesting any and every
complication.' In a fourth article,[1] written twenty-five years after
Whistler's death, he put the whole of this indictment into one simple
sentence. 'Whistler accepted', he said, 'why, I have never understood,
the very limited and subaltern position of a *prima* painter.'

> [His] paintings were not what Degas used to call *amenées*', he continued,
> 'that is to say, brought about by conscious stages, each so planned as
> to form a steady progression to a foreseen end. They were not begun,
> continued and ended. They were a series of superimpositions of the
> same operation. . . .

I have quoted Sickert's criticisms of Whistler at some length for
two reasons. Whistler and all that he stood for may be taken as
Sickert's point of departure, and his progressive repudiation bears
a precise relation to his own development. This repudiation,
thoroughgoing though it was, was not absolute. There were qualities
in Whistler which he continued to revere and which moved him to
pay him this ardent yet discerning tribute:

> I imagine that, with time, it will be seen that Whistler expressed the
> essence of his art in his little panels – pochades, it is true, in measure-
> ment, but masterpieces of classic painting in importance. . . . The
> relation of and keeping of the tone is marvellous in its severe restriction.
> It is this that is strong painting. No sign of effort with immense result.
> He will give you in a space nine inches by four an angry sea, piled up
> and running in, as no painter ever did before. The extraordinary beauty
> and truth of the relative colours, and the exquisite precision of the
> spaces, have compelled infinity and movement into an architectural
> formula of eternal beauty. . . . It was the admirable preliminary order
> in his mind, the perfect peace at which his art was with itself, that
> enabled him to bring down quarry which, to anyone else, would have
> seemed intangible and altogether elusive.[2]

Nor was it only Sickert's admiration that outlasted his friendship
with Whistler; his personal devotion survived it also.

[1] 'The Daily Telegraph', 25 April 1925.
[2] 'Review of Life of J. McN. Whistler', by J. and E. R. Pennell, *The Fortnightly Review*, December 1908.

The diary of the painter's mother [he wrote] depicts the child the same as the man I knew; sunny, courageous, handsome, soigné; entertaining, serviable, gracious, good-natured, easy-going. A charmeur and a dandy, with a passion for work. A heart that was ever lighted up by its courage and genius. . . . If, as it seems to me, humanity is composed of but two categories, the invalids and the nurses, Whistler was certainly one of the nurses.[1]

If Whistler was Sickert's point of departure, Degas, for the greater part of his life was his ideal. 'The greatest painter of the age' is how, in a personal account, he described him.[2] This account is remarkable in several respects, in none more than for being a portrait entirely credible and entirely delightful, yet painted without a single shadow. I mean that for Sickert Degas was a being without defects. I am far from having the good fortune to have read everything that Sickert has written or even all his published writings, but I cannot recall a single instance of adverse criticism of Degas. He did not regard him, I take it, as of the stature of Turner or of Millet but, within narrower limits, as the perfect artist. Sickert reverenced Degas for his achievements, but there was one question of method over which he was passionately convinced, and it is impossible to read his writings without coming upon frequent references to it, just as it occurred frequently in his conversation. This was the question whether large pictures of more or less complex subjects should be painted on the spot, direct from life, or in the studio from preliminary studies or photographs. His opinion was, I think, first expounded at length (and with admirable pungency) in a book published in 1892 on Bastien-Lepage and Marie Bashkirstev. This has long seemed to me to be among the best of Sickert's writings, and I was surprised to find it omitted from Sir Osbert Sitwell's judicious selection.[3]

To begin with, [he said] it was thought to be meritorious . . . for the painter to take a large canvas out into the fields to execute his final picture in hourly tête-à-tête with nature. This practice at once limits your possible choice of subject. The sun moves too quickly, you find that grey weather is more possible, and end by never working in any other. Grouping with any approach to naturalness is found to be impossible. You find you had better confine your composition to a single figure . . . that the single figure had better be in repose. Even then

[1] 'The Burlington Magazine', December 1917.   [2] Op. cit.
[3] 'A Free House', 1947.

your picture necessarily becomes a portrait of a model posing by the hour . . . your subject is a real peasant in his own natural surroundings, and not a model from Hatton Garden, but what is he doing? He is posing for a picture as best he can and he looks it. That woman stooping to put potatoes into a sack will never rise again. The potatoes, portraits every one, will never drop into the sack. . . .

With these melancholy procedures Sickert contrasted those of Millet, based upon the conviction that, in the master's own words, '*Le nature ne pose pas*'. 'Millet knew that if figures in movement were to be painted so as to be convincing, it must be by a process of cumulative observation . . . he observed and observed again . . . and when he held his picture he knew it, and the execution was the singing of a song learned by heart, and not the painful performance in public of a meritorious feat of sight-reading. . . .' 'To demand more than one sitting for a portrait is sheer sadism' is a saying that recurred in both his writings and his conversation. That the method of Millet and of the old masters should also be in this regard the method of Degas was a source of constant satisfaction to Sickert. There was no conviction that he held more fiercely than that there was no fundamental difference between the old art and the new, and that the history of art was therefore a history of additions, not of revolutions. 'There is no new art', he wrote. 'There are no new methods. . . . There can no more be a new art . . . than there can be a new arithmetic . . . or a new morality.'[1] Not even the painter who carried a large canvas into a field so much provoked him as critics who treated the new as though it superseded the old.

> You are not to consider [he admonished them] that every new and personal beauty in art abrogates past achievements as an Act of Parliament does preceding ones. You are to consider these beauties, these innovations, as additions to an existing family. How barbarous you would seem if you were unable to bestow your admiration and affection on a fascinating child in the nursery without at once finding yourselves compelled to rush downstairs and cut its mother's throat, and stifle its grandmother. These ladies may still have their uses.

Sickert's sympathies towards artists who attempted new themes was readily kindled, but he remained steadfast in the conviction that the

---

[1] 'The International Society', *The English Review*, May 1912.

classic or academic method constituted the only durable framework.

Oddly enough, Degas, whom Sickert venerated, probably influenced him less than the master whom he abjured. In particular, the low tones which Whistler taught him to use continued to distinguish his painting until after 1903, but his ready acceptance of the accidental elements in life as subjects for painting, no less than his preference for subjects drawn from popular life, it may reasonably be assumed that he derived from Degas.

During the years 1899-1905 when Sickert, as already noted, was living abroad, he sent a number of his best pictures to the New English Art Club, which, as he observed, set the standard for painting in England. The Club was founded in 1886, in opposition to the Royal Academy, by artists who had studied in Paris, for the purpose of establishing a platform for realistic painting. Its earliest members worked chiefly under Barbizon influence, but since about 1889 the more enterprising among them had applied a colour vision derived from the Impressionists to themes in general already accepted in England. The preference of leading members, notably Sickert himself, for 'low-life', no less than that of others, notably Conder and Beardsley, for exotic and 'decadent' subjects outraged academic opinion. Not since the earliest days of the Royal Academy had so preponderant a part of the keenest and ablest talents of England been gathered in a single institution, and the resulting interaction of one temperament upon another issued in a widely diffused spirit of audacity. Notwithstanding the diversity of temperaments which found a welcome in the New English Art Club, the Club became identified with a distinctive method of painting, which Sickert thus described:

> Technically we have evolved, for these things are done by gangs, not by individuals, we have evolved a method of painting with a clean and solid mosaic of thick paint in a light key ... and ... a whole generation holds it in common. .... [1]

Sickert here voices, incidentally, an opinion rare among artists – namely, that art is largely a collective pursuit. Most artists have a sense, often a blinding sense, of their individual uniqueness, and of the solitary character of their struggle with refractory material and

[1] 'The New English and After', *The New Age*, 2 June 1910.

the buffets of Fortune, but to Sickert, who was always learning and always teaching, the collective aspect of their vocation was constantly present.

> It is well to remember [he declared] that the language of paint like any other language, is kneaded and shaped by *all* the competent workmen labouring at a given moment, that it is, with all its individual variations, a common language, and not one of us would have been exactly what he is but for the influence and the experience of all the other competent workmen of the period.

It is related that, when some pictures alleged to be by Sickert were coming up for auction, an interested person who doubted their authenticity telegraphed to him: *Did you paint the pictures signed with your name and at present on view at such and such auction rooms?* Other wits might have sent the reply; *No, but none the worse for that.* Sickert is the only artist known to me who might have meant it.

During the early years of the new century Sickert's painting underwent a gradual change. Previously many of his best works had had something of the character of coloured drawing. If we examine *Gatti's Hungerford Palace of Varieties, second turn of Katie Lawrence,*[1] of about 1888, *The Old Hotel Royal, Dieppe,*[2] of 1900, *The Horses of St. Mark's, Venice,*[3] of 1901, *The Statue of Duquesne, Dieppe* (Plate 1),[4] of 1902, *Rue Notre-Dame, Dieppe,*[5] of the same year, they are all of them, in spite of the elaboration both of their design and their colour, essentially drawings in paint. Their outlines are emphatic; the paint is lightly applied. The best works of the immediately following years reflect the movement, widespread among European painters, towards a certain massiveness, achieved by a more deliberate, more concentrated design, and by a thicker application of paint. Such paintings as *The Lady in a Gondola,*[6] of about 1905, *Mornington Crescent*[7] and *The New Bedford* (Plate 2),[8] both of 1907, *The Juvenile Lead,*[9] of about 1908, all show how closely Sickert shared its aims. With the exception of the first (which was, however,

[1] Coll. Mr. J. B. Priestley.   [2] Coll. Mr. Alfred de Pass.
[3] Coll. The Earl of Crawford and Balcarres.
[4] The City Art Gallery, Manchester.
[5] The National Gallery of Canada, Ottawa (Massey Collection).
[6] Whereabouts unknown.   [7] Whereabouts unknown.
[8] Coll. Dr. Robert Emmons.   [9] Whereabouts unknown.

3. WALTER RICHARD SICKERT. *Portrait of Victor Lecour* (1922).
Oil, 23½ × 31½ in. The City Art Gallery, Manchester.

4. PHILIP WILSON STEER. *Girls Running: Walberswick Pier* (1894).
Oil, 24½ × 36¾ in. The Tate Gallery, London.

5. PHILIP WILSON STEER.
Chepstow Castle (1906).
Oil, 35½ × 47½ in.
Coll. Her Majesty
Queen Elizabeth
the Queen Mother

6. PHILIP WILSON STEER. *Portrait of Mrs. Raynes* (1922).
Oil, 27 × 22 in. The Tate Gallery, London.

painted in London), the subjects of all these later paintings were taken from Camden Town, where he settled on his return from abroad. This grim and often fog-bound but roughly genial neighbourhood of small, square, late Georgian or of tall, early Victorian long-windowed houses, soot-encrusted and built in crescents or straight rows, was one in which he delighted. In accordance with his habit, he rented odd rooms for working in. The nearby Caledonian Market was among his favourite haunts. One day he was seen there (according to an account which has reference to a later day) in an old trench-coat and a straw hat with a broken brim, with his trousers stuffed into brown leather Army boots that reached almost to his knees, and as the boots had no laces the uppers jumped backwards and forwards as he walked. He came upon an old piano. 'Mind if I try it?' he asked the owner of the stall. 'Go ahead, guv'-nor', was the reply. Thus encouraged, he rattled off an old music-hall tune and then spun himself round several times on the revolving stool. 'Very fine tone', he gravely assured the owner and wandered off into the crowd.[1] Of the four places where Sickert painted most, Camden Town, Dieppe, Venice and Bath, the first was the one which he most intimately understood. Yet Mr. Wilenski can bring himself to write:

> In painting these [the Camden Town] pictures Sickert was no more recording life in Camden Town than he was recording life in Chinatown. He let his North London cronies think that the locality had something to do with it. But in fact when he was painting, his mind was not in North London but in North Paris.[2]

The artist's mind, surely, is always upon his subject, and Sickert himself has repeatedly affirmed that 'serious painting is illustration, illustration all the time'. Sickert's sayings were sometimes paradoxical, but here he was voicing a tenaciously held conviction which had immediate reference to his own work. The quality which gives such peculiar fascination to the North London paintings is the application to subjects conspicuously shabby and anecdotal of procedures which resume, with consummate erudition and taste,

[1] 'Sickert', ed. and with an essay on his life and notes on his paintings, by Lillian Browse, and with an essay on his art by R. H. Wilenski, 1943, p. 17.

[2] Op. cit.

the distilled wisdom of the foremost masters of the age; not only of Whistler and Degas, but of Pissarro, Vuillard and Bonnard. And not of his own age only: his colour, especially his muted but resonant pinky-carmines, shows to what good purpose he had lately spent his time in Venice. When I applied, just now, the attribute of *taste* to Sickert, I was aware that it was an attribute which he himself would have disclaimed with aversion, as also, at his behest, would certain among his admirers. Sickert's own view of taste – that it is the death of an artist – I have already noted. He spoke constantly of painting as 'a rough and racy wench'.

> The more our art is serious [he declared with studied deliberation] the more will it tend to avoid the drawing-room and stick to the kitchen. The plastic arts are gross arts, dealing joyfully with gross material facts. They call, in their servants, for a robust stomach and great powers of endurance, and while they flourish in the scullery, kitchen, or on the dunghill, they fade at a breath from the drawing-room.[1]

Except where this question of taste is concerned I believe all the opinions of Sickert's which I have cited hitherto to have been objective opinions, which may be accepted at their face value. But about this question he protests too much. It is true that an artist cannot relish a tasteful 'arrangement' he has thought up for himself as keenly he can something suddenly perceived (either by the outward or the inward eye), any more than a man can fully enjoy, as Sickert used to say, a meal that he has cooked himself. It is true that many of the greatest artists have ennobled some of the grossest subjects; but that there is any necessary connexion between serious art and – even in the broadest meaning of the word – the kitchen, is a notion which the history of art shows to be false. The great Italians, from Giotto to Tiepolo, to whom we owe so disproportionate a number of the masterpieces of the world, had scarcely a glance to spare for scullery or kitchen; nor had Van Eyck, El Greco, Poussin, Watteau, Delacroix or Turner. The cooks of Velazquez are not finer than his infantas or his *Virgin of the Immaculate Conception*. To persuade us of the truth of the view he had propounded, Sickert wrote as though the drawing-room were the only conceivable alternative to the kitchen, but this is no more than a dialectical device, and a transparent device at that. Why should

[1] 'Idealism', *The Art News*, 12 May 1910.

Sickert, a critic of the rarest insight, have persisted in so questionable a generalization? He gave us, I believe, a clue when he wrote:

> To the really creative painter, it must be remembered, the work of other men is mainly nourishment, to assist him in his own creation. That is our reason why the laity are wise to approach the criticism of art by an artist with the profoundest mistrust.[1]

The answer to this question is, I believe, that Sickert was himself essentially a man of taste, and, in consequence, acutely aware of the vitiating effects of taste once it becomes predominant in a man's work. The acerbity and the frequency of his warnings against the dangers of taste suggest that Sickert had had personal experience of them. An artist of robust stomach, wholly at ease in dealing with gross material fact, a Rubens or a Rowlandson, would be disposed to regard taste not with animosity, but rather as a minor, but on the whole an enviable sensibility. The circumstance which, as I understand the matter, so peculiarly exacerbated Sickert's animosity towards taste, was his own discipleship of Whistler. He came gradually to realize that he had come near to worshipping, in his first master, the very quality against which he should have been most vigilant. And was it not this circumstance, too, that gave eventually a personal twist to his especial dislike of the predominance of taste in Whistler himself? May not his feeling have resembled the gradual and galling recognition by a child of a defect in a parent from which he also suffers? It was not that Sickert was lacking in robust qualities, but detested Taste was always at his elbow with his plausible ways. . . . You have only to look at his painting and drawing to see how strongly sheer taste was always working in him; the delicate slates and violets, and the lemons, and the muted carmines of Tintoretto. And there were occasions when he capitulated altogether to his taste: he forgot his sarcasms about the 'august site' motive, and took a ticket to Venice, and painted St. Mark's under a star-hung midnight heaven. Could any paintings be remoter from the scullery than Sickert's Venetian subjects, whether they be St. Mark, Santa Maria della Salute, or for that matter La Giuseppina herself. It would be difficult, I believe, to show that Sickert's paintings of Venice – and, one might add, of 'august sites' in Dieppe, aspects

[1] 'The English Review', March 1912.

of the venerable Church of St. Jacques, or of the stylish hotels along the seafront or of the spacious arcading by the harbour – were inferior to the shabby interiors of Camden Town. An intensely observant, or, as he himself said, 'a breathlessly listening' artist, he divined the history, the social ambience and everything which goes to make up the distinctive 'atmosphere' of a place, which enabled him to paint and draw it – 'beautiful' or 'ugly' – with extraordinary comprehension.

It was, I suppose, in the best of his Camden Town pictures that Sickert came nearest to realizing his aims as a painter. His criticism of Whistler for accepting the subordinate position of a prima painter, for persisting in the 'trial and error' method, has already been noted; also his corresponding praise of Degas for his deliberateness, resulting in the growth of the power to begin, continue and end pictures according to a minutely pondered plan. Sickert's abhorrence of the sketcher's attitude towards painting, and in particular of this attitude in Whistler, like his abhorrence of taste, derived, it is reasonable to suppose, from the knowledge that he himself shared with his first master something of the sketcher's temperament. The summary character of a considerable part of his early work would suggest that this was the case. I have already drawn attention to the fact that several of his largest as well as his finest Venice and Dieppe pictures have the character of drawings rather than of paintings. They may be said to be impressions rather than constructions. Constructions are precisely what the best of the North London pictures are. The *Mornington Crescent* already mentioned and *The New Home*,[1] of about 1912, are pictures of this different kind: there is nothing summary about them; they are deliberate, compactly designed and thickly painted. Painting of this kind probably did not come easily to Sickert; it was the result of a prodigious effort of will, inspired by tenacious conviction. In general, it was the more summary method that he employed, but even with this he experienced difficulties the existence of which it is at present unfashionable to admit. Sickert is freely spoken of as a master of his craft, and, more especially, as a master draughtsman. He was an artist of the highest intelligence and, in consequence, of the most exacting standards, but not, it seems to me, a natural master. Drawing

[1] Coll. Mr. A. J. M. McDonnell.

did not come to him as it came, for instance, to Augustus John, as a gift of the fairies. How poorly, even at the height of his powers, he could on occasion draw is apparent not only in acknowledged failures, but in such a widely admired picture as *The Camden Town Murder*, of about 1907.[1] The torso of the recumbent woman, a confusion of clumsy planes which fail to describe the form, would do no credit to a student; the hands of both woman and man are shapeless. This picture shows in its extreme degree the innate weakness as a draughtsman and summariness as a designer against which he fought a lifelong, but in the main a glorious battle. That by the exercise of constant self-discipline and of his superb intellect he made many splendid drawings, and painted pictures which are marvels of reflective construction, is an indication of how powerfully the creative will worked in Sickert – a will which ever draws strength from the difficulties which it overcomes.

In the course of Sickert's Camden Town period, which lasted about nine years, and ended with the outbreak of the First World War in 1914, his work underwent a radical change. This may be considered as a manifestation of the increasing influence in England of Cézanne, van Gogh, Gauguin, Seurat and those other artists who repudiated important parts of the teaching of their revered Impressionist masters. The manner, or, more precisely, the timing of this change was singular, for the Continental Post-Impressionists were familiar to Sickert long before their influence was felt in England. Why should he have continued year after year uninfluenced by it until it began to attract the excited attention of his juniors? Sickert's was a highly complex, and, in many respects, a secretive character, and this question is one to which I would hesitate to give a confident reply, but upon which I would offer an opinion. One of the mainsprings of Sickert's actions was love of change – of change simply for its own sake. From his childhood to his old age he would abruptly sever relations with old friends and companions, and welcome new ones; the variations in the character in which he presented himself to the world are legendary. In the conduct of his life he responded with a freedom that verged upon irresponsibility to his love of change. In his work this love is sober and discreet, unobtrusive, but manifest. Sickert had the habit of making friends

[1] Whereabouts unknown.

younger than himself. This was in part due also to the desire for change, in part to his passion to teach and to lead the young, and in so doing, perhaps, to renew the illusion of youth. When he settled in North London he began to gather about him a new group of young friends which included Spencer Gore, Harold Gilman, Henry Lamb and a contemporary, Lucien Pissarro, and later on Charles Ginner and Walter Bayes.[1] The interest of all these in one or another aspect of Post-Impressionism was electrified by the Post-Impressionist exhibitions held in London in 1910 and 1912. Sickert, I surmise, was excited by his two-fold love of change and of leadership into a belated (as well as a reserved and transitory) participation in the Post-Impressionist movement. When I say 'excited' I am far from meaning 'stampeded' : the article he wrote on the Post-Impressionists[2] – which contains a noble tribute to Gauguin – shows all his accustomed independence and wisdom.

Sickert's relations with the English Post-Impressionists eventually became embittered, and he left them. The association had, however, lasting effects upon his own work: it led him to heighten his tones, to observe colour in shadows, and to lay on his paint in small mosaic-like patches instead of long strokes and large patches, hitherto characteristic features of his style. To the end of the Camden Town period belongs one especially notable work: *Ennui*,[3] of about

---

[1] Painter, principally within the tradition established by Sickert; also a teacher and critic. Born 31 May 1869 in London. Attended evening classes at the City and Guilds of London Institute, Finsbury, 1886–1900, and at the Westminster Art School under Frederick Brown, for a few months about 1902. Taught at the City & Guilds Institute, at Camberwell School of Arts & Crafts; Headmaster of the Westminster Art School from 1919 until 1934. As a critic he rendered to his fellow artists what Sickert called 'the incalculable service of speaking the truth as he conceives it'. In 1906 he succeeded Fry as art critic to 'The Athenæum', a position he held until 1916. He was a contributor to 'The Outlook', 'The Saturday Review' and 'The Week End Review'. His writings are pugnacious but sometimes obscure. 'I have read your Athenæum article', Sickert would tell him, 'read it three times and I believe, I am proud to believe, that I understand it.' He has also written three books, 'The Art of Decorative Painting' (1927), 'Turner, a speculative Portrait' (1931), and 'Painter's Baggage' (1932). He has also occasionally designed for the theatre. He has held one-man exhibitions at the Leicester Galleries (1918 and 1951) as well as the Goupil Gallery and Carfax.

[2] 'The Fortnightly Review', January 1911.

[3] The Tate Gallery, London. Smaller versions in the coll. of H.M. Queen Elizabeth the Queen Mother and at the Ashmolean Museum, Oxford.

1913. This, although it is lightly painted and has a certain superficial appearance of slightness, is a scrupulously composed and a highly finished work: a work which could in no way be altered or added to without loss. An air of deceptive simplicity veils the artist's mastery, rather as the unaffected manners of the man of the world may veil his accomplishments. In this picture, too, with even more than his customary skill, the artist has disguised his own weaknesses; first of all his difficulty in coming to close grips with form – in describing it with fulness and precision. Its large scale and noble proportions, however, and the economy of means with which so much is forcefully conveyed, make *Ennui* the culmination of the entire Camden Town series. Only once again did he achieve so splendid a major work. This is the *Portrait of Victor Lecour* (Plate 3),[1] of about 1922, in which Sickert's finest qualities, his rich, sardonic sense of human dignity; his power of conveying, not only the atmosphere of a room, but the life which has been lived in it; his adroitness as a designer; and his vivid understanding of the essence of the European tradition – all are radiantly present. I know of no late Sickert to compare with it; I detect, in fact, a steady decline in his powers after the beginning of the First World War, and *The Soldiers of Albert the Ready*,[2] of 1914, I take to be the first symptom of it. There is much to suggest that his vital powers were waning. There was a change in his method of painting which was profoundly symptomatic of decline. About 1914 he began to rely upon photographs and old prints rather than upon his own drawings and cumulative observation. In the early nineteen-twenties he began gradually to abandon drawing, although now and then he produced a drawing or an etching, such, for instance, as *The Hanging Gardens of Islington*, which show all the old mastery. In a letter to 'The Times'[3] he asserted that 'a photograph is the most precious document obtainable by a sculptor, a painter or a draughtsman', but he had many years earlier expressed the qualifying opinion that

> the camera, like alcohol ... may be an occasional servant to a draughtsman, which only he may use who can do without it. And further, the healthier the man is as a draughtsman, the more inclined will he be to do without it altogether.[4]

[1] The City Art Gallery, Manchester.   [2] Coll. Mr. G. P. Dudley Wallis.
[3] 15 August 1929.   [4] 'The English Review', January 1912.

The decline in Sickert's power did not show itself in a steady diminuendo, but in wild fluctuation. At no time did he paint or draw more finely than in the *Portrait of Victor Lecour* or in *The Hanging Gardens of Islington*, but there are also among his later works paintings in which no trace of his rare spirit is apparent. I do not refer to the failures which every artist abandons or destroys, but to works exhibited, frequently reproduced and authoritatively praised. What, for instance, has *Sir Nigel Playfair*, of 1928[1] – a work without a single merit – in common with the other works hitherto discussed in these pages? What are the *Echoes* – with one specified exception – of the late nineteen-thirties, but trivial pastiches barely held together by Sickert's knowledge and taste? Yet so responsible a critic as Sir Osbert Sitwell has said that there are among them 'paintings more magnificent than any that the artist had hitherto achieved'.[2]

The cause of the acceptance by many people, ordinarily of independent judgement, of any work by Sickert, however ill-conceived and ill-executed, as a masterpiece can only be the extraordinary power and fascination of his personality.

It was indeed an elusive personality, remote and detached, yet also entirely of the world, needing alternately to hold himself aloof and to enjoy the bustle of the world and the influence and affection that his manifold gifts ensured. Solitude was necessary for his work; he must also have been conscious that his withdrawals made the enchantment of his presence the more enjoyed – an enchantment which he heightened by his legendary changes of 'character' – from dandy to fisherman, from gamekeeper to chef, each one perfectly sustained. Latterly he preferred a free and fantastic version of his 'workaday' self. I recollect, for instance, his coming to meet me at Margate Station in the summer of 1938 wearing a huge, long-peaked grey cap, a suit of bright red, rough material (the coat with long tails and the trousers egregiously ample) and an outsize pair of khaki bedroom slippers. The taxi in which he drove me to his house at St. Peter's-in-Thanet resembled, in construction and even in smell, an ancient brougham.

Sickert's presence, which seemed to hold out the promise of the sunniest intimacy, conveyed simultaneously the threat of ruthless sarcasm and cold displeasure. What a fabulous subject for a Boswell!

[1] Coll. Lady Playfair.   [2] 'A Free House', p. liv.

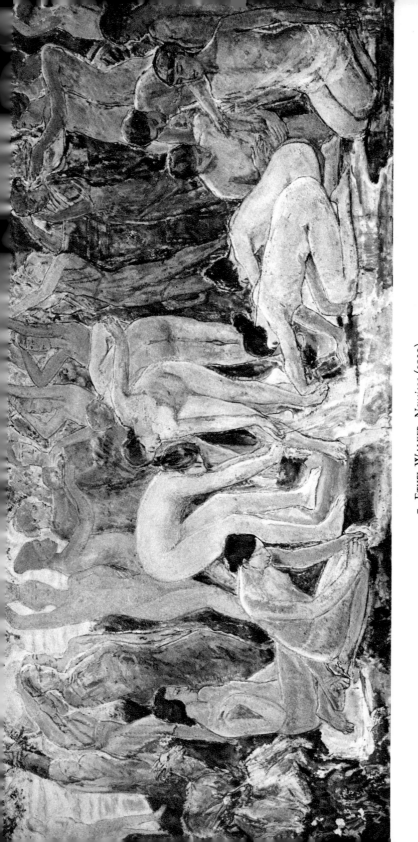

7. Ethel Walker. *Nausicaa* (1920).
Oil, 72 × 144 in. The Tate Gallery, London.

8. ETHEL WALKER. *Portrait of Jean Werner Laurie* (1928–30).
Oil, 23¼ × 19½ in. The Tate Gallery, London.

But Sickert had no Boswell, and he moved elusively from one to another of the painting rooms he collected, and showed constantly differing aspects of his own subtle complex self. In spite of an ultimate heartlessness, he was capable of intimacy – I have rarely read letters so self-revealing as two or three among those he wrote to my father in the late 'nineties – but intimate relations between him and his friends were apt to be transitory or intermittent. With this power of disconcerting by mingled charm and threat, he possessed an extraordinarily retentive memory. In consequence he was able to quote at length and minutely describe in a manner which held his listeners spellbound, the artists, actors and writers, as well as low-life 'characters' he had known, and to discourse upon the most fascinating aspects of their private lives or their most abstruse ideas and their loftiest achievements. It enabled him to draw easily upon a wide range of reading, for he devoted, I suppose, as many hours each day to reading as to painting and drawing. (He was as familiar with the classical writings of Italy and Germany as of Greece, Rome and England.) His personal ascendency is now being prolonged by the republication of his writings. The incisiveness, independency and dry, racy wisdom of these have equipped him to advocate the traditional values in the arts, as Chesterton advocated the traditional values in theology and morals, so as to delight, even if not to convince, a generation which has grown up in the belief of the inevitability of continuous revolution and is apt to confuse novelty with progress. But the effect of his writings upon his reputation as an artist may prove deleterious. For his prestige is now such that to criticize his work with candour is considered scandalous. But his reputation as an artist must ultimately depend upon the best of his Dieppe, Venice and Camden Town paintings, of his Degas-inspired music-halls, upon *Victor Lecour* and his best etchings and drawings. The inclusion of reproductions of such pictures as the wretched *Camden Town Murder* and *Sir Nigel Playfair* already referred to and the (by any standards) derisory *Signor Battistini*[1] in serious publications does his memory a grave injustice. For Sickert was at his best a master: a master of sober and exquisite colour, who could suggest the atmosphere of places with a certainty and fulness which none of his contemporaries has been able to approach, as none has been able to perceive beauty so

[1] Private Collection.

abundantly in places and objects generally considered ugly. Without a trace of idealization, Sickert has the power of showing us, in a row of sooty Islington houses, a piercing beauty. That is true glory. To claim that he portrayed with exceptional insight the life of the ordinary man is the starkest nonsense. He produced (I am now considering his work as he, like Hogarth or Keene, wished it to be considered, as illustration) merely intriguing vignettes: incidents which provoke our curiosity. But he could do no more than this, for, as Roger Fry observed, 'things for Sickert have only their visual values, they are not symbols, they contain no key to unlock the secrets of the heart and spirit'. Sickert lacked the emotional power that would have given reality to his figures. As it is, they are inert puppets, though marvellously, sometimes touchingly, resembling human beings, but they feel neither hunger nor thirst, neither love nor hate, only, perhaps, indifference, which at bottom was his own attitude towards his fellow men.

PHILIP WILSON STEER

1860–1942

THE generalization made in the Introduction of this book upon the neglect of English artists does not apply to Steer. MacColl's authoritative and spirited biography, tightly packed with information and pertinent comment, is but the epitome of a vast Steer legend. The innumerable authors of it range from George Moore to fellow artists and students who break for the first and last time in their lives into print to add yet another to the formidable sum of recorded anecdotes about the idiosyncrasies of Steer: his solicitude for his health, his modesty, his love of cats and his inarticulate wisdom. I do not refer to the existence of this legend to call in question its essential truth, but because the dense aura of 'respect' which it engenders has made more difficult the just appreciation of the artist's work. What is of far greater consequence is the possibility, even the probability, that it had adverse effects upon the artist himself. George Moore's portrait, for example, gives several indications of how heavy with solicitude and adulation the atmosphere around Steer became. Upon the completion of Steer's portrait of his old housekeeper, *Mrs. Raynes* (Plate 6),[1] Moore describes[2] how, as he and Tonks stood before it, he asked if the blue vase on the shelf did not seem a trifle out of tone, and Tonks 'said in an awed voice: "It will go down" and begged me not to mention my suspicion to Steer. . . .' Moore speaks, too, of friends who 'bring an abundance of love and admiration somewhat disquieting to the master', and he surmises that, in the recesses of Steer's mind,

> If not a thought at least a feeling is in process of incubation that perhaps Ronald Gray's appreciations lack contrast, the humblest sketch being hailed in almost the same words as the masterpiece that has taken months to achieve.[2]

It is no part of my purpose to provoke scepticism as to the general verisimilitude of the huge, composite portrait of Steer (to

---

[1] The Tate Gallery, London.
[2] 'Conversations in Ebury Street', 1924 and 1930.

which I have myself contributed a detail here and there) which so many of us cherish with affectionate admiration. Personal acquaintance with Steer, extending over a number of years, and the circumstance that a warm friendship subsisted between him and my parents for the greater part of their lives have given me opportunities of comparing fact and legend, and observation and direct report have for me confirmed and rounded out the portait which can be discovered in the pages of Moore, MacColl and its other delineators.

From these there emerges a big, small-headed, slow-moving, comfortable man, a lover of the quiet and the familiar, an impassioned valetudinarian ('Steer dreads getting wet even as his cat', wrote Moore, 'and he dreads draughts; draughts prevail even in sheltered nooks, and draughts are like wild beasts, always on the watch for whom they may devour'). A man with his feet planted firmly upon the material world: an assiduous and successful follower of the fluctuations of the stock market, and an economical man. Yet one who did not allow his preoccupations with property to impinge upon his paramount preoccupation. An instinctive and disinterested collector

> instigated [to quote Moore once again] by a love of beautiful things, so pure, that he would collect Chelsea figures and Greek coins though he knew of a certainty that no eyes but his own would see them.

A man of chaste life but of a Rabelaisian humour, usually cosy, but illumined on occasion by a flash of wit. At an evening party an artist who had lately been charged with an attempt upon the virtue of a servant entered leaning upon a stick. A lady asked Steer what was wrong with the new arrival; 'Housemaid's knee' was his reply. But above all Steer emerges as an instinctive man, according a superficial wondering respect to the intellectual processes of his friends, but fundamentally sceptical of the value of ideas: indeed, for Steer ideas were hardly realities at all. Notoriously, when the talk of his intellectual friends departed from familiar ground – the technique of painting, connoisseurship, gossip – and took a philosophic turn, Steer slept. By instinct he was a Tory, insular, independent, incurious, unimpressionable. As a student in Paris he seems to have had little liking for the French, almost no interest in their language, literature, or in their history. He did go to see

Gambetta lying in state, 'which', he characteristically reported, 'was not anything much'. The ignorance of French, by which he was insulated from Parisian life, and which even prevented him from becoming aware of the very existence of the Impressionist school of painting, eventually brought his studies to a sudden end. In order to bring about a reduction in their numbers, the Ecole des Beaux-Arts imposed upon its foreign students the obligation to pass an examination in French, for which Steer felt himself unqualified to sit, with the result that, in 1884, he returned to England. Such, in brief, is the legendary Steer. It is an authentic but a superficial likeness, which does no more than hint at an infirmity in him which is manifest in his art, a radical infirmity of which his aversion from the processes of conscious thought, from what Rossetti called 'fundamental brainwork', and his sheer incuriosity were symptoms. This infirmity was a strain of laziness, and it was perhaps his instinctive consciousness of it which disinclined him from any activity, intellectual or physical, liable to divert his limited energies from his painting. His other activities were conducted in an easygoing fashion. He read desultorily. Social intercourse, being invariably the one 'qui se laisse aimer', he was able satisfactorily to sustain with the minimum of sacrifice and effort.

His duties as a teacher from 1893 until 1930 at the Slade School made even slighter calls upon him. There are stories of students awaiting the criticism of their teacher seated behind them, and turning round at last to find him asleep. If a student said, 'I'm in a muddle', he would reply, 'Well, muddle along then'. Because he was apt to go to sleep and to make comments of such a kind, he was not without value as a teacher – in fact, the contrary was the case. He showed at moments a power of imparting, by a benevolent, homely phrase, something of his own instinctive wisdom; and his fame as a painter and the massive integrity of his presence made what he said memorable for his students. Like his agreeable social life, his teaching was conducted with the least possible exertion.

Steer's habitual lethargy of mind, and, to a lesser degree, of body also, exercised a far-reaching effect upon his human relations. He possessed most of the qualities which make a man lovable: a benign largeness, an instinctive modesty, a slow, unaggressive geniality, an impressive calm; he also possessed, from early days, the prestige accorded to extraordinary powers. In most times and places such a combination of qualities would by themselves have assured him a sufficiency of affectionate regard; his lethargy immeasurably enhanced their appeal, for it put to sleep that most deadly source of contention between artists, the spirit of rivalry. In spite of his manifest superiority over the majority of the artists with whom, in the course of his long life, he was associated, he probably excited less jealousy than any artist of his generation. It often happens that the evident satisfaction which a successful rival derives from the exercise of his superior powers is even more provoking to his friends than his possession of them. Steer not only disclaimed possession of superior powers; he persisted, sometimes beyond the verge of absurdity, in denying that anybody had ever supposed him to possess them. The lengths to which he was prepared to carry his pretensions were exemplified in connection with his appointment, in 1931, to the Order of Merit. He was at first unwilling to accept it, but after much persuasion on the part of friends he agreed. On the morning when he received the royal offer he took it to show to Tonks, whom he greeted with the enquiry, 'Have *you* received one of these?'

With equal resolution, Steer disclaimed higher ideals than his fellow artists. He referred habitually to his own activity as 'muddling about with paints' and let it be understood that he regarded painting as an ordinary 'job', like any others, in connection with which the expression of any high ideal was out of place. He once complained of my father, whose exalted sense of the artist's vocation sometimes irritated him: 'Will Rothenstein paints pretty much like the rest of us – but from higher motives, of course.'

Steer's egalitarianism sprang partly from a genuine sense of his own shortcomings confronted with the infinite and never-diminishing difficulties of painting, partly from his instinctive wisdom in withdrawing as far as possible from the field of contention the huge bulk of his talent, and thereby preserving it against distracting animosities. This difficult manœuvre could hardly have been executed more adroitly: Steer, who was scarcely more inclined to put himself out for his brother artists than he was to criticize them, became the personification of benign modesty. So much is apparent from the various authoritative writings about Steer. What has been, so far as I am aware, totally ignored is the question whether his intellectual lethargy, which involved a reluctance to recognize the value – it might almost be said, the very existence – of ideas, was detrimental to his life as an artist. I am persuaded that it was.

Not until Steer's life had neared its end did it occur to me that neither the familiar legend nor the accepted estimate of his art, according to which he was the Constable of our day – a Constable who had studied Gainsborough and Turner to some purpose – accounted fully either for his character or his art.

One day in 1942 Mr. G. E. Healing, the possessor of a collection of Steers, called at the Tate Gallery with a picture which he was prepared to sell. The picture was *The Beach, Walberswick*, of 1890. I can see it clearly still, propped up against the pink hessian of the sandbagged temporary quarters into which the staff had been driven by the bomb-wrecking of our permanent offices; I can see it clearly and well remember the electric effect it had upon me. Could anything, I asked myself, be more different than this from the green, opulent, complacent pictures generally accepted as characteristic Steers? There was no hint of greenness, opulence or complacency about the three intent, lanky but rather stylish young girls with their backs towards the spectator and gazing out across a boldly curving spit of sand to a sparkling sea. The elegance and the poetry of the scene had something of Whistler about it, yet more of Elstir, but nothing of the later Steer. And there was a suggestion of Lautrec in the incisively drawn boots of the girl on the left, and the indication that the long legs of this at first glance ethereal creature are planted on the sand with an almost startling energy. The picture revived the vague admiration I had felt on seeing reproductions of some early Steers in the collection of the late Sir Augustus Daniel, and, upon my earnest recommendation, *Walberswick Beach* was purchased for the Tate. A further visit to the Daniel Collection, and above all the opportunity which this afforded of seeing his *Girls Running*: *Walberswick Pier* (Plate 4), of 1894, convinced me that here surely was the masterpiece of what I had come to regard as the most important period of Steer's production. It is not one of those pictures that imparts a considerable volume of information. It does not touch any of the deeper chords of human experience; still less does it contain any intimation of the life of the spirit. It represents, on the contrary, a spectacle in itself in no way extraordinary: two young girls

running swiftly along a pier away from the sea. Yet the whole
scene has been apprehended with an almost apocalyptic intensity.
It has been seen as though by a blind man vouchsafed the gift of
sight the moment the two girls started to run towards him; it has
been set down with visionary splendour. The composition is unremarkable, nor are the figures finely drawn, yet there they are,
animated by an odd, incredible energy, racing towards us across the
wide planks, the white, broad-sashed, rather formal dresses touched
with the glory of the day. They are strange girls; so much is at once
apparent; and why are they running so fast? There is something
memorable about this picture. Had Renoir painted it, the effect
might have been of greater breadth and resonance; if Lautrec, the
strangeness of the girls might have been defined for us, yet as it is
there is a freshness, an immediacy, an angular, unsophisticated grace
which, added to the intensity of feeling manifest in every inch
of this picture, make it memorable. Compared with works by
either of these or by any of the other great Impressionists, it is
marked by something of the lanky candour of adolescence, but it
springs direct from the same vital source. The owner of this picture
rejected the overtures I made with a view to its purchase for the Tate,[1]
but this made me the more determined to strengthen the Gallery's
representation of Steer's early work. It was not long before other
and only slightly less dazzling opportunities presented themselves.
The Bridge at Etaples, of 1887, a small oil, of two figures against a
luminous background of lemon and grey river and sky, the Tate
had purchased the year before, but this work, for all its pensive
beauty, had not at the time struck me as expressing anything of the
audacious vision of the painter of Girls Running: Walberswick Pier
and The Beach, Walberswick; later it seemed to me their reticent,
less positive counterpart. From the Steer sale at Christie's the
Gallery acquired The Swiss Alps at the Earl's Court Exhibition, a
sketch in which echoes of Whistler and of Japanese colour prints
are dashingly blended, and a much more personal work, Southwold.
Both pictures were painted in 1887. Although it is not in quite the
front rank of the artist's early pictures, this Southwold does more
conspicuously than any other early Steer manifest the exulting spirits,
the extremism, by which most of them are marked, and which most

[1] It was however presented to the Tate Gallery in 1951 by Lady Daniel.

sharply distinguishes them from all his later work – so conspicuously, in fact, that there was a moment when I wondered whether
it could indeed be by Steer's hand. The theme of this picture too is
figures against the sea. The way in which the brilliant colours are
laid on in ribbons, rapidly and thick, in immediate response to
strong, uncensored emotion enables us to compare *Southwold*
without absurdity with a van Gogh. Steer's emotion was slighter
in volume, less deep and purposeful in its nature, and the ribbons of
paint were appropriately thinner, but at the moment when he
painted this picture the two artists were not remote from each
other. There is something of a trumpet-call of defiance in the
excessive size and redness of the head of the schoolgirl on the left:
a sign of how little he cared for the aggressively complacent opinion
of the British public. In MacColl's biography the principal critical
chapter is headed by a remark made by Steer to an interviewer:
'They said I was wild.' The biographer's intention in prefacing with
such an opinion his final summing up of his friend's achievement
and place in history was evidently ironical. Yet what sign of
wildness could be plainer than this oversize, empurpled, intrusive
head?

During the same year protracted negotiations were in progress for
the acquisition of yet another early Steer. *The Swiss Alps at the
Earl's Court Exhibition* and *Southwold* I purchased quite simply on my
own initiative at the Steer sale at Christie's, relying upon the enlightened mercy of the Trustees of the Tate to confirm my action
at their next meeting, but *Boulogne Sands*, of 1892, was elusive from
the first.

When Frederick Brown, Steer's frequent summer painting
companion, Tonk's chief at the Slade, a gruff old survivor of the
early days of the New English, died in 1942, I paid a visit to Or-
monde House, Richmond, where he had spent the latter part of his
life. My expectation of finding some remarkable pictures in the
house of this old incorruptible of somewhat circumscribed but
intense loyalties was not disappointed. The walls of the dark but
finely proportioned room were covered with paintings and drawings by his friends and associates of the New English and the Slade.
Two of these at once attracted my attention: a small self-portrait
by Gwen John, to which I shall refer later on, and a large beach scene

by Steer. This was in a lamentable condition, but between innumerable cracks and beneath a heavy coat of yellowed varnish could still be discovered what MacColl had thus beautifully described just fifty years before when the picture was first shown in its pristine brilliance:

> The children playing, the holiday encampment of the bathers' tents, the glints of people flaunting themselves like flags, the dazzle of sand and sea, and over and through it all the chattering lights of noon – it is like the sharp notes of pipes and strings sounding to an invitation by Ariel.

I told Miss Ellen Brown that I was convinced that this picture ought to hang in the Tate, and she allowed me to show it to the Trustees, who were of the opinion that it represented an opportunity on no account to be missed. After many setbacks the Tate Trustees successfully appealed to the National Art-Collections Fund, by whom, in November 1943, the picture was at last presented to the Gallery. The audacious and sparkling character, the overtone of tense, mysterious exaltation manifest in the early paintings of Steer of which I have been speaking, *Girls Running: Walberswick Pier*, and in those acquired by the Tate Gallery between 1941 and 1943, is shared by a number of other pictures by Steer painted between 1887 and 1894. Among the most notable of these are *On the Pierhead, Walberswick*,[1] of 1888, *The Ermine Sea, Swanage*, of 1890, *Beach Scene, with Three Children Shrimping, Boulogne*, of 1890 and *Children Paddling, Swanage*, of 1894, all three of which belonged to Sir Augustus Daniel, and *Cowes Regatta*,[2] of 1892.

Now whether these works, according to the accepted opinion, are considered to constitute the awkward exploration, under the fugitive spell of Manet and the Impressionists, of a blind alley, or, as I suggest, a splendid beginning precipitately and mysteriously abandoned, the differences between them and the most characteristic works of the artist's later life are so radical as to be apparent to the least practised eye. Indeed, so radical that it would be difficult to distinguish any qualities common for example to *Girls Running: Walberswick Pier* and the characteristic masterpieces of his maturity,

[1] Coll. Mr. Hugo Pitman.   [2] Coll. Mr. C. J. Scaramanga.

Richmond Castle,[1] of 1903, and *Chepstow Castle* (Plate 5),[2] painted two years later, apart from a certain looseness of handling which had become widely prevalent with the diffusion of Impressionist influence. Yet this almost total transformation of Steer's outlook, which appears to me to be the most important event in his life, has remained – so far as I am aware – unnoticed or ignored by all those who have written on his work. This is the case even in the authoritative biography by his lifelong intimate, D. S. MacColl. Perhaps the very closeness and continuity of the relations between the two rendered the changes in his subject almost imperceptible to the biographer. MacColl seems almost unaware of the revolution in Steer's vision; a hint here and there, however, suggests that, in spite of his deeply convinced and comprehending defence of Steer's early work when it was first publicly shown, he regarded most of it as slight compared with that of his maturity. He alludes to the collection of the artist's work built up by Charles Aitken at the Tate as having been enlarged and – evidently with reference to the acquisitions already described – 'even diluted'. Elsewhere he notes with surprise the interest evoked by the early work in the memorial exhibition of 1943. Even granted the fullest allowance for the inevitable difficulty in distinguishing the changes which succeed one another in the life of an intimate contemporary, there is something singular in the failure of the possessor of so sharp a critical faculty as MacColl, as he looked intently backwards over his friend's life, to note the change in the whole character of his art which took place about 1900; MacColl, who justifiably reminds us of his critical severity towards his friends. How can he have failed to note the contrast between the profoundly purposeful spirit which informs these early works, the intensity of the running girls, the vivacity of the paddling children, the intentness of the seaward-gazing girls, the subdued tension of the couple on the bridge, and the inanity of his later figure subjects? A predilection for inane gestures and vaguely allusive subjects showed itself early. In *The Pillow Fight*,[3] of 1896, the girl with the solemnly lethargic face aiming the pillow wide of its archly posturing target has been 'posed'

[1] The Tate Gallery, London.

[2] Coll. H.M. Queen Elizabeth the Queen Mother. There is another version in The Tate Gallery, London.

[3] Coll. Mr. C. J. Scaramanga.

so as to be incapable of throwing it at all. For this 'promising romp' MacColl complacently notes that he was in part responsible, having sent the artist a reproduction of a Fragonard as an incentive. In *The Mirror*,[1] of 1901, described by MacColl as one of Steer's two most memorable double-figure compositions, the attention of the woman reflected in the mirror is elsewhere, nor is that of the woman holding it engaged in what she is doing. In *Golden Rain*,[2] of about 1905, and *Reclining Nude*,[3] of 1905 (to mention two at random), naked women – who are never anything but studio models – loll inconsequently in incongruous or indeterminate surroundings. In writing of these pieces, Steer's biographer extenuatingly alludes to his 'disinterest in event'. Artists have at all times exercised the right of modifying history and nature in the interest of their creations. Veronese could hardly have pushed to a greater extreme of improbability his huge representation of *The Supper at the House of Simon the Pharisee* at the Accademia in Venice; Turner declared that no one should paint London without St. Paul's, or Oxford without the dome (*sic*) of the Bodleian. It is nevertheless true to say that the most serious artists have in general modified objective fact for the purpose of making their representation of it more not less convincing. Steer's later figure compositions, however, were the merest pretexts for representing one of those aspects of nature in which he most delighted – soft, rounded female bodies. So did Renoir, but Renoir's nudes, while they are hardly more purposefully employed than Steer's, are adolescent girls, with lips parted for an eager intake of breath, or who you would know are smiling notwithstanding their averted faces, or great elemental women, who might be the mothers of the human race; while Steer's are usually Chelsea models; old man's pets, not made for generation and love.

It would be difficult, on account of the sporadic character of Steer's development and the scarcity of evidence as to his innermost convictions about painting, to trace with anything like precision the radical change and, as I believe, the deterioration, of his creative faculties which unmistakably showed itself around the year 1900; yet its causes, principal and accessory, are tolerably clear. It may reasonably be supposed that in Steer's early years the effects of his

[1] Coll. The late Sir Augustus Daniel.
[2] Coll. Mrs. E. J. Hesslein, New York.   [3] Coll. Mr. René MacColl.

lethargy of mind (and to less conspicuous degree of body also) were minimized by the exuberance of youth, and by the quickening sense of adventure which belongs to the beginning of the career of an artist of exceptional powers, and by the invigorating wind blowing from Paris. Even in those years he seems, as one critic has observed, to have responded to the achievements of other masters in much the same manner as he responded to nature. Many of his early paintings clearly indicate the source of their inspiration: the paddling pictures, Monet, *A Procession of Yachts*,[1] of 1893, Seurat, probably by way of Pissarro, *Mrs. Cyprian-Williams and Children*,[2] of 1891, and the *Self-Portrait with Model*,[3] of 1894, Degas. In all these pictures, and still more conspicuously in the *Girls Running: Walberswick Pier* and others noticed earlier, Steer took the work of other painters as points of departure, but in every instance, in spite even of a naïve imitation of idiosyncrasies (witness the truncation of the artist's head, Degas-fashion, in the *Self-Portrait with Model*), it may fairly be said that he has made what he borrowed unquestionably his own. But by 1900, when Steer passed his fortieth year, his youth lay behind him; painting, if still a continual joy and a continual agony, was a breath-taking adventure no longer. The fruitfully disturbing proximities of Degas, Manet, Monet, Pissarro and Seurat were only memories to be faintly stirred by the endless, reminiscent monologues of his friend, George Moore. The fact was that Steer had entered another world, a closed world in which the air was stuffy with adulation. Here there was nobody to temper the intellectual sloth which so firmly asserted itself, or the lazy, good-natured contempt for all investigation into the causes of things. There were, on the contrary, friends ready for ever to see something impressive in his defects, and their continual bluff, bachelor jokes depicted him as the great man of action properly indifferent to the chatterings of theorists. Steer's propensity for being sent to sleep by the serious conversation of his friends was a favourite theme: it was indeed an endearing trait. The harm done to Steer was not the work of sycophants – he was quick to discount anything they said – but of intimates of high intelligence and high integrity, ardently devoted to his interests, whose

[1] The Tate Gallery, London.
[2] The Tate Gallery, London. [3] Coll. Viscount Moore.

pervasive attitude could hardly have been without effect. At a critical moment in his life, Steer was surrounded and jealously guarded by friends who made of his deadliest weakness an engaging virtue. His very supineness excited a species of possessiveness in them, fierce and enduring. I remember conversations with several of them in the course of the organization of the Memorial Exhibition at the National Gallery in 1943 (for which I was the official responsible) not long after his death, and how anger kindled in them at the idea of anyone outside the little closed circle of 'cronies' concerning themselves in any way with Steer: they had staked out their own claims over the big, immensely gifted but supine personality. In conversation with some of these, a sudden, envenomed hiss would warn the unwary that he had unwittingly touched a vested interest in some episode of the artist's life, some personal characteristic or opinion. The impassioned possessiveness of 'Steer's friends' clashed in the extensive but closely contested 'no man's land' of the artist's personality.

From the time when I first became convinced of the extraordinary merits of Steer's early paintings until the first of a short series of visits which I paid him shortly before his death on 21 March 1942, the problem of the change in his outlook remained only vaguely present to my mind. Two of these visits I partially recalled in a note in 'The Burlington Magazine'.[1] Some years had elapsed since I had been to his house, and I was at once aware of changes in him. His eyesight had grown worse; but although he was almost blind it was wonderful to see the ease with which his large figure moved on the narrow stairs and in and out of the rooms, very dark that winter's morning, crowded with pictures and with the miscellaneous pretty objects he had accumulated in a lifetime of collecting. This ease was evidently due to his intimacy with the house where he had lived and worked for more than forty years. I had heard, of course, of his increasing blindness, and the courage with which he accepted it did not surprise me. I was, however, unprepared for the comprehensiveness of his interests and still more for his detachment from the opinions and attitudes attributed to him in the legend that has grown up about his name. He showed the liveliest interest in public affairs, especially in the conduct of the war, in history, in literature and music. Unable

[1] 'Two Visits to Steer', August 1944.

to paint, he listened to the news on the wireless, to discussions, to concerts, and daily to the evening service. 'Flo', his devoted house-keeper, and his friends read to him constantly. And, unlike other illustrious men in their old age, he seemed interested in the present rather than the past. To a lady who had said to him that she would like to see the strange world which would take shape after the war, Steer responded with an emphatic 'So should I'. And the satisfaction he took in exercising his mind and reaching his own conclusions without the intervention of his clever friends was gradually borne in upon me, by what stages I cannot now recall. One incident remains clearly fixed. I had come to see him, to discuss the question as to who should write the introduction to the volume to be devoted to his work in the series on British artists that I was editing for the Phaidon Press, and I told him that I believed that this work should be undertaken by one of the younger critics, who would attempt to make a fresh assessment of his work in a spirit more detached than would be possible for one of the intimates who had so early discovered and so consistently proclaimed his merits. The energy with which he expressed his concurrence came as a surprise. 'My old friends', he declared, 'have written well about me, and I'm grateful for their encouragement, but they've written enough.' I then explained that the person I had in mind had hitherto made no special study of his work, and would even approach it in a positively critical spirit, but he was excellently equipped to consider it against a broad background of European painting. 'He sounds to me just the man', Steer said, his face lighting up. 'Who is he?' I explained that he was Robin Ironside, a colleague at the Tate. 'Very well then: bring him to lunch, any day you like.' Then, as though welcoming an occasion for speaking about matters which had troubled him, he referred to the project, which I knew had been under consideration for some time, for an authorized biography. 'The idea of my life being written doesn't appeal to me', he said. 'Lives have a way of leaving out what's really important. Perhaps they have to.' Referring to various writings on Tonks, he said:

'Tonks was a big man, and big men have conspicuous faults as well as conspicuous virtues; but there seems to have been a sort of conspiracy to discount Tonk's faults. In any case, my own life has been very pleasant, but not very interesting. But my friends tell me that something of the sort will eventually be done, and that it had better be done by someone I don't disapprove of too much, and I expect they're right. There's one thing, though, I'm clear about: I don't want it done by someone who's already said his say about me. I'm tired of the old opinions, the old stories. In the last years, when I've been more alone, I've come to see many things differently; there are things I've only just begun to think out.'

The impression his attitude made upon me at the time was that, in spite of his affection and admiration for Tonks, Steer derived a conscious satisfaction from his present independence of the influence of a friend whose energy, strength of purpose and intellectual grasp so far exceeded his own. This I placed on record in my 'Burlington' note, but on account of Steer's recent death, the occasion seemed to me inappropriate for dwelling upon imperfection in a complex of friendships of a singularly wholehearted and enduring character. Nor would I do so now were I not convinced that Steer had come to recognize the source of these imperfections, to realize that certain of his intimates, by flattering his own supine attitude towards the 'fundamental brainwork' necessary to the perfection of the work even of the most instinctive artists, and by persistent argument, had impaired the activity and narrowed the range of his mind, and had imposed their own ideas upon him, to the detriment of his art. Certainly he seemed to lose no opportunity of qualifying his affectionate loyalty to his old friends by an attitude of marked detachment from them, and most emphatically from their opinions. To me, familiar ever since I was of an age to speculate about human relationships with the solidarity and the exclusiveness of the circle in which Steer was enclosed, these utterances were a surprise. It was they which caused me to call in question those parts of the legend which represent him as an artist so unerring in his intuition as to have no need for a reasoned apprehension of things. It became clear to me that Steer, no longer able to paint and brooding upon the past, had become aware of the baleful part which certain of his friends had played in fostering his intellectual inertia.

Even if the jealously possessive circle in which he lived after the 'cronies' had closed in upon him, and the numbing blend of adulation and bluff fun disposed him to ignore the causes of things, even the causes of the effects in which he most delighted, and robbed his figure painting, especially, of the vivid purposeful character which had distinguished it, he remained nevertheless a memorable figure, and one of the great landscape painters of our time. This, indeed, is the opinion of his painter friends, of the critics, accepted by a substantial part of the public which concerns itself with painting. Steer's reputation is so high, and the fervour of his advocates so fierce, that to dwell upon the shortcomings of his art is still to invite the imputation of questionable taste. For those prepared to brave this imputation it is necessary to insist that he lacked the artistic will of the greatest masters, and that he was tempted too readily to see nature in terms of other painters. I remember how easily visitors at the Memorial Exhibition of 1943 recognized which master he had had unconsciously in mind in representing given subjects. The absence of a consistent personal vision left him without a firm basis for logical and sustained development, while his lack of intellectual convictions and his delicate receptivity were apt to leave him at the mercy of chance memories. Few phases of his art, therefore, bear a logical, necessary relation to those which precede or follow them. But though a highly personal vision and logical growth may be said to be characteristic of the great masters, the relative want of both in Steer does not invalidate the high claims put forth on his behalf. The art of Delacroix was affected not less than that of Steer by the art of other masters; the unfolding of Turner's vision, owing among other causes to his love of emulation, would seem to have been as arbitrary at many points. There were moments when Steer, inspired not by particular works but rather by the spirit of Constable and Turner, painted landscape in which piercing observation goes hand in hand with a splendid poetry. I have in mind, besides such masterpieces as *Chepstow Castle* and *Richmond Castle,* already mentioned, *In a Park, Ludlow,*[1] of 1909, and the two versions of *The Horseshoe Bend of the Severn,*[2] both of 1909. Turner taught him to see the majestic, the rhythmical and the glowing qualities in landscape; Constable the beauty of noonday light, of the glistening surfaces of wet foliage

[1] Coll. Mrs. Geoffrey Blackwell.
[2] The City Art Galleries, Manchester and Aberdeen.

and grass, and of the contrast between white cloud and angry sky, between rainbow and thunder-shower – in fact, of the living texture of nature. In these majestic, darkly tempestuous or glowing landscapes can be caught traces of a devoted discipleship of Rubens and Gainsborough also. Around his middle fifties, a change of style, corresponding to an inevitable ebb of physical energy, became apparent in his work. The epic mood and the massive mottled surface were slowly dissolving into something approaching the opposite of them: a long series of landscapes frankly inspired by the lyrical, thinly and limpidly painted sketches made by Turner as a result of his last visit to Rome twelve years before his death. Of the scenes Steer made at Harwich, at Bosham in 1912–13, of Shoreham, 1926–7, misty, subtly coloured visions, it would be no exaggeration to say that they are a worthy tribute to the miraculous originals of the master to whom he was faithful to the end. These subjects are nearly related to his productions in water-colour. This medium he used from about 1900, at first occasionally; then, as he abandoned the practice of completing large canvasses outdoors, he made use of it as a means of accumulating material for works to be completed in the studio. He became entranced, however, by the medium itself, and gratified by the success it brought him. Eventually he evolved a remarkable style, compounded of Turner, Alexander Cozens, Claude, with a faint but intriguing touch, as Tonks noted, of the Oriental, and dependent upon an astonishing dexterity.

Towards the close of his life, his water-colours had come to be widely regarded as his principal achievement. In spite of the almost miraculous quality of the finest of them I believe this to be a mistaken view, and that his fame will ultimately rest securely upon three phases of his paintings in oils: namely, his early figure subjects, the epic landscapes of his early middle years, and the liquid, lyrical visions of his old age, and a single portrait, the tenderly wrought face and figure of his grim housekeeper, *Mrs. Raynes*.

ETHEL WALKER

1861—1951

C AMILLE PISSARRO was quoted earlier in these pages as describing Impressionism as a way of seeing compatible with the free play of the imagination. But he expressed this opinion at a time when, under the promptings of Seurat, he had lately become convinced that the *original* Impressionism, by its acceptance of the scene accidently come upon, and of the necessity for completing the picture on the spot, before the light changed, in a word, by its acceptance of the *sketch* as the highest artistic ideal, did of its very nature circumscribe the imagination. He made the assertion, in fact, with the new, consciously constructive Impressionism in mind, of which he was just then a transient advocate, rather than the earlier movement. It was clear enough that this latter was not readily compatible with a deeply ranging imagination. After its first wonderful flowering and within the lifetimes of its founders, it was rejected by the most imaginative of the younger painters, and it dwindled eventually into the most tepid and unexacting of academic traditions.

Ethel Walker was the first in point of seniority of those English painters who were impelled, by an imaginative temperament, to reject Impressionism; or, rather, to modify it radically to suit her own highly personal ends. In her sense of the primacy of light she was innately Impressionist, but the Golden Age of her highest imaginings could not be represented with sufficient clarity by a system of tones; it demanded contours.

In the chapters on Sickert and Steer I was able to proceed quickly to the consideration of their work. Both were well known personalities; both are the subjects of illuminating biographies, as well as of extensive mythologies. Ethel Walker was certainly 'the best-known woman artist', but there has been no serious attempt to appraise either her art or her personality; or even, so far as I have been able to ascertain, any attempt at all. In order to find out what had been written on this artist, I visited the two principal art libraries

75

in London. The subject index of one recorded the existence of four catalogues of one-man exhibitions, the other of a single sketchy article in a recent issue of a monthly periodical. Not much after nearly ninety years' original, aggressively independent living, after more than sixty years of increasing and effective dedication to painting. And now, it is too late to obtain from her certain important facts about her life and opinions. The last time I saw her, during the early days of 1950, it was plain that her memory had failed. She was able to recollect little and confusedly, except for a few incidents which she cherished rather as landmarks in the gathering darkness than for their intrinsic worth. One such was connected with the first occasion when she exhibited a picture. I had picked out from among the many curled and yellow photographs that were propped against the mirror above the mantelpiece one of an interior with a girl wearing a long white dress turned away from the spectator. It was from a painting, I explained, which I had long regarded as one of her best, but of which I had never seen the original.

'Oh, I'm glad you like that,' she said, 'it's very beautiful. It belongs to a relative of mine, to——I can't remember his name. It was the first oil painting I ever made. There was an exhibition in Piccadilly. At the private view George Moore came in and looked attentively at something of mine. "You've got somebody new who's good," he observed to Steer. "There she is," Steer answered. "Come over and meet her." At that time I had no studio, so Moore invited me to his flat at Victoria Street, and told me I might work there whenever I wished. So one day soon afterwards I brought a model from Pulborough in Sussex, where I was living, and took her to Moore's flat. No sooner had we arrived than a dense fog closed down. We tried a pose or two, but it was almost dark. "It's no good," I said to the model in despair. As she turned away she took so beautiful a pose beside the fireplace, with her full white dress flowing away behind her, that I was inspired, and set feverishly to work in spite of the darkness.'

Where the exhibition was she was unable to recall. It was probably at the Dudley Gallery, where this picture, entitled *Angela*, was shown in 1899. This is not only a beautiful but a mature painting, and cannot possibly (quite apart from her admission that Moore had been attracted by a previous work) have been her first. I would have liked to ask her about this and other matters, but I was reluctant to tax her failing memory.

I shall not forget that last sight I had of Ethel Walker. The previous November she had held, at the Lefevre Gallery, the last exhibition of her work in her lifetime. She was very old; she was illustrious; she had not long since ceased to paint, but the exhibition was virtually ignored both by the public and the Press. I had learnt that she was ill and indigent. But I should have been surprised to find her discouraged, for no artist I have known has ever felt so assured of the immortality of her work – or of the salvation of her soul.

When I came into her studio, unannounced and for a moment unheard, the scene before me epitomized the confident delight of Ethel Walker in the work of her hand. Beside an iron stove in which a large fire glowed, she crouched, in order to keep warm, but sideways, so that she could look out into the room. All round, upon easels, propped against chairs, upon chairs, in fact upon every level space with some kind of support behind it, every one of them turned towards their creator as a flower towards the sun, stood a dense and various assembly of her own paintings and drawings. At them she was gazing enrapt, with pride and wonder. For her, in that dark afternoon they shone like stars in the firmament. The scene lasted for but a moment. Seeing me, she got up and welcomed me, as though she had received an eagerly awaited visit from an intimate friend, instead of an unexpected visit by an old acquaintance. Presently, forgetful of her age and infirmity, she was lifting and moving her pictures to enable me to see them in the best light, just as she had when I first called upon her in that same house nearly twenty years before. Perceiving the admiration which her activity aroused, she abruptly told me her age. 'I'm eighty-six. I was born on 9 June'. 'Were you eighty-six last birthday', I enquired. 'Last birthday', she said. That made 1863 the year of her birth; hitherto she had given it as 1867. She was born in fact in 1861.

Except for the orientation of the pictures, the large L-shaped studio overlooking the river, on the first floor of 127 Cheyne Walk, which she had occupied for the past forty years, was little changed. It had silted up with her miscellaneous possessions, odds and ends of china, medicine bottles, photographs, letters, and the like, and the dust had settled still more thickly upon them. It was typical of the room that the reflections yielded by the few mirrors it contained, although these were not particularly old, were foggy and reluctant. The room had changed little because its occupant had changed little. She had grown smaller and forgetful and infirm, but these were superficial changes: the deep voice, the courage, the benevolent indifference towards other people, the restless energy and above all the unquestioning conviction of her own greatness were as conspicuous as always. That conviction was always expressed so frankly that each new manifestation of it had long been received with a partly admiring and partly malicious enjoyment. As a member, for instance, of a hanging committee of an exhibition, she would remove pictures already hung in favourable positions, replace them with her own, and walk out with an air of satisfaction at having contributed rather more than her share to the collective wisdom of the assembly. She would write to me from time to time to suggest that this or that other picture in some current exhibition would be a particularly appropriate addition to the national collection. 'I would remind you', she wrote on one occasion, 'that every purchase of my work strengthens and enriches the sum of good pictures at the Tate Gallery.'

The declaration, several times repeated during this last visit of mine, of her belief in reincarnation gave me a less unsympathetic insight into her limitless vanity. In support of it she quoted Walt Whitman: 'As to you, Life, I reckon I am the leavings of many deaths'; she urged it as the only valid explanation of genius, of all superior qualities. Therefore she regarded herself not so much as a unique phenomenon, but as the last of a long succession of previous 'incarnations', to whose remarkable merits she owed her own. Her pride, as I now understand it, resembled the family pride of the aristocrat rather than the wholly self-regarding pride of the upstart. But how constantly and how candidly she displayed it! I have never seen anyone so transported with delight by pictures as Ethel Walker by her own. Such exclamations as 'That's beautiful, isn't it?' or 'Even though that is a little sketch, it has the scale of a great picture' formed a continuous pæan of praise. She was sublimely confident that the admiration of others equalled her own. When one of her aunts died, the widower reproached her for neglecting to send a letter of condolence. When at last she wrote, it was to say that she was 'very sorry that Aunt Maud did not live to see my *Resurrection*, as she would have loved it so'. And when Steer died she said, 'Now he and Sickert are gone I'm the only artist left'.

Late on the afternoon of my last visit the fire of life died down in her, and I prepared to leave.

'I owe a good deal to Sickert,' she observed: 'he confirmed me in the habit of working fast. I've always worked fast, especially when I'm painting the sea. Sometimes, at Robin Hood's Bay, I've waited for weeks for a certain effect, a harmonious fusion of water and cloud. When it comes I rush to my canvas and paint furiously with the tide, for the sea and the sky won't wait for me, and, when the effect has gone, I never touch the canvas again. And Sickert taught me to paint across my forms, and not into them. I once said he was generous with his knowledge. Sickert, hearing of it said, "But she never takes any notice of what I say."'

The deep voice died away and we said goodbye. As I stood by the door and turned for a last look at the small figure in the red jacket and gilt buttons, white blouse and black bow tie crouched once again over the fire, at the amphitheatre of pictures and all the disorderly accumulations of forty years, scarcely visible now in the failing light, she spoke again, quietly, without looking round: 'A painter must be brave, must never hesitate. Timidity shows at once. I've always been brave – but now I've given away my palette and brushes.' She had nothing more to say and I went quietly out. I never saw her again. She died in that house on 2 March 1951.

◦ ◦ ◦

When we consider her character, her freedom from the ordinary conventions, her fanatical independence, her habit of uttering her uncensored thoughts and her domineering ways, it is perhaps odd that she led so relatively tranquil a life. It is now the fashion to assume that artists live entirely for their work, which constitutes their only relevant biography. I remember hearing H. G. Wells assert that the life of the average commercial traveller was more eventful than that of the most adventurous artist. But that is not invariably the case. The life of Sickert, for example, would make a fantastic saga comprising half a dozen secret lives, fascinating relationships with the illustrious and the forgotten; nor has the life of Augustus John been barren of event. Even Delacroix, who led, if ever a man did, a life dedicated to art, confessed that in his earlier days 'What used to preoccupy me the least was my painting'.[1]

That Ethel Walker's impact upon her generation has been slight (the only influence she has exercised has been upon the gifted spinsters, the 'matriarchs' of the New English Art Club) and her life little more eventful than Steer's is due to the completeness of her self-absorption. People affect others principally because, consciously or not, they wish to. Such was her self-absorption that, given models and the sea to paint and a generous ration of admiration (and some dogs), she could have lived happily, so to speak, in a vacuum. She has looked attentively at reproductions of the cave paintings at Ajanta, at the Blessed Angelico, Botticelli, Whistler and, longest of all, at Puvis de Chavannes, the Impressionists and Gauguin. And she has looked with tender respect; yet these works have been important in her eyes not so much on their own account as incitements to her own imaginative life. She speaks of her friends, however interesting their personalities, solely in relation to herself. Of George Moore, for instance, I once heard her say: 'He was in love with me; he tried to get into my bedroom and I threw him down the stairs. "You have the affection of a porcupine", he protested, "unconscious of its quills as it rubs against the leg of a child."' But her profound self-absorption was not inconsistent with constant and practical kindness to the afflicted and to animals. Of all religious bodies she most approved, I think, of the Salvation Army, on account of its special solicitude for the poor.

◌   ◌   ◌

Ethel Walker was the younger child of Arthur Abney Walker, a Yorkshireman, and his Scottish second wife Isabella, born Robertson, widow of a Presbyterian minister. At the time of Ethel's birth her parents resided in Melville Street, Edinburgh. One of her ancestors, Hephzibah Abney, had assiduously practised the art of water-colour; his daughter, Elizabeth, married her first cousin, Henry Walker, of Blythe Hall, Nottinghamshire, and Clifton House, Rotherham,

[1] 'Journal', 11 October 1852.

and their son, born in 1820, was Ethel Walker's father. The Walkers were ironfounders, and built old Southwark Bridge. About 1870 Arthur Walker left Clifton House, the large, bleak building where he was born and which now serves as Rotherham's municipal museum, and settled with his family at Beech Lodge, Wimbledon. Ethel attended a strict but excellent school kept by the Misses Clark in the then rural neighbourhood of Brondesbury. At this academy she attracted the particular attention of Hector Caffieri, the drawing-master, who was the first person to encourage her tentative but growing interest in painting. His connection with the school came, however, to a sudden end. A train in which the Misses Clark, accompanied by a number of favoured pupils, were travelling with edifying purpose happened to draw up beside another train, in which Mr. Caffieri was observed seated in a third-class compartment and smoking a pipe. There could be, of course, no question, the Misses Clark thereupon decided, of a person capable of such conduct being permitted to continue as a member of their staff. But about this time Ethel formed an intimate friendship with a girl named Claire Christian, whose family were neighbours of the Walkers in Wimbledon. Claire Christian shared Ethel's principal interests, and one consequence of their friendship was a heightening of their preoccupation with the arts. About 1878, in the company of an aunt, Ethel paid her first visit to France. In the early 'eighties, with Claire Christian, she attended the Putney School of Art. By this time art was her vocation: after a day's work at the school the two girls assiduously studied anatomy and drew from casts of Greek sculpture. Later they visited Spain together and made copies after Velazquez in the Prado. On their homeward journey they stopped in Paris, and, prompted by George Moore,[1] saw for the first time the work of Manet and the Impressionists.

There comes early in the life of most artists the miraculous moment when they look with understanding upon the work of a great master. I have more than once heard Ethel Walker declare that Velazquez taught her to paint. It does not appear to me that Velazquez affected her painting in any perceptible sense, and I am inclined

[1] Both Ethel Walker and Claire Christian, and their relations with George Moore, are described at some length and often in the latter's 'Hail and Farewell' under the pseudonyms of Florence and Stella.

to think that her often repeated avowal of her indebtedness was a recognition, not of any specific debt, but of her awakening to a realization, under the first impact of his genius, of all that painting could signify.

The atmosphere of Beech Lodge, although she was adored by her mother and her old nurse, was not conducive to her studies: with Claire Christian she went into lodgings in Wimbledon and later rented a cottage at Pulborough in Sussex. She worked under Frederick Brown at the Westminster School, and she followed him in 1892 to the Slade School when he was appointed to the Professorship, where she remained for two years.

The early life of Ethel Walker presents one curious feature. She seems to have been talented. From an early age she seems to have been possessed by the idea of becoming a painter. Her family's circumstances made her free of the necessity to support herself. She was endowed with a singular power of will. How was it, then, that, in these highly propitious circumstances, her beginnings were desultory and she came to maturity late? She had reached her late twenties before she went to the Putney School of Art; she was over thirty when she followed Brown to the Slade. The painting which she described to me and to others as her first, *Angela*, was probably done, as it was certainly shown, in 1899, when she was nearly forty. To this question I can offer no answer. But once she had reached the degree of maturity represented by *Angela* she developed rapidly in a highly personal direction, and won an increasing measure of recognition among her fellow painters.

Angela is an example, although an admirable one, of a kind of painting that was being done at the New English rather than an individual creation. The subject, a girl in a white dress, comes straight from Whistler, the Club's irascible patron saint, only it is represented, quite consciously, in a rougher, more homely style than the Butterfly's: the interior is less deliberately arranged, the thick paint is more loosely applied. It would not be difficult, in fact, had it borne their signatures, to accept it as the work of Steer, of Tonks or of several other leading members of the Club.

It was not long before Ethel Walker abandoned her pre-occupation with the representation of figures solidly modelled in sombrely lit Victorian interiors. The best of these paintings exhibited a truth of tone, a grasp of form, a grace, and a bold, easy handling of paint which gives them a place only just below the best of their kind, Brown's *Hard Times*[1] or Steer's *Music Room*,[2] for instance. But they are no more than admirable essays in a kind of painting already fully evolved, and even displaying symptoms of exhaustion.

The paintings of Ethel Walker's maturity differed in every important respect from those of her apprenticeship. Instead of representing facets, shadowy or shady, of the real world in terms of what might be termed the common vision evolved by the New English Art Club, she became absorbed in the contemplation of a Golden Age of full if gentle light, which she represented after a highly personal fashion. Instead of the building up of solid form, she aimed now at the creation of forms which were delicately shimmering and evocative, rather than descriptive, and, more generally, at an art not based directly upon observation but upon observation frankly transformed by a poetic imagination. Here I am thinking chiefly of what I consider to be her principal works: namely, her figure compositions, for in a considerable part of her painting – in a quantitative sense, indeed, the larger part – she continued to represent the visible world. But like her compositions, her later portraits of girls and her paintings of the sea, her two favourite subjects, reflected the radical changes which transformed her outlook during the first decade of the new century. Like the compositions, they are no longer modelled in terms of light and shade, but in delicate and brilliant colour; her preoccupation with surface design is more, and with design in depth less marked.

The transformation in her art was due to two factors: the impact of Impressionism[3] from without and the steady growth within of her vision of a Golden Age. From Impressionism she learnt how to illuminate the groups of virginal figures in their vernal settings which became more and more the focus of her most intense imaginings. Although the influence of the Impressionists upon her was mainly technical, the contemplation of their sunlit landscapes must also have illumined her inward vision. In her pictures painted directly

[1] The Walker Art Gallery, Liverpool.   [2] The Tate Gallery, London.

[3] The love of brilliant colour which she first learnt from the Impressionists was strengthened by her contacts with the Belgian painters Leon de Smet, Marcel Jeffreys, Emil Claus and Marcel Hess when they were refugees in England during the First World War.

from life – the long, enchanting series of portraits of girls and of agitated seas off the Yorkshire coast – she showed herself a disciple of the Impressionists, but in her imaginary compositions too she used certain of their technical methods, direct painting in small disjointed brush strokes of pure colour without subsequent retouching, besides modelling in colour instead of tone, but for purposes remote from theirs. Her frankly ideal visions of a Golden Age, elaborately constructed and painted in her studio from studies, had little in common except their colour with the objective studies of the Impressionists in which the thing seen was accepted with slight modifications and completed on the spot. What I have called the Golden Age of Ethel Walker's imagining was not in itself an original conception; it had haunted the imaginations of numerous European painters ever since the Renaissance. Of Ethel Walker's older contemporaries, Puvis de Chavannes had portrayed it with most conviction, and he must therefore be counted among the chief among her masters.

The two paintings in which this vision is most completely expressed are *Nausicaa* (Plate 7),[1] of 1920, and *The Zone of Love*,[2] of 1931–33, both imaginative compositions. Like all her compositions, these were based upon numerous drawings made from carefully posed models, freely transposed into an imagined world of beauty: a rainbow-hued springtime world peopled by slender young girls, naked, dreamy and innocent. These two big tenderly wrought paintings are original creations.

In this ideal world, the spirit of Ethel Walker was ecstatically at home, but how delightful a contrast it made with the studio in which her earthly body had its being – with the accumulated disorder, the long-gathered dust. How much nearer to reality that other world was in her eyes, how oblivious she herself of her earthly surroundings was suddenly revealed to me when she exclaimed: 'I can't work to-day. I'm like the old Chinese artist who couldn't work if the smallest particle of dust in the air annoyed him.'

[1] & [2] The Tate Gallery, London.

HENRY TONKS

1862—1937

A CONVERSATION which took place in 1892 between Frederick Brown, the recently appointed Slade Professor of Fine Art at University College, London, and a thirty-years-old doctor named Henry Tonks, to whom he presently offered the post of Assistant at the Slade School, had important results. The doctor abandoned his profession and became instead a painter and draughtsman, also a teacher of drawing – the most inspiring and influential, in fact, of his generation. This alone would entitle him to a place in the history of English art. But I make no apology for noticing Tonks in these pages as an artist in his own right as well.

Tonks was a phenomenon that has become rare almost to the verge of extinction – namely, an academic artist. And by an academic artist I do not mean one who supinely accepts whichever of the well established conventions happens currently to prevail but one whose art is based upon traditional canons, clearly apprehended. Academies during the past century or so have become more and more conspicuous for the disregard they have shown for the fundamental traditional values; it is therefore no accident that when the real academic artist, the Alfred Stevens, the Henry Tonks, does appear, he is rarely counted among their members. Always traditional and scholarly in his orientation, Tonks deliberately chose his side when values upon which the art of Europe had hitherto been based seemed to him to be challenged. Throughout his life as an artist he was an assiduous and a reverent student of the methods of the great masters.

Tonks was a late-comer to art, and the road he followed, as he himself has told us, was a strangely devious one. He was born of a solid, cultivated family, the proprietors of a brass-foundry in Birmingham, at nearby Solihull, the fifth of eleven children, on 9 April 1862. There must have been many illustrated books in his father's library, as the son claimed to have been familiar 'from infancy' with the draughtsmen of the 'sixties, with Charles Keene and Wilhelm Busch and, thanks to the catalogue of the 1857 Exhibition at Manchester, with the Pre-Raphaelites. Sadistic ill-treatment at the High Church preparatory school to which he was sent left him with a lasting aversion to dogmatic religion; at his public school his career was undistinguished and he was scarcely less unhappy. 'I only began to live', he declared in old age, 'when I left that damnable Clifton.' His interests shortly turned towards medicine, and in January 1880 he entered as a pupil the Sussex County Hospital at Brighton. At school he was sensible of a vague attraction to the artist's life, but there is no record of his having shown a special predilection for drawing. One faculty invaluable to an artist he early possessed: a retentive visual memory. How precisely and how vividly this enabled him to evoke, years later, incidents from boyhood and youth! The particular use, for instance, of the cane by the headmaster of his preparatory school:

He was a tall, powerful man, and he had an ingenious way of lifting the boy up the better to adapt his clothing to the punishment, and swinging him round at the same time, so that all could see the result of his prowess.[1]

Or the early stirrings of romantic sensuality:

If I had met you, as I did not, as a little girl going for a walk in Kensington Gardens, that spot would have remained sacred for me, just as the sea end in Montpellier Road, Brighton, has a meaning for me, because once I saw up the street a girl who excited my passions (my word, she was a dull girl really but just like a ripe peach).[2]

At Brighton he made drawings, which he attempted without success to sell at half a crown apiece from the window of a small shop; he also made his first attempt at painting, which he quickly abandoned in discouragement. Eighteen months later he transferred to the London Hospital, where he remained for three years, devoting himself to anatomy and physiology. During all this time he became more and more absorbed by drawing, taking as his subjects both the living and the dead, until it gradually became his ruling passion.

[1] 'Notes from Wander-Years', by Henry Tonks, *Art Work*, Winter, 1929.

[2] From a letter to a friend, quoted in 'The Life of Henry Tonks', by Joseph Hone, 1939, p. 22.

One winter he visited Germany. At Christmas in Dresden occurred one of the critical moments of his life.

One of my family sent me as a present 'The Life of Randolph Caldecott' [he wrote, recalling it]; the flat in Moscincksy Strasse, my room, the position in it of the bed, and the moment of the night when I read how he had, almost by chance, from being a bank clerk, found the way to become the charming artist he was, come back to me with extraordinary vividness. I will not say that I registered a vow at that moment, but the determination of making myself into an artist then became fixed.[1]

On his return, although he won his Fellowship of the Royal College of Surgeons and was appointed Senior Resident Medical Officer at the Royal Free Hospital, he quickly found his way to the 'truly comic and dirty little studio', as he described it, 'which under Frederick Brown became the centre of a revolution which has done much to destroy the powerful vested interests of those days', the London County Council's Technical Institute, Westminster. The association between Tonks and Brown led shortly to the appointment, earlier referred to, which had a decisive effect upon the career of Tonks and upon the draughtsmanship of several generations of students in England.

For the rest of his life Tonks was obsessed by his having reached the age of thirty before he was able to devote his whole energies to drawing and painting. The disadvantage under which he fancied himself to labour on account of a late start in his chosen vocation seems to have aggravated his innate diffidence, and the strain of irascibility he inherited from his father, for he became, especially where his drawing and painting were concerned, a secretive and touchy man. Criticism of any kind was liable to provoke his resentment and to bring him to the verge of despair. No doubt, unknown to them, his angry suspiciousness must have been provoked continually by three of his most intimate friends: by Steer, on account of his wonderful natural gifts, by George Moore, notorious for a strain of obtuseness in his human relations, and by D. S. MacColl, most inveterately critical of men. Moore's criticisms corroded the friendship of Tonks, to whom his death, as he confessed to his intimates, came as a relief. MacColl's more deeply informed judgements

[1] 'Notes from Wander-Years.'

sometimes caused coolness between the two, but they also bore positive fruit in a series of water-colours, *Mr. MacColl visits Heaven and Criticizes*,[1] made during the First World War, which exhibit Tonks's satirical humour and flexible draughtsmanship.

Irascible suspicion, an ingenuity in finding pretexts for offence, with its issue in coolnesses, quarrels and separations, pronounced though they were, did not dominate Tonks's human relations. He possessed, on the contrary, a particular talent for friendship. In social contacts of a casual or routine order, he was inclined to be sarcastic and aloof; he was mostly content to reserve his sociability for the friends of his choice. These he met constantly; with them he maintained a regular correspondence, sometimes, late at night, pursuing by letter the subject of a conversation only just ended. During the latter part of his life he set aside a part of each day, often as much as two hours, for correspondence with his friends. Of them, the closest was Steer, for whom he showed a devotion which never wavered. Among others with whom, at one time or another, he was particularly intimate were, besides Moore and MacColl, Sir Augustus Daniel, already mentioned as the possessor of the finest of Steer's early paintings, for whose judgement he had an exceptional regard, the brothers Laurence and Leonard Harrison, Sargent's sister, Mrs. Ormond, and my father – for whom his friendship turned suddenly to enmity, apparently upon the unwarranted suspicion that he had written a flattering letter to Sargent with a view to securing his election to the Royal Academy[2] – C. H. Collins Baker, and, towards the end of his life, St. John and Mary Hutchinson.

The duality in his nature, which revealed itself in a capacity for friendship of the most constant and intimate kind, together with a proneness to suspicion, secretiveness, jealousy, touchiness and even malignity, was evident in other apparent contradictions. A dour, puritanical strain, revealed by the thin-lipped, sour mouth, the chilly stare, and a fussiness in the ordering of his daily life (he smoked, for instance, at fixed times of day, usually with reference to his watch), seemed incongruous with his sometimes Rabelaisian humour, the faint strain of impropriety apt to reveal itself in his conversation, and the sheer prettiness of much of his art.

[1] Coll. Mrs. St. John Hutchinson.

[2] 'Men and Memories', by Sir William Rothenstein, Vol. II, 1932, pp. 192–3.

With his students his relations were mostly as happy as they were fruitful. The famous sarcasms, which provoked so continuous a profusion of tears among the women students, and for which he has sometimes been blamed, caused little lasting pain, and were, in fact, a characteristic expression of an exhilarating personality whose impact upon the Slade was that of a bracing wind. To students whom he considered to be of promise, in particular, his kindness was proverbial, although his ability to distinguish great talent from promise was far from unerring. He recognized with reluctance the genius of Augustus John (whose influence as a student at the Slade exceeded his own), while the modest geese whom he acclaimed as swans were many.

Tonks was so quintessentially, so almost, on one side of him, parochially English that the discovery that he read with diligence the French intellectual periodicals, and was conversant with the ideas of Valéry and Proust, seemed to me, in spite of the voracity of his intellectual appetite, as hardly less odd than the knowledge that one of the most intense and solemnly high-minded of my painter friends not only never missed the now discontinued Radio Rhythm programme, but was familiar with the careers of even minor composers of swing music.

During the years 1910 and 1912 there occurred events, which will be described at a more appropriate place in these pages, which had a decisive effect upon the outlook of Tonks, and upon perhaps the majority of his generation. These were the two exhibitions of Post-Impressionist painting held at the Grafton Galleries, at which the work of van Gogh, Matisse and Cézanne was first introduced to the British public. Until that time, Tonks's eager intelligence had ranged freely among the arts, in general taking a logical and rather detached view of things. The New English Art Club, where he first showed in 1893 and with which he was closely identified, although conservative by Parisian standards, had been a rallying point, since shortly after its formation, for the most brilliant and adventurous talents. Tonks therefore inevitably counted himself a man of 'progressive' affiliations and sympathies. The presence of serried ranks of Post-Impressionist pictures, fiercely coloured, vehement, harsh, and, to an even greater degree, I imagine, the general aesthetic theories deduced from them by Roger Fry and their other sponsors and supporters, provoked in Tonks a violent revulsion of feeling which resulted in a settled antipathy towards contemporary art, and the conviction that it was the negation of the traditional values to which he had pledged his loyalty. 'I don't believe', he confessed to Daniel, 'I really like any modern development.'[1]

By 1910 Tonks was nearly fifty years old, and the character of both his art and his teaching had assumed a rigid pattern. Had he been content to allow that the new modes of expression were outside his province and even his sympathies, as one who had made up his mind long since upon fundamental principles, and that they posed problems to which younger generations must apply themselves, he would have ridden, with dignity and without adverse effects for himself, the storms which Post-Impressionism raised. But he was not content with an attitude, however critical, of detachment: instead, with sour monotony he elected to condemn. I am not at this point concerned with the degree of justification he had; only with its effects upon himself. These I believe to have been harmful, in that his attitude of condemnation raised a barrier between himself and the most gifted of his younger contemporaries. The last twenty-two years of his life – he died on 8 January 1937 – were spent in an exasperated insulation from the issues which agitated the most creative minds. Was he not, he once disarmingly enquired, 'a crabbed old hopeless piece of wood that had been taken by the flood into a backwater'? Tonks constantly talked and occasionally wrote in denigration of the new directions in the arts; he never, I think, defined his own attitude so lucidly as he did in the course of some reflections upon Proust:

> Artists are perhaps as likely as any to come nearer to the meaning of life: why I hate Post-Impressionism or any form of subjectivity is because they, its followers, do not see that it is only possible to explain the spirit as long as we are in the world, by the things of the world, so that the painting of an old mackintosh (I don't pretend to explain how) very carefully and *realistically* wrought may be much more spiritual than an abstract landscape. There is no short-cut to poetry, it has to be dug by the sweat of his brow out of the earth, and it comes to a man without his knowing it; in fact one must never look for it. Of course it sounds absurd seeing the dreadful things we do, but a painter who is not a poet ought to be put in the stocks.[2]

[1] Hone, p. 191.   [2] Op. cit., p. 272.

One great quality Tonks possessed in common with his friend Moore: an inflexible will to succeed. Both were almost without natural talent; both, by sheer effort of will, made themselves serious artists. The early works of Tonks, drawings and paintings alike, were dry, slight and affected, self-conscious Pre-Raphaelite echoes, *A Lady in her Garden*, for example, of 1894, which belonged to Frederick Brown, is characteristic of his work during his early years at the Slade. The late start, which he so frequently lamented, was, I suspect, the spur that pricked him remorselessly onwards. He drew, he painted, he studied the methods of the masters; he was never satisfied, no artist was less complacent than he. Slowly his drawing began to express his hardly won grasp of construction and gesture, and his painting the solidity and the variety of light-suffused colour and the vernal, romantic atmosphere for which he struggled. Among his own paintings I fancy that *The Crystal Gazers*,[1] of 1906, was the one in which he considered that his aspirations were most nearly fulfilled. Most, perhaps, of Tonks's admirers would incline rather to agree with Mr. Collins Baker that none of his works stands so surely for his highest endeavour as *Spring Days*,[2] of about 1928-9. In any case, the two pictures have much in common. The themes of both are pairs of young girls in sunlit rooms, of whom one is absently engaged upon a domestic task, the other withdrawn in dreamy meditation. Both pictures the artist has succeeded in endowing with a certain enchantment. The enchantment fades a little, it seems to me, under close scrutiny. In the earlier picture, for instance, the figure of the girl holding the crystal is perceived to constitute a vast and shapeless mass, in itself ungainly to the point of absurdity and bearing no proportion to the shapely head and shoulders. In drawing this figure, the artist, evidently working close up to the model, has been mesmerized by his ruler and has neglected to use his eyes. The effect of the foreshortening of the corresponding figure in the later picture, although less flagrant, is to make it awkward and bunchy; and the two figures, moreover, have only the most perfunctory formal relation to each other. It is not, however, errors in drawing and other technical defects, serious as they are, which arrest the spectator's delight in pictures which abound in obvious beauties; it is something more radical than these. In the passage just quoted

[1] Formerly Coll. Mr. Leonard Harrison.   [2] The Tate Gallery, London.

from Tonks's writings, he observes with wisdom that 'there is no short-cut to poetry . . . it comes to a man without his knowing it; in fact one must never look for it'. How interesting an anthology could be made of wise precepts, and of instances of their authors' neglect to observe them! For surely in no two pictures has poetry been looked for with so obvious and, it may be said, with so laborious a pertinacity; never has every short-cut been more assiduously explored, lovely girls young and dream-rapt, enveloped in an atmosphere of sunlight and elegance. Nor is there any earth for the poetry to be dug from. Even Mr. Collins Baker would hesitate to claim that the hardly-won poetry in these two pictures came to the artist 'without his knowing it'. Superior to both these pictures is, I think, a cracked ghost of a picture, *The Hat Shop* (Plate 9),[1] of 1897. In this work, so ardently admired by George Moore, from the earth, so to speak, of an ordinary hat-shop the artist has dug up authentic poetry, compounded of elegance and a mysterious, almost haunted spaciousness. Another and much later picture in which he has wonderfully succeeded in a similar feat is *An Advanced Clearing Station in France*,[2] of 1918, a monumental work in the authentic academic tradition.

Tonks cherished a passionate belief in poetic painting. ('A painter who is not a poet ought to be put in the stocks.') There would seem to be something in common between the strenuous aspirations of Tonks after poetic painting and the sense of obligation felt by many English artists of the late eighteenth and early nineteenth centuries to paint historical pictures. If only they had been content to represent closely observed contemporary subjects instead of personified virtues and vices, how much anguished perversion of talent to unsuitable ends and how many pretentious failures – even from the brushes of Hogarth and Reynolds – would have been avoided. *Spring Days* is a far better picture than *Sigismunda Mourning over the Heart of Guiscardo*, or the various versions of *The Snake in the Grass*, yet when I see one of the too rare examples of the kind of painting for which Tonks's qualities best adapted him, it seems to me that these poetic pictures are the fruit, if not of their perversion, at any

[1] Formerly Coll. Sir Augustus Daniel, acquired and restored by the City Art Gallery and Museum, Birmingham, 1951.

[2] The Imperial War Museum, London.

rate of their diversion from their proper ends. I refer to the small series of interiors with figures of friends or familiars, such as *Steer at Home on Christmas Day with Nurse*,[1] of about 1928, *An Evening at the Vale*,[2] of 1929, and *Sodales: Mr. Steer and Mr. Sickert*,[3] of 1930. These paintings, which are closely related to his own caricatures, derive from the satirical group-portraits of Hogarth, Reynolds and Patch. The satire is gentle, almost tender, in *The Evening at the Vale*, although Moore wrote angrily that he had been represented as 'a flabby old cook' and the artist himself as 'an elegant young man striking an attitude like a demi-god against the mantelpiece, and he is nearly as old as I am'. In *Steer at Home on Christmas Day with Nurse*, where his friend is shown pouring tea for his formidable house keeper, Mrs. Raynes, and for her friends, the satire is broader but not less affectionate; in *Sodales* it is uproarious.

All these paintings abound in 'earth', from which the artist has dug to good purpose, and, in unaffected innocence, has discovered abundance of genial and acutely perceptive poetry. Because he has worked in a vein so entirely natural to him, and because he has followed so closely his own wise precepts, the spectator is conscious of nothing of the painful strain under which he laboured in order to create, or rather, perhaps, to piece together, the various beauties in the ostensibly 'poetic' pictures. The figures, on the contrary, fall so easily into place that they seem to be real people, inevitably, indubitably present. The three more elaborate pieces, on account of the expressive and harmonious formal relations between the sharply contrasting and incisively characterized personalities, and of the intimate atmosphere which unites them, take their places among the best conversation-pieces of our time. *Sodales* presents the critic with a more difficult task, in that there is a puzzling disproportion between the means and the effects which they produce. The means in the 'poetic' pictures are of a formidable elaboration. In *Sodales*, they are elementary and at points frankly imperfect. The drawing of Steer is woolly; Sickert is incompletely related to his background, and the whole composition is too shallow for comfort. Yet how little these imperfections appear to compromise the effect of richness,

[1] The Slade School, London.
[2] The Tate Gallery, London. Another version exists.
[3] Formerly Coll. Mrs. Ormond.

energy and character that the picture unquestionably has! Perhaps it is, after all, the very detachment of Mr. Sickert from his surroundings which so eloquently depicts him as a bizarre wanderer who, just for an hour or two, has blown into the snug world of Mr. Steer. It is my own belief, at all events, that it is upon these too few conversation-pieces that the reputation of Tonks as a painter will principally rest.

LUCIEN PISSARRO

1863—1944

THE path of Lucien Pissarro was as straight and untrammelled as Tonks's was circuitous and beset by chance. Of all contemporary painters at work in England, Lucien Pissarro was the most completely prepared for his profession. From his infancy it was assumed, in the face of the stubborn opposition of his mother, that there existed only one vocation for him, and as soon as he was able to hold pencil and brush he was taught by Camille Pissarro, his father. Whenever the two were separated, the father addressed to the son a stream of letters, which, when they were first published in 1943, were immediately recognized as documents of the first importance to students of nineteenth-century painting.[1] In these almost daily letters written for the instruction and encouragement of his son, Camille spoke with perfect candour and illuminating insight of his contemporaries, especially his great fellow Impressionists, and with unrivalled authority of the problems of vision and technique which preoccupied them all. So that when most of his own contemporaries were groping in provincial obfuscity, Lucien was the recipient of a continuous inner history of the art world of Paris during the most brilliant epoch of modern painting from the pen of one of its masters.

Lucien Pissarro was born in Paris on 20 February 1863, the eldest of seven children, of whom all five brothers became artists, but he spent his boyhood at Osny near Pontoise, where his parents lived. All the boys showed at an early age powers of observation and draughtsmanship in which their father frankly delighted, but their mother, too familiar with the privations and griefs which harass the lives of materially unsuccessful artists, was bitterly averse to their following her husband's vocation. In order in a small measure to alleviate his family's poverty, Lucien left his school at Pontoise at the age of fifteen and went to work in Paris for a firm which sold English fabrics, but his employer eventually told his father that he

---

[1] 'Camille Pissarro: Letters to His Son.' Edited with the assistance of Lucien Pissarro by John Rewald.

was an excellent boy, but lacking any trace of talent for business. In 1883 he was sent to London to learn English, where he lodged at the house in Holloway of his uncle by marriage, Phineas Isaacson, whose wife was half-sister to Camille Pissarro, and supported himself by working with Messrs. Weber & Company, music publishers, at 84 New Bond Street. This employment stimulated his musical taste: he regularly attended concerts and gained a fair knowledge of the works of the classical composers. He did not continue long in this occupation, for in the following year his parents moved from Osny to Eragny, a village not far from Gisors, and they required his help, both in this undertaking and on account of their unusually straightened circumstances. Not long after the family was established in their new home, he went to work in Paris with the lithographers Manzi Joyant. This experience proved invaluable, for in the studios of the firm he became familiar with the various processes of colour reproduction. In the evenings, with his friend, the artist Louis Hayet, he either drew from the model at an obscure school in the Rue Brequel, or frequented cafés and music-halls to make studies; in addition, he continued to paint. Slowly he began to make a modest reputation. In 1886, for instance, he was commissioned by the editor of 'La Revue Illustrée', F. G. Dumas, to make four woodcuts as illustrations for 'Mait' Liziard', a story by Octave Mirbeau. These woodcuts clearly show the influence of Charles Keene, who was admired in the Impressionist circle and whose engravings for 'Punch' Lucien collected.

It was in that same year that Lucien, together with his father, came to be intimately linked with Seurat and Signac, and an enthusiastic participant in the Neo-Impressionist movement of which these two were the originators. Already in the following year, Camille Pissarro – deeply implicated in the Impressionism of which the new movement was in some measure a repudiation, and the possessor of a temperament too spontaneous and a hand too vigorously expressive not to feel cramped by its rigid procedures – began to recede from it. But it was not until some years later that he abandoned the practice of divisionism. Upon Lucien the impact of Neo-Impressionism was lasting in its effects. He belonged by birth to the generation which was acutely conscious of the disorderly, fugitive elements in the earlier, in what his father termed

9. HENRY TONKS. *The Hat Shop* (1897).
Oil, 26×36 in. The City Art Gallery & Museum, Birmingham.

10. LUCIEN PISSARRO. *Ivy Cottage, Coldharbour* (1916).
Oil, 20¾ × 24½ in. The Tate Gallery, London.

'romantic', Impressionism; his personal relations with Seurat, Signac and Félix Fénéon, the principal literary advocate of Neo-Impressionism, were close. What is more important, Lucien was without the particular qualities which the discipline of the movement repressed. He was thus able to continue in harmony with the most vigorous and fruitful impulse of the time – that of restoring the imagination and conscious architectural design to their rightful places in painting – and in harmony with his friends. And in harmony, above all, with his own particular vision. But he was not infected by the air of pedantry which hung about the movement. It is to be expected that the son of a master, especially when he has much in common with him, should be dismissed as a shadow of his father. Lucien Pissarro, on account of his innate affinities with a father who inspired in him an unreserved and unclouded devotion and his own modest, unassertive character, was particularly exposed to denigration of this sort. In comparison with those of Camille, his gifts were of a secondary order: he was an altogether tamer, less creative figure, but to call him a mere shadow is to do him much less than justice. His father, for all his devotion to his favourite son, praised him sparingly. He told him, however, that delicacy and distinction were his outstanding qualities, and that he possessed naïve good faith and a discreet reserve. These certainly are not the supreme attributes of a painter, but, cultivated with the single-heartedness and sober judgement of Lucien Pissarro, they produced an art which was sensitive, dignified and consistent. In the best of his paintings the forms, thoughtfully disposed, scrupulously realized, scintillate with a sober, even luminosity. This artist's vision had reached its maturity by the time he was in his early twenties, and he spent the remainder of his life in the unremitting effort to strengthen and purify it.

Lucien Pissarro was represented with his father, Degas, Mary Cassatt, Berthe Morisot, Gauguin, Redon and Seurat at what was, in fact, the eighth and last Impressionist Exhibition (although, on the insistence of Degas, the word 'Impressionist' was omitted from the announcement of it), held above the Restaurant Doré at the corner of the Rue Lafitte and the Boulevard des Italiens from 15 May to 15 June 1886.

In November 1890 he took the decisive step of settling permanently in England; in 1916 he became a British subject. The most compelling of the several reasons which prompted this migration was fear of his father's influence. Letters show how the effects of Camille's mighty talent upon theirs, tentative and unformed, preoccupied both father and sons: 'I know you fear my influence, but there is such a thing as going too far'; 'It has to be England, for here I am a hindrance to you all'; 'I feel you are still too close to my work'. But Lucien was also moved by other considerations, of which the chief was his want of success in Paris as an illustrator of books. Only the commonplace in conception and the mechanical in execution, it seemed to him, were acceptable in France. England, on the contrary, he regarded as the country where the inspiring revival in the making of books, which originated with William Morris, was still in progress. From this movement he expected to learn and to it he aspired to make his contribution. He took a small painting-room and tried, without success, to support himself by giving lessons in drawing and engraving to private pupils. Thanks to introductions from Fénéon and Mirbeau, he met English writers and artists. One of these was the poet John Gray,[1] author of 'Silverpoints', who was soon to enter the priesthood of the Catholic Church. Gray performed a valuable service to Lucien by introducing him to Charles Ricketts, for many years his closest English friend and most influential mentor. Through Ricketts the world of book illustration, typography and binding was immediately open to him. Ricketts and his intimate friend, Charles Shannon, invited him to contribute to their elegant and esoteric journal, 'The Dial', illustrated with woodcuts, the first number of which was published in the previous year. Woodcuts by Lucien appear in the second number, published in February 1891. In 1892 he married Esther Bensusan, a distant relative, and Camille Pissarro came over for the wedding. After a visit to France, the young couple settled in April 1893 in Epping, at a house in Hemnall Street which he called Eragny, in honour of his father. Here, in 1894, he established the Eragny Press. He had already printed two folios of woodcuts, of which the second, *Les Travaux des Champs*, contained six subjects designed and drawn upon the wood by his father. The first book to issue from the Eragny Press,

[1] Erroneously described by John Rewald as an artist. 'Camille Pissaro: Letters to His Son Lucien', p. 137.

'The Queen of the Fishes', was handwritten and the text reproduced by process. Of the thirty-five books produced by the Press, a series of sixteen was printed in the Vale type, designed by Ricketts, who lent it to the Pissarros (for Esther quickly showed herself a conscientious and skilful assistant), and a later series, similar in number, appeared between 1903 and 1914, in the Brook type that Lucien designed.

It was not long before he took an honourable place in the small group of artist-craftsmen-printers, of which Morris was the first and Ricketts, at the time of Lucien's arrival in England, the most active. 'Unity, harmony, such are the essentials of fine book building', Ricketts declared. 'A work of art is a whole in which each portion is exquisite in itself yet co-ordinated.' Of them all, Lucien strove the most uncompromisingly after the unity of which Ricketts spoke. In his later books, he not only designed and cut the type, but he designed and, with the help of his wife, engraved the illustrations and embellishments, thus dispensing with the services of the professional wood-engraver (upon whom even Morris had depended), and he made their bindings.

This is not the place to dwell upon the achievements of Lucien Pissarro as a designer and maker of books, but the feature of it most nearly related to his painting calls for mention – namely, his use of colour. It would have been surprising if an artist so deeply imbued with Impressionism had not expressed it in his books as well as his painting, and in fact the distinguishing feature of the products of the Eragny Press was their delicate colour and tone. His double preoccupation with unity and with colour led him on occasion to knit his coloured woodcuts closely to his text by printing it, instead of in black, in muted greens and greys. His successful use of colour as a primary element within a completely harmonious whole was his most enduring achievement in this field.

The Pissarros remained at Eragny House, occupied chiefly with the making of books, until 1897, when they moved to London, living at 63 Bath Road, Bedford Park, until 1900, when they settled at a house known as The Brook at Stamford Brook, where they made their home until the death of Lucien on 10 July 1944 at Hewood, Somerset. The stables at The Brook, a pleasant Georgian house, were adapted for a studio.

During its earlier years the Eragny Press absorbed the greater part of his energies, but he was continuously active as a painter. At Epping his contacts with his fellow painters were comparatively few, but his establishment in London marked a change – gradual, but eventually notable – in the position he occupied among them. As a young man he was inclined at times to be irresolute in his aims and fitful in his habits of work. In the 'Letters' there is evidence of his father's awareness of these defects. After Lucien's illness in the spring of 1897, for instance (when Camille had come to England to bring him, Esther and their daughter Orovida back to Eragny), it seemed to him that his eldest son was prolonging his convalescence unduly. 'I hope that now you are back in your own circle', he wrote,[1] 'you will be able to work. You must give proof of will-power; it is also a question of habit. With a little courage you will succeed.' But as Lucien passed from youth to middle age his self-confidence and his industry increased. As the fame of the Impressionists grew steadily in England, the son of one of the most illustrious among them came to be regarded with a kind of reverential respect. Before, however, he was able to speak with authority as his father's son and out of his own experience as a painter, a valued friendship had to be broken. Increased knowledge of Impressionism, while it inspired the ablest among the younger painters, confirmed in their seniors a bitter prejudice against it. Among the militant sharers of this prejudice was Ricketts. Camille Pissarro was concerned at the 'Italian influence of Ricketts' over his eldest son: '. . . you give me the impression that you listen only to him', he complained.[2] The influence of Ricketts over Lucien as an engraver and a maker of books, as a typographer above all, was constant and valuable; as a painter it was negligible. The eager susceptibility Lucien showed on the one side and the indifferent imperviousness on the other has puzzled certain of his admirers, but I think with little cause. He was consistent in each instance in that he adhered to the more vigorous tradition, but his course was determined by consistency upon a deeper level than that where conscious judgements are formed. As a boy he had given himself heart and mind to the Impressionism taught him by his father. As a young emigrant in England, he had also identified himself, and with scarcely less reserve, with the

[1] 23 October 1897.   [2] 12 July 1900.

tradition of William Morris as an engraver and a maker of books.
To have abandoned either would have been at variance with the
unyielding constancy of his nature. Lucien's quiet adherence to the
principles of an eminent father was understandable, a trait even to be
respected in a young man, especially as they long continued to be
little understood. But as gradually these principles made more of a
stir in the world, and gained numerous adherents, and Lucien, no
longer a reserved youth, became their respected advocate, the days
of his friendship with Ricketts were numbered. How easy to understand the growing coolness towards his young friend of the dictatorial Ricketts, hostile to realism as the enemy of the imagination,
and impatient of rival preachers, especially young disciples of his
own who set themselves up in middle life as preachers of heresy!
It is not therefore surprising that the day came when Ricketts passed
Lucien by without recognition.

Lucien continued, as I have said, to produce books until the
closure, in 1914, of the Eragny Press, but for the better part of a
decade painting may be said to have been his most constant preoccupation. His vision was steady and sensitive rather than original,
and his technique was solidly adequate rather than brilliant, but
everything he did was marked by a delicate perceptiveness and a
gentle candour. A certain unworldliness, a detachment from intrigue,
are somehow mirrored in his art. The paintings of Lucien did not
excite either passionate admiration or passionate censure, but they
were held in a constantly growing regard. And the artist himself,
his earlier hesitancies and want of urgency gradually outgrown,
exerted a positive and fruitful influence, not only upon Sickert, but
upon the chief personalities of a younger generation. But as learning
is more important than teaching, I will defer treating of his influence
until I come to write of the school of painters which he helped to
establish.

After his first penurious years in England, he never consented to
give formal instruction in drawing or painting, but he used to invite
serious students who approached him to bring their work to his
studio. His quick and accurate discernment of the needs of students,
and his quiet, modest fashion of responding to them, spread his
influence among a widening circle of younger painters.

From the time of the return of Sickert to England from Venice in 1905 and for several years afterwards Pissarro and he were on close and friendly terms. The focus of their association, the focus, too, of the activities of the most gifted among the younger generation, was the memorable meetings at 19 Fitzroy Street. Each member of the group which formed here around Pissarro and Sickert had the right to a rack to store his pictures and to an easel upon which to show them to the numerous persons who became interested in this novel point of contact with honoured exponents of the Impressionist tradition and a group of young painters of conspicuous talent, in this novel means of circumventing the dealers with their burdensome commissions and the exhibiting societies with their rigid and undemocratic constitutions. Saturdays were the days when the 'members' entertained their friends, showed and sometimes sold their work. At lunchtime they would adjourn to the Etoile in neighbouring Charlotte Street. These 'Saturdays', Ricketts's and Shannon's 'Friday evenings', and the second and fourth Sundays in every month when Lucien entertained his friends at The Brook (in fair numbers for tea; a smaller company of the more intimate were privily invited to remain to supper), became the principal events of his social life. At his own somewhat studious but hospitable evenings, spent in serious talk and study of his excellent collection of prints and illustrated books, among the most regular guests were his associates of 19 Fitzroy Street, Thomas Sturge Moore, the poet, Campbell Dodgson, Keeper of the Print Room of the British Museum, Ethel Walker, William Rothenstein and, until the final breach, Ricketts and Shannon. Pissarro exhibited with the Camden Town Group (which grew out of 19 Fitzroy Street) in 1911, with the New English Art Club from 1906, at the Allied Artists, and his first one-man exhibition was held at the Carfax Gallery in May 1913. The last considerable exhibition of his work to be held during his lifetime at Millers in Sussex, 'Three Generations of Pissarros', in which his father and his daughter Orovida were also well represented, I had the privilege of opening. I remember how proud I was to have been invited to perform the ceremony, and how he behaved as though it were they who were indebted to me. I can see him very clearly against the Pissarro paintings and drawings, among the crowd which had gathered in Lewes from all parts of Sussex, his short, stout figure, his full white beard shot with black, his cloak, his black wide-brimmed hat, and, behind the thick lenses of his spectacles, his slightly protuberant dark eyes; I remember the grave and gentle expression they radiated. Just as he had nothing of 'the melancholy, harsh and savage' elements which his father noted in his own temperament, or of his pungency as painter or writer (it would never, for instance, have occurred to Lucien to say, with reference to his politics, 'Gauguin . . . is always on the side of the bastards'), so his art differed from that of Camille. The father's was fluent and direct; the son's was conscientious and constructive. Lucien derived his palette from his father as a boy at Eragny, and his conception of design – the forthright, somewhat rigid system of design partly imposed upon, partly discerned in nature – from his Neo-Impressionist contemporaries, Seurat and Signac, but he gradually modified the uncompromising divisionism which they taught him. No new impulse would seem to have affected his tranquil, sensitive and deeply honest development of an outlook and of methods acquired early in his life. His painting therefore changed little – his brush strokes became rather shorter, less vigorous, but more sensitive as he grew older, and the quality of his paint a trifle drier – but the centre of gravity remained precisely where it was: no painter at work in England during the present century showed a greater consistency of aim than Lucien Pissarro.

JAMES PRYDE

1866—1941

THERE are certain painters about whom I find it difficult to determine whether they succeeded in expressing some important element in human life, or whether they produced, with whatever integrity and accomplishment, what are, in the last analysis, mere variants of existing works. I catch myself peering, as it were, into the faces of artists living or remembered, whose works I have pondered, and trying to read there the answers to my doubts – doubts which a future historian will find it easy to resolve – into the venerable face of George Clausen,[1] nobly marked by sixty years of humble and devoted dedication to painting, or at the fresh handsome face of Charles Shannon,[2] which carried even into old age the same unsullied spiritual look it had worn when he was a youth, I am conscious of a painful sense of arrogance in ignoring in these pages their solid, honourable achievements. But I am compelled to the conclusion that the art of the one is an unreflective projection of the art of Bastien-Lepage and that of the other of the art of Watts,

[1] *Sir George Clausen*, 1852–1944, figure and landscape painter of scenes of rural life, influenced by the French plein-air school and Impressionism; also author of occasional decorations. Born in London, 18 April 1852, son of a decorative painter of Danish descent. Studied at South Kensington under Edwin Long, and in Paris at the Académie Julian. Also visited Belgium and Holland. An original member of the New English Art Club, 1886; A.R.A., 1895; R.A., 1908; R.W.S., 1898. Professor of Painting in R.A. schools, and author of 'Six Lectures on Painting', 1904, and 'Aims and Ideals in Art', 1906. Knighted, 1927. Died 23 November 1944 at Cold Ash, near Newbury, Berks.

[2] *Charles Haslewood Shannon*, 1863–1937, painter of figure subjects and portraits, illustrator and connoisseur. His paintings often reveal a scholarly indebtedness to the Old Masters, especially to the tradition of Titian and Giorgione. Born at Quarrington, Lincolnshire, 26 April 1863, son of the Rector. Studied at the Lambeth School of Art, where he met Charles Ricketts, his lifelong companion, with whom he collaborated in the Vale Press and the *Dial*. A.R.A., 1911; R.A., 1920. Incapacitated after a fall from a ladder in 1929. Died at Kew, near London, 18 March 1937. The greater part of the works of art he and Ricketts had collected was left to the Fitzwilliam Museum, Cambridge.

both of which lack the principle of organic growth; that they belonged to that category of artists whom Northcote described as
cisterns rather than living streams. I am the more conscious that my
judgement may be at fault in that I propose to consider an artist
who, in comparison with Clausen and Shannon, was deficient in
creative power and in skill and, what was worse, in belief in his own
vision – in fact, a failure, James Pryde. My justification is the
originality and the consistency of the vision that was his, which,
however, he lacked both the intellectual power to organize and the
energy to develop.

James Ferrier Pryde was born in Edinburgh on 30 March 1866.
The circumstances of his early life conspired to foster, if not to
stimulate unduly, a highly romantic imagination. Every important
element in his vision derived from his earliest days, and it is no
exaggeration to say that no subsequent experience changed or added
to it. The house in which Pryde was born, and where he spent his
first two years, was as tall and sombre as a building in one of his
own paintings. After an eight-year suburban interlude, his parents
established themselves in Fettes Row, where they lived for twenty
years, first at No. 22, moving two years later to No. 10. This house,
also high, narrow, dark, was lit by a chilly north light; its narrow
staircase mounted steeply up and up through a sombre half-light.
This narrowness, gloom and perpendicularity made an impression
which deepened with the passage of the years. At either end of
Fettes Row stand two churches which would further have encouraged his predeliction for the tall and the impressive, and made him
aware of the dramatic possibilities of columns and steps. Although
it offers the sharpest contrast in architectural style to the New Town
in which Pryde passed his boyhood, the Old Town, with its narrow
streets of gaunt and gloomy tenement buildings and washing flutter-
ing from the windows, ministered to his same abiding sense of the
beauty of grandiose dereliction. There was one particular object, the
great four-poster bed of Mary Queen of Scots at Holyrood, that
haunted his imagination for at least as long as he was able to paint.
The importance of Edinburgh in the shaping and furnishing of his
mind, apparent to any student of his art, is acknowledged in a brief
autobiographical fragment. 'To me,' he wrote, 'it is the most
romantic city in the world. . . . I was very much impressed with the

spirit of Holyrood, the Castle, and the old houses and Close, in the High Street.'[1]

But there must have been thousands of young men and women in Edinburgh whose imaginations were stirred by the sombre architecture of that wonderful city; environment moves readily enough to poetic imaginings, but rarely, of itself, to their transmutation into art. There was one improbable circumstance of Pryde's home life which made him familiar with the idea of transmutations of such a kind: his whole family, from his father, Dr. David Pryde (from 1870 Headmaster of the Edinburgh Ladies' College) downwards, was stage-struck. Irving had played in Edinburgh in the 'fifties, and the admiration which Dr. Pryde then formed for him, communicated to his wife and children, became a hysterical family cult. There is reason to suppose that James Pryde, besides participating in the solemn rites of Irving worship, was addicted to more popular devotions in the shape of attendance of the 'penny gaffs', the boisterous shows held in street booths behind the Royal Scottish Academy. Besides giving him an insight into a living art which made the prospect of his becoming an artist appear an immediate possibility instead of a perilous voyage into the unknown, his associations with the theatre made a deep and manifold impression upon both his life and his art. They inspired in him the ambition, intermittently and lamely realized, of becoming an actor himself; they began a connection with the theatrical world which lasted until the end of his life, and they stamped his personality with something of the actor, and his painting with the character of stage scenery.

By his early twenties he would seem to have been possessed of almost all his assets as an artist. At what periods of his life he became familiar with Hogarth, Velazquez, Guardi and Piranesi is unknown. The study of the work of all these artists was of manifest value to him. From them he must have gained an enhanced confidence in his own highly personal way of looking at the world; from them he evidently learned much about the making of pictures, and, it must be said, a repertory of pictorial mannerisms. Pryde's biographer discovered, for instance, that he possessed a photograph of Velazquez' *View from the Villa Medici: La Tarde*, and he considers it

[1] 'James Pryde', by Derek Hudson, 1949, p. 20.

probable that it was from this picture that Pryde appropriated several of his favourite themes, notably the high archway, boarded up in a manner to give it a look of dereliction, the tall cypresses, the eroded statue, the balustrade with the drapery hung over it. But although by his twenties he had reached the fulness of his growth, the time was not yet come for him to blossom in his fulness as a painter. How gifted and serious an artist he was is apparent from the charcoal drawing he made about 1886 of *Miss Jessie Burnet*,[1] a study of a young girl which puts one in mind of a Gwen John, only it is fuller, and finished with the conscientiousness of a beginner.

After the end of Pryde's desultory studies at the Royal Scottish Academy School and a brief visit to Paris without apparent consequence to his art, he settled in 1890 in England. Chance, however, at first directed his energies not towards painting but to the designing of posters. Mabel, one of his five sisters, an original character, met William Nicholson, a fellow student under Herkomer at his imitation Beyreuth school at Bushey, and after a singular courtship the two were married, and they established themselves in the spring of 1893 at The Eight Bells, a small former public-house at Denham, Buckinghamshire. A day or two after their arrival James Pryde came for a week-end and remained for two years. The visit led to the fruitful collaboration of Pryde and Nicholson as 'J. & W. Beggarstaff', who designed the best posters that had been seen in England. There is a sharp division of opinion as to whether Pryde or Nicholson was the dominant partner. That question is outside the scope of this book. The chorus of well-merited praise of the Beggarstaffs' posters has obscured the probability that the collaboration was prejudicial to Pryde's prospects as a painter. Pryde was lazy, and the habit of imagining in such broad, simplified terms as poster-designing demanded and his dependence upon his energetic brother-in-law to do the greater part of the executive work must have fostered a laziness which showed itself in the emptiness of much of Pryde's later painting, and in a disposition never to do for himself what he could persuade others to do for him.

In the autobiographical fragment earlier referred to, Pryde observed that the early impressions gained in Edinburgh did not affect his work until considerably later. It was about 1905 that the

[1] Coll. Mrs. G. K. Menzies.

emotions with which his early years in Edinburgh had charged his mind began to show themselves – emotions which, during the fifteen years or so since his departure, had been growing, as it were underground, in strength and clarity. With a curious suddenness, they fused into a vision romantic, dignified, sombre and highly personal, which, for the next twenty years, was expressed in a series of paintings of imaginary architectural compositions with small figures. Owing to Pryde's habit of giving the same title to several pictures, which may have been due to carelessness, perhaps even to a deliberate intention to mystify, the dates of his pictures are difficult to ascertain. The earliest of his architectural compositions was probably *Guildhall with Figures*, first exhibited in 1905, purchased by Sargent and subsequently lost. The architectural compositions are beyond question Pryde's original contribution to painting. Thirteen of them had as their principal feature a great bed, based upon his early memories of the bed of Mary Queen of Scots at Holyrood.

At first sight there is something deeply impressive about the best of these compositions; there is something about them which, even after the critical faculty has been provoked, lingers in the memory. It would hardly be possible to forget the way of seeing which Pryde for a few moments compels even the most recalcitrant to share. For to Pryde belonged one of the qualities of a great imaginative artist of imposing his vision by the force of sheer conviction. Augustus John, in the course of a brief description of his visits to Pryde's studio, indicates the particular character of these architectural pictures.

This studio [he wrote] had the lofty, dignified and slightly sinister distinction of his own compositions. Upon the easel stood the carefully unfinished and perennial masterpiece, displaying under an ominous green sky the dilapidated architectural grandeur of a building, haunted rather than tenanted by the unclassified tatterdemalions of Jimmy's dreams.[1]

The tall, derelict buildings, the high rooms, darkly painted and harshly coloured, convey a powerful suggestion of a malignant and inescapable fate overhanging man. Pryde has been likened to Poe, but he is closer to Hardy. But even the best of Pryde's paintings will not

[1] 'James Pryde', by Derek Hudson, p. 82.

withstand scrutiny. The general impression they leave is lasting, because there was something memorable and unique about his way of seeing, but it may be fairly said that never, in one single instance, did he succeed in giving it form which will long satisfy an exacting eye. I remember years ago saying of a picture in the presence of Gordon Craig that it was too theatrical for my taste, and how sharply he rebuked me with the words, 'And why shouldn't it be theatrical?' The answer which I was too slow to give is, I suppose, that the quality of theatricality, with its appeal to ephemeral emotions, is proper to a play, because when the curtain is rung down nothing remains, but improper in a work of art intended for prolonged scrutiny. And the defect of Pryde's painting is its theatricality: it is designed to make only a momentary impression. The spectator, suspicious of the degree to which his emotions have been played upon, becomes coolly critical, and his attitude hardens as he notes, one after another, the crude devices the artist has employed. The unvarying and excessive disparity in scale, for instance, between his buildings and his human beings is perceived to be grotesque. The doors are so vast that nobody could push them open. He notes, too, the slipshod manner in which these crude devices are constructed, the poverty and flimsiness of forms which at first seemed so imposing, and the way in which most of the pictures are designed, according to a formula, in three planes parallel to the picture surface, each separated from the other by a pace or two, like drop-scenes in a theatre. The art of Pryde, in fact, is lacking in all the qualities of good, let alone of great painting, except for the vigorous and consistent vision which he was never able fully to realize. Or, rather, which he was not equipped fully to realize in paint. Pryde's gifts fitted him ideally for the theatre, where his particular defects would not have mattered. The theatre was alive to his talents: both Gordon Craig and Lovat Fraser were deeply in his debt, and after he had all but ceased to paint, his theatrical sense was recognized by an American producer, Miss Ellen Van Volkenburg, who induced him to design the scenery for Paul Robeson's 'Othello' at the Savoy Theatre in 1930. Pryde himself was always drawn to the theatre; from time to time he played a small part himself. In the summer of 1895 he toured with Gordon Craig, taking the part of the priest in the last act of 'Hamlet', and another priest in 'Villon', a one-act play.

As an actor [wrote Craig] he never really existed: but the idea of acting, the idea of the theatre – or rather the smell of the place – meant lots to him. Yes, I think he got much 'inspiration' from the boards – and the thought and feel of it all, as of a magical place. . . . There were little moments when in a bar or in the street he would put on the actor, as it were. He thought well of his own 'stage personality' off the stage: on it, it all vanished. But I'll swear he saw into the marvellous possibilities.[1]

Pryde not only thought well of his stage personality; he came to regard the world as a stage. Four sentences from Augustus John's account of him, already quoted from, bring back to abounding life the Pryde of the later years:

Jimmy had been an actor and he still seemed to be playing a leading part in some robust old melodrama. Whatever his role might have been, it was a congenial one and he hadn't seen fit to remove his make-up. The performance in fact was non-stop and must have put a strain on even his constitution. When I last saw him in 'Rules', Maiden Lane, it looked as if it were almost time to ring the curtain down.[2]

My father has noted his passion for dressing up as Pierrot, and another friend described him so dressed and playing the harmonium on Southwold beach. His everyday appearance continually engaged his attention: his attitudes were studied and practised, and his dress was the product of serious thought. He took pleasure in the contrast between the bohemian appearance of his brother artists, sporting ear-rings and hobnailed boots, beards and cloaks, and his own dandified and dignified but not less distinctive appearance in a long maroon overcoat with enormous buttons, and a velvet collar and a plush top-hat such as cabbies wore.

The contrast which Gordon Craig observed between Pryde's inability to act and his enchantment with the idea of acting and his sense of the theatre as a magical place, is in some degree paralleled by his inability to find forms to express, nobly and exactly, his sense of the grandeur of a towering dilapidated building or of a high, curtained bed and the littleness of the human figures which they overshadow. In a moment of exultation, his biographer acclaimed Pryde as the greatest painter since Turner. For making this and other high claims for his subject, Mr. Hudson was taken to task by various

[1] Op. cit., pp. 37–8.   [2] Op. cit., p. 82.

reviewers. The suggestion that Pryde could hold his own with
Turner as a painter will not, of course, bear an instant's calm reflection, but a comparison between Pryde the painter and Turner the
poet, would not be irrelevant; between the series of high, derelict
buildings and rooms and beds, sombrely shadowed and gloweringly
lit, and the inept and never completed 'Fallacies of Hope'. To press
the comparison would be unfair to Pryde, but the painting of Pryde,
like the poetry of Turner, conveys, for all its imperfection, intimations of a vision more powerful and more deeply felt than its maker
was able to express. It is for the occasional glimpses they afford of a
harsh, gloomy but authentic poetry that the best of Pryde's paintings
deserve to be remembered.

The comparative study of the careers of artists shows how little,
by themselves, even high gifts of mind and hand are able to achieve
unless they are directed by an unfailing purpose. In every generation
many artists gifted – and gifted sometimes abundantly – with the
first two, but who lack the last, vanish without trace. Pryde lacked
it totally, so that neither the power and consistency of his vision nor
his skill as a draughtsman availed to arrest his premature decay as an
artist. Very early in his life he showed a broad vein of irresponsibility
not only towards his obligations as a citizen, but also as an artist. It
mattered little that he upset coffee-stalls upon their owners and
patrons, that he engaged in street fights or that he was frequently in
hiding from his creditors or that he drank heavily. Artists who have
been guilty of all these and more, from Benvenuto Cellini to our
own time, have succeeded, notwithstanding the diversion of creative
power involved. But Pryde neglected to cultivate with assiduity
that sombre, grandiose vision of his. To name a single instance of
this neglect, though possibly the gravest: he was a painter of architecture, yet, his biographer informs us, he only admitted having
painted a single building 'from the life'. This may not have been
literally true, but the repetitiveness, the absence of development, an
airlessness and a want of definition at key points are clear indications
of his neglect to refresh his vision by the study of nature. At the
heart of his failure lay, I think, the simple and awful fact that he
slowly lost interest in painting.

Between 1915 and 1918, in the middle of that period of his life
which his biographer calls his 'years of achievement', which extended

from about 1905 until about 1925, a friend of mine saw Pryde frequently. She was one of a small circle of intimates of which Pryde was the focus. The members met several times a week at the houses of one or another of them, and often at his studio at 3 Lansdowne House, Holland Park – lent to him by Sir Edmund Davis, a wealthy patron of the arts – where he settled in 1914 after his separation from his wife. The studio, dark and lofty as one of his own compositions, was furnished like them with deep-red hangings and ornamental columns, and elaborately arranged to give an impression of careless, opulent profusion. On an easel stood the 'carefully unfinished and perennial masterpiece' noted by Augustus John, which, my friend assured me, during those three years underwent no perceptible change. His friends, she said, exerted as much pressure as they dared in the face of his aversion from talk about painting to revive his manifestly languishing interest in his vocation, but he gave at times the impression of positive boredom with painting, and of awaiting, with eager anticipation, the hour when he would foregather with his friends. He accomplished nothing of consequence, and during the last ten years or more of his life he appears to have done nothing at all. His languishing energies were directed towards dignified and gentlemanly forms of begging, whether it was writing to friends to purchase a picture or choosing, at public gatherings, the company of those most likely to stand him drinks or to drive him home. On rare occasions, when pressed for debt, and unable, for some reason, to extract the requisite sum from a friend, he would take up his brushes as a last resort.

By a curious stroke of fortune, it happened that early in the nineteen-twenties, at the very time when his creative energies began to fail, his reputation blossomed. Perhaps this combination of circumstances was not so curious after all. His most productive and fruitful years lay immediately behind, and the fact that he spent his time at the Savage Club, bars in the Strand and other places much frequented by journalists instead of at his easel, resulted in the widespread fanning by gossip-writers of a merited reputation. He became a sort of legendary king of bohemia. When sober he was inclined to be taciturn, at other times his conversation delighted those privileged to hear it. He showed occasionally flashes of wit. One night some years earlier, at the National Sporting Club, a friend, indicating

Augustus John, who looked a Christlike figure in those days, asked Pryde, 'How old is Gus?' Pryde looked across the ring. 'I don't know', he answered, 'but it must be getting dam' near time for his crucifixion.'

His friends, devoted and exasperated by turns, expected, his biographer tells us, to find him one day lying dead in his own four-poster with the curtains in tatters around him and the cobwebs spread over his special possessions: a last great dramatic tableau. But when he described himself as having 'one foot in the grave and the other on a banana skin', he showed greater prescience than his friends. Early in 1939, infirm in mind and body, he was taken to St. Mary Abbots Hospital, Kensington. Here he spent his last two years in a ward for old men, sucking sweets and reading detective stories. Here he died on 24 February 1941, aged not, as his friends supposed, seventy-one, but seventy-four. The old actor had consistently lied about his age. The Providence which ordained that he should not die in his four-poster had prepared a stupendous tribute to the vestiges of greatness in the lazy old inebriate who had lost his memory. As he lay dying, the earth trembled under the impact of falling bombs, black smoke covered the city and flames leapt up the shattered buildings. For an apocalyptic moment, nature, whom Pryde had neglected to his infinite cost, was transformed according to his vision.

FRANCES HODGKINS

1870—1947

IN the late nineteen-twenties the public was made aware of a new talent by an exhibition held at the now defunct Claridge Gallery. The works shown were oils and water-colours in a handwriting assured, sometimes to the verge of carelessness, and marked by arresting combinations of colour. It was not easy to decide whether they were the emanations of a simple or of an artfully sophisticated mind. Original some of them evidently were. It was presumed that an artist hitherto unknown and so easily familiar with contemporary modes of seeing must be young. This impression was strengthened by the appearance of work by the same hand in exhibitions representative of the avant-garde, and it was deliberately fostered by the artist herself. It was, however, erroneous: the dashing arrival was almost sixty years old. In her determination to preserve unimpaired her identification with the younger painters whose ideas, after a lifetime of painting, she had come to share and whose admiration she deeply valued, Frances Hodgkins was inclined to suppress and distort the facts about her life before she was, so to speak, reborn. These attempts to mislead the inquisitive were deliberate, but not systematic. After the acquisition of her first picture by the Tate Gallery in 1940, I asked her for certain biographical facts, which she readily gave, and, I believe, accurately. These included the precise date of her birth, which has not, I think, been recorded, not even in Miss Myfanwy Evans's excellent essay.[1]

Frances Hodgkins was born in Dunedin, New Zealand, on 28 April 1870, the second daughter of William Matthew Hodgkins, a solicitor born in Liverpool, who had gone out as a young man, spending some years in London and Paris on the way. In the artistic and intellectual life of the colony he played a zestful part: he helped to establish the Art Gallery, was founder and first President of the Otago Art Society, and well known as a topographical water-colour painter in a politely modified Impressionist style. He also gave

[1] 'Frances Hodgkins', The Penguin Modern Painters, 1948.

lectures, and he and Mark Twain, Miss Evans has told us, once changed platforms without warning; 'a joke', she cryptically adds, 'that was not as successful as they had hoped'. Her father taught both his daughters to paint in water-colours, but it was not Frances who was considered to have the talent, and not until the 'nineties, when her sister married, did she inherit the status of 'the artist of the family'. The presence in New Zealand of Girolamo Nerli, a dashing Italian portrait-painter, had the effect of setting up a professional standard and of sharpening the discontent of artists with the pleasant but still amateurish culture of New Zealand. Nerli had twice painted Robert Louis Stevenson in Samoa and been a quickening influence upon Charles Conder and other painters in Australia. At Dunedin he taught at the art school, but his instruction was dilatory and intermittent. 'In the morning I open the student', he said, 'and then I go over to the public-house and rest. In the afternoon I shut the student up. Good to get the salary, but I do not like the Accademia – too much work.' Her occasional contacts with this bizarre person seem to have been without profit, but a certain conventional competence, by one means and another, she evidently acquired, for a picture of hers, *Maori Woman*, painted in 1900, was bought by the National Gallery of New Zealand. I have never seen this painting, but I understand that it is capable but commonplace and affords no hint of the direction in which her art eventually developed.

Before the end of the century, her father had died, and she had made up her mind to go to Europe. Although he had lived well, he died poor, and she had to exert herself in order to earn sufficient for the expensive journey. She gave lessons in water-colour painting and piano lessons, and she drew illustrations for the 'Otago Witness', her first published works. According to Miss Evans, these 'manage to show both her distaste and her capacity'. In 1900 she went to Europe, and spent two years in travel, visiting Brittany, Holland and Morocco. It was in Morocco, she used afterwards to say, that she had her first glimpse of her way ahead. Here she found the subjects that she had drawn with her father, in the mountains and the bush at home, moving figures in bright light, but in Morocco the moving figures were strange and more vivid than any she had seen before and they made a sharper impression. (The circumstances of the life she led were of a kind to exercise a bracing effect upon a temperament as adventurous as hers. With a woman friend, she joined a native caravan and went to Tetuan, where she had to remain for three months because the place was besieged by bandits.)

The work of her first dozen years or so in Europe is scattered, lost and difficult to see, but the impression I have of it (based, let me insist, upon very little evidence) is that it reflects a personality bold, energetic, eminently capable, but lacking entirely the delicate poetry of her later years. And lacking more than this, for I also detect a distinct strain of vulgarity. It was a symptom of this insensibility, I fancy, that Miss Evans had in mind when she wrote (of her work of a slightly later period) that Frances Hodgkins 'had felt the influence of the gipsy-caravan storm – that purely English-bohemian thunderstorm . . . that was still shaking such diverse trees as . . . Brangwyn and Lovat Fraser'.

In 1902 she settled in Paris, where her particular qualities won her considerable success. She was asked to join the staff at Colarossi's (where no other woman has taught, I believe, either before or afterwards, and where there have been few teachers who have never themselves attended any school) as a teacher of water-colour. Eventually she opened a school of her own. Her work seems to have been welcomed wherever she chose to send it, the 'Internationale' (which was traditionally reluctant to accept work by women) and the 'Société des Aquarellistes' among others. Sudden, unexpected success (I am not speaking of the success that crowns a life or a great achievement) is an experience that enslaves certain temperaments by a process of intoxication, but others it repels. Those others seize the chance of seeing it at close quarters, and decide that they do not want it on the terms on which it is to be had. It is significant that Frances Hodgkins's progressive isolation from the world and her living more intensely within herself began with her first taste of success. But it often happens that success, when treated with reserve, redoubles its attentions. In 1912 she returned to New Zealand, and held exhibitions there and in Australia. The work of 'the girl from "down under" who conquered Paris' (as she was called by Australian newspapers) was purchased for public collections and was presently sold out altogether. After her visit home, she returned to Paris to her painting and her teaching, but it was not long before the First World War was declared, and she left for England, where she made her home. She lived in St. Ives from 1914 until 1919; after the war she travelled, living at various times in London, the Cotswolds, Bridgnorth, and also abroad, chiefly in France and Spain. From 1922 until 1926 she lived in Manchester, where she worked without any notable success as a designer for the Calico Printers' Association, and conducted a painting class. The fact that she had joined so whole-heartedly in everything that was going on made her regard the rejection of her works, when the City Art Gallery organized a large inclusive exhibition, with a bitterness, Miss Evans has told us, out of proportion to its consequence. But there were compensations at hand. After many vicissitudes, she began at last to discover the peculiar angle and range of vision, the strangely singing colour, the fluid composition from which sprang the seemingly artless poetry (which was in fact the result of calculation and industry) that became so memorably her own. All this was plainly apparent to discerning visitors to her first one-man exhibition in London, especially (to her delight) to the younger painters. It consisted of twenty-five water-colours, four drawings and nineteen oil paintings, and was held at the Claridge Gallery in the spring of 1928.[1] The enhanced status that the exhibition conferred upon Frances Hodgkins was confirmed the following year by her election to the membership of the Seven and Five Society, a small group, notably free of dead wood, to which the ablest of the younger artists belonged. From this time onwards she was so completely identified with her much younger contemporaries that new acquaintances perceived with astonishment her approximate age.

The change in the character of her work that led to her identi-fication with a school of much younger artists had nothing of the nature of the sudden 'conversion' to which academy painters are occasionally subject. Although not yet easy to trace in detail, it was beyond question a process of steady growth.[2]

During the First World War an observant spectator might have noticed, besides the dashing proficiency of her work, a note of intensity and a complicated but certain sense of colour. Both these are perceptible in her first oil painting, *Two Women with a Basket of*

[1] 23 April until 12 May.

[2] A chronological list of the artist's works is included in 'Frances Hodgkins: Four Vital Years', by Arthur R. Howell, 1951–2.

Flowers, of about 1915,[1] aesthetically a strange blend of vice and virtue. One of the women, for instance, but for a touch of robustness, resembles one of those arty masks in white china made for the decoration of suburban walls, yet the colour, suggested by Vuillard, one would suppose, has been subtly and personally transposed. (We know that she looked with attention not only at Bonnard and Vuillard, but at Cézanne, Derain, Dufy and other Parisian contemporaries, and even attended the opening of the first Futurist exhibition.) This picture was purchased by the Tate in 1944. The following summer I wrote to her to ask for certain facts regarding it. I give her reply in full, as it shows that she began to paint in oils some years earlier than is generally believed (according to Miss Evans, this was about 1919), and, more generally, gives an indication of the warmth and impulsiveness of her character:

STUDIO,
CORFE CASTLE,
DORSET.

Belated reply to letter   Oct. 7th 1945.
dated July 13 1945.

DEAR MR. ROTHENSTEIN, – This is the letter that should have been written 2 months or more ago, rather late, indeed *very* late and I am filled with remorse that such an important event for me as the acquisition of my earliest painting should go unacknowledged by the artist. My excuse must be for not replying earlier to your letter, is that I was in Wales painting at the time.

Please accept my apologies.

I was absolutely overcome by the high honour paid me – and I greatly appreciate the recognition of my worthiness as creative artist.

In reply to your request for the date when *Two Women with a Basket of Flowers* was painted I think 1915 St. Ives is sufficiently accurate – I remember Mr. Moffat Lindner liking it so much that he bought it as soon as it was finished and from then on it hung in his beautiful house among the Elite – Sickert, Steer, etc.

It would be interesting to know how it came to the Tate Gallery – and when.

(2) It gives me intense pleasure to know my picture is enshrined in glory at Millbank. I hope I shall soon see it. I was delighted with the copy of 'Windmill' and the excellent reproduction. It gave me a thrill – a nostalgic one. Will you convey my grateful thanks to the Editors from me – and the great pleasure it has given me.

---

[1] The Tate Gallery, London.

Thanking you for the warm sympathy and interest you have shown my work.

> Yours sincerely,
> FRANCES HODGKINS.

In reference to the Drawing of a Woman that you mention I believe it belongs to me. I shall verify this when I am next at the Lefevre Gallery. If this should be the case I would like to present it to the Gallery.[1]

The drawing mentioned in the postscript is a big half-length of a seated woman made probably during the 'twenties, which is so complete a statement in the formal sense that a sculptor could carve from it (indeed, it has the look of something carved out of a tree trunk). Its noble, clearly defined forms make it to my thinking one of the finest drawings of our time. But it is neither for such a painting, intriguing as it is, as *Two Women with a Basket of Flowers* or the somewhat similar *Portrait of Moffat Lindner*,[2] a tempera of 1916, or even the drawing I mentioned just now, that Frances Hodgkins is chiefly to be valued, but for the intimately personal poetry of her last years, when she had shed the last of her borrowed plumage. Writing in December 1929 to Mr. Arthur R. Howell from the South of France, she described the panoramic splendour of what she saw.

> But let me tell you [she added] that in my humility I have not lifted up my eyes higher than the red earth or the broken earthenware strewn about making such lovely shapes in the pure clear light . . . you may hear them clink as you unroll the water-colours I am sending along to you by this same post.

To-day she has found favour with fashionable opinion: she is even spoken of as a great master. But of course she was not that: she lacks the scale, the range, the variety, the purposefulness. What Frances Hodgkins succeeded in doing, after twenty years of ceaseless experiment, was so to attune her eye and train her hand as to enable her to respond 'to the broken earthenware strewn about making such lovely shapes in the pure clear light', and to make out of such things

[1] It proved to be the property of Messrs. Reid and Lefevre, from whom it was purchased by the Tate Gallery in 1948.

[2] Coll. the late Moffat Lindner.

fantasies intimate and lovely, yet so convincing that, in her own words, we can hear them clink. This, in picture after picture, was what she had succeeded in doing, when, on 13 May 1947, in Purbeck, where for the last fifteen years of her life she had made her home, she died. Neither her talents nor her industry, nor even the admiration of people of influence, enabled her to make more than a precarious living, and latterly not even that. In 1942 she was granted a Civil List pension

WILLIAM ROTHENSTEIN

1872–1945

BIOGRAPHIES, memoirs and journals always fascinated my
father, but he used to complain of the disproportionate attention often given to childhood. Yet I have never known anyone whose own childhood so manifestly and so decisively shaped his
character. First and most potently the countryside around Bradford,
Yorkshire, where he was born, at 2 Spring Bank, Horton, on 29
January 1872, the third of the six children of a wool merchant.

> Above Saltaire, a couple of miles from home [he wrote fifty years
> afterwards] were the moors, and one could walk, I was told, as far as
> Scotland, without taking the road. In winter sometimes when the
> moors lay under snow, no footmarks were to be seen; one walked
> through a landscape strange, white and virginal, while above one's head
> the peewits wheeled and uttered their haunting cry. The low stone
> walls on the moor looked black against the snow . . . the mill chimneys
> along the valley, rising up tall and slender out of the mist, would look
> beautiful in the light of the setting sun.

Again:

> These old quarries had a great fascination for me; there was a haunting
> stillness and a wildness about them. . . . A deserted old quarry, not
> more than fifteen minutes' walk from our own house, was a favourite
> playground. It lay off a path, a hundred yards from a canal, among
> black and stunted trees; there hung about it that haunted atmosphere
> peculiar to places where men have once been quick and busy, but
> which, long deserted, are slowly re-adopted by the old earth.

And here and there over the stark and sombre earth stood the stone
skeletons of the great medieval abbeys, in those days not restored and
tidied up, but grass-tufted, masonry fallen, weed-choked, widely
scattered over the surrounding land. Of these the nearest were Kirkstall
and Bolton; beside this last was the famous 'Strid' across the Wharfe,
which became a sacred place in my father's eyes when he knew that
Wordsworth had written a poem about it. And at nearby Haworth

the presiding genius of the region was still a living memory: my father heard old people there speak of 'Miss Charlotte'. The two sons of Mr. Brontë's successor were in his form at school, and he used on a Sunday to walk across the fields to the church where Mr. Brontë had lately ministered and spend the day with his friends at the Vicarage which had been the Brontë's home. 'The Vicarage, the church and churchyard, and the Black Bull close by', he noted, 'and the steep grey street with the austere stone-roofed houses were all much as they were in the Brontës' time.' Of all these places he made his first childish drawings.

A man of sensibility born and reared in this grim, twilight region is likely to respond in one of two ways: he may shudder and recoil and depart, as soon as may be, for some tamed, mellow place; or he may take the starkness and the grimness to his heart. In the material sense, my father did, at the age of sixteen, leave Yorkshire for ever, but it is my conviction that the Yorkshire landscape, its dour, smoke-blackened buildings, yes and the stubborn, unsmiling people, strong in their frankness, and in their conscious rectitude, nurtured the most fruitful as well as the most enduring element in his personality. There was in his bewilderingly many-sided personality much more than this; but it is my conviction that these made its core. And it was a core of unusual strength, ever predisposing him towards an assertive and an unyielding independence and against compromise of any kind.

The quality of the Liberalism which he imbibed at home, besides fostering in him a natural love of justice, a natural humanity, also sanctioned an openness of mind even sometimes in those spheres where decisions are imperatively called for. He would often observe, for instance, that it was possible for a man to lead a life of virtue, no matter what religion he professed, or even if he professed none at all, but from this truism he was disposed to draw the conclusion that all religions were therefore equally true. This disposition derived partly from his abiding sense of the unchanging nature of man, and of the identity of the predicaments in which in all ages he has found himself, of the need, for instance, for reconciling the desire of the artist for perfection with his needs and duties as a social being, while the problem whether the man who desires the perfection of his own soul ought to retire from the world or remain in it, to struggle with deadly and multifarious temptations was one which constantly preoccupied him. It derived no less directly from that indeterminate quality in the heart of Liberalism that declares itself in a shrinking from sharp-edged definitions. This is less noticeable in its operation in the political sphere, where the loosely but generously conceived principles which it prefers have often compared well with opportunism to the Right and pedantry to the Left, but in the quest for the absolute they are apt to prove equivocal guides. My father was apt to regard any precisely formulated principles with suspicion, and to discount them as arbitrary theories to which men must, in his own words, 'conform or be damned'; religious dogma he discounted with that bland incomprehension common among Englishmen. He never saw it as possibly an assertion, in its starkest, most enduring form, of objective truth, but, at the best, as a perhaps necessary but artificial construction. I remember how, as a schoolboy, when I contended that the doctrines of the Catholic Church were either (as I believed) true or else they were false, but that in either event they treated of realities, he insisted that 'the Church needs dogma as a garden needs walls to enclose it'.

Such, besides a passion for drawing, a responsiveness to beauty and an eagerness for experience, were, I think, the most important emotional and intellectual features of the sixteen-year-old boy who, in 1888, left Bradford for the Slade School and a year later for a four years' stay in Paris. In addition, he possessed immense energy and a power of concentration to match it. For the rest he was a striking combination of moral earnestness and high-spirited wit, of shyness and audacity.

The year he spent at the Slade was of value to him on account of the personality and methods of Alphonse Legros, the Professor. 'We really did *draw* at the Slade', my father used to say, 'at a time when everywhere else in England students were rubbing and tickling their paper with stump chalk, charcoal and indiarubber.' Legros, whose earliest exhibited work had attracted the favourable notice of Baudelaire, had settled in England on the advice of Whistler, where he became friendly with Rossetti. In the true but almost forgotten sense of the term, Legros, who had studied under Ingres, was a fine academic draughtsman, a disciple of Mantegna, Poussin and Rembrandt.

He taught us [said my father] to draw freely with the point, to build up our drawings by observing the broad planes of the model . . . he would insist that we study the relations of light and shade and half-tone . . . this was a severe and logical method of constructive drawing.

This method of drawing was one to which my father wholeheart-edly responded; thenceforward constructive drawing became for him both an incitement and a discipline. From Legros he had also an immediate sense of contact with the great succession of European draughtsmen: he listened rapt while he quoted sayings of his master, Ingres, and spoke of Millet and Courbet with a familiarity tempered with reverence. But by the late 'eighties Legros had grown tired of teaching, and my father, oppressed by the spiritless atmosphere of the Slade, was easily persuaded to go to Paris.

In Paris he who scarcely more than a year before had been a provincial schoolboy and who at the Slade had vainly longed to speak to one of the older students, aroused the benevolent interest first of his professors at the Académie Julian, and not long afterwards of Whistler, Pissarro, Lautrec and Degas. Whistler one day paid an unexpected early-morning call at his studio, and thereby began a close friendship and, on my father's side, an ardent discipleship, which continued for some years until the friendship was suddenly extinguished in one of the Butterfly's most envenomed quarrels. My father's drawing in those days was lighter in touch and feeling, more stylish, than it afterwards became, yet Whistler showed an almost prophetic insight into the underlying weight and intensity of his nature when he used to say of him that he carried out right to the end what with others was mere gesture. The effect of the friendship of Whistler was conspicuous, but not enduring. It is manifest in a series of portraits of men painted in the early 'nineties, such as *L'homme qui sort*,[1] of 1892 (a portrait of Conder, shown at the Salon du Champ de Mars), another portrait of *Conder*,[2] and portraits of *Gordon Craig*,[3] *Max Beerbohm*[3] *and Marcel Boulanger*,[4] in all of which the subject is represented as a tall frock-coated figure in elegant silhouette against a low-toned but slightly lighter background.

The friendship of my father with Degas and Pissarro resulted from

[1] Coll. Mrs. Robichaud.   [2] Musée d'Art Moderne, Paris.

[3] Coll. writer.   [4] Lost.

his first exhibition, held with Conder in 1891 in a small gallery in
the Boulevard Malesherbes which belonged to a courageous dealer
named Thomas, whom Lautrec had interested in their work. Degas
sent word by a model of his that my father might, if he cared, pay
him a visit. Pissarro came to the exhibition with his son Lucien.
With Degas my father's relations were never so intimate as they were
with Whistler, but I think their effects, if less apparent, struck
nevertheless a deeper chord. Creative powers of the highest order,
united as they were in Degas with austerity and an uncompromising
integrity, commanded his utmost admiration. That such a man
should admit to his friendship a boy hardly nineteen years old
aroused his gratitude. The long evenings in the Rue Victor Massé
(where Degas lived in two flats, the walls of the lower hung with
the French masters he collected and the upper with his own works),
spent in detailed discussion and close examination of works of art,
did more to broaden and sharpen my father's critical faculties than
any other experience in his early life. He delighted in Degas's deadly
wit, the phrases that deflated or drew blood; in his stories about
his master, Ingres, and the great men of his age. For all his veneration
he was unable, in one important respect, to profit by Degas's
advice. Degas not only seldom painted direct from nature, but was
apt to ridicule this practice as an odious outdoor sport, and
he urged my father to paint only from studies, and showed him
how to correct and simplify these by redrawing on tracing
paper pinned over them. But my father's visual imagination
was weak; he was dependent upon the immediate presence of
nature, which alone incited his faculties to function at their highest
pitch. In the course of his life he carried out a number of elaborate
figure compositions. These called for the redrawing, often the
radical modification, of studies made from nature, but it is true to say
that everything most living in his work was done in the heat generated by direct contact with his subject. Degas's belligerent nationalism expressed itself in various ways, but in none so consistently as
in his hatred of the cosmopolitanism that had already begun to
supplant the culture of France, the disintegrating effects of which he
continually deplored. In so speaking, he strengthened my father's
own innate antipathy for cosmopolitanism, above all for its frequent
concomitants, the exotic and the smart.

The effects of his contacts with Pissarro are difficult to isolate from those of Impressionism as a whole. For some years before my father's arrival in Paris, this movement had put a powerful spell upon students, especially upon English students. The influence of Whistler, with his insistence upon low tones and severely selective composition, and of Degas, with his insistence upon precise drawing and his continuous praise of Ingres, however, combined to postpone the day when my father had to reckon with Impressionism.

After he had lived for four years in Paris, chance, in the guise of two commissions, led him home to England. Lord Basil Blackwood, son of the British Ambassador, invited him to stay at Balliol to draw his portrait, and some drawings he did there attracted the attention of John Lane, the publisher, who commissioned him to make a set of twenty-four Oxford portraits. These commissions he interpreted as signs that his life in Paris was drawing to its close, and as good omens of a new life in his own country. He possessed the talent for applying himself with such passionate industry to any work he had in hand, and for experiencing any phase of life to the utmost, that when the call came to undertake something fresh he was able to make changes without regret. 'You have gathered in your sheaves', I remember MacColl saying to him, towards the end of both their lives. But when the time came to give up his studio he was troubled by doubts as to whether he was wise to leave Paris, for his four years there had been years of achievement and experience. His drawing had become expressive and elegant; his sense of character vivid and humane; his intellect had been enriched and sharpened in the quickest thinking, the most critical and creative society there was. He had won the respect and the friendship of those whom he most ardently admired, and all this by the age of twenty-one. Whistler, Wilde and Conder urged him to remain. Reflection confirmed his intention to return to England and, with a brief interlude painting landscape at Montigny, he went from the society of Lautrec and Verlaine to that of the Common Rooms of Balliol and Christ Church. At Oxford, and in London where he settled a year later, he added to the already extensive gallery of portraits, begun in Paris with Verlaine, Zola and Rodin, likenesses of Pater, Swinburne and Henry James.

Soon after the beginning of the new century a radical change, involving both loss and gain, began to be manifest in his work. It was a change due perhaps mainly to intellectual conviction, but it may be in part the consequence of some psychic disturbance possibly unconnected with painting. I know nothing of the cause of such a disturbance, but I offer it as a possible explanation of a change of outlook more radical than an intellectual re-orientation would be likely to effect. Before about the year 1900 his work was distinguished by an eager curious insight into character, whether of face, of figure, or of locality, which expressed itself, notwithstanding his obvious high spirits and irrepressible humour, with a grave, disciplined detachment. His drawing, elegant and tenuous though it often was, showed a surprisingly sure grasp of form. The intellectual motive for the change is clearly expressed in my father's own words. Of the years after his return to England he wrote:

> My sympathies were with the Realists; but I felt there was something accidental, a want of motive and of dignity, in contemporary painting. To achieve the vitality which results from direct contact with nature, with nature's final simplicity and radiance, how unattainable! Yet only by aiming at an impossible perfection is possible perfection to be reached.

A few lines later he expressed what was, I think, the central article of his own belief:

> . . . I was possessed with the faith that if I concerned myself wholly with appearance, something of the mystery of life might creep into my work. . . . Through devotion to appearance we may even interpret a reality which is beyond our conscious understanding.[1]

The Wordsworthian conviction that form is the discipline imposed by God upon the universe, and that by subjecting himself to it, the artist may approach the innermost realities, is one which again and again finds expression in his critical writings. Such reasoning was cogent enough, yet there is something mysterious about the transformation of my father's outlook. He had always been serious and always industrious, but in the course of the early nineteen-hundreds he became increasingly marked by an extraordinary earnestness and intensity, an almost fanatical industry and an increasing severity with

[1] 'Men and Memories', 1931, I, p. 325.

himself. This heightened earnestness showed itself in every one of his many activities. 'Your father is far more interested in religion than the average parson', Eric Gill said to me. There was an occasion when a French Benedictine, perceiving this preoccupation, tried to persuade him to enter the Order's house at Flavigny. He was strongly affected by the writings of Tolstoy. He was shocked at the impoverishment of English provincial life by the progressive concentration of civilization in London, and he struggled to arrest it. The revival of fine traditional craftsmanship and the recognition of the undervalued art of India were other active preoccupations. And for the recognition of the achievements of those artists whom he most admired, especially of his younger contemporaries, his efforts were unremitting. Of Steer, Augustus and Gwen John, Stanley Spencer, Paul Nash his praise was constant, and if occasion required it, no exertion on their behalf and on that of many others at different times was too great. I have never known an artist whose generosity towards his fellow artists was so positive and so unstinted. But it is with this heightened earnestness and intensity as it showed itself in his work that I am chiefly concerned. So far from wavering in his conviction that for him Realism was the inevitable means of interpreting nature, it seemed to him on the contrary that the defect of all but the greatest Realists, Rembrandt, Velazquez, Chardin and a handful of others, was that they were too easily satisfied, that they stopped complacently when they should have pressed audaciously forward to pierce the baffling complexity of the appearance of nature so as to approach more closely the innermost truth. So it was without illusions as to his own shortcomings that he attempted with the whole force of his own passionate nature to come to closer and closer grips with the world of appearance. The attempt resulted, broadly speaking, in a vast increase of power at the expense of grace. It seems to me that nothing he did after the change approached in noble elegance of style his lithographed drawings of *Henry James*, of 1898, of *Fantin-Latour* or of the big double portrait of *Ricketts and Shannon*, both of 1897, or even the pastel *The Model*,[1] 'made when he was eighteen years old. He renounced, or rather, the more exigent ideal which possessed him involved the renunciation of, certain felicities of style. The grimness of his determination to be faithful to this ideal

[1] Lost. Reproduced in 'L'Art français', 2 April 1892.

11. JAMES PRYDE. *The Red Ruin* (c. 1916).
Oil, 60¾ × 55½ in. Coll. The Rt. Hon. Viscount Cowdray.

12. FRANCES HODGKINS.
Two Plates (1940).
Water colour, 16×27 in.
Coll. Sir Kenneth Clark.
K.C.B.

exposed him to serious temptation. First, on account of his conviction that he ought always to be ready to take advantage of every spark of inspiration, he worked too continuously and always under the highest pressure. This led to a species of recurrent imaginative exhaustion, a recurrent aridity; and this in its turn led, as he himself confessed, to much painting for the sake of painting. Second, his ardour to probe his subject to its very depths, to resolve its complexities and to achieve final simplification led him, as Sir Charles Holmes complained, to 'aim to put too much into each canvas'. What was still worse, there were occasions when, in his eagerness to 'intensify' (the term was continually on his lips) some aspect of his subject, he would take insufficient care with his composition.

About this time, another artist, some seven years his junior, a man infinitely remote from him in temperament and convictions, made an observation which was curiously relevant to my father's predicament.

I shall have to disappoint people at first [Paul Klee noted in his diary in 1903]. Things are expected of me which a clever fellow could easily simulate. But my consolation must be that I am more handicapped by the sincerity of my intentions than by any lack of talent or dispositions.

I have expressed my admiration for my father's earliest work: I have called attention to the principal defects of the later; but I do not suggest that the total effect of the change was for the worse. The change itself may be interpreted as the determination on his part to face all the risks of total failure in an attempt to paint greatly, rather than to continue as a minor artist; 'to aim,' in his own words, 'at what was beyond me rather than to achieve an easier and more attractive result'. To this attempt – to vary a famous naval order – to engage nature more closely, to wring the very utmost out of his subject, he brought an inflexible will and extraordinary powers of concentration, and an inability to compromise.

The effect of this rededication, daily – indeed, hourly – renewed, was by its very earnestness, by its very strenuousness, in part self-defeating. The grace and ease that distinguished the work of his boyhood and youth gave way to a dourness, an almost aggressive 'probity' (to use one of his own highest terms of approbation), even on occasions when his subjects, young women, children, sunlit orchards or fields of ripe corn, would seem to call for lighter handling. But if dourness and aggressive probity dried up much of his later work, this passionate rededication was not in vain, for when inspiration came, there he was, alert and disciplined, with the pent-up energy of a coiled steel spring. At such times, as though in compensation for the months of humble and dutiful effort so grudgingly rewarded, he painted pictures which – it seems to me – possess qualities of greatness. I mean that they realized Baudelaire's artistic ideal ... 'The creation of a suggestive magic containing at one and the same time the object and the subject, the world outside the artist and the artist himself.' ... Of these I would name *The Quarry*,[1] of 1904, *Aliens at Prayer*,[2] of 1905, *Farm in Burgundy*,[3] of 1906, *St. Seine L'Abbaye* (Plate 14),[4] of 1906, *Cliffs at Vaucottes*,[5] of 1909, *Morning at Benares*,[6] of 1911, *St. Martin's Summer*,[7] of 1915, and *Portrait of Barnett Freedman*,[8] of 1925. There is at least one painting which anticipated the later attitude, *Vézélay*,[9] of 1896, while the earlier one persists in two of the best of his later paintings – namely, *Mother and Child*,[10] of 1903. *Portrait of Augustus John* (Plate 13)[11] and *The Doll's House*,[12] both of 1899, show him in happy transition.

The effects of his enhanced seriousness of purpose might have been oppressive had it not been for another but apparently unconnected change in his vision which also occurred in the early years of the century. This was a sudden preoccupation with full daylight, with a consequent intensification of his own palette. Its chief cause was probably his increasing interest in landscape. He worked, almost always, not from studies but in front of his subject, which brought him up at once against the problems of the representation of open-air light. Another cause was the delayed influence of Impressionism, from which he had been temporarily immunized by Whistler's

---

[1] The Cartwright Memorial Hall, Bradford.
[2] The National Gallery, Melbourne.   [3] Coll. Mr. Edward le Bas.
[4] The City Art Gallery, Manchester.   [5] The Tate Gallery, London.
[6] The City Art Gallery, Manchester.   [7] The Tate Gallery, London.
[8] The Tate Gallery, London.   [9] Coll. the late Robert Baring.
[10] Coll. Mrs. E. J. Hesslein, New York.
[11] The Walker Art Gallery, Liverpool.   [12] The Tate Gallery, London.

advocacy of low tones. Rejection of Whistler's dandyism, I surmise, led naturally to the end of this immunity, and his eye was gradually filled forthwith by dazzling light. But the twentieth century had begun, and it was impossible for an artist of sensibility to respond, quite simply, to the original Impressionism of Monet. The emphasis on conscious design, on structure, and on poetry and drama, which crystallized in the Post-Impressionist movement, accorded too closely with my father's own predilections not to make it inevitable that the Impressionism that so richly coloured his vision should be an Impressionism transformed. Although the theories of Seurat attracted him as little as those of Monet, in so far as he attempted to unite hard structure with brilliant colour he may properly be regarded as something of a Post-Impressionist, but the appellation would have surprised him. For far from being associated with Post-Impressionism, he was widely regarded as hostile to it; but his positive alienation from it was due to a personal clash with Roger Fry, the promoter of the movement in England. Fry was a warm admirer of my father's work, and had written in forthright praise of it, and, perceiving, perhaps, the elements which it had in common with that of the avowed Post-Impressionists, he urged him to associate himself with them. Want of respect for the work of some of the Post-Impressionists, a certain mistrust of Fry's leadership and a sense of loyalty to the New English Art Club with which he had exhibited since 1894 impelled him to decline. His refusal eventually aroused in Fry an enmity which was as active as it was lasting. The critical opinions expressed by my father with regard to several aspects of Post-Impressionism, and the personal hostility towards him, within the movement, fomented by Fry, opened a breach between him and painters whose principal aims he shared. Certainly he showed no sympathy at all for one derivative of Post-Impressionism – namely, Abstraction – which he regarded as a cardinal heresy, because it seemed to him to involve nothing less than a new atheism: implying a denial of the material world, and the reliance of artists on their intellects rather than on their eyes. Nor had he any particular sympathy for the work of van Gogh or of Gauguin, yet he shared the sense these artists had of the inadequacy of the Impressionists' aims. He held that the urge to express form and colour was the first among the painters' impulses,

but the minds of artists [he wrote] are not so limited, so poorly furnished, that they cannot associate their sense of form with those touching
elements in man's pilgrimage through life which bring the arts within-
the orbit of common experience.

It seems to me that there was a certain inconsistency that marked at
one point his attitude towards the subject of a work of art. Although
the subjects to which he responded most naturally were faces, figures,
buildings and the things fashioned by man for his use such as were
beautiful or interesting in themselves, he had a clear apprehension
that no object in itself is trivial, and that only trivial treatment can
make it so. He spoke often of Rembrandt's making so noble a work
of art out of the split-open carcase of an ox, and of Chardin's power
of representing a knife and a loaf and Cézanne a dish of apples with
similar breadth and force. Yet for all his own passionate preference
for subjects that pertained, as he put it, to 'man's pilgrimage through
life', and his indifference to subjects that were fortuitous or slight, he
showed, nevertheless, an odd reluctance to make due allowance for
the power of the noblest of all subjects – namely religion – to
inspire great works of art. Of the early Italians he wrote:

> The notion that these were great religious artists because all painters
> and sculptors believed in the stories they were hired to illustrate, is a
> fallacy . . . such . . . subjects . . . allowed the artist to paint the streets
> and buildings of the towns which they lived in. . . .

Granting the element of truth contained in this contention, the
suggestion that Giotto and Duccio, Piero della Francesca and Fra
Angelico were the Courbets and Manets of their times, drawing their
inspiration solely from the life around them, is to deny the main-
spring of their art. To regard the world as a complex of forms to be
æsthetically related to one another seems to me to imply a pitiably
impoverished vision, but at least a consistent one. But if subject
is to be regarded as significant, where is the logic of praising Chardin
and Cézanne for their belief in their loaves and apples, and calling in
question the belief of the great religious artist in the Incarnation? And
where the logic of extolling nobility of subject, if the noblest is not,
in fact, held to be inspiring at all? It is easy, however, to insist too
much upon this contradiction, for it arose from his deeply felt conviction that both the fundamental concern and the most vital

inspiration of the artist was the beauty of the visible world. Later in life, he experienced in altered form a renewal of the intermittent religious impulse of his childhood and youth, heightened later by his contacts with Indian mystics. But his sense of his obligation as an artist to interpret this beauty was so overwhelming as to confuse his vision of the religious life which nevertheless increasingly absorbed him. Towards the very end he drew near to the Catholic Church, but the final act of entry into her communion was inhibited by his abiding conviction that all of himself that was of any account had already been offered to God in the only way in which he certainly knew how to offer it – namely, to the praise of the world which God had created. Two priests of the Society of Jesus followed the inconclusive struggle with respectful sorrow. To the last there remained an inner recess of his consciousness where he still believed, like Dubedat, that the great artists were his saints, whose creative activities were the only activities of any abiding significance. Even the understanding of these, he used to maintain, was a mere social amenity – as though works of art are not created to be understood; as though they are not fulfilled by comprehension.

This habitual opinion did nothing to mitigate the recurrent bitterness that seared his later years, arising from the precipitous decline in his own reputation as an artist. That he did not suffer oblivion was due to the impossibility of ignoring so formidable a personality. To one who in youth won the admiration of Degas and Pissarro, who in middle age was regarded without question as one of the most representative English artists, who had exerted himself so continuously in the service of his fellow artists, who had been the teacher of so large a proportion of the ablest among his juniors, the neglect of his paintings was a grief – a grief sharpened, if anything, by the undiminished respect paid to him as a writer, as an authority, and as a person. There was something particularly ironical in his eyes in the praise which he continued to receive for everything except his painting, for almost all his other activities, with a single important exception, were then confined to those hours when the light was insufficient for painting. To his writings in particular no time was allowed which he could have given to his art. A grave illness, which made work impossible during the middle twenties, seemed to me to be aggravated by his enforced inactivity. I therefore urged him to set down his recollections. He made a beginning during his convalescence, but after his recovery he wrote the remainder of three large volumes of his 'Men and Memories', amounting to about half a million words, before rising in the mornings, and, rather less frequently, after nightfall. During these hours he was also occupied with a vast correspondence. The important exception was his teaching; the Principalship of the Royal College of Art, which lasted from 1920 until 1935, inevitably involved continual interruption of his painting. In the same way, his passionate advocacy of the art of India and the formation of his own collection of Indian paintings, of the revival of wall painting, of local craftsmanship, farming, and many other activities at Far Oakridge, the Gloucestershire village which, apart from a brief interlude, was his home from 1912 until his death, were all the occupations of what, in another man, would have been his leisure hours. And as though these and, at one time or another, many more were insufficient to absorb his energies, he used to rise with the sun at Far Oakridge, and, with axe and billhook, clear acre after acre of overgrown woodland. And he possessed the capacity of experiencing, with an extraordinary intensity, all his activities and his friendships; and above all, the various phases of his own art. From each he extracted all that he was capable of extracting. The sustained exaltation with which he experienced a new subject is expressed most explicitly, I think, in the chapter on India in the second volume of 'Men and Memories'. During both World Wars, in the first, as an artist on the Western Front, in the second with the Royal Air Force, his comrades, bored, uncomfortable, exasperated, noted with incredulity the entranced activity of a man for whom every instant of those dreadful days was manifestly precious.

The bitterness of his last years must not be exaggerated: cheerfulness kept breaking in. At work, in spite of the almost inevitable falling-short of the exacting standards he set himself, in spite of the grimness of the struggle, his happiness was intense. It was not only painting and drawing that he enjoyed to the end, but the various incidental experiences which they involved. When the Second World War broke out he was sixty-six years old. On account of his age and of his unfashionable reputation, his chances, he rightly considered, of official employment as a regular war artist were small, and he resigned himself to serving, at the best, upon some appropriate committees. I persuaded him to offer his services as an artist directly to the Royal Air Force, which offered subjects as inspiring as they were novel. Neither he nor I was unaware of the dangers which would attend such a course of action, for he had suffered, for more than twenty years, from a heart gravely weakened by overwork.

So it was that he had the delight of working as an artist to the end. We did not meet often during the war, but I shall always carry with me the memory of the slight, straight-backed, energetic figure in a sky-blue uniform, carrying his portfolio of paper, setting eagerly off for some airfield, or else returning with a sheaf of drawings and innumerable stories of new-made friends. What a strange conjunction there was of two remote periods of time when this small figure, mentioned in the 'Goncourt Journals', the familiar of Verlaine, Pater and Oscar Wilde, was out over the North Sea in a Sunderland flying-boat, with a crew not a member of which was less than half a century his junior.

Want of success had reduced his income to minute proportions, yet he gave his services to the Royal Air Force, and presented all the work that he did on his own account while on active service to the nation. But he gave even more than his work. The ordeal of constant air flight, the draughty messes, the indifferent food imposed a strain upon his injured heart heavier than it could withstand; he became ill, and after a year or two of restricted activity he died.

Portraits had formed the largest part of his production, but when he sat on the terrace of his house at Far Oakridge knowing that he had only a little time to live, it was not faces, illustrious or beautiful, that occupied his thoughts; it was the Stroud Valley with its severely defined contours, its sonorous depths. It was as though he saw all the loveliness of nature gathered in between its steep, wooded declivities. As he sat and watched it with rapt attention hour after hour under the changing effects of light, marvelling at its beauty, more deeply than ever was he convinced that by yielding himself up humbly and absolutely to the attempt to represent this beauty the artist might reveal, here and there, a glimpse of the reality behind it. Strong in this faith, but able no longer to act in accordance with its dictates, he died on 14 March 1945.

When I learned of his death and looked back over his benevolent and industrious and amazingly full life, in the mass of memories one incident, trivial at first glance, disengaged itself from the rest, and stood forth as peculiarly typical of my father's daily conduct. Not many years before, he and I together visited an exhibition, where he was attracted by an example of the later work of Sickert, of which he was in general highly critical. Presently he was engaged in conversation with a lady, to whom I heard him say: 'That small study is absolutely enchanting, and it's delightful to be able to praise it. Certain of Walter's recent works have made it difficult for his old friends to look him in the face.' As we were leaving, I warned my father, whose often untimely candour provoked resentment, against speaking in such terms in public, 'How can you place,' I asked, 'the slightest reliance on that lady's discretion? Incidentally, who was she?' In sombre tones came the reply: 'Mrs. Sickert, John.'

13. SIR WILLIAM ROTHENSTEIN. *Portrait of Augustus John* (*c.* 1900).
Oil, 29½ × 21½ in. The Walker Art Gallery, Liverpool.

14. SIR WILLIAM ROTHENSTEIN. *The Abbey Church of St. Seine* (1906).
Oil, 29½ × 21½ in. The City Art Gallery, Manchester.

WILLIAM NICHOLSON

1872—1949

WHEN William Nicholson was twenty-one years old he made a woodcut portrait of Queen Victoria which, published in 'The New Review', then edited by W. E. Henley, made him famous in a day. Among its numerous admirers was Whistler. 'A wonderful portrait, Mr. Nicholson', he said. 'Her Majesty is a wonderful subject', Nicholson modestly replied. 'You know,' rejoined Whistler, 'Her Majesty might say the same of you.'

Nicholson was a wonderful subject, but, in my estimation at least, for reasons different from those voiced by the friends who have written about him from the most intimate knowledge. In a biography[1] as vivacious in tone as it is pious in intention, Miss Marguerite Steen tacitly endorses the opinion of certain unnamed authorities whom she quotes that 'William Nicholson is the greatest master of Still-Life of his own or any other age'. In the most discerning appraisal[2] of his art that has yet appeared the late Robert Nichols asserts that 'a Nicholson, albeit surrounded by twenty other paintings, can be instantly recognized across a room on first entry to a gallery'. One has only to think of the still-lifes of Chardin, of Velazquez, of Manet, of a dozen others to see that Miss Steen's claim will not bear an instant's scrutiny. Nor is Nichols's claim justified. A dandy is rarely conspicuous, and William Nicholson, artist and man, was a dandy. He was not a great master, and as a painter he was as little original as a man of high gifts and undeviating independence could well be. (His originality showed itself in his woodcuts and to a lesser degree in the posters over which he collaborated with Pryde.) William Nicholson the painter seems to me to be something quite different; something rare, especially in England – namely, a little classical master. As a little master, he would in several periods of history have been acclaimed. But our own is not interested in modest perfection. To-day van Gogh is the most popular painter.

[1] 'William Nicholson', 1943.
[2] 'William Nicholson', Penguin Modern Painters, 1948.

The heroic failure is preferred to the completely achieved but minor success. The vehement, unstudied utterance is preferred, and infinitely preferred, to the polished epigram. (The very expression 'polished epigram' has become as incongruous with what is most admired in contemporary art as a frock-coat or a heavily tasselled malacca cane with contemporary fashion in dress.) The little master is, then, of all kinds of artist the least fashionable; to such an extent unfashionable that those who loved and admired William Nicholson will, I am afraid, regard this description of him as disparagement.

The dandy, as Baudelaire noted, has his special discipline to follow, his special sacrifices to make, and William Nicholson was no exception. He needed a measure of success to enable him to develop his small but perfect talent, sufficient to bring up a family early established and quickly increasing and thereby to place him beyond the caprices of patrons. In addition to his talent, he possessed three invaluable assets. First, a remarkable capacity for work – a capacity not so much the product of will power or of a sense of moral obligation as of a restless creative activity. He could never be idle. Second, an acute business sense, which brought him early and increasing material success. Third, and most important, an intimate understanding of the nature of his own talents. Many artists waste half a lifetime in the vain pursuit of objects unattainable through their particular gifts; Nicholson early understood what he should be about, so that, wasting no time, he took every opportunity of learning what he needed to learn. There is, in consequence, a close-knit coherence about his fastidious life-work.

Nicholson was born on 5 February 1872, at 12 London Road, Newark-on-Trent, and christened William Newzam Prior, the second son and third child of the second wife of William Newzam Nicholson, the proprietor of the Trent Ironworks and Member of Parliament. Exceptionally observant and continuously active, Nicholson was without any power of concentration upon anything which did not engage his interest, and at Magnus Grammar School, Newark-on-Trent, which he attended, nothing except drawing engaged his interest. His schooldays were unfruitful and unhappy and he attempted in after years to erase the memory of them. But now and then the nightmare would come seeping back through the doors he supposed he had bolted and barred upon it, and he would describe how he and the other boys scraped off their bread the loathsome grease they were given in place of butter, and pushed it through the iron grating which covered the heating pipes in the floor, and how the rats swarmed to eat the grease, and the deadly stench given off by the combination of grease and rat when the furnace was lighted. 'Greek before breakfast', he used to say, 'on an empty stomach, after breaking the ice in the washbowl, prevented me from ever wishing to visit Greece.' Yet these years were not utterly unfruitful, utterly unhappy. They were redeemed by the presence in the school of a drawing master named William H. Cubley.[1] This humane and perceptive man was a pupil of Sir William Beechey, who was a pupil of Reynolds. So it came about that in this malodorous wilderness was an old man giving precise but unheeded instruction in the technical methods of Sir Joshua. Cubley not only gave his pupil an insight into traditional methods of oil painting, but he persuaded his father to allow him to study art, and enabled him to escape from a school which offered him present misery and no prospect of success.

Herkomer's art school at Bushey, to which his father sent him at the age of sixteen, if less positively disagreeable to him, was hardly more profitable than the Magnus School. The instruction perfunctorily given in Herkomer's grandiose Bavarian castle was based upon no rational principles, and it was not long before Nicholson realized that he was learning nothing – nothing, at least, from Herkomer. One day the life-class was aroused from its apathy by the noisy intrusion of a flock of geese, driven in from an adjacent common by a student. This spirited and whimsical act, so incongruous with the portentous atmosphere of the school, attracted the attention of Nicholson to the boisterous, intractable girl responsible. Her name was Mabel Pryde; she was, as she proudly informed him, sister to James Pryde, who presently himself arrived at Bushey. The company of a brother and sister as original and exhilarating as Herkomer was dull made Nicholson more and more refractory to his teaching and intermittent in his attendance at the classes. Relations between master and student became tense. One day, it being Nicholson's turn to arrange the model, he brought in a woman from

1 Born 1814; died 1896; twice Mayor of Newark-on-Trent.

the village and posed her with an open umbrella behind her head. Of her he made a lively sketch. This Herkomer described as 'a piece of Whistlerian impudence' and dismissed Nicholson from the school for 'bad attendance and bad work'. The displeasure of Herkomer put an end to his profitless pupillage, but an incident of a strangely similar kind a little later embittered his relations with his father. He painted a portrait of his mother, and his father, invited by his diffident son to look at it in the studio by himself, came out speechless with uncomprehending rage. There followed a short period of study in Paris at the Académie Julian. The particular problems which preoccupied his French contemporaries had no special relevance to Nicholson, who made few intimate contacts, and remained, in fact, a somewhat solitary figure. A chance visit to Ridge's bookshop in Newark shortly after his return to England had consequences more important for his life as an artist than the sum of his Parisian experience, even though this included the copying of a painting by Velazquez, a master whose combination of the most searching realism with the most exquisite taste must have helped Nicholson to a knowledge of himself. Ridge's was an old-established firm which had published some of the early work of Byron, and possessed a large and interesting collection of old woodblocks. Excited by what he saw, Nicholson went home, secured a piece of wood, planed it down, and with nails and a penknife he cut a block from which he printed his first woodcut. Nicholson's work as a wood-cutter lies outside the scope of these pages, but it radically affected his work as a painter.

Not long after his return from Paris Nicholson's courtship of the girl who had driven the flock of geese into the life-class at Herkomer's culminated in marriage. The Prydes were a violently opinionated, quarrelsome and eccentric family, and Nicholson, sensible, shy, a hater of 'scenes', conducted his unobtrusive courtship of Mabel largely in the coal-cellar of the Prydes' house in Bloomsbury, where the family had migrated on Dr. Pryde's retirement. Mrs. Pryde, under the spell of one of her successive enthusiasms, had installed in the cellar a vapour bath, wherein the victim sat, the lid closed firmly over his head, while steam was raised by an interior lamp. So long as this enthusiasm lasted, the interior mechanism of this formidable apparatus was shown to the more privileged visitors to the house. One day, when William and Mabel were chattering among the coalsacks, Mrs. Pryde – whose disapproval of the courtship was notorious – descended the steps followed by a body of visitors; embarrassed, he jumped into the vapour bath and held down the lid, to the disappointment of Mrs. Pryde when her utmost efforts failed to raise it.

The unpredictable temper of the Pryde household persuaded the young couple that it would be prudent to make their plans without consultation with the parents of either. They were accordingly married in secret at Ruislip on 25 April 1893.

Nicholson's marriage led immediately to an association more momentous for his work than his marriage itself. Within a few days of his settling with his wife into the first of their many houses – 'The Eight Bells', a small former public-house at Denham – James Pryde arrived for a week-end and remained with them for two years. The collaboration of the brothers-in-law as the Beggarstaffs, for the designing of posters, briefly treated earlier in these pages, was the chief consequence of this prolonged visit. The estrangement of Nicholson and Pryde in later life has led to a tendency on the part of the advocates of each to belittle the contribution of the other to the illustrious partnership. To assess with any degree of precision the contribution of these two would be, after so many years, as difficult as it would be unfruitful. Pryde's was the more mature and the more audacious personality. Edinburgh had not yet dwindled into a repertory of conventional formulae; memories of her high sombre buildings, her dark history, still haunted his dreams. If he was lazy and irresponsible, the reckoning was yet to come. Nicholson's personality had the greater potentiality for growth, but at this time he seemed no doubt, in comparison with Pryde, a diffident, pedestrian being, which no doubt accounted for the condescension discernible in Pryde's attitude towards him. But about Nicholson's industry, his manual dexterity and his business capacity there was no doubt. If the original conceptions were, perhaps, mostly Pryde's, their translation into finished designs was chiefly due to the skill and pertinacity – doubtless heightened by his responsibilities as a married man – of Nicholson. But if the assumption of Pryde's readier invention is justified, Nicholson's work of the immediately ensuing years as a wood-cutter proclaims him an apt pupil. Like

Pryde, Nicholson learnt two obvious but important lessons from their joint experience as designers of posters; clarity and economy of statement, and effective distribution of light and shadow.

The Beggarstaffs were so intimately identified – as collaborators and as brothers-in-law – that the radical differences between them have sometimes been overlooked. They had, indeed, very little in common. They were alike in possessing little of the humbleness of most serious artists. Pryde's pride, which proclaimed itself in grandiose talk, was obvious enough; Nicholson's was masked, but it went deeper. To boast, like Pryde, would have been repugnant to the dandyism which governed Nicholson's conduct of his life as well as of his art, but somewhere in his innermost being there was, I suspect, a hard core of spiritual complacency. But not the kind of complacency that ever excused him from the utmost exertion. He was never a facile artist: the suavity, the cool vivacity, the truth of tone, the buoyancy, the character in his portraits – all these were purchased at the price of an agony of effort, sustained throughout a lifetime. With Pryde there was little agony of effort, or none. So long as his Edinburgh memories were sufficiently fresh to stir his imagination, he exploited the consequent ferment. When they faded, he exploited his prestige, his dignified handsomeness, his odd engaging humour instead – in a word, he cadged. He trod the broad path as inevitably as Nicholson trod the narrow. Potentially, Pryde was, perhaps, the larger artist, as he was the larger human being; he was built upon a scale more ample and generous than Nicholson, but he lacked Nicholson's capacity for growth. Even the latter's most conspicuous qualities – his taste, his sense of perfection – were not 'gifts', but endowments painfully acquired and improved. Those who admire the work of Nicholson are apt to be impressed so deeply by his most perfect achievements that they can scarcely perceive his defects. Yet could anything show the tastelessness of art nouveau more clearly than the landscape backgrounds of his several paintings of Morris dancers, made during the first years of the century? Could anything be worse drawn than the obtrusive near thigh – too long, too flat and a ludicrous match for the far one – of *Carlina*,[1] of about 1909? Or a more ostentatious display of dexterity than the famous

[1] The Kelvingrove Art Gallery, Glasgow.

Hundred Jugs,[1] of 1916? I cite these examples of failure (which, incidentally, have found places in the principal exhibitions and publications devoted to the work of this artist) to support my contention that his perfection, like the perfection of the prose of George Moore's maturity, was the outcome (but at no time the certain outcome) of anguished effort. Yet than his best paintings none look more effortless. In these he shows a suave and assured perfection or an insight into character which will, I fancy, enable them to offer an effective resistance to the blind but mercilessly probing assaults of Time. Of the still-lifes for which I would claim the relative perfection possible in an age which cares little for perfection, I would name *The Lowestoft Bowl*,[2] of 1900, *The Marquis Wellington Jug*,[3] of 1920, *Glass Jug and Fruit*,[4] of 1938, and *Mushrooms* (Plate 15),[5] of 1940; of portraits *Miss Jekyll*,[6] of 1940, *Walter Greaves*,[7] of 1917, and *Professor Saintsbury*,[8] of 1925, and of intimate landscapes *Black Swans at Chartwell*,[9] of 1932.

Nicholson was at his best when he responded directly to a simple subject (in so far as any subject might retain its simplicity under the subtle scrutiny of this being whom Robert Nichols aptly compared to a sophisticated child), for he seems to have been little interested in the deeper implications of the appearance of things. His mind, like his eye, was preoccupied wholly with the intimate segments of the surface of the world that came under his minute and affectionate observation (with foreign or unfamiliar subjects he had no success). Never was there a less enquiring or reflecting, or, in the best sense, a more *superficial* mind. Very occasionally he did probe beneath the surface. For instance, in the amusingly contrasted double portraits of *Mr. and Mrs. Sidney Webb*,[10] of about 1927, and *The Earl and Countess of Strafford*,[11] of 1940, he has made, in the words of Miss Steen,

an almost Hogarthian commentary on the new and the old aristocracy. In the one [she notes] with its ugly modern fireplace of a suburban villa, its litter of documents, the earnest shapelessness of Lord Passfield's

[1] The Walker Art Gallery, Liverpool.   [2] The Tate Gallery, London.
[3] Coll. Miss Vivien Leigh.
[4] Coll. The Rt. Hon. Vincent Massey, Toronto.
[5] The Tate Gallery, London.   [6] The National Portrait Gallery, London.
[7] The City Art Gallery, Manchester.   [8] Merton College, Oxford.
[9] Coll. Mrs. Winston Churchill.   [10] The London School of Economics.
[11] Coll. The Earl and Countess of Strafford.

trousers, his carpet slippers, his wife's hand clawing absently towards an economical fire, epitomizes low living and high thinking as thoroughly as the other epitomizes high living and as little thinking as possible. . . . Lady Strafford changing one of the cards of her Patience, Lord Strafford dangling 'The Times' from one drowsy hand.

Miss Steen's claim is justified: the artist has summed up and contrasted two ways of life and thought with extraordinary acuteness. But ordinarily he is content with an almost wholly visual regard – a regard not simply retinal, as Monet's sometimes was, but a vision disciplined by his sense of style and amplified by knowledge. 'Painting isn't only sight', he observed to Nichols; 'it's knowledge. In addition it's capacity to remember.' Nicholson's intimate, civilized vision is a highly traditional vision, for it perceives clearly defined objects, and has little in common with that newer vision evolved by Rembrandt, Turner, Constable and Delacroix, according to which appearances are composed of planes and contours which change continually under the influence of light. Now and then not only in his landscapes, but even in such a still-life, for example, as the *Glass Jug and Fruit* referred to above, he was conspicuously affected by it, but he was most himself among objects which existed tangibly, so to speak, in their own right. This remained essentially though less emphatically the case, it seems to me, until the end, even though he moved steadily from the umbrageous glossiness of *The Lowestoft Bowl, The Marquis Wellington Jug*, to the light-suffused *Gold Jug*,[1] of 1937.

The relation between the art and the personality of William Nicholson was not complementary or in any sense paradoxical: the one was, quite simply, an extension of the other. There was about this personality, as both Miss Steen and Nichols have observed, something childlike: he lived in the present, without much troubling himself about past or future. He delighted in what was civilized – for preference, in the intimate, the highly finished, the whimsical – he was alienated by anything which might be regarded as pretentious, but he occasionally condemned as pretentious persons and achievements authentically great. When he served as a Trustee of the Tate Gallery, he was sparing in his praise of his contemporaries, but when he praised, he praised with an endearing conviction and pugnacity,

[1] Coll. H.M. Queen Elizabeth the Queen Mother.

and I recall with gratitude his advocacy of two painters, favourites of mine, whose art had nothing in common with his own, Walter Greaves and Edward Burra. Dandyism, in his case a desire for an unobtrusive yet original elegance, was, I believe, the strongest and most enduring motive of his actions: such elegance he also aspired to achieve, though with less passion, in his clothes, in his houses – in fact, in everything with which he was intimately concerned. He would wear white duck trousers and patent leather shoes in his studio. He was the pioneer, I believe, of the spotted collar worn with the spotted shirt. When collars were worn high, he, 'seeking glory', he admitted, 'even in the cannon's mouth', wore higher collars than anyone else. I cannot recall his appearance in such early days, but I well remember the small, neat figure in the olive-green coat and white trousers, and the 'ivory-coloured, enquiring little face, with a hat cocked at a knowing angle' which impressed Miss Steen when she first met him in the middle nineteen-thirties. No. 11 Apple Tree Yard, St. James's, the stable which he took in 1917, he gradually transformed into a studio that was efficient, a delight to live in, and a monument – a miniature monument – to his taste, filled with the whimsical precious accumulation of years: lustre jugs, sporting prints, caricatures by Max Beerbohm, Callot maps, military drums, a top-hat to hold his brushes. . . .

About 1947, following a stroke, he experienced a sudden failure of his mental powers. Miss Steen, with whom he lived since shortly after their first meeting in 1934, took him to Blewbury, the Berkshire village where she had a house, and devoted herself to a vain attempt to restore him to health. It was suggested that he should continue to paint, on account of the tranquillizing effect of this occupation. Rather than fall below the severe standards which he had always set himself, he renounced the possibility of recovery and the greatest pleasure which life had to offer him. His health continued to decline, and he died on 16 May 1949.

HAROLD GILMAN

1876–1919

MENTION has been made earlier in these pages of the co-operative activities of a group of friends radiating from 19 Fitzroy Street, one of Sickert's accumulation of odd painting rooms. Sickert, whose opinions underwent frequent changes, never changed his prejudice against the selection by jury of works of art for exhibition – a prejudice shared by his Fitzroy Street friends. There was no no-jury exhibition in London in those days. In 1907 the art critic Frank Rutter undertook to organize one. The Allied Artists' Association, a body similar in organization to the Société des Artistes Indépendants in Paris, was consequently formed. The new Association gained enthusiastic support in Fitzroy Street. At the General Meeting held in the spring of 1908, in response to a plaintive proposal by an obscure member that 'the best works by the best artists' should be given the best places in the exhibition, Sickert thus voiced the prevailing sentiment: 'in this society there are no good works or bad works: there are only works by share-holders'. The Association's first exhibition – a huge assembly of pictures by some 600 members – was opened in the Albert Hall in the July of the same year. The Association, although open to anybody who cared to join, in fact replaced the New English Art Club as the rallying point for adventurous talent, and as the most effective rival to the Royal Academy. The attitude which members of the new society maintained towards the old was exemplified in the reply of a member of the hanging committee, Theodore Roussel, to a lady who asked him how he could hang such dreadful pictures. 'Madam', he said, 'we have the same privilege, as at the Royal Academy, of hanging bad pictures; only here *we have not the right to refuse the good.*' But there was in general a geniality about their disapprobation. 'You're going to tell me', said Walter Bayes to Rutter, who had invited him to become a member, 'that your exhibition will be better than the Royal Academy.' 'I'm not', Rutter said. 'It's going to be bigger and worse.' 'In that case', Bayes said, 'I'll join with pleasure.'

In accordance with the democratic constitution of the Association, all members were eligible to serve on the hanging committee, and invitations were sent out in alphabetical order. By the third year, 1910, it was the turn of the Gs. This system brought together Harold Gilman, Charles Ginner and Spencer Frederick Gore. The result of this fortuitous meeting was to give a new impetus and a new direction to English painting. Not since the earlier years of the New English Art Club had there been so quickening a centre of energy and enquiry as was presently provided by the intimate association of these three painters. The outlook of the New English, though ferociously attacked in academic circles, was, in fact, sufficiently temperate to remain content to develop the ideas which had animated the Barbizon painters and the Impressionists – ideas which, for Paris at least, had long since ceased to be a novel focus of interest. It was not, however, the principles of its most articulate members, nor even the brilliant performance of its most gifted, that enabled the Club to play so singularly fructifying a part in the history of English painting. This part it was enabled to sustain for more than two decades by the discriminating liberality of its management, and the resulting interaction of temperaments issued in a widely diffused impulse to creativity.

The movement generated by Gilman and his friends was more firmly anchored to principle, and its impact, though sharper, was necessarily more limited both in duration and extent.

Gilman was a massive, confident figure, tenacious and fond of argument, with the kind of presence suggested by a contemporary journalist, who wrote of his 'bald head and regal mouth'. Ginner, one of the most consistent painters of the time, possessed a knowledge of Parisian theory and practice approached by very few of his English contemporaries. Gore fostered a wonderful talent for reconciling all honourably reconcilable attitudes.

Gilman and Gore were already old friends who had studied together at the Slade and were also friends of Sickert and Lucien Pissarro, and frequenters of 19 Fitzroy Street. Gore had admired the paintings that Ginner sent over from Paris to the first exhibition of the Allied Artists' Association two years before and asked Rutter who he was. Rutter knew nothing of him except that he lived in Paris. In 1910 Ginner came over especially to serve on the hanging committee. Gilman and Gore introduced themselves, and told him they liked his work.

Harold Gilman was the second son of the Rev. John Gilman, Rector of Snargate with Snave, Kent, a son of Ellis Gilman, head of the firm of Hamilton, Gray & Co., of Singapore. He was born at Rode, Somerset, on 11 February 1876, and educated at Abingdon, Rochester and Tonbridge schools. In 1894 he went up to Brasenose College, Oxford, but ill-health compelled him to terminate his studies before he could take his degree. The year 1895 he spent in Odessa. In 1896 he decided to become a painter, spending a year at the Hastings Art School and the four following years at the Slade, working under Brown, Steer and Tonks. The year 1904 he spent in Spain, he visited the United States in 1905 and Norway shortly before the First World War. At the Slade he seems to have learnt little and made no mark. The important event in his early life as a painter was his study of Velazquez at the Prado, of several of whose works he made careful copies.

I have seen few of the paintings which resulted from his attempts to apply the principles of Velazquez, but they appear to have been mostly portraits, often life-size, low-keyed harmonies of greys and browns, and smooth in texture and in general somewhat Whistlerian in intention, with something about them of Manet and the Belgian Stevens. I recently saw a landscape, a crepuscular, weakly drawn Whistlerian essay, *The Thames at Hammersmith*,[1] of, perhaps, 1909, which is, though far from undistinguished, a tidy compendium of the very qualities which, but a few years later, he was most fiercely to abjure. The real significance of his discipleship of the Spanish master was not, however, apparent in these paintings, but in the insight he gained into the mind of one of the supreme realistic painters. Gilman's was one of those powerful temperaments which mature slowly, but however unconvincing its first-fruits, it is clear that prolonged contact with Velazquez strengthened his own innate realism. It is reasonable to suppose that it was from him that he learnt that the pursuit of nature could not be too close. Next he came into the orbit of 19 Fitzroy Street. At this time he was still preoccupied with tone values, but his admiration for Lucien Pissarro, and through him for the Impressionists, led him to an enhanced sense of the attrac-

[1] Coll. Reid and Lefevre.

tions of pure and brilliant colour. At the same time, Sickert opened his eyes to the poetry of popular subjects, of public-houses, of Camden Town 'interiors' with their chests-of-drawers and iron bedsteads, and showed him how to extract poetry from the near and the familiar. Camden Town, for Gilman, was, of course, the near and the familiar, for he spent the greater part of his life as a painter in this neighbourhood, first in the Hampstead Road by the railway bridge, later at 47 Maple Street, Tottenham Court Road. (The last time I saw this square Georgian house, the rooms of which Gilman depicted in such brilliant colours, it had become a blackened ruin, and the wooden shutters were being furiously banged by the cold night wind.) From Sickert he also adopted the broken brush stroke but he used rather lighter tones than this friends, and his touch was already more deliberate. It was at this point in his development that he and Gore met Ginner. Immediately afterwards, Ginner called on him, and found him painting the portrait of the wife of his friend, R. P. Bevan. Gilman, although he was very much aware that there had been momentous movements on the Continent since Impressionism had passed its climax, had no precise idea of their nature.[1] The discovery that his new friend Ginner was familiar with the work of those fascinating but, so far as London was concerned, mysterious leaders of the younger generation, Gauguin, Cézanne and van Gogh, still further enhanced in Gilman's eyes the value of his friendship.

There took place at this time an event that provoked differences more radical and widespread, perhaps, than any single event in the history of art in England. This was the exhibition 'Manet and the Post-Impressionists' – generally known as 'The first Post-Impressionist Exhibition' to distinguish it from the 'Second Post-Impressionist Exhibition' held in the same place from 5 October until 31 December 1912 – organized by Roger Fry, and held at the Grafton Galleries, Grafton Street, from 8 November 1910 until 15 January 1911. For it was through this exhibition that the British

---

[1] Works by contemporary Continental masters had occasionally been shown in London before 1910: Sixty paintings and twenty drawings and lithographs by Lautrec at the Goupil Gallery in May 1898. Cézanne was represented (with Boudin, Degas, Manet, Monet, Morisot, Pissarro, Renoir and Sisley) at the International Society's first exhibition in the same year, and by ten works in a Durand-Ruel Exhibition at the Grafton Galleries in 1905, and again with Rodin in 1906, and Matisse and Gauguin at the New Gallery in 1908.

public (including almost the entire body of British artists) first received the full impact of Cézanne, van Gogh and Matisse – and a shattering impact it was. When the ensuing controversy died down, it was seen that this exhibition had changed the face of the art world of London. Here, as everywhere else, there had always been conflict between 'progressive' and 'conservative' opinion. 'Progressive' opinion upheld, while 'conservative' opinion condemned, for instance, Benjamin West's use of contemporary, in place of the traditional classical, costume in the painting of 'history', Pre-Raphaelitism, and the 'Impressionism' of the New English Art Club. Yet it was also the case that 'progressive' and 'conservative' had always merged by insensible degrees one into the other. One of the principal consequences of the first Post-Impressionist Exhibition was to sharpen the differences between the opposing factions. Thenceforward one had to be for or against 'modern art', without qualification. Another was that British painting assumed a less insular character. A third was the emergence of Fry as the most influential English art critic and politician in the place of D. S. MacColl, the severe and eloquent theorist, champion and chastener of the New English and scourge of the Royal Academy.

Gilman and Ginner visited this momentous exhibition together. At first sight Gilman was captivated by Gauguin, in particular by the richness of his colour and his variety as a designer, but he was unable to accept van Gogh as an entirely serious painter. What he saw at the Grafton Galleries impressed him so deeply as to call for a complete examination of his own fundamental convictions. For a nature so scrupulous, so deliberate, so confident in the validity of ideas as Gilman, this was a serious process. Ginner took him to Paris, where they saw everything that could be seen: the room decorated by van Gogh at Bernheim's; Pellerin's fabulous assembly of Cézannes; the great collection of Impressionists at Durand-Ruel's, and the work of painters of more recent growth, the Douanier Rousseau, Bonnard, Vuillard and Picasso at the galleries of Vollard and Sagot. On his return, his judgements were compared, in the course of innumerable discussions, with the maturer judgements of Ginner. As Gilman reflected and talked, his original enthusiasm for Gauguin cooled into respect. Cézanne he deeply admired, but it was van Gogh who in the end emerged for him as the greatest of modern masters, and as the master who could teach him most of what he wished to learn. ('Letters of a Post-Impressionist, being the familiar correspondence of Vincent van Gogh', which was constantly in his hands, might be termed his Bible.) These discussions, in which Gore often joined, and assiduous experiment, crystallized in a distinctive aesthetic, to which all three artists subscribed.[1] Ginner eventually formulated the general idea which formed the heart of it when he declared:

> All great painters by direct intercourse with Nature have extracted from her facts which others have not observed, and interpreted them by methods which are personal and expressive of themselves – this is the great tradition of Realism. . . . Greco, Rembrandt, Millet, Courbet, Cézanne – all the great painters of the world have known that great art can only be created out of continued intercourse with Nature.

The arch-menace to the great tradition of Realism, he contended, is always

> the adoption by weaker commercial painters of the creative artist's personal methods of interpreting nature and the consequent creation of a formula, it is this which constitutes Academism. . . . It has resulted in the decadence of every Art movement . . . until it finally ended in the 'debacle' of Bouguereau, Gérôme, of the British Royal Academy. . . .

He then proceeded to the analysis of the form which the arch-menace had assumed at the time at which he wrote. Although

> the old Academic movement which reigned at Burlington House and the Paris Salon counts no more . . . there is a new Academic movement full of dangers. Full of dangers, because it is disguised under a false cloak. It cries that it is going to save Art, while, in reality, it will destroy it. What in England is known as Post-Impressionism – Voilà l'ennemi! It is all the more dangerous since it is enveloped in a rose-pink halo of interest. Take away the rose-pink and you find the Academic skeleton.

[1] This was set forth by Ginner on various occasions, most comprehensively in an article entitled 'Neo-Realism', which first appeared in 'The New Age' and was reprinted as the foreword to the catalogue of an exhibition of paintings by Gilman and Ginner at the Goupil Gallery, held in 18 April–9 May, 1914.

Those who adopted the superficial aspects of the work or the teaching of Cézanne, whether straightforward imitators or Cubists, were singled out for particular condemnation. A sharp distinction was drawn between the Romantic Realism of Gauguin, who himself went to the South Seas, and his personal interpretation, and the formula created by Matisse and Co., 'to be worked quietly at home in some snug Paris studio. . . .' He attacked the idea that Decoration is the unique aim of art, and spoke of the importance of subject to the realist:

> Each age has its landscape, its atmosphere, its cities, its people. Realism, loving Life, loving its Age, interprets its Epoch by extracting from it the very essence of all it contains of great or weak, of beautiful or of sordid, according to the individual temperament.

Impressionism in France, he concluded, was beyond question the latest and most important realistic movement, for 'the Impressionists, by their searching study of light, purified the muddy palettes by exchanging colour values for tone values'. The Neo-Impressionists neglected, in their scientific preoccupations,

> to keep themselves in relationship with Nature. . . . On the other hand, we find Cézanne, Gauguin and van Gogh, all three children of Impressionism, learning from it, as a wholesome source, all that it had to teach, and with their eyes fixed on the only true spring of Art: Life itself.

I have quoted from Ginner's essay at some length not because it adumbrates a theory – albeit at points somewhat summarily – to which I can subscribe, but because it provided a basis for the practice of three serious and gifted painters and general guidance for a number of others.

The close association of Gilman, Gore and Ginner affected Ginner relatively little, as his own highly personal style was already mature when he came to England in 1910, but it resulted in the formation of something approaching a common style. This left the widest latitude to the individual eye and hand: it would hardly be possible, that is to say, to mistake any single canvas by any of these three for one by either of the others. The most noticeable consequence of their study of the Impressionists, of Cézanne and of their two great successors was their adoption of a brighter palette. This involved, for Gilman

15. Sir William Nicholson.
Mushrooms (1940).
Oil, 13¼×17⅜ in.
The Tate Gallery, London.

16. HAROLD GILMAN.
Eating house (1914).
Oil, 17½ × 23½ in.
Coll. Mr. Edward le Bas.

and Gore, an end of their discipleship of Sickert, who continued to use the sombre colours which they came to regard as anathema. Wyndham Lewis has described how Gilman

> would look over in the direction of Sickert's studio, and a slight shudder would convulse him as he thought of the little brown worm of paint that was possibly, even at that moment, wriggling out on to the palette that held no golden chromes, emerald greens, vermilions, *only*, as it, of course, should do.[1]

Equally important was their repudiation – most emphatic with Gilman and least with Gore – of the Impressionist conception of a painting as having something of the character of a sketch, of something begun and completed under the same ephemeral effect, or of having that appearance. Gilman was determined to give his work the qualities of permanence and dignity. To this end he broadened his planes, simplified his masses and gave his designs firmness to the point of rigidity. And he rejected the light brush strokes of the Impressionists and Sickert: he painted with slow deliberation, putting the utmost thought into every touch. And his colour assumed a splendid and forthright brilliance. In the course of his struggle to obtain these qualities, and on the advice of Sickert and Ginner, he worked less from life and relied more upon his admirable pen-and-ink drawings. Ardently as he rejoiced in broad planes, firm designs and deliberate brush strokes, which made mosaics of brilliant colour, he never painted for painting's sake, nor was he moved solely by the aesthetic impulse. On the contrary, he was intensely moved by the human significance of the spectacle of surrounding life: he did not paint his mother, and Mrs. Mounter, the landlady whom he has made immortal, or his rooms in Maple Street, or even his massive teapots, as Cézanne painted apples, because they were accessible and they stayed still. He painted them because he loved them. Discussing Daumier's series of Don Quixotes, Gilman confided to his friend Sir Louis Fergusson that one of his greatest ambitions was to create a character, or rather to seize the essence of a character in real life and exhibit it on canvas in all its bearings. His love for the persons and things nearest to him grew with his growth as a painter.

[1] 'Harold Gilman: An Appreciation', by Wyndham Lewis and Louis F. Fergusson, 1919, p. 13.

The consistent growth of his powers of heart and eye and hand can be traced by comparing four paintings of different periods of his maturity: *The Little French Girl*,[1] of about 1909, a delicate work, beautifully true in tone, in greys and pinks plainly derived from his study of Velazquez. The girl herself is affectionately portrayed; so too is the furniture. When we set this beside *The Artist's Mother*,[2] of 1917, it seems to lack personality and candour: we become aware that the touch of pathos in the little girl is a consequence of the expedient of placing her, by herself, in a big room. The dignity and repose of his mother are obtained, as Americans put it, 'the hard way', by the most direct rendering in deeply pondered, immediately arrested, brush strokes. But next to *Mrs. Mounter* (Plate 17),[3] of 1917, even his mother, splendid painting though it is, looks small in form and confused in colour. *Mrs. Mounter*, with its majestic design in broad planes, its intensely brilliant colour and its tender insight, in my opinion is one of the great English portraits of the century, one among perhaps a dozen. I do not think that Gilman ever surpassed this portrait, but his last big painting, of a subject panoramic and entirely unfamiliar, which called for a composition infinitely more complex, showed that he had not reached the limit of his development. This picture was the radiant and stately *Halifax Harbour after the Explosion*,[4] of 1918, which, when I last saw it, shed an incongruous lustre in a dark, neo-Gothic gallery in the New World, above the door of which, unless my memory is playing tricks, was carved the word FOSSILS. Although this must take a place among his finest paintings, he did not require, in order to obtain grandeur of form, a subject grand, as Halifax Harbour is, in any ordinary sense. A picture which it is instructive to compare with this great work is one scarcely inferior to it which represents the interior of a small *Eating-House* (Plate 16),[5] of about 1914. Here, three wooden partitions against walls of pitch-pine and wallpaper and casual glimpses of nondescript diners have been transformed by Gilman's robust affection into a noble design in which harshly glowing colour is fused with closely knit form.

[1] The Tate Gallery, London.   [2] The Tate Gallery, London.
[3] The Walker Art Gallery, Liverpool. There is a smaller version, of 1916, in the Tate Gallery.
[4] The National Gallery of Canada, Ottawa.   [5] Coll. Mr. Edward le Bas.

By 1914, when he was thirty-eight years old, Gilman had evolved a way of seeing and a way of drawing and painting which enabled him, when circumstances were propitious, to produce masterpieces. Five years later he and Ginner caught Spanish influenza in the great epidemic of 1919 and were taken to the French Hospital, where he died on 12 February.

The death of Gilman was a grave loss to English painting. He was the acknowledged leader of a group of friends who had infused a new vigour into a great modern tradition. His character, in particular the union of intense seriousness with exuberant goodwill, endeared him to a wide circle of friends. Something of the flavour of this character is caught in this description by Wyndham Lewis:

> The Gilman tic was a thing prized by his friends next to the sternness of his painting. He was proud of a pompous drollery, which he flavoured with every resource of an abundantly nourished country rectory, as he was proud of his parsonic stock. He was proud of his reverberating pulpit voice: he was proud of the eccentricities of his figure. He was also proud of a certain fleeting resemblance, observed by the ribald, to George Robey, the priceless ape. But, above all, he was proud to be a man who could sometimes hang his pictures in the neighbourhood of a picture postcard of the great modern master, van Gogh.[1]

Unlike many, possibly the majority of artists, Gilman was deeply concerned for the wellbeing of the art of painting in general. He favoured working with a small, cohesive group of other painters, partly because he believed that new methods are evolved not by individuals, but, as Sickert used to say, by gangs, partly because he regarded such a group as an effective means of propagating sound methods. He was also an able and earnest teacher.

The Allied Artists' Association was recognized by Gilman and his friends as a valuable means of enabling artists, especially independent and lesser-known artists, to show their work, but its exhibitions were on altogether too vast a scale to exert influence in any particular direction. The more clearly their opinions crystallized, the more aware did they become of their need for a platform from which to proclaim them. The question as to how they were to obtain one was the occasion of numerous discussions among them. This question

---

[2] 'Harold Gilman: An Appreciation', pp. 13–14.

quickly resolved itself into a simple issue: whether to try to capture the New English Art Club or to form a new society.

> . . . I doubt if any unprejudiced student of modern painting will deny [wrote Sickert in 1910] that the New English Art Club at the present day sets the standard of painting in England. He may regret it or resent it, but he will hardly deny it.[1]

This estimate of the Club's importance was shared by Gilman and his friends, but of recent years his own work and that of the painters whom he most admired had been rejected by its juries. Sickert was of the decided opinion that they stood no chance of obtaining control of the New English, and Gore (who had become a member the previous year) was reluctantly convinced that it had tacitly renounced the pioneering policy for which it had earlier been conspicuous, and had become, in fact although not in profession, an academic force, and that its capture was therefore not even to be desired. Augustus John firmly maintained the view that the New English stood for the highest prevailing standards, and it would be wrong to secede, especially for him who owed everything to it. The climax of these discussions came early in 1911 when, over dinner at Gatti's, it was decided to form a new society. Gilman, innately uncompromising, who had favoured this course from the first, was jubilant, and Sickert, leaving the restaurant ahead of the others, grandiloquently exclaimed, 'We have just made history.' A meeting to settle details was held at 19 Fitzroy Street. There were further meetings at the Criterion Restaurant, and, finally, in May, at a restaurant long since demolished, off Golden Square, the new society was formed and appropriately christened by Sickert 'The Camden Town Group'.[2] Gore was elected President. The Group held only three exhibitions, in June and December 1911 and December 1912, all at the Carfax Gallery in Bury Street, St. James's. None of these was a financial success, and Arthur Clifton, the director of the Carfax Gallery, was not prepared to continue them. Members of

---

[1] 'The Allied Artists' Association', *The Art News*, 14 July.

[2] The original members were: Walter Bayes, R. P. Bevan, Malcolm Drummond, Harold Gilman, Charles Ginner, Spencer Gore, J. D. Innes, Augustus John, Henry Lamb, Wyndham Lewis, M. G. Lightfoot, J. B. Manson (Secretary), Lucien Pissarro, W. Ratcliffe, W. R. Sickert, Doman Turner. Duncan Grant joined after the first exhibition.

the Group then approached William Marchant, proprietor of the Goupil Gallery, with the view of transferring their exhibitions to his premises. He was sympathetically disposed, but he objected to the title of the Group for the very reason that had led Sickert to choose it – namely, that a sensational murder had given Camden Town an ominous reputation. He also favoured an enlarged society in order to ensure that his more capacious galleries should be filled.

By 1913 there was a spirit of fusion abroad. Of the various groups active in the region about Tottenham Court Road – of which the membership was largely identical – each had its particular difficulty. All suffered from insufficient resources and the consciousness of being too small to be effective. The Camden Town Group fused with 19 Fitzroy Street, and successfully sought the adherence of the Vorticist Group led by Wyndham Lewis, of which Frederick Etchells,[1] William Roberts and Edward Wadsworth were the principal members. After protracted negotiations, a meeting was held on 15 November 1913 at 19 Fitzroy Street, with Sickert presiding, at which it was decided to form yet another and more comprehensive society, and to call it the London Group. Gilman was elected President, and continued in office until his death. The new group represented a fusion not only of the three groups already mentioned, but also of the Cumberland Market Group which came into being on the initiative of Gilman and Bevan[2] as a successor to 19 Fitzroy Street. Shortly afterwards Spencer Gore died, and with his death the tensions within the London Group, latent in the presence of his disinterested benevolence, his tact and his charm, caused dangerous rifts. The outbreak of the First World War brought further confusion, and when it cleared away, the Group fell under the control of Fry whose aims were totally opposed to those of its founders.

More satisfying to Gilman than all this formation and amalgamation of groups – for he lacked the adaptability, the guile, the

[1] After the First World War he devoted himself mainly to architecture.

[2] Robert Polhill Bevan, painter of horses, market scenes and landscapes. Born in Hove, Sussex, 5 August 1865. Studied for a short time at the Westminster School under Brown, then in Paris at Julian's. Met Gauguin 1894 at Pont Aven. Married S. de Karlowska 1897. An original member of the Camden Town Group 1911, and of the London Group 1913; member of the New English Art Club 1923. Died 8 July 1925 in London.

ambition and the talent for intrigue, all, indeed, of the political talents except clarity of aim, persistence and the more doubtful asset of courage – was his teaching. For a time he taught an evening life-class at the Westminster School. The class had for some time been taught by Sickert, who resigned shortly after the outbreak of war, and Gore was appointed in his place. On the death of Gore, or possibly earlier, the class was taken over by Gilman. Before long Sickert, wishing to resume his teaching at Westminster, secured Gilman's dismissal. This caused a breach between him and his friend and teacher that was never healed. Gilman's evening classes, both at the Westminster and at the small school at 16 Little Pulteney Street, Soho, that he afterwards ran with Ginner, were attended by admirers of his painting who, in the words of one of them, 'wished to learn to see colour as he saw it'. The usual subjects were nudes and charwomen. Gilman, who shared Sickert's disapproval of the painting of figures in isolation from their environment, used to fit up a screen with a boldly patterned wallpaper for a background. The method of painting he taught was, of course, that which he had himself evolved. In accordance with this method his students made no under-painting or anything of the nature of a preliminary sketch, but instead they built up their pictures in separate brush strokes, each carefully considered and rightly related to the rest. They began with the highest lights and worked downwards to the darker passages, looking rather for colour than tone relations, for he did not subscribe to the widely held belief that if tone relations were right, right colour relations would inevitably follow. They were taught that there was no such thing as a uniform surface that could be represented by a wide sweep of the brush; that all surfaces that presented this appearance at first glance proved under scrutiny to have infinite subtle variations. Although they were enjoined to aim at finality with each brush stroke and never to be content with less, it was recognized that this was a counsel of perfection, and they were bound to err, especially at first, but it was infinitely preferable to err on the side of overstatement of a colour's strength and purity, and the grossest error was to take refuge, when in doubt, in some indeterminate colour such as brown. Colours inclined to be neutral must be forced to confess a tendency to a positive colour, and this intensified. The colours of the spectrum and white were the colours they used. Gilman said one day, after some deliberation, that an occasion *might* arise when, say, raw sienna was the proper colour to use, for one touch, but this he thought most unlikely, and he advised them (for the hundredth time) to avoid, if they were to escape the danger of muddiness, all earth colours. The scraping off of any paint from their canvases he never favoured, but advised them instead to add fresh touches on top of the old, nor did he mind how thick, in consequence, they painted, observing that some of Rembrandt's canvases must originally have been very heavily loaded.

Gilman gave his students the strong impression of *seeing* the clear, pure greens, lilacs and yellows he used in painting flesh, and of being unable to see in any other way. Inevitably they themselves came to see nature in terms of pure colour relationships. Certain of his methods evidently derived from Signac and Seurat, but his aims, unlike theirs, were in no way affected by their scientific preoccupations: with him the emphasis was always on the *beauty* of the colour in the subject. He shared Sickert's opinion that even a knowledge of perspective and anatomy was superfluous to someone able to render tone and the direction of lines with sensibility and precision. He surprised one of his students by telling him to begin the drawing of a nude with an outline silhouette. So confident was he that he tempered his own dogmatic approach by taking any observations a student ventured to make with the utmost seriousness, and by an openness to new ideas. This combination of certainty and modesty made him an admirable teacher. He did not work on his students' canvases, and their familiarity with his own work made 'demonstration' un-necessary. His criticism generally took the form of a searching analysis of the subject in terms of colour relations.

In spite of the brevity of his professional life and of his restricted scope as a teacher, and of the prompt diversion to ends with which he could have had no sympathy of the organization that represented the culmination of his political activity, there are signs that the reputation and influence of this single-minded and uncompromising painter stand higher than at any time since his death. Higher, certainly, in one particular: during his lifetime scarcely anybody except his friends bought his modestly priced pictures; now they are year by year more difficult to acquire.

GWEN JOHN

1876–1939

GWEN JOHN was in almost every respect the opposite of
her brother Augustus. He is an improviser; she developed
methodicity, as he has told us, to a point of elaboration
undreamed of by her master, Whistler. He is expansive; she was
concentrated. He is exuberant; she was chaste, subdued and sad. He
is Dionysian; she was a devoted Catholic. He enhanced or troubled
the lives of those whom he touched; she stole through life and out of
it almost unnoticed.

Neither in France, where she mostly lived, nor in her own
country, did her work arouse sufficient interest during her lifetime
to inspire, so far as I am aware, a single article. In 1946, seven years
after her death, a Memorial Exhibition, consisting of 217 works
in various mediums, was held in London.[1] This was received with
marked respect, but a few months later, if she was not quite forgotten,
she occupied only a tiny niche in the public memory. Its most
memorable consequence was the arresting evocation of his sister's
memory in Augustus John's foreword to the catalogue.

Yet few of those privileged to know her work fail to receive from
it a lasting impression. Many of them are moved to compare it with
that of her brother, to his disadvantage. The expressions of personalities so opposite as Gwen and Augustus John are hardly comparable;
we can only note the contrasts between them. About this there
would be nothing invidious, for he is his sister's most ardent advocate.
The very extremity of the contrasts between these two children of
the same parents has always seemed to fascinate Augustus John:
I have seen him peer fixedly, almost obsessively, at pictures by Gwen
as though he could discern in them his own temperament in reverse;
as though he could derive from the act satisfaction in his own wider
range, greater natural endowment, tempestuous energy, and at the
same time be reproached by her single-mindedness, her steadiness

[1] At the Matthiesen Gallery, from 17 September until 12 October; a selection
was shown under the auspices of the Arts Council in several other cities.

160

17. HAROLD GILMAN. *Mrs. Mounter at the Breakfast Table* (1917).
Oil, 36×23 in. The Walker Art Gallery, Liverpool.

18. GWEN JOHN. *A Corner of the Artist's Room in Paris* (1900–05?).
Oil, 12½ × 10½ in. Coll. Mrs. Augustus John.

of focus, above all by the sureness with which she attained her simpler aims.

The case of Gwen John provides a melancholy illustration of the neglect of English painting. I am not expressing an original opinion in saying that I believe her to be one of the finest painters of our time and country, yet – apart from her brother's eulogy and a discerning article on the Memorial Exhibition by Wyndham Lewis[1] – her work has received no serious consideration whatever; indeed, it can scarcely be said to have been noticed at all. Outside the Tate, which possesses a dozen of her paintings and drawings, she is insignificantly represented in public collections and there are relatively few of her works in private hands. Gwen John is, in fact, in danger of oblivion. It would be unjust to her contemporaries to suggest that they are solely to blame. She herself deliberately chose a life of seclusion. After her death a number of her paintings disappeared from the little room she occupied. No work by her later than 1932 is known, and so withdrawn was her life during the closing years of it that it is uncertain whether she ceased to paint or whether the paintings she made were lost. Not many of her friends survive, and those who do recollect curiously little about her. One of them invited me to his house not long ago, telling me that he saw her often during that last obscure decade. When I arrived he confessed that his memory retained nothing precise. Even her family's recollections are meagre. So it is an elusive personality that I am trying to reconstruct.

Fortunately, thanks to the kindness of Mr. Edwin John, her favourite nephew, I have had access to a number of important documents. During her last years she possessed a little shack on a piece of waste land where she lived and worked, and an attic room in a neighbouring house, which she had previously occupied but used latterly for the storage of her effects, both at Meudon. After her death her nephew, who is also her heir, went to Meudon, where he found in the attic room, besides a number of pictures, a mass of papers, covered with dust, that had lain for years there undisturbed. These include a few letters from Rilke, a number from her father, and a long series of intimate brief letters from Rodin. The letters addressed to her are largely complemented by

[1] 'The Listener', 10 October 1946.

copies that she made of others of which the originals are missing (several evidently from M. Jacques Maritain, for example), by numerous drafts or copies of her own letters to Rodin and others, and copies of prayers and meditations and extracts from the writings of the saints and other Catholic writers, as well as from Bertrand Russell, Baudelaire, Dostoievski, Oscar Wilde and Diderot. There is something puzzling about these copies. It is understandable that she should wish to preserve copies of such of her letters as she valued and make drafts of letters difficult to compose, but this does not account entirely for the number of such copies. There is one meditation of which there are seven, several of them identical. From all these papers I have had permission, through the kindness of her brother and her nephew, to quote, but in view of the most intimate character of many of them and of Gwen John's extreme reticence about her own life, I shall avail myself of it as sparingly as the requirements of my narrative allow.

Gwendolen Mary John was born on 22 June 1876 at Haverfordwest, Pembrokeshire, the second of the four children of Edwin William John, a solicitor, and his wife Augusta, born Smith, of a Brighton family. Not long after her birth the family moved to 5 Lexden Terrace, Tenby. Here, in an attic, Gwen and Augustus, in both of whom their vocation early declared itself, had their first studio. An extraordinary capacity for devotion was also early evident in Gwen, who was always, her brother relates, 'picking up beautiful children to draw and adore'. In 1895 she followed Augustus to the Slade and they shared a series of rooms together, which they constantly changed, living solely on fruit and nuts. The intensity of Gwen's friendships at times made the atmosphere of the group of which the two of them were the focus 'almost unbearable', according to her brother, 'with its frightful tension, its terrifying excursions and alarms'. The break in one such friendship brought a threat of suicide. But the excursions and alarms did not interrupt the progress of her art. How beautifully she drew while she was still a student is apparent from her *Self-portrait at the Age of About Twenty*[1] (in which she looks considerably younger). One of her passionate attachments, in fact, was invaluable in fostering her technical knowledge of painting, for Ambrose McEvoy imparted to her the results of his

[1] In a private collection. No. 57 in the Matthiesen Exhibition.

researches into the methods of the old masters. Without his help, she could hardly have painted the *Self-portrait*[1] (Plate 19) in a red sealing-wax coloured blouse, which, although I am unable to date it precisely, was probably done soon after she left the Slade. This portrait – to my thinking, one of the finest portraits of the time, excelling in insight into character and in purity of form and delicacy of tone any portrait of McEvoy's – owes the technical perfection of its glazes to his knowledge, as generously imparted as it was laboriously acquired.

On leaving the Slade in 1898 she lived in a little room over a mortuary in the Euston Road, and later in a cellar in Howland Street, where she made water-colour drawings of cats. After leaving Howland Street, she lodged for a time with a family, father, mother and two sons, one of whom became a celebrated painter, in a house where the shutters were always closed, for they paid no rates. Before long she left England and settled in France, returning only for occasional visits. How bleak the interlude was between the Slade and Whistler's school in Paris to which she presently attached herself is clear from a letter to her brother.

> I told you in a letter long ago that I am happy [she wrote]. Where illness or death do not interfere, I am. Not many people can say as much. I do not lead a subterranean life (my subterranean life was in Howland Street) . . . If to 'return to life' is to live as I did in London – *Merci, Monsieur*! . . . There are people like plants who cannot flourish in the cold, and I want to flourish. . . .

At Whistler's school, taking to heart her master's saying, 'Art is the science of beauty', she proceeded, her brother has told us, to cultivate her painting in a scientific spirit. She used to prepare her canvases according to a recipe of her own, and invented a system of numbering her colour mixtures which, however helpful to her, makes her notes on painting and schemes for pictures unintelligible to anyone else.

> . . . She had [he added] no competitive spirit and rarely went out of her way to study her contemporaries, but was familiar with the National Gallery and the Louvre.

[1] The Tate Gallery, London.

When asked her opinion of an exhibition of Cézanne water-colours, her reply, scarcely audible, was 'These are very good, but I prefer my own.'[1]

Whistler's school was not a school at all in the current sense, but a class, managed by a former model named Carmen, which Whistler visited once a week. A comment by Whistler on the work of Gwen John is related by her brother, who met him in the Louvre and introduced himself as the brother of one of his pupils:

Mr. Whistler with great politeness asked me to make Gwen his compliments. I ventured to enquire if he thought well of her progress, adding that I thought her drawings showed a feeling for character. 'Character?' replied Whistler, 'Character? What's that? It's the tone that matters. Your sister has a fine sense of *tone*.'

Her attendance at Whistler's school was confined to the afternoons. She lived in a top flat in the Rue Froidveau, which she shared with two fellow students, Ida Nettleship, who was shortly to become the wife of Augustus John, and Gwen Salmond, some years later the wife of Matthew Smith. The three girls practised the most rigorous economy, and, although Gwen John outdid her companions in this respect, she was not able, out of her tiny allowance, to save sufficient to pay the small fees required to attend Whistler's school. By a benevolent act of intrigue, Gwen Salmond secured her admission as an afternoon pupil. 'I've written home', Gwen John delightedly exclaimed, 'that I've got a *scholarship*.' In spite of her dedication to painting and drawing, she seems to have done little of either at this time. An incident related by a friend who was a witness of it may explain this singular circumstance. Some time after she had gone to Paris, her father arrived on a short visit. By way of welcome, she arranged a small supper to which she invited several of her friends, at which she wore a dress copied from one in a picture by Manet. It was a dress to the making of which she had given infinite trouble; it had been purchased at the price of many frugal meals foregone. 'You look like a prostitute in that dress', was her father's opening observation. 'I could never accept anything from someone capable of thinking so', she answered, and my informant believes that in order to replace the rejected small allowance she posed regularly

[1] Introduction to the Catalogue of the Memorial Exhibition.

as an artist's model. For this she was qualified by a grave dignity and a beautiful, slender figure, 'un corps admirable', as Rodin, an authority on the subject, called it some years later. The incident left no bitterness, to judge from the long series of unintimate but prosily friendly letters from her father which she preserved.

Dates are difficult to establish, but it was probably in the autumn of 1898 that she first settled in Paris. A year or so later she was in London again. For a time she shared what my father described as 'comfortless' quarters with her brother in Fitzroy Street; then they moved into a house lent to them by my parents. My father, having to return to London for a night in the middle of the following winter, telegraphed to the Johns to warn them of his arrival, which he thus described:

> When I reached Kensington I found the house empty and no fire burning. In front of a cold grate choked with cinders lay a collection of muddy boots. . . . Late in the evening John appeared, having climbed through a window; he rarely, he explained, remembered to take the house-key with him.[1]

(In this house, 1 Pembroke Cottages, Edwardes Square, I was born eighteen months later.) Recalling, in the winter of the present year (1951) the events of that earlier winter, Augustus John observed confidentially: 'I'm afraid Will did not find Gwen and me very satisfactory tenants. . . .' He married in 1900, and Gwen must have remained in England for a while, for Ida, his first wife, wrote to my mother many months later saying: 'I long for Gwen; have you seen her lately?'

One autumn early in the new century, probably in 1902, she returned to France in circumstances which should enable me to fill in a little the tenuous outlines of the portrait that I am trying to draw – a portrait which nevertheless I shall find it difficult to bring clearly into focus. She was accompanied on a journey to Paris, by way of Bordeaux and Toulouse, by Dorelia, whom her brother married shortly after the death of his first wife, and to whom I am indebted for some details about both the journey and her companion. The two girls travelled by boat to Bordeaux, whence they walked to Toulouse. Their first night in France they spent in a field on a bank of the Garonne, and they were wakened in the morning by a

[1] 'Men and Memories', Vol. I, 1931, p. 352.

boar. They intended to walk on to Italy, but after spending three months or so in Toulouse and visiting Montauban they went to Paris instead. Here Gwen stayed for the rest of her life, apart from a few brief visits to England and to the French coast, for she loved the sea, and from time to time she needed, with a curious urgency, the refreshment she was able to draw from no other source. On their journey they lived spartanly. In Toulouse they lodged in two bare rooms which they rented for two francs a week; they subsisted upon bread, cheese and figs, which cost them fifty centimes a meal, and which they ate in the fields; and they bathed in the river, maintaining themselves meanwhile by making portrait sketches in cafés for three francs each. The person who emerges from Mrs. John's description was attractive to men and susceptible to their admiration; reserved and quiet-voiced; pale and oval-faced, her hair something in colour between mouse and honey, done with a big bow on top; with a slender figure, and tiny, delicate hands and feet, yet of exceptional strength, able to carry heavy burdens over long distances at speeds which her companion found excessive. 'I shouldn't like to carry *that*', shouted a sturdy Montauban workman, indicating the big bundle on her back. While not unsociable, she loved solitude; indifferent to mankind as a whole, she was passionately attached to her few friends, and apt to form other strong attachments that quickly cooled. Beneath a reserved friendliness occasionally varied by moodiness, Mrs. John was aware of a strain of censorious puritanism. She disapproved, for instance, of the theatre; she spoke angrily of the 'vulgar red lips' of a beautiful girl whom they used as a model. She rarely spoke of painting or other serious matters, but when they became subjects of conversation she was able to express herself with ease and conviction.

A few days after Mrs. John had given me the foregoing information, I received from her the following note, evidently intended to correct the rather too austere impression she thought she had given:

FRYERN COURT,
FORDINGBRIDGE, HANTS.
Jan. 19th/51.

DEAR JOHN,

. . . You asked me how Gwen dressed and though I cannot remember what she wore she always managed to look elegant, and though I cannot remember what we talked about I do remember some very light-hearted evenings over a bottle of wine and a bowl of soup. She wasn't at all careless of her appearance; in fact, rather vain. She also much appreciated the good food and wine to be had in that part of France, though we mostly lived on stolen grapes and bread.

Yours sincerely,

DORELIA.

During her three months in Toulouse, Gwen John worked steadily. She painted at least two portraits of her companion, the lamplit *Dorelia at Toulouse*[1] and *Dorelia in a Black Dress*,[2] both from life, directly on to the canvas without preliminary studies. She both drew and painted quickly, her brother told me, 'with an intensity you could scarcely believe'. *Dorelia at Toulouse* is one of her best portraits. The beautiful young woman reading at night, facing the full lamplight that casts her shadow big on the wall behind, is painted with extraordinary tenderness, as though in pity for a being trustfully unaware of the scarring realities of life. Yet it is not with a sentimental, but a serenely detached, an almost impersonal pity that the beautiful reader is portrayed.

By 1902, when she was twenty-six, the art of Gwen John had reached maturity. It may indeed have matured still earlier, but I am unable to assign a definite date to any painting done before *Dorelia at Toulouse* (my surmise that the Tate *Self-portrait* was painted some three years earlier is based upon slender evidence). I have examined a number of her paintings with her brother, her nephew Edwin, Mrs. Matthew Smith and others who knew her, but I was able to elicit, with regard to dates, few opinions and no facts. *A Lady Reading*,[3] *Nude Girl*[4] and other paintings of the same character would seem to be among the earliest that survive, but what of the lovely *A Corner of the Artist's Room in Paris*[5] (Plate 18). This picture, an ultimate expression, surely, of the Intimiste spirit, by its tiny perfection reminds us not of any other picture so much as of the song of a bird. When was it painted?

The art of Gwen John shows throughout an extraordinary consistency and independence. There are few painters whose origins do

[1] Coll. Mrs. Augustus John.
[2] The Tate Gallery, London.
[3] The Tate Gallery, London.
[4] The Tate Gallery, London.
[5] Coll. Mr. Augustus John.

not appear, or, rather, obtrude themselves, in their early works (if not their later). But where outside her own imagination are the sources of this artist's inspiration? There are artists wider in range (indeed, there are few narrower), but I can think of none in our time to whom the term 'original' can more properly be applied. Nothing could be more restricted than her subjects: a handful of women: her sister-in-law Dorelia, a girl called Fanella, a few nuns, a few orphan children, herself; some cats; but beyond these – except for an occasional empty room or view from a window – she scarcely ever went. Nor was her treatment of them various: all are represented singly and in simple poses; all (except the cats) are chaste and sad.

So deep were the roots of her art that it seems hardly to have been affected by two events, one of which whirled her, she said, like a little leaf carried by the wind, and the other eventually transformed her life. The first of these events was her long intimacy with Rodin; the second her adoption of the Catholic faith. The circumstance that they were to some extent coincidental made the years of her life affected by them a time of extraordinary anguish.

Their correspondence suggests that she met Rodin in 1906. At their first encounters at all events there was no trembling of the leaf. In an early letter she even alluded to her lack of respect for his work. In another undated but evidently later letter she wrote with bitter reproach: 'Quel vie vous me donnez maintenant! Qu'est-ce que je vous ai fait mon Maitre. Vous savez toujours que mon cœur est profonde. . . .' We may surmise that Rodin quickly overcame her indifference and tapped the deep wells of her adoration, and, having reduced her to a condition of helpless dependence upon him, found her single-hearted devotion, when the first excitement ebbed away, an added complication that his already complicated life could hardly sustain. In 1906 he was already sixty-six years old and constantly, he complained, 'enrhumé' or 'grippé'; he was the most illustrious sculptor of the modern world, and deeply involved in a wide complex of relationships, professional, social, amorous and financial. But it would be unjust to depict him as a man who under the spell of a superficial attraction recklessly established an intimacy that he soon regretted. The numerous brief letters he wrote to her testify to a friendship that was close and enduring, and that certain

19. GWEN JOHN. *Self-portrait* (*c.* 1900?).
Oil, 17⅝ × 13¾ in. The Tate Gallery, London.

20. GWEN JOHN. *The Convalescent* (1925–30?).
Oil, 16 × 12¾ in. Coll. Mr. Hugo Pitman.

of them should be evasive in the circumstances need be no matter for surprise. They speak of his appreciation of her painting and drawing, but above all of his concern at her neglect of her health. In one of the earliest, written in 1906, he says. 'Il faudrait changer de chambre [her room at 7 Rue Ste. Placide] qui est trop humide et n'a pas de soleil.' Continually he urges her to eat well, to take exercise. There is a sentence in a later letter that sums up their relations: 'Moi je suis fatigué et vieux. Vous me demandez plus que je peux mais j'aime votre petit cœur si devoué, patience et moins de violence.' A singular, if unimportant, fact about their friendship is Rodin's continuing vagueness about her name. He addressed her letters 'Mademoiselle John Mary', 'John Marie', sometimes simply 'Mary'. Anguishing though Gwen John's friendship with Rodin evidently became, it was incomparably the largest and most deeply felt friendship of her life.

Not comparable in its intensity or indeed in its character with her relationship with Rodin was that which she formed with Rilke, probably the most enduring friendship she had. There is a letter from him dated 17 July 1908, in which he offered to lend her books, and expressed regret that since the previous year she had not wished to remember him, and there is a brief, cool reply from her, written in the third person. But their friendship grew, and a letter from her dated April 1927 shows how much she came to rely upon his guidance and affection:

I accept to suffer always [it runs], but Rilke! hold my hand! you must hold me by the hand! Teach me, inspire me, make me know what to do. Take care of me when my mind is asleep. You began to help me. You must continue.

It was her concern for Rilke's soul that caused her, the day after his death, to call on the Maritains (who also lived at Meudon) to ask whether she should pray for it there or at the place where he died.

Precisely when Gwen John was received into the Catholic Church I have been unable to discover, but it must have been early in 1913. On 10 October 1912 she wrote to the Curé of Meudon to excuse herself for not attending an instruction, and on 12 February of the following year she noted: 'On Saturday I shall receive the Sacrament for the 5th time'; but it would seem that her relations with Rodin had not changed. Her religious life therefore began in circumstances of extraordinary difficulty, but the courage and the implacable clearsightedness with which she faced them made her will, already exceptionally strong, into an instrument of formidable power. But the process was one of prolonged, unmitigated anguish. 'A beautiful life', she wrote, 'is one led, perhaps, in the shadow, but ordered, regular, harmonious.'

The many prayers and meditations she left do not reveal an aptitude for speculation, or an intellect of exceptional interest, but she possessed, in a high degree, the quality of *immediacy* by which we are constantly arrested in the writings of Newman and Pascal. 'Do not think', runs one of her notes, 'that you must wait for years. In to-night's meditation God may reveal himself to you.' She was relentless with herself in her determination to transform her life.

> I have felt momentarily [she wrote] a fear of leaving the world I know, as if I should be loosing [*sic*] something of value, but I cannot tell what there is of value in it that I should be loosing [*sic*]. It is because I cannot criticise the world I know, because I have not been able to criticise it that it appears to have a value [she wrote in English or French according to her fancy; inaccurately in both].

In the notice of her Memorial Exhibition from which I have quoted, Wyndham Lewis asked how she could have isolated herself so successfully from the influences of her age. 'Part of the answer', he wrote, 'is that one of her great friends was Jacques Maritain: she belonged to the Catholic Revival in France.' Apart from the question whether the friendship of M. Maritain would be likely to isolate an artist from contemporary influences, the fact is that neither of the scorching and exalting experiences she underwent appears to have had any immediate effect on her art; they would seem to have neither hastened nor retarded its serene progress. She was protected from the effects of current modes of feeling and expression, just as she was protected from the unsettlement that such experiences bring to shallower natures, by her extraordinary, though wholly unassertive, originality and independence. I do not mean that her painting did not change; in its unhurried fashion, it changed greatly. In her early paintings, the Tate *Self-portrait* and the other probably rather later and equally fine *Self-portrait* belonging to her brother, she used glazes or else thin fluid paint, gradually and delicately correcting until the picture corresponded with her vision of her subject. In her later painting her method was the opposite of this: she used thick paint, and was reluctant to touch her canvas more than once in the same place, preferring, in the event of failure, to begin again. She gradually abandoned the use of dark shadows – shadows sometimes almost black – and kept her tones light and very close together. As with advancing years her tones grew lighter, so her austerely simplified forms attained still greater breadth. But these changes were never accompanied, as they have been sometimes, even in the work of as considerable a painter as Monet, by diffuseness. Her later work, on the contrary, is distinguished by a heightened intensity. And the delicate colours – they look as though they were mixed with wood-ash – applied with touches so modest but so sure, and the firm draughtsmanship beneath produce an impression of extraordinary grandeur, no matter on how small a scale she worked. The wisdom she gained from her emotional and spiritual ordeals was little by little embodied in her deeply rooted art. In the later years her goodness, which had earlier been instinctive and unfocused, became radiantly manifest.

The last twenty-five years of her life or thereabouts were spent at Meudon, whither she had no doubt followed Rodin not long before her reception into the Church. For some years she occupied the attic room in which her pictures and her papers were found after her death at 29 Rue Terre Neuve, but in the summer of 1927 she acquired a small piece of ground in the Rue Babie, at the back of which stood a garage. In this secluded and rather dilapidated structure, the trees and shrubs growing up to shield it, she lived and painted. Without any of the domestic arts (she could scarcely cook the simplest dishes), she existed in what to an ordinary mortal would have been un-endurable discomfort, eating scarcely anything (although never neglecting to feed her cats), sleeping in summer in the open in her flowering wilderness. Cats were her constant companions, and she experienced in their acutest form the anxieties from which those who have animals for friends are never immune. 'Fearful anguish because of the cat', runs one of her little notes. 'All equilibre lost.' It was on their account that she so rarely revisited England during these years. 'The cats more than my work make it too difficult for me to come over', she wrote to a friend. 'I've had so many tragedies [*sic*] with them, now I'm afraid to leave the two I have now.' Nor was she easily persuaded to send her pictures for exhibition in London or New York, where, in spite of her indifference to the opinions of anyone except her friends, she had a few deeply convinced admirers. My father was one of the few whose praise she valued. In an undated letter to my mother she wrote: 'You say my pictures were admired. I tell myself since reading that, that Will admired them. I do not care for the opinions of others.'

The innumerable pieces of paper upon which she wrote down her drafts and copies of letter, prayers, meditations, notes on painting tell the story of her later life. The notes on painting are the rarest. Some of them are indecipherable, others unintelligible, but a few vividly evoke her palette. 'Smoky corn and wild rose', runs one of them, 'faded roses (3 reds), nuts and nettles faded roses and vermilion roses in a yellow basket . . . cyclamen and straw and earth. . . .' Another, in a draft of a letter to a friend, recalls her loving intimacy with nature: 'At night I used to pluck the leaves and grasses in the hedges all dark and misty and when I took them home I sometimes found my hands were full of flowers.' But most of these random notes concern the religion which shared her life with painting: 'Ma religion et mon art, c'est toute ma vie', she said to her neighbour in the Rue Babie. She took Holy Communion daily, but when she reached a point in the painting of a picture when her undivided attention was demanded she would work continuously and absent herself from Mass for as long, sometimes, as a month. Reproached gently by her neighbour about these absences, she consulted the Curé:

> . . . un prêtre en qui elle avait la plus entière confiance, très éclairé et de grande largeur d'idées. [I quote from an unpublished account[1] of Gwen John written by her neighbour.] Il savait qu'il avait à faire à une artiste, qu'il ne pouvait traiter comme tout le monde, aussi, elle revînt toute joyeuse: 'il ne m'a rien dit, il ne m'a pas dit que j'avais fait un péché'. Je compris a mon tour, et je ne lui en parlai plus.

Although she lived a devout, even a saintly life, Gwen John preserved, in all the spheres where it was appropriate, her independence unimpaired, and never felt, like many others, in

---

[1] Written in 1947.

particular, perhaps, English converts to the Church, the need to make excessive demonstrations of piety.

Sous un certain angle, elle était restée protestante [as her neighbour quaintly put it]; j'en eus un bel échantillon le jour de la mort du Pape PIE XI. Outre qu'il était le chef des catholiques, c'était un ami de la France, et nous avions été tres émus de sa disparition. Je l'apprends à Mlle. John qui me répond 'qu'est-ce que vous voulez que ça me fasse', et à son tour, elle m'apprend la mort d'une vieille voisine, assez peu sympathique que nous connaissions à peine l'une l'autre. Vexée de la réponse je lui dis : 'mais vous semblez plus fâchée par la mort de Mme. M. que par de celle du Pape.' Elle part d'un éclat de rire franc, prolongé, qui m'interloque 'Bien sûr que je suis plus fâchée par la mort de Mme. M. . . . un million de fois plus. Elle je la connaissais, je passais tous les jours devant sa porte, mais le Pape ! Il y en aura un autre, et puis voilà ?' C'est tout le regret que j'en pus tirer.

During her last years her passion for solitude grew more imperious than ever, but she was friendly with the several orders of nuns in Meudon, in particular the Dominican Sisters of the Presentation. The Sisters, and the orphans who were their care, became her principal subjects. She did nothing better than her best portraits of these nuns, *Mère Poussepin*[1] (the Mother Superior, and her special friend), for example, and *Portrait of a Nun*,[2] in which her uncompromising search for visual truth is beautifully balanced by her affection for her friends.

But her way of life was one that could not last for long. For a person of her temperament the price of such entire independence and solitude as she demanded was increasing ill health. The self-neglect against which Rodin had ceaselessly protested ended her life.

To go to a doctor inconvenienced her [her friendly neighbour complained], to take solid nourishment inconvenienced her also, and without comfort, without ease, treating her body as though she were its executioner, she allowed herself to die.

In the early autumn of 1939 she became ill, and too late felt a sudden longing for the sea. She took train for Dieppe, but on arrival she collapsed, and was taken to the hospital of a religious house, where she died on 13 September. She neglected to take any baggage with

---

[1] Coll. Mr. Hugo Pitman.   [2] The Tate Gallery, London.

her, but she had not forgotten to make provision for her cats in her absence. 'This retiring person in black', as her brother once described her, 'with her tiny hands and feet, and soft, almost inaudible voice', died as unobtrusively as she had lived. He has also related how narrowly she missed having a part in a great public monument:

> Commissioned by the Society of Painters, Sculptors and Engravers to execute a memorial to Whistler, Rodin produced a colossal figure for which my sister posed, holding a medallion of the painter. This was rejected by the Society, following the advice of the late Derwent Wood, on the grounds of an unfinished arm, and instead a replica of the *Bourgeois de Calais* took its place on the Embankment.[1]

Her brother came upon it years later, he told me, neglected in a shed in the grounds of the Musée Rodin.

[1] Catalogue of the Memorial Exhibition.

AUGUSTUS JOHN

1878–

NOT long ago I was discussing the relative merits of contemporary English painters with one of the most serious and influential of English art critics. 'I suppose', he said, gazing into the distance, and speaking with the conscious open-mindedness of a man to whom no field of speculation is closed, 'I suppose there *are* people who would place John among the best.' Future ages, I am convinced, will marvel at the puny character of an age when even the most highly regarded critical opinion is so little able to distinguish between average and outstanding stature.

There are, of course, obvious reasons why John should not, for the time being, greatly excite the curiosity of the young. His aims are not theirs, and in any case he has been illustrious for so long as to provoke their impatience. So to-day, so far as critical opinion is concerned, he is on the way to become 'the forgotten man' of English painting, and his fanciers are the old and the ageing for whom his work was the inspiration of their formative years, or else 'outsiders', intelligent stockbrokers and the like, with the wit to consult their eyes rather than their ears when buying pictures. The withdrawal of the aura of fashionable approval leaves a man's faults exposed, and many of John's paintings and drawings expose him to legitimate criticism. There are paintings which, owing, perhaps, to some want of constructive power, he is unable to finish and compelled to abandon, wastes of paint which his utmost efforts have failed to bring to life. And there are paintings in which, under the spell of El Greco, he has coerced his own robust forms into a kind of parody of the gaunt and rhetorical forms of the great Cretan. There are paintings which manifest a vulgarity unredeemed by any positive merit, such, for instance, as *Rachel*.[1] Nor are his drawings always beyond criticism. It is not difficult to discover instances of a figure's being marred by a forced or a purposeless posture, or a face 'improved' into conformity with a type which momentarily monopolizes his admiration. The

[1] The Tate Gallery, London.

occasions for criticism offered by such defects are genuine enough, and it would be wrong to discount them, but considered in relation to the magnificence of the life's work of Augustus John they furnish material for, if not a negligible, at least a comparatively tame indictment.

Contemporary critics, from a nice aversion from dwelling upon the obvious, end by ignoring the obvious altogether. It is therefore necessary to say that, according to the accepted canons whereby an artist can be judged, elusive though these admittedly are, Augustus John – to make no higher claim – is a considerable painter. He has been able, not sometimes but again and again, to fuse, by the intensity of his imaginative heat, the four ingredients of painting so well and simply defined by Allan Gwynne-Jones as drawing, design, colour and a sense of space.[1] And he has done this, not only often, but with an audacity and a majestic sweep that I believe to justify my use just now of the term 'magnificence' to describe the sum of his achievement.

I propose to say little about the landmarks of the painter's life. I have not had the advantage of seeing his as yet unpublished autobiography, and the extracts that appeared in 'Horizon', he tells me, have been radically revised. Furthermore, although I expect this book to be of absorbing interest and written in the evocative and poetic prose of which he possesses the secret, I shall be surprised if it contains very many of those basic facts that must form the framework of any biography, even of the briefest sketch. This supposition I base upon the knowledge that, although the memory of the artist retains innumerable images of rare interest and beauty, it does not so easily retain the sequence of events, their dates, or even their causes. Nor does he preserve, except by accident, letters or documents of any kind. I remember a few years ago, when I was engaged upon my 'Phaidon' monograph on this artist, I called at his studio in the faint hope of his dating certain of his paintings. There was one in particular, a portrait of one of his sons, of which I required the date. 'Dodo will be able to help you', he suggested, and we consulted his wife forthwith. 'It oughtn't', I said, 'to be so difficult. He might, mightn't he, be about six in the portrait? When was he born?' His parents, so eager to help me, looked at each

[1] 'Portrait Painters', 1950, p. xiii.

other with abysmal blankness. They could not remember. This would be no great matter had the artist's life been an uneventful affair, a life of uninterrupted toil in a garret, say, or a quiet pastoral life. It has, however, been a many-sided life, deeply implicated in many other lives, adventurous, bold, robust and long: in fact, a saga. Like the life of Sickert, it is too vast a subject to be attempted, however briefly, in these pages. Nor is it likely to suffer neglect. John, like Sickert, will be lucky if he escapes his Thornbury.

Augustus Edwin John was born at 5 Lexden Terrace, Tenby, Pembrokeshire, on 4 January 1878, the third of the four children of Edwin William John. In the combination of powerful impulses which form his temperament, the chief is a passion for personal liberty and entire independence. To judge from a letter,[1] written on revisiting his birthplace, to my father more than forty years after he had left it, John was from very early days painfully aware of his temperamental incongruity with the constricted life of Tenby. 'I am.... suffering again from the same condition of frantic boredom and revolt', runs the letter, 'from which I escaped so long ago.' But he and his sister Gwen formed a close alliance to make their escape into the world of art of which they knew themselves citizens. First Augustus, and shortly afterwards Gwen, entered the Slade School, where Augustus remained from 1894 until 1898. The phenomenal mastery of John's drawing at the Slade has been generally acclaimed. Before he was twenty he had become the first draughtsman in England. The admiration his drawings evoked among his fellow students is described by Spencer Gore in an unpublished letter to Doman Turner:[2]

I think [he wrote] that John when he first went to the Slade started making the very slightest drawings; when I went there he was making hundreds of the most elaborate and careful drawings as well. I have seen sketch-books full of the drawings of people's arms and feet, of guitars and pieces of furniture, copies of old masters, etc. He used at that time to shift his rooms occasionally, and people used to go and collect the torn-up scraps on the floor which was always littered with them and piece them together. I know people who got many wonderful drawings in that way.

The best of his student drawings can hang without dishonour in any company. In the expression of form and movement, they are not

[1] 6 May 1939.   [2] 25 January 1909.

inferior to the drawings of Keene, nor in energy to those of Hogarth, while their combination of lyricism, robustness and strangeness make even the poetry of Gainsborough's drawings a little tame and expected. Palmer could at his rare best draw with a greater imaginative intensity, but how very rare that best was. With John the power of drawing splendidly endured for decades, changing its character, flickering, faltering and slowly sinking, but always present, and even in old age apt to blaze suddenly up.

The moment when he seems first to have shown his extraordinary talent was attended by a singular circumstance. My father used to relate a story which also finds a place in his memoirs, which he heard, he said, from Tonks, according to which John was 'quiet, methodical and by no means remarkable' when he first came to the Slade, but while diving at Tenby struck his head on a rock, and emerged from the water 'a genius'. This story he occasionally told, not, I fancy, because he thought that it had any basis in fact (he was inclined to be severely sceptical about occurrences that appeared to involve the suspension of natural laws), but because it seemed to him amusingly in keeping with the fabulous personality of his friend. Not long ago I happened to read some memoirs in MS. by John Everett, a close friend of John's and his contemporary at the Slade. In this MS. – an extremely candid and detailed record – the same story is related by someone who believed in its literal truth, and who, although not a witness of the dive, was a witness of the transformation of John, after the visit to Tenby, from a plodding student into a. commanding personality with a genius for drawing. The Gore letter just quoted also suggests that his early Slade drawings were unimpressive.

Though at the Slade he drew like a master, he painted like a gifted student. He had studied the painting of Rembrandt and Rubens at the National Gallery, and on his first visit to the Louvre, in 1899, in company with my father, he received from Puvis de Chavannes impressions of an idealized humanity, and of the beauty of the relation between figures and landscape, so strong that they never left him. The inspiration of this painter is manifest in many of his own figures in landscape, whether in big compositions, such as the *Lyric Fantasy*[1] (Plate 22), of 1911, or the small, brilliantly coloured paint-

[1] Coll. Mr. Hugo Pitman.

ings he made in company with Innes in the years preceding the First World War. One other painter on this first visit to the Louvre made an impression upon him which, though perhaps more powerful still, was less enduring. This was Daumier, who reinforced with immense authority the lesson he had begun to learn from Rembrandt, of seeing broadly and simply, and who taught him to interpret human personality boldly, without fearing to pass, if need be, the arbitrary line commonly held to divide objective representation from caricature. *The Rustic Idyll*,[1] a notable pastel of about 1903, was made under the immediate inspiration of Daumier.

Whatever its effect upon his draughtsmanship and his personality, John's dive at Tenby did not make him a painter. The *Portrait of an Old Lady*,[2] of 1899, the year after he left the Slade – which the artist told me was his first commissioned portrait – is probably a fair example of his painting of this time. In grasp of character as well as in drawing it is far inferior to the best of the drawings he did at the Slade. The hands, for instance, are without form or the power to move. When, having found his hesitant essay in a dealer's gallery in 1941, I brought it to his studio for identification, he did not at first recognize it as his own.

Only three years later, however, his *Portrait of Estella Dolores Cerutti*[3] proclaimed him a master in the art of painting. Certainly he has not often surpassed it, but then neither have most of his contemporaries. A comparison between these two portraits gives the measure of his progress. The earlier is niggling in form; the later is clearly stamped with that indefinable largeness of form characteristic of major painters, but, except for occasional youthful accidents, scarcely ever of minor. The paint of the earlier laboured almost in vain; that of the later powerfully radiates a cool light. The old lady is modelled hardly at all; the young lady as plastically and as surely as a piece of sculpture. The earlier can be taken in at a long glance; the later indefinitely holds the spectator's interest, without, however, yielding up the secret of the artist's power.

From the time when he painted the Cerutti portrait John must be accounted a masterly painter as well as draughtsman, but his painting is most masterly when it approximates most closely to drawing. Most

---

[1] Coll. Mr. Bernard Falk.   [2] The Tate Gallery, London.
[3] The City Art Gallery, Manchester.

of his finest paintings have the strong contours and the clearly defined forms that belong particularly to drawing. Especially is this true of his early and middle years. The vision of painters tends to grow broader and more comprehensive with age. One need only compare the later with the earlier work of those who in other respects have so little in common as Titian, Rembrandt, Turner and Corot to see how pronounced this tendency is. Of recent years John's vision has undergone a similar change. Not only his painting but his drawing has grown broader, more comprehensive, more 'painterly', though he has remained essentially a draughtsman.

During the past century there has been a widespread decline in technical accomplishment, and the wisest painters have felt obliged to try to compensate for this loss of manual skill with greater thoughtfulness, above all by giving their utmost attention to design.

Almost from the beginning of his life as an artist, John has commanded immense technical resources; never, therefore, has he been aware of any need for a compensatory concern with composition (still less for the cultivation of an esoteric taste or – in spite of possessing an intellect of exceptional range and power – of protective aesthetic theories). Little hampered by technical obstacles, his art has grown freely, and it reveals with an extreme directness the personality of the artist. For the style of the man who is able to set down his emotions, his intuitions, his ideas, without greatly troubling about the means he employs, reveals more than that of the man who organizes, minutely qualifies, polishes; in fact, a style of such a kind may hide almost as much as it reveals. 'Do not be troubled for a language', said Delacroix; 'cultivate your soul and she will show herself.' Confidently trusting in his preternaturally gifted eye and hand, John has implicitly followed this injunction. Like the periods of a great natural orator, John's designs are improvisations. Organization and theory would stultify John's vision and the flow and flicker of his wonderfully expressive natural 'handwriting', just as the classical conventions so integral to the drama of Corneille and Racine would have stultified the poetic impulse of Hugo, Lamartine, Baudelaire or Whitman. There is, of course, a weakness inherent in the very nature of the improviser. Spontaneous invention depends upon intense emotion; and intense emotion notoriously fluctuates. In a work of art that has been meticulously planned, and its every detail worked out in advance, the conversion, at a critical moment, of failure into success may be achieved by some slight adjustment; but in an improvisation a mistake can be redeemed as a rule only by a painful struggle of which the outcome is uncertain. Often John carries all before him in a first impetuous assault, and produces masterpieces almost without effort, but there are times when no efforts, however tenacious or prolonged, suffice to avert the results of some apparently insignificant error.

Later in these pages I say something of the contrast between two categories of artist: between him whose work is an obvious extension of the man, and him whose work is a compensation for what the man is not. John belongs unequivocally to the former class: the people whom he represents (with the inevitable exception of the subjects of many commissioned portraits) are the people who attract or interest him as human beings, and the landscapes are the places where he most enjoys living. His work, that is to say, is in the most intimate sense an extension of himself.

Nature is for him like a tremendous carnival [Wyndham Lewis once wrote in 'The Listener'] in the midst of which he finds himself. But there is nothing of the spectator about Mr. John. He is very much a part of the saturnalia. It is only because he enjoys it so much that he is moved to report upon it – in a fever of optical emotion, before the selected object passes on and is lost in the crowd.

The love of liberty that is John's strongest passion is not a remote, political concept (although in so far as he is interested in politics he is libertarian enough), but personal liberty. The almost physical urge from which it springs is expressed in an undated but very early letter to my father:

. . . You know the grinding see-saw [he wrote] under a studio light cold formal meaningless – a studio – what is it? a habitation – no – not even a cow-shed – 'tis a box wherein miserable painters hide themselves and shut the door on nature. I have imprisoned myself in my particular dungeon all day to-day, for example all day on my sitters' faces nought but the shifting light of reminiscence and that harrowed and distorted by an atrocious 'skylight' . . . this evening at sun down I escaped at last to the open to the free air of space, where things have their proportion and place and are articulate. . . .

It was thus neither chance nor casual romanticism that drew John to the gipsies – those nomads in whom the spirit of personal liberty burns most obstinately – but his apprehension of a community of outlook between himself and them. 'The absolute isolation of the gipsies seemed to me the rarest and most unattainable thing in the world', he wrote.

The early part of John's life was devoted mainly to the subjects in which this spirit was plainly manifest. At the Slade he used to discover, among tramps and costers, as well as gipsies, strange characters whom he took for models. In summer holidays in remote parts of Wales he sought out primitive peasants, the unconscious purveyors of strains of wild poetry that come singing out in his drawings of them. In Liverpool, where in 1901 he spent about a year as a teacher of art, it was the homeless wanderers by the docks, wayward old men, in whom he discovered a novel and expressive magic. In his early days he discovered people such as these, but later he has had mostly to content himself with emphasizing such aspects of the gipsies' spirit of 'absolute isolation' as he is able to discern in the faces of the sitters who have knocked at his studio door. For in England to-day every painter without means who wishes to make a living by the practice of his art must paint portraits. If John had been able to continue to devote himself to the portrayal of the types of men and women who have resisted the pressure of urban civilization and preserved their primitive way of life, we should possess a dramatic and unique portrait of an aspect of England and Wales that has almost vanished from our sight. But life is not kind to artists, and John will never complete this portrait, but we must be thankful that with brush, pencil and etching-needle he has enabled us to share his haunting vision of a freer, braver and more abundant way of life than that which most of us know.

The art of John has always been marked by an audacious and independent but not with a revolutionary character. His own debt to the past he has always readily admitted. 'I am', he wrote in an early letter[1] to my father 'about to become a *mother*. The question of paternity must be left to the future. I suspect at least four old masters.' His chosen masters, besides Puvis de Chavannes and Daumier, are Rembrandt, Goya, Gauguin; among his contemporaries, the two from whom he learnt most were Conder and Innes. At all times, however, he has taken freely according to his needs, but

[1] 4 May 1901.

there has been little danger of the integrity of a personality so positive and so robust being impaired by what it assimilates. There is one master, however, from whom he has taken much that has resisted assimilation. This, as I have already noted, is El Greco; working under the spell of whose ecstatic rhetoric John is not entirely himself.

'Advanced' movements in painting he is inclined to regard with sympathetic curiosity, but also with detachment. A sentence in an early undated letter to my father, evidently written from Paris early in the century, gives an indication of his attitude. 'The Independents', he wrote, 'are effroyable – and yet one feels sometimes these chaps have blundered on something alive without being able to master it.'

The introductory chapter of this book deals at some length with the diminished attraction exercised by the visible world over the minds of artists of the Post-Impressionist era, which has led to the virtual abandonment of the traditional European ideal of representing in something of its fulness the world to which the senses bear witness. This disinterest, although it has affected at one time or another many, even perhaps the greater part, of the most original painters of our time, has never touched John. Every one of his paintings and drawings, be it failure or success, testifies to his passionate response to the world that his eyes see, but it may nevertheless be of interest to quote a passage from a letter that also speaks, as vividly, I think, as any of these, of the quality of his vision, with its combination of frank enchantment with the nearest and most obvious material realities and of a mysterious apprehension of deeper realities beneath. The passage comes from the letter, already quoted, about studios:

> Never have the beauties of the world [it runs] moved me as of late. Our poultry run I see to be the most wonderful thing – so remote, so paradisaic, so unaccountable it seems, under the slanting beams of the Sun, and loud with the afflatus of a long day's chant of love. The birds move automatically, like elaborate toys, but with a strange note from the East (subdued now, their wild flight forgotten on the long journey) amidst dappled gold under gilded elders, old medicine bottles, broken pots and pans and cans; the unseemly debris – the poor uncatalogued treasures – of a midden.

Three short sentences in a letter written many years later succinctly sum up his confidence in his preoccupation with what is at hand, with what he likes and, above all, with what is alive:

I find the country better to live in than the town [he wrote to my father]. One comes across thrilling things which don't take place in the studio. In art one should always follow one's nose, don't you think?[1]

John's small figures in landscape, his pure landscape, his still-lifes and above all his portraits, however boldly idiosyncratic, however romanticized, are firmly based upon what he sees, but he engages in one kind of painting which primarily depends not upon observation but on invention. This is the big composition. No kind of painting interests him so deeply. I remember his saying when he opened the exhibition of photographs of contemporary British wall paintings at the Tate Gallery in 1939, 'When one thinks of painting on great expanses of wall, painting of other kinds seems hardly worth doing', and shortly afterwards, in a restaurant: 'I suppose they'd charge a lot to let Matt Smith and me paint decorations on these walls.' In a monograph[2] on the artist published some years ago, I spoke with some indignation of the neglect of his powers of painting upon a great scale. Although the world would beyond doubt be a more beautiful and inspiring place if there were a number of public buildings embellished by big completed wall paintings by John, I now think that I a little overestimated his capacities as a painter on a monumental scale. Certain important qualities he does possess: a rich and abundant creative impulse, extraordinary powers as a draughtsman, and above all a noble largeness of style. In all his essays in painting on such a scale, these are luminously apparent. I spoke earlier in this study of the weakness inherent in the improviser's temperament: it follows that the larger the scale of operations the greater the likelihood of their being frustrated by this weakness.

The small improvisation can be abandoned without regret and started afresh. How many thousands of failures Guys or Rowlandson must have crumpled up! But in a large picture too much is at stake from the first; such a work can be brought to a successful conclusion by the science and intellectual discipline that alone can compensate for the inevitable fluctuations of intense emotion. Genius is rightly held to be the capacity for taking infinite pains, but there is a kind of genius capable of taking infinite pains only while it is, as it were, in action. In fact, a special kind of genius is required to

<hr/>

[1] 6 May 1939.   [2] 'Augustus John' (Phaidon British Artists), 1945.

21. AUGUSTUS JOHN. *Robin* (*c.* 1909?).
Oil, 18×14 in. The Tate Gallery, London.

22. Augustus John. *Lyric Fantasy* (*c.* 1911).
Oil, 92×185 in. Coll. Mr. Hugo Pitman.

take infinite pains by way of preparation. John belongs to the first order: he enjoys painting pictures rather than planning them, and while no effort is too strenuous while he has his brush in hand, he lacks all those qualities that go to make a great organizer. I doubt whether any human achievement on a monumental scale is possible without a pre-eminent capacity for organization. And so it is that John's monumental paintings, even the finest of them, remain unfinished, dazzling sketches abandoned with their difficulties unresolved. The *Study for a Canadian War Memorial*,[1] of 1918, an immense and complex composition in charcoal, peopled by scores of figures, was never carried out. *Galway*,[2] of 1916, for all its brilliance is no more than a gigantic sketch. (Its 400 square feet were covered, the artist told me, in a single week.) The vivid and animated *Mumpers*[3] (of about 1914?) could have been carried further. So also the *Lyric Fantasy*, of about 1911, which is more highly charged with a mysterious poetry than any of his other works of this order. The subject is a group of wild, lovely girls, to whom he has given something of the fierce and lofty isolation that he envied in the gipsies, and some ravishing children in an arid, Piero-haunted landscape. John is acutely regretful of its unfinished state. Their incompleteness is not, of course, due solely to the want of this capacity in the artist. The times are uniquely unpropitious. Artists cannot be expected to undertake works that call for great expenditure of time and energy without any assurance of being able to sell them, and neither governments nor private corporations give painters or sculptors opportunities remotely comparable with those which their predecessors enjoyed of working on a heroic scale.

Perhaps the most notable quality of the monumental paintings – in particular, the *Lyric Fantasy* – is the poetic relation between figures and landscape. This he developed, less magnificently but with more completeness, in a whole series of paintings on a relatively miniature scale. As a young man he became friends with Innes, a painter with an original and lyrical vision. In him a passion for mountains – those of his native Wales and the South of France, for preference – and for pure, vivid colours burned with a heat particular to men conscious of having a short time to live, for he was

[1] The National Gallery of Canada, Ottawa.
[2] The Tate Gallery, London.   [3] The Detroit Institute of Arts,

consumptive, and he died at the age of twenty-seven. Innes's intense and romantic vision of mountain country was an inspiration to John, who assimilated and enhanced it, for among glowing, exotic Innes-conceived mountains he placed brilliant and evocative but summarily painted figures in peculiar harmony with their surroundings. When Innes died and the focus of John's interest shifted, something went out of English painting that left it colder and more prosaic. The importance of the group of poetic paintings inspired by the association of John, Innes and the delightful but much less gifted Derwent Lees has yet to receive full recognition.

During the course of his immensely productive life he has been attracted by a wide range of subjects, but portraiture has remained his principal concern. England is the portrait-painter's paradise: from the sixteenth century onwards she has given not only to native portrait-painters, but to a long succession of foreigners also, full scope for their talent. The death of Lawrence seems to mark a singular change in the history of portrait-painting. Until about 1830 the best exponents of this art were professionals. No amateurs rivalled Holbein, Van Dyck, Lely, Kneller, Gainsborough, Reynolds or Lawrence himself, but since then amateurs have painted the outstanding portraits. Few portraits by professionals are comparable with Stevens's *Mrs. Collmann*, Watts's gallery of great Victorians, Whistler's *Miss Cecily Alexander*, Sickert's *George Moore*, Steer's *Mrs. Raynes*, Wyndham Lewis's *Miss Edith Sitwell* and *Ezra Pound*, or Stanley Spencer's early *Self-portrait*. Like his contemporaries McEvoy and Orpen (who began as genre painters and turned professional portrait-painters later on) John, especially during the latter part of his life, has painted great numbers of portraits, but, unlike these two, he may be said (though the distinction is a fine one) to have remained something of an amateur, for he is constantly at work on compositions large and small, flower-pieces, landscapes and drawings of the figure, and from time to time he loses interest in commissioned portraits and abandons them, a course which a professional would be unlikely to adopt. Change of subject preserves the spontaneity of his response to the drama of faces.

The portrait-painters of the epoch which Lawrence brought to an end were sustained, during spells of lassitude and indifference (to which most artists are subject), by the momentum of a workmanlike and dignified tradition: but the waning of that tradition left the painter face to face with his sitter, dependent, to an extent which his predecessors never were, on his personal response to the features before him, on his power to peer deeply into the character which they mask or reveal. Very rarely is a man's response to faces, or his understanding of them, sufficiently powerful and sustained as to enable him to make it his whole profession, and he who paints little or nothing except portraits deadens by exploiting this response. To paint portraits supremely well, it would seem to be wise to refrain from painting them too often. A passionate preoccupation with portraiture has only occasionally tempted John to over-indulge it, or to exploit it for the benefit of those who are eager to purchase the immortality which at certain moments it lies in his power to confer. At such auspicious moments he gives splendid expression to the qualities of nobility, strength, courage, wisdom, candour and pride in his sitters, but should they happen to possess none of these, he is able to make little of them. But his portraits are not therefore merely romantic tributes to the elements of greatness which he discerns; they rarely suffer from the absence of the critical spirit; they are free from the touch of personal approbation that marks Watts's portrait of his great contemporaries. John's portraits are the products of a more sceptical nature and a less reverent age. Watts portrayed select spirits, as almost wholly noble; John, whose sitters are more arbitrarily chosen, portrays the noble qualities in men and women whose natures on balance are as often base as noble. And where Watts brought a grave and exalted mind to bear upon his sitters, John comprehends his with a flame-like intuition, as in the miraculous *Joseph Hone*[1] (Plate 23), of about 1926, *Robin*[2] (Plate 21), of about 1909, and *David*,[3] of about 1918.

Genius which is intuitive and spontaneous is of necessity uneven in its achievement. If John's crowded annals have failures to record, in his inspired moments no living British painter so nearly approaches the grandeur and radiance of vision, the understanding of the human drama, or the power of hand and eye of the great masters of the past.

[1] The Tate Gallery, London.   [2] The Tate Gallery, London.
[3] Coll. Mr. A. Chester Beatty.

CHARLES GINNER

1878—1952

GILMAN and Gore I had not the privilege of knowing. I always climbed the stairs that led to Ginner's little painting room at 66 Claverton Street with the pleasurable anticipation, not only of seeing a friend, but of entering a presence for whom these two others were living memories. They have been dead for more than thirty years, and Claverton Street is miles away from Camden Town, yet something of the way of life which all three lived in intimacy together in North London was still gently sensible in these rooms in Pimlico: the way the landlady loomed large, the way the landlady's choice in wallpapers was accepted, and the way the streets outside receded in long, grey, symmetrical vistas, down which, on certain auspicious evenings, one made one's way with Ginner to some 'eating-house' with shabby, comfortable red-plush seats. I live only a few minutes' walk away, but I mostly see chromium and neon lighting, except when I walked with Ginner along streets which are, or seem in recollection to be, gas-lit. Sickert used to say that English artists live like gentlemen, but Ginner lived with a simplicity that put one in mind of a Continental artist: two small (meticulously tidy) rooms, adorned by half a dozen studies given to him by friends, a small library consisting of a few score well read classics, half English and half French, an annual 'painting holiday' – that represented about the extent of my friend's needs.

No biography has been written of Ginner, nor has there been published a collection of reproductions of his work. So far as I am aware, he is not even the subject of an informative article.[1] I propose therefore to preface this brief study of his art by giving the principal landmarks of his life.

Charles Ginner was born on 4 March 1878 in Cannes, the second

---

[1] The nearest approach is the generous tribute in Frank Rutter's 'Some Contemporary Artists', but this very slight sketch – which contains a number of inaccuracies – was published as long ago as 1922.

son of Isaac Benjamin Ginner, an English physician practising on the Riviera. Dr. Ginner came originally from Hastings; his wife was a Londoner of Scottish descent. Ginner's grandfather was a mysterious figure: meagre vestiges of legend attribute to him a propensity for smuggling and a detailed knowledge of the Bible. Of his grandfather's six sons, all left England, and one was murdered in China. Ginner attended the Collège Stanislas at Cannes. For as long as he could remember he wished to be a painter, but he had to overcome the opposition of his family. At the age of sixteen his health broke under the combined assault of typhoid and double pneumonia. For almost a year, in a successful attempt to restore it, he sailed the South Atlantic and the Mediterranean in a tramp steamer belonging to an uncle. On his return he spent some time in an engineer's office, and when he was twenty-one he left Cannes for an architect's office in Paris. In 1904 his family withdrew their opposition to his becoming a painter and he entered the Académie Vitti, where Henri Martin was teaching, but he worked mostly under Gervais. From the first he used bright colours; Gervais expressed sharp disapproval and used to hide them beneath coats of umber. The year following he entered the Ecole des Beaux-Arts, but in 1906, after Gervais had left, he returned to Vitti's, where his principal teacher was the Spanish painter Hermens Anglada y Camarasa. At that time the art schools of Paris were being slowly permeated by Impressionism, but the Post-Impressionists were still officially regarded with contempt. When Ginner confessed his admiration for van Gogh, Anglada replied, 'A man who'd paint his boots can't be an artist.' He left Vitti's in 1908 and worked on his own for two years in Paris, where he took van Gogh, Gauguin and Cézanne for his guides. In April 1909 he visited Buenos Aires, where he held an exhibition, thus introducing Post-Impressionism into the Argentine. In January 1910 he came to London to serve, as already noted, on the Hanging Committee of the Allied Artists' Association's third exhibition. It was owing to his friendship with Gilman and Gore, and to their urgent persuasion, that he decided to settle in London. At first his mother kept house for him at Prince of Wales Mansions, Battersea, and he had a studio in Tadema Street, Chelsea, near the World's End, but later he took rooms on his own in Chesterfield Street, by King's Cross Station, in the heart of the 'Camden Town Country', where Gilman and Gore were near neighbours. These three met constantly in one another's studios, at the Etoile Restaurant, at the Café Royal and at the Saturday afternoons at 19 Fitzroy Street, which were also regularly attended by R. P. Bevan, John Nash, Albert Rothenstein, C. R. W. Nevinson, Jacob Epstein and Walter Bayes, Sickert and Pissarro presiding.

The four years between his arrival in London and the two events that brought this period to a melancholy close – namely, Gore's death and the outbreak of the First World War – were the happiest of his life. Although he had neither the authority of Gilman nor the charm of Gore, he enjoyed affection, influence and respect. He had many qualities to warm the hearts of his friends, among which modesty, benevolence, generosity and candour were conspicuous. His own work, which was at first more mature than that of his two friends, showed qualities that they were eager to emulate. He was, furthermore, familiar with the work of Continental masters who for almost all his English contemporaries were distant demigods. This made him something of an oracle among them, although Bevan had worked with Gauguin at Pont Aven. And he possessed the capacity – too rarely exercised – for expressing himself in lucid, energetic prose.

The essay on Neo-Realism, for instance, quoted at length in the chapter on Gilman, aroused considerable interest and was the subject of a long review by Sickert.[1] All these circumstances combined to give Ginner during these years the exhilarating consciousness of playing an honourable part in one of the chief artistic movements of his time and country.

War, however, brought about the disruption of their circle, and with it their intimate and delightful collaboration, and presently the death of Gilman intensified for Ginner the sense of loneliness that had followed the death of Gore.

Ginner was called up about 1916, serving first as a private in the Royal Army Ordnance Corps, but his knowledge of French (he was completely bilingual) resulted in his transfer to the Intelligence Corps. He was promoted sergeant and stationed at Marseilles, and later recalled to England to work for Canadian War Records, with the honorary rank of Lieutenant. This involved an eight weeks'

[1] 'Mr. Ginner's Preface', *The New Age*, 30 April 1914.

visit to Hereford, to make drawings of a powder-filling factory for
an elaborate painting. Back in London, he took studios in the
Camden Road and at 51 High Street, Hampstead, living meanwhile
above the Etoile. In 1937 he moved to 66 Claverton Street, where he
lived until his death on 6 January 1952. In the Second World War
he served as an official artist, specializing in harbour scenes and
bomb-damaged buildings in London.

Ginner's faith in the value of friendly co-operation between artists
had been expressed by membership of many societies. Soon after he
settled in London, he was invited to become a member of 19 Fitzroy Street; he was a foundation member of the Camden Town, the
Cumberland Market and the London Groups. The New English
Art Club he joined in 1920, and he was elected an Associate of
the Royal Academy in 1942, where he consistently advocated the
admission of younger contemporaries of talent.

The most conspicuous attribute of Ginner as an artist is the
stability of his vision. Such an attribute, in itself, of course, affords
little indication either of high qualities in an artist or of their absence. It may accompany deep convictions, or mere laziness, sterility
or the determination to exploit a market. Ginner's achievement as
a whole offers no evidence of laziness or of sterility, and in the
changeable circumstances which prevail to-day a market is more
readily exploited by politic change than by stability. In fact, stability
has become as much the exception as it was the rule in, for example,
fourteenth-century Siena. Constant changes in aesthetic fashion –
the result of the absence of an authoritative tradition and of prevalent curiosity, restlessness, and the unprecedented accessibility of
examples of the art of other civilizations – in fact conspire to make
stability difficult to maintain. Therefore it may fairly be taken to-day
as a sign of a convinced and independent mind. The stability of
Ginner's vision, at all events, is so pronounced as to be phenomenal.
I have never seen a painting of Ginner's Paris period, but those he
sent over to the first Allied Artists' Association Exhibition in 1910
seem to have resembled those of later date. (According to Rutter,
they were a nuisance to handle because the wet paint stood out in
high ridges.) The practice of painting thick was at this time fairly
general, both on the Continent and in England. 'We have evolved
a method of painting with a clean and solid mosaic of thick paint

in a light key', Sickert wróte of the New English Art Club in 1910.[1]
Ginner's practice in this respect was, however, based upon that of
van Gogh: he applied the paint in strips. (It was from Ginner that
Gilman learnt this method of painting.) In other and more fundamental respects his style was already what it has remained since. In
The Café Royal,[2] of 1911, there is, for instance, the extremely
complex yet entirely firm and logical construction, the mass of
detail severely disciplined to the requirements of the design as a
whole, that mark, though still more emphatically, the work of his
later years. There are also the same defects. His pictures lack atmosphere, and they often, in consequence, have an archaic look, as
though they were conceived before Constable and Turner showed
that the accepted distinction between the solid objects of nature
and the atmosphere through which they were seen, between, say,
tree-tops and clouds, from the point of view of the painter, is not
invariably a real distinction. There is an evident want of interest in,
and an incapacity to represent, the human figure, weaknesses the
more felt in view of the artist's unvarying preoccupation with the
environment of man, usually, indeed, his own actual habitation. And
his touch is without either subtlety or variety. But these weaknesses
are far outweighed by his qualities. If he largely ignores atmosphere,
few of his contemporaries have represented urban landscape or
individual buildings with such intimate insight. The shabbiest of
them, under his minute but tender scrutiny, reveals beauties at a
casual glance scarcely conceivable. His representation of even so
apparently monotonous a structure as a brick wall or a tiled roof –
which are among his most favoured subjects – will be seen to present
surfaces of astonishing variety, and each brick or tile to have its own
identity. If, like Turner, he has little aptitude for portraying men
and women, he creates an ineffable impression of their unseen
presence: his steps are worn by their tread, his walls are blackened
by the smoke of their fires, his flags are put out to declare their
rejoicing or their mourning; there is little indeed in his pictures that
does not refer, and always with an implicit affection and respect, to
his fellow men. And if his touch inclines to monotony, is there not
adequate compensation in what Sickert called his 'burning patience'?

[1] 'The New English and After', *The New Age*, 2 June.
[2] The Tate Gallery, London.

23. AUGUSTUS JOHN. *Portrait of Joseph Hone* (*c.* 1926).
Oil, 20 × 16 in. The Tate Gallery, London.

24. CHARLES GINNER. *Flask Walk, Hampstead, under Snow (c.* 1930).
Oil, 26 × 16 in. Coll. Mr. Edward le Bas.

His earlier paintings were all done from oil sketches made in front of his subject. During a visit to Dieppe in 1911, Sickert showed him how to work from squared-up drawings. After 1914 he relied entirely upon detailed drawings of this character, accompanied by elaborate written colour notes. I am inclined to think that the words 'burning patience' go to the heart of his achievement. Ginner did not possess a tithe of the genius of his master, van Gogh, or even a tithe of the natural capacity of his exact contemporary, Orpen, yet this 'burning patience' enabled him to create, both in oil and pen and ink and water-colour, a long series of pictures which reflect the continuous growth of a personality entirely humane, honourable and modest.

SPENCER GORE

1878—1914

SPENCER GORE died at the early age of thirty-five, and only a few months before the outbreak of the First World War, an event that obliterated the memory of many merely delicate talents. His paintings might be mistaken by an inattentive observer for essays, tentative and lacking in decided character, in the manner of the French Impressionists. And Gore himself might have been discounted, too, by a casual acquaintance, as a cultivated genial person, a shade too genial, perhaps, to be an entirely serious person. Yet after his death Sickert, in an article entitled 'A Perfect Modern',[1] paid a tribute to his work and character in terms of higher praise than I recall his using in respect of any other English painter of the time. Gore's obituary in 'The Morning Post' expressed the opinion that 'his personal character was so exceptional as to give him a unique influence in the artistic affairs of London in the last dozen years'. Those who meditate to-day upon the achievements of those last years of the Indian summer of European civilization, if they do not entirely subscribe to the opinions of Sickert and the unknown obituarist, weigh them, at any rate, with sympathetic comprehension.

Spencer Frederick Gore was born on 26 May 1878 at Epsom, the youngest of the four children of Spencer Walter Gore, Surveyor to the Ecclesiastical Commissioners and holder of the first Lawn Tennis Championship held at Wimbledon in 1877 (and brother of Charles Gore, Bishop of Oxford), and his wife, Amy Smith, daughter of a member of the firm of solicitors who acted for the Ecclesiastical Commissioners in Yorkshire. Spencer Gore's boyhood was spent at Holywell, his parents' house in Kent. He went to Harrow, where his vocation declared itself, and he won the Yates Thompson Prize for drawing. After leaving school he entered the Slade, where he worked for three years under Brown and Steer and Tonks, whose teaching he always recalled with gratitude, and he formed a lifelong friend-

---

[1] 'The New Age', 9 April 1914.

ship with Gilman. About the time of his leaving the Slade his parents suffered a financial reverse, and after his father's death his widow took Garth House, a much smaller place, at Hertingfordbury in Hertfordshire, where then and later he painted many landscapes.

At the beginning of the new century there was not much to distinguish Gore from other Slade students. Certainly the few Steer-like landscapes of about 1905 that I have seen give no indications of special promise, nor do the landscapes of the following years, which show that Corot and Sisley had displaced Steer as the principal objects of his study. It was in the summer of 1904 that he first met Sickert. The meeting was effected by my father's younger brother Albert, who was a fellow student of Gore's at the Slade. The two of them went to Dieppe and spent two days continuously in Sickert's company. So began an intimate friendship that was to end only with Gore's death. The meeting had other consequences. After years of wandering abroad, Sickert, always disposed for change, always interested in what his friends were about, had begun to grow tired of his self-imposed exile. In London the New English Art Club had entered upon the most brilliant and influential period of its history. The illustrious painters of mature talent – with two exceptions, every one of those treated in these pages was associated with the Club, most of them as members, a few as exhibitors only – were being joined by the most talented of the younger generation. The enthusiasm of his two visitors for what was happening at the New English, and at the Slade, from which its membership was so largely drawn, focused the interest of Sickert upon London and sharpened his desire to return there. As already noted, he settled in Camden Town in 1905. That year Sickert lent his house at Neuville to Gore, where he stayed from May until October. Of the paintings he did there – the Corot-Sisley inspired essays already mentioned – none of those that I have seen reflects a personal vision, but what they convincingly show is a deepened understanding of the science of painting, and, in particular, of the methods of the French Impressionists. His sympathies with Impressionism were not only, nor, perhaps, even principally aroused by his six months' intensive painting in France, for it was about this time that he formed an intimate friendship with Lucien Pissarro. This friendship was of cardinal importance for Gore, however, not for what it enabled him to learn about Impressionism

– by this time the movement, even in England, was widely known among the intelligent – but for the insight it gave him into Impressionism's ultimate development. Reference has already been made in these pages to the double part played by the younger Pissarro in substituting knowledge of Impressionism among English painters for rumour, and often alarmist rumour at that, and in explaining the activities of those, of whom Cézanne and Seurat were the chief, by whom Impressionism had been 'remade'. By none of the younger painters was this body of knowledge more intelligently assimilated than by Gore. His knowledge of Continental painting – like that of many of his generation – was notably enlarged by the first Post-Impressionist Exhibition. It is significant of the temperamental difference between Gore and Gilman that Gore was most attracted by Matisse, whose impact, coming after that of Gauguin, excited him to bolder experiments in colour and pattern, while Gilman received an impetus that lasted to the end of his life from the burning realism of van Gogh. During his time at Neuville he visited Paris and saw the big Gauguin exhibition at the Salon d'Automne. The Renoirs he saw at the Durand-Ruel exhibition at the Grafton Gallery that year had particularly impressed him, and after studying the Cézannes, the first probably that he had seen, he observed to a friend that 'there was something in them'. It was not until three or four years later that he arrived at a full understanding of the art of Cézanne.

It was in 1905, too, that the results of his always grateful yet independent discipleship of Sickert and Pissarro, and his own meditations upon the nature of painting and his assiduous practice, revealed themselves in a series of paintings of music-hall and ballet subjects that were both personal and mature. These subjects continued to occupy him until about 1911. It may be presumed that Sickert first drew his attention to the beauties of the theatre, but his treatment of them derives from Lucien Pissarro. Gore used to spend every Monday and Tuesday night, over long periods, at the Alhambra Ballet. After seeing the Russian ballets produced for the first time in London by Fokine, with Nijinsky and Karsavina in the leading parts, he turned to a friend and said, 'I've dreamt of things like this, but I never thought I should see them'. His method was to visit the theatre, always occupying the same seat, equipped with a small note-book, conté chalk and a fountain-pen. Thus stationed and equipped, he would add a stroke or two, at the relevant moment, to a study of a transient pose or relationship of figures. A tight-rope walker involved a succession of visits to capture a pose held only for an instant. 'Every time she got to a certain spot', he wrote, 'I had my pencil on the spot where I left off and added a little. It took some time.'[1] From the numerous resulting studies oil paintings were built up. Gore, like Gilman and Ginner, observed a strict distinction between paintings and drawings made in front of the subject and those made in the studio.

> I think [he wrote] that when in front of nature what you produce should be exactly what you see and not touched except out of doors. If you set out to arrange or compose, it should be done entirely away from the subject, making of course as many studies from nature as you want.[2]

Gore painted few portraits, but in one of them, *North London Girl*[3] (Plate 25), of 1912, his sense of colour and tone, as well as a strong sense of character, are happily combined. (The subject is the girl who served tea at the 19 Fitzroy Street 'at homes'.)

In 1907 he visited Yorkshire, where he painted several landscapes which showed that he was able to handle outdoor subjects maturely also. Although it was, for technical reasons, impossible to paint directly in the theatre, Gore did not share Sickert's belligerently held conviction that to paint in front of the subject was a cardinal error, and that pictures ought to be painted from studies. He always worked as directly from nature as circumstances allowed. His method was to draw his subject on the canvas in paint, next putting in the cool and the warm colours, keeping the range both of tones and values as narrow as possible, for he believed that fine distinctions were more 'telling' than violent contrasts. Upon this foundation he slowly built up a mosaic of paint unmixed with medium. It was his aim to define form in terms of colour. To Sickert's warnings against the dangers of overstatement he found it easy to pay attention, for overstatement was foreign to his nature and contrary to his up-bringing: his statements about the form and colours and relations

---

[1] Unpublished letter to Doman Turner, July 1909.   [2] Ibid.
[3] Coll. Mr. J. W. Freshfield.

of things were never, like those of his friend Gilman, challenges.

Up to about 1906 Gore was scarcely more than a serious and gifted student, but he had already begun to exert 'the unique influence in the artistic affairs of London' noted by 'The Morning Post'. Of the several qualities that combined to give him special authority among his fellow artists the chief was a combination of disinterestedness and charm. Disinterestedness without charm might have provoked exasperation, and charm without disinterestedness liking without esteem. It was the spectacle of this tall, young man of distinguished bearing, whose extreme carelessness of his personal appearance seemed to symbolize a carelessness of his personal interests, devoting himself wholeheartedly to the general good, in particular to the reconciling of differences that could honourably be reconciled, that won him this special degree of authority and affection. In addition he possessed an integrity that was not questioned and an unassertive assurance. Sickert wrote: 'I never heard him complain of anything.' No one was more emphatic in his recognition of Gore's qualities than Sickert. In reply to those who spoke of Gore's indebtedness to him, he used to insist upon what he had learnt from Gore, and after Gore's death he wrote of his career as 'the most complete object-lesson on the conduct of a life and of a talent that it is possible to have experienced'.[1] Gore had a quality which only reveals itself in his work upon the closest scrutiny – namely, extreme intelligence. By the kindness of the artist's widow, I have had the privilege of access to a remarkable series of letters written by Gore at odd moments snatched from his own laborious hours of work or from those of exertion on behalf of his friends, at moments, often, when he was too tired to paint or draw or organize, which shows how concentrated, supple, uncompromising, and above all how lucid his intelligence was. These letters were addressed to Doman Turner, a deaf fellow artist to whom Gore undertook to teach drawing. The first of them is dated 8 June 1908 and the last 24 November 1913. They give a clear insight into Gore's beliefs and his practice as a painter and draughtsman, and although they are impersonal in tone, they reveal almost as much of the character of him to whom they are addressed as of the writer's. They show

[1] Introduction to the catalogue of an exhibition of thirty-six of Gore's works held in February 1916 at the Carfax Gallery.

that, while he was satisfied with his pupil's technical progress, he is dismayed to discover that he did not value his own talent as a serious artist must, and that he suffered from a radical apathy. 'From your letters', wrote Gore, 'I always have a kind of suspicion that the things you do interest me more than they do you.'[1] The correspondence therefore lost its didactic character. I hope that one day it will be published in full. Here in the meanwhile are a few characteristic extracts:

Don't think about making patterns but of drawing objects in such a way that a sculptor could model from them. . . . Contours and light and shade have no value of themselves, it does not matter whether the lines are clumsy and the shadow ragged so long as they both help to explain the size or shape of some form in relation to the other forms which go to make up the object or objects you are drawing. What one asks of a draughtsman is What is your personal view of this head or figure or landscape? not how neatly or how smoothly you can cover up so much paper with lines and shading making up a pattern, even to imitate fairly accurately the general features of the thing seen.[2]
In drawing, everything must grow out of something else – be in relation to it and everything else be referred back to it. . . . The interest is in what you see not what you know.[3]
Drawing deals with the forms of things alone. Directly you go outside this you get to painting. That is to say, relations of tone or colour. And I think that drawings of effects are absolutely uninteresting or only interesting on account of the form and not of the effect. . . . Drawing from memory always leads to some kind of mannerism which may be good if it has enormous knowledge and purpose behind it as in J. F. Millet or Lionardo [sic], but it is interesting to notice in Millet and in Daumier and others who did not always get their facts first hand, that such things as the folds of a coat are never very interesting however magnificent the whole figure may be. . . . Whistler was a great artist . . . but he made the great mistake of setting up a standard of beauty derived from other painters. . . . If you compare this attitude with that of Renoir Degas Manet Monet Pizzarro [sic] Siseley [sic] . . . or Courbet . . . who all went to nature like children to find new beauty and whose work points to the fact that beauty exists everywhere; then you will find that Whistler like a backwater leads you nowhere while they are like a river carrying you wherever you want to go.[4]
A drawing is an explanation of an observation. If you observe nothing special your drawings will have nothing to them. . . .[5]

[1] 9 September 1910.   [2] 26 June 1908.   [3] 28 August 1908.
            [4] 8 September 1908.   [5] undated.

These brief extracts from Gore's notes for his pupil will give, I think, an indication of one reason at least for the fruitful character of his influence – namely, his capacity for giving lucid and practical expression to the convictions that formed in his mind as a consequence of continuous practice and long meditation. They also show how firmly his own art was rooted in the visual world. It has been a disposition among those who, especially of recent years, have mentioned Gore to suggest that he began as an Impressionist and ended as a Neo-Impressionist. This would be an overstatement altogether. His vision underwent no transformation; there was only a change of emphasis. Gore was a close and perceptive observer of the work of the masters whose art was so radically affecting most of his generation, fully aware of the contributions of Cézanne and Seurat to European painting, and interested in Cubism from its beginnings. (There exist several of his own paintings which may be regarded as essays in a modified Cubism.) All these interests served to stimulate his preoccupation with design and with the structure of things. But with what detachment he regarded Neo-Impressionism years after he had become familiar with the movement from Lucien Pissarro and others is clear from an allusion to one aspect of it in a letter to Doman Turner.

> Neo-Impressionism [he wrote] was the name given to people who tried to reduce the system of divided colour to a science. . . . The two chief exponents were Signac and Seurat. . . . Lucien Pissarro learnt to paint in this manner. It was not a great success because it made a painting very mechanical. . . .[1]

Gore was in fact nearer to this movement in his ballet and music-hall scenes – the *Inez and Taki*,[2] of 1910, than in his last Richmond landscapes. His Post-Impressionist sympathies showed themselves in an enhanced awareness of the structural elements in nature, and of the designs they formed, hidden from the inattentive eye. To the end his procedure was one of discovery, a seeking out of the design already there, never the imposition of a design upon nature. Gore's evolution has been succinctly described by his friend Ginner:

I have a fine example of a broad-minded artist who was ready to learn from the various modern schools. Spencer F. Gore, who was first

[1] 11 June 1910.   [2] The Tate Gallery, London.

influenced by Mr. Walter Sickert, corrected in himself his master's degraded colour by absorbing the influence of the Impressionists through Mr. Lucien Pissarro. Later on he did not close his eyes to the Cubist and Vorticist movements, but learned much from them while remaining a realist in his outlook on life. He had received from these schools of painting a stronger sense of design [and] saw it in nature. . . .[1]

From the time, about 1906, when he may be said to have reached maturity until his death was a span of only eight years. These he devoted first of all to painting, but he was constantly concerned with the welfare of the art of painting, and the service of his painter friends. 'He discovered and encouraged', wrote Sickert, 'any talent that came his way with devotion and sequence. . . .'[2] He was a founder-member of the Allied Artists' Association, of 19 Fitzroy Street, the unanimously elected President of the Camden Town Group (he selected and arranged the Group's comprehensive exhibition at Brighton[3]), a member, from 1909, of the New English Art Club (on its juries, Sickert has also told us, 'he exerted a salutary influence') and an active founder of the London Group.

Nothing as a rule can be less interesting than the small politics of the formation and conduct of artistic societies [wrote the obituarist already quoted]. Mr. Gore saw the necessity for these activities. . . . It was often asked . . . what was the bond of union which enabled the Camden Town and London Groups to hold together. . . . It is hardly an exaggeration to say that it was simply the character of Gore, so liberal in his enthusiasms, so incapable of petty jealousy. . . .

I never had the privilege of knowing Gore, but everything that I have heard from those who had confirms the justice of this tribute. His year of teaching, in 1914, at the Westminster School has already been noted, and in 1912 he supervised and carried out decorations at a highly intellectual night-club, the Cabaret Theatre Club, at 9 Haddon Street. Among the collaborators he secured were Wyndham Lewis, whose large panel won for Cubism its first success in England, and Eric Gill. At the height of his activity, at the moment when his work was showing a new breadth and firmness of structure, without sacrifice of the delicacy that had earlier

---

[1] 'Modern Painting and Teaching', *Art and Letters*, July 1917.

[2] Introduction to catalogue of Memorial Exhibition at the Carfax Gallery, 1916.

[3] At the Public Art Galleries from 16 December 1913 to 14 January 1914.

distinguished it, he died. In the early summer of 1913 he left Camden Town – where he had spent the greater part of his working life, first at 31 Mornington Crescent, now demolished, and later at 2 Houghton Place – for Richmond, where he settled at 6 Cambrian Road, in order to be near the Park. On 25 March 1914 he got wet while out painting, contracted pneumonia and forty-eight hours later, on the 27th, he was dead.

Small memorial exhibitions were held in February 1916 at the Carfax Gallery and in October 1920 at the Paterson Carfax Gallery, and in April 1928 a fully representative one at the Leicester Galleries.

He drilled himself [Sickert wrote] to be the passive and enchanted conduit for whatever of loveliness his eyes might rest upon. . . . But it is not only out of scenes obviously beautiful in themselves, and of delightful suggestions, that the modern painter can conjure a piece of encrusted enamel. Gore had the digestion of an ostrich. A scene, the drearyness and hopelessness of which would strike terror into most of us, was for him a matter for lyrical and exhilarated improvisation. I have a picture by him of a place that looks like Hell, with a distant iron bridge in the middle distance, and a bad classic façade like the façade of a kinema, and two new municipal trees like brooms, and the stiff curve of a new pavement in front, and on which stalks and looms a lout in a lounge suit. The artist is he who can take a flint and wring out attar of roses.[1]

[1] 'A Perfect Modern.'

AMBROSE McEVOY

1878—1927

THE branch of the McEvoy family to which the painter Ambrose belonged has no history. His father, a man as gifted as himself, emerged suddenly on a dark night in the eighteen-fifties from a turbulent sea upon the coast of one of the southern states of North America. After a quarrel with his parents, two shadowy Irish emigrants to New England, Charles Ambrose McEvoy ran away from home and embarked with a few companions in a small sailing ship. Overwhelmed by the waves, the vessel broke up, and he and two Negroes succeeded in reaching a small lighthouse. They were the only survivors. After being cared for for a short time by the lighthouse keeper, he was adopted by a cotton millionaire. A few years later, the War between the States broke out. Young McEvoy, who seems to have sympathized with the emancipation of the Negroes, assisted, nevertheless, in the capture of John Brown and fought for the state of his adoption. He served first in the Army of the Confederacy, but was disabled from further service by a wound received at the Battle of Bull Run, which was tended by Dr. Whistler, brother of the illustrious artist. He next placed at the service of the Confederacy his audacious resourcefulness as an inventor. Certain of his ideas were embodied in the construction of the primitive ironclad, the *Merrimac,* others in the fantastic *David,* a submarine vessel consisting of two immense concentric iron balls, which, setting out to raise the blockade of Charleston, moved out along the sea-bed with a 25-foot spar bearing a torpedo projecting from her bows. The Federal sloop, *Housatonic,* was marked out for destruction. The *David,* submerged, rammed her with her torpedo. There was a devastating explosion. The blockader and the *David* both sank. From this disaster to his own vessel, he evolved the principle of the depth-charge, with which, with extraordinary prescience, he predicted that the submarine would eventually be fought.

After the defeat of the Confederacy, Captain McEvoy and Dr.

Whistler both settled in England. Here he evolved and sold to the British Admiralty his principal invention, the first submarine-detector, the hydrophone. Science and engineering did not, however, absorb the entire energies of this prodigiously ingenious and versatile man, for he was interested in music and the visual arts. He was the first to discover the unusual talent for drawing of his elder son, Ambrose. Instead of treating it as an effeminate propensity, after the fashion of the usual prosperous Victorian parent, he had nothing but joy in watching its development.

Ambrose McEvoy was born on 12 August 1878 at Crudwell, Wiltshire. Shortly before the birth, a year later, of his brother Charles, the future playwright, the family moved to London, and settled at 51 Westwick Gardens, West Kensington. Both brothers attended, without notable results, a long-defunct school known as Elgin House.

Through the friendship between his father and Dr. Whistler, Ambrose McEvoy enjoyed the privilege of knowing Whistler, who showed a sympathetic confidence in his talent. He used, in after life, to recall how Whistler took him as a boy to Hampton Court, and, stopping before Tintoretto's *Five Muses of Olympus,* enjoined him to 'drink it in,' and how they stood in front of it for a long time in silence. It was on the advice of Whistler that his father sent him, in 1893, to the Slade School, where he remained for three years.

Those for whom the name McEvoy evokes the dashing creator of fashionable beauty in a nimbus of rainbow-coloured light may be surprised to know that at the Slade he was a slow and laborious worker and an impassioned student of the technical methods of the old masters. Upon this subject, at this time and later, he kept copious and detailed notes.

At the Slade he became engaged to be married. A fellow student, Mary Spencer Edwards, had watched him at the National Gallery while he was making a copy of Titian's *Noli me tangere,* and had been so moved by the tall young man with the poetic and gentle expression that marriage to the man to whom she was engaged became impossible any longer to contemplate. She wrote to him to break their engagement. A few days later, in front of the Titian, she and Ambrose McEvoy were introduced by Augustus John. A few days later she saw him again, at John's Fitzroy Street studio, and she watched him attentively, as, talking to a group of fellow students, he pushed with long fingers his hair out of his eyes. She was too shy to speak to him, but that day, he told her afterwards, he loved her also. Immediately afterwards they became secretly engaged. Marriage for the time being was a remote prospect. Captain McEvoy had met with financial disaster the year his son entered the Slade, and Colonel Edwards, her father, would have regarded marriage to an artist with repugnance.

When McEvoy left the Slade, he lived for several years in extreme poverty, continuing at the National Gallery and the Soane Museum his intensive study of the methods of the old masters, in particular of Titian, Rubens, Rembrandt, Claude, Gainsborough and Hogarth. In order to give the requisite time to his studies, he produced little. He was determined to give his painting the soundest possible technical basis, whatever the sacrifice of present comfort or reputation. In the course of his studies, he pondered his findings and slowly discovered the methods best suited to the fulfilment of his own aims. In the several notebooks in which, mostly between 1898 and 1902, he wrote down his miscellaneous observations upon the methods of the old masters, his æsthetic philosophical reflections, his injunctions to himself with regard to his procedures over a given painting or painting generally, there is nothing to suggest that he evolved either a consistent system of painting or a comprehensive æsthetic outlook. How deficient he was in the necessary intellectual power his dull disjointed writings clearly show. But they show also a habit of close, first-hand observation, especially of the various methods of glazing, and constant preoccupation with the capturing upon his canvas of the utmost that was possible of the harmony which he saw everywhere in nature. 'Harmony produced by all the means at our disposal,' he wrote, 'is the most interesting subject of thought to me. . . .' But he was a painter and not a writer, and if his notebooks suggest that as a thinker he was pedestrian and incoherent, his paintings and drawings of those early years proclaim him to be an artist of exceptional sensibility and insight.

His principal works were figures in interiors, low in tone, tranquil in mood. In spite of their beautiful, pensive quietness. McEvoy did not emerge as a quite distinct personality. Frederick Brown, his master, in *Hard Times,* and other members of the New English Art Club had painted pictures which contained, in a somewhat robuster form, most of the elements of McEvoy's. In method McEvoy's were based, more deliberately than theirs, upon his studies of Rembrandt and Rubens: that is to say, the composition was put in black and white and the local colour added to it. They are, in other words, not original pictures, but there is a quality in their mood of shadowy, pensive quietness, and in the delicate deliberation with which each form is defined precisely without impairing in the slightest the total unity, that raises them above mere school pieces. The most characteristic of them, *The Engraving*,[1] of 1900, was bought the following year by Frederick Brown for £25. The sale of two other pictures in the same year, *The Thunder-Storm*,[2] a not very successful attempt at a dramatic subject, and a landscape, enabled him on 16 January 1901 to marry Mary Spencer Edwards. For a time they lived in Jubilee Place, Chelsea, but he developed an almost obsessive desire to acquire 107 Grosvenor Road, a house overlooking the river, which he bought in 1906 and which remained his home for the rest of his life and provided the background for many of his pictures. Others he began elsewhere, often in his studio in Trafalgar (now Chelsea) Square; they were mostly finished in the big studio he built at the back of his riverside house.

The years immediately following his marriage were industrious, penurious years. He worked almost continuously, and, though he gave more time to painting than he had as a student, he still spent two evenings a week at the South Kensington Museum in the study of the methods of the masters. Before long the self-discipline, which enabled him to resist the temptation to hurry in the face of actual want, was rewarded by the appearance of a discriminating patron in the person of Sir Cyril Kendall Butler. From him McEvoy received very small prices, but he and his wife were maintained for more than a year in a cottage near their patron's house at Bourton, near Shrivenham. Gradually he received a more valuable reward: the laboriousness so irksome to sitters was transformed into an extraordinary facility. Confident in having evolved methods whereby his pictures would last, this slowest of painters became the most rapid. Mrs. Archibald Douglas, the wife of his most generous and

[1] Coll. the late S. D. Bles.   [2] Coll. Mrs. Bishop.

constant patron, told me that his *Portrait of Lady Tredegar*,[1] of 1919, was completed in twenty minutes.

The absence of a clearly defined personality, of deeply felt convictions, is apparent upon close scrutiny of the subdued and tranquil interiors of McEvoy's first decade. How impressionable he was is shown by an incident which occurred in 1909. At the annual exhibition of the New English Art Club, there was a painting of a favourite Dieppe subject of Sickert's, painted in that artist's highly personal style. This painting brought Sickert much commendation. 'Better than anything you've ever done', remarked a brother artist with a fulsome smile. 'I'm afraid', Sickert answered, 'it is', and referred him to the catalogue. The painting was the work of McEvoy, done in the course of a visit to Sickert at Neuville. Nothing could be more different than this picture from his interiors, or from his own earlier landscapes, *The Orchard*,[2] of 1904, a highly artificial fusion of memories of Gainsborough and Claude, or the more closely observed and genuinely poetic *Winter*,[3] of 1905. During the few years following the painting of the Dieppe picture, changes in the character of his art proclaimed even more plainly that his interiors and his landscapes offered inadequate means of expressing what became his most passionate, his almost exclusive preoccupation, beautiful women. Such in all probability had always been the case, for such passionate and exclusive preoccupations, although they may show themselves suddenly, are rarely of sudden growth. This hypothesis would account for the element of reserve which prevents McEvoy's early interiors and landscapes – distinguished and poetic as they are – from carrying complete conviction. In painting them McEvoy was making beautiful pictures as a craftsman makes a beautiful object, but one look at any of the fashionable beauties of the later years – sometimes, by comparison, ill-considered and even vulgar – makes it clear that his interest was fully engaged. Although fashionable women came at last to absorb his energies entirely, and although his portraits of them could be, indeed, what his *Portrait of Lady Tredegar* so unabashedly is, examples of the vulgarest display, his habitual attitude towards his subjects was far removed from vulgarity.

The radical change in his outlook became apparent in 1913. Two

[1] Coll. Mrs. Archibald Douglas.   [2] Coll. Mrs. Archibald Douglas.

[3] Whereabouts unknown.

years earlier he had painted the best of his interiors, *The Ear-ring*,[1] which, in so far as it is, in essence, a study of a woman and only formally an interior at all, foreshadows the change to come. In 1912 he painted what I believe to be the last of his interiors, *La Reprise*.[2] This is an elegant and tender but listless work; for comparison between it and *The Engraving* or *The Book*,[3] of 1902, shows how far his interest in the representation of rooms was exhausted. It was the model for *The Ear-ring* and *La Reprise* – a Basque governess who came in 1911 to look after the two McEvoy children and who subsequently married the portrait-painter, Gerald Brockhurst – who provided the occasion for the change. In 1913 he painted a portrait of her which he called *La Basquaise*.[4] This, shown at the New English Art Club's autumn exhibition that year, brought him popular success, which two other portraits shortly confirmed. These were *Madame*, of 1914, an un-noteworthy portrait of his wife, purchased by the French Government for the Luxembourg, and *Lydia*,[5] of the same year, an entirely wretched portrait of the wife of the painter Walter Russell. The success of these three pictures was such that by 1916 this laborious and almost starving painter of reticent interiors was besieged by fashionable ladies determined to have their portraits painted.

McEvoy made a reputation as a fashionable portrait painter with three inferior works, but it was abundantly justified by others.

The opinion has been for many years pretty widely accepted that McEvoy began as a serious and sensitive painter of interiors and landscapes and that, dazzled by the glamour of fashionable women, he degenerated into an audacious, even a flashy sycophant. I have already intimated that this is an opinion from which I dissent. Even were the early works still more distinguished and the later more frequently as bad as the artist's detractors claim they are, I would be reluctant to rate orthodox variants of existing works, however impeccable in taste and however sensitive, which reveal the fundamental dullness from which all such works must suffer by their nature, more highly than original works called into existence by an ardent emotion. These last are the creations of Ambrose McEvoy;

[1] The Tate Gallery, London.   [2] The City Art Gallery, Aberdeen.
[3] Coll. Mrs. Bernard Yarrow.   [4] Coll. Mrs. P. G. McFadden, Philadelphia.
[5] Coll. Mrs. Archibald Douglas.

25. SPENCER GORE. *North London Girl* (1911).
Oil, 24×20 in. Coll. Mr. J. W. Freshfield.

26. AMBROSE McEVOY. *The Hon. Daphne Baring* (1916).
Oil, 42½ × 32½ in. Coll. The Hon. Mrs. Arthur Pollen.

27. AMBROSE McEVOY. *Portrait in Black and Green* (1923).
Water colour, 26×18 in. (sight). Coll. Mrs. K. Dyson.

28. Sir WILLIAM ORPEN.
The Play Scene from 'Hamlet'
(1899).
Oil, 69¼×87½ in.
Coll. The Marquess of
Cholmondeley.

the earlier, in the last analysis, of his teachers and his older contemporaries. He suffered, let it be conceded without delay, a number of egregious, indefensible failures of method, failures of taste, but no more, I think, than might be expected of any artist working in an audacious manner beset by the many trials – capricious and unpunctual sitters, exacting social obligations, the frequent necessity of working in unfamiliar environments and the like – to which the fashionable portrait-painter is always subject. But there are other and, it seems to me, most notable works to McEvoy's credit.

In McEvoy's miscellaneous writings the expression 'beauty' is of frequent occurrence, in contexts which suggest that his conception of this attribute was strictly confined to things pleasing in themselves, a conception remote, for instance, from that of Sickert or Stanley Spencer, artists largely concerned with the discovery of beauty in things – iron bedsteads and amorous octogenarians – not in themselves beautiful. Among things in themselves most eminently pleasing – especially to men – are, quite obviously, women. Upon them, in his interiors of the very early 1900s, he fixed a scrutiny searching but reticent. After the passage of some years, this had grown franker: in an unconvincing *Interior*,[1] of 1910, one of them, for instance, is represented nude. After 1912 his interest in the women he paints was undisguised: the rooms in which in former times he had so carefully placed them, withered away, and they emerged as the sole subject of his pictures. On the comparatively rare occasions when he painted portraits of men, it is reasonable to suppose that his successes – as in *Viscount d'Abernon*,[2] of 1916, and more notably *The Rt. Hon. Augustine Birrell*,[3] of 1918 – owed much to the enhancement of his sensibilities in the face of a subject of a different kind. The last ten years of his life were devoted, almost exclusively, to painting beautiful and fashionable women. Had he been unconscious, had he not been, indeed, acutely perceptive, of their desirability as women and scarcely less of the distinction of the positions they occupied in the social system, he could have had no success as a painter of fashionable portraits. These two qualities must always be emphasized by the successful portrait-painter, whether his

[1] Coll. Lady Butler.   [2] Coll. Viscountess d'Abernon.

[3] The National Gallery of Canada, Ottawa.

subjects are hieratic and remote infantas or princesses pretending to be milkmaids.

For McEvoy his sitters' allurements as women and as fashionable women never included overt sensuality, anything remotely corresponding to the wet, sensual mouths and the bare bosoms of Lely's ladies, or any traditional aristocratic symbolism, the vista of park, the fluted column. McEvoy's intention was, in fact, an extremely subtle one and the allurements and the social distinction of his sitters merely formed part of the raw material to be transmuted into an ethereal likeness in which direct allusion to such qualities would be intrusive and entirely destructive of the effect at which he aimed. This was to paint a beautiful woman as a man in love with her would see her: to paint her transformed into an unearthly being, her most exquisite qualities of body and mind projected in a radiant, many-coloured nimbus. (He could not bear to hear, his daughter Anna told me, the slightest disparagement of any sitter while her portrait was in progress, lest the spell which he wove about her should be broken.) Such an aim, impossible to realize in terms of the muted tones and the meticulously rendered detail of the early works, called for technical methods of an entirely different kind. The change in the focus of his interest was accompanied by reliance upon brilliant lighting, often from below, besides the very loose, very rapid way of painting already noted. In a book entitled 'The Technique of Portrait Painting', the author, the portrait-painter Harrington Mann, in the course of a eulogistic comparison between McEvoy and Botticelli, tells us that in the work of the former 'the design and the drawing are unimportant'. His brother artist had evidently looked with insufficient care at McEvoy's later portraits – for instance, at *The Hon. Daphne Baring* (Plate 26),[1] of 1917. McEvoy's design and drawing were relatively unimportant, except at the principal point of focus. Here – and it is precisely this that gives the poetry and the delicate distinction to the best of his portraits – the features, or certain of them, are drawn with extreme sensibility and precision. Without this point of lucid definition, a late portrait by McEvoy would be a mere iridescent chaos; and that, in fact, is just what his failures are. But *Daphne Baring* is far from being a failure. It is one of the best portraits he ever painted. The drawing of the face, the mouth in

---

[1] Coll. The Hon. Mrs. Arthur Pollen.

particular, and even, at certain points, the Botticelli-inspired dress, is beautiful and exact. The farther removed, however, from such delicately wrought points of intrinsic interest, the broader, the less decisive, was the artist's touch, until, as he approached the margin of his canvas – or of his paper – the scarcely defined forms dissolve entirely.

In one respect, McEvoy's procedure in his later portraits was similar to that in the early interiors. Both were painted, not 'directly', in opaque colour, but usually in thin glazes over an almost monochrome sketch of yellow ochre, black and white, a procedure used by few of his contemporaries, and the result of his studies of his chosen masters of the seventeenth and eighteenth centuries, among whom it was general.

It was inevitable that a painter who sought for such elusive aims should suffer failures, and a number of McEvoy's society portraits, for all his taste and all his application, are garish and in the worst sense 'dated' things. But there are his successes. Besides *Daphne Baring*, these include *Mrs. Charles McEvoy*,[1] of 1913, *Lady Gwendoline Churchill*,[2] of 1917, *Viscountess Wimborne*,[3] also of 1917, and *Miss Violet Henry*,[4] of 1918. But in none of his paintings in oils has he achieved so high a degree of perfection as in his water-colours. In this medium, so much more readily adapted to realize his particular aims, he did his finest work. Unfortunately for him, the painter of society portraits must carry these out in oils. But he has left *Black and Green*[5] (Plate 27), a magical portrait of a young girl in which he realized his highest aims, that could hold its own beside a Gainsborough; the only slightly less lovely *The Artist's Wife*[6] and two *Portraits of Zita*,[7] all of 1923. In the early 1920s he began to use the lighter medium more and more often, but he had by then only a few years left to live. Pneumonia cut short his life as Big Ben struck four on the morning of 4 January 1927.

[1] Whereabouts unknown.   [2] Whereabouts unknown.
[3] Coll. Viscount Wimborne.   [4] Coll. Mr. Philip Henry.
[5] Coll. Mrs. K. Dyson.   [6] Whereabouts unknown.
                    [7] One, coll. Mrs. James.

WILLIAM ORPEN

1878–1931

THE story of Orpen's life is a story of material success more spectacular and continuous than attended that of any of the other subjects of these pages. In terms of material success he is to be ranked, in fact, with the most successful painters who have ever worked in England – that is to say with Van Dyck, Kneller, Reynolds, Lawrence and Sargent.

In my own early memories (he was my uncle by marriage), he survives clearly as a small man with a pale, high-cheek-boned face, light grey eyes that observed much and revealed little, a figure without a trace of the atrophied staidness that marks most adults, but slim and active as a boy's. I remember an occasional sense of embarrassment when, having missed something he said on account of the rapidity of his speech, I had to ask him to repeat it. He was always ready to join in any game or sport, always as an equal – that is to say, without making facetious references to his age or arrogating to himself any authority as an adult – and he always excelled. One night we were playing table tennis at his house in Chelsea; he said: 'I'm going to ask one of the best players I know to come round.' Presently we were joined by a pale, small, old man in his middle twenties, whose name I did not hear, who beat us all without exertion. Many years later, when I met Ben Nicholson, I recognized him as the masterly player.

Orpen seemed to enjoy discussing, sometimes long afterwards, games we had played, which he was able to recall with surprising minuteness. Not long ago I came upon a copy of his book, 'An Onlooker in France', which he gave me inscribed 'In memory of a bathe at Groom's Farm, March 1921' – an occasion when we had played water-polo at a house in Buckinghamshire where the Orpen family spent a summer.

As a painter I was at first aware of him as a member of an as yet not sharply differentiated group of members of the New English Art Club which included Sickert, Steer – all the painters, in fact, about whom I have been writing. I can just remember my father's being challenged for maintaining that John was a more considerable artist than Orpen. Presently I was aware of him as the most successful painter in England, and as one esteemed by many as the best. In those days his success seemed both glittering and firmly based. There were the Rolls-Royces waiting beyond the paved forecourt of his magnificent studio in South Bolton Gardens, and there was the adulation of critics. But there was also the admiration, or at least the respect, of his fellow artists. If voices were raised in criticism of the forced lighting and obvious interpretations of character that marred certain of his portraits, these could be silenced by an allusion to one of his classic portraits, or, if that did not suffice, to some prodigy of drawing of his student days, or to the triumphant *Play Scene in 'Hamlet'* (Plate 28). To this impression of success built upon rock-like foundations the personality of the artist also contributed. His industry was prodigious; and in my own home I was able to apply the severest standard of comparison. There was always a sitter, or, in case the sitter should fail to arrive, a self-portrait in progress. His pretensions – within my hearing always – were of the most modest: to be a good craftsman, to paint what was in front of him, not blindly accepting its appearance, but making the fullest use of his knowledge. And whether in his high white studio, or the small house, long since demolished, in Royal Hospital Road, Chelsea, in which the little rooms resembled, in their subdued light and the polished high-lit quality of their furnishings, his own early 'interiors', there were always drawings – late as well as early – of which any artist might be proud, and which seemed to proclaim the fundamental soundness of his art.

Now, twenty years after his death, hardly anything remains of that vast reputation. Orpen is a fading 'period' memory. When his name is mentioned it is, more often than not, as a symbol of the hard, glossy portraiture patronized by successful public men in the second and third decades of the century.

Orpen was born on 27 November 1878 at Oriel, Stillorgan, County Dublin, the fourth son of Arthur Herbert Orpen, a Dublin solicitor, and christened William Newenham Montague. The Orpens are a respectable Protestant family, who claim descent from a Robert Orpen, who came to Ireland from Norfolk in the seventeenth

century. William Orpen's mother was the eldest daughter of
Charles Caulfield, Bishop of Nassau.

Membership of an Anglo-Irish family, the exceptional happiness
of his childhood, lack of any formal education, and attendance at an
art school as a full-time student while still a boy were four circumstances which, in their particular combination, chiefly determined
his character.

From his Anglo-Irish inheritance and upbringing he derived those
divided loyalties which always set him a little apart from his fellow
citizens, whether Irish or English. His Protestantism, his English
descent, and his residence in England during virtually the whole of
his adult life made him an unquestioning member of the British as
distinct from the Irish social system, yet he had a strong sense of
being an Irishman, and although without the most cursory interest
in politics, he regarded several of the Irish leaders with an affection
and veneration such as he never accorded to any public figure in
England – with the exception, towards the end of his life, of Lord
Derby. In a letter to my father he wrote: 'Larkin is the greatest man
I ever met.' I remember how particularly his three daughters, my
first cousins, maintained as children that they were 'Irish', even
though born in England of a mother with no traceable strain of any
blood but English. Until the First World War, he often took holidays in Ireland, taught occasionally at the Dublin Municipal School
of Art, and retained touch with fellow countrymen, notably Hugh
Lane, but also George Moore and others. It would be true, I think,
to say that Orpen's Irish life bore the sort of relation to his English
life as the unconscious does to the conscious. Had he received more
than the most elementary education, or intellectual discipline of any
kind, he might have reconciled his sentimental love for his native
country – for her most ardent aspirations he had no trace of
reasoned sympathy – with his effective identification with his
adopted one, but he left school at twelve, and never formed any habit
of reading great or even serious literature, and therefore grew into a
man, in the deeper sense, without a country. The early possession
of extraordinary dexterity as a draughtsman, and a consuming
ambition to develop it to the utmost, seem to have disposed him to
discontinue, with his departure from school, an education that may
hardly be said to have begun, which issued in lifelong intellectual

dyspepsia. Finally, his exceptionally happy childhood combined with this want of education to give him a kind of resentment against 'growing up', an instinctive sense of identification with the irresponsible spontaneous child as against the pompous adult.

At the age of seventeen he entered the Slade School, where he remained for four years, leaving in 1899. He was fortunate in that during his time there the School was at the climax of a period of extraordinary brilliance: the result of fierce and continuous competition between contending talents of a high order. Among his contemporaries were Wyndham Lewis, McEvoy, Edna Waugh and Augustus John. If on his arrival his drawing, although distinctly above the average and remarkable for a boy of his age, was not phenomenal, nothing that impassioned ambition could do to transform capability into brilliance was left undone. He drew, and shortly afterwards painted, with an intense and disciplined industry, and every moment he could spare from these labours he applied to the study (not like McEvoy, of the methods, but of the style) of the old masters. He was discovered at three o'clock one morning at work upon a Sketch Club composition by a fellow student, who afterwards observed: 'I have little doubt that he was punctually in his place at the School the same morning.' Whether he was looking at a model or at the work of an old master, he assiduously cultivated his exceptional powers of observation.

This combination of talent and industry did not have long to wait for its reward. Orpen shortly became one of the most accomplished draughtsmen in what was at the time probably the leading academy of drawing. By the staff – Brown, Steer and Tonks – he was enthusiastically acclaimed as the prodigy he was, and the attitude of many of his fellow students was accurately reflected in the opinion of one of them, who wrote not long after Orpen had left: 'When I was at the Slade, it was a one-man show; that man was Orpen.'[1]

However that may have been, there is no doubt that at the Slade Orpen made drawing after drawing of extraordinary brilliance. In my opinion, Orpen in his student years was within the first dozen draughtsmen that these islands have produced. Others have drawn with deeper insight and loftier imagination and greater originality,

[1] 'The Artist', August 1901.

but only very few have possessed so full and easy a command of the
full possibilities of drawing. By many such an opinion will be
dismissed – especially by my younger contemporaries – as fantastic,
but I should be surprised if a comprehensive exhibition of British
drawing did not confirm it. But Orpen did not only excel at drawing
at the Slade: he painted one picture which seems to me, in a curious
way, to be a masterpiece. This is *The Play Scene in 'Hamlet'*,[1] the
'Summer Composition' which won him the £40 Slade Prize in 1899.
Hamlet was the subject set, but Orpen understood that the play scene
alone offered scope for his exuberant whimsicality. It may be
regarded, his biographers tell us, as 'an undisguised avowal of the
sources from which he took nourishment'. It would be truer to say
that it was a distillation of all his arduous and well-memorized
studies. The lighting, at once dramatic and unifying, was derived
from Rembrandt (of whose works there had been a great exhibition
at Burlington House the previous winter), and the nude figure in the
foreground was an ingenious theft from the same source, but the
fruits of this young student's intense scrutiny of Goya, Daumier,
Hogarth, Watteau, Rowlandson, Velazquez, Hals, Conder, Augustus John and a dozen others – most, in fact, of the romantic-
realist masters of Northern Europe and of Spain – are easy to
discern.

The notebooks which he filled during these years with detailed
copies of every conceivable manifestation of art and craftsmanship
to be found in the art galleries and museums of London and, to a
lesser degree, of Paris and Dublin – Renaissance jewels, Gothic
fan-vaulting, Assyrian reliefs, mediaeval works – testify to a
fanatical determination to master the elements of style of all periods
and races, and, most positively of all, of the great European draughtsmen, Rembrandt, Rubens, Michelangelo, Watteau and Hogarth for
preference. But to take note of the huge extent of Orpen's debt is by
no means to suggest that the picture lacks originality. On the contrary,
it is highly original. The saying current in Oxford that to copy
from one book is plagiarism, but to copy from several is research,
has a certain applicability to this strange, precocious little masterpiece. There is an odd sentence in an essay on Orpen[2] published a
few years after the picture was painted which conveys something of

[1] Coll. The Marquess of Cholmondeley.   [2] 'The Slade, 1893–1897', 1907.

the quality of the picture's strangeness. 'The workmanship', wrote a fellow student, 'is so vigorously unhealthy as to appear to prove that refined morbidity is the only road to rude health.' *The Play Scene in 'Hamlet'*, organized and executed with extraordinary skill and informed with a spirit in which irrepressible wit blends harmoniously with mysterious grandeur, holds the spectator's attention, even now, as few pictures of the time can hold it. It is an astonishing achievement for a twenty-one-year-old student: it was also the culmination of Orpen's career as a painter. From this point the history of his life as an artist is the history of decline. The 'Summer Composition' picture raised his already brilliant reputation among artists to one of eminence. It was agreed that a new star had risen; no one suspected that it had already reached its zenith. There seemed no occasion for the slightest misgivings; in fact, the three principal paintings which he exhibited at the New English Art Club the following year set at rest the doubts of those few disposed to discount his *Hamlet* as a happy accident and won him a place among the leading painters of the day. These paintings were a romantic *Portrait of Augustus John*,[1] of that year, frankly based on Whistler's *Carlyle*; *A Mere Fracture*,[2] of 1900, an admirable conversation-piece, inspired, I think, by my father's domestic interiors (one of which, *The Browning Readers*,[3] of 1900, shows my mother with her sister, Grace, whom Orpen married in 1901), and *The Mirror*,[4] also of 1900.

It was this last work that was decisive in the establishment of Orpen's reputation. I know nothing about the particular circumstances in which it was painted, but it seems to me to mark a change in Orpen's outlook as decisively as it did to his contemporaries at the time. To them it marked the settling down to a steady mastery of a brilliant but wayward student, but in retrospect it seems to mark rather the rejection by a precocious master of precisely the qualities that gave significance to his vision, of the exuberant but slightly sinister humour, of the vivid if not yet steadily focused sense of satire, and, notwithstanding his innumerable quotations – and long, familiar quotations they often are – from the works of the old masters, of the capacity to see life from a queer, unexpected angle. *The Mirror* marks the rejection of all this, and more than this, in

---

[1] Whereabouts unknown.   [2] Coll. Mrs. Geoffrey Blackwell.
[3] The Cartright Memorial Hall, Bradford.   [4] The Tate Gallery, London.

favour of a mastery that was a mastery without compelling purpose. Orpen's biographers exaggerate no more than pardonably when they write of it as being 'painted with the minute precision of a Terborch or a Metsu',[1] for it is beyond question a highly accomplished display of painting, though, compared with that of the two Dutchmen, the handling is cold and brittle. I have referred to this picture, notwithstanding the entirely unassuming character of the subject – a model named Emily Scobel seated beside a circular, convex mirror in which the artist is reflected at his easel with a woman looking over his shoulder – as a 'display' of painting, for it is no more than a brilliant essay in a style perfected centuries before. Orpen has not taken Dutch seventeenth-century subject and style as, for instance, Delacroix the style and subjects of Rubens, or even Haydon the Elgin Marbles, as incitements or as points of departure, but simply as a convenient and popular means of exercising his conspicuous skill.

The culmination of his biographers' eulogy of *The Mirror* is their claim that it is 'a picture that would have gained the whole-hearted applause of an Academy jury'. The claim is but too well founded, for it is one of the ablest manifestations of the moribund and therefore aimless academism of our times.

The Mirror is a melancholy portent, for the greater part of Orpen's subsequent endeavour was given to unreflective representations of aspects of the real world – representations which, with the passage of the years, first grew commonplace and at last on occasion shamelessly vulgar. But this did not exhaust his energies, for there was a part of him which so commonplace an activity did not satisfy, and which clamoured for expression as long as he was able to hold pencil or brush. *The Play Scene in 'Hamlet'* expressed the whole of Orpen: in this painting his skill, his memory, his observation are the faithful and wonderfully efficient servants of a personality full of wit and fantasy and the sense of mystery. But after the dedication of his talents to commonplace purposes the imaginative elements in his nature were without adequate means of expression. As he became ever more preoccupied with painting portraits of fashionable and highly placed persons, these elements were apt to obtrude themselves ineptly, even absurdly, in the products of the few working hours he

[1] 'William Orpen : Artist and Man', by P. G. Konody and Sidney Dark, 1932.

spared from the execution of his innumerable commissions, in such pointless whimsies as *Myself and Venus*,[1] of 1910, *On the Irish Shore: Fairy Ring*,[2] of 1911, and *Leading the Life in the West*,[3] of 1914. By this last year it seemed as though the submerged imaginative side of his nature had sufficiently atrophied to need no stronger expression than whimsies of this kind, but the First World War stirred it into violent animation. All through the war he continued to record, with all his customary industry and skill, if with little of his former distinction, the faces of generals and statesmen. The urge to comment upon life as well as to record it, the urge to satirize, to protest, to laugh, to mourn surged up irresistibly. What moved him most deeply and most continuously (as it moved the other war painters and poets) was the contrast between the men at the Front, who were torn and burnt, blinded and crazed, and who suffered these things and the fearful prospect of them with such stoicism and even cheerfulness, and the people at home – above all, those in authority and those who in some way profited by the war – who accepted with complacency and even with cynicism sacrifices beyond description. This contrast, though he himself was in certain respects a hard man, caused him an anguish which at the Peace Conference, where he was the principal British painter, in daily contact with the peace-makers, became an obsession. The only occasion when I can recall his speaking with vehemence upon a serious theme was one night in 1920 when we were sitting alone after dinner at his house. He talked, more than he habitually talked, incoherently and faster, about the sickening impact of the callousness and the petty self-interest of the peace-makers in Paris, above all of their forgetfulness of the millions of mangled, rotting corpses in the Flanders slime. He took out of his pocket a copy of Maurice Baring's poem 'In Memoriam' to his friend, Lord Lucas, which he read out, his jerky diction obscuring its qualities as a poem, but giving an enhanced intensity to its meaning.

'This poem', he declared, 'is the greatest work of art that's come out of this whole war. I got Maurice Baring to copy it out for me. Maurice Baring said to me: "I'm mad, but nobody's noticed it yet." That's true of us all: the whole world's mad.'

[1] The Carnegie Institute, Pittsburgh. [2] The Johannesburg Art Gallery.
[3] The Metropolitan Museum, New York.

These words, spoken at that particular time by any one else, I might easily have forgotten. Spoken by Orpen, who had, his biographers justly note, 'few prejudices and no opinions', and whom 'any sort of serious talk bored', they were memorable. It is necessary to insist upon the earnestness of his obsession because this earnestness is not convincingly manifest in the pictures that he painted under its spell. Of these the chief was *To the Unknown British Soldier in France*. It was arranged that he should paint a group of the victorious Allied politicians, generals and admirals in one of the great rooms in the Palace of Versailles.

> I painted the room [he said at the time] and then I grouped the whole thirty-nine, or whatever the number was, in the room. It took me nine months' incessant painting; hard work. And then, you know, I couldn't go on. It all seemed so unimportant, somehow. In spite of all these eminent men, I kept thinking of the soldiers who remain in France for ever . . . so I rubbed all the statesmen and commanders out and painted the picture as you see it – the unknown soldier guarded by his dead comrades.[1]

The picture as originally painted showed the flag-draped catafalque standing at the entrance to the room, shown in significant darkness, where the Peace Treaty had been signed; on either side stood the two guardian figures based closely upon a study, *Blown up – mad*, done during the war. The arty pose of the legs (feet in the 'fifth position') and the length of classic drapery, calculated a shade too precisely to answer the requirements of modesty, gave these figures an air of utter incongruity with the grimness of the tableau in which they play the leading parts. The air of incongruity struck by these two wan, artificial figures was transformed into one almost of mockery by the presence above their heads of two frolicsome little Cupids on the wing. The exhibition of the picture at Burlington House in 1923 provoked a public outcry, which led to its rejection by the Imperial War Museum, for which it had been destined.[2]

It may perhaps be asked why I should dwell at some length upon one of the failures of an artist who painted other pictures of exceptional merit. I would answer that the weaknesses that made *To the*

---

[1] 'William Orpen: Artist and Man', p. 254.

[2] The Imperial War Museum finally accepted it after the artist had deleted the guardian Tommies and the winged Cupids.

Unknown British Soldier in France so conspicuous a failure are just the weaknesses that betrayed the extraordinary combination of talent and industry which at first seemed so surely destined for triumphant achievement. The defects of this picture are the defects of his achievement as a whole writ large.

In writing of Orpen's early life, I noted a combination of four circumstances which, as it seems to me, were the principal agents in the formation of his character. I noted how the divided loyalties to which the Anglo-Irish are liable made Orpen sentimentally an Irishman and practically an Englishman: a man who put down no deep roots anywhere; his removal from school at an age so early that his innate intellectual incuriosity never had to meet the challenge of education, his total dedication to drawing and painting when he had scarcely emerged from childhood, which increased beyond the possibility of redress his predilection for manual skill as opposed to a developed mind; and the happy childhood, with which in the course of his journey through life he unconsciously compared the disappointing present, thereby feeding his antipathy to the operations of the intellect as activities distinctively adult.

These four circumstances combined to make him, and to an extraordinary degree, a man wanting in settled principles or convictions; a man wanting, above all, in the means whereby settled principles and convictions could be forged – namely, an enquiring and a disciplined mind.

I have seldom known any man, and never a man of superior talents, with so little intellectual curiosity and so feeble an intellectual grasp, or with so contemptuous an attitude towards the life of the mind as Orpen. 'He had nothing but scorn', say his biographers, 'for the lesser intelligentzia', but the truth is that his attitude towards those whom they would perhaps have called the greater intelligentzia was not very different. It is true that he revered Maurice Baring and entertained an affectionate regard for George Moore, but it was the personalities of these two, I fancy, rather than their intellects which appealed to him. His biographers note that he was unable to read Ruskin. He used to say, with a touch of pride, that he was brought up on the Irish Question, but what it was he had no idea. Yet this ignorance precluded the slightest rational sympathy for the aspirations of a people with whom, upon a certain level of consciousness, he felt intimate ties. Except for the occasion I have referred to, I never heard him speak at length upon any serious subject. He could not, of course, avoid allusions to serious subjects, but they were in general of the nature of epigrams, staccato but ambiguous, and an instant later the disjointed, machine-gun talk had rambled far away. Games – lawn tennis, table tennis and billiards for preference – were the subjects about which he talked most consecutively, and now and then he evoked a vivid image. For instance, W. M. Hughes, the Australian Prime Minister, coming sullen and reluctant to a sitting, reading 'The Times' throughout the grudgingly conceded hour, then at its conclusion folding the paper up and walking out without having spoken a word. My own experience of his aversion to serious discussion, of his total intellectual incuriosity, is paralleled by the experience of others who knew him better. But what, I shall impatiently be asked, has intellectual curiosity to do with the creative faculties? Little or nothing, according to the opinion which strongly prevails today. Art with an intellectual basis is contemptuously condemned in Academic circles as an 'art of "-isms" ' (so runs the current cliché), while in avant-garde circles it is often quite deliberately rejected; Picasso, for instance, has declared in an interview with Christian Zervos,

> I don't know in advance what I am going to put on the canvas, any more than I decide in advance what colours to use. While I work, I take no stock of what I am painting on the canvas. Everytime I begin a picture, I feel as though I were throwing myself into the void. I never know if I shall fall on my feet again.[1]

And the influence of such opinions is clearly reflected in an aggressive preference shown by the avant-garde for the art of children, primitives, the insane over that of rational men, and by the contemptuous belittlement of the most intellectual of all the great periods of art, that of the Italian Renaissance.

So long as Orpen was content to make the 'straightforward' representation of the human face and figure his principal concern, his dismissal of intellectual preoccupations as mere pretentiousness had no conspicuous consequences for his art. Even such accomplished

[1] Cahiers d'Art, nos. 3-5, 1932.

paintings as *The Mirror* and *Charles Wertheimer*,[1] of 1908 (an expertly Sargentesque portrait of the well-known art dealer, the first picture he sent to Burlington House), involved little intellectual exertion. A year later, in 1909, Orpen painted a conversation-piece so admirable in its complex design and distinguished by such penetrating insight into character as to suggest that even then he might, by a great effort of will, have recognized upon what a broad and downward road *The Mirror* and *Charles Wertheimer* were signposts and have returned to the other and narrower way that he had left after *Hamlet*. This picture was *Hommage à Manet*[2] (in fact, homage to his friend, Sir Hugh Lane), in which George Moore, Steer, MacColl, Sickert, Lane and his own master, Tonks, are gathered round a tea-table beneath Manet's *Portrait of Eva Gonzales* at the house in South Bolton Gardens which then belonged to Lane and which Orpen afterwards acquired and used as a studio until his death. This (Plate 29) seems to me beyond question his best picture after *Hamlet*, and among the best conversation-pieces of the time. But evidently the day for the retracing of steps was past, and *Hommage à Manet* proved to be his Ave atque Vale to his own most exacting standards as a painter, and to his old friends of the New English circle. Already commissions for portraits, attracted by the *Charles Wertheimer* and others, were pouring in. By 1910 Orpen was the most successful portrait-painter of the age. There was no time for reflection; it was the golden treadmill for him.

When I said just now that Orpen's failure to recognize the potential contribution of the intellect to the creation of a work of art had no conspicuous consequences for his portrait-painting, I did not mean that it had none. On the contrary, it declared itself in an increasing obviousness in his interpretation of character. There were splendid exceptions. In particular, the Moore in *Hommage à Manet*. There are a number of others sufficiently well known, and a retrospective exhibition would no doubt bring yet more to light. But it can hardly be denied that, as the years passed, Orpen's magnates became more obviously magnates personified, his aristocrats more

[1] Whereabouts unknown. Its exhibition the same year at Burlington House led to Orpen's election as an Associate of the Royal Academy in 1910 and as a full Member in 1919. Before 1908 he had shown his principal work at the New English Art Club, of which he became a member in 1900.

[2] The City Art Gallery, Manchester.

obviously aristocrats, in the sense that heroes were quite simply heroes and villains were villains in Victorian popular drama. The effects of this increasing reluctance to meditate, to probe, and his increasing willingness to accept the most superficial aspect of a sitter and approximate it to that of some stock type, he made the more conspicuous by fierce and obviously artificial high-lighting and the virtual suppression of backgrounds. How rapid was the change may be seen by comparing the 'Moore' painted with such intimate satire, such comprehending affection, and the Lord Spencer[1] of seven years later, the personification of stagy hauteur, spot-lit. Neither the superficiality of interpretation, nor the forced and arbitrary lighting, nor the arbitrary sundering of heads from their backgrounds can obscure, however, the extraordinary sureness and vigour with which the best – even, perhaps, the majority – of Orpen's portraits were painted.

It was when he was under the necessity of representing not something material that could be observed but an intellectual perception that the consequences of his neglect of the intellectual values were shockingly apparent. The contrast between the heroism that animated the soldiers at the Front and the selfish complacency that prevailed at home, which stirred in Orpen such depths of indignation and pity, was a contrast grasped by the mind. To give it convincing visible form called for the exercise of intellectual powers far beyond his resources. His indignation and pity therefore did not move him to scathing utterance, but to incoherence. It is not surprising that the man who was brought up on the Irish Question, but who had no notion as to what it was, proved incapable of understanding or disentangling the complex question of the comparative conduct of those at the Front and those at home. To Orpen there was on the one hand 'the simple soldier man', than whom (I quote from his poem, 'Myself, Hate and Love'[2])

No man did more
Before.
No love has been
By this world seen
Like his, since Christ
Ascended.

[1] Coll. Earl Spencer.   [2] 'William Orpen: Artist and Man', p. 86.

On the other there was the petty, bickering, profiteering, and callous 'frock'. The fact that the men at the Front and the others elsewhere, however different their conduct may have been, were parts of a single whole, inextricably bound up together, entirely escaped him. He forgot that those at home were the fathers and mothers and brothers and sisters and children of those who served, and that returned soldiers could be profiteers, that even profiteers in khaki were sometimes heroes.

Orpen in the grip of a sympathy at once generous and bitter for the ardours and endurances of the inarticulate serving soldier – the most deeply felt emotion, I believe, of his entire life – is a subject tragic to contemplate. He possessed the emotional force, above all the capacity for indignation, the satiric spirit, a singular gift of incisive, expressive draughtsmanship and high competence as a painter – almost all the qualities needful to produce memorable works upon this theme. Yet with these almost superabundant talents he was able to accomplish scarcely anything, because he was unable to understand the nature of the events which so deeply moved him. It was inevitable that he should fail to express what he could not understand. Instead of memorable works, his indignation and pity spent themselves – except, of course, when he was recording what was before him – on tasteless incoherencies, such as *To the Unknown British Soldier in France, The Thinker on the Butte de Warlencourt*[1] and *Adam and Eve at Péronne*[2] – on these and in ludicrous verse.

During the epoch of peace-making in Paris, the small, whimsical, prodigiously gifted figure who, though he moved familiarly among the great statesmen of the day, was well known to hold them and their doings in small esteem, became a legend. When the satirical panorama of the feverish and glittering scene he had observed so closely and which was so expectantly awaited failed to take shape, his reputation waned.

Failure to express what he had felt most deeply caused him to respond with a growing apathy to the unending succession of sitters who presented themselves at South Bolton Gardens. But if he could no longer be moved, he determined to give everything that he had it in him to give. Driven by bitter conscientiousness, he harnessed all his energies, all his will to the single end of securing perfect

[1] The Imperial War Museum, London.   [2] The Imperial War Museum, London.

'likeness' of face and figure. What he produced was something akin to what we may expect of the mechanical brain when it is adjusted to paint portraits. Of these post-war mechanical marvels, *The Surgeon: Ivor Back*[1] may stand as an example.

The succession of portraits of this character hardened the scepticism about his stature engendered by his inability to exploit the possibilities offered by Versailles to his satiric talents and his angry mood, and at his death his reputation, which was once so solidly based, looked imposing only to those who took little notice of professional opinion, or else were ignorant of it. Coming out of St. James's Church, Piccadilly, after the memorial service, I remember the florid Chairman of the Walker Art Gallery in Liverpool exclaiming, 'We have lost the greatest artist England ever had', and I remember the unresponsive faces of Orpen's painter friends. Yet abilities so ample, matched by a sense of life so vivid and personal as Orpen's – even though, for want of a lucid and enquiring mind, incapable of that 'fundamental brain-work' which Rossetti postulated as necessary for the artist – resulted in work of more merit than current opinion is disposed to allow. The best of his painting is likely to be valued more highly than it is to-day, and his drawing more highly still. He continued to draw well long after his painting was in decline. Certain of his war drawings I would place not far below his best work at the Slade, and the pen-and-ink sketches with which he used to illustrate his letters are often brilliant revelations of a wit and imagination absent from all but his earliest painting.

Orpen died on 29 September 1931. I have tried to suggest something of the spiritual barrenness which he experienced as a consequence of harbouring deep emotions to which, as an artist, he was unable to give coherent expression. During the years between his return from Paris after the signature of the Peace of Versailles and his own death his malady showed itself in an almost desperate reluctance to speak of, or even to hear, anything that was not trivial, as though it might turn his thoughts towards the aridness within. It declared itself, in the presence of the slightest threat to triviality, in outbursts of horseplay (to which he had earlier been more moderately addicted). He would get down from the dinner table to bark at a dog, or he would bring out a mechanical toy. But it declared

[1] Coll. Mrs. Ivor Back.

itself most plainly in the trivial relations which he cultivated with those with whom he came in contact, a symptom of which was his habit of speaking of himself, in the third person, as 'little Orps' or even as 'Orpsie boy'. It would be difficult to imagine a more effective protection against intimacy. Whether such a reading of the inner life of his last years would find favour with his friends at the Arts Club, where he used to take me to lunch, or the Savile Club, where we often met, I am inclined to doubt, for in these places his total freedom from pretentiousness, innumerable small acts of kindness, and above all his staccato yet rambling conversation, half inaudible yet strangely vivid, won him an aura of popularity that masked the sterility within.

A few days after his death I saw on the easel in his studio a recent version of *Lord George Hell*, a picture he had painted years before as an illustration to Max Beerbohm's *Happy Hypocrite*. This he painted when, forbidden to work, he escaped to his studio from time to time from the nursing-home where he spent the last months of his life. His biographers assert that his 'last pictures do not mark a final step in his artistic evolution . . . and without hesitation may be eliminated from the sum-total of his achievement'. This judgement can hardly be questioned, but this picture testifies that the last act of the dying man, amid the failure of his mental and physical powers, was an attempt, however feeble, to recapture the imaginative qualities of his earliest years.

MATTHEW SMITH

1879—

THERE are certain artists whose work is an extension, direct and obvious, of their personalities. No friend of Rubens or of Byron would have been surprised by the painting of the one or the poetry of the other. There are others whose work is the expression of a part, sometimes a hidden part, of their personality. Shakespeare, for instance, does not appear to have impressed his contemporaries as a great man as distinct from a great dramatist. The painting of Rossetti and of Whistler respectively, while not incongruous with their personalities, discloses nothing of Rossetti's robust sense of humour or of his robuster tastes and appetites, nor of the combative arrogance that was Whistler's most conspicuous characteristic. Then there are the artists whose work is in entire contradiction to all that they seem personally to be: men and women whose art represents, in the psychological jargon of to-day, a 'compensation', an ideal which they cannot realize in their lives. Nothing could have been more incongruous with Pater, the fusty don, the zealous follower of the fortunes of his College on river and playing-field, than Pater the author of 'Marius'. It is in this last category that we must place Matthew Smith.

How completely the painter seems to differ from the man will emerge in the course of this brief study: a study in which I shall attempt to give something more than biographical landmarks. If facts about the man are of any value, as in my opinion they are, in the study of his art, facts concerning a man who appears to differ from his art are evidently of more value than those which relate to a man of whom his art is an unmistakable projection of himself. Furthermore, very little is known about Matthew Smith. He constitutes the outstanding example of the paucity of writing about English painters to which I have earlier referred. At the present moment Matthew Smith is probably the most admired painter in England, more especially among his fellow artists, yet, so far as I am aware, the elementary facts concerning him have never been put down. Even the admirably informed and highly patriotic 'Yorkshire Post', the leading newspaper of his native county, once published the statement that he was born in Manchester.

Matthew Arnold Bracy Smith was born at Elm View, Halifax, on 22 October 1879, in the West Riding of Yorkshire, the third of the five children of Frederic Smith, a wire manufacturer, and his wife Frances, born Holroyd, who came from Edgbaston, Birmingham. Frederic Smith was a cultivated man and an amateur of the arts. He wrote occasional verse, a collection of which, 'A Chest of Viols', was published in 1896; he collected pictures of the kind then in vogue with northern manufacturers, representing monks fishing or carousing and similar subjects, by Dendy Sadler and other painters of popular genre. The principal interest of his leisure hours was violins, of which he seems to have been an impassioned and discerning collector. He possessed two or three by Stradivarius, and his house became a place of pilgrimage for those who shared his interests. A memorial of his preoccupation with pictures and violins survives in the form of a painting, *Stradivarius in His Studio*, which he commissioned Seymour Lucas to make and which was shown at Burlington House a few years before the First World War.

At about the age of ten, Matthew Smith began to show a vague interest in painting. He collected invitation cards when they bore reproductions of drawings on them and stuck them into a book, and he copied elaborately a portrait of Lord Leighton out of 'The Pall Mall Gazette'. But he took no interest at all in the paintings by the popular academic artists that hung on the walls of his father's large, gloomy house. His preoccupation with painting grew in intensity, but it brought with it no definite aspirations, but only a growing sense of isolation. He yearned to speak to someone about painting. One day a successful painter named Prescott Davis called to see his father. As he was about to leave, the shy boy formed the desperate resolution of showing him his sketch-book, but the drawer in which it reposed stuck fast. After this humiliating, although unwitnessed defeat, his sense of isolation reached a pitch where he could hardly endure it. Believing that a business-man ought to have intelligent interests to occupy his leisure, his father at first encouraged his predilection for painting, but so soon as it threatened to exclude all other interests, he began to regard it with hostile apprehension. Presently, by means of an occasional reproduction, news of the Impressionist painters found its way into the grim twilight of the West Riding. At once it filled Matthew Smith with an unfamiliar agitation which his father recognized as subversive of what he himself believed. From that time relations between father and son were strained. If he suffered from a sense of isolation at home, his school life, at Halifax Grammar School, at Hilderthorpe, Scarborough, and, worst of all, at Giggleswick, was one of misery unredeemed.

The unhappiness of his early years was no doubt aggravated by want of sympathy at home with his vague aspirations towards painting and by the conditions which prevailed at the schools he attended, but it would be unjust to his parents at least to conceal the fact that he was a neurasthenic child, and his ailment heightened an extreme natural sensibility. At the age of seven he had the misfortune to see another boy suffer from a fit in a Halifax Street, and for years the memory of the struggling figure at the foot of a lamppost, his contorted face picked out from the surrounding darkness by the yellow gaslight, was one he was unable to suppress.

After he left Giggleswick, about the age of seventeen, he was sent to Bradford to work in the firm of Empsall and Firth, and although then he showed no aptitude for business his father took him into the family concern. When he was about twenty the family moved to Bowden in Cheshire. His by now constant preoccupation with the arts and his manifest incapacity for business brought about some modification in the attitude of his father, who agreed to his entering the Manchester School of Art, but only for the purpose of learning industrial design. The four years he spent there were wholly wasted except for a short period towards the end, when he managed to insinuate himself into the life-class. By this time it was evident to his father that he was no more fitted to become an industrial designer than a business-man; he resigned himself, but without a vestige of confidence, to his son's attending the Slade, where he remained for two years. Tonks shared the opinion of his father respecting his talents, and took every opportunity of giving it humiliating expression. On one occasion, in front of the whole school, he said to him, 'What in the world made *you* think of taking up painting? I give you six months to see what you can do.' The fear aroused by the threat to expel him, to proclaim his failure to his family, brought

about the complete breakdown of his health. He had to leave the
Slade for a doctor's care. When he had partially recovered, he
secured his father's consent to his studying abroad, on condition
that he did not go to Paris. A London friend had often talked to him
of Brittany, and the knowledge that Gauguin had worked there
quickened his interest. To Brittany therefore he went in 1908
and settled in Pont Aven, where Gauguin had lived. 'Here', he once
said to me, 'my life began; my mind began to open out.' At Pont
Aven he made two friends, Guy Maynard, an American painter and
the most interesting personality it had yet been his fortune to meet,
who thought much as he did, only more maturely and in the light
of a wider experience, and Madame Julia, the proprietress of the
Hôtel Julia, where he lodged, who enjoyed doing kindnesses to the
young man in whose face and bearing she discerned perhaps something of his bleak and troubled life. He remained at Pont Aven from
September 1908 until June the following year, when he migrated
to Etaples, which, besides a change in landscape, possessed for him
the yet stronger attraction of relative proximity to Paris. It was at
Etaples that he painted a *Self-Portrait*,[1] one of the few surviving
examples of his work of this period, and the earliest known to me.
It represents a shy, friendly young face, with blinking eyes that peer
out at you with an expression of mild surprise. When Matthew
Smith first showed me this picture in the winter of 1949, I was at
once reminded of another, not only curiously similar in character,
but which occupies a similar position in the œuvre of a painter as
dissimilar as possible from him. A few months previously, in Léger's
studio in Paris, I had noticed a portrait of an elderly man,[2] painted
throughout with the same short strokes with brushes heavily loaded
with the same drab colours. It expressed, too, the same diffident
honesty. When I asked Léger what it was, he said: 'But that's where
I started from.'

On 10 January 1910, having sold his bicycle in order to be able to
pay the fare, Matthew Smith went at last to Paris. Here he
attended Matisse's school in the Boulevard des Invalides, but his

[1] Coll. the artist.
[2] Coll. Mme. Jeanne Léger, Paris. This picture was included (No. 1) under the
title of *Portrait of the Artist's Uncle* in the Léger exhibition arranged by the Arts
Council at the Tate Gallery in 1950.

pupillage was of brief duration, for the school closed after he had been there for a month. Matisse himself went round on Saturday mornings, and any student who wished for criticism might leave out his work, but Matthew Smith was too shy to invite this ordeal. It has sometimes been stated that he was closely associated with Matisse, but this is not the case. He attended none of the 'open Sundays' that Matisse held for students and others; he saw him, in fact, only on the three occasions when he visited the school. On one of his visits, Matisse put up a copy of a drawing of four figures by Signorelli and analysed its structure with an acuteness which delighted his diffident English student. 'Voici l'architecture', he concluded, and walked out. For the rest Matthew Smith worked by himself in a small, impossible studio in the Avenue du Maine (steel tramlines were hammered into shape on the floor below), existing on the £6 a month that his father allowed him. For the first time, life assumed for him an aspect at once benign and settled: his own work and his studies in the Louvre (where he made an elaborate copy of Ingres' *Madame Rivière*) and at the galleries where contemporary art was to be seen were giving him the beginnings of confidence in his powers and clarity to his ideas. In February 1912 he took a step which seems to have had the effect of bringing this tranquil period to an end. That is to say, he married Gwen Salmond, one of the ablest Slade students of her time, whom he had met the previous year at a holiday painting class at Whitby. They moved from place to place, living successively in Fontainebleau, Grez-sur-Loing (where he formed a lasting friendship with Delius) and finally London, in a flat at Grenville Place, Kensington.

When the First World War broke out he was rejected as unfit by the Artists' Rifles and the Honourable Artillery Company. In 1916 he was called up and joined the Inns of Court Officers' Training Corps, with which he spent a desolate winter training at Berkhamsted. The first morning he arrived on parade with the evidence showing too clearly in his face and bearing of the party (attended by members of 19 Fitzroy Street) at which he had spent the previous night. When his commanding officer told him to 'fall out', he dropped his rifle. The misery of his situation kindled in the mind of this pacific and almost pathologically shy young man the determination to become an officer. He applied for a commission. When asked if he had any experience in the control of men he answered, 'Yes'. 'What sort of men?' the interviewing officer enquired. 'Yorkshiremen', said Matthew Smith. He was promptly gazetted second lieutenant. Although harassed by his military duties and other difficulties, he managed, at irregular intervals, to paint. In 1913 he had taken a room in Percy Street, but he soon settled at 2 Fitzroy Street in an attic room that he retained, and occupied whenever he was able, until the end of the First World War.

In these, the least propitious circumstances he had ever known, the art of Matthew Smith underwent an extraordinary transformation. This art, that had been as tentative and diffident as the painter himself, suddenly attained an aggressive maturity first noticeable in the fine *Lilies*,[1] of about 1914, but which was resoundingly manifest in two big nudes, both seated in chairs, which he called after the room where they were painted – *Fitzroy Street I*[2] (Plate 30) and *Fitzroy Street II*.[3] Both were painted in 1916 direct and from the same model in the same pose. Both are painted with a startling violence of colour derived immediately from Fauvisme. These two nudes, especially considering the hesitancy of the artist's long apprenticeship, are astonishing productions: astonishing in their strident boldness and in their powerful draughtsmanship. They are among the most vivid and the strongest of all his paintings, yet they are hardly, in the full sense of the term, paintings at all: they are powerful drawings, coloured with a harsh, disciplined violence. For a moment it seemed as though the artist were concerned primarily with problems of form. Both paintings were rejected by the London Group, at that time closely controlled by Fry. But work of such exceptional power could not remain unknown. They made an impression upon several artists who happened to see them. The girl who sat for these two pictures introduced the painter to Sickert, who called at the attic room. 'You paint', he said, 'like a painter and you draw like a draughtsman.' For a time a close friendship subsisted between them. Sickert encouraged Matthew Smith, who found him wonderful company and 'full', he told me, 'of uncommon sense'.

In 1919 Matthew Smith was demobilized and his health collapsed. The immediate occasion of his breakdown may have been the sudden

[1] The City Art Gallery, Leeds.   [2] The British Council.
[3] Coll. Mrs. Dorothy Searle.

relaxation of the wartime tension that had given temporary cohesion to temperaments, coalitions and organisms of many kinds. Whatever the immediate occasion, the cause was the unhappiness of his childhood, deepened, in the years that followed it, by the obstructions placed in his way to becoming an artist. It was as though the effort to become an artist was so exacting that, having achieved his purpose and having, with the two *Fitzroy Street* nudes, triumphantly proclaimed it, the tax upon his overstrained mind was greater than it could endure. He used to remain shut up for days together at 2 Fitzroy Street, making copies from reproductions of paintings by Delacroix and Ingres, unable to face without apprehension contacts with the world outside. About this time he painted several still-lifes of fruit. One of these, *Apples on a Dish*,[1] of 1919 (Plate 31), is as fine, I think, as any of the numerous paintings of similar subjects that he has made since. It too often happens that contemporary artists represent 'simple' subjects because elaborate ones would be beyond their powers, but in this still-life Matthew Smith has followed the injunction of the dying Crome to his son to dignify whatever he painted, and his apples have an almost breathtaking nobility of form, and, fused with it, colour that is both audacious and delicately astringent.

Early in 1920 he left London and spent half the year at St. Columb Major in Cornwall. At first he could accomplish nothing; he remained there alone after his wife and sons had left, and eventually became absorbed by landscape. This was a fruitful time, in which he produced a group of small landscapes, low and rich in tone, which express a sombre, sometimes even an almost anguished joy in the dour Cornish countryside. In these pictures, although they are built up upon a basis of firm drawing, which in certain cases the artist has not attempted to disguise, he showed, in his representation of atmosphere by the use of a wider range of colours and tones and by the closer fusion of colour and form, that he had begun to see as a painter rather than a draughtsman. I have called his stay in Cornwall a fruitful one because he made, for the first time, a group of pictures in which he painted, in fact, like a painter (for the first half of Sickert's compliment was simple flattery). These Cornish landscapes are still regarded as among his best paintings. But, like

[1] The Tate Gallery, London.

certain paintings of Constable's later life, stormy canvases such as *Hadleigh Castle* or *Stonehenge*, whose sombre and troubled splendour reflected the artist's distress of spirit, the Cornish landscapes of Matthew Smith, with their black oppressive skies and trance-livid fields, roads and trees, were the products of a darkening mind, a mind engaged in a losing struggle to maintain its equilibrium. He went to Brittany, where he collapsed into a distracted melancholy in which he wandered from Grez to Paris, from Paris to Lausanne, from Lausanne to Lyons, in search of a doctor who could cure him. Whether it was that his infirmity had run its mysterious course, or whether the specialist at Lyons was more skilful than those many others who had passed him, pessimistically, from one to another, at Lyons, in 1922, he began to emerge from the shadowy limbo in which he had lived for about two years. He was able to work: he made a copy of the El Greco in the Lyons Museum. The next year he was back in London, where he remained for about two years in a room at 115 Charlotte Street. The two following years he spent mostly in Paris, in a studio at 6 bis Villa Brune.

Between 1922 and 1926, Matthew Smith evolved in all essentials both the way of seeing and the highly individual method appropriate to its expression that he has developed consistently ever since. For all their violence, the *Fitzroy Street* nudes seem to express a vision intellectual, constructive, and, as already noted, a draughtsman's. His later paintings, mostly still-lifes and nudes – that is to say, by far the larger and most important part of his life's work – have expressed a vision in every respect the precise opposite of all this, an attitude in which passion and intuition play the dominant parts, and in which the operations of the intellect count for little; the vision of an impassioned painter and an indifferent draughtsman.

At the Mayor Gallery in Sackville Street from 7–28 April 1926, Matthew Smith held his first one-man exhibition. During these four years his work had come to be regarded with a respectful interest by his fellow artists and by discerning critics, but this exhibition placed him in the front rank of the younger English painters.

The most important sign of recognition was an article by Roger Fry that appeared on 1 May in 'The Nation'. This article was the first attempt at a considered estimate of the work of Matthew Smith, and, slight though it is, it remains one of the best.[1] How just a notion he had formed of what Matthew Smith was about is plain from the two following passages:

> It is evident [wrote Fry] even from the first that his intention is neither to achieve dramatic expressiveness, although a certain almost melo-dramatic mood seems at times to result as an accidental by-product, nor to create decorative harmonies. He is clearly after some more intimate and significant interpretation of vision. . . . And one sees that it is upon colour that he lays the task of situating his planes in the spatial and plastic construction. Upon colour, too, he relies to achieve the suggestions of chiaroscuro. In all this he is pushing to the furthest limits the essentially modern view of the functional as opposed to the ornamental role played by colour in pictorial design.

Although generous in his praise, Fry did not overlook one of the painter's besetting weaknesses: 'I mean', he observed in gentle admonition, 'his tendency to define his volumes with too uniformly rounded, too insensitive a contour.'

In December the year following he held a second one-man exhibition at the Gallery of Alex. Reid and Lefevre in King Street. On this occasion he was treated not as a promising beginner but as a painter with an established position. The position he had gained after so long and painful a struggle was reflected as clearly in the prices which his pictures commanded as in the respectful attitude of the critics. *The Girl with a Rose*[2] (Plate 32), painted in 1925 (to my thinking one of those works in which his finest qualities are fully realized), priced in the 1926 catalogue at £30, reappeared as *Femme à la Rose* at £150. Ever since 1926 his reputation has grown steadily until, at the time when I write these words, there is probably no English painter so widely admired among those who care for the plastic arts. It is interesting to recall that Mr. Churchill once publicly reproached the Royal Academy for its failure to exhibit his work.[3] But the highest tribute he has yet received came some six years earlier, from the pen of his admirer and close friend, Augustus John.

[1] As originally published, it formed part of a review entitled 'The Mayor and Claridge Galleries', and it was later incorporated in a longer essay, 'Plastic Colour', and published in 'Transformations', 1926.

[2] Coll. Dr. J. W. Halliday, and now known as *Model à la Rose*.

[3] 'The Daily Mail', 16 May 1934.

With a cataract of emotional sensibility [he wrote], he casts upon the canvas a pageant of grandiose and voluptuous form and sumptuous colour, which are none the less controlled by an ordered design and a thoroughly learned command of technique. This makes him one of the most brilliant and individual figures in modern English painting.[1]

The decisive growth in self-knowledge during the early twenties which allowed him to develop, at long last, so personal and so consistent a vision of things was partly instinctive and partly deliberate.

Matthew Smith was very much aware that the *Fitzroy Street* nudes and the Cornish landscapes represented an immense stride forward, and even that they were, in their way, formidable productions, but the more he considered them the more he was convinced that, whatever their qualities, they were not true reflections of his own innermost intuitions. He became convinced, on the contrary, that by his close study, his sedulous imitation even, of Post-Impressionists, of Fauves, of Cézanne above all, he had built himself what he described to me as a spiritual prison. His dissatisfaction at last became unbearable. Certain that his earlier works were the products of this prison, and false, he determined at no matter what cost to cultivate a sensibility entirely his own and to search for the means of giving it appropriate expression. Under the stress of his dissatisfaction, he actually called upon himself aloud to be himself. The consequent renunciation of the firm, constructive way of painting, the strident or gloomy colouring he had evolved during the first five years or so of his maturity, was no easy gesture. Until his middle thirties he had struggled and groped, an unconsidered failure. Then, in four years, he seemed to be justified, was sought out and praised by Sickert and others, and, far more important, he had seemed at last to have earned the right to be confident in himself. It was bitter to have to discount all this as, at best, a false dawn. Deeply despondent, he started to roll up his stone again. But he was rewarded with a strange promptitude. Having by a sustained effort of will expelled the fruits of years' intensive study of other painters, he made the exhilarating discovery that he was able to paint, whether from the model or from flowers, with a fluency he had never known, and, what was of greater consequence, that when he painted with

[1] 'Vogue', 5 October 1928.

mind, as it were, swept and garnished, he could express what he exultingly recognized as uniquely his own.

His natural approach to things was not intellectual; he was not deeply preoccupied with the problems of their structure, and, released from the necessity of concern with what did not really interest him, he became with extraordinary ease what he fundamentally must always have been, a man moved by passion, guided by intuition rather than by the operations of the intellect. By 1926 all this was fully apparent, and during the quarter of a century since, his work has undergone extraordinarily little change. This gain in self-confidence, which brought with it the release of his creative faculties, although it led with a surprising promptitude to the formation of a relatively unvarying style, has never been accompanied by a vestige of complacency. The discontent of Matthew Smith with his own work is acute and continuous. And not without reason, for an art so reckless, pursued in an age that does not possess a tradition, cannot be otherwise than uneven. It distresses him that after painting a picture resonant and beautifully expressive in colour and with a noble largeness of form, he is liable to find himself struggling with what obstinately remains no more than so much paint, with forms that no less obstinately remain insensitive, monotonous and confused. Matthew Smith is well aware of the relative facility of his orchestration of colour and the precariousness of his grasp of form and composition. Upon these he lavishes endless care, and suffers depression that lifts only when, through some providential alchemy, colour, form and composition fuse into a masterpiece.

This exasperated discontent with his own work – not so much with his drawings and preliminary studies as with the results of sustained effort – is one by which the serious artist is peculiarly afflicted. Ethel Walker is the only painter treated of in these pages to take a frank delight in her own work, and even her habit of self-praise may have sprung from a determination that others should admire it. There are modest minor artists and Sunday painters, but they are, I think, more liable, if not to the sin of pride, at any rate to the disabling error of complacency. Of this last I recall an extreme yet not uncharacteristic example. When I was Director, in the middle nineteen-thirties of the City Art Galleries in Sheffield, the members

of the art club of a neighbouring city came to see, under the guidance of their President, an exhibition of contemporary painting. The
President, a locally well-known Sunday painter of garish, rigid
figures who fixed one with an epileptic stare, stopped in front of one
of the most masterly of Steer's Cotswold landscapes. 'All I can say
about this', he observed to his expectant disciples, 'is, it's not *my*
method.'

Matthew Smith's prestige with critics and collectors and his
hardly won fluency brought him personal difficulties and disillusions
of a kind he had not earlier encountered. As a failure, he had met
much neglect, but also much kindness. As a success, he inspired
professional jealousy and interested friendship.

The two men to whom, perhaps, he owed most – Sickert for his
encouragement, and Fry for his advocacy – were conspicuous
among those whom he had to count among his enemies. The first
time they met after the publication of Fry's article, Sickert was
unable to conceal his resentment. The following year Matthew
Smith said to Sickert: 'I've sent you a card for my show. But you
needn't go; it's only complimentary.' 'You may be sure', answered
Sickert, 'that my visit won't be complimentary.' After this encounter
they rarely met again.

It was believed by some artists that one of the constant objects
of Fry's continuous intrigues was the exaltation of Duncan Grant.
In earlier days Matthew Smith had shared with certain other artists
the impression that in the interests of Duncan Grant their reputations
were 'played down' by Fry; then, to his surprise, there appeared the
article in 'The Nation'. This was followed by an invitation on the
part of Fry to join the London Artists' Association. The gratitude
that Matthew Smith felt for Fry did not eradicate his earlier impression that he was a crafty politician who issued, whenever he returned
from Paris, new orders, fresh variants on the party line; and he
therefore declined the invitation. Fry's response was to cut him in
the street.

In the meanwhile his restless habit of moving from place to place
had become an established feature of his way of life. After his
departure from Paris in 1926, he paid a long visit to Dieppe; in 1927
and 1928 he was in Fitzroy Street again. In 1929 – the year of his
retrospective exhibition at Tooth's Gallery from 16 October to

16 November – he moved to the Grove End Road, St. John's Wood, and spent some time at Arles. From 1930 until 1932 he was in Paris, living in the Passage Noirot. During 1931, 1932 and 1933 he also lived partly in Cagnes. In 1934 he settled in Aix-en-Provence, where he remained until 1940. At Aix he was happier, and as a consequence less restless than at any time in his life. He visited Paris in 1936, living at the Villa Seurat and in 1939 he spent Christmas in London, the first Christmas of the Second World War. From Aix he was finally driven by the ominous events of the spring of the following year that culminated at Dunkirk. He flew from Marseilles to Paris, where he found himself for the time being trapped. In Paris no telephones worked, but bad news travelled, it seemed, the faster. Eventually, on 8 June, the British Embassy was able to arrange for him to be flown to London. In England, he continued to move, with accelerated speed, from place to place. The Cumberland and the Royal Court Hotels, studios in Regent's Park and Maida Vale followed in quick succession. It was during this, for him, more than usually restless period that I first came to know him.

We used to meet, after the manner of bees who return to hover about a ruined hive, in the hideously transformed brasserie of the Café Royal, attracted by the prospect of seeing others who similarly hovered about the ochre-and-scarlet room in the raw glare of the art nouveau hanging lanterns. To me, as to most of them, the historic and oddly beautiful earlier room walled with mirrors set in slim gilt pilasters, the painted ceiling supported by ornate gilt columns, in which everything but the glass was toned by generations of tobacco smoke to the colour of a meerschaum pipe, was no more than a boyhood memory, yet its ghost retained vestiges of magnetic power still.

I was at first surprised to observe how often Matthew Smith dined alone, and the more so when, after I had the privilege of dining with him, I discovered that this illustrious and affectionately regarded man was often lonely. But this caused me less wonder than the effect of his society upon myself. After our first dinner together, as I walked home exhilarated by the awareness of having spent one of the most enjoyable of evenings, I tried to recollect precisely what it was that had afforded me so much pleasure. But I scrutinized the evening's impressions without

29. SIR WILLIAM ORPEN. *Hommage à Manet* (1909).
Oil, 62 × 51 in. The City Art Gallery, Manchester.

30. MATTHEW SMITH. *Fitzroy Street, No. 1* (1916).
Oil, 34×30 in. Coll. Mrs. Dorothy Searle.

31. MATTHEW SMITH. *Apples on a Dish* (1919).
Oil, 18 × 21½ in. The Tate Gallery, London.

32. MATTHEW SMITH. *Model à la Rose* (1926).
Oil, $35\frac{7}{10} \times 25\frac{1}{2}$ in. Coll. Dr. J. W. Halliday.

reaching an adequate conclusion. The clearest impression was of a melancholy man of about sixty, very pale, wearing a grey check suit of rather formal cut, who read the menu from very near through thick-lensed spectacles, who spoke in an even voice so quiet that it seemed to come from far away, who repeated sentences to which he wished to give emphasis twice over, in precisely similar tones. The principal subject of our conversation, if my memory serves, was the problem – acute for everyone in those bomb-ravaging times, but, as I was later to discover, a constant preoccupation with Matthew Smith – of living and working accommodation. He occupied at that time a room in a large, dilapidated and not entirely reputable boarding-house in Piccadilly and a studio with a leaking roof in Maida Vale, for both of which he had formed a gnawing aversion. The studio I never visited, but one day as we were leaving his room in the house in Piccadilly there emerged like a great bat from the murk of the corridor, into which she noiselessly disappeared again, the Countess Casati wearing a triple cloak, leopard-skin gloves and a hat that framed a face in which I could discern no features but the huge dark eyes. 'Oh, hullo, hullo', whispered Matthew Smith mildly into the unresponding gloom.

'But there was a studio in Dieppe', he said with feeling, 'on which I had an option, but I gave it up to somebody else, a friend, you know, who didn't really want it, but the owner wouldn't give me another chance. I was terribly disappointed over that studio. I could have worked there. I could see my future pictures stacked there in rows. Stacked there in rows, you know.'

Often the conversation ranged more widely, but whatever its subject, I have never left Matthew Smith without the same sense of exhilaration as I experienced that first night, although later intensi-fied with gratitude for the privilege of his friendship. The charm of his presence arises, I think, from the fact that almost any subject of conversation, or even silence, suffices to reveal the qualities of the man, the courage of a nature constitutionally timid and without a vestige of an aggressive impulse, and the active but masked benevo-lence, but a benevolence that does not compromise his candour. I never remember his saying a gratuitously cruel thing, nor failing to express himself with perfect frankness when occasion required it. His conversation reveals, too, another of his qualities: an extreme but entirely unassertive love of independence. He avoids all commitments which would restrict his freedom to live and to paint in accordance with the dictates of his own nature, and he would, I think, accept no honours or distinctions liable to compromise this freedom. The conduct of life, he finds, I fancy, sufficiently complicated in itself to make him wary of all needless entanglements. Earlier on I referred to my surprise at finding how often, in spite of being liable to loneliness, he dined alone. Many men, as they advance in their professions, form the habit, whether from preference or a sense of obligation, to associate with successful confrères and successful or at least established persons in general. In this they are moved by a vague sense of the appropriateness of such associations, of their value, above all, to the consolidation of their positions. From all such considerations Matthew Smith is entirely free. But he has positive reasons for avoiding associations of this kind: for he takes a spontaneous delight in eccentric characters and persons of wit and talent – above all, perhaps, in beautiful women – whatever their position or occupation. In consequence, he is bored as readily as a child by those whose 'importance' is their chief recommendation, as well as by casual companions who do not arouse his interest. He has no ambition, I think, to be the focus of attention, but I have seen him taking as much pleasure in a party at three in the morning, as he would if he were a very young man who had never been to one before. It is not surprising that he inspires the same degree of friendship as a man as he does admiration as a painter.

I have written nothing about his development since he formed his highly personal language of painting in the early nineteen-twenties, because in essentials it has varied extraordinarily little. In a detailed study there would be fluctuations of style to be recorded, and periods when nudes, faces, flowers, fruit or landscapes monopolized his interest. There is also discoverable an increasing emphasis upon bold and emphatic linear rhythms, but this emphasis is already pronounced by 1925, in, for instance, *La Femme du Cirque*.[1] If we compare, for example, *Flowers*,[2] of about 1920, the earliest example

---

[1] Formerly Coll. Mr. G. P. Dudley Wallis.

[2] The City Art Gallery, Leeds.

of his mature style known to me, with his *Blue Jug*,[1] of 1937, or his *Peaches*,[2] of about 1940, this change is evident, but it is by similarities rather than differences that we are impressed. Nor, since he evolved his mature style so slowly and in the face of so much difficulty, has he altered his technical procedure. Almost invariably he paints direct from his subject, only very rarely making use of preliminary studies. First he draws in his composition on a blank canvas in thin paint (well diluted with oil) so that it may easily be washed off. Deeply imbued with the classical idea that design is more important than colour, and aware that he has a natural sense of colour, but a sense of design cultivated by the sweat of his brow, he labours upon his composition until it satisfies him. Often he spends an anguished morning or, if need be, a whole day getting his composition right, but once he has succeeded he is able to work at great speed and the picture is soon finished.

'A picture', he explained to me, 'should be "finished" from the start. In painting the gravest immorality is to try to finish what isn't well begun. But a picture that is well begun may be left off at any point. Look at Cézanne's water-colours. . . .'

Matthew Smith does not begin a picture until he sees it in his mind's eye in its completeness.

He has not the advantage of working, like Poussin, for example, in an age in which the practice of painting is ordered by certain generally accepted rules. That nothing of importance can be achieved by the mere observance of rules, however sound, scarcely needs saying, but what is widely forgotten to-day is that by wise observance errors may be avoided. Every original work of art must be a perilous adventure, but in such anarchic times as our own it is a leap in the dark. Matthew Smith is a passionate and an instinctive painter, naturally impatient of rules and suspicious of them as tending to compromise individuality; and, as already noted, his grasp of structure is fluctuating. ('His linear drawings', Paul Nash once observed, 'hardly suggest the consummate painter he is.') It is not therefore surprising that he should be the most uneven of living painters of his stature.

'He does not often hit the nail on the head', wrote an anonymous

[1] Coll. Mr. A. J. L. McDonnell.
[2] The Tate Gallery, London.

critic, 'but you should just see the wood all round' – but, I hastily add, he *does* sometimes hit it, and then you should just see. . . !

These words were written many years ago, but true though they are, the sum of the nails hit on the head with resounding blows is now considerable. These paintings, reckless and rhetorical hymns of praise to the colour and warmth and ripeness in the world, give him an assured place among the major English painters of the age.

BIOGRAPHIES

GILMAN, HAROLD, 1876-1919

Painter of interiors, portraits and landscapes. Born 11 February 1876 at Rode, Somerset, son of a clergyman. Educated at Abingdon, Rochester and Tonbridge Schools, and, for one year, at Brasenose College, Oxford. 1896 entered the Hastings Art School to study painting; in 1897 transferred to the Slade School, where he met Spencer Gore. Visited Spain in 1904 and copied Velazquez and Goya. Entered Sickert's circle in Fitzroy Street, helping to found the Camden Town Group 1911. Stimulated by the first Post-Impressionist Exhibition at the Grafton Galleries 1910; visited Paris with Ginner; adopted a more brilliant palette under the influence of van Gogh, Gauguin and Signac. Exhibited jointly with Gore in 1913, and in 1914 with Ginner, when they called themselves 'Neo-Realists'. First President of the London Group 1913. Taught at Westminster School, then at a school founded by himself and Ginner. Painted, 1918, a picture of Halifax Harbour, commissioned by the Canadian Government for the War Memorial at Ottawa. Died in London, 12 February 1919.

GINNER, CHARLES, 1878-1952

Painter of intimate landscape and urban subjects. Closely associated with Spencer Gore and Gilman. Born at Cannes, Alpes Maritimes, France, 4 March 1878, of English parents. Went to Paris 1900 to study architecture, but soon turned to painting, which he studied at the Académie Vitti under the Spaniard, Anglada y Camarasa, and at the Ecole des Beaux-Arts. In 1909 visited Buenos Aires, where he held an exhibition which helped to introduce Post-Impressionism to South America. Settled in London, 1910, his style already largely formed. Exhibited with Gilman 1914; reprinted, as foreword to the catalogue, essay on 'Neo-Realism'. Published appreciations of Gilman after the latter's death in *Art and Letters*, 1919, and elsewhere. Member of the Camden Town Group 1911, of the London Group 1913, and of the New English Art Club 1920; A.R.A. 1942. Official War Artist in both world wars. C.B.E. 1950. Died in London, 6 January 1952.

GORE, SPENCER FREDERICK, 1878-1914

Painter of landscapes, music-hall scenes, and interiors, usually with single figures. Born at Epsom, Surrey, 26 May 1878; studied at the Slade School, a contemporary of Gilman. Was introduced to Sickert in Dieppe by Albert Rutherston, 1904. Subsequently associated in Fitzroy Street with Sickert, Lucien Pissarro, Gilman and Ginner. Contributed an article to *The Art News* 1910 on 'The Third London Salon of the Allied Artists'

Association'. Member of the New English Art Club 1909; co-founder and first President of the Camden Town Group 1911; member of the London Group, 1913. His late works show an increasing concern with pictorial construction under the influence of Post-Impressionism. Died 27 March 1914 at Richmond, Surrey. An obituary notice in *Blast* by Wyndham Lewis put Gore's paintings of the theatre above those of Degas: 'Gore gets everything that Degas with his hard and rather paltry science apparently did not see.' Small Memorial Exhibitions were held in 1916 and 1920, and a fully representative one at the Leicester Galleries in 1928.

HODGKINS, Frances, 1870–1947

Painter chiefly of landscape and still life, and for a short period designer of textiles. Born in Dunedin, New Zealand, 28 April 1870. Received instruction in water-colour painting from her father, an amateur artist, but attended no art schools. Came to Europe, 1900. Travelled in Holland, Italy, France and Morocco. Settled in Paris 1902, where she acquired a reputation as a water-colourist in a plein-air manner, teaching for a year at the Académie Colarossi and afterwards at a school of her own. 1912, visited New Zealand and Australia, holding one-man shows of her Continental work. Began to paint in oils 1915 and, returning to France 1919, after the war-years spent in Cornwall, was influenced by Matisse and Derain. Evolved a highly personal style characterized by diffusion of the formal emphases and a poetic 'mobility' of colour. Made a reputation with work in this style with her first one-man exhibition in London at the Claridge Gallery in 1928. Member of the Seven and Five Society. Owing to the Second World War, spent her last years in England and Wales. Died at Purbeck, Dorset, 13 May 1947.

JOHN, Augustus Edwin, b. 1878

Painter mainly of portraits, but also of big figure-compositions, landscapes and flower-pieces; draughtsman and etcher. Is sometimes indebted to the example of the old masters, most notably Rembrandt and El Greco. From *c.* 1910 he was influenced for a few years by the bright colours and simplified forms of Post-Impressionism. Born at Tenby, Wales, 4 January 1878. Studied at the Slade School, where his extraordinary ability, especially as a draughtsman, attracted attention. 1901–2 Professor of Painting, Liverpool University. Member of New English Art Club, 1903. Has painted much in France and in Wales, where he camped with gipsies. Several of his painting expeditions 1911–14 made in company with J. D. Innes and Derwent Lees. A.R.A. 1921; R.A. 1928; resigned 1938; re-elected 1940. Received the Order of Merit 1942. Trustee of the Tate Gallery 1933–40. Travelled widely in Europe, and has visited the U.S.A. An exhibition of his drawings was shown at the National Gallery 1940, and, in a reduced form, at Temple Newsam, Leeds, 1941.

JOHN, GWENDOLEN MARY, 1876–1939
Painter chiefly of portraits and single figures. The sister of Augustus John. Born in Haverfordwest, Pembrokeshire, 22 June 1876. Studied at the Slade School and at Whistler's School in Paris, where mostly lived after 1898. Intimate friendship with Rodin (from c. 1906); friend of Rainer Maria Rilke and Jacques Maritain. Received into the Catholic Church 1913. Latter part of her life spent at Meudon. Exhibited occasionally at the New English Art Club 1900–11, and had one-man show at the Chenil Gallery 1926; but her work otherwise seldom seen in her own lifetime. The Memorial Exhibition at the Matthiesen Gallery, 1946, established her reputation. Died in Dieppe, 13 September 1939.

McEVOY, ARTHUR AMBROSE, 1878–1927
Painter of figure subjects, portraits and occasional landscapes. Born in Crudwell, Wiltshire, 12 August 1878. 1893, encouraged by Whistler to enter the Slade School, where he met Augustus John. Later worked with Sickert in Dieppe. Began by painting landscapes and interiors with figures, in low tones; c. 1915, gained success as a portrait-painter, mainly of women and often in water-colour. 1916–18 attached to the Royal Naval Division, and painted a number of distinguished sailors and soldiers, now in the Imperial War Museum. A member of the New English Art Club 1902; A.R.A. 1924; R.P. 1924; A.R.W.S. 1926. Died in Pimlico, London, 4 January 1927.

NICHOLSON, SIR WILLIAM NEWZAM PRIOR, 1872–1949
Painter of still-life, landscape and portraits, wood-engraver and designer for the theatre. His art is remarkable for an agreeably capricious fancy in the choice and arrangement of his subject-matter and for an exquisite sense, particularly in his still-lifes, of colour and texture. Born at Newark-on-Trent, 5 February 1872. Educated at Magnus, where he was coached by an art-master who had been a pupil of Sir William Beechey. Studied briefly under Herkomer, when he met James Pryde, and afterwards at Julian's in Paris. 1893–c. 1898 collaborated with Pryde, whose sister Mabel he had married, in designing posters under the name 'The Beggarstaffs'. First exhibited as a painter at the International Society, of which Whistler was President. Designed the original settings for Peter Pan 1904 and other plays, together with woodcut illustrations for a number of books. A large retrospective exhibition of his work was held at Nottingham in 1933; and there was a joint exhibition with J. B. Yeats at the National Gallery in 1942. Knighted 1936; Trustee of the Tate Gallery 1934–39. Died in Blewbury, Berks, 16 May 1949.

ORPEN, SIR WILLIAM NEWENHAM MONTAGUE, 1878–1931
Painter of portraits and genre, the latter often whimsical in character. Born 27 November 1878 at Stillorgan, Co. Dublin. After studying at the

Dublin Municipal School of Art, 1892–6, came to London and entered the Slade School, where precocious ability won him a brilliant reputation. A member of the New English Art Club 1900; A.R.A. 1910; R.A. 1919. Knighted 1918. Official War Artist 1917–18, and Official Artist at the Peace Conference in Paris 1919. Presented a large collection of his war pictures to the Imperial War Museum. His later work consisted mainly of portraits of fashionable and eminent sitters. Died 29 September 1931 in London.

PISSARRO, LUCIEN, 1863–1944

Landscape painter and, during the earlier part of his career, designer and printer of fine books. An important link between English art and the French Impressionist movement. Born in Paris, 20 February 1863, eldest son of Camille Pissarro. Studied under his father; influenced by Seurat and Signac and exhibited with the Impressionists 1886, and from 1886–94 at the Salon des Indépendents. Came first to England 1870; again in 1883–4. Settled here 1890, met Ricketts and Shannon, and contributed woodcut illustrations to the *Dial*. Founded the Eragny Press 1894, and printed books until 1914 with the help of his wife, Esther L. Bensusan. Associated with Sickert in Fitzroy Street. A member of the New English Art Club, 1906. Naturalized 1916, but called himself a 'Channel painter'. Exhibited R.A. 1934–44. Died in Hewood, Somerset, 10 July 1944.

PRYDE, JAMES FERRIER, 1866–1941

Imaginative painter, principally of architecture and interiors. In the works of his characteristic style (attained *c.* 1905), figures are almost invariably dwarfed by their surroundings, while the atmosphere is redolent of mystery and drama. Born in Edinburgh, 30 March 1866. Studied at the Royal Scottish Academy and briefly at Julian's in Paris. Afterwards settled in London, where he led a bohemian existence. Took up acting for a time, and designed posters, 1893–*c.* 1898, in collaboration with his brother-in-law, William (later Sir William) Nicholson, under the name 'The Beggarstaffs'. Designed scenery and costumes for *Othello*, 1930; but painted little after 1925. Died in London, 24 February 1941. A Memorial Exhibition organized in 1949 by the Arts Council and shown in Scotland was subsequently shown in a reduced form at the Brighton Art Gallery and the Tate Gallery.

ROTHENSTEIN, SIR WILLIAM, 1872–1945

Painter, portrait draughtsman and writer. In his paintings he 'sought to combine austerity of design and unflinching research into drawing with radiance of tone'.[1] Born 29 January 1872 in Bradford, Yorkshire. Studied at the Slade School and at Julian's in Paris. Encouraged by Degas and

[1] Allan Gwynne-Jones, 'Portrait Painters', 1950, p. 33.

Pissarro, and formed friendship with Whistler. Began making portrait-drawings, many of persons who became famous in the world of art and letters. Member New English Art Club 1894. Visited Italy 1906, India 1910, U.S.A. 1912. Official War Artist 1917–18. Held various official positions: Professor of Civic Art, Sheffield, 1917–26; Principal Royal College of Art 1920–35; Trustee of Tate Gallery 1927–33. Author of *Men and Memories* 1931–32, etc. Knighted 1931, Hon. D.Litt., Oxford, 1934. Attached to R.A.F. 1939–41. A special exhibition of his work was shown in the British Pavilion, Venice Biennale, 1930, and there was a Memorial Exhibition at the Tate Gallery in 1950. Died at Far Oakridge, Gloucestershire, 14 March 1945.

SICKERT, WALTER RICHARD, 1860–1942
Painter of figures and urban scenes and etcher. Born in Munich, 31 May 1860, son of Oswald Adalbert Sickert, painter and illustrator, of Danish descent. Settled in England 1868. Studied for a short time at the Slade School and under Whistler. Knew, and was influenced by, Degas. Exhibited at Royal Society of British Artists 1886–88; Member of New English Art Club 1888. Lived at Dieppe 1900–5; then settled in Fitzroy Street, where his studio became a meeting-place for artists – Gore, Gilman, L. Pissarro and others. A founder of the Camden Town Group 1911; member of London Group 1919. Frequently visited Venice. Lived in Bath 1916–19 and after 1938. Married Thérèse Lessore 1926, as his third wife. President Royal Society of British Artists 1928. A.R.A. 1924; R.A. 1934; resigned 1935. A lifelong teacher, generally at private classes. His early work is sombre in colour and often ironic in its treatment of music-hall scenes and drab interiors. Latterly he made use of photographs and Victorian engravings as themes for his pictures, working in brighter tones. An exhibition of his work was held at the National Gallery 1941. A selection of his acute, independent and amusing occasional writings on the arts, *A Free House*, was published in 1947. He died 22 January 1942 at Bathampton, Bath.

SMITH, MATTHEW ARNOLD BRACY, b, 1879.
Painter of nudes, still-life and landscape. The sharp oppositions of colour of his early manner, developed under the influence of the Fauves, have given place to richer and more varied harmonies, while the forms have tended to become more opulent and freer in design. Born in Halifax, 22 October 1879, the son of a wire-manufacturer. Worked for four years in the family factory before entering the Manchester School of Art to study design; from 1905–7 studied painting at the Slade School. After working for a year in Brittany, arrived in Paris 1910, where he attended the short-lived school run by Matisse. Lived alternately in France and England until 1939. His output up to the early 'twenties was small; first one-man show at Tooth's Gallery 1926. Retrospective exhibitions of his

work were held at the Venice Biennale in 1938 and 1950, and at Temple Newsam, Leeds, in 1942. Member of the London Group 1920. C.B.E. 1949.

STEER, PHILIP WILSON, 1860–1942

Painter of landscape and occasional portraits and figure studies; a leading figure in the English Impressionist Movement. Born in Birkenhead, 28 December 1860, the son of Philip Steer, a painter and drawing master. Studied at the Gloucester School of Art and in Paris at Julian's and the Ecole des Beaux-Arts. Influenced principally by Whistler, the French Impressionists, Boucher, Gainsborough, Constable and Turner. Exhibited R.A. 1883–5. In 1886 became a foundation Member of the New English Art Club, where he continued to exhibit regularly. Lived in Chelsea and painted in the summer mainly in Yorkshire, in the Cotswolds and the West Country, and on the south and east coasts, e.g. Walberswick, Richmond (Surrey and Yorks), Knaresborough, Chepstow, Ludlow, Dover, Malden, Bridgnorth, Corfe. Teacher of painting at the Slade School 1893–1930. Received the Order of Merit 1931. A large retrospective exhibition of his work was shown at the Tate Gallery in 1929; and there were Memorial Exhibitions at the National Gallery 1943 (organized by the Tate Gallery), at Temple Newsam, Leeds, 1944, and at Birkenhead 1951. He died in London, 21 March 1942.

TONKS, HENRY, 1862–1937

Draughtsman and painter of figure subjects, chiefly interiors, with interest in effects of light; also author of lively caricatures. Born at Solihull, Warwickshire, 9 April 1862. Studied medicine, but from 1888, when F.R.C.S., attended Westminster School, under Brown, in the evenings. In 1893 finally gave up medicine to join staff of the Slade School. Professor at Slade 1918–30. As a teacher had notable influence on English draughtsmanship. Member of the New English Art Club from 1895. Practised plastic surgery during 1914–18 War and went to Archangel, Russia, as Official War Artist 1919. An exhibition of his work was held at the Tate Gallery in 1936. Died in London, 8 January 1937.

WALKER, DAME ETHEL, 1861–1951

Painter of portraits, flower-pieces, sea-pieces and decorative compositions. Influenced by Impressionism, Puvis de Chavannes, Gauguin, and by Oriental art. Born in Edinburgh, 9 June 1861. Attended Putney School of Art. Visited Madrid and copied Velazquez. Worked under Fred Brown at Westminster School and followed him to the Slade School when he was appointed to the Professorship in 1892. Afterwards attended evening classes under Sickert. A member of the New English Art Club 1900; A.R.A. 1940; D.B.E. 1943. Worked in London and at Robin Hood's Bay. Died in London, 2 March 1951.

VOLUME TWO

LEWIS to MOORE

★

FOR VINCENT

Par ce que c'estoit luy,
par ce que c'estoit moy.

PREFACE

WHEN these two volumes of studies were originally planned, it was intended to bring the series down to my younger contemporaries and to include such painters as Francis Bacon and Lucian Freud, and this intention was advertised on the dust-jacket of the first volume. But I am grateful to the distinguished painter of my acquaintance who emphasized the difficulty of maintaining the same perspective in treating of men who have completed, or have largely completed, their life's work, and men whose work is both too incomplete and too near; and he urged me to include no one born later than 1900. To this plan I propose, at any rate for the present, to adhere. This volume, then, deals with painters all of whom were born before the turn of the century; like its predecessor it treats of them in the chronological order of their birth-dates.

On a later page I shall explain why there is no study here of the work of such distinguished painters as Ivon Hitchens and Allan Gwynne-Jones, and why there is, on the contrary, a chapter on Nevinson. There is one other serious omission about which I cannot but say a word at once. The present volume contains no essay on Henry Lamb, although it is enriched with a reproduction of his *Lytton Strachey* (Plate 37), one of the best portraits painted in England in this century. In 1955 I approached Mr. Lamb with a view to seeking material for a study of him; initially, however, although most charmingly, he deprecated any such study and in the event time was pressing and the opportunity passed. But I am conscious that the absence of any account of him, and particularly of the portrait that I reproduce, is an impoverishment of my book.

There was a time when the distinction between the painter in oils and the water-colourist was a rigid one, when, that is to say, a painting meant a painting in oil and a water-colour, quite strictly, a water-colour drawing. But the days of such and similar strict nomenclature are passing, and for my purpose the title of painter embraces both kinds. Both David Jones and Henry Moore, therefore, find a place in these studies of English painters.

Henry Moore, the last of my studies, was born some eighteen months before 1900. I need not say that the decision to write only of men born before this date does not imply that I consider their life's work to be done, that they are fit objects of study because they are as good as dead. The inclusion of Henry Moore is enough of itself to nullify such an implication, and indeed I shall argue that it is in the most recent years, within the last decade, that his work has developed most markedly.

Designed as the successor of my first volume, this book carries no separate Introduction. The general method, too, is the same. Whereas the groups into which from time to time artists band themselves turn out to be short-lived and more fortuitous than they at first seemed to be, the distinctive characteristic of English painters, as it appears to me, is their extreme and highly developed personality. In consequence, if I may quote what I wrote in the Preface to the first volume, the chronological arrangement of these studies is deliberately intended to emphasize the individuality of their subjects by cutting them off from all such fortuitous and ephemeral groupings.

In one respect my treatment of my subjects is less uneven than it was in my first volume. At the time of writing none of the painters whose life and work I discuss was the subject of an adequate biography; indeed the great majority are still living. And although much has been written about the work of some of them and little or nothing about that of others, I found that any attempt to do them justice meant, in every case, a discussion of their work from its beginning to its end or to its maturity. In consequence it was possible for my treatment to be more uniform.

I am under heavy debts, for information and help, for permission to quote from letters and other sources, for permission to reproduce pictures. So heavily am I indebted that I cannot fully list all my obligations. By gracious permission of Her Majesty Queen Elizabeth the Queen Mother I am able to reproduce Paul Nash's *Landscape of the Vernal Equinox*. I wish to thank for their kindness the custodians of public collections and private owners who have allowed me to reproduce their pictures. To the artists themselves of whom I treat and almost all of whom I was able to approach directly I owe much gratitude for their ready and kindly response to my queries and requests. I am particularly indebted to Mr. Thomas Balston for his careful and patient assistance in my chapter on Mark Gertler. A special word of thanks is due to Mrs. Nevinson and to Mrs. Wadsworth, as also to Miss Kate Lechmere, Mr. John Piper, Mrs. Grove, and Count Vanden Heuvel.

JOHN ROTHENSTEIN.

Newington.
October 1955.

WYNDHAM LEWIS[1]
1882–1957

AFTER spending some seventy years on this earth Wyndham Lewis has not assumed in the slightest degree the colour of his surroundings. He remains unweathered in our terrestrial climate; he stands out as harsh and isolated as a new machine in a field. It should occasion little surprise if research were to establish that this was the guise in which he first in fact appeared upon our planet: a defiant and heavily armoured mechanical man newly descended from Mars. There is a mystery about his beginnings. Nobody ever claims kinship with Wyndham Lewis, or to have been at Rugby with him, and no one seems to be certain where, or when, he was born. For instance in 'The Art of Wyndham Lewis',[2] a most careful survey undertaken with his help and approval, it is stated that he was born in 1884 in Nova Scotia. A few months later, in a letter to 'The Times',[3] he gave the United States as his birthplace. Nor has the precise date of his birth been established. It may be that he has some reason for the strict secrecy about his origins and his personal life that has always been so conspicuous a feature of his conduct; however this may be, such an attitude accords very well with his general sense of his vocation. He believes in the face of the prevailing adulation of the specialist mind of the scientist, and has declared it throughout his writings, that the independent critical mind is still the supreme instrument of research. And he believes that the functions of a mind of this sort can best be exercised in relative isolation, and in a posture of candid and aggressive challenge, free, above all, from any pretension to 'impartiality', that 'scientific impersonality' which he has always repudiated as treacherous and unreal. In the editorial to the first of the two issues of 'The Enemy',[4]

---

[1] This chapter was written in the artist's lifetime (he died on 7 March 1957) but I have left all tenses unaltered. I have ascertained, however, that in the Rugby School register Lewis was entered as having been born on 18 November 1882, the only son of Captain Charles Edward Lewis, of Amhurst, Mount Avenue, Ealing.

[2] Edited by Charles Handley-Read, 1951.   [3] 9 January 1952.

[4] January and September 1927.

one of several hard-hitting but short-lived periodicals that he has called into being to advertise his ideas, he dilated upon the advantages of isolation.

> My observations [he wrote—with immediate reference to his own withdrawal from the art arena of London–Paris] will have no social impurities whatever; there will be nobody with whom I shall be dining tomorrow night (of those who come within the scope of my criticism) whose susceptibilities, or whose wife's, I have to consider. If the public is not aware of the advantages it derives from such circumstances as these, it is time it awoke to its true interest. Why does it not exact of its chosen servants some such social, or unsociable, guarantee?

His conduct of his life, in this respect at all events, has been led in general accord with his convictions, and to-day there is, among figures of comparable stature, no figure so isolated as he. Reputations are made, and to an extent far greater than the public appreciates, by members of gangs acting in close support of one another. I doubt, for instance, whether more than a few people are even now aware how closely knit an association 'Bloomsbury' was, how untiring its members were in advertising one another's work and personalities. Most people who came into casual contact with members of this gifted circle recall its charm, its candour, its high intelligence; few of those who were impressed by the openness of mind and the humane opinions proclaimed by 'The Nation', afterwards 'The New Statesman and Nation', their parish magazine, suspected how ruthless and businesslike were their methods. They might well have been surprised had they known that not a few painters—some of whom are subjects of these chapters—were convinced that there were hardly any lengths to which certain of the 'Bloomsburies' were not prepared to go to thwart or ruin the careers of young painters who showed themselves too independent to come to terms with the canons observed by 'Bloomsbury', or, more precisely, with the current 'party line' that their leader deemed to be implied by what he judged to be the most 'significant' trends prevailing in Paris. There is indeed a surprising contrast between the civilized personal relations that obtained between the 'Bloomsburies' themselves and the standards of conduct that some distinguished men seriously believed they applied to their relations with those outside their sphere of influence and recalcitrant to it. Four of the

33. Wyndham Lewis. *A Battery Shelled* (1919).
Oil, 72 × 125 in. The Imperial War Museum, London.

34. WYNDHAM
LEWIS. *Portrait of
Edith Sitwell*
(1923–35).
Oil, 34×44 in.
The Tate Gallery,
London.

painters, for example, whose work I am discussing felt 'Blooms-bury' malevolence and intrigue as a shadow that at least darkened their lives; one of them, on the last occasion on which I saw him before his death and in private, said that it had ruined his life and that, had he known what it would be like, he would have been most careful not to antagonize them. One of these days it will be possible to arrive at a clearer idea of 'Bloomsbury' art criticism by considering it in the light of the personal relations of certain of its leading mem-bers to the artists whose works came under the notice of 'The Nation' and its successor; but this, for obvious reasons, is a question that cannot yet be publicly discussed.

Quite early in his career Lewis clashed sharply with Roger Fry in circumstances which I will presently relate. Thereafter he was to be traduced when he could not be ignored. In view of the pervasiveness of 'Bloomsbury' influence his activities were therefore ignored often. 'There really is no occasion to apologize for a great insistence on this point', he wrote in an unsigned editorial comment,[1] 'not in the Age of The Great Log-Rollers–for insisting upon the fact that *Mr. Lewis has never yet been rolled by the hand of man.* NO ONE HAS EVER ROLLED MR. LEWIS–who, as well, is not a log, and so does not consort horizontally with logs and so physically cannot be rolled.' For years, 'by a sneer of hatred, or by a sly Bloomsbury *sniff*',these people have done their worst with the subject of this study; yet it would be unjust to attribute his isolation solely or even mainly to their activities, whose power to injure has in any case waned somewhat of late. There are two more radical sets of causes for it, psychological and intellectual. Lewis's radical suspicion of his fellow men, his habitual assumption that almost all men almost all the time are moved solely by their own interests, and that they are scarcely capable of dis-interested actions or even emotions, which causes him to be ever vigilantly on guard, does not seriously impair his quality as a private person as much as might be supposed: he can be an enjoyable com-panion, as willing to listen as to talk, considerate, and polite, some-times to the point of courtliness, and a constant friend. But, although he happens to be a very interesting individual, Lewis has always insisted that as artist and thinker he is a public not a private person. In this role he is certainly more candid, most *himself* in fact. His view

[1] 'Enemy Pamphlets: No. 1 Satire and Fiction', 1930.

of human nature declares itself, in particular in his writings, with utter candour and repellent power. I remember D. H. Lawrence, on the only occasion I met him, saying of Lewis's characters 'How they every one of them stink in his nostrils.' That his writings, both in intention and effect, have been beneficial to his fellow men I am firmly persuaded, but I doubt whether he regards them with any positive affection.

Want of affection, however, even when candidly declared, need not isolate a man. But Lewis adopts no such supine attitude: he is possessed by a satiric demon of extraordinary power and virulence. Most men delight in exercising their powers, and Lewis's satiric demon imperiously demands exercise, both in and out of season. Consider a random instance from his 'Art of being Ruled'.[1] This book constitutes the most ferocious and the most shrewdly directed attack I know upon the falsity and the drabness of the 'revolutionary' doctrines almost universally accepted to-day. 'Revolutionary politics, revolutionary art, and oh, the revolutionary mind, is the dullest thing on earth', he says . . . 'Everything is correctly, monotonously, dishearteningly "revolutionary". What a stupid word! What a stale fuss.' Immediately afterwards he refers to 'reactionary' journals as being like breaths of fresh air, worth their weight in gold, and Catholicism as essential to our health. Yet we turn the page to discover that he has switched the attack from the revolutionary, from '. . . the detestable crowd of quacks—*illuminés*, couéists and psychologists', to those who oppose them. This entertaining vignette of the 'Reactionary' represents him as a figure no wit more attractive than his scarlet counterpart. 'The "Reactionary", a sort of highly respectable genteel quack, as well, with military moustaches and an "aristocratic" bearing,' he writes, 'is even more stupid—if that were possible—than the "Revolutionary". We listen to him for a moment, and he unfolds his barren, childish scheme with the muddle-headed emphasis of a very ferocious sheep.' If any part of the theme of 'The Art of Being Ruled' were the predicament of the common man between revolution and reaction this impartial lampooning would of course be entirely consistent, but that 'revolution' is its target is obvious from the start.

Lewis is one of those rare beings, among whom Leonardo was

[1] 1926.

incomparably the greatest, in whom the intellectual and artistic impulses are of equal intensity. Whenever Lewis writes, however severely intellectual his subject (and however careless his writing), he is always the artist as well as the philosopher or critic. As an artist, as a literary artist especially, he is virulently satirical, liable, when dwelling upon almost any person, or class of persons, Englishmen, stockbrokers, women, the rich, as well as revolutionaries and reactionaries, to envisage them not as intellectual abstractions, but as artistic creations, that is to say, as satiric creations. As a private individual, Lewis nourishes no more rancour, I believe, than the average man; but he satirizes as naturally and as inevitably as G. F. Watts, for example, ennobled. It need scarcely be said that this propensity to satire does not endear him to his victims, more especially when these have had reasons for counting themselves among his not very numerous friends and benefactors. An intractable independence of mind, a belief in the value of a detached, uncompromised status as best suited to the exercise of criticism, an innate or early acquired secretiveness, a clash with incomparably the most influential intellectual gang at the outset of his career and an inveterate tendency to ferocious satire almost as readily directed at his intimates as at his enemies, are the principal causes for the isolation of Wyndham Lewis–an isolation for which I can recall no parallel among his contemporaries of comparable stature. With regard to his stature there is as yet no sign of an accepted opinion; instead the widest diversity of view. I have heard several of those few whose learning and judgment have won them the highest esteem refer to him, both as painter and writer, in terms of scarcely qualified contempt. There are circles who would regard the opinion that his contribution to art criticism was not less valuable than that of Fry not only as ludicrous but in some perhaps not readily definable way as unpleasant.

There also exists an opposing body of opinion, no doubt considerably smaller, but perhaps even more deeply convinced. Included in the company are Mr. Roy Campbell, H. G. Wells, W. B. Yeats, Miss Rebecca West and J. W. N. Sullivan, while Mr. T. S. Eliot once wrote of him, in a review of his novel 'Tarr', 'Mr. Lewis is a magician who compels our interest in himself; he is the most fascinating personality of our time. . . . In the work of Mr. Lewis we recognize the thought of the modern and the energy of the cave-man.'

Lewis's command of the written word has freed the visual artist in this strange but remarkable prophet from the impulse to preach with his brush or his drawing pen, and makes it possible to isolate his paintings and drawings from the productions of his typewriter. But to isolate too rigorously an art that represents only one of the activities of a being who is as closely integrated as he is versatile would serve no serious purpose. With him the eye and the intellect are intimately related, and he himself has never regarded himself as a pure 'visual' or indeed shown much respect for the artist with pretensions to being a pure visual, with no preoccupations except form and colour. 'The best artist,' he has written 'is the imperfect artist. The PERFECT artist, in the sense of "artist" *par excellence*, and nothing else, is the dilettante or taster.'[1] The art of Lewis needs to be considered in a larger context, and above all, it seems to me, in that of his ideas. The art of painting is probably his first preoccupation, but the predicament of the artist in the modern world has driven him, as it has driven other artists of intellect, to a close analysis of the elements of his situation. There is an obvious parallel in this respect between Lewis and Ruskin: both, originally concerned almost exclusively with the arts, ended by taking vast areas of speculation for their province. At the very outset of his career as a writer Lewis dealt with the predicament of the serious painters of his generation, and showed powers of analysis and exposition of a rare order.[2] His words are as enjoyable and as relevant as they were the day when they were written. Of how pitiably little art criticism can this be said! Briefly his argument is that Impressionism involves a disabling subservience to Nature's 'empiric proportions' and 'usually insignificant arrangements', and is conducive to a new and shallow academism.

The alternatives he considers are: *Cubism*, which he shows to be as closely concerned as impressionism with naturalism, no less 'scientific' in its methods, and which 'tempts the artist to slip back into facile and sententious formulas, and escape invention'. *Futurism*, which is always 'too tyrannically literary, . . . too democratic and subjugated by natural objects, such as Marinetti's moustache'.

[1] 'Blast II', 1914.   [2] Ibid.

Expressionism-in which he includes abstraction-which is disabled by its ambivalent attitude towards the natural world. 'If you do not use shapes and colours characteristic of your environment, you will only use some other characteristic of somebody else's environment, and certainly no better. And if you wish to escape from this, or from any environment at all you soar into the clouds, merely', is how he states his basic criticism.

Lewis's art and his thinking provide his answer. The first thing to notice about him is the decisive and consistent externality of his approach. 'Give me the *outside* of all things,' he wrote. 'I am a fanatic for the externality of things.'[1] And, more explicitly, '. . . what made me, to begin with, a painter, was some propensity for the exactly defined and also, fanatically it may be, the physical and the concrete'.[2] Precisely what he was *not* is defined in some notes on Kandinsky, whom at the time when he wrote he regarded as the only purely abstract painter in Europe.

> Kandinsky, docile to the intuitive fluctuations of his soul, and anxious to render his hand and mind elastic and receptive, follows this unreal entry into its cloud-world out of the material and solid universe. He allows the Bach-like will that resides in each good artist to be made war on by the slovenly and wandering spirit. He allows the rigid chambers of his Brain to become a mystic house haunted by an automatic and puerile spook, that leaves a delicate trail like a snail.[3]

He has always been much preoccupied by the distinction between the fashionable subjective method used by Kandinsky and Klee, and by Henry James and James Joyce, and the 'external' method of which, in our day, he is one of the few exponents. Early in 1939, discussing 'The Apes of God' with Lewis, I pointed out the traits in his victims that he had most precisely caught and most grotesquely parodied. To keep the record straight he occasionally issued a little formal denial that my identifications were well-founded (as of course they were), and growing tired, or even perhaps apprehensive of the turn the conversation had taken (for the air was heavy with threats of libel actions), he abruptly turned the conversation to the philosophy behind the book. No sooner had he begun to expound it than it was time for me to leave. A few days later there arrived through the post 'Satire and Fiction', an inscribed copy of the pamphlet he

[1] 'Blasting and Bombardiering', 1937, p. 9.
[2] 'Time and Western Man', 1927, p. 129.   [3] 'Blast II'.

composed and published concerning the rejection by 'The New Statesman and Nation' of Mr. Roy Campbell's review of 'The Apes of God'. The author had marked several passages that served to complete the exposition which my departure had cut short. As these define something fundamental in Lewis's outlook, and as the pamphlet is difficult to come by I will transcribe a few sentences from it.

In another book [by Lewis], the outlook, or the philosophy, from which it derived, was described by me as a 'philosophy of the EYE'. But in the case of 'The Apes of God' it would be far easier to demonstrate . . . how *the eye* has been the organ in the ascendent here.

For 'The Apes of God' it could, I think, quite safely be claimed that no book has ever been written that has paid more attention to *the outside* of people. In it their shells, or pelts, or the language of their bodily movements, comes first, not last.

In my criticism of 'Ulysses' I laid particular stress on the limitations of the *internal* method. As developed in 'Ulysses', it robbed it . . . of all linear properties whatever, considered as a plastic thing–of contour and definition in fact. In contrast to the jelly-fish that floats in the centre of the subterranean stream of the 'dark' Unconscious, I much prefer, for my part, the shield of the tortoise, or the rigid stylistic articulations of the grasshopper. . . . The ossature is my favourite part of a living organism, not its intestines.

In the last marked passage he speaks of 'the polished and resistant surfaces of a great externalist art'.

Near the beginning of the first volume of this work I contrasted the arguments employed by Mr. R. H. Wilenski and others to make us believe that the modern movement in the arts is synonymous with a revival of classicism with the scarcely deniable absence of any classical characteristics from the art that it actually produced. In a world which, however classical its patter, had in action so unmistakably 'declared for Dido against Aeneas and Rome', Lewis is one of the few artists who makes a serious attempt to carry fashionable classical theory into practice. That his sympathies are fanatically classical he has repeatedly stated:

I always think of something very *solid*, and I believe it is a sensation I share with many people when the term 'classic' is employed, and of something very dishevelled, ethereal, misty, when the term 'romantic' is made use of. All compact of common sense, built squarely upon Aristotelian premises that make for permanence–something of such a public nature that all eyes may see it equally–something of such a

universal nature that to all times would it appear equal and the same—
such is what the word *classic* conjures up. But at *romantic* all that drops
to pieces. There is nothing but a drifting dust . . . which no logical
pattern holds together. . . .[1]
   The 'classical' [he adds] is liable to incline to be objective rather than
subjective . . . to action rather than to dream . . . to the sensuous side
rather than the ascetic: to be redolent of common sense rather than
metaphysic . . . to lean upon the intellect rather than the bowels and
nerves.[2]

I have quoted at some length from the contrast Lewis has drawn
between the classical and romantic attitudes not as a lucid and forceful restatement of a rather threadbare theme, but as a concise
declaration of his own convictions as an artist.

Lewis regards himself as a classical artist, but this implies no special
degree of discipleship of Raphael, Poussin or Ingres. No slightest
suspicion of revivalism attaches to the classicism of Lewis; he is, for
good and ill, to a degree rare in a man of high intelligence, uninterested in the past. But his claim to classicism is very relative, and
made with a strict qualification. He recognizes that an art that is
impersonal and public can exist in its fullness only when it has an
audience which shares common values, and that no 'highbrow' set
in a great metropolis like London or Paris, still less such enormous,
sprawling proletarianized societies as ours, can for a moment supply
the same order of framework that was forthcoming for the artist of
the Augustan age, or the homogeneous, compact society behind
Dryden, Pope and Swift.

On account of this and other conditions which characterize our
civilization he has declared that 'It would be mere buffoonery, in an
artist of any power among us . . . to say "as an artist I am a classicist".'
But however unfavourable the circumstances Lewis has consistently
tried 'to be impersonal rather than personal; universal than provincial; rational rather than a mere creature of feeling; to act as the
rational animal, man, *against* the forces of nature', for such, he concludes, 'is the dramatic role of the classical consciousness'. I have said
enough to give an indication of the character of the strange, tough,
heavily armed and heavily armoured being who seems to have
dropped from nowhere.

∿   ∿   ∿

[1] 'Men without Art', 1934, pp. 187–8.   [1] Ibid., p. 190.

I have already referred to an uncertainty about the place where he first appeared. It seems reasonably certain that this was on the other side of the Atlantic, and the date somewhere about 1884. It is worth mentioning that in 1951, in the course of a conversation about other matters, I asked him a question about his early life, and he refused an answer saying, 'now that I'm blind and unable to paint, writing is my only means of support, and my recollections of my own life are my chief material, and I don't see why I should give away a single fact; and I don't intend to, to anybody'. He went to Rugby School, and according to Mr. Handley-Read's book, 1897 and 1898 were the years he spent there. In 1898 he went to the Slade School, where he remained for three years. No work of his student years seems to have survived, but at the Slade are preserved three drawings, one signed and dated 1902 and two others of similar character. These proclaim him a draughtsman of no ordinary gifts, content, for the time being, to accept academic discipline. They are precise, elegant studies, marked by a reticent yet unmistakable masculine strength and hardness. The next six years he passed abroad, visiting France, Germany, Holland and Spain. In his autobiographical writings these wander-years are treated with characteristic reserve. He spent six months at the Heimann Academy in Munich, and occupied a studio in Paris in the rue Delambre. At the Slade, in spite of the hostility of Tonks, he acquired a firm grasp of drawing; to this invaluable accomplishment he had added, by the time he returned to England in 1909, a formidable education, both intellectual and artistic. It is reasonable to assume that the austere hardness of Spain strengthened those qualities in himself; how closely he observed certain aspects of the German character was brilliantly manifest in his novel 'Tarr'. It was his desire to pierce behind the enigmatic façades of the Russian students he met in Paris, he told me, that first led him to search, in a long course of reading Russian novels, for the sources of their arrogant and mystical confidence in their country and themselves. Little as is known about his years abroad, from the many and significant allusions to them in his conversation, I believe that it was largely in the course of his travels that he developed his highly personal attitude to life.

No example of the considerable quantity of work that he is believed to have done abroad has apparently survived, but there is sufficient evidence to show that by 1909 he was also beginning to evolve a correspondingly personal style as a draughtsman. Whether because he produced little-which is unlikely-or because he destroyed much and most of what survived has been lost, examples of the work of the years immediately following his return to England appear to be rare. There are, however, several in the Baker Collection in the Victoria and Albert Museum. His association with the Camden Town Group, of which he was a foundation member, must have been due to his friendship with Gilman and personal ties with other members, and perhaps to his apprehension that the Group was the most serious and active nucleus of painters in England. Certainly there was no community of aim between Lewis and his fellow members, and he played no part in the Group's brief but influential history. But from 1911, the year of its foundation, dates the earliest of a fairly extensive group of drawings in which Lewis for the first time consistently strikes a note that we recognize as unmistakably his own. For the most part they represent rocklike men and women standing or seated in landscapes of lunar aridity and harshness. These massive, primitive persons are depicted sometimes making gestures of incoherent protest against some malign fate, sometimes in attitudes of hopeless passivity. The drawings are carried out in varied combinations of mediums, which include pen and ink, water-colour washes (often mushroom pink, brown and grey), pencil and chalk. The artist's preoccupation with these massive incoherent primitives was intense but not enduring. During the following year, he began to make drawings of a character afterwards recognized as Vorticist. The term Vorticist was first used by Ezra Pound in 1913. Lewis was, inveterately, a theorist, but it was, I think, the sensational impact of Marinetti, preaching his gospel of Futurism, that first provoked Lewis to formulate his own counter-gospel and brought out the inveterate pamphleteer in him. Unlike Surrealism Vorticism was not a clearly formulated canon, but an expression of Lewis's own convictions-temporarily adopted by a small group of associates-promulgated with a violence and pungency which he had learnt from the Futurists. The movement has often been treated as an English version of Futurism. Apart from their propaganda techniques and the fact that they were both extreme and noisy manifestations by truculent young men contemptuous of the near past, above all of an Impressionism that had become a pervasive and bone-less academism, Vorticism had little in common with Futurism; in fact the English movement rejected the principal tenets of the Italian. In 'Notes and Vortices: II', Lewis has given in some detail his reasons for his inability to accept Futurism. While applauding the 'vivacity and high spirits' of the Italian Futurists he condemns them as too much theorists and propagandists, as too mechanically reactive, too impressionistic, and unable to master and keep in place their ideas. What most repels him is their hysterical insistence upon ACTION. 'The effervescent Action-Man, of the Futurist imagination, would never be a first-rate artist', for, he says, 'to produce the best pictures or books it is possible to make, a man requires all the peace and continuity that can be obtained in this troubled world, and nothing short of this will serve'. Finally, he was impatient with the attempt to represent figures or machines in violent motion, which was to represent a blur. *Je hais le mouvement qui déplace les lignes*, he quoted at Marinetti, when they found themselves over adjacent washbasins in a London restaurant. There were clashes between Futurists and Vorticists during Marinetti's visit to London: Lewis, Gaudier-Brzeska, T. E. Hulme, Edward Wadsworth and others barracked the Futurist Leader as he delivered a lecture at the Doré Gallery in New Bond Street. Lewis used to claim that he owed his equanimity when subjected to heavy gunfire in Flanders to having been 'battle trained' by hearing Marinetti imitating on the lecture platform, with the aid of Richard Nevinson with a drum, the noise of a bombardment.

One characteristic a number of Lewis's Vorticist drawings do share with the work of the Futurists is violent action. Among the earliest of them are the *Centauress*[1] drawings of 1912, in pen and ink and water-colour. The centauress herself bears some resemblance to the primitive figures of Lewis's preceding phase, but the later drawings bear the stamp of a very different character. The earlier are spontaneous, and, if the adjective would not be inappropriate to forms so massive, even sketchy. The later are emphatically deliberate, and their most conspicuous feature is their angular, rectilinear character. They clearly have an intimate affinity with the international Cubist movement. But Lewis was a Cubist with a difference. 'The Cubists,

[1] Examples in Coll. Charles Handley-Read and the Mayor Gallery.

especially Picasso,' he wrote, 'found their invention upon the posed model, or the posed Nature-Morte, using these models almost to the same extent as the Impressionists.'[1] This practice he repudiates as an absurdity and a sign of relaxed initiative. According to Lewis the Cubists either took apples or mandolins as the basis of their designs or if, on the other hand, they 'departed from what was under their eyes, they went back to the academic foundations of their vision, and reproduced (in however paradoxical a form) an El Greco, a Buonarotti'.[2] In either case they avoided invention: that was his contention. This is not the place for an analysis of Cubism, but the rapid collapse of a movement so brilliantly staffed and which promised to fufil the highest hopes of the most adventurous painters of the age for the establishment of a new classical art suggests that there may have been radical defects in the ideas upon which it was based. It is characteristic of Lewis that, a self-confessed, indeed an aggressive revolutionary, he should have subjected the great revolutionary movements of his time to the most searching criticism. When most of his contemporaries had climbed on to the bandwagon and most of his seniors were throwing brickbats (and how wide of the mark!) Lewis analysed with exemplary independence the revolutionary tendencies that he most respected.

Lewis's Vorticist drawings were either totally abstract inventions, such as *Planners*,[3] of 1913, a pen and ink, crayon and water-colour drawing, or the designs for *Timon of Athens*,[4] of 1913–14, in which he made use of a modified Cubist technique, with a frankness rare if not unknown among continental Cubists, in order to enhance the intensity of the representation of an invented scene. For Lewis the years immediately preceding the war were times of intense and many-sided activity. During 1913 he carried out four decorative paintings in oil, in The Cave of the Golden Calf, an intellectual nightclub run by Mrs. Strindberg, in the Eiffel Tower restaurant, in the house of Lady Drogheda,[5] and in South Lodge, the house of Violet Hunt, all of which have been destroyed. This last, according to my own imprecise recollection, was inferior to most of his Vorticist

[1] 'Blast II'.   [2] 'Wyndham Lewis, the Artist', 1939, p. 77.
[3] The Mayor Gallery, London.
[4] Lewis's first publication, The Cube Press, 1914: a folio containing twenty drawings, six in colour.
[5] Of which a reproduction was published in 'Blast', No. 1.

drawings known to me. On the very eve of the war Lewis created two agencies for the propagation of his ideas and the advertisement of his activities. These were the Rebel Art Centre, the seat of what he called 'The Great London Vortex', and the periodical 'Blast'.

The Rebel Art Centre was brought into existence as the result of his stormy departure from the Omega Workshops, the centre established in July 1913, at 33 Fitzroy Square, by Roger Fry, where a group of his friends undertook, in Fry's words,

> almost all kinds of decorative design, more particularly those in which the artist can engage without specialized training in craftsmanship. . . . Actuated by the same idea of substituting wherever possible the directly expressive quality of the artist's handling for the deadness of mechanical reproduction, they have turned their attention to hand dyeing and have produced a number of dyed curtains, bedspreads, cushion covers, etc., in all of which they employ their power of invention with the utmost freedom and spontaneity of which they are capable.
>
> In furniture they have not attempted and will probably not attempt actual execution, but they believe that the sense of proportion and fitness and the invention, which are the essential qualities of such design, can be utilized to create forms expressive of the needs of modern life with a new simplicity and directness.[1]

When Lewis came in one day he was told by Fry that the Omega had been given 'a wonderful commission' by 'The Daily Mail' to design and carry out the furnishing and decoration of a Post-Impressionist room at the Ideal Home Exhibition, and that the principal tasks were already allocated. 'But you, Lewis,' Fry said after a moment's reflection, 'might carve an overmantel.' Carving in the round is not one of Lewis's many talents, and he addressed himself gloomily to his task. A few days later he happened to meet P. G. Konody, art critic of 'The Daily Mail' and art adviser to Lord Rothermere, its proprietor. Konody asked him how the Post-Impressionist room was shaping, and Lewis told him that, apart from his languishing overmantel, he knew little about it. 'As the designer I think you *ought* to know,' Konody complained. 'The *designer?*' Lewis asked. Then Konody told him that he had called to see him at the Omega Workshops, been told he was out, that Fry had offered to take a message, and he had asked him to convey to Lewis and

[1] From a prospectus, undated, of Omega Workshops Ltd. Artist Decorators.

Spencer Gore an invitation from 'The Daily Mail' to design the Post-Impressionist room.

Talking with me years later about the episode, Lewis said that if he had known what protest would cost him he would have kept silent. But he did not know: so there was an angry interview, followed by the trailing of a coat, in the form of a letter that may one day find place in the anthologies of invective. 'The Round Robin', as Lewis called it, not only charged that 'the Direction of the Omega Workshops secured the decoration of the Post-Impressionist room at the Ideal Home Exhibition by means of a shabby trick', and that it had suppressed 'information in order to prevent a member from exhibiting in an exhibition *not* organized by the Direction of the Omega', but it attacked the policy of the Omega and the character of its director.

> As to its tendencies in Art, they alone would be sufficient to make it very difficult for any vigorous art-instinct to long remain under that roof. The Idol is still Prettiness, with its mid-Victorian languish of the neck, and its kin of 'greenery-yallery', despite the Post-What-Not fashionableness of its draperies. This family party of strayed and dissenting Aesthetes, however, were compelled to call in as much modern talent as they could find, to do the rough and masculine work without which they knew their efforts would not rise above the level of a pleasant tea-party, or command more attention.
>
> The reiterated assurances of generosity of dealing and care for art, cleverly used to stimulate outside interest, have then, we think, been conspicuously absent from the interior working of the Omega Workshops. This enterprise seemed to promise, in the opportunities afforded it by support from the most intellectual quarters, emancipation from the middleman-shark. But a new form of fish in the troubled waters of Art has been revealed in the meantime, the Pecksniff-shark, a timid but voracious journalistic monster, unscrupulous, smooth-tongued and, owing chiefly to its weakness, mischievous.
>
> No longer willing to form part of this unfortunate institution, we the undersigned have given up our work there.

The circular, which bore the signatures of Frederick Etchells, C. J. Hamilton, Wyndham Lewis and E. Wadsworth, was widely distributed, especially among patrons of the Omega and also sent to the Press. According to his biographer[1] Fry decided not to take up the challenge. 'No legal verdict,' as he observed, 'would clear his

[1] Virginia Woolf, 'Roger Fry, a biography', 1940, pp. 193-4.

character or vindicate the Omega.' But he had other means of visiting his rancour on the principal challenger. Of these he did not neglect to make unremitting use.

Brief and unhappy though his experience at the Omega was, it would seem to have impressed Lewis with the advantages to be drawn from a centre of the kind. A friendship that he had formed not long before with Miss Kate Lechmere gave him the opportunity of realizing his ambition to control such a centre himself.

Miss Lechmere he had met at the house of Mrs. R. P. Bevan, probably in 1912. At a chance meeting a few days later he invited her gruffly to dinner. Throughout dinner he spoke not a single word. Over coffee he apologized and explained that he was upset and distracted by some hysterical letters that he had lately been getting. But soon he was able to revert to his normal interests. Had she read Gorki? he inquired; he talked at length about the 'Tales of Edgar Allen Poe' which he was reading in Baudelaire's translation. Thenceforward they often met.

When he was in the grip of the resentful mood that followed his departure from the Omega, she wrote to him from Paris to propose the formation of an atelier, like a French one. So, in the spring of 1914, the Rebel Art Centre was established, where it was intended that classes, lectures, exhibitions should be held. Premises were taken in a fine Georgian house, 38 Great Ormond Street, of which the first floor provided the rooms for the Centre's own operations. The Rebel Art Centre stirred into full activity the politician in Lewis. He refused to allow 'membership', in any formal sense, to any of those who were, for all practical purposes, its members. Of these the chief were Etchells, Gaudier-Brzeska, Wadsworth, Epstein, Nevinson, Roberts, Bomberg, T. E. Hulme and Ezra Pound. At the opening meeting Nevinson said, 'Let's not have any of these damned women,' and Lewis confessed with embarrassment that the Centre was entirely financed by Miss Lechmere. Nevinson's aversion to women's participation in public affairs was shared by Lewis, who was invariably reluctant to admit that the Rebel Art Centre owed its existence to a woman. Another instance of Lewis's prejudice against women was his refusal to allow the artists who, in imitation of the procedure followed at 19 Fitzroy Street, brought their work to be seen by friends, to hand round tea. At 19 Fitzroy Street the artists

waited upon their guests; at the Rebel Art Centre this menial task
was strictly reserved to women.

Unlike many other projects undertaken in 1914 the Rebel Art
Centre was not extinguished by the war; after an existence of some
four months it came to an end, principally because it was unable to
withstand the stresses imposed upon it by the possessiveness and
suspiciousness of Lewis. His conduct of its affairs was audacious and
enterprising, but his suspicion of his associates, his fondness for
intrigue, his uncertain temper, his jealousies and the strains that
inevitably ensued within the Centre, quickly overwhelmed an
institution that his conduct had prevented from acquiring necessary
support. Its activities, effectively publicized, gave it and Lewis much
prominence, but it accomplished little. Ford Madox Hueffer (afterwards Ford) and Marinetti lectured there, but its teaching activities
were restricted, for only two students presented themselves for instruction: a man who wished to improve the design of gas-brackets
and a lady pornographer. The day came when Miss Lechmere
declined to bear further expense and Lewis moved out.

The most fruitful consequence for Lewis of his connexion with
the Rebel Art Centre was his association with Hulme. Scattered
references to Hulme occur in Lewis's writings; in 'Blasting and
Bombardiering' he is the subject of a chapter. It is there conceded
that he was a remarkable man, with a sensitive and original mind,
but the entertaining and condescending account of this man gives
no hint of the extent to which Lewis is in his debt. 'All the best things
Hulme said about the theory of art,' he claimed, 'were said about
my art';[1] he refers, too, to the influence of his own pronouncements
upon Hulme, and sums up in the words, 'what he said should be
done, I *did*. Or it would be more exact to say that I did it, and he
said it.'[2] That Lewis possesses an intellect of immeasurably greater
range and penetration than Hulme is not open to question, yet there
are reasons for thinking that in the association between the two men
it was not Lewis but Hulme who played the dominant part. If Hulme
had spoken and written earlier he would have been one crying in
the wilderness; if later, one uttering commonplaces; but his coming
was providentially timed and the ideas he propounded proved
salutary, energizing and influential. He was neither an original

[1] 'Blasting and Bombardiering', p. 106.   [2] Ibid.

thinker – there can be scarcely an idea in his writings that he had not come upon in his reading of Pascal, Sorel, Bergson, Worringer, Lasserre or Husserl – nor an accomplished writer, although there is something attractive about his forthright muscular style.

At the heart of Hulme's system of ideas was his disbelief in the perfectibility of man. There are, he held, two prevailing views about man's nature:

> One, that man is intrinsically good, spoilt by circumstance, and the other that he is intrinsically limited, but disciplined by order and tradition into something fairly decent. To the one party man's nature is like a well, to the other like a bucket. The view which regards man as a well, a reservoir full of possibilities, I call the romantic; the one which regards him as a very finite and fixed creature, I call the classical.[1]

I do not propose to follow in any detail the arguments by which he associates the romanticism of the generations immediately preceding his own with the progressive supersession of classical by romantic principles in the political and every other sphere of activity following the triumph of Rousseauism in the French Revolution. The root of all romanticism was for him this notion that man the individual is an infinite reservoir of potentialities, and that the destruction of order, which is oppressive by its very nature, will release these potentialities and 'progress' inevitably follow. Against the naturalistic, 'vital' art produced by the romanticism of the modern world he sets up the classical ideal of the archaic Greeks, the Egyptians, Indians and Byzantines 'where everything tends to be angular, where curves tend to be hard and geometrical, where the presentation of the human body, for example, is often entirely non-vital, and distorted to fit into stiff lines and cubical shapes of various kinds'.[2] He insisted upon the impulse towards abstraction discernible in the later works of Cézanne which makes them 'much more akin to the composition you find in the Byzantine mosaic (of the Empress Theodora) in Ravenna, than it is to anything which can be found in the art of the Renaissance'.[3] Abstract art:

> exhibits no delight in nature and no striving after vitality. Its forms are always what can be described as stiff and lifeless. The dead form of a

[1] 'Speculations, Essays on Humanism and the Philosophy of Art', by T. E. Hulme, edited by Herbert Read, 1936, p. 117.
[2] Ibid., p. 82.   [3] Ibid., p. 101.

pyramid and the suppression of life in a Byzantine mosaic show that behind these arts there must have been an impulse, the direct opposite of that which finds satisfaction in the naturalism of Greek and Renaissance art.[1]

By far the greater part of the art of his own and the immediately preceding centuries Hulme regarded as sharing the same naturalistic and vital impulses as those of Greece and the Renaissance from which it derived. Hulme was not a diehard concerned to defend or revive any existing or past social order. Nor was he an enemy of progress, but he believed on the contrary that the prevailing trust in an inevitable process called Progress vitiated the creative efforts of the individual and sacrificed the right of moral judgment. In the words of his informed and fair-minded biographer Hulme believed that 'the liberal and romantic outlook coloured nearly all political and philosophic thought in England; and he claimed that this outlook was mistaken and could be abandoned without any sacrifice of generosity and intellectual integrity'.[2] Hulme–who was born on 16 September 1883 at Gratton Hall, Endon, Staffordshire, and educated at the High School, Newcastle-under-Lyme and St. John's College, Cambridge–seems to have begun his brief career as a writer in 1911 with a series of articles on Bergson in 'The New Age'. The following year[3] there appeared in the same journal five 'Imagist' poems under the heading 'The Complete Poetical Works of T. E. Hulme'. It was not so much by his writings, however, as by his talk that Hulme disseminated his ideas, not from the lecture platform–where both he and Lewis were conspicuously ineffective –but in café, college common-room and at the Rebel Art Centre.

The fact that Hulme expressed himself most persuasively in conversation and that Lewis published nothing on the philosophy or criticism of art before the appearance of 'Blast' makes it extremely difficult to assess with any degree of precision the intellectual relationship between Hulme and Lewis. We know that it was shortly after the influence of the ideas propounded by Hulme began to make itself felt in London that Lewis's own drawing assumed a geometrical, non-vital character. On the other hand we know that on his own long sojourn on the Continent Lewis observed much and read much, and Hulme's biographer has told us that 'he had become

[1] Ibid., p. 85.   [2] 'T. E. Hulme', by Michael Roberts, 1938, p. 12.
[3] 25 January.

interested in the new geometrical art of Picasso, Wyndham Lewis, David Bomberg, William Roberts and Jacob Epstein'.[1]

What is most likely, I think, to have occurred is that Lewis had acquired some familiarity with the ideas Hulme propounded–it is most improbable that a man of his curiosity should have known nothing of continental philosophical ideas, and he had listened to Bergson lecturing at the Collège de France–but that they were sensibly clarified, vivified and expanded by contact with the more impressive personality of Hulme. How splendid a head he had is apparent from the portrait of him Epstein modelled.[2] A combination of knowledge, conviction, critical sensibility, charm, brilliance, humour and a sense of fantasy enabled him to dominate any conversation. 'To hear Hulme develop general ideas and abstractions was like studying an elaborate pattern whose inner lines and texture emerge gradually as you gaze.'[3] I myself had the good fortune to hear at second-hand Hulme's description of a free fight that broke out in the Ethical Section at the Philosophical Congress held at Bologna in 1911. In addition Hulme was courageous and extremely tough. On one occasion when Lewis showed reluctance to continue a discussion Hulme lifted him up and held him upside-down against the railings of Soho Square and continued to develop some intricate theme at leisure. The extreme jealousy that Lewis showed where Hulme was concerned suggests that he was conscious of his debt to a man whose greatest capacity was for the stimulation and direction of the creative faculty in others, whom he regarded somewhat in the light of mediums. It was certainly in such a light that he regarded Epstein, who ought, he considered, to carve instead of modelling and whose carving *The Rock Drill* may well owe something to Hulme. Epstein told me that Hulme, tireless in his efforts to inspire others, was apt to be lazy where his own work was concerned, assuming that he had a long life before him. In this he erred: he joined the Honourable Artillery Company shortly after the First World War began and was killed on 28 September 1917.

For Lewis 1914 was a year more productive and eventful than any he had known. By the loan of £100, and an order for fifty copies

[1] Michael Roberts, op. cit., p. 20.
[2] The only cast is still in the National Gallery of Canada, Ottawa.
[3] 'Caravansary and Conversation', by Richard Curle, 1937.

on behalf of the Rebel Art Centre, Miss Lechmere enabled Lewis to publish 'Blast', the spectacular periodical which brought Lewis an ephemeral notoriety. This outsize periodical with the raspberry cover, and the combative introductory manifesto in huge black type, was read with eager curiosity, mixed with derision at what was taken to be the irresponsible extremism of the robust 'blasts' and 'blesses'. Like so much of Lewis's writing–except for signed contributions by Ford Madox Ford and Rebecca West, some poems and a manifesto by Ezra Pound and another by Gaudier-Brzeska, and a review by Wadsworth, almost the whole text was his work–it not only withstands the assaults of time but flourishes upon the ordeal. *Timon of Athens*,[1] a folio of drawings, rectilinear in character, of figures in energetic movement, also appeared that year. Beyond comparison his most important achievement of 1914 was the composition of 'Tarr', his first novel and in certain respects his best. It is a work of extraordinary energy, which uncompromisingly manifests his 'externalist' convictions. It was not published in book form until four years later. It was in 1914 that he completed his first *Portrait of Ezra Pound*.[2] Towards the end of the year he was ill, and on his recovery in 1915 he joined the army.[3] The Vorticists[4] held their only exhibition in March, at the Doré Gallery, organized by Lewis, who wrote a 'note' for the catalogue, in which he thus defines the movement.

> By Vorticism we mean (a) ACTIVITY as opposed to the tasteful PASSIVITY of Picasso; (b) SIGNIFICANCE as opposed to the dull or anecdotal character to which the Naturalist is condemned; (c) ESSENTIAL MOVEMENT and ACTIVITY (such as the energy of a mind) as opposed to the imitative cinematography, the fuss and hysterics of the Futurists.

In that year appeared the second, and final, number of 'Blast'.

Army training entirely arrested Lewis's activities as draughtsman and painter during 1916, but he found time to revise 'Tarr', which appeared month by month in 'The Egoist'–then under the editorship of Harriet Weaver, Richard Aldington and Dora Marsden–from

---

[1] Undated but published in 1914. [2] Lost.

[3] Lewis has described in 'Blasting and Bombardiering', his first volume of memoirs, published in 1937, his life during the war and post-war periods.

[4] The Vorticist exhibitors included Jessie Dismorr, Etchells, Gaudier-Brzeska, Roberts, Helen Saunders, Edward Wadsworth and Lewis. Six other artists, among them Bomberg, Duncan Grant, Kramer and Nevinson, were also invited to exhibit.

April until November the following year. A barren period was
ended by his secondment as a war artist to the Canadian Corps. This
appointment not only released, but stimulated, a flood of creativity.
Besides giving a constantly industrious artist the leisure to draw and
paint, it provided him with a subject to which he responded ardently.
Although vividly conscious of the calamitous character of war, and
of the shallowness of the machine-worship of his Futurist associates,
Lewis was enraptured by the physical splendour of mechanized
warfare. Big guns in particular–he served in the artillery–possessed
the characteristics of hardness, bareness, purposefulness, power and
unqualified masculinity that marked his own temperament. In the
presence of big guns the place of satire is usurped by romance.

> Out of their throats [he wrote] had sprung a dramatic flame, they had
> roared, they had moved back. You could see them, lighted from their
> mouths, as they hurled into the air their great projectiles, and sank back
> as they did it. In the middle of the monotonous percussion, which had
> never slackened for a moment, the tom-toming of interminable
> artillery, for miles around, going on in the darkness. . . .[1]

The sense of romance that this description conveys is present in an
intenser degree though in a less obvious form in his gun paintings.
In these he, who had for so long observed, theorized, experimented,
now emerged as an artist assured, weighty and highly individual.
The most considerable are *A Battery Position in a Wood*,[2] a drawing
of 1918, *A Battery Shelled*,[3] of 1919 (Plate 1), *A Canadian Gunpit*,[4]
of 1918. These and a number of subsidiary studies well illustrate an
aim which took an increasing hold upon him, that of reducing the
flux of nature to something simpler, more rigid, more tense and
angular. Impersonal figures move like automata at the compulsion
of some irresistible force.

Lewis may be said to have belonged to the international Cubist
movement, but like much else he wore his Cubism with a difference.
His criticism of the Cubists for avoiding creation by organizing their
compositions upon a natural, posed model I have already noticed.
He also criticized them for the triviality of their subjects, for their
failure to attempt the grandness that Cubism almost postulated.

[1] 'Blasting and Bombardiering', p. 120.
[2] The Imperial War Museum, London.
[3] The Imperial War Museum, London.
[4] The National Gallery of Canada, Ottawa.

'HOWEVER MUSICAL OR VEGETARIAN A MAN MAY BE, HIS LIFE IS NOT SPENT EXCLUSIVELY AMONGST APPLES AND MANDOLINES. Therefore there is something requiring explanation when he foregathers, in his paintings, exclusively with these two objects.'[1]

Neither reproach is applicable to his own Cubist works. His abstractions, such as the *Planner* drawings, are inventions, not based upon nature, and the *Timon of Athens* designs and the paintings and drawings of the First World War represent an attempt to apply Cubism to subjects of wider scope and deeper human concern. The chief effect of his service as a war artist was to sharpen a discontent with the restrictions imposed by pure Cubism. The effect of his confrontation with a subject so overwhelmingly compelling as the theatre of war, which, as already noted, had an especial appeal for him, was to sharpen his sense of the inadequacy of pure Cubism to express the full content of his vision.

The geometrics which had interested me so exclusively before [he wrote] I now felt were bleak and empty. *They wanted filling.* They were still as much present to my mind as ever, but submerged in the coloured vegetation, the flesh and blood, that is life. . . .

There was his programme, and one which he shared with the best of his contemporaries. No work by Lewis shows the wonderfully subtle perception of the use of Cubism in defining form of, for instance, Picasso's *Femme à la Mandoline*[2] or *Femme Assise*,[3] Duchamp's *Nude descending a Staircase*,[4] or certain Braques, but he put it at the service of a wider purpose. Pure Cubism constituted a position which others, unable to see their way ahead, tacitly abandoned, but from which Lewis marched out with colours flying.

Lewis's suggestion that he was filling his geometrics gives an inadequate notion of the extraordinary power of expressing natural forms which he acquired during the latter part of the war. *Red Nude*,[5] of 1919, for instance is equally powerful whether it is considered as a design or as a representation–in which contempt is curiously fused with something near to veneration–of a massive standing woman. What a splendid drawing this is! During these years his powers as a draughtsman came to maturity, and although he was able to draw

[1] 'Blast II'.   [2] Coll. Mr. David Rockefeller.
[3] The Tate Gallery, London.   [4] The Philadelphia Museum of Art.
[5] The British Council.

well throughout his life, at no other time did his drawings exhibit such abounding vitality controlled by so classical a discipline. And he drew finely with ease, and admirable drawings done round about nineteen-twenty are not uncommon–drawings of the quality, for example, of *Girl in a Windsor Chair*,[1] of 1920, or the *Portrait of Ezra Pound*,[2] of the same year. After the early 'twenties his drawing done from life lost something of its quality as the extraordinarily tense equilibrium between powerful thrusts–between the force of gravity and that of muscular effort, between horizontals and verticals–gradually relaxed. It inclined to become decorative, and lines, though they charmed by the distinction of their fancy, lost their former suggestion of stark inevitability. They were no longer lines of force. The extent of the process of relaxation can be judged by comparing with the two drawings just mentioned–which hold their own, in my opinion, with any drawings made anywhere within a similar range of years–say, *Portrait of the Artist's Wife*,[3] of 1936, or with *Lynette*,[4] of 1948, in which the forms are loosely defined. Now and again something of the old energy seems to revive, but the revival is more apparent than real, as may be seen by a comparison of the Pound portrait with *Head of Ezra Pound*,[5] of 1938, in which, in spite of the aggressively forceful character of the lines the forms are not defined with anything approaching the precision of the earlier drawing. No such relaxation is discernible in his imaginative drawings–powerfully evocative, and, in spite of the obvious debts to African, Oceanian and other primitive arts, highly personal works. From their black, bristling forms a species of primitive magic emanates. In the 'forties, however, their forms became more open, and relaxed, but however weakened they still convey something of the same potent magic. A characteristic example is *What the Sea is like at Night*,[6] which was made as late as 1949 when his sight was seriously impaired.

I have made it clear that I regard Lewis as one of the first draughtsmen of his time, and a word on his methods of drawing would not be superfluous. Although a visitor to several of his successive studios

[1] The City Art Galleries, Manchester, Rutherston Collection.
[2] Whereabouts unknown: reproduced in 'Blasting and Bombardiering', facing p. 28c.
[3] Coll. the Artist.   [4] Coll. the Artist.   [5] Coll. Mr. Wyndham T. Vint.
[6] Coll. Mr. and Mrs. W. Doge Hutchinson.

I have never seen him at work; with the exceptions of his wife and those who have sat for their portraits I doubt whether more, at the most, than a very few have been accorded this interesting privilege. It is possible, nevertheless, to form some notion of his procedure. Mr. Handley-Read has pondered the available evidence and given so clear and workmanlike an account of his findings that I cannot do better than quote from it.

> There are no sketches, [he wrote] if a drawing goes wrong it will be done again, or the faulty area will be cut out, the paper replaced, and the passage redrawn. There is no scaffolding in pencil . . . there is no attempt to hide preliminary lines. He draws first of all the horizontal and vertical lines, which give a firm basis to the structure . . . the weight of the arm rests on the last joint of the little finger which acts as a kind of ball-bearing runner when the long straight lines are being drawn, and as a pivot or compass-point for the curves. . . . With the addition of heavier shading the essentials of the drawing are before us . . . and then comes the detail. A little shower of pen strokes, like sun-flower seeds, is stabbed and scattered. . . .[1]

If Lewis was unable to retain intact the extraordinary powers of drawing that he possessed around 1920, his powers as a painter were maintained if not increased for the better part of two decades. As his paintings are rare in comparison with his drawings, it is hardly possible to trace his development precisely, but a few of the best were painted on the eve of the Second World War. There is nothing inconsistent in this divergence: drawing is apt to reflect, with an immediacy that cannot be disguised, the personality and condition of the artist; painting, a more calculated procedure, reflects it at several removes. If ill-health, for instance, affected the delicate adjustment between Lewis's hand and eye, any deleterious effect it might have had upon his drawing could have been offset in his painting by greater concentration. Lewis's reputation as a painter in oils will depend upon a small group of works. The chief of these I take to be, in addition to *A Battery Shelled, Bagdad: a panel*,[2] of 1927, *Portrait of Edith Sitwell*[3] (Plate 34), painted between 1923 and 1935, *The Surrender of Barcelona*,[4] of 1936, *Portrait of T. S. Eliot*,[5] and *Portrait of Ezra Pound*,[6] both of 1938, and, ranking somewhat below these,

---

[1] 'The Art of Wyndham Lewis', p. 59.   [2] The Tate Gallery, London.
[3] The Tate Gallery, London.   [4] The Tate Gallery, London.
[5] The Municipal Art Gallery, Durban.   [6] The Tate Gallery, London.

The Red Portrait,[1] of 1937, of which the subject is the artist's wife. These works form a group remarkably consistent in quality and style; all are conspicuously original. Apart from *Bagdad*, a near-abstract by a more adult, more masculine but less lyrical and less sensitive Klee, all represent persons and events belonging wholly to the real world, although the *Barcelona* deals with a subject from history, and the artist's aim in each case would seem to have been to evolve forms, colours, compositions, gestures, expressions, all calculated to represent the essence of each subject with the utmost force and clarity. Someone–I cannot remember who–once aptly described his forms as 'vaulted and buttressed, fretted and smoothed'. These metallic forms–hard, reinforced, smooth-curling and polished –are animated by abrupt, dynamic rhythms. The *Portrait of Edith Sitwell* is probably the work in which Lewis most nearly approaches achieving the breadth, clarity and solidity of classical art. The *Pound*, although less noble in conception and less complex in form, is free from the laboured quality that is just apparent in certain details of the long-worked earlier portrait. Compare, for instance, the conventional sheet of paper at her knee with the watch-spring energy of the papers at his elbow. Both portraits manifest his prophetic faculty with the same certainty as the best of his writing: he seems to have discerned in Edith Sitwell the great poet she became, and in Ezra Pound the victim of some horrible destiny. The *Eliot* is a less communicative affair than either of the others; not a sensitive likeness, for of his strained conscience-hauntedness and of his humour there is no trace, and none of a yet more obvious characteristic, the grave distinction. As an interpretation of character it is of little interest, but it is a likeness of a seated man at once tense and solid, and every part of its tightly integrated complex of forms sculptured as if out of some hard material holds the attention. In one respect the artist has registered a success of a specifically contemporary order. During the past century artists have combed the surface of the world–some have even dredged its depths–for objects in themselves unattractive from which they might distil some element of beauty. Barely two centuries ago beauty was held to be restricted to a narrow range of subjects, and only since then have the whole contents of the world (including man's dreams and the uncensored

[1] Coll. Mrs. Eva Handley-Read.

contents of his unconscious mind) been regarded as proper subjects for a work of art. This inclusiveness was an inevitable consequence of the growth of the belief that beauty resides not in any subject but in the eye of the beholder. It has long seemed to me – and the notion is strengthened in me by every visit to an exhibition of contemporary portraits – that of all the vast variety of products of our industrial civilization the most refractory to treatment by painter or sculptor is the *lounge suit*. I know of no lounge suit, certainly no new smart lounge suit, that has been transformed – without loss of verisimilitude – into a seemlier, indeed a nobler object than the one worn by Mr. Eliot in Lewis's portrait of him. Such a transformation called for the exercise of exceptional artistic power, and deep insight into the character of our shabby civilization.

Lewis often speaks as though the relative fewness of the paintings he has produced is due to the particular circumstances of the age, which compel the original artist to dissipate his energies in defending and justifying his creations by articles, pamphlets and the like, and in painting 'pot-boilers' to enable him to afford to undertake his serious projects. The circumstances he has had in mind are certainly not the products of his fancy. They are real enough, but I think he exaggerates their special relevance for himself. Most of the original painters of his time have written little or nothing in justification of their work; when they have written at all, it has more often than not been in response to pressure from an enterprising publisher. Contemporary painting, with its repudiation of traditions and of the reality perceptible to the average eye, has indeed brought into being a vast expository literature, but this is pre-eminently the work of professional art critics and art historians. Had Lewis not been so apt to show himself mistrustful towards those who have written about his work, and on occasion dictatorial, it would have found effective advocates, and relieved him of any obligation to take up the pen in his own defence. In one sense such advocates might well have been more effective than he: effective in the sense of winning sympathy and patronage for his painting. But in another sense he was his own most effective advocate.

Upon appropriate provocation, armed and armoured like some massive tank, he would roll into action, and the opponents would be crushed beneath the vehicle's steel tracks, would be withered by blasts of heavy dialectical gunfire and suffer final agonies from his secondary armament of satiric invective. I have met no polemical engine more deadly in all English literature; it seems to me to surpass even that of Swift. Magnificent, but it enabled him to win only Pyrrhic victories. A society with higher literary than pictorial traditions was quick to accord him recognition–although in my opinion not adequate recognition–as a writer; but this recognition was astutely used to disparage his painting. Nobody that I know of has suffered death from invective; every one of Lewis's mangled enemies lived to fight–mostly from secure ambush–in other days. The modicum of respect and the harvest of resentment his polemical writings reaped won him few friends and fewer patrons.

Of 'pot-boiling' Lewis has never made any success. Considering that a formidable, even a menacing character marks his best painting and drawing, a deliberate attempt to ingratiate involved a filleting process which could result only in the elimination of the very qualities for which his work is most to be valued.

In the preceding pages there will have been afforded some explanation of why, in an age in general so ready to recognize merit, there is so little disposition to concur in Mr. T. S. Eliot's opinion that Lewis is 'the most fascinating personality of our time'. For myself, I am convinced that the 'mists of winter' which in 1951 thickened into an impenetrable fog before the eyes of Lewis ended the career of a painter and draughtsman whose best work will stand beside the best done in his time. It is in the best sense masculine and positive, the product of one who acts, not, like most contemporary art, of one to whom things merely happen, of one who looks arrogantly forward without nostalgic glances backward, one who–if humanity by a miracle escapes a third world war–may be looked back upon as a great primitive of a nobler, clearer and more rational way of seeing.

Lewis has lived a continuously industrious life; and has produced a phenomenal volume of work of a variety unsurpassed by any Englishman of his time. In addition to his paintings and drawings he has produced volumes of satire, philosophy, art and literary criticism, contemporary history and three volumes of autobiography.

Lewis is among the most articulate men of his generation and, with the full realization of the difficulties opposed by the traditionless character of his age to such a programme, it has been his constant endeavour to address himself, in all his work, to a public as wide as is consistent with a fair measure of responsibility. Although therefore in this respect he has nothing in common with such 'iceberg' men as Acton, who published no more than a small fraction of his speculations and researches, or the philosopher Wittgenstein; none the less, there is a private Lewis not readily perceptible in his work.

In the Introduction which prefaces the first volume of these studies I stated my belief that there is a sense in which the artist transcends his work, and that it is difficult to think of any fact about an artist, or of any circumstances of his life, that might not have an effect upon his work. From this belief I was led to the conclusion that an obligation falls upon those to whom has fallen the privilege of knowing artists to place on record something about their personalities and their opinions.

The seriously held opinions of Lewis I would suppose to be fully elaborated in his writings, and less explicitly in his painting and drawing. But his works, designed to express his opinions with the utmost clarity and the utmost pungency, also act as masks for his private personality. In consequence I have treated, in the course of this study, almost exclusively with the public personality. By way of discharging the obligation to which I just now referred I propose to conclude by a few comments on the man not easily discernible in the work of the artist. This man is an eccentric, whose attitude towards the surrounding world is political and, to an extraordinary degree, defensive. He is actuated, I believe, by an overmastering impulse to record, in all its aggressive sharpness, the vision of his outward and his inward eye, his prophet's apprehension of the real and the false. It is the case that the antagonism of 'Bloomsbury' and the British aversion for what is stark, uncompromising and truculently stated have exposed him to hostility and criticism; but both have done so in far smaller measure than he habitually assumes. Suspicion and trigger happiness with his armament of satire have done more to isolate him than the nature of his opinions, or even the manner in which they have been proclaimed. However that may be, his habitual attitude is one of militant resistance to impending martyrdom. At restaurants he insists upon sitting with his back to a wall. At Adam and Eve Mews, where he lived when I knew him

first in the early 'twenties, his rear was secured by a high wall; at
29A Kensington Gardens Studios, Notting Hill Gate, where he has
mostly lived during recent years, the narrow many-cornered
approach, leading eventually to an inner fastness, might have been
constructed with a professional eye to defence. To the sequestered
and fortress-like character of the places where he has lived is added
an extraordinary secretiveness, as an elaborate security measure. Not
for years after his marriage, for instance, did he admit to the existence
of his wife. It was probably during 1938 or 1939 that I had dinner
with him at Kensington Gardens Studios. Dinner was elaborate and
the studio impeccably tidy. I was reminded of the earlier occasion,
when I had been entertained by my host. Then we had sat on pack-
ing-cases in front of a red-hot iron stove, from whose angry rays
we must have suffered painfully had we not been shielded by a yard-
high range of cinders encircling the fearful source of heat. Only a
feminine hand, I reflected, and a feminine hand of more than usual
authority could so have transformed the environment of so formidable a man. Suddenly I knew that Mrs. Lewis—of whose existence
I had vaguely heard—was somewhere present, concealed somewhere
in the tiny studio flat. Not long afterwards, during the winter of
1939, on a visit to the United States, I met Lewis in New York and
Buffalo. In the latter city he introduced me to his wife, and proposed
that they should spend Christmas at the house of my wife's parents
in Lexington, Kentucky. My wife wrote gently reproaching Lewis
for having neglected to bring his wife to our house in London,
where he himself had been a visitor from time to time. In a long and
regrettably lost reply he wrote that the Romans were never accompanied by their wives on their campaigns but that the Gauls and
other barbarians sometimes were, and that he varied his own practice
in accordance with the exigencies of the campaign upon which he
was engaged. In Europe therefore he followed the Roman fashion;
in America, the Gallic, sometimes even, he concluded, actually riding
into battle with his wife. To our regret, the exigencies of a campaign
of wider scope impeded our reunion in Kentucky.

I recall a characteristic circumstance of his last visit, just before
the war, to our London house. Lewis having accepted an invitation
to dinner at short notice, my wife then telephoned to Margaret Nash
to ask her and Paul to dine with us also. 'We should love to come,'

Margaret Nash said, 'love to.' 'By the way,' said my wife, 'Wyndham Lewis is coming.' 'Oh, Wyndham Lewis? Just a moment, I must speak to Paul.' And then, a few moments later, 'I'm sorry, but Paul's asthma is bad to-night, and besides–Wyndham Lewis–Paul doesn't feel inclined. There were some letters, and Paul has not been very well since.' That night my wife asked Lewis what he had done to offend Paul Nash. 'Nothing at all,' Lewis answered. 'Paul is a real pro. One of the few we've got in England. I'd not dream of doing anything to Paul. Besides, I've not seen him for months.' 'Nor written to him?' 'Not that I can remember.'

'Margaret Nash seemed to think you had.'

'Now I do remember writing him a letter–Paul and I had a trifling difference as a matter of fact.'

'And you wrote him a letter? Surely you did more than that?'

'It comes back to me now. After this difference I wrote to Paul. He didn't answer. I wrote again, and again no answer, so I wrote to him every day.'

'How long did your difference last?'

'Nearly three weeks.'

'And how did the matter end?'

'With a letter from Paul's solicitor explaining that his doctor wished our correspondence to cease.'

DUNCAN GRANT

b. 1885

AN anonymous reviewer of the first volume of these studies
took me to task for referring to my own relationship with
their subjects. Writers who treat of contemporary subjects
work under manifest disadvantages: they are likely to be ignorant
of relevant documents, documents of the kind which come to light
only after a lapse of time, and they find the utmost difficulty in seeing
persons and events in their just proportion, which for those who
write later is relatively easy. It may justly be objected in fact that the
contemporary historian 'cannot see the wood for the trees'. But he
does have opportunities of observing the trees, and since these
studies are, so to speak, about trees rather than about woods, I regard
it as useful on occasion to make clear in what circumstances I have
made my own observations. Biographies of artists are apt to contain
accounts of events and alleged sayings which are of little value simply
because nothing is known of their origin: whether they come from
friends or enemies, or whether they are hearsay or else fabrications.
Therefore the writer who is able to say, 'I heard the artist say this',
or 'I saw that', may be making a contribution, however modest, to
the sum of facts out of which history is made. It also follows that the
possible value of a fact will be enhanced if something is known of the
relation of the observer to the observed. The anonymous reviewer,
in any case, took a naïve view of the question of detachment. He
chose to forget that there exists no such quality as perfect detachment.
All writers worth reading have an attitude towards their subject,
and the more plainly this attitude is manifest the less likely are they
to deceive. If the reader knows where a writer stands, he will be able
to make the necessary allowance for his bias. The deceiver is he who
claims, explicitly or by his manner, a detachment that he cannot
possess. What malevolence, on the other hand, may be masked from
the casual reader of certain learned journals by a bland manner,
numerous footnotes, meticulous citation of authorities!

I have chosen to preface my study of Duncan Grant with these general observations because I do in fact stand in a particular relation to the society of which this artist is a central figure. It is a relation that I have, quite simply, inherited. Following the resounding success of 'Manet and the Post-Impressionists', that is to say the so-called 'first' Post-Impressionist exhibition organized by Roger Fry at the Grafton Galleries in November 1910, the directors offered him the control of their galleries during the autumn months. This opportunity Fry hoped to use to bring together all the serious tendencies in English painting and to show them side by side with French, which, if successful, might, in the words of his biographer, 'unite groups; destroy coteries and bring the English into touch with European art'.[1] In pursuance of this aim he wrote several letters to my father giving at some length his reasons for his belief in the fruitfulness of the projected exhibition and appealing urgently to my father to participate. In spite of his admiration for Fry's wide knowledge, the perennial freshness of his outlook and his gifts of lucid and persuasive exposition, he decided, for reasons already briefly noted, to refuse.[2] Fry regarded this refusal as a betrayal of the progressive forces in English painting by a friend whose place was in their ranks. He never forgave my father, and he communicated his rancour to a wide circle of the Bloomsbury group. Not only were the most venomous attacks made on any artist of the time made on my father in the columns of 'The New Statesman and Nation', but I myself, years later, was, in one way and another, made aware of Bloomsbury hostility.

If there should be an arm's-length character or any want of fairness in my treatment of any member of 'Bloomsbury', it will be due to a constraint in my relations with them of which I shall have given a summary indication of the cause. Let me, however, make unequivocally clear that, so far as I am aware, Grant has never associated himself with the vendettas and intrigues so ruthlessly pursued by certain of his friends, or indeed been actively concerned with art politics of any kind.

Fear has stamped my first meeting with Grant vividly upon my memory. One hot afternoon in the summer of 1922 I found myself with two companions, likewise Oxford undergraduates, in a house

[1] 'Roger Fry: a biography', by Virginia Woolf, 1940, pp. 165-6.
[2] p. 131.

where none of us had been before, pausing at an open french window that gave upon a lawn, at the farther end of which a tea-party was in progress. We paused because the lawn was not so large that we could not discern among the tea-drinkers the figures of Lytton Strachey, Aldous Huxley and Duncan Grant, as well as that, so awe-inspiring upon a first encounter, of our hostess Lady Ottoline Morrell. At that moment, however, this modest patch of grass seemed to us an alarmingly large area to cross beneath the gaze of so many august eyes. So it is that I can still picture the group: Lytton Strachey inert in a low chair, red-bearded head drooped forward, long hands drooping, finger tips touching the grass; Aldous Huxley talking, with his face turned up towards the sun; Duncan Grant, pale-faced, with fine, untidy black hair, light eyes ready to be coaxed from their melancholy, and Lady Ottoline wearing a dress more suitable, one would have thought, for some splendid Victorian occasion, and an immense straw hat. In the course of the afternoon I heard Grant speak, but one had to be alert to catch his scarcely more than whispered words which, towards the close of his sentences, became almost soundless. The friendliness he showed did not, however, disguise even from my inexperience his membership of some society with a means of communication very special to itself. After listening to the discourse of Lytton Strachey and several others I vaguely apprehended that in this Oxfordshire village were assembled luminaries of a then to me almost unknown Cambridge world.

At this time Grant was thirty-seven years old, having been born at Rothiemurchus, Inverness-shire, on 21 January 1885, the only child of Major Bartle Grant, and his wife Ethel, born MacNeil, from Kircudbrightshire. The Grants had for centuries been lairds of Rothiemurchus, but as both Duncan Grant's grandmothers were English his ancestry was as much English as Scottish. From the age of two until the age of eight he lived in India, where his father's regiment was serving, with home leave every second year. Even in this early period of his life his responsiveness to what he saw was sufficiently developed for him to experience a conscious joy, he told me, in the colour and movement of Indian life, especially in the life of the bazaars, of which he even made childish drawings. Back in England he attended a private school at Rugby, and at the age of fifteen he entered St. Paul's as a day boy, and being destined for a

35. **Duncan Grant.** *Pour Vous – Portrait* (1930).
Oil, 34 × 29 in. Coll. the Artist.

36. DUNCAN GRANT. *Green Tree with Dark Pool* (1926).
Oil, 30 × 24 in. Coll. Lady Keynes.

military career he was placed in the Army class, where mathematics was the principal object of his study. But of mathematics he understood nothing and during his unhappy years at both schools a long-cherished ambition to spend his life in drawing and painting took an ever firmer hold. (At Rugby he prayed that God would make him paint like Burne-Jones.) However little such an ambition would have recommended itself to his father, his London home was with a family whose outlook was radically different. His father's sister was married to Sir Richard Strachey, at whose house in Lancaster Gate he lived during his parents' continuing absence abroad. It soon became evident to Lady Strachey that Duncan Grant was without either the qualifications or the disposition for an army career, and she persuaded his parents to allow him to go, in 1902, to the Westminster School of Art. Neither here, however, where he spent upwards of two years, nor at the Slade which he briefly attended later on did he make any particular mark nor did he derive much benefit from the instruction he received. The somewhat negative response to his art schools of this young man who during a youth shadowed by the prospect of an army career had longed to be an artist was due to the character of his second home. From it he received the heightened consciousness and the intellectual stimulus that many other students owe to the art schools they attend. As well indeed he might, for it must have been one of the most intelligent houses in England. The five Strachey brothers and their five sisters all shared a passion for learning, a bracing scepticism, and a wit which made membership of their circle an adventurous and exacting education. One of the brothers, Lytton, became a lifelong intimate of his cousin Duncan.

On leaving Westminster, after having failed to gain admission to the Royal Academy Schools, he visited Italy, where he made copies of the Masaccios in the Carmine, and studied with wondering awe the Piero della Francescas at Arezzo: works now invariably acclaimed as masterpieces but which at that time attracted comparatively little notice.

A French painter, Simon Bussy, engaged to Dorothy Strachey, was a visitor at his second home, and it was he who suggested that Duncan Grant would profit by study in Paris. To Paris he accordingly went to spend a fruitful year as a pupil of Jacques-Emile

Blanche, who taught at La Palette. I once asked him what paintings most impressed him in those days and he said that at the Westminster School he knew comparatively little about the work of his
older contemporaries. An occasional reproduction of a Degas or a
Whistler was passed from hand to hand. Paris, he said, did not enlarge his knowledge as much as might be supposed. It was less easy
than it became a few years later to see the work of contemporaries
at the dealers' galleries, but it was from the Caillebotte Collection of
Impressionists, then hung at the Luxembourg, that he first received
the full impact of modern painting. He also studied the older masters,
especially Chardin, at the Louvre. Living at an hotel with English
students his contacts with the French were few. Upon his return to
London he spent a few weeks at the Slade before settling into a
studio in Fitzroy Square.

It was during these years that the group which became known as
'Bloomsbury' was in the process of formation. Bloomsbury came
into being as a consequence of the establishment in London of
members of a group of Cambridge men of several generations
drawn together by friendship–one of the most attractive characteristics of the group was the high value which its members put upon
friendship–and a community of ideas. The intellectual climate of the
group at Cambridge was analysed with penetration and candour in
the first of 'Two Memoirs' by Maynard Keynes, an original lifelong member of it, in the essay entitled 'My Early Beliefs'. Among
the places where members of the group foregathered was the house
of Duncan Grant's cousins, the Stracheys. On account of the friendship between him and them it was natural that he should enter the
Bloomsbury circle. Although, even perhaps because, one of its least
publicly articulate members, he became one of those most generally
liked and respected: for he was highly intelligent, full of a high-
spirited enjoyment of life, and of a pale dark handsomeness, yet unassertive, free from the rancour and virulent partisanship that marred
the characters of some of his friends. A still more important place of
meeting of the group was the house of Sir Leslie Stephen whose
daughters Virginia and Vanessa, with their husbands Leonard Woolf
and Mr. Clive Bell, constituted the centre of the circle of friends.
Into this house Duncan Grant was introduced by Lytton Strachey,
and with the Bells in particular has formed an intimate and lasting

friendship. Other notable members of this circle of friends were Roger Fry, Maynard Keynes, Desmond MacCarthy, E. M. Forster and Lowes Dickinson. Fry Duncan Grant had first met at the age of sixteen or seventeen at the Strachey's, and had been strongly impressed by his intellectual powers, but it was not until 1909, when he again met him through the Bells, who already knew him well, that the two men became intimate friends. In the Bloomsbury circle Duncan Grant quickly became 'the painter' (with Vanessa Bell an admired second), just as Fry became 'the art critic and expert' (with Vanessa Bell's husband Clive his truculent suffragan), and Maynard Keynes 'the economist and man of affairs'. The effect upon the artist of the somewhat uncritical admiration and powerful advocacy of so highly organized and so influential a body of friends is a matter which I shall examine briefly later on. Duncan Grant's establishment at the centre of this self-conscious, esoteric and highly intellectual society placed him in an environment which exercised a strong and continuing effect upon his art. It was, in fact, the decisive event of his life.

There has been a disposition among some of those who have written about Duncan Grant to represent him, in quite early days, as an apostle of the revolution made by the painting of Cézanne and even of Picasso and Matisse. He can have known little about them, however, before the Post-Impressionist Exhibition of 1910. Even Fry confessed, as late as 1906, 'to having been hitherto sceptical about Cézanne's genius'.[1] It was not until two years later that Duncan Grant saw for the first time works by Picasso and Matisse in the collection of Gertrude and Leo Stein in Paris. The experience had no immediate effect upon his own work, for in 1910 he painted the *Portrait of James Strachey*,[2] a characteristic 'New English' picture, if better composed than most, but the work, surely, of an eye innocent, for all practical purposes, of Cézanne, a work in close accord with that of the soberest spirits of the Club and as remote from that of Picasso and Matisse as anything painted anywhere that year. This portrait, like the early *Still Life*,[3] of three years earlier, show him as an intelligent and serious traditional painter, with an eye for construction and for the texture of things.

[1] Virginia Woolf, op. cit., p. 112.
[2] The Tate Gallery, London.   [3] Coll. the late Lord Keynes.

The events which changed the direction of Duncan Grant's art were the Post-Impressionist Exhibitions of 1910 and 1912. An account of these two exhibitions, their effect upon individual painters and the direction of painting in England and the resounding sensation they provoked could make an illuminating and entertaining book. Duncan Grant once told me that he received no shock from these exhibitions, even though they introduced him to some painters whose work he had not previously seen. The change in his own work suggests that when he saw Picassos, Matisses and other contemporaries at the Stein's he saw them with the eyes of an intelligent sightseer, but that the impact he received from them at the Post-Impressionist Exhibitions was so violent as to make it an intimate part of his own experience. The ensuing change in his outlook declared itself at once. Even in such a picture as *The Lemon Gatherers*,[1] of 1911, painted, Mr. Mortimer tells us, from Sicilian memories[2] (from memories, he might have added, of Florence and Arezzo as well), even in a picture in which he aimed at frankly monumental form in the manner of the Italian masters, a certain audacity and freedom testify to the pervasive influence of Post-Impressionism. The difference between this and the other pictures referred to, painted before he felt the impact of Post-Impressionism, and those painted under its spell is conspicuous. After 1910 he painted for a time with the fervour, but also at times with something of the subservience, of a convert. Mr. Mortimer describes the early Post-Impressionist paintings of Duncan Grant as 'without parallel in the history of the British School'.[3] The possibility of being able to catch in them 'references to . . . Matisse, to African sculpture . . .' he does concede. 'References' is too ladylike a word, however, to meet the occasion. *Still Life*[4] (apples), of about 1912, is almost pure Cézanne. *Head of Eve*,[5] of 1913, is Picasso of the *Demoiselles d'Avignon* period; *The Tub*,[6] of the same year, would be unimaginable without Matisse and *Background for a Venetian Ballet*,[7] of 1922, is a belated essay in Fauvism, in the manner of Derain.

[1] The Tate Gallery, London.

[2] 'Duncan Grant.' Penguin Modern Painters, 1944, p. 7. Mr. Mortimer is in error in dating this picture 1908. The artist, accompanied by Maynard Keynes, visited Sicily and Tunis in 1911.   [3] Ibid., p. 9.

[4] The Courtauld Institute, London.   [5] Coll. Mr. David Garnett.
[6] Coll. Mrs. Vanessa Bell.   [7] Coll. Mrs. B. Mayor.

What are difficult to catch in these essays are references to Duncan Grant. And it cannot even be said that they are distinguished essays. In the *Head of Eve*, for instance, Picasso's energetic hatching technique has been closely imitated, but Picasso's austere adaptation of the grim, impersonal masks from the Congo or the Ivory Coast has been softened into a baby face with oversize eyes and a little pouting mouth. Lest it should be supposed that I have drawn these examples from the penumbra of admitted failures, it should be stated that all have been selected for reproduction in either one or the other of the two books devoted to the artist.[1] It was not until Grant's elation at the discovery of the direct and audacious language of the Parisian Post-Impressionists had somewhat subsided that he began to find his own distinctive way of seeing and the means to give it form. In 1913 there came an opportunity for a wide extension of his range, and the process helped him towards the discovery of what he was best fitted to do. This opportunity he owed, as so much else, to his friend Fry. In my study of Wyndham Lewis I had occasion to refer to the organization by Fry of the Omega Workshops, inspired by the dual purpose of enabling artists to live, without having to teach, by making designs for furniture, pottery, textiles and the like, and making a constructive protest against the timid design and mechanical finish of current factory products. A precursor of the Omega venture was the assembling of the artists who collaborated in 1911 in the decoration of a room at the Borough Polytechnic.[2] Before

[1] Mortimer, op. cit., and 'Duncan Grant', with an Introduction by Roger Fry, 1923.

[2] On the initiative of the Chairman of the House Committee, Basil Williams, a friend of Roger Fry, a group of painters was commissioned to decorate a students' dining-room. Williams's intention was to show how halls and refectories could be made attractive by murals at comparatively low cost. Besides Grant the artists were Fry, who played the leading part in the project's organization, Bernard Adeney, Etchells, Macdonald Gill and Albert Rutherston. The theme chosen was *London on Holiday*. 'We decided,' wrote Adeney in a letter to a member of the Tate Gallery staff (31 December 1953), 'to employ the technique of graduating the colour tones to a dark contour to increase the rhythm of the design–as in Byzantine Mosaics.' At Fry's suggestion the paintings were made in a wax medium on canvas so that they could be removed in the case of rebuilding. The total cost to the authorities was about £100. The scheme, which consisted of seven panels (Grant was responsible for two), aroused considerable interest as an example of native Post-Impressionism on a grand scale, although it appears to have made no appeal to the staff or students, who considered the murals lugubrious. Rebuilding necessitated their removal in 1929 and they were offered to various institutions, but were declined. Eventually they were purchased by the Tate Gallery in 1931 for a nominal sum.

this time the Bloomsbury circle was an academic group composed chiefly of Cambridge men of a philosophic inclination; thenceforward Bloomsbury possessed a wing concerned with the visual arts. For Duncan Grant participation in the Omega project was as fruitful as it was embittering for Wyndham Lewis. The opportunity of designing and decorating a wide variety of objects revealed both to him and to others that he possessed a richly inventive faculty hitherto hardly suspected. He quickly showed himself a designer with a fresh and lyrical touch, with a touch, too, of fantasy, and a designer of resource, so that he quickly came to set the tone of the Omega products. The 'handwriting' of their decoration was essentially the 'handwriting' of Duncan Grant. There was one conspicuous feature, however, which they derived from Fry. One of Fry's marked characteristics was an innate hatred of what was smooth, facile or mechanical. The suave facility of Sargent, for instance, provoked in Fry a particular antipathy, exacerbated by the esteem in which these qualities were held. (It is my belief that Sargent was a far more considerable artist than Fry allowed, but his paintings certainly possess the character for which Fry had so consistent a distaste.) Another object of this innate antipathy was the smooth regular finish of machine products, which led him to persuade his artist friends to exaggerate the irregularities which characterize the hand-made object. Exaggerated irregularity, a touch, even, of wilful clumsiness, suggestive of the intelligent and sensitive amateur beloved by Fry, and subtly reproachful of the smoothly mechanical professional whom Fry detested, remains, as a consequence of Duncan Grant's months at the Omega, a permanent characteristic of his work. If this be a defect it is a small and rather engaging one to set against the gains in confidence, versatility and self-knowledge which he owed to the experience. It was not long before his enhanced resourcefulness found varied use. Jacques Copeau invited him, in 1914, to design the costumes for his production of 'Twelfth Night' at the Vieux Colombier Theatre in Paris. Occasional designs for the theatre became a feature of Duncan Grant's activity. 'The making of designs for the theatre is a sheer pleasure,' he told us, 'and a necessary rest from painting, but I dislike the incidental work it involves, especially the visits to the dressmaker.' Among the other theatrical productions for which he has designed costumes, scenery, or both, are 'The

Pleasure Garden' by Beatrice Mayor, at the Stage Society; 'The Postman', a short ballet in which Lopokova danced, at the London Coliseum; Aristophanes' 'The Birds', at Cambridge, and 'The Son of Heaven' by Lytton Strachey, at the Scala. Before the First World War he began to decorate rooms in the houses of his friends, and in the course of his life many different kinds of rooms have been enlivened by his fantasy, as well as the room at the Borough Polytechnic, which with a group of other artists he decorated in 1911.[1] It was before the war that he enjoyed the first of his rare meetings with Matisse, the living painter whom he most admired and whose example has counted for much in his own growth as an artist. With a letter from Simon Bussy he called on Matisse at his house on the route de Clamart, near Issy-les-Moulineaux. He is unable to recall any words spoken by the master but he does remember that he was engaged upon a still-life with goldfish and that the celebrated *La Danse*[2] was in the studio, though he distrusts a little this latter memory. But as Matisse moved to this suburban house in 1910, where *The Dancers* was painted in the same year, Duncan Grant may well have seen it there. The first of Matisse's six goldfish subjects[3] was painted in this or the previous year and the last in 1915.

For Duncan Grant, as for thousands of others, the outbreak of the First World War interrupted a way of life in which much had been fulfilled but much more promised. Denied by his convictions the harsh satisfaction of fighting for his country and in consequence the opportunity of serving as a War Artist, these years were for him relatively barren. For a time he worked on a farm in Suffolk. In 1916 Keynes bought the farm-house named Charleston, near the village of Firle in Sussex, 'to provide', he said, 'a country house where Duncan Grant and David Garnett . . . could discharge their obligations under the National Service Act by doing agricultural labour,'[4] but he referred to it with characteristic generosity as 'Duncan's new country house.'[5]

As a young man Duncan Grant showed extraordinary high spirits. The most striking manifestation was his participation in the

[1] Grant's panels are *Bathing* and *Football*. The Tate Gallery, London.
[2] Museum of Western Art, Moscow.
[3] Statens Museum fur Kunst, Copenhagen.
[4] 'Maynard Keynes', by Roy Harrod, 1951, p. 217.
[5] Ibid.

'Dreadnought' hoax of 1910. With Horace Cole, the instigator, Adrian Stephen and his sister, Virginia, he spent two or three hours in the first great battleship, then shrouded in highly publicized secrecy, disguised as an Abyssinian notable, after a telegram, purporting to come from the Admiralty, advised the Captain of the visitors' arrival. They were shown the wireless, then regarded as a species of 'secret weapon', but owing to their make-up did not dare accept an invitation to luncheon. The exploit startled the whole country and echoed round the world. Duncan Grant apologized to the First Lord of the Admiralty, Reginald MacKenna. King Edward was greatly distressed and expressed the hope that none of the culprits would ever come to Court. In spite of such high spirits and the respect that has been widely accorded to him on account of his detachment and intelligence, his wide interests and the combination of an eager flow of spirits with a dignified reserve, he rarely played any part in public affairs. On one occasion he did, however, use his influence with Keynes–who since about 1908 had been perhaps his closest friend– to propose that the National Gallery should make some purchases from the Degas sale of 1918. Keynes persuaded the Chancellor of the Exchequer, Bonar Law, of the wisdom of such a course and the sale was attended by Keynes himself, representatives of the Treasury and members of the staff of the National Gallery. 'Do buy Ingres portrait of self Cézanne Corot even at cost of losing others', Duncan Grant urged Keynes by cable. In consequence of his timely intervention the National and Tate Galleries were enriched by the purchase of works by Ingres, Corot, Delacroix, Forain, Gauguin, Manet–including his *Firing Party*–and others.

With the coming of peace Duncan Grant was able to settle down, without serious interruption, to the doing of the greater part of his life's work, taking a studio at first in Hampstead, then one that had been occupied by Whistler, Sickert and John at No. 8 Fitzroy Street, later dividing his time between Charleston, occasional visits to London where he usually takes an annual holiday, and, between 1927 and 1938, spending some months each year at Cassis near Marseilles.

Free, by the early nineteen-twenties, from the spell of Post-Impressionism he began to find a way of seeing very much his own, or, to be more precise, two complementary ways: the way of a decorator and the way of a realist. The first was the earlier to reach maturity. The comprehendingly affectionate essay by Fry published in 1923 makes it clear that his friend and tutor was of the opinion that his true talent was for decoration.

> He pleases because the personality his work reveals is so spontaneous, so unconstrained, so entirely natural and unaffected, [he wrote] . . . he has . . . a great deal of invention . . . the peculiar playful, fantastic elements in it which remind one occasionally of the conceits of Elizabethan poetry. . . . Gifted as he is with a particularly delightful rhythmic sense and an exquisite taste in colour, he is particularly fitted to apply his talents to decoration.

Fry emphasized this opinion by noting regretfully that 'at a time when the movement of creative artists was in favour of insisting almost exclusively upon the formal elements of design, he should have tended to suppress his natural inclination to fantastic and poetic invention. . . . The effort to create complete and solidly realized constructions in a logically coherent space, which has succeeded of late to the more decorative conception that derived from Gauguin, has, I think, hampered rather than helped his expression. Duncan Grant co-ordinates form more fully on the flat surface than in three dimensions.' In considering this opinion it should be remembered that it was formed in 1923, when Duncan Grant had enjoyed numerous opportunities—at the Omega, in the theatre and on the walls of friends and patrons—to exercise his talents as a decorator, but that he had as yet paid little attention to the creation of 'complete and solidly realized constructions in space' and his most serious attempts in this direction were made after the publication of Fry's essay.

Long before 1923 Fry had become the impassioned apostle of the idea that everything of value in a work of art resides in its formal harmony, and he had become a victim of a mystique of pure form. Content was of no consequence except in as much as it favoured formal harmony. 'I want to find out what the function of content is,' he wrote to Lowes Dickinson in 1913, 'and am developing a theory which you will hate very much, viz. that it is merely directive of form, and that all the essential aesthetic quality has to do with pure form.'[1]

Duncan Grant was far the most gifted artist in the closely knit

[1] Virginia Woolf, op. cit., p. 183.

Bloomsbury circle, the court painter and designer, so to speak, so that an admission that he was so far in his own work from exemplifying the cherished doctrine of pure form as even to 'remind one occasionally of the conceits of Elizabethan poetry' must have been one that Fry made with reluctance. It is evident that he made it with the utmost conviction. An anonymous critic once wrote to Fry that he seems to have felt that ' . . . in cases of maladjustment between artist and critic the fault was almost always on the artist's side'. Brueghel and Hogarth and Turner lay in their graves, all their manifold shortcomings beyond the critic's correction. But Duncan Grant lived, so to speak, within point blank range. Fry had a passion for acting the mentor and Duncan Grant was the continuously praised 'star turn'. I do not know how insistently the critic played the mentor in this case and there must be two or three informed upon the matter. I once discussed with Duncan Grant to what extent he regarded himself as affected by aesthetic theories. 'I've had to pay attention to many theories,' he answered, speaking with deliberation, 'but I don't believe I've adopted any. With me it's been rather a question of picking one's way *through* theories. I could hardly help being interested in theories, but my interest doesn't go very deep.'

Standing open to correction I would hazard the guess that Duncan Grant did 'pay attention' to the prevailing insistence upon the exclusive value of the formal elements of design, especially when supported by Fry's extraordinarily persuasive argument, with the result that the preoccupation of this born decorator was largely diverted from decoration to the creation of 'complete and solidly realized constructions in a logically coherent space'. Just as, in the age of Reynolds, the painter who was not a painter of 'history' was inferior to him who was, so, in the Bloomsbury circle, the painter who did not realize such constructions was inferior to him who did.

Because it would have given Fry such satisfaction to praise the purely formal qualities in his art, his praise of him as a decorator should be received with particular respect. Fry extols his decorative qualities, the elegance of his handling, the singular charm of his manner, his lyrical joyousness and his enjoyment of what is beautiful –in the ordinary sense–in nature. None the less he seems to me to lack one of the essential qualities of a great decorator, namely the power to enhance the act of living by exhilarating those who see his works with a vision of a humanity and its environment idealized, either by the creation of an Olympus, a Parnassus, an Arcadia, or even–to descend to a commonplace level–a humanity'glamourized'. Unless, in fact, by its exuberance, wit, gaiety, and style, a decoration affords us a glimpse of a world of greater nobility, delight or amenity than that with which we are familiar, it cannot be said to have realized its principal purpose. It is easy to recognize in the decorations of Duncan Grant the engaging qualities which delighted Fry, and others besides. Take, for instance, *Decoration on a Cupboard*,[1] of 1921, or *Long Decoration–Dancers*,[2] of 1934. The earlier shows fantasy and wit and a feeling for the poetry of homely objects, and the later is rhythmic in movement, clear and gay in colour, the whole lyrical in feeling. Yet in spite of its manifold beauties neither is really intended to enhance life; the heavy boneless limbs of the dancers, their flabby hands, their thick humourless feet suggest that the painter was not quite in earnest about this all-important purpose. Sir Kenneth Clark once wrote of Duncan Grant's concern with 'the earthly adventures of amorous gods'. But for the sake of which of his dancers would Jupiter have given himself the trouble of changing into a bull? It may be that beneath his gay lyricism lurks a melancholy that makes him sceptical about the prospects of enhancing man's condition. It does not seem to me, as it seemed to Fry in 1923, that the artist co-ordinates form less fully in three dimensions than he does on a flat surface. Whatever forces persuaded him to attempt to 'create complete and logically realized constructions'–whether Fry himself or the consensus of opinion among the artists of his acquaintance–it appears difficult to deny to Duncan Grant a substantial measure of success, especially in his portraits of women. Of a longish series there are at least two which take their places with the fine portraits of our time: *Miss Holland*,[3] of 1930 (Plate 35), and *Vanessa Bell*,[4] of 1942. In the earlier a design which beautifully combines great breadth with great subtlety, animated by sweeping movement, is carried out with a masterly ease and precision. Nothing is omitted or scamped, but the detail takes a subordinate, though

[1] Coll. the late Lord Keynes.
[2] The City Art Gallery, Birmingham.
[3] Coll. the Artist. Reproduced in Mortimer, op. cit. under the title *Pour vous*.
[4] The Tate Gallery, London.

enriching, place in the largely seen scheme of things, and the portrait is evidently a penetrating likeness. The later portrait is remarkable for a combination of all his decorative resources—figure, draped curtain, high chair, screen, cloak and patterned carpet are related in a harmony at once opulent and of great dignity—with the creation of a wholly convincing presence. Such a combination is rare in contemporary portraiture. *Vanessa Bell* is a modest descendant, as it were on a scale appropriate to our time, of the great portraits of the past in which stateliness and insight into character marched naturally together. How appropriate that so admirable a portrait should have for its subject the artist with whom he has been most constantly associated: who has worked so often simultaneously from the same models and from whose talent, at once distinguished and robust, his own has derived nourishment. These two portraits and a handful of others will outlast, I think, any of the purely decorative paintings of Duncan Grant.

There is another theme which has on many occasions brought his highest faculties into play, namely the nude. To my thinking Duncan Grant has made nothing more beautiful than these pastels from the nude model and a few are among the most lyrical drawings of the time. I have particularly in mind a *Nude*,[1] of 1934, and a *Nude study*,[2] of 1935. The owner of these two lovely drawings accurately described the artist's vision as 'so instinctively and unhesitatingly chromatic that he can build up a passage of modelling with strokes of pure colour'.[3] The words were written before these two drawings were made, but this ability was never more perfectly exemplified than in the second of them.

Some ten years ago Duncan Grant put his hand to an undertaking of a different character from anything he had done hitherto. When I received an invitation from the artist in the summer of 1943 to go down to Sussex to see a series of wall paintings which Vanessa Bell, her son Quentin and he himself had carried out in the parish church at Berwick, a village not far from Firle, I took the journey with interest tempered by misgiving. It did not seem to me that he was well equipped either in mind or hand for such an enterprise.

[1] Coll. Sir Kenneth Clark, K.C.B.   [2] Coll. Sir Kenneth Clark, K.C.B.
[3] 'Drawings by Duncan Grant at Agnew's', in 'The New Statesman and Nation', 17 June 1933.

Neither the sceptical, or rather the in general positive hostility of the Bloomsbury circle to Christianity–hostility, let it be said at once, not so much to the Christian ethic as to the Christian Church, more particularly in its supernatural aspects–nor the decorative method of wall painting he had evolved for the evocation of the philandering of nymphs and satyrs, seemed to promise anything but failure. It was apparent when I entered the church that my apprehensions were groundless. *The Nativity* and *The Annunciation* were represented by Vanessa Bell, *The Parable of the Wise and Foolish Virgins*, by Quentin Bell, and *Christ in Glory* by Duncan Grant himself. There was no mistaking that the series was the work of three different hands, but they all radiated the same mood of noble gravity. The figures were solid, clearly defined, yet not without a becoming touch of mystery. The one defect that I noticed was that the solidity of certain of the figures was insisted upon to a degree which caused them to project from the walls and thereby to break the unity of surface of the series as a whole. Even if the Berwick paintings bear no comparison with those at Burghclere they must, I think, be accounted among the best paintings to be made in church or chapel in England during the present century.

With characteristic delicacy of feeling the artists arranged that I should visit the church alone. My visit ended, I joined them and Mr. Clive Bell for lunch at Charleston. It was a curious experience, and for several reasons, chiefly because it was the first occasion since I had stayed with Roger Fry as a schoolfriend of his son Julian that I had been in the house of a member of the inner circle of Bloomsbury. Duncan Grant is not a good hater, and he took no part that I know of in the Bloomsbury vendetta against my father, who was, I believe, one of the first artists to give him encouragement. In any case the cohesion of the group had loosened and its influence waned, and I sensed, mainly from the conversation of Mr. Clive Bell, that certain younger artists now provoked greater antipathy than a son of my father. Certain sharp comments he made about younger contemporaries gave me a sudden realization of the extent to which the survivors of a circle regarded when I was young as aggressive advocates of 'significant form' and other 'advanced' ideas had become 'Old Bolsheviks' who showed less sympathy towards younger artists accounted 'advanced' than my older painter friends such as Matthew Smith and Charles Ginner who were their seniors. In fact, having vaguely expected to be made delicately to feel reactionary, I found myself in an environment fascinating for its 'period' interest though for other reasons, of course, as well. There were the pieces of Omega furniture and carpets and the textiles designed by my hosts, their slightly clumsy yet distinguished pottery embellished by swirls and hooks in their deliberately irregular, their unmistakable calligraphy; also the iron stove, the mustard-coloured wall-paper and other objects made familiar by their pictures. All this and the gentle voices, dying away often, of the artists and the booming voice of the critic expressing opinions in which an urbane liberalism blended oddly with unexpected rigidities, strong prejudices more easily sensed than defined. Here I was in the only corner of this vanishing society to survive intact: people and environment, everything: even, out of the windows, could be glimpsed the subjects of so many of the two artists' landscapes.

At the conclusion of this brief study of Duncan Grant's painting it might be useful if I were to put together and set down what I remember his saying about his method of painting. Landscapes and still-lifes he does direct from life, beginning with very summary indications in charcoal on the canvas but generally without preliminary studies,

> but I begin to paint [he explained] as soon as I possibly can. It's not only that painting is such a delight, but as I paint with difficulty I want to come to grips with it with the least delay. When I first came to know him at the Stracheys [he continued] Simon Bussy urgently impressed on me the value of making copies and I've always followed his advice. I don't try to make exact copies but interpretations. I agree with Bussy that there is a great deal to be learnt from this practice. It isn't the painting that one does before another painting that teaches one. The real idea behind copying is to induce one to look at a picture for a long time. Even if you're a painter and deeply interested, it is difficult to look for very long and it is much easier if one is doing something.
>
> I usually have several pictures going at the same time—too many I'm inclined to think—sometimes compositions, at others realistic works. I don't often work on pictures of both kinds at the same time: my interest in imaginative works and in realistic ones runs in phases. . . .

I am very conscious that these brief studies of mine, although perhaps not wholly without value as reports of an eye-witness or of a witness at one remove, omit much of importance, and that they will all of them be quickly superseded. But none, I fancy, so quickly as this study of Duncan Grant. The circle to which he belonged included some of the most articulate persons of their generation: they have left, and will leave, innumerable letters and other records which will vastly amplify our knowledge of the lives and works of its members and possibly lead to radical reappraisals. There is a classic waiting to be written on this circle full of interest, indeed unique in its time, although in certain respects so malign in its influence.

For the moment, however, although there clings to the name of Duncan Grant an aura of respect, interest in his work declines. From one generation to another the focus of interest inevitably shifts, but this alone does not account for the neglect of an artist of gifts so considerable and so various. There is another, a more readily perceptible cause. When Bloomsbury was a power in the intellectual and artistic life of England and its nominees held or dominated most strategic critical positions, praise of Bloomsbury's court painter became the rule. Most people have by now forgotten to what lengths these routine paeons went. Take, for instance, these words by an ordinarily sensible critic, Mr. William Gaunt:

> Duncan Grant is an artist in the full sense of the word–as opposed to the typical English artist who never grows up–in the Constable tradition. . . . I do not think, however, it is too much to say that he combines some of the masculine English quality with a wider and more imaginative outlook than the man of Suffolk.[1]

More significant still are some sentences in an article by an extremely conservative critic, Mr. Adrian Bury, who in the course of what is plainly intended as a severely critical notice described Duncan Grant as 'a sort of nephew of Cézanne, but with more discipline than his uncle, a painter who has made Post-Impressionism logical'.[2] Sporadic praise of this kind, however lacking in discrimination, did little harm. Entirely different was the praise that issued forth, almost week by week in the vastly influential Bloomsbury 'parish magazine' 'The Nation', after 1931 'The New Statesman and Nation'. Its most regular art critic was Mr. Clive Bell who contributed to the first and was the art critic to the second from 1933 to 1943. This

[1] 'Drawing and Design', May 1927.
[2] 'The Saturday Review', 20 August 1931.

critic's praise of his wife and of his intimate friend Duncan Grant was as continous as it was excessive. Take a characteristic passage in an article in which allusion is made to Duncan Grant's 'genius': 'Here is the most important exhibition yet given', wrote Mr. Bell, 'by the living artist whom many good judges consider the best... after seeing these pictures none will be at pains to contradict.'[1] In the course of the article Picasso, Bronzino, Constable, Piero della Francesca and Gainsborough are mentioned by way of comparison. The harm caused by this routine spate of such injudicious praise—more especially when it contrasted so sharply with the treatment accorded to other artists–involved twofold, and, as I am persuaded, threefold injury to Duncan Grant. It wearied a whole generation with his name; worse still, it sowed the suspicion in the minds of other artists that they were belittled in order that his reputation might be enhanced, and thereby bred dislike of a man of integrity and charm of character; and, as I believe, it had a deleterious effect upon the artist himself. With all his qualities as an artist he has one insufficiency: an insufficiency of passion. Compare one of his landscapes with one by Gainsborough, Constable, Courbet or Corot or any great landscape painter, and what is usually at once apparent is that his subject has mattered less to him than theirs to them: where they have manifest passion he has a tasteful intelligence. Usually–not always: there are conspicuous exceptions to this generalization, such as *Green Tree with Dark Pool*,[2] of 1926 (Plate 36). But for a man with an insufficiency of passion few things can be more enervating than the lifelong echo of 'genius, genius, genius' in his ears. But the effects of overpraise, however reckless, will pass and Duncan Grant will be recognized for a painter with a sense of beauty matched by a sense of actuality, and for a decorator of extraordinary resource.

[1] 'The New Statesman and Nation', May 1934.
[2] Coll. Lady Keynes.

JAMES DICKSON INNES
1887–1914

EW, if any, more painters are able to maintain themselves by the practice of their art than were able to do so before the Second World War. But if they cannot live as artists, their existence–the existence of a fortunate few among them–is at least recognized. The exhibition of their work abroad is believed to make a modest contribution to British prestige, and it is officially sponsored. It is also believed that some good may come of its exhibition within the shores of these islands, and this too receives official support.

Before this last war, however, a painter, unless spectacularly successful or else notable for something besides his work, was ignored. In the Introduction to these studies, which prefaces the first volume, I referred to an acquaintance's having told me that she was engaged upon a study of Innes, and I made the comment that, although this painter had been dead only thirty-eight years, the materials for this undertaking would be assembled with infinite labour. Some time has passed, and I have heard nothing further, but I fancy the undertaking has been abandoned, and I doubt whether material adequate for anything more than a sketch any longer exists. A sketch has indeed been written, and well written, by a friend who was a fellow student of Innes's and whose intimacy ended only four years before his death. But except for Mr. Fothergill's few illuminating pages,[1] Innes the man, so to speak, has sunk into his grave almost without trace. His death passed virtually unmentioned in the Press, although it has been said that his friend and patron Horace Cole managed to secure the insertion of a few lines about him in one of the weeklies.[2] Nor has Innes been judged

[1] 'James Dickson Innes', with an Introduction by John Fothergill to the reproductions collected and edited by Lillian Browse, 1948.

[2] The authority for this statement is the late Randolph Schwabe, Slade Professor, University College, London, from 1930 to 1949, who published an article 'Reminiscences of Fellow Students', relating principally to Innes, but with references to John Currie, Derwent Lees and a few others, which appeared in

sufficiently important for mention in 'The Dictionary of National Biography'.[1]

James Dickson Innes was born on 27 February 1887 at Llanelly, where his father, a Scot, had an interest in a brass and copper works. His grandfather and great-grandfather both served in H.M. Customs and Excise. Both his brothers distinguished themselves, Alfred as a biological chemist, and Jack, who died in 1931, as a naval architect. 'It was a well-bred family at Llanelly,' Mr. Fothergill tells us, 'four serious and almost silent males, and Mrs. Innes the life of it.' Innes attended Christ's College, Brecon, and from 1904 until 1905 the art school at Carmarthen, winning a scholarship which took him to the Slade, where he remained until 1908. He spent his vacation in 1906 at Oxford and Plymouth, and in 1907 at Chepstow, a painting ground favoured by Steer, his own favourite teacher at the Slade, and in the same year, while still a student, he first exhibited at the New English Art Club. In the year following his death-knell sounded: he was ill, and his illness was diagnosed as tuberculosis by Dr. Tebb, who was for a time our own family doctor. I clearly recall his thin pale face, his reddish hair, but still more clearly how much more interest he showed in discussing painting and literature than in medicine.

It is difficult to make out how much talent Innes's work showed before he came to the Slade. It was without character, Mr. Fothergill declares, 'all save the grandiose conception, *The Quarry, Llanelly*'.[2] But this picture is dated, in the volume to which he contributed the essay already cited, as 1906, that is, when he was already a student at the Slade. To judge by the reproduction in this book–I have not

'The Burlington Magazine' in January 1943. I already possessed, in briefer but rather more candid form, the facts set forth in the 'Burlington' article. On 24 March 1941, I spent an afternoon with Schwabe at Oxford. At that time neither Mr. Fothergill's essay nor, of course, Schwabe's own article had appeared, and concerned at the probability that almost every vestige of the life and personality of an artist of extraordinary gifts should be irreparably lost, I responded warmly when he spoke of Innes, and made notes immediately afterwards of what he told me. I think it must have been my insistence upon the duty of someone who knew him to put down what he remembered that prompted the 'Burlington' article.

[1] Among the subjects of these studies those in the previous volume who qualify for inclusion, ten years having elapsed since their death, the following are included: McEvoy, Orpen, Tonks; the following are not: Gilman, Gwen John, Gore.

[2] The Parc Howard Museum, Llanelly.

seen the original–it is a 'New English' landscape of what Sickert used to call 'an august site', but it showed aspirations after monumentality based upon hard structure not commonly to be met with at the Club's exhibitions.

In spite of his originality he was easily led, and what I take to be the principal painting he made during his Slade years, *The Wye near Chepstow*,[1] of about 1907, was an elaborate–and highly successful– essay in the manner of Steer of one of his master's favourite motives, in which, however, the luminosity of grass and foliage does not disguise his greater delight in the rocky elements in nature or his concern with design.

Figure drawing he found both difficult and distasteful, and it was an exercise which he often avoided. Oddly enough he was awarded a prize for a figure competition with *Death of the Firstborn*, but according to Mr. Fothergill this was an imaginative landscape in which 'the first born themselves, a muddled little group of three figures, were relegated to a shadow in the middle distance'. Either towards the end of his term at the Slade or shortly afterwards he painted a small group of figure pieces, of which the two most successful are *Moonlight and Lamplight*[2] and *Resting*.[3] The first represents a subject which offered many difficulties, in particular the harmonizing of the genial but prosaic lamplight which fills the room and the blue and silver moonlight seen outside the window. The figure seated beside the window is Innes's friend and follower, the Australian-born painter Derwent Lees. If this figure is featureless, that in *Resting* is inept, with her huge head and tiny face and supporting arm too feeble for its function. More interested in inanimate nature than in his fellow men, in these and similar interiors still-life takes precedence over figures. In the first picture the landscape outside the window gives occasion for a muted expression of his most passionate love, but the furniture and even the clear-cut shadows were the objects of a more affectionate scrutiny than the artist's friend. In the second the most vividly realized features are the curling prints hanging on the wall framed with black bands of shadow along two edges.

But Innes's short painting life began, Mr. Fothergill has told us, when in 1908 the two of them went to France together, first to

[1] Coll. Mr. Hugo Pitman.   [2] Mr. and Mrs. Arthur Crossland.
[3] Mr. and Mrs. Arthur Crossland.

Caudebec, then to Bozouls, near Rodez and last to Collioure, near Perpignan. At the second place he painted *Bozouls near Rodez*,[1] a 'New English' picture with an added crispness and sparkle, and a group of water-colours, of which *Bozouls, near Rodez*,[2] the only one of them known to me, is somewhat summary and empty. It was, Mr. Fothergill wrote, at Collioure with its 'Saracenic church . . . and gem-like with fishing boats of antique build and scarlet sails', and its heat and light, that Innes's sense of colour was awakened, but not until he was back to England did this transforming experience become apparent in his painting. 'But for this visit', concludes Mr. Fothergill, 'we might have had in Innes just one more exponent of pale English sunshine and veiled charm.' Within the next two years he had evolved a way of expressing what he saw and felt, and about 1910, working consciously against time, he began to paint his finest pictures.

The art of Innes was a singular art. Mountains were his theme, yet his representation of them was not grandiose or monumental. A critic's jibe that he made molehills out of mountains is justified to that extent, but his eminences were spacious, rhythmical, often noble and sometimes menacing. If there was nothing vast about them, equally there was nothing small or mean: perhaps on account of his disinterest in man they are oddly scaleless. According to Mr. Fothergill he was an unsophisticated lover of nature, who even pretended to know all about trees and butterflies, yet the reflection of his knowledge in his pictures is a faint one. We learn from the same authoritative source that he was an impassioned student of Turner, Constable and Cotman, but that he owed nothing to French painters. To his English predecessors, Cotman in particular, his debts are evident, but his approach to his subjects, especially as manifest in his pure, vivid colour, his sparing use of neutral tones, his hard, clear-cut forms, associates him with Gauguin and other Post-Impressionists. Had Innes consciously admired these French masters, Mr. Fothergill would hardly have given so explicit a denial that he owed them nothing. There was a channel, however, through which their influence might have reached him and taken a hold upon his unconscious mind. Like Augustus John, Innes was associated with the Camden Town Group. The differences between these two and the

[1] The Tate Gallery, London.   [2] The Leicester Galleries, London.

members of this group of painters of urban landscape were conspicuous, yet close personal relations subsisted between them; indeed John and Innes were titular members of it. It is likely that the passion for strong, pure colours and the contempt for neutral tones which animated Gilman (a disciple of Van Gogh) and to an only slightly lesser degree Bevan (who knew Gauguin) and Ginner (who had long been familiar with the painting of the Post-Impressionists working in France) should have communicated itself in some degree to Innes.

That French influence, if it played any part in the formation of Innes's painting, played a part of which the painter was unaware, receives some corroboration from Matthew Smith. The two painters went together, he told me, in 1908 or the following year, to the house of Leo Stein, where Innes showed himself not only entirely unresponsive to the works of Matisse and other Post-Impressionists so finely represented there but even to those of Cézanne. (There was another occasion when Matthew Smith, regretting Innes's apathy if not dislike, took him to Vollard's gallery, but the dealer, less sympathetic towards students than dealers in general are to-day, unceremoniously turned them out.) The exotic character of his art and in particular his rosy mountain-peaks may owe something to the study of Japanese prints, too, which were commonly met with in his day: the British Museum, which he often visited, housed, then as now, a splendid collection of them. International art movements are notoriously pervasive, their slightest manifestations, only unconsciously received or half understood, are often sufficient to serve their inscrutable though imperative purposes, for they may be seed falling upon soil ready to receive them. Whether on account of some elusive interplay of influences or else through spontaneous generation, the art of Innes is in fact closely related to that of the Post-Impressionists, and has little in common with that of Steer or of the others whom he regarded as his masters. In spite of his talk about botany his art was not primarily a descriptive art. The contemplation of mountains induced in him a mood of exaltation, which he expressed most eloquently in terms of conscious design, sometimes, as in his celebrated *Waterfall*,[1] of 1910, of a very elaborate character, and of pure, strong, even violent colour.

[1] The Tate Gallery, London.

If Innes was unaware of the effects of Post-Impressionism upon himself, he was certainly aware of a strain in himself recalcitrant to Ruskin's injunction 'to go to nature with all singleness of heart, selecting nothing, rejecting nothing'.. At Bozouls, on his momentous first journey to France, he expressed misgiving to Mr. Fothergill at his impulse 'to try for something more or better than nature'. 'I'll go and be moral,' he said, and spent the next three afternoons making a precise study of a green boulder in a stream. Later he showed him a big canvas, which in the course of three laborious but fruitless weeks he had covered with thousands of representations of leaves, but he quickly came to understand that for him this kind of exercise was immoral. From St. Ives, where he went the following year, he wrote to Mr. Fothergill, 'An artist came to see some of my latest pictures. "That's a good slap at nature," said the man wishing to be encouraging. "I think, rather, it's a good slap in the face," I replied.'

It was to St. Ives that his mother took him for a longish stay at 'The Retreat' in order that he should fight, in the healthiest circumstances, the disease that had fastened upon his lungs, but he knew that he stood no chance. 'Really I am entirely happy now here . . . my mind is, I think, fairly disconnected from the body which is not so strong as might be but the mind seems all right, so don't say, "You flatter yourself".' And late that year or early next he wrote for Mr. Fothergill a parody of Blake's poem to Flaxman, of which he gives these lines in his essay:

. . . Pneumonia and drink appeared to me and terror appeared in heaven above
And Hell beneath and a mighty and awful change threatened my earth
And the germicidal war began, all its dark horror passed before my face,
And my angels told me that seeing such visions I could not subsist upon earth

Innes's first love was always his painting, but he was also a romantic lover of life, and the knowledge that he had only a little time left, a few years at most, led him not only to intensify his efforts as a painter but disposed him the more to live, after his easy, casual fashion, still more fully. From quite early days he had showed some disposition to depend, for forgetting what he wished to forget and for heightening his pleasures with a rosy aura, upon alcohol. The nearer prospect of death increased this dependence.

About this time the friendship between Innes and Mr. Fothergill came to an end, and they never met again, and one consequence is that with it ends the slight record which, nevertheless, remains the chief source of information about the artist and the man. The narrative suddenly breaks off and little is added about either the painting or the life of Innes during the four final years. About the former he offers only one comment of substance, namely that he was in a hurry. 'Earlier he had worked,' he writes, 'with the same charming leisure with which he had walked and talked, but latterly, I was told, he angrily regretted all that work as wasted and began to work at top speed.'

It does not seem to me that this stricture is justified by Innes's work. Both his earlier and his later life had their failures, but it was during the years 1910–13–after the breach with Mr. Fothergill–that he painted the pictures by which he is likely to be remembered. There was a time, certainly, around 1912, when his touch became swifter and more fluent, but his best paintings of that time, in which speed and fluency are apparent, cannot be said to show signs of haste. Such, for instance–to name only a few, illustrations of which accompany his essay–are *Tan-y-Grisiau*,[1] *Mediterranean*,[2] *Ranunculus*,[3] and *In the Welsh Mountains*.[4]

It is unfortunate that Innes should have foregone the company of his close friend and brief chronicler at the very moment when he was entering upon the most fruitful period of his short life. In 1910 and the two years following he visited in Wales, where, applying his now fully awakened sense of colour to the interpretation of the splendid landscape of his native country, he painted the greater number of his finest pictures. The innate understanding he had of the mountains of Wales gave a reassuring credibility to his most exotic conceptions: Mount Arenig and Bala Lake, however unearthly from a momentary effect of sunlight their colouring may be, are always of the earth. Some, though by no means all, of his Mediterranean landscapes have by comparison the look of pure fantasies.

The most remarkable picture he made during that first year of full maturity was *The Waterfall*[5] (Plate 38), a water-colour. There are

[1] Coll. Captain Peter Harris.   [2] Coll. Mrs. Arthur Gibbs.
[3] The Contemporary Art Society (Sir Edward Marsh Bequest), now in the Walker Art Gallery, Liverpool.
[4] The City Art Gallery, Manchester.   [5] The Tate Gallery, London.

other pictures by his hand which glow with a richer or a more scintillating light, but in none known to me does he show such mastery of intricate design. It is a picture that maintains a delicate balance–and it is chiefly this which gives it an unearthly air–between abstraction and representation. At one moment it presents itself to our gaze as a complex of forms and movements which, from whatever angle one may regard them, hold us under their spell. (I know of few small modern pictures which invite–or repay–so prolonged a scrutiny.) At another, it represents, and most convincingly, a wide stream which flows out of the far distance towards the spectator between strangely formed rocks and beneath a menacing sky, descending here and there over shallow falls until, in the foreground, it abruptly precipitates over black rocks into two big falls, and it is full face and from midstream that he witnesses this fascinating culmination of a quiet journey. *The Waterfall* is an exercise in design, more especially in the silhouetting of one form against another derived from Cotman, of a complexity which gives it a place apart among the works of Innes. There is another particular in which it differs from his most characteristic works, in which the focus of interest is the far distance: the point where mountain-peak stands up black against an opal sky or else emerges sharp and clear above a fleecy wreath of cloud, and the foreground is summarily handled or even on occasion dispensed with altogether. In *The Waterfall* the spectator is compelled to share the artist's fascination with a foreground which, however, is intimately linked, both formally and dramatically, with the farthest background. Preoccupation with the distant–in this picture the meeting-point of sombre peak and menacing sky–marks another but less splendid work of this year, *The Dark Mountains: Brecon Beacons*.[1] In one respect the best of his landscapes of the following year make a new departure. The outlines of *The Dark Mountains: Brecon Beacons* are lacking in the character of rock: they are a little soft in modelling and texture; but those which so nobly rise in the two of the *Bala Lake*,[2] of about 1911, have all rock's density and hardness. These, more especially that with the high central peak, are beautifully classical in their lucid harmony. Fine, too, is an *Arenig*[3] in its combination of radiance with weight,

[1] Temple Newsam, Leeds.   [2] Coll. Mr. Louis G. C. Clarke.
[3] The National Gallery of Canada, Ottawa (Massey Coll.).

but a *Tan-y-Grisiau*,[1] of about the same time, is a fluffy pastiche of Constable's *Weymouth Bay*.

Round about 1911, too, the increased swiftness and fluency of handling to which I alluded just now became a marked though intermittent feature of his work, and more conspicuously in the Mediterranean landscapes than in the Welsh. It would seem that the heat and the brilliance of the South of France, which first excited his audacious sense of colour, also stimulated him to the use of this rapid and summary way of painting, and that the Welsh mountains favoured a serener although a still more exalted mood. It was particularly in his interpretations of these that he seemed to be haunted by a highly personal conception of the ideal landscape which also haunted the imaginings of Puvis de Chavannes and Gauguin. The ideal landscape of Innes, unlike that of these two, was not an idyllic setting for man, but a wild landscape generally austere in form though in colour glowing with a romantic radiance, and peopled, only latterly and then with reluctance, by a lone figure or at most a couple.

One of the marks of Innes as a colourist was the audacity with which he used purple. Schwabe told me that Innes reproved him for speaking disrespectfully of the representation of purple heather, and was unimpressed when reminded of Ruskin's warning against the free use of purple. This was a colour generally avoided in English painting until the Pre-Raphaelites used it and regarded it indeed almost as an emblem of their emancipation from subserviency to outworn, but still tyrannically enforced, conventions. 'And then about colour', Holman Hunt reports his young self saying to Millais in criticism of prevailing methods,

> why should the gradation go from the principal white, through yellow, to pink and red, and so on to stronger colours? With all this subserviency to early examples, when the turn of violet comes, why does the courage of the modern imitator fail? If you notice, a clean purple is scarcely ever given in these days. . . .[2]

Innes could easily have seen, indeed so regular a visitor to art galleries could not well have avoided seeing, work by the Pre-Raphaelites, but I have found no evidence that they were objects of

[1] Coll. Rt. Hon. Vincent Massey, P.C., C.H.

[2] 'Pre-Raphaelitism and the Pre-Raphaelite Brotherhood', by W. Holman Hunt, O.M., D.C.L. Two vols, 1905, Vol. I, p. 88.

his particular study, and it is no more possible to say whether Innes was affected by the deep evocative purple of Hunt and Hughes-'the colour of Amethysts, Pageantry, Royalty and Death'-and by the jewel-like colours of the Pre-Raphaelites than whether he was by the forthright, audacious colours of the Post-Impressionists. Some day, perhaps, the discovery of letters written by Innes, more informative than those at present known, will enable us to form a clearer notion of the external influences that contributed to the formation of his art.

Innes's most successful works were in water-colour, although he painted from the first in oil as well, but towards the end he came to prefer the heavier medium. Ill health and awareness of how little time was left to him brought a feverish quality to his work. The large *Arenig*,[1] of 1913, which at a distance seems to be a kind of summing up of Innes's achievement, on closer inspection reveals forms loose and unfelt, and colours, like the colours of a poster, designed to make an immediate impression rather than to give prolonged delight.

The work of his last years was marked by an innovation: the introduction into his landscape of figures. Interiors with figures had long been a subject of occasional interest to him, but of an interest conspicuously less intense than that inspired in him by landscape. As a consequence, however, of the ripening of his friendship with Augustus John-which began probably about 1910-with whom he spent much of the spring and summer of 1911 and 1912 in North Wales, during the latter year the presence of a female figure or two, of somewhat Johannine aspect, became a feature of his landscape. *Mountain Pool*,[2] of 1911, *Tan-y-Grisiau: The Green Dress*,[3] *The Van Pool*,[4] both of 1912, and the splendid *Mountain Lake*,[5] of 1913, all contain figures. When John introduces a figure into a landscape it is apt to become a focus of interest, but unlike his friend Innes was not a humanist, and his figures, as Mr. Fothergill observed, are blended with or growing out of his rocks and mountains. If Innes-who revered John-owed the presence of figures in his own landscape to his example he imparted his own vision of landscape to his friend.

---

[1] The Tate Gallery, London.   [2] Coll. The Hon. Lady Ridley.
[3] Coll. Major Peter Harris.   [4] Coll. Mr. Hugo Pitman.
[5] Coll. Mr. Hugo Pitman.

During the last two or three years of his life he was haunted by the knowledge of how near the end must be, and that, in consequence, he would have almost no time to realize in its fulness the vision of landscape which he must have known, modest as he was, to be both original and poetic, and that, moreover, his avid sense of experience must be largely unsatisfied. The twofold urge to create and to experience was sharpened by the stimulating nature of his illness, and because he spent his time among companions who, however devoted in other respects, had little care for his health, or none at all, his thirst for alcohol encountered no restraint. Unable to live and work in quiet he spent his evenings at the Café Royal, musichall and theatre, and his expedition on the way home from the Pyrenees to Marseilles for an assignation with so unusually robustly constituted a companion as Augustus John was bad for his health. John, who took him to the Hotel Bozio, at Ste. Chamas, on the Etang de Berre, seeing how ill he was, advised him, he tells us, to return to England, which he did.[1]

Innes's admirers could wish that John had given a fuller account of him in 'Chiaroscuro', but the few pages he devotes to his friend are excellent. He begins with a description of him:

> He himself cut an arresting figure, [it runs] a Quaker hat, a coloured silk scarf, and a long overcoat set off features of a slightly cadaverous cast, with glittering black eyes, a wide sardonic mouth, a prominent nose and a large bony forehead, invaded by streaks of thin black hair. He carried an ebony cane with a gold top, and spoke with a heavy English accent, which had been imposed on an agreeable Welsh sub stratum.[2]

This description is amplified by Schwabe:

> He was of middle height, black haired and thin featured, handsome to many people, though others must have regarded him differently, since, when I was away from London for a while, and lent him my rooms in Howley Place, my charwoman, on my return, assured me that he was, literally, 'the devil', and she was undoubtedly terrified of him.[3]

Mr. Fothergill calls his voice 'low and melodious', and himself 'affectionate and easily led as one who wanted help to get through life's effort'.

[1] 'Chiaroscuro, Fragments of Autobiography', First Series, 1952, p. 205.
[2] Ibid., p. 202.   [3] 'The Burlington Magazine', January 1943.

John proceeds to a revealing account of an expedition he made in the Spring of 1911 at Innes's invitation to the Arenig valley north of Bala.

> Our meeting at Arenig [John recollects] was cordial, yet I seemed to detect a certain reserve on his part: he was experiencing, I fancy, the scruples of a lover on introducing a friend to his best girl–in this case, the mountain before us, which he regarded, with good reason, as his spiritual property. . . . At this time [he continues] Innes' activity was prodigious; he rarely returned of an evening without a couple of panels completed. These were, it is true, rapidly done, but they usually meant long rambles over the moors in search of the magical moment. Perhaps he felt he must hasten while there was time to make these votive offerings to the mountains he loved with religious fervour.[1]

They left the inn, Rhyd-y-fen, and took a cottage, a few miles distant, by the brook called Nant-ddu, which looked out on Arenig. Here they returned the following year and yet again.

Innes's extreme susceptibility to beauty made him hardly less responsive to women than to mountains, though to no woman, I think, was he as constant as to Mount Arenig. Of his romantic attachments John has several stories to tell. He describes Innes's enchantment, in a bar at Corwen, with Udina, a lovely young gypsy of the rare tribe of Florence, and how next day he rose early to rejoin the Florences, and finding them gone followed on foot until, on the outskirts of Ruthin, he was discovered collapsed by the roadside. More characteristic still is the account he gives of Innes's relations with a singer known as 'Billy', a girl who 'had some beauty, much good nature, and an American accent contracted in Soho'. To her Innes became very much attached, though his feelings, in John's opinion, were more chivalrous than passionate.

> At this time [he relates] he had acquired a caravan from a gypsy, and this was resting in the yard of an inn in the remote village of Pen-machno. Burning with romantic zeal, he resolved to extricate Billy from a life in which the Café Royal played too great a part, and at last gained her consent to accompany him to North Wales, where they would take to the open road, and travel the world together in healing contact with Nature and the beneficent influences of his beloved mountains. They were approaching their destination: Dick, greatly moved, pointed through the carriage window, crying 'Billy, look, the mountains of Wales!' but Billy, immersed in 'Comic Cuts', was not

[1] Op. cit., p. 203.

to be disturbed. They reached Penmachno and spent several days at the inn. From time to time Dick would suggest a visit to the yard to inspect their future wheeled home, but Billy, refusing to budge, only called for another whisky and soda.

They soon returned to London and the Café Royal. Some years later, being at Penmachno, I saw Innes's van or what was left of it. It had never been moved: some fragments of its wheels still protruded from the ground.

But his last and deepest attachment was to Euphemia Lamb. They met in a Paris café, and Innes at once responded to the beauty of her pale oval face, classical in feature yet animated by a spirit passionate, reckless and witty, and the heavy honey-hued hair: a beauty preserved in many paintings and drawings by her artist friends, most notably, perhaps, in a tiny drawing in pen and ink[1] by John, but even now not extinct. Together Innes and Euphemia made their way, largely on foot, to his favourite resorts on the foothills of the Pyrenees, and back to London, he contributing to their support by making drawings in cafés and she by dancing. Their attachment lasted until his death. He used to write verse in her honour and design and make jewellery for her adornment.

Innes himself was alternately depressed and exhilarated, idle and industrious, and as soon as he emerged from a period of sterile melancholy he was prone to recklessness. One day when Horace Cole, noted as a friend of painters and the great practical joker of the age, was on his way abroad, he was accompanied to the Victoria Station by Innes and, according to Schwabe's published account, 'one or two intimates'.

In the taxi-cab [it proceeds] they bethought themselves of the rite of 'blood brotherhood', and at once put it into practice. They mingled their blood freely enough. Innes drove a knife right through his left hand. One of the others stabbed himself in the leg and was laid up for some time afterwards. Cole made a prudent incision, sufficient to satisfy the needs of the case. The driver was indignant when he saw the state of his cab and its occupants, but the rite had been performed and no lasting damage was done.

The 'one or two intimates' of the published account of the incident, and he who stabbed himself in the leg, according to Schwabe's verbal account earlier referred to, were the same person,

[1] Coll. Mrs. Edward Groves.

namely Augustus John, who was also the instigator of this revival of
the rite. An impulsive quixotism used to involve Innes in brawls.
A mutual friend told me that he once accompanied him to some
Parisian night-haunt, out of which he was thrown a few moments
afterwards and presently arrested, and that he had gone to the
magistrate and managed to secure his friend's release. Parted from
every franc with which they had set out, and ravaged by the night's
adventures, the two friends sat morosely together–feet to head–on
a divan in the friend's studio. 'Well, I shall simply lie here,' said
Innes, 'until funds arrive from London.'

During his last years 'his teeth suffered', wrote Schwabe, 'and I
doubt if he could masticate properly'. In Fitzroy Street, where he
lived for a time, he was so low that he seemed incapable of getting
out of bed in the morning without a stiff dose of brandy which a
friend would fetch from 'The Yorkshire Grey'. His paintings and
drawings, according to Schwabe's account, were neglected no less
than his health: he left them about in improbable places, and they
were bought only by a few friends and admirers.[1]

Even within hailing distance of death, at Mogador in North
Africa, where he had been taken by his friend Trelawney Dayrell
Reed in a last desperate attempt to arrest the progress of his malady,
Innes occupied himself in experimenting with various combinations
of tobacco.[2]

In 1914 he went to Brighton where he was nursed devotedly by
his mother. With Horace Cole John visited him there; the war had
broken out, and John recalls the general excitement over it, and the
indifference of Innes, who took no interest in anything except his
medicine. At last he was moved to a nursing-home at Swanley in
Kent. Here also the two friends went to see him in company this
time with Euphemia Lamb.

> The meeting of these two was painful, [wrote John] we left them alone
> together: it was the last time I saw him. Under the cairn on the summit
> of Arenig Dick Innes had buried a silver casket containing certain
> correspondence: I think he always associated Euphemia with this
> mountain, and would have liked at the last to lie beside the cairn.[3]

[1] 'The Burlington Magazine', January 1943.
[2] A Short Appreciation, by Augustus E. John, in the 'Catalogue of Watercolour
Drawings and Paintings', by the late James Dickson Innes, Memorial Exhibition,
The Chenil Galleries, April–June 1923.   [3] 'Chiaroscuro', pp. 205-6.

When he died on 22 August 1914 at the age of twenty-seven he was buried instead at Whitechurch, Tavistock, along, now, with both his parents.

Innes died too early to infuse his own poetic spirit into English painting. He had one disciple, the Australian-born and Slade trained painter Derwent Lees, whom he took with him to Collioure. Lees left at least one work of great beauty in the Innes tradition, *Pear Tree in Blossom*,[1] of 1913, but he was ambitious of quick success and to this end adapted himself to the styles of John and McEvoy as well as Innes, and before he could form a personal style his mind became deranged.

[1] The Tate Gallery, London.

L. S. LOWRY

b. 1887

IHAVE introduced the artists considered in these pages in the order of their birth, as I explained in the Preface to the first volume, so as to avoid groupings, which are more apt to obscure than to clarify. But had I decided to consider them instead as members of groups, and had associated Steer and Sickert as 'English Impressionists', say, and Lewis, Roberts and Wadsworth as 'Vorticists', there would be no group in which Lowry could appropriately be placed. He occupies, in most respects, a position as remote from any contemporary as Gwen John; in fact farther removed, for however personal her treatment of them there is nothing novel about her subjects, whereas his constitute a modest landmark in the history of the concept of the beautiful. Lowry's remoteness from his English contemporaries does not arise from any want of harmony with his surroundings. When Sickert wrote 'The artist is he who can take a flint and wring out attar of roses,' he had Spencer Gore in mind, but his words apply more forcibly to Lowry. One of the most persistent characteristics of the whole modern movement in painting, traceable as far back as Rembrandt's *Slaughtered Ox* and *Anatomy Lesson* and beyond, has been a continuous extension of those aspects of life deemed to constitute permissible subjects for art, of the conception of 'the beautiful' in short. Step by step the idea that beauty resided in the artist's vision asserted itself against the classical view that beauty was an attribute, sometimes a measurable attribute, of things themselves. The classical ideal, supported by the authority of Greek and Renaissance art, did not die. It remains, coherent and comprehensive, and it still retains a hold, obscurely recognized, over the hearts and minds of civilized men. It would be foolish to dismiss the possibility that a day may come when that appeal will once again be imperative, but for the present the tide still runs in the contrary direction, and artists are more preoccupied with the discovery of beauty in subjects hitherto regarded as ugly – with wringing attar of roses from flint – than in the representation of subjects

37. HENRY LAMB. *Portrait of Lytton Strachey* (1914).
Oil, 91½ × 70 in. The Tate Gallery, London.

38. J. D. INNES.
The Waterfall
(1910).
Water-colour.
10¼×14½ in.
The Tate Gallery,
London.

beautiful-in-themselves. Sickert's description applies to Lowry with peculiar aptitude because Lowry has not, like Gore, simply subscribed to the widely held view expressed by Sir Winston Churchill that 'once you begin to study it, all Nature is equally interesting and equally charged with beauty',[1] but with an audacity that should appeal to Sir Winston he has annexed to the kingdom of beauty what are probably the ugliest regions that have ever disfigured the surface of the earth, the industrial suburbs of Manchester and Salford. It was in the North of England that the Industrial Revolution began. As the dark satanic mills sprang up in dense clusters along the valleys of South Lancashire and South and West Yorkshire, the traditional life of the surrounding country underwent a rapid process of disintegration and whole populations were drawn into the industrial vortex. The problem of their housing was mostly left to the uncontrolled activities of the speculative builder. The kind of building that these circumstances brought into being in Manchester in the 1840's is thus described in a contemporary official report:

> An immense number of small houses . . . of the most superficial character . . . are erected with a rapidity that astonishes people unacquainted with their flimsy structure. They have certainly avoided the objectionable mode of forming underground dwellings but have . . . neither cellar nor foundation. The walls are only half a brick thick . . . and the whole of the materials are slight and unfit for the purpose. . . . They are built back to back; without ventilation or drainage; and, like a honeycomb, every particle of space is occupied.

In order to accommodate the rapidly growing population whole great areas of the industrial north were densely covered by rows of such houses, divided from one another by what a contemporary called 'that mass of filth that constitutes the street'.

As the nineteenth century drew towards its close successful efforts were made to ameliorate conditions in this densely packed mass of rotting rat-infested houses. Typhus and cholera are gone and the old houses replaced, and efficient drainage and innumerable other amenities have been introduced. Yet those areas which felt the first horrifying impact of industrialization bear to this day the seared imprint of it, and they will in all probability continue to bear it for generations. This imprint, which reveals itself in an architecture

[1] 'Painting as a Pastime', 1948.

bleak, meagre and disorderly, in an atmosphere sombre and grimy, in a humanity that serves the forges, the looms and the glowing furnaces of the great mills, this imprint is the subject of Lowry's art. His distillation of beauty from the shabbiest and meanest subjects that the world has to offer is in harmony with the spirit of his age, but his choice of the locality in which he performs this remarkable operation is an anachronism. The prevailing tendency towards centralization is faithfully reflected in the world of art. Most artists who regard themselves as 'avant-garde', no matter whether they belong to Salford or Sioux City, are affiliated (if only on a 'country-member' or even a correspondence-course basis) to the huge and brilliantly advertised School of Paris. This school has no accepted style. The principal requirement for membership is to-day little more than the ability to imitate the superficial elements in the style of one or other of its original masters–Picasso or Braque, Matisse or Gris. It is desirable that the imitation should be carried out, at any rate for a time, *in Paris itself*. Should this prove impossible, then it should be done in London or New York but *on no account* in Salford or Sioux City. Centralization is now so complete that even members of lesser, more traditional schools, no longer practise their art in the places where they happened to be born. As soon as they can afford to do so they take the journey to London (or Paris or New York) from which few of them ever return. When they have established their reputation they may safely and even profitably settle in some picturesque rural dependency of the capital.

So compelling are the attractions for artists of a few great cities and so pitifully meagre the patronage of provincial cities that it is in these few major centres that the fine arts to-day are exclusively produced, and for the most part, it need scarcely be added, in the closest conformity with the styles and sentiments that prevail there. Regional art–except as practised by those who, in these bitterly competitive days, have been unable to 'get away' and been compelled to stay disconsolately where they are–no longer exists in England, except in the person of Lowry. He was born in Manchester. He has never been to Paris, or anywhere abroad, comes only occasionally to London which, though he regards it with affection, leaves him, as an artist, entirely untouched. Let me place on record the basic facts of his quiet life.

Laurence Stephen Lowry was born at Old Trafford, Manchester, on 1 November 1887, the only child of Robert Stephen Lowry, an estate-agent and a native of the same city, and his wife Elizabeth, born Hobson. He attended the Victoria Park School, and at about the age of sixteen, not long before he left, he began to draw, and presently he realized that he had no wish to do anything else. Aware of his shyness and his love of home (and knowing nothing of the hardships of a painter's career) and sympathizing with his serious quiet pursuits, his parents raised no objections to his attending the Manchester School of Art. Here he had the good fortune to meet a painter named Adolphe Valette, who had come to Lancashire as a designer to a textile firm and who used to attend the School of Art, where he was eventually invited to take the life class. 'I can't over-estimate the effect on me at that time,' Lowry once said to me, 'of the coming into this drab city of Adolphe Valette, full of the French Impressionists, aware of everything that was going on in Paris. He had a freshness and a breadth of experience that exhilarated his students.' In 1909, three or four years after he began to attend the Manchester School of Art, Lowry's parents moved out and he with them (for so long as either of them lived he remained at home) to 117 Station Road, in Pendlebury, an industrial suburb. The move was to enable them to be near friends, but the friends died. They none of them liked the place, and planned to move away, but they never did, and Lowry continued to live in the house until 1948. Presently he transferred to the nearer though inferior art school at Salford. Speaking of the effect upon artists of the pictures they see in early life, he said to me: 'As a student I admired D. G. Rossetti and, after him, Madox Brown. The queer thing is, I've never wavered; they're my two favourite artists still.' 'Yet your admiration for neither of them is even faintly reflected in your work,' I said. 'No. I don't believe it shows; nor if you were to ask me, could I tell you why these two artists are constantly in my mind.'

I am unable to form a clear notion of what Lowry's work was like during his earliest years. Fragments come upon in his studio suggest that it was characterized by the scrupulous notation of low, rather muddy tones. It must, I think, have been the painting of a serious student, but lacking in purpose. In 1916 he had an experience – on the surface of it a characteristically commonplace experience – that

gave him, in the winking of an eyelid, a sense of vocation that has
never left him. After his parents' removal to Pendlebury, his dislike
for the place took the form of a half-conscious determination to
ignore it, and he ignored it for seven years. One day he missed a
train from Pendlebury, and as he left the station he saw the Acme
Spinning Company's mill. The huge black framework of rows of
yellow-lit windows stood up against the sad damp-charged afternoon sky. The mill was turning out and hundreds of little pinched,
black figures, heads bent down (as though to offer the smallest
surface to the whirling particles of sodden grit) were hurrying across
the asphalt square, along the mean streets with the inexplicable
derelict gaps in the rows of houses, past the telegraph poles, home-
wards to high tea or pubwards, away from the mill without a backward glance. Lowry watched this scene (which he had looked at
many times without seeing) with rapture: he experienced an earthly
equivalent of some transcendental revelation. Recalling the experience more than thirty years later he exclaimed to me with wonder,
'And to think that it had never occurred to me to do Manchester
subjects.'

Those moments of illumination at the station in 1916 formed him.
From that time he has made it the purpose of his life to represent the
grimmest regions of industrial Manchester and Salford with the
same clarity with which he was privileged to see the Acme Mill. It
is characteristic of his patient and laborious spirit that certainty about
his vocation did not lead him to leave the Salford Art School; there
he remained for a further ten years, assiduously drawing from the
antique and the life in order to fit himself the better to pursue it.
'I always enjoyed the antique: there's a nobility about it,' he said to
me, 'but the life: I never was so stirred by that.' This lack of interest
is reflected in his work. When he represents human figures as
distant marionettes he is able to endow them with a bleak but highly
expressive animation, as they loiter in the neighbourhood of a street
accident or at the door of a surgery or chapel or as they mill around
a playground, but when he represents them 'close-up', on account
of his want of interest in the living human body, as well as his uncertain grasp of form, he invariably fails. But his is also a radically
lonely spirit; as he once said, he feels cut off from normal human
communication.

During all these years at art schools he worked only at what seemed to him to be of value, equipping himself as a painter, but he never completed a set course. Immediately after his eyes had been opened to their esoteric yet touching beauties he began to make paintings of the industrial suburbs of Manchester. Although his dedication to these subjects has remained almost constant–indeed his occasional aberrations have served to emphasize his constancy–his way of treating his subject has changed. Writing about a Lowry exhibition in 1945 the art critic of 'The Times' expressed the opinion that in other circumstances the artist might have been 'a Wiganish kind of Corot'. This telling phrase precisely describes not his potentialities but what in fact he had already been. His early landscapes, instinct with a kind of gloomy lyricism, put one very much in mind of Corot. Lowry's colours are smoky instead of limpid or silvery like Corot's, but there is the same reticent candour, the extraordinarily precise perception of values, the refinement in colour, and something too of the same humility of spirit. In these early canvasses he shows one characteristic which has become very uncommon: a way of handling paint as though it were precious.

Contemporary painters are apt to be suspicious of 'quality' too deliberately sought and made an end of instead of accepted as a happy but almost accidental consequence of the successful pursuit of larger aims, in the same way as contemporary writers are of 'fine writing'. No painter was ever less 'precious' in his outlook than Lowry, freer from preoccupation with 'finish'; or with pigment for its own sake, with the 'cookery' of painting. He handles paint as though it were precious because respect–respect for the rights, the talents, the convictions, the privacy of his fellow men, for nature and for the objects of daily use–is a sentiment that deeply colours his outlook. No painter whom I have known has been more consciously aware of a sense of privilege, amounting almost to a sense of wonder, at being a painter, and any attitude but one of respect for his medium would be out of harmony with his thinking and his feeling.

During his years as a 'Wiganish Corot' he painted Manchester and Salford subjects very tenderly, showing, as already noted, an extraordinarily sensitive perception of values, and a power of exquisite modulation within a narrow range of colours and tones: a few drab greens, burnt sienna, umber, all seen as it were through a light screen of industrial smoke. His subjects were often taken from the less ugly aspects of these cities; he showed a preference for those areas where a few trees might belatedly put forth a little frost-bitten foliage, or a few blades of grass push hopefully upwards through the smooth-trodden black earth. Good examples of the 'Wiganish Corot' period are the *Salford Art Gallery*[1] and *Peel Park, Salford*,[2] both of 1924. But as the vision he had at Pendlebury eventually permeated every part of his being, the search for foliage and blades of grass seemed to him a little absurd. If he wanted to paint foliage and grass, he reflected, he could take a tram out to where they grew unstunted; if he wanted to paint Manchester and Salford why should he take for subjects what, of all things, was least characteristic of them? So he looked these two appalling places full in the face, and concerned himself more and more exclusively with their most characteristic features: the massive mills and the contrastingly flimsy dwellings of those who worked in the mills; the grim twilight areas of disorderly dereliction; the chapels, the pubs, the sweetshops, where they try to forget their work. It is significant that he rarely painted the most modern mills, and never, I think, the new housing estates, for his real subjects are the bleak pervasive vestiges of the Industrial Revolution. Lowry never represents what he has not seen, yet what he shows us is not a portrait of our own age of equality and planning, when the impact of relievable misfortune is pillowed by social security, when a drab uniformity is replacing squalid disorder. Squalid disorder is what he constantly depicts, and the poverty that accompanied the production of wealth on a scale incomparably greater than any previous age had known – a poverty measured not only in terms of wages but in terms of life itself. There were no splendid church services or civic spectacles – no symbolic marriage of the Mayor of Manchester to the Ship Canal; no civic games, no complex of beautiful public buildings such as ameliorated the harshness of life in earlier civilizations.

The traditional belief that emotions are best expressed by colour and ideas by line does roughly correspond to the truth. So long as he was impelled by a vague desire to represent the seemliest fragments of a hideous environment – a corner of a park, or the classical

[1] Whereabouts unknown.   [2] The City Art Gallery, Salford.

portico of a public building–Lowry could rely upon his delicate sense of colour and tone. But once he came to see Manchester and Salford as creations of *man*, huge complex industrial organisms, his subject became not scenes sought out because they were pleasant, but man in his environment. It was a subject that called, inevitably and imperatively, for the expression of ideas. For such a purpose even the most delicate perceptions of colour and tone are of little help. What he required was a more expressive and, above all, a more exact language of paint, and first and foremost the ability to draw.

When I began to meditate upon the work of Lowry with the view to writing these pages about him, I looked forward to doing justice to a man dedicated to a forbidding subject and personally lonely and obscure. To a man for whom I feel affection; to painting which I believe has a unique place in the art of its time. Such, however, are the difficulties of writing about living men that I find that, in the case of Lowry, doing justice involves initially a degree of depreciation. Singularly enough, in the course of the little that has been written or broadcast about him, he has been unwisely praised. Mr. Eric Newton, for example, has said of him, 'He is not an artist of the first rank; that is to say, he is not a Titian, a Rembrandt or a Velazquez ... but he is among the first of the artists of the second rank,' and he proceeded to link him with Constable and Brueghel.[1] On another occasion he wrote that 'Lowry's Pendleton [as Mr. Newton here and elsewhere calls Pendlebury] is as positive and convincing as Constable's East Bergholt.'[2] Such excessive praise is a consequence of a generous impulse, but I know of no standard of values according to which Lowry could be placed among the first in a class which would include Goya, Degas, Botticelli, Poussin, Dürer, Brueghel or Constable. Or of any according to which he would stand in relation to such masters otherwise than as a domestic cat to tigers. He has the misfortune to be born into an era of decline, when great traditions have been lost. It is, I think, oubtful whether there is a single painter now alive to whom we could assign without misgiving a foremost place in the second rank. It is possible to do justice to Lowry only if such indefensible claims are taken not as criticism but as gestures of encouragement.

[1] At opening of the artist's first Exhibition in Manchester, 25 October 1948.
[2] 'The Sunday Times', 18 February 1945.

In his search for a means of expression adequate to his enlarged and intensified vision of surrounding life Lowry made two discoveries: that his drawing and his composition were elementary. He was unable to make his forms solid or exact, and his arrangement of them were often marred, for example, by intrusive horizontals, sometimes along both foreground and horizon, that are not only clumsy but destructive of any illusion of space. His paintings often looked like back drops.

There was no second revelation: Lowry's highly personal style is the product of his unceasing struggle with two radical shortcomings. The full power of creating solid form he has never acquired, but he has so far overcome his inability to compose, except with the simplest forms, as to enable him in happy moments to represent even panoramic subjects spaciously and variously.

Art is a mysterious pursuit, without laws (except, perhaps, for a few bye-laws), and I cannot explain how it comes about that in the heat of his encounter with what ought to have been crippling disabilities Lowry is able to forge the means of giving the most convincing form to what he divined that afternoon at Pendlebury station. 'The essence of poetry with us in this age of stark and unlovely actualities,' wrote D. H. Lawrence in 1916 to a friend,[1] 'is a stark directness, without a shadow of a lie. Everything can go, but this stark, bare, rocky directness of statement, this alone makes poetry today.' I think there could be no better description of the fundamental virtue which makes the best of Lowry's work memorable. As memorable, in its way, as that of Utrillo, one of the very few of his contemporaries with whom he is at all closely comparable. The colour of Utrillo (in his earlier days) was far richer and more various than Lowry's ever was, his sense of form subtler, larger; but Lowry, with his narrower means, evokes the life of a city even more pungently and more completely, and with a richer humanity—a city, it must be remembered, almost formless, almost colourless, and so far more refractory than Paris as a painter's subject. The more abysmal the ugliness, it might be said, the greater the beauty that may be distilled from it. From time to time Lowry has been classed as a 'Sunday painter', a species of amateur that is to say. An amateur may achieve something in constantly depicted cities like Paris or London,

[1] Catherine Carswell.

39. L. S. Lowry.
The Football Match
(1949).
Oil, 28×36 in.
Coll. Mrs. H. D.
Walston.

40. PAUL NASH.
Meadow with Copse:
Tower Hamlets
District (1918).
Water-colour,
10 × 14 in.
Coll.
Mr. G. H. Nevill.

Venice or New York, but to transmute into art a huge featureless tract of industrial dereliction, and without the guidance of predecessors, is a feat beyond amateur powers.

On account of the stony directness of his statements about what Lawrence called 'stark and unlovely actualities', Lowry is sometimes regarded as a satirist moved by indignation or a social reformer moved by pity. In fact he is neither. 'People in Manchester,' he has said to me more than once, 'are as happy as people anywhere else.' He stands in a singular relationship to his subject; a relationship which he could not, I think, put into words, and which I confess I do not fully make out. I have never heard him express any particular opinion about Manchester or Salford. On one occasion we were speaking of an article which attributed to him pity and other sentiments towards his subjects. He turned towards me in emphatic protest: 'I don't feel anything. Anything at all. I simply paint. Of course,' he continued, 'I must have unconscious feeling.' With characteristic modesty he disclaims the intellectual power to analyse his feelings, much more to expound them. He is a man who feels and meditates but who forms few decided general ideas. He has reached, for instance, no conclusions about religion or politics, 'though I spend a lot of time,' he said, 'thinking about them'. 'Occasionally I like to see pictures,' he said in answer to some question of mine, 'but only occasionally.' But I have never known a painter quicker than Lowry to discern the good qualities in any pictures in which they are to be found. What he lacks in the way of intellectual penetration is made up by the most intense and affectionate observation of his subject. In a general sense his subject is the industrial area of South Lancashire, and by extension poor industrial regions anywhere, but it exists for him in its most compelling form in a particular, a strictly local sense, namely an area immediately adjacent to the Oldham Road, formed by Rockford Road, Apollo Street, Livesey Street, Mozart Square, Butler Street, Elizabeth Street, Woodward Street, Kemp Street (late Prussia Street) and Redhill Street (late Union Street) beside the canal. To this district he goes every day except Saturday and Sunday, and spends the middle hours walking the streets, making pencil notes on the backs of envelopes, occasionally a careful drawing, but mostly just observing. 'I don't know a soul in this district, but I love it more than any place I can imagine,' he said, 'especially this street' (it was along Union Street that we were walking at the time), 'and Woodward Street and the footbridge over the canal. And when the idea for a painting has come to me, I hurry home and put it down.' He usually spends few hours painting; a short time early in the morning, longer at night. Sometimes he works through the night 'without getting tired,' he said; 'at night I lay in my design and put down my colour in a general way, but I never work on detail or *finish* anything by artificial light.' His method is to paint straight on to a white canvas without an undersketch. Sometimes he improvises out of his vast detailed repertory of observations, 'without the slightest idea of what I'm going to do'. More often he works from drawings made in the street. Some of his paintings are transpositions, others faithful renderings. *Dwellings, Ordsall Lane, Salford,*[1] of 1927, for instance, was made from a fairly detailed chalk drawing.[2] How faithful a rendering the painting is I was able to see one midsummer afternoon in 1951 when I stood, with Lowry, lashed by rain from a slaty sky on the place where the drawing was made.

Usually Lowry is occupied with about twenty subjects at the same time. A big painting, worked on intermittently, takes him about eighteen months to complete. Only rarely does he paint directly from his subject. After the main lines of the composition have been drawn in black paint, he puts in the colour, mixed with a little medium, gradually building up to the required quality and pitch, always keeping on the light side.

Mr. Newton once said that 'Lancashire is to him what a crippled child is to a devoted mother. . . .'[3] This is a matter about which it would be unwise to be dogmatic, but so far from sharing Mr. Newton's opinion I believe that far from regarding his subject with pity Lowry is to an extraordinary degree dependent upon it. He is entirely aware of the ugliness of this region, but I have never heard him allude to it in terms of pity. (A few pages back I noted his insistence that Manchester people were as happy as people anywhere else.) His attitude appears to me to be one simply of fascination and love, that has grown year by year until it has him almost enslaved.

[1] The Tate Gallery, London.
[2] The Tate Gallery, London, presented by the artist.
[3] L. S. Lowry, a broadcast by Mr. Eric Newton, 14 November 1948.

Not only is he drawn into the Oldham Road district every day when there is a bus service from Mottram in Longendale, the nearby village where he has lived since 1948, but in times of despondency he is able to regain his tranquillity only by walking its streets.

> There's one street, [he told me] Juno Street, that I couldn't paint, as it has no distinctive feature at all. Yet in my studio my mind turns to it constantly. I don't know why, but I am grateful to that street that I shan't ever paint. In fact, it's not too much to say that in bad times it's this district that keeps me going.

For many years he has been aware of his singular dependence.

In the middle 'thirties Pendlebury, where he had spent almost all his working life, ceased to have any interest for him, but he found that the attraction of Oldham Road was undiminished. 'After a little time in the country or by the sea,' he said, 'I have to go back.' One of his attempts to break the spell of the Oldham Road added to the range of his art. In 1944 he went to Anglesey. 'I was bored almost to death. I couldn't work. I could hardly even look at anything. A month after I had got home I started to paint the sea that I'd seen, nothing but the sea. But a sea with no shore and no boat sailing on it–only the sea.' Just as he goes in times of depression to the Oldham Road, so in times of loneliness away from home he finds comfort in the poor quarters of any industrial town. 'I go round quite a bit, and I know the poor quarters of many English cities and of Glasgow, but it's only round the Oldham Road that I am entirely alive. I wish,' he said, looking round the sitting-room of 'The Elms', his little stone house in Stalybridge Road, Mottram, 'there was a week-end' bus service into Manchester. Mottram's a nice place, but I'm lost in the country.'

Lowry's sea-pieces–featureless stretches of smooth water–reveal as no other of his pictures the exceptional directness and intensity of his perceptions. The work of so many painters is marked by a false simplicity, a simplicity that results not from an authentic breadth of vision, nor from a tension between the desire to include and the necessity to exclude, but simply from emptiness of mind, from an unjustifiable esteem of simplicity as an end in itself. The sea-pieces of Lowry are models of simplification; not only ships and shores and clouds but even big waves are excluded so that the artist may press nearer to expressing the essential nature of the sea. With this subject he is troubled neither by his uncertain draughtsmanship nor his difficulty in composing: his exact perception of tone and colour is enough, and the little canvasses, half sky, half sea with neat lines of blackish ripples, exert a mesmeric effect.

In the Spring of 1951 I spent an afternoon visiting dealers' galleries with Mr. Graham Greene. In one of these we were shown paintings by Tintoretto, by Degas, and by other illustrious masters, but his attention remained upon a tiny canvas, divided almost exactly in two by a horizontal line, the upper half stained with a faint grey and the lower with a dusky green, an early seascape by Lowry which he bought and insisted on carrying promptly away.

In Manchester Lowry has a few close friends, and in the Salford Art Gallery he has found intelligent and loyal support, for in this institution is assembled the best collection of his work in public possession. Nevertheless he leads a lonely life, 'with fourteen clocks for company'. Departure from the neighbourhood would, however, be impossible, so dependent is he on the Oldham Road, and this not only for his subjects but as a point of contact with the world. This is the world, and the only one, in which he has roots. I have already commented that Lowry's is an essentially lonely spirit and intimated that this personal characteristic it may be which, more than a simple lack of interest in the living human body, accounts for his failure in the depiction of the figure. He feels himself unable to communicate in the normal ways with other human beings and confesses himself correspondingly unhappy; it may be that here is a clue to the explanation of the bleakness of the human elements in his pictures. The industrial north is indeed, or was, no less bleak and grim and chilling in all its non-human environment than it is in them. Among the people who live there, however, these qualities are conspicuously lacking; instead there is warmth and easy gregariousness and an abundance of community feeling. But in Lowry's work, as a writer in 'The Observer' has commented, there is a wistful and melancholic quality.

> His figures are often pathetic—not because they are poor or stunted or shabby but because they are lost souls, unable to communicate. The Lowry landscape, though it has a pale sad beauty of its own, is a lost landscape. . . . Places are transmuted in his mind and come out strange and far away.[1]   [1] 14 August 1955.

He has no other world; he could never leave it. In his earlier years, even had he had the wish, departure would have been difficult: outside the Manchester region he was unknown, and even within it, in spite of the encouragement of the 'Manchester Guardian', he remained little known until the early 'thirties when the circle of his admirers widened. It was not until 1939 when Mr. McNeill Reid, of Messrs. Reid and Lefevre, happened to see some pictures of his at a framer's, and was so impressed by their originality that he arranged an exhibition of Lowry's work, that his name came to be known outside his own locality. I well remember the impression that Lowry's pictures made on myself, for whom a six-year sojourn in a region that had much in common with his Salford had ended only the year before. Six years in the West Riding were long enough to get to know it and not long enough for the sharpness of the impression to blur. I stood in the gallery marvelling at the accuracy of the mirror that this to me unknown painter had held up to the bleakness, the obsolete shabbiness, the grimy fogboundness, the grimness of northern industrial England. It was as a connoisseur of all this that his pictures held me fascinated; only when the fascination of the subject had a little subsided were the beauties of these scenes as paintings borne in upon me. I chose for submission to the Tate Trustees the picture that summed up remorselessly yet with tenderness the industrial north I knew so well. This was *Dwellings, Ordsall Lane, Salford.*

The exhibition brought Lowry a modest national reputation that has grown steadily since. It is a reputation that is surely merited: out of the ceaseless struggle of this man with no more than moderate natural abilities to express, with 'the stark directness' of which Lawrence spoke, his vision of surrounding life, has come an art singularly dignified and, above all, singularly human.

PAUL NASH

1889—1946

BARELY ten years have passed since Paul Nash died, and his reputation has scarcely had time to assume its final form. Yet already touches are added, year by year, to a portrait of the artist which portrays him as more certain of his way, more sustained and logical in his growth, than the facts would seem to suggest. 'Nash's development as a painter remained singularly consistent throughout his life,'[1] wrote his friend E. H. Ramsden, and a little earlier in the same essay she alludes to him as a water-colourist 'who must be acknowledged to have been supreme'.[2] Of the sequence of four pictures which were his last works, she wrote that 'with the sublime melancholy of the first and the splendid exaltation of the second, the life of the painter moves to its triumphant close'. I think that the assured, rather Olympian genius of Ramsden's study, who belongs to the great tradition of English landscape painting and to whose style belongs the quality of grandeur, differs in important respects from Paul Nash as he was. He differs, at all events, both from the Paul Nash whom I knew, well but not intimately, for many years, and, as it seems to me, from the artist as experienced in his work. It is with some diffidence, however, that I will try to outline the lineaments of a figure which does not strikingly resemble the hero of Ramsden's and other studies, for his personality was more complicated, more allusive than the clear-cut memories suggest, and his taste was so subtle that it is not always easy to distinguish between the works which are the outcome of deep convictions and those which he has manufactured out of a tasteful blend of experience undergone in the shallows. If I seemed just now to suggest that Ramsden had invented a Paul Nash larger and more perfect than Paul Nash as he was, I did her an injustice. Her portrait was derived from another, namely the self-portrait which the artist had constantly

[1] 'Paul Nash, Paintings, Drawings and Illustrations', edited by Margot Eates with Essays by Herbert Read, John Rothenstein, E. H. Ramsden and Philip James, 1948, p. 30.　　　　　　　　　　　　　　　　[2] Ibid., p. 23.

in his mind–a portrait clear and complete down to the smallest detail–which it was his purpose to leave behind him. But may I say at once that this self-portrait was not conceived as a disguise? He was both too much of an artist and too much a man of integrity for that. The clue to his motives is contained in the following observation by Sir Herbert Read. After noting that his clothes, although not conventional, were always well cut, and his studio orderly as a chart-room, he concludes: 'He always dominated his environment. . . . His work was a part of his environment–not an unrelated activity relegated to some graceless workshop.' If this exceedingly just observation were understood to include not only the artist's immediate environment such as clothes, house furnishings and the like, but also his reputation, as artist and man, that is to say his situation–living or dead–in the minds of his fellow men, it brings us nearer to an understanding of Paul Nash's ambition. In her preface to the memorial volume already quoted from, the editor, Miss Margot Eates, explaining how it came into being wrote:

> When, therefore, the burden of increasing ill-health enforced on him considerable periods of inaction during the last two years of his life, he devoted himself in these times of unlooked for, and unwanted, leisure to the task of compiling from his photographic records a 'Picture Book' . . . which should provide a co-ordinated survey of his paintings and drawings.

According to my own understanding of Paul Nash he would as soon have considered leaving the world without leaving, as a lasting memorial, a Picture Book in which his best work would be assembled and arranged and presented with all his resources of taste and skill as a pharoah would have contemplated leaving it without his pyramid. He did in fact compile a list of the pictures which he wished included in any posthumous retrospective exhibition.

Paul Nash compiled his picture book not because he was ill but because he knew that he was going to die.

Paul Nash was born on 11 May 1889 at Ghuznee Lodge, now 2 Sunningdale Gardens, in the region of Earl's Court, London, the elder son of William Harry Nash, Recorder of Abingdon, and his wife Caroline Maud, daughter of Captain Milbourne Jackson, Royal Navy. His upbringing was strict. Their father permitted, for example,

Paul and his brother Jack–John Nash the painter and illustrator–to draw on Sundays, but, in order to mark the difference from other days, forbade them to paint. In later years the father deplored their working on that day, troubled by the thought that a picture made on the Sabbath might afterwards be sold. The three years, 1904–6, which Paul Nash spent at St. Paul's School, were years wasted. 'I was seventeen,' he has told us, 'when the long and complicated purgatory of my school life came to an end. I emerged from it impaired in body and spirit, more or less ignorant and equipped for nothing. My education,' he added, 'only began when I was at liberty to learn for myself.'[1] He put that liberty to good use. His purposeful and inquisitive mind not only made itself master of an unusually wide range of techniques useful to an artist but equipped itself to move easily in various intellectual spheres as well.

After he had failed to pass the Naval entrance examination and after his father had failed to enlist him in the respectable professions of architecture and banking, for which his inability to understand elementary mathematics disqualified him, he was allowed, and with his father's blessing, to try to earn his living as an illustrator. In order to undergo some elementary training he attended the evening classes at the London County Council technical school at Bolt Court in Fleet Street. It was thus, through prolonged misery and successive failures, that Paul Nash found his vocation–a vocation which had for some time had a vague attraction for him. There is symbolic significance, although probably no other, in that it was this same year, 1909, that on a visit to an uncle who lived near Wallingford he first saw those memorable twin grove-surmounted hills, the Wittenham Clumps, which later in his life were to become for him an image of compelling force. But even then they impressed. 'They were,' he said, 'the Pyramids of my small world.'

From the time when he was a child Paul Nash showed an acute responsiveness to what was strange, and began, as he has told us, 'to exaggerate forms and sounds. So many innocent things . . . began to have a sinister nature.'[2] Of this his unfinished memoirs and his conversation afforded many instances. There was a time, for instance, when he was frightened when the light was put out at night by the

---

[1] 'Outline, an autobiography and other writings', by Paul Nash, 1940, p. 72.
[2] Ibid., p. 44.

sound of far-off galloping overhead. One night he cried out to one of the maids and made her listen. Presently a distant drumming went softly thudding over their heads. 'It's the rats,' whispered the maid, 'they're hunting, have you heard their horn?' For a long time he was haunted by the sound, high, thin and faint, of the rats' horn, just as, years afterwards, he was haunted by the strange words and strange forms which induced the prolonged periods of agitation so fruitful for his art.

At the time when he may be said to have begun his life as an artist his mind was suffused not so much with the strange or sinister as with the romantic. It was, in particular, subject to the spell, which he came later to regard as disintegrating, of D. G. Rossetti. He read Tennyson and Morris, Keats, Whitman, Blake and Coleridge; and the discovery of each was a fresh, disturbing shock, but Rossetti-about whom he said he had read everything that had been written, and whose pictures and poems he knew almost without exception-remained his mind's presiding genius. He wished to become another Rossetti, whose example led him for a time to write verse. Such a work as *The Crier by Night*,[1] of 1912, and the figure with the pale rapt face of Beata Beatrix enfolded in mysterious shadows, is the work of a Rossetti-intoxicated youth. Slowly, however, Blake replaced Rossetti as the painter-poet. To Rossetti Paul Nash owed beyond question a strong imaginative impulse, but upon inanimate nature, the subject of almost all of Paul Nash's work, Rossetti had little light to show.

Of recent years the word 'literary' used in reference to the plastic arts has become an adjective so opprobrious that a writer must hesitate to use it about a painter unless he is prepared to face an outcry from the painter's friends. In the present inflamed state of opinion it would avail a writer nothing to plead the undoubted fact that many of the masters-Rembrandt and Delacroix to mention two conspicuously important examples-were literary painters. 'So you'd try to *justify* yourself, would you?' he would be likely to be asked, and his offence long held against him. But if the truth about Paul Nash is to be told, then there is no avoiding the currently opprobrious adjective, for he was, and to a marked degree, a painter whose vision was directed and stimulated by literary conceptions and even

[1] Coll. Mrs. Paul Nash.

by evocative phrases. It is my intention later in these pages to try to define more closely the nature of the literary incitements; for the present it is sufficient to state the fact of their positive existence.

Although he was born in London Paul Nash had his roots in the country, for the Nash family had long been established in Buckinghamshire. From about the age of twelve he lived mainly in his ancestral county, but it was not so much the country itself—responsive as he was to its beauties—that made him see it intensely as a subject for his art. This revelation he owed, characteristically, to a book. It was about 1909 or 1910 that he read 'Lavengro', and the effect of it was immediate and decisive. Paul Nash has described it in a passage of special insight and beauty.

To live in those little close rooms of Rossetti's, so charged with the intense atmosphere of romantic love, produced in me a tingling sensation in sympathy with his mood. I felt the anguish of those imprisoned lovers. . . . I, too, counted the heart-beats in the silence:

> . . . when in the dusk hours (we two alone)
> Close-kissed and eloquent of still replies . . .

But I began to realise that my fixed attention was wandering, that with the succession of Lancelot and Guinevere, Hamlet and Ophelia, Paolo and Francesca, a feeling of constriction was invading me and that my tingle was the exquisite but crippling sensation of pins and needles. Very slowly, as one must in that predicament, I began to stretch my cramped limbs and then, very softly, for I felt a renegade, I crept from the room. I might have spared my caution. No one and no thing noticed either my presence or its departure. The lovers stayed locked in their anguished embrace, the chained monkey continued to pick the rose to pieces, the boarhound of unsure anatomy still slept by the side of the lance and the shield. On the window-sill the dove lay dead. Outside the door I passed the frenzied eavesdropper among the shadows.

I emerged into open spaces. Led by the voice of Lavengro I followed on to the heath.[1]

And on the heath he remained, representing it by day and by night, in winter and summer, tenderly cultivated and hideously scarred, concerned sometimes with its surface, at others with some presiding spirit, ever responsive to change in mood and season. There were several reasons why 'Lavengro' should have held a fascination so strong for him as to draw him away from all his earlier

[1] Op. cit., pp. 78-9.

preoccupations out on to the heath, but it is reasonable to suppose that the strongest was the intimations the book has of an English countryside before it had been tamed: a countryside about which there was something intractable, wild, mysterious. The book inspired at least one illustration, a drawing *Lavengro and Isopal in the Dingle*,[1] of 1912, a drawing so deeply felt that the poetry of the effect far transcends the ineptness of the means apparently used to produce it. In the process of leading Paul Nash out on the heath 'Lavengro' had an improbable ally in the shape of Sir William Richmond. When he showed one of his drawings partly imagined and partly observed, this elderly academician suddenly exclaimed, 'My boy, you should go in for Nature.'

Like those of most artists the earliest drawings of Paul Nash are essays in the manner of others, but at Bolt Court he began to see things in his own way, and to exercise his imagination. He made among many others a series of drawings showing a wide prospect of undulating fields backed by a long low range of wooded hills, above which was suspended a huge girl's face with hair streaming out like wings on either side. How one of these drawings had far-reaching effects Paul Nash has himself related. One evening . . . 'there seemed to be an air of excitement among the students. But before I had time to investigate, the door opened and a remarkable-looking small figure entered abruptly. . . . The expression of (his) head was one of acute intelligence and the carriage almost imperious, as of a person accustomed to command . . . from the moment that wide judicial mouth opened a stream of easy, persuasive and ingenious talk flowed out, full of shrewdness and wit . . . the unerring gaze swept the room. . . .'[2] The imperious figure was my father: the result of his visit, the award of the maximum marks to Paul Nash's drawing. Some months later he brought a sheaf of his drawings to my father. After a little consideration he gave his opinion. 'You should go to the Slade,' he pronounced, 'and learn to draw.' The suggestion was accepted as a sound one but Paul Nash pointed out that he could not expect his father to find the fees. 'Well, then, why not make them for yourself?' replied Rothenstein without hesitation. My father had high expectations for the future of this beginner–truly self-described as 'without *apparent* natural talent . . .'–and a friendship

[1] Coll. Sir Gerald Kelly.   [2] Op. cit., pp. 32, 83.

grew up between them that was to last until my father's death. It was Paul Nash's habit to turn to him often for help and advice. To Selwyn Image, a late survivor of the Pre-Raphaelite movement, afterwards Slade Professor of Fine Art at Oxford, and to the benevolent poet Gordon Bottomley,[1] he also owed much for their encouragement in those tentative days.

Assiduity and luck enabled him to enter the Slade in 1910. This school, by the way, described by so many as the very fountain of bohemian life, the home of liberty, conviviality and eccentricity, 'differed very little', according to Paul Nash, 'from St. Paul's at its chilliest'.[2] (He himself contributed to its formality by appearing in contrast to the prevailing sartorial bohemianism with close-clipped hair, dark suit, stiff collar and bowler hat.) During the time he spent there the Slade was in one of its periodic spates of talent, and Stanley Spencer, Mark Gertler, William Roberts, Edward Wadsworth and C. R. W. Nevinson were all fellow-students. His first encounter with Tonks he has thus admirably described. 'With hooded stare and sardonic mouth, he hung in the air above me, like a tall question mark, backwards and bent over from the neck, a question mark, moreover, of a derisive, rather than an inquisitive order. In cold discouraging tones he welcomed me to the Slade. It was evident he considered that neither the Slade, nor I, was likely to derive much benefit.'[3]

If in spirit he had followed Lavengro on to the heath, his body was not able to leave the 'close rooms of Rossetti's, so charged with the intense atmosphere of romantic love', in an instant. At the Slade he certainly became more and more preoccupied with nature, yet he continued for some time to lack the means to represent landscape. *Spring at the Hawk's Wood*,[4] of 1911, fairly gives the measure of his incompetence at rendering natural appearance. *The Bird Garden*[5] of the same year, although it shows hardly more grasp of form, does give a hint of the special poetry that later on was to animate drawing after drawing.

In spite of his apparent want of talent and the downright silliness

---

[1] The letters which passed between them were published as 'Poet and Painter', being the correspondence between Gordon Bottomley and Paul Nash (1910–48), edited by Claude Colleer Abbott and Anthony Bertram, 1955.
[2] Op. cit., p. 90.   [3] Ibid., p. 89.
[4] Coll. Miss Barbara Nash.   [5] Coll. Mr. C. St. J. G. Miller.

of some of his drawings–*Pyramids in the Sea*,[1] of 1912, for instance, which he considered good enough for reproduction in 'Outline'–the note of strange beauty that, usually in vain, he attempted to utter could occasionally be heard. And when heard it impressed and lingered in the memory. Within a year of leaving the Slade he held his first exhibition at the well known but now long defunct Carfax Gallery in Ryder Street. Although the purchases had mostly been made by friends it was a modest success. Of the purchase by my father Paul Nash has given a touching account which concludes, For me at that point in my career it seemed, as if by magic, to change the aspect of my first real venture from something accorded a hesitating acceptance into a distinguished triumph and one that had been recognised by the highest award.'[2] The main acquisition, *Falling Stars*, of 1911, which duly took its place on our walls, was the first work by Paul Nash that I had seen. What is more important is that, unless I am mistaken, this beautiful drawing is the first in which the artist's extraordinary responsiveness to the peculiar character and drama of trees is fully realized. These two trees are, moreover, enfolded by darkness, with which, in his early years he was deeply preoccupied.

In the summer of the year following his exhibition, when he spent a day at my parents' house in Gloucestershire, I made the acquaintance of the artist himself. Most clearly I remember his cold very blue eyes, which on first meeting seemed unfriendly–but after a few minutes his good will was evident. They were exceptional eyes: their blueness, the steadiness of their gaze, and the habitual closeness of the pupils to the upper lid gave them the far-ranging look of the eyes of sailors. His hair was so dense and wavy as almost to resemble some exotic piece of headgear. He was extremely neatly dressed. At that time there was no particular contact between us. If he had been a sailor–so far as we children were concerned–he would have had a better claim to our attention, but he was simply one more young artist, bringing his drawings to be looked at, examining the pictures on the walls, seeking advice. Besides it was evident that he was uninterested in children, and entirely intent upon fulfilling the purpose of his visit. Later on when I came to know him it became apparent to me why in the course of this visit and one or two others

[1] Coll. Mrs. Gerald Grimsdale.   [2] Op. cit., p. 128.

I vaguely recall the relations between him and us remained so tenuous. Driven by their passionate absorption in their work artists are more than commonly industrious. Intense application with some is followed by periods of idleness, dissipation or recreation; others. merely vary their work. Corot delighted in fishing for its own sake, but when Delacroix listened to an opera or a play he deliberately subjected his imagination to the stimulus that charm afforded. Paul Nash was one of those who was constantly occupied with his work. It was not that he drew or painted for more hours at a stretch than others, but he was interested in every possible aspect of his work, and when he was not drawing or painting he would photograph some subject likely to be of use in a composition, he would study some object he had found—a twisted piece of wood, a stone worn into a fantastic shape, the skeleton of a leaf—which might serve a similar purpose; he would project albums of his works, plan for exhibitions or reproductions, or again he would plan the formation or the actions of groups of fellow-artists. The most celebrated example was Unit I, an ephemeral, ideologically bound group of painters, sculptors and architects, including Wadsworth and Burra, of which he was the driving-power and whose manifesto he wrote.[1] With such activities and many others of a like kind he was endlessly occupied. With him the living of life and the pursuit of his profession were inseparably fused. His life as an artist had style: 'He carried over, with his actual career,' as Sir Herbert Read aptly observed, 'some of the swagger of the rejected career—art, for him, was to be the Senior Service.' At the time of Paul Nash's first visit to my parents' house none of us children could have had any relevance at all. Some of those who read these pages may think that if my account of him is correct he was an ambitious man. Ambitious he undoubtedly was, but before they condemn him on that account they should reflect upon how harshly life bears upon painters and what a difficult business even the most gifted—portrait painters apart —find it, at times, even to survive.

During the few years bounded by his departure from the Slade and his involvement in the First World War the work of Paul Nash assumed a distinct character, almost as dissimilar from that which preceded it as from that which followed. Which of the traditional

[1] Cp. 'Unit I', edited by Herbert Read, London 1934.

English painters in water-colour pointed the way is uncertain, but during those years his work assumed a traditional character. He was too personal an artist to imitate an old master but what he did was to assimilate something of the spirit of Girtin, Cotman and others, and to evolve a free contemporary version of traditional idioms. He seemed destined to follow closely, with intelligence and taste, a conventional course. English Landscape, his chosen subject, he represented in its most park-like aspect: green lawns, formal hedgerows and farms and the elegant intricacies of lofty elm trees were features which he dwelt on with a peculiar tenderness and comprehension. In the best of these clearly drawn, firmly if lightly constructed, brightly but coolly coloured water-colours he struck an original note. In the less happy are to be readily detected the facile rhythms of 'art nouveau', which produced so widespread an effusion of billowy clouds, waves and vegetation, and highly coloured bubble-like formations of undefined matter. It is odd that a man of taste ordinarily so discerning should have chosen one such work *Landscape at Wood Lane*,[1] of 1914, for inclusion in his autobiography.

During the same years his life opened out in a number of directions: his reputation steadily grew: he became engaged to be married, and he made many new friends. The outbreak of the First World War brought this epoch of his life and art to an abrupt end. He enlisted as a private in the Artists' Rifles in August 1914 and was detailed for service at home. In the winter of that year he married Margaret, daughter of the Rev. N. Odeh. In 1916 he was gazetted 2nd Lieutenant in the 3rd Hampshire Regiment, and in February of the following year he went abroad and was stationed in the Ypres Salient. What he experienced in that place of desolation made him an artist as decisively as the scenes of his boyhood by the River Stour made Constable an artist. When he entered the Ypres Salient he seemed to be an artist of modest range, who had largely outlived a somewhat boyish romanticism, which expressed itself in nocturne, with pyramids, palm trees, shadows of unseen figures, falling stars and the like, and had become a painter of park-like landscapes, to the essentially conventional character of which he gave a poetic and stylish turn. When we look back at the artist of those days with the knowledge we have of his later work, this originality and stylishness

[1] The City Art Gallery, Manchester (Rutherston Coll.).

are more conspicuous than they were to his contemporaries, but they were sorely inadequate to ensure the most fleeting survival of his reputation. There can be little doubt that had he been destined to take his place among the unnumbered thousands who died in the Ypres Salient he would have been unremembered, but surviving the bitter desolation of the place immeasurably deepened his perceptions.

Certain friends of his have from time to time expressed surprise that an artist who had been so consistently drawn to dwell upon landscape in its most cultivated and most benign aspects should have responded to such purpose to the Western Front. It was precisely this preoccupation that so well prepared him for the fruitful contemplation of that overwhelmingly, perhaps even uniquely, terrible spectacle. For an artist brought up in such a time as the present, familiar with bomb-scarred cities and multitudes of refugees 'bombed out', or also, dispossessed of home and property, wandering without hope along the unfriendly highroads of the world, the Western Front would be no more than an impressive reminder of the evil in man. The impact upon the imagination of a Paul Nash of this vast desolation of tortured country, churned to mud, pitted with shell-craters, the grass scorched and trampled, was of the utmost violence. An artist accustomed to handle nature more arbitrarily, or familiar with her harsher aspects, might have taken the spectacle less hardly, but he, who had treated her with such tender respect, was pierced by a sense of outrage. The man who loved the intricate tracery of elms had now to contemplate the shattered stumps of trees without names.

From the first, therefore, almost inevitably the idea took root in his mind that here was a subject that must be drawn and painted, and in particular by him, but it would seem that it was in the course of a conversation with my father that he first envisaged it as within the bounds of the possible.

I have just got home [he wrote to him on 20 May 1916] and sit down at once to write to you . . . my wife . . . upbraided me for not jumping at your idea of drawing in France. I *did* jump inwardly. . . . Will you let me know if you have a definite scheme. . . . The idea has dwelt so long in my mind and always seemed so impossible that a hint of its realization excited me tremendously. Please write to me for I am really roused.

41. PAUL NASH.
Winter Sea
(1925-37).
Oil, 29 × 38 in.
Coll.
Mrs. Charles Grey.

42. PAUL NASH.
*Landscape of the
Megaliths* (1937).
Water-colour.
19¾ × 29¼ in.
The Albright Gallery,
Buffalo, U.S.A.

Soon after he went to the Western Front he began systematically to charge his memory and, in snatched moments, to make studies.

In April 1917 he went into the front line. After three months in France and only a few weeks at the Front he had 'the curious fortune', he reported in a letter to my father, 'to fall suddenly down a narrow trench and break my twelfth rib. . . . I brought back some twenty drawings from France . . . and . . . have arranged . . . to have a show. . . .'[1] The impression made by this handful of drawings upon such persons as John Buchan, Edward Marsh, Campbell Dodgson, C. F. Masterman and my father, as well as Paul Nash's own unceasing and adroitly conducted campaign in support of his ambition, resulted in November in his being sent back to France as an Official Artist. At the Front again, and this time free from military duties, Paul Nash applied the whole of his time to his work as painter and draughtsman. The Official Artists held their appointments for strictly limited periods, but during those few weeks in the autumn of 1917, densely packed with experience, he worked with extraordinary industry, making the very utmost of the facilities placed miraculously but transiently at his disposition.

> Yesterday I made twelve drawings, [he wrote to his wife on 13 November] nine of different aspects of one of the most famous battle-fields in the war. I just missed the battle. . . .[2] I start off directly after breakfast and do not get home until dinner-time and after that I work on my drawings until about eleven o'clock at night when I feel very sleepy and go to bed.[3]

Yet such in these times was his exaltation of spirit that he had the superabundant energy to write letters to his wife which are at points nothing less than verbal equivalents of his drawings. The following passage from the letter just quoted constitutes perhaps the most expressive of these verbal equivalents, and a statement, too, of what he conceived to be the current purpose of his work.

> I have just returned, last night, from a visit to Brigade Headquarters up the line, and I shall not forget it as long as I live. I have seen the most frightful nightmare of a country more conceived by Dante or Poe than by nature, unspeakable, utterly indescribable. In the fifteen drawings I have made I may give you some vague idea of its horror. . . . Sunset and sunrise are blasphemous, they are mockeries to man, only the black

[1] The exhibition, 'The Ypres Salient', was held at the Goupil Gallery in July.
[2] Passchendaele.   [3] 'Paul Nash: Paintings, Drawings and Illustrations', p. 18.

rain out of the bruised and swollen clouds all through the bitter black of night is a fit atmosphere in such a land. The rain drives on, the stinking mud becomes more evilly yellow, the shell holes fill up with green-white water, the roads and tracks are covered in inches of slime, the black dying trees ooze and sweat and the guns never cease. They alone plunge overhead tearing away the rotting tree stumps, breaking the plank roads, striking down horses and mules, annihilating, maiming, maddening they plunge into the grave which is the land; one huge grave and cast upon it the poor dead. It is unspeakable, godless, hopeless. I am no longer an artist interested and curious. I am a messenger who will bring back word from the men who are fighting to those who want the war to go on for ever. Feeble, inarticulate will be my message, but it will have a bitter truth and may it burn their lousy souls.[1]

The time which Paul Nash spent at the Front, as soldier and as Official Artist, amounted in all to little more than two months, but during that brief spell he experienced life more deeply, more intensely than most men during the full term of their allotted span.

When he first went to France what most touched him was the incongruity between the hell of blasted and poisoned earth and manifestations of an ultimately unconquerable nature:

> ... in a wood passed on our way up, [he wrote to his wife] a place with an evil name, pitted and pocked with shells, the trees torn to shreds, often reeking with poison gas–a most desolate and ruinous place two months back, today was a vivid green, the most broken trees even had sprouted somewhere and, in the midst, from the depth of the wood's bruised heart poured out the throbbing song of a nightingale.[2]

But it was the hellish aspect of things that quickly filled his mind: he became ecstatically absorbed in its sinister beauty.

The contemplation of it excited in him–as in thousands of other soldiers–an insistent preoccupation with the moral issues involved. He never arrived at a consistent attitude towards the war. At certain moments he was sickened by its wastage and corruption, and the moral obliquity that made it possible; at others he was exalted by its terrible splendour.

In May 1918 the work he had completed as a War Artist was shown at the Leicester Galleries, under the title 'Void of War'. The impact of the new works was sharper and wider than that of those shown at the Goupil the year before; it was generally recognized that a new figure was now to be numbered among the foremost

[1] 'Paul Nash: Paintings, Drawings and Illustrations', p. 18.   [2] Ibid., p. 15.

English artists. The workmanlike preface which Arnold Bennett contributed to the catalogue fairly reflected the impression the drawings made.

> The interpretative value is, to my mind, immense, [he wrote] Lieutenant Nash has seen the Front simply and largely. He has found the essentials of it—that is to say disfigurement, danger, desolation, ruin, chaos—and little figures of men creeping devotedly and tragically over the waste. . . . Their supreme achievement is that in their sombre and dreadful savagery they are beautiful.

When Paul Nash, led by the voice of Lavengro, had left the little close rooms of Pre-Raphaelite romanticism and emerged on to the heath he was impelled, first and foremost, by his need to find a style. A style serviceable, evocative and personal, was what he was looking for, rather than the exceedingly genteel prettinesses of the heath on which he found himself. There can be no question of the genuineness of his response to the beauties of landscape. They richly nourished his imagination, but they were more important to him in that they provided the materials out of which he hoped to evolve a style, and when he arrived in France he had evolved a somewhat tentative one that promised to become an instrument well fitted to the representation of the park-like and garden-like aspects of landscape which all but monopolized his attention. The spectacle of the theatre of war transformed almost instantly his whole conception of style. He was in the presence of something so vast, of such sombre magnificence, that the idea of using it as the material for a style seemed to him a puny blasphemy. Accordingly, in excitement and exultation, he gave himself up to the humble representation of the awful spectacle about him. He was scarcely conscious of the problems of style, but his former preoccupation with them enabled him to select, as it were instinctively, from the vast chaos extending on every side, precisely those elements that enabled him to make drawings which embody the very essence of it, and which live so vividly in the memory. I know of no works of art made by any artist working there who saw the splendours and miseries of the greatest of all theatres of war so grandly. Out of infinite horror he distilled a new poetry. The best of these war studies, in pastel, water-colour, ink and chalk or in a combination of them, *Canadian War Memorial, Vimy,*[1] of 1918,

[1] The National Gallery of Canada, Ottawa.

Spring in the Trenches, Ridge Wood,[1] of 1917; *Sunrise, Inverness Copse,*[2] of 1918; *Dawn, Sanctuary Wood,*[3] of 1918; *Meadow with Copse: Tower Hamlets District,*[4] of 1918 (Plate 40); *Nightfall, Zillebecke District,*[5] of 1918; *Ruined Country, Old Battlefield, Vimy,*[6] of 1918, and *The Menin Road,*[7] of 1918, the large painting in which he elaborated in tranquillity themes stored up in his memory or else summarily noted down–these will take their place among the finest imaginative works of our time.

In a letter which he wrote from the Front line there occur the words 'I have seen things . . . that would last me my lifetime as food for paintings and drawings.' Certain of the images that formed in his mind in the course of his ecstatic contemplation of these desolate, unearthly landscapes, long outlasting his preoccupation with them, became permanent features of his vision.

'The headless trees white and withered, without any leaves, done, dead,' which he had noted in Flanders, transformed by time and the imagination, became the megaliths, the tree-trunk monsters, fossils, fungi and other features of the still and timeless country of his later imaginings.

Chapter VII of the synopsis that he left of his uncompleted autobiography begins with the words 'struggles of a war artist without a war'. These words mark no more, perhaps, than his intention to enlarge upon the difficulties attendant upon changing from an officially sponsored artist to a demobilized artist left suddenly at large in a strange unsettled world. It is possible to read in them a deeper meaning. The change from war to peace production offered no serious difficulties to a man so resourceful and so determined to succeed and so newly crowned with laurels. He turned his hand to new kinds of work: wood engraving, textile designing, writing; he executed designs for Barrie's 'Truth about the Russian Dancers'. These activities and many others were interrupted, in 1921, by a serious illness. To recuperate he settled at Dymchurch in Dorset. The allusion to struggles of a war artist without a war seems to me to have reference not so much to the immediate problem of finding

---

[1] The Imperial War Museum, London.   [2] The Imperial War Museum, London.
[3] The Grundy Art Gallery, Blackpool.   [4] Coll. Mr. G. H. Nevill.
[5] The Imperial War Museum, London.   [6] The Imperial War Museum, London.
[7] The Imperial War Museum, London.

employment as to the way in which his vision, deepened and intensified by an overwhelming experience, could be realized without the magnificent subjects which had formed it. To express his response to the Western Front he had forged an instrument too powerful, too stark for the depiction of elegant elm trees, neatly fenced fields and other features of the well ordered and smiling landscape that had earlier engrossed him. Was he to allow it insensibly to shrink, to relax? If not, upon what subjects should he direct it without incongruity? To the first question, for an artist so tenaciously aspiring, there could be only one answer; to the second I do not believe he ever discovered an answer that gave him lasting satisfaction. That is why, near the beginning of this study, I called in question E. H. Ramsden's claim that his 'development as a painter remained singularly consistent throughout his life'. To me his development seems on the contrary to have been rendered erratic and fitful by a lifelong search for the inspired harmony between form and subject that marked the best of his war pictures. The search was full of difficulty, and only from time to time was it successful. On the Western Front a subject was presented to him which his gifts ideally fitted him to interpret, but later he was preoccupied with the realization that in these favoured circumstances he had made works of art which bore perhaps marks of greatness, and it was therefore with anxiety as well as delight that he was driven constantly forward in search of some new illumination. The problem did not present itself abruptly, because the principal subject of his attention— the Kent coast about Dymchurch—although without the spectacular character of the Western Front, was a dramatic theme and one susceptible of fruitful treatment by similar methods and in a similar spirit. The water-colours he made of that nobly curving coast are to be regarded rather as the completion of an earlier phase than the beginning of a new. They are less intense in feeling, but the conditions in which they were made allowed him a wider choice of viewpoint and longer time for contemplation. In that the element of consciously imposed design is more strongly marked than in anything he had done hitherto they give an indication of the general direction he was to follow. A whole series of water-colours came into being as a consequence of his visit to this stretch of coast, designs calculated with exquisite precision to express the rhythmic sweep of the shore, the infinite spaciousness of sea and sky. Such a work as *Dymchurch Strand*,[1] of 1922, shows a power of comprehending an immense area of landscape with the unstrained certainty of Girtin. And it does not stand alone: *Dymchurch Wall*,[2] of 1923, and the more abstract *Coast Scene*,[3] of 1921, and *Winter Sea*,[4] of 1925-37 (Plate 41), are surely among the finest designs of their time. How enduring the images formed in his mind during the fruitful years of preoccupation with the coast of Dymchurch can be appreciated by comparing *Winter Sea* with *Totes Meer*,[5] another oil painting made in circumstances entirely different and fifteen years after the earlier painting was begun. The cold tones, the folded and undulating forms, the informing spirit are to an extraordinary degree the same.

The bracing and elevating effect of the shore near Dymchurch in helping him to solve, for a time, the problem of how a war artist could adapt himself to peacetime themes became apparent when he left Kent. He paid a two- or three-week visit to Paris–his first–in 1922, spent the winter of 1924-5 at Cros de Cagnes, near Nice, visited Florence and Siena, and, in 1925, settled at Iden near Rye. The consequence of these various moves was that his work lost something both of purposefulness and momentum. I would be reluctant to dogmatize about this early visit to Paris, but it is my belief that direct contacts with contemporary French art confused him. The great international movements in the arts–Fauvism, Cubism and the others–as they radiated outwards from Paris were all-pervasive, affecting some artists without their being aware of it and others who were fully aware. Paul Nash, it needs scarcely be said, was always aware of the movements which played upon his consciousness. For him, however, there was a difference between taking Parisian modes of seeing as it were out of the air, and being in immediate contact with Parisian art and artists. In the one case he was simply drawing upon what had become a common heritage; in the other he was subjecting himself to a distracting influence.

The work he did on the Western Front and at Dymchurch owed much that is most precious in it to the Cubist sentiment that strongly

---

[1] The City Art Gallery, Manchester (Rutherston Coll.).
[2] Coll. Major D. Fairfax Harvey, M.C.   [3] Coll. the Hon. Mrs. St. Leger.
[4] Coll. Mrs. Charles Grey.   [5] The Tate Gallery, London.

affected a whole generation of artists everywhere, but visits to
France, contacts with French artists, even visits to exhibitions of
contemporary French painting, were apt to agitate him to the disadvantage of his work. The agitation was a subtle one and is not
easy to convey. It was as though, confronted with French painters
and their works, he felt the presence of a tradition which both drew
and repelled him. He was drawn to it as the tradition which was
central and in comparison with which all others were in varying
degree 'local', and as a tradition which fostered audacity and sparkle
and was as remote as possible from what he used to call 'the cold
middle-class Sunday lunch' character that summed up all that most
repelled him in the tradition of his own country. As a man and artist
deeply fastidious it seemed natural to belong to 'the best' tradition,
but he had seriously meditated inhibitions. Even when most tempted,
he was conscious of the depth of his English roots, of the nourishment he had drawn from the English water-colourists, the English
poets, from Rossetti and Borrow and Blake, and from the sights and
sounds of the English countryside. And he was, to judge from odd
remarks I heard him make, afraid that all this delicate and complex
English inheritance might be ironed out flat in the abstraction that
so predominantly formed the character of the Parisian tradition. He
used to say that he was 'for, but not with' the advocates of a wholly
abstract art, and he once precisely staked the limits of his own
participation in an art of this kind.

> The hard cold stone, the rasping grass, the intricate architecture of trees
> and waves [he wrote] I cannot translate altogether beyond their own
> image, without suffering in spirit. My aim in symbolical representation
> *and* abstraction, although governed by a purpose with a formal end in
> view, seeks always to give life to a conception within the formal shell.[1]

It was during the late 'twenties and the early 'thirties that he was
most sensitive to the attractions of the abstract—an attraction that
was heightened by the exhaustion of his purely visual response to
nature. This exhaustion is conspicuous in such naturalistic works as
French Farm,[2] of 1926, *Balcony, Cros de Cagnes*,[3] *Cros de Cagnes*,[4] and
Mimosa Wood,[5] all three of 1927. He needed to rely more and more

---

[1] From an article published in 'Axis', January 1935.   [2] Coll. Miss Winifred Felce.
[3] Coll. Miss Winifred Felce.   [4] The Italian Ministry of Education.
[5] The National Gallery of New South Wales, Sydney.

upon a formal structure, and his most successful works were those in which a clear-cut geometric design was elicited from or imposed upon his subjects, works of which *Chestnut Waters*,[1] of 1924-38, and *Pond in the Fields*,[2] of 1927, are characteristic examples. Presently the geometric design came first to dominate and eventually to constitute the picture. This development may be charted by comparing *Landscape at Iden*,[3] of 1928, *Kinetic Feature*,[4] of 1931, and *Poised Objects*,[5] of 1933. My own reading of his predicament during these years is that his vision had grown languid: bored with nature and uninventive in the field of pure abstraction, he was without compelling purpose, and it is my belief that a sentence come upon in a book would stir his imagination and momentarily restore the purpose he lacked. To-day few epithets would be likely to be regarded as more derogatory than 'literary', but it is necessary to say that Paul Nash was, in the most intimate sense, a literary painter. He was haunted by fragments of prose and poetry until, as he used to say, they 'grew enormous' for him. In 1930, for instance, he began his illustrations to Sir Thomas Browne's 'Urne Buriall' and 'The Garden of Cyrus',[6] and reading the first he came upon a sentence that became a treasured possession.

> Before *Plato* could speak [it read] the soul had wings in *Homer* which fell not but flew out of the body into the mansions of the dead.
> This idea [he wrote many years afterwards] stirred my imagination deeply. I could see the emblem of the soul—a little winged creature, perhaps not unlike the ghost moth—perched upon the airy habitations of the skies which in their turn sailed and swung from cloud to cloud and then on into space once more.[7]

This inspiring idea gave lightness, spaciousness and an aerial poetry to the illustration in the book and the preliminary water-colour.[8] To the reading of the works of Thomas Browne Paul Nash owes much more than a single compelling image. The potent strangeness of Browne's personality, projected by his solemn, fantastic, luminous prose, prose that is poetry in everything but form, impressed itself deeply upon Paul Nash's nature, already well prepared to receive it.

---

[1] The National Gallery of Canada (Massey Coll.), Ottawa.
[2] Coll. Mrs. Raymond Asquith.   [3] The Tate Gallery, London.
[4] Private Coll.   [5] Private Coll.   [6] Published in 1932.
[7] 'Aerial Flowers', written in 1945 and published posthumously two years later.
[8] Coll. Mr. Rex de C. Nan Kivell.

43. PAUL NASH.
Landscape of the
Vernal Equinox
(1943).
Oil, 28×36 in.
Coll. Her Majesty
Queen Elizabeth the
Queen Mother.

44. C. R. W.
Nevinson.
La Patrie (1916).
Oil, 23¾ × 35½ in.
Coll.
Mr. L. J. Cadbury

The sonorous sentences echoed in his head; they charged it with a teeming imagery. From his childhood, when he began to exaggerate forms and sounds, he had been peculiarly susceptible to the charm of strangeness; and who stranger than the man of whom Coleridge wrote that 'so completely does he see everything in a light of his own, reading nature neither by the sun, moon, nor candlelight, but by the light of the faery glory round his head'?

During the 'thirties another incitement to his delight in strangeness strengthened the spell laid upon him by the reading of Browne: the dream imagery of Surrealism. To this imagery a nature such as Paul Nash's was inevitably responsive. He had contacts with Max Ernst, André Breton and Paul Eluard, and he took part, both as a member of the committee and as an exhibitor, in the International Surrealist Exhibition held in London in 1936. The imagery permeated his life as well as his art. Soon after he moved into a newly acquired house, 3 Eldon Road, Hampstead, that same year, I went there to luncheon and, being about to sit down in a certain chair, was warned by Mrs. Nash that it was already occupied, as indeed it was, by a stuffed hawk; the same bird, I think, as figures in his *Landscape from a Dream*,[1] of 1938, a characteristic example of the artist's surrealist painting. Thomas Browne and the surrealists evoked from the imagination of Paul Nash a dream world of strange juxtapositions, of cryptic symbols–the moons, tumuli, fossils, monoliths, fungi and the like–all vaguely allusive to mystic numbers, occult correspondences belonging to the veiled childhood of the world, the world devoid of organic life or else the habitation of primitive man.

> There is the same attention to oddities, to the remoteness and *minutiae* of vegetable objects, the same entireness of subject, [wrote Coleridge of Browne] you have quincunxes in earth below, and quincunxes in the water beneath the earth; quincunxes in deity, quincunxes in the mind of man, quincunxes in the optic nerves, in roots of trees, in leaves, in petals, in everything.

Add to all this the symbolism of surrealism and a perceptible Parisian accent and you will have a fair verbal equivalent of the principal work of Paul Nash during the period immediately preceding the Second World War. Characteristic examples of this odd crossing, so to say, of Thomas Browne and André Breton are

[1] The Tate Gallery, London.

Landscape of the Megaliths[1] (Plate 42), and *Wood of the Nightmares' Tails*,[2] of 1937, and *Nocturnal Landscape*,[3] and *Circle of the Monoliths*,[4] of 1938. During the same years he made, too, a number of paintings and water-colours of a slightly different character, in which the emphasis is upon the surrealist element in an existing landscape rather than, as in the first group, upon the incongruity of the objects represented, such, for instance, as the large wooden lattice structure in *Nocturnal Landscape*. Of these more realistic works *Stone Sea*,[5] of 1937, and *Monster Field*,[6] of 1939, are outstanding examples; the latter of them he regarded with as much satisfaction as any work of his last decade.

Early in this essay I took issue with the Paul Nash legend that is beginning to take shape. I must now challenge one of the attributes that is on the way to being accepted as being his in a supreme degree –imagination. To E. H. Ramsden he is an 'imaginative and inventive' artist who can take us 'from time into eternity, from the sensible realities of the visible world into the supersensible of a world that is above the visible'.[7] That such might be the effect of the impact of certain of his works it would be impertinent to question; but I would suggest that the effect would be due not to imagination or invention but to some other quality. Painters are an exceptionally, even a notoriously, observant class, for ever looking, constantly noting down. The habit of observation springs from the threefold necessity of stocking the mind with fruitful images, of finding inspiring subjects and of discovering the laws of nature whereby the selected images or subjects may be most convincingly represented. With different artists the emphasis is upon different aspects of this necessity: Blake, for instance, rarely took subjects from nature direct but used observation as an imaginative incitement, and Constable, little concerned with imagery, applied himself to a close study of the laws of nature with scientific detachment. But the involvement of mankind in his environment is so intimate that the most imaginative artists cannot dispense with a working knowledge of natural laws, or the most realistic with imagery distilled from the contemplation of nature.

[1] The Albright Gallery, Buffalo.   [2] Coll. Miss Elfrida Tharle-Hughes.
[3] The City Art Gallery, Manchester.   [4] Coll. The Rev. F. R. Holmden.
[5] Coll. Mrs. Malcolm L. McBride.   [6] The City Art Gallery, Durban.
[7] 'Paul Nash, Paintings, Drawings and Illustrations', p. 27.

It is generally assumed by those who have written about Paul Nash that he belongs unequivocally to the imaginative tradition, the tradition of Blake, and that he was detached to an unusual degree from the scientific tradition of which Constable was the first and most authoritative English advocate. 'A great imaginative artist: that was established decades ago,' a critic wrote of Paul Nash, as though it were a truism, a critic the most read of our day and upon an important occasion.[1]

It is not my purpose simply to deny so much as to qualify this assumption. It is true that his own sympathies were ranged ardently with the imaginative tradition: his intentions were imaginative. He was not deeply concerned–and as he grew older his concern diminished–to represent aspects of nature; he was determined to create an imagery out of his inner vision. That inner vision, at its happiest moments, crystallized in pictures of a rich strangeness, glowing with the heat of the sun or of a lunar pallor. How much the poorer the art of our century would have been without Paul Nash's last visionary landscapes! Were they to suffer destruction they would be missed, of so special a kind is the beauty they manifest. Of how few individual works can the same honestly be said! Works such as *Pillar and Moon*,[2] of 1932-42, *Landscape of the Vernal Equinox*,[3] of 1943 (Plate 43), *Nocturnal Flower*,[4] of 1944, and *The Eclipse of the Sunflower*,[5] of 1945, most particularly the first, appear to me to be works of great and original beauty. The fact that he was able only occasionally to create works of this quality was due to the fact that unlike his masters Rossetti and Blake Paul Nash imagined with painful laboriousness. Neither general imaginative conceptions, nor the precise imagery in which they might most vividly and precisely be expressed, came to him without effort. To his dependence upon the incitement of the haunting fragment from poetic literature I have already alluded. The *Landscape of the Vernal Equinox* and the other sunflower pictures of the 'forties, for instance, were inspired by a literary image for long the subject of his meditation, first come upon, I fancy, in 'Urne Buriall': 'the noble flower of the sun . . .

---

[1] Eric Newton–Introduction to the catalogue of the Paul Nash Memorial Exhibition at the Tate Gallery, 1948.
[2] The Tate Gallery, London. [3] Coll. H.M. Queen Elizabeth the Queen Mother.
[4] Private coll., U.S.A. [5] Coll. Mr. R. C. Pritchard.

wherein in lozenge-figured boxes nature shuts up the seeds and balsam that is about them', and intensified by Blake's memorable lines:

Ah, Sunflower! weary of time,
Who countest the steps of the sun.

No less was his dependence upon close observation of nature for the appropriate clothing of his imagery. The most conspicuous feature of the only two of Paul Nash's many domiciles with which I was familiar–the house at 3 Eldon Grove, Hampstead and the flat at 106 Banbury Road, Oxford, where he lived principally from 1939 until his death–was his collection of found objects, curiously shaped stones and fragments of wood and bark, skeletons of leaves, shells and the like. These became more and more necessary as stimulants to his imagination and, more important, as providing a repertory of forms with which to express his ideas. A camera was his constant companion,[1] and in addition he would buy and borrow photographs. I was the witness of a comical encounter between him and a fellow painter with whom I stayed during 1944 in a beautiful house he rented not far from Oxford. Here Paul Nash occasionally sallied from his flat in the Banbury Road. The garden contained a shady grove of trees in which statues were romantically disposed. The sight of these lichen-covered foliage-shrouded figures–touchingly evocative of the ancient world–stimulated in him a delightful agitation. Just as a sportsman in the presence of game instinctively brings his gun to bear, so did Paul Nash attempt to focus his camera upon stone fawn and dryad. But every attempt was baffled by some adroit movement of his vigilant host. 'After all,' he explained when Paul Nash, unable to bear his frustration, had returned prematurely home, 'it is *my* grove: I don't really see, do you, why it should be the theme of a whole series of Paul's pictures?' So complete at times was his dependence upon photographs and found objects in the making of his 'imaginative' pictures that he was unable even to assimilate and transmute them by the exercise of imagination, but instead introduced them direct on to the canvas or paper. Most of those who knew him were well aware of this procedure and there is written confirmation of it from a friend who frequented his studio. 'Natural

[1] A selection of his photographs was published as 'Fertile Image', and a retrospective exhibition was organized by the Arts Council, 1951.

objects, e.g. shells, wood-fragments, fungi, leaves, etc., were taken
into the studio for closer examination and were there painted into
the composition from direct observation,' wrote Dr. Richard
Seddon in his 'Notes on the Technique of Paul Nash', giving two
examples of pictures, *Ballard Phantom* and *Nest of Wild Stones*, in
which this procedure had been followed.[1] There follows an observation more significant still. 'When the objects were too big to be
taken home (e.g. the tree forms in *Monster Field*) they were (1)
sketched *in situ* in water-colour or (2) photographed.' What this
passage makes clear is the actual preference of the artist for painting
found objects or photographs of them into his imaginative compositions. A picture which contains some elements painted from
direct observation and others that are imagined–whether ostensibly
realistic or imaginary makes no difference–is particularly liable to
enfeebling tensions and to a lack of unity of style. These are, I think,
the besetting weakness of the less successful of his later imaginative
pictures, but that is by the way. My purpose in considering this
aspect of his art was not to make this criticism but to attempt
to shed some light upon the larger question of the character of his
imagination.

Paul Nash, it seems to me, was not, in the fullest sense, an imaginative artist at all, in the sense, that is to say, of possessing an innate
image-making faculty, a mind from which imagery flowed naturally.
Instead it was a mind which became deeply versed in and deeply
devoted to the imaginative tradition. Its leaders were the objects of
his utmost veneration; its minor practitioners of his amused, acutely
discerning appreciation. To this tradition he bound his most urgent
preferences, emotional and intellectual. Paul Nash possessed an
indomitable will. In default of a natural image-making faculty he
evolved–when the inspiration he derived from the Western Front
had waned and left him without clear direction–the procedure
already noted. He developed his intense receptivity and systematically exposed his mind to the poetry, the prose and the visual arts
that were most evocative of the earth's oldest memories, that echoed
most strangely in the corridors of the mind. Then when there arose a
responsive ferment in himself he set about to find objects which
would give lucid expression to his vague imaginings. His acute and

[1] 'Paul Nash, Paintings, Drawings and Illustrations', p. 43.

calculating intelligence, his poetic insight and his exquisite taste made Paul Nash a wonderful agency for transmuting literary emotions into the most sharply defined forms, for providing perfect visual equivalents for Mansions of the Dead and Sunflowers weary of Time. Sometimes the process had a mechanical quality evident in the resulting pictures; at others that fine mind, steeled by that indomitable determination, was rewarded by the power to make out of borrowed elements something most lyrical and wholly his own. The mind of an artist is a complex instrument, and in attempting to describe the creative operations of the mind of Paul Nash I am aware of having over simplified, but I believe that my description is a little less remote from the unattainable truth than the declaration that he was a great imaginative artist.

During his latter years his will had to contend not only with imaginative dryness but with increasing ill health: for from 1932 until his death thirteen years later his life was made periodically burdensome by asthma. The difficulties of these years were sensibly increased by his involvement–first as an artist attached to the Royal Air Force and later to the War Artists' Advisory Committee–in a war that made no specific appeal to his imagination. To the eye it offered nothing remotely comparable to the Western Front: his man-made monsters flying out of the moon through cloud landscapes represented no new departures but were the products of an earlier phase of seeing. The idea of *The Rose of Death*, the name the Spaniards gave to the parachute in their Civil War, haunted his mind, but to no great purpose. It was not the white flower but *Totes Meer*, the Dead Sea of crashed German bombers beneath the icy light of the moon, that suggested that in other circumstances he might have created out of the Second World War an art as memorable as that inspired by the First. But the needful effort was beyond his strength, for he had already begun to die.

◦   ◦   ◦

This essay was already in proof in 1955 before Mr. Anthony Bertram's 'Paul Nash: the Portrait of an Artist' appeared. It was, therefore, too late for me to avail myself of the wealth of new information provided in this patient biography. There is one matter, however, which by way of conclusion I shall select for an allusion, since it qualifies an incomplete statement of my own and a part of the Nash legend which, as I have complained, tends to obscure both the real man and the nature of his achievement.

On an earlier page I referred to Paul Nash's reading, at the beginning of his career as an artist, as comprising, with Rossetti, Tennyson, Morris, Keats, Whitman, Blake, Coleridge. The evidence for this was Nash's unfinished autobiography. Mr. Bertram's researches into Paul Nash's letters of the time, however, show that these great names were not relevant until a later date. In 1909, when Nash was just short of twenty, 'there was great enthusiasm for "The Beloved Vagabond" by W. J. Locke. "I think if I failed in this life (and I don't mean to)," Nash said, "I should ... take to the High Road. ... Think of such a glorious existence if you really loved the open air and knew about the woods and fields, as I do a very little."[1] But of course vagabondage was not Nash's line at all, though the influence was not to disappear at once; it was later to be more respectably derived from Borrow.'[2]

There was an enthusiasm for E. F. Benson's 'Angel of Pain' and a very considerable one for the works of Algernon Blackwood. 'Nash first particularly praised "John Silence", which certainly contains a good deal of what was to be characteristic Nash imagery . . . haunted woods, Druidic circles, mystic flying and again the curtain which threatens to lift on the hidden presence.'[3] There was an even more intense enthusiasm for 'The Education of Uncle Paul' ... 'the book has helped me and done me good'[4] ... 'it is amazing,' comments Mr. Bertram, 'that this twaddle should have fed an imagination so athletic as Nash's. But it certainly did: we cannot fail to be struck by that accumulation of images from nature, which is also almost a list of his themes. And the white wings were also to play their part.'[5]

In 1912 came an admiration for, it would seem, Arthur Machen and 'The Hill of Dreams'. In a letter of 5 March he quotes: 'Long, long ago, a white merle flew out of Eden. Its song has been in the world ever since but few there are who have seen the flash of its white wings thro' the green gloom of the living wood, the sun splashed, rain drenched, mist girt, storm beat wood of human life.' And he goes on: 'but today, as I came thro' the wood, under an arch of tempest and led by lightnings, I passed into a green sun splashed place. There, there I heard the singing of a rapt song of joy! here and there I saw the flash of white wings.'

Paul Nash referred to the 'Hills of Dream', but there is no such book. ' "The Hill of Dreams" by Arthur Machen,' writes Mr. Bertram, 'seemed a likely guess, but the passage is not to be found in it. And yet the book corresponds so exactly at many points to Nash's imagery and imaginative life at that time that he must certainly have read it, and confused the title and source of his quotation. ... There are many passages which are almost

[1] 9 March 1909. [2] Bertram, op. cit., pp. 42–3. [3] Ibid., p. 43.
[4] 6 May 1911. [5] Op. cit., p. 44.

descriptions of certain pictures. The following extract is assembled from three of them:

> In the hedge of the lane there was a gate on which he used to lean and look down south to where the hill surged up so suddenly, its summit defined on summer evenings not only by the rounded ramparts but by the ring of dense green foliage that marked the circle of oak trees. . . . The image of it grew more intense as the symbol of certain hints and suggestions. . . . The streaming fire of the great full moon glowed through the bars of the weird oaks, and made a halo shine about the hill.'[1]

The book contains descriptions of trees, too, as 'forms that imitated the human shape, and faces and twining limbs that amazed him . . . here and there an oak stripped of its bark, white and haggard and leprous'. As Mr. Bertram again comments, 'these are Nash's Monster Trees and the subjects of many photographs in "Fertile Image".'[2]

These passage I quote not primarily because they manifest the literary nature of Nash's imaginative painting, concerned though Nash was for a time, under the influence of fashionable aesthetic theory, to deny any such literary inspiration. Still less do I quote them to his discredit. There is no suggestion that Paul Nash took images that he used throughout his painting life from books such as these. There was, after all, something innate that responded to such literature and such romantic imagery, and although such literature represented, in a sense, the most deplorable elements in romantic writing, although it was imprecise and thoroughly messy, full of what Mr. Eliot calls 'undisciplined squads of emotion', it is better to be moved even by stuff such as this than not to be moved at all. But it seems to me a remarkable and significant achievement for a man, whose early literary tastes were of this character, to be able to discipline and refine a thing so intimate as imagination into something both more clear-edged and more deeply moving. The First World War did much; it helped to rinse him of what Mr. Bertram calls 'the pseudo-poetic and second-hand romanticism of his long adolescence'.[3] But above all there was what I have already called his indomitable will.

I have said that the Paul Nash legend tends to obscure not only the real man but also the nature of his achievement. For what Paul Nash achieved was to make, out of an innately slender talent, a substantial body of distinguished painting—just as, out of an innately poor talent for the writing of English, he made the excellent prose of 'Outline'—and distinguished not least in the quality of the imagination that in it he became able so hauntingly to express and evoke. It is an achievement of assiduous industry and discipline, and it is a considerable one.

[1] Op. cit., pp. 49–50. [2] Ibid., p. 50. [3] Ibid., p. 90.

C. R. W. NEVINSON
1889–1946

AS this series of studies has grown the question of which painters to include and which not becomes more troubling. Sometimes the answer is simple: to have ignored Sickert or Augustus or Gwen John or Stanley Spencer, or, as an extraordinary intellect at work among the arts, Wyndham Lewis, would be palpably absurd. At other times the answer is not simple at all. There are painters one aspect of whose work seems to me to have a chance of proving durable, and the rest to have little. Again there are painters whose qualities I am able to apprehend, yet with insufficient comprehension to enable me to appraise them. Ivon Hitchens, for example. I have been delighted by the glimpses he affords into the enchanted depths of a vernal or an autumnal wood–glimpses I remember gratefully like something vividly seen in childhood or a few bars of a haunting, almost forgotten tune. But this is not enough: my mind is insufficiently attuned to be able to appraise the elusive irridescence of the art of Ivon Hitchens.

Other painters there are on whose work I shall have nothing to say in these pages because the excellence that it uniformly maintains is that of a tradition which is well understood and has been abundantly written about, so that to-day critical explanation is superfluous. A notable example of such an art is the portraiture and still-life of Allan Gwynne-Jones, who, in sharp contrast to the highly idiosyncratic subjects of these studies, works with serene consistency in the finest academic tradition. It is an uncommon achievement. The present is a time when extremely individualistic art is almost the rule among serious independent painters in England; on the other hand the art that is popularly termed academic and is described by its advocates as traditional–and sometimes as that which alone is 'sane' or 'competent' or 'healthy'–is far indeed from any seriously maintained academic tradition. In fact, the genuine academic painter, the painter who is able to express himself fully within a great tradition and with a complete understanding of its possibilities and limitations,

361

is a very rare bird indeed, and a fortunate one. But such a painter is Gwynne-Jones. With no inclination to extend the frontiers of his art or to pioneer in the forests, he has cultivated the gardens of his choice with no less distinction than consistency. It is difficult to think of a work more impeccable than his *Peaches in a Basket*,[1] of 1948.

C. R. W. Nevinson is a painter who belongs to the first of these three categories, is a painter, that is to say, one part only of whose work seems likely to endure. During a brief period of years he painted pictures which demand a place in any account of English painting during the present century, and for the rest of his life paintings which, notwithstanding certain excellent qualities, seem to me to have no title to such a place. It was Nevinson's misfortune that his finest pictures had for their subject something that everyone was under an almost irresistible compulsion to expel from their memory: the First World War's Western Front. The memory of mile upon mile of earth dissolved into deep slime or else burnt and torn, the scene of death on a scale without precedent, is a memory which, even for those who never saw it and even after a second and more hideous world war, cannot be recalled without a painful effort. It was a further misfortune that during the ensuing years his work acquired a repute that was widespread rather than firmly established. The neglect that often follows an artist's death has been with him unusually severe. Few names, among those well known in Georgian times, occur less frequently in conversation, I should say, among painters and writers about painting. If now and then the name of Nevinson is mentioned by some young student of art history, it is likely that it is not the painter but the solitary English Futurist, the friend of Boccioni and Soffici, the man who beat the drum at the Doré Galleries while Marinetti declaimed his verse, who has aroused his passing interest.

◇   ◇   ◇

Christopher Richard Wynne Nevinson was born on 13 August 1889, the only child of Henry Woodd Nevinson and his first wife Margaret Wynne, daughter of the Rev. Timothy Jones, a Welsh-speaking Welshman and classical scholar, in John Street, Hampstead, since renamed Keats Grove. The Nevinsons occupied a house, now

[1] The Tate Gallery, London.

demolished, which stood opposite to the elegant white villa where Keats lived.

Henry Nevinson was a celebrated war correspondent, and his wife made a career for herself in education and politics, playing an active part in the campaign for Women's Suffrage and the reform of the Poor Law. The home they made was a disturbing place for a boy to grow up in. The father was inclined to be a radical both in his thinking and his feeling, who yet delighted in army life. The mother, a shingled, sandalled progressive in home affairs, was also an ardent jingo, and when Mafeking was relieved she and her small son, he relates in his memoirs, 'draped in red, white and blue . . . wandered from Ludgate Circus to Piccadilly ringing a dinner bell'.[1]

This conflict in both his remarkable parents, arising from their emotional attachment to the established order of things, represented by the Empire, the Army, the older public schools and universities, and their attachments, equally emotional, to progressive causes of many kinds was inherited, in an acute form, by their son, who was at once ardently institutional in his loyalties, yet something of a revolutionary too, but the conflict in father and son took a precisely opposite course. The father, who began with traditional class sympathies and wished his son to follow him to Shrewsbury and Oxford, ended as a passionate socialist. I remember a discussion taking place at my own parents' house during the General Strike of 1926, on its rights and wrongs, but nothing of what was said except Henry Nevinson's passionate exclamation: 'The People: right or wrong!' The son, after being among the very first among English painters to be fully conscious of the revolutionary ferment on the Continent in the years just prior to the First World War, and taking a leading and energetic part both in proclaiming Futurist and Cubist ideas and in making them a part of his way of seeing, was soon declaring that 'The immediate need of the art of today is a Cézanne, a reactionary, to lead art back to the academic traditions of the old Masters, and save contemporary art from abstraction, as Cézanne saved Impressionism from "effects".'[2] Yet just as his father continued to delight in army life so did the son preserve until the end something of his early challenging attitude towards art and life.

[1] 'Paint and Prejudice', 1937, p. 7.
[2] 'The Studio', December 1919.

There was another way in which the personalities of his parents affected him, and wholly adversely. Both in their different ways were champions of under-dogs, turbulent pioneers, indifferent if not contemptuous of public opinion. Unpopular causes were their vocation, and their challenging character and progressive temper were as defiantly manifest in the home as they were outside. The walls, distempered instead of papered, were ornamented with reproductions of Italian primitives and Pre-Raphaelites, and with English water-colours. These departures from the prevailing taste of the middle-class neighbourhood, in which Nottingham lace curtains and a cosy profusion of knick-knacks were the rule, deepened the suspicions engendered by Mrs. Nevinson's shingled hair, and, as a consequence, her son relates, he was booed in the streets. This and other manifestations of hostility implanted in him an enduring sense of being an innocent victim of the world's ill-will, indeed of its persecution. At the height of his success as a painter, with his massive figure and booming voice Nevinson presented to the world an imposing, even a formidable aspect; yet those who knew him were, I fancy, uncomfortably aware that only just beneath the surface worked an inordinate horror of ill-will and a readiness to see it even where it was not. This vulnerability was made the more acute by unhappy experiences at school. At the age of seven he was 'publicly flogged . . . for giving away some stamps which I believed to be my own'.[1]

After a happy interlude at University College School he was sent, in 1904, to Uppingham, where persistent ill-treatment left him, he relates, 'septic in mind and body' and led to a serious operation and his removal from school. It was after his illness, in the course of a tour in Spain, North Africa and north Italy, that he began to draw. On his return he went back to Uppingham for one term, but his health was still so bad that it was plain that there was no longer any question of his going to Balliol as his father wished. During his tour he had decided to become a painter. When he left Uppingham he entered, in 1907, the St. John's Wood School of Art.

It was the bicycling tours on which his mother used to take him that developed the visual side of his nature. They visited churches and colonies of artists.

[1] Op. cit., p. 3.

In the art colonies at Pont Aven, Concarneau, Quimper, St. Pol, Caudebec, and St. Michel we always associated with the painters. The name of Monet had been familiar to me for some time. As my mother had been in Paris from about 1870 she was particularly versed in the Impressionist school; and I had already devoured, by the age of fifteen, the books of Camille Mauclair on Renoir, Manet, Degas, Sisley, and Pissarro, and had heard of Gauguin and Cézanne. I had even heard of the 'mad' paintings of Van Gogh some five years before their 'discovery' by Roger Fry and the dealers.'[1]

By the time he left Uppingham he had not only a lively interest in painting. He had a point of view.

I was [he relates] a modernist. The plethora of artistic training and my revolt against public-school traditions made me bored with old masters; in Venice an international exhibition of contemporary art had interested me more than anything I had ever seen. I really was excited about it, although it is significant that now I can recall no single picture I saw there except those which introduced me to the technique of a Neo-Impressionist, Signac.[2]

As he is writing of the time before he left Uppingham, it is unclear to what 'the plethora of artistic training' refers. The only training he appears to have had was occasional instruction from John Fulleylove, the architectural draughtsman and water-colour painter. The description of his discovery, while a student at St. John's Wood, of the drawings of Augustus John and Orpen, in a publication entitled 'The Slade', and of how they 'completely upset my applecart' and precipitated 'a period of doubt', suggests that his memory was at fault, and that the continental masters whom he named had remained little more than names, or that he came upon them a little later on. Had he been, in fact, as familiar with them as he claimed, his 'apple cart' would hardly have been upset by reproductions of drawings so closely formed upon the old masters as those of John and Orpen. Nor would his 'period of doubt' have been ended as it was when Sargent 'the god of St. John's Wood' stated that John was 'the greatest draughtsman since the Renaissance'. To a student 'familiar with all French art,' as he claimed to be,[3] neither the drawings of John and Orpen nor the opinions of Sargent, worthy of note though they be, would offer so shaking an experience as to lead to the overthrow of all his values.

[1] Op. cit., p. 9.   [2] Ibid., p. 13.   [3] Ibid., p. 19.

Nevinson was, I fancy, more accurate when he insisted on the academic aspect of the school and recalled his laborious days in the 'antique', chalk stump and pointed indiarubber in hand, his drawing from the model at night, his concentration upon head and figure painting and the interest in the old masters which it brought, more especially in Dürer, Holbein and Antonello da Messina. The impact of the drawings of John and Orpen showed him that the Slade tradition had an energy and an expressive power unknown to his teachers. Accordingly in 1909 he left St. John's Wood for the Slade, where he remained for three years.

Nevinson was fortunate in going to the Slade during one of its liveliest periods. Stanley Spencer, Gertler, Currie and Wadsworth were among his fellow-students, and these, with Allinson, Claus, Ihlee, Lightfoot and Nevinson himself, formed a gang which wore uniforms of black jersey, black hat and scarlet muffler and which roved the streets of Soho in search of trouble. They did not, according to various accounts, have far to look. While he was at the Slade Nevinson studied sculpture with Havard Thomas. Like a number of other beginners of promise he was given his first opportunity of showing his work, in 1910, by the Friday Club, and some of it earned the favourable notice of serious critics. Two of his urban landscapes, paintings in the impressionist tradition, were singled out for their exceptional promise by 'The Sunday Times'. Sickert had spoken some words of encouragement to him and Gilman and Gore had welcomed him into the Camden Town circle. For the first time Nevinson felt the ground firm beneath his feet. He was happy in the consciousness of making progress. His feeling of unhappy singularity was waning. Then Tonks told Nevinson as he had told Matthew Smith a few years earlier that he was without talent and unqualified to be a painter. For students with whom he was in sympathy and numerous others Tonks was a great teacher of drawing–one of the few great teachers of the time–but there were always certain students for whom he formed inveterate dislikes and whom he harried without mercy. In certain cases–and Nevinson was one–he pursued his victims long after they had left the Slade. So cogently did Tonks frame his advice to Nevinson to abandon painting that it was temporarily accepted: the Slade student became for a short time a Fleet Street apprentice. Nevinson enjoyed interviewing Little Tich and Marie Lloyd, but the episode was baleful in its effects. The hostility of Tonks revived and intensified his crushing sense of the world's ill-will, a sense which from that time onwards was ever on the alert. Moreover his brief term in Fleet Street taught him at once too much and too little about the Press. From it he learnt its extraordinary power and how to harness it, but little of its attendant dangers. Even after he left Fleet Street he knew how to secure the widest publicity for his work and for his opinions. This doubtless contributed to his material success, but it also provoked the jealousy of other artists, vulgarized his reputation and involved him from time to time in situations which would have been distressing to most men but which were particularly injurious to the constitution of a man of his temperament. In spite of its undesirable consequences Press publicity appealed to Nevinson. He took a frank pleasure in being a celebrity and a popular oracle on any topic of the moment, and his Fleet Street experience suggested to him that this pleasure was not at all uncommon, especially among eminent persons who insisted that they were superior to such vulgar satisfactions. Such hypocrisy was repellent to his own candid nature. Later on he came to attach a moral sanction to his belief in publicity.

My Futurist training [he wrote] had convinced me that a man who lives by the public should make his appeal to that public and meet that public, and that all hole-and-corner cliques, and scratch-a-back societies are disastrous to the artist and his output. A coterie becomes a tyrant, falsifying a man's standards. Consciously or unconsciously he trims. When he is dealing with a wider and perhaps a more undiscriminating public there is always the chance that his point of view may appeal to an unknown individual. In the past it has been the expert, the critic, and the "artistic" who have been wrong, and stray members of the public always right.[1]

A visit to Paris in 1911–at perhaps the most creative moment in the history of modern painting–restored his sense of vocation. In the mornings he worked at Julian's in the rue du Dragon and at the Montmartre Julian's in the evening, and occasionally at the Circle Russe where Matisse taught. After a return to London he was back in 1912 for a further and still more fruitful stay in Paris, for it was then that he received the impact of Cubism. 'I felt the power of this

[1] Op. cit., pp. 91–2.

first phase of Cubism,' he wrote, 'and there was a desire in me to reach that dignity which can be conveyed pictorially by the abstract rather than the particular.'[1]

Nevinson gives a fairly extensive account of his visits to Paris, but because of the small number of his early works which appear to survive, and the inaccuracy of his writing, it is difficult to assess with any degree of precision the nature of the impact upon his ideas or his practice. The general direction of his development was away from the tradition of Renoir, Monet and other Impressionists towards the newer tradition which Picasso, Matisse and a crowd of others were forging out of the legacy of Cézanne, and he was conscious of the attraction of Gauguin and of Van Gogh, whose example, · he has told us, encouraged him to use outline to simplify his form and to emphasize his planes, and of abstract art, more especially of that of Kandinsky. But these were forces that were animating a whole generation of painters. Even the influence of Cubism, which he acknowledged so explicity and which at first glance seemed so completely to dominate the work of his most creative period, seems ambiguous under scrutiny.

The account he gives of the artist's Paris, though lively, throws no new light upon the personalities or ideas which were contributing to the formation of what was nothing less than the matrix of a new art. He was gregarious, voluble, alive to what was going on around him; he was acquainted with a number of leading artists; he even shared a studio with Modigliani. The assurance of his writing is, however, hardly justified.

> The works of Picasso, Matisse, Derain and Vlaminck were by now well known to me if to no one else. The Fauviste school, through the influence of Gauguin, was reacting against the prettiness and technical accomplishment of French art. They were trying to introduce into their work a harsher or wilder note, a more intense expression, although of course, Picasso was still swayed by Toulouse-Lautrec and was only just leaving his blue period. . . .[2]

The year was 1912: Fauvism, far from being, as he implies, a new movement, had fulfilled its aims some four years earlier, and the former Fauves were currently engaged in adventures of a quite different kind; Picasso had left his blue period some eight years earlier, and he could not have been said to be 'swayed by Toulouse-Lautrec' since the beginning of the century.

Wherever he went every manifestation of life presented itself to Nevinson as an object of fascination. To have his creative interest aroused, he had but to look. Whether it was the gaunt silhouette of a factory at night, brightly dressed girls in punts on the Thames, 'any London street' (the title of one of his paintings)–it scarcely mattered. The work of most painters is empty because they do not love life enough, and because a great master, on account of the burning patience of his dedication, needing a natural object to paint which was immobile and relatively unchanging, painted apples, these lesser men–however rapid their execution–have made still-life a pretext for ignoring life. (I can just hear their supercilious question, 'but isn't an apple as much "life" as anything else?'.) Nevinson's eye was too voracious, especially of the dramatic, the exciting, the sinister and the pretty, and its voracity tended to carry the hand with it too fast, to demean it into a mere recorder. The discipline of Cubism enabled him to impose a style upon the variegated prey of his voracious eye. For many artists who adopted Cubism it was an experiment, another set of principles; for Nevinson, at the most creative period of his life, Cubism was the thing needful to give to his work the simplicity and the dignity he desired to reach. Yet his debt to Cubism being made plain it is necessary also to draw a sharp distinction between the Cubism of the pioneers of Cubism, Picasso and Braque during the years 1910, 1911 and 1912, and the later Cubism of Nevinson. 'Cubism,' declared Picasso, 'is an art dealing primarily with forms.'[1] This is true both of the earlier phase of dissection and reassembly of the forms of nature generally known as Analytical, and of the later, more inventive, remoter from a point of departure in nature, generally known as Synthetic. For Picasso and Braque, although Cubism was primarily an art of form, it was not a wholly abstract art, it was also an art of representation.

Always there were vestiges of 'nature', [as Alfred H. Barr observed] whether a landscape, a figure or a still-life. And these vestiges however slight remained essentially important, for they revealed the point of departure, the degree of transformation undergone by the original image; they supplied the tense cord which anchored the picture to

[1] 'Picasso Speaks'. 'The Arts' (New York), May 1923.

common reality yet gave the measure of its daring distance. In this sense a cubist picture was not only a design but a precisely controlled and far-fetched metaphor.[1]

To Nevinson the subtle analysis of natural forms of Picasso and Braque would have been incomprehensible; with the principles of Cubism or any other contemporary movement he was unconcerned. He was an artist of superb adaptability and resource, who saw in contemporary movements expedients adapted to the representation of certain subjects. 'I maintain,' he asserted, 'that it is impossible to use the same means to express the flesh of a woman and the ferro-concrete of a sky-scraper. . . .'[2] But Picasso, for whom within a certain span of years Cubism was not an expedient but a natural evolving language, did precisely that, painting *Factory at Horta*, in 1909[3] and *Girl With a Mandolin*,[4] the following year, in a style in all essentials the same.

During the three years before the First World War Nevinson kept in close touch with Paris, but in 1913 London became the principal theatre of his activities. These were years when the art world of London, like that of Paris, was deeply but optimistically agitated by the new movements that were continually germinating, clashing, intermingling, changing direction; continually affected, too, by the ebb and flow of ideas from Paris, at that time a white-hot crucible of ideas eagerly discussed, bitterly fought over, and wafted promptly away to the ends of the artistic earth to bring inspiration or resentment, but at all events passionate interest, wherever they lodged. Although London was not as significant a centre as Paris, a city where those concerned with the visual arts are more visual and less literary than they are apt to be in London, more audacious and more extreme in their thinking, and, above all, the place where the revolutionary masters congregated, nevertheless London on the eve of the First World War was a centre where a quite unusual number of men of talent were active in painting and sculpture, in thought about the arts, in writing and discussion, and where, in consequence, foreigners of talent such as Gaudier-Brzeska came to live and many

[1] 'Picasso: Fifty Years of his Art', 1946, p. 74.

[2] 'Catalogue of an Exhibition of Paintings, Etchings, Lithographs and Woodcuts' by C. R. W. Nevinson at the Bourgeois Galleries, New York, 10 November to 4 December 1920.

[3] Museum of Western Art, Moscow.　　　　[4] Coll. Mr. Roland Penrose.

more to propagate their ideas and to see what was in progress. The bracing and optimistic character of the climate brought forth and was in turn heightened by a series of exhibitions of the works of continental painters and sculptors, by the inauguration of Frank Rutter's Allied Artists' Association–a London version of the Paris 'Independents'–and by the formation of more or less revolutionary exhibiting groups of many kinds.

Nevinson's adventurous predilections and his exceptional knowledge of movers and shakers of the Parisian art vortex led him quickly into its London equivalent. He contributed in 1910, 1913 and 1914, to the Allied Artists' exhibitions at the Albert Hall, which, vast and inchoate though they were, generated much heat and led to fruitful associations, and he was included in the Post-Impressionist and Futurist Exhibition brought together by Frank Rutter at the Doré Galleries in the autumn of 1913, a lively survey of revolutionary painting from Pissarro, Cézanne, Van Gogh and Gauguin to the generation of Nevinson himself. Among the fine paintings contributed by Nevinson was *The Departure of the Train de Luxe*,[1] which was a frankly Futurist work, and owed much to Severini, whose paintings, more especially *The 'pan-pan' Dancers at the Monico* in the Exhibition of Works by the Italian Futurist Painters at the Sackville Gallery in March 1912, had provoked wide interest. This picture stirred Nevinson to an extraordinary enthusiasm. When he met Severini at lunch with Roger Fry and Mr. Clive Bell he was fascinated not only by the Futurist painter himself, but by the Futurist gospel in general and more particularly by its insistence upon dynamism and the beauty of modern life, especially the teeming life of great cities, of machinery.

> We choose to concentrate our attention [wrote Severini] on things in motion because our modern sensibility is particularly qualified to grasp the idea of speed. Heavy, powerful motor-cars rushing through the crowded streets of our cities, dancers reflected in the fairy ambience of light and colour, aeroplanes flying above the heads of an excited throng. . . . These sources of emotion satisfy our sense of the lyric and dramatic universe, better than do two pears and an apple.[2]

[1] 1913. Whereabouts unknown.
[2] The artist's introduction to the catalogue of Gino Severini's Exhibition, Marlborough Gallery, which had no connexion with the existing gallery of the same name, April 1913.

The two painters became close friends, and Nevinson accompanied Severini back to Paris, where he was introduced into Futurist and Cubist circles. When Marinetti, the founder and leader of Futurism, told Severini that he had it in mind to revisit England, Nevinson asked Severini to persuade him to carry out his intention,[1] and when he arrived in the autumn of 1913 Nevinson joined with Wyndham Lewis in organizing the dinner of welcome at the Florence Restaurant.

This dinner at which about sixty painters, writers and others were assembled was an event of which Nevinson has given a lively description:

> It was an extraordinary affair. Marinetti recited a poem about the siege of Adrianople, with various kinds of onomatopoeic noises and crashes in free verse, while all the time a band downstairs played, 'You made me love you. I didn't want to do it.' It was grand if incoherent. I made a short speech in French and Lewis followed, then jealousy began to show its head. Marinetti knew of me through Severini and he understood my French better, so he paid more attention to me. He did not know, poor fellow, that he was wrecking a friendship that promised well. His French was good, having nothing of the Italian accent or phraseology I associated with Severini or Boccioni. It certainly was a funny meal. Most people had come to laugh, but there were few who were not overwhelmed by the dynamic personality and declamatory gifts of the Italian propagandist; while still the band downstairs tinkled on: 'You made me love you.' It seemed incapable of playing anything else. This was my first public appearance before the Press. It was also my first speech of any kind. The men who covered it for the papers knew little of what was said, but from a sensational point of view they got all they wanted, and for a time my name seemed always to be in print.[2]

Some months after the long remembered dinner in his honour Marinetti paid a further visit to London and with Nevinson issued 'Vital English Art. Futurist Manifesto'. This first appeared in 'The Observer' on 7 June 1914, but was subsequently printed in other newspapers, and Nevinson used to shower copies of it from the galleries of theatres. In order to distinguish it from earlier pronouncements of the kind issued by the Futurist movement since the original Futurist Manifesto, which was published in 'Figaro' on 20 February 1909, this has become known as the English Futurist

[1] Nevinson, op. cit., pp. 56, 57.   [2] Ibid., p. 57.

Manifesto. Like its predecessors, it was a violent denunciation of the worship of tradition, of 'the pretty-pretty . . . the sickly revivals of mediaevalism, the Garden Cities with their curfews and artificial battlements, the Maypole Morris dances, Aestheticism, Oscar Wilde, the Pre-Raphaelites, Neo-primitives and Paris'; against 'the sham revolutionaries of the New English Art Club'; against 'the old grotesque idea of genius–drunken, filthy, ragged, outcast . . . the Post-Rossettis with long hair under the sombrero, and other passeist filth.' ('Passeist filth' became, for a time, a stock term of denigration applicable to any work of the past or to any work of the present in which the influence of the past was too obviously manifest, of which the speaker wished to register disapproval.) It was not, however, its denunciations of passeist filth–lively copy though this furnished for the Press–as its commendation of England's 'advance guard of artists' that provoked the uproar that followed its publication. 'So we call upon the English public', runs the final paragraph of the manifesto, 'to support, defend and glorify the genius of the great Futurist painters or pioneers and advance-forces of vital English Art –Atkinson, Bomberg, Epstein, Etchells, Hamilton, Nevinson, Roberts, Wadsworth, Wyndham Lewis.'

In appending his name to the manifesto Nevinson committed an egregious error–an error that had unhappy consequences for himself. The manifesto, as the *pronunciamento* of a foreigner, would probably have been treated as a spirited display of fireworks, but, appearing over the signature of an Englishman as well, several of its targets seemed ineptly chosen. The Pre-Raphaelites, for instance, had never been less influential than they were in 1914, and people wondered which garden city was protected by artificial battlements, and were amused that anyone should see a menace to progress in the activities of the scattered tiny groups of intellectuals who were attempting, a little forlornly, to revive ancient folk dances. People wondered, too, why a statement which opened with the words, 'I am an Italian Futurist poet,' and ended with a call 'to support, defend and glorify the genius' of, among a small number of artists, Nevinson himself should have been signed by Nevinson at all. More informed readers were also aware that he was eager to have his own works accepted by the 'sham revolutionaries' of the New English Art Club. Of his election to its membership in 1929 he wrote, 'I think no honour gratified me more.'[1] He disclosed in the same paragraph that he had allowed himself to be put up for membership 'fifteen years before', that is to say, in 1914, the year of the manifesto's issue. These errors of judgment were small matters and would have been quickly forgotten, but he was guilty of a greater. Nevinson was a bold, outspoken man, ever ready, in the best traditions of his family, to speak out in support of what he considered to be right. He was a friend of Marinetti and Severini, and a painter of precocious talent. All this gave him a deserved prominence among 'the pioneers and advance forces of Vital English Art'. But it did not make him their leader, and it did not make him an art philosopher. By signing a manifesto jointly with Marinetti he made what many interpreted as an assertion of leadership, an assertion the more explicit on account of the description of the eight other artists named in the manifesto as Futurists. If Nevinson, an avowed Futurist, had allowed no allusion to these others, the manifesto might have been regarded as an exclusively Futurist affair: as things were, it was easy for these eight to see an attempt to subordinate them to his leadership. Above all, it looked like a direct challenge to a man who was an art philosopher of extraordinary power and originality, and who was the directing power in the Rebel Art Centre, which Nevinson, with his propensity for associating himself with institutions, thoughtlessly gave as the address beneath his signature. Moreover Lewis would not have forgotten that Nevinson owed something to his early encouragement, and more to his ideas.

The reply to this real or fancied challenge was not long in coming. A week later 'The Observer' published the following reply, which, considering Lewis's provocation and his formidable powers as a pamphleteer, is a document less savage than severe, and wounding chiefly by the omission of any reference to the manifesto's English signatory:

> DEAR SIR, – To read or hear the praises of oneself or one's friends is always pleasant. There are forms of praise, however, which are so compounded with innuendo as to be most embarrassing. One may find oneself, for instance, so praised as to make it appear that one's opinions coincide with those of the person who praises, in which case one finds oneself in the difficult position of disclaiming the laudation or of even slightly resenting it.

[1] Op. cit., p. 186.

There are certain artists in England who do not belong to the Royal Academy nor to any of the passeist groups, and who do not on that account agree with the futurism of Signor Marinetti. An assumption of such agreement either by Signor Marinetti or by his followers is an impertinence.

We, the undersigned, whose ideals were mentioned or implied, or who might, by the opinions of others, be implicated, beg to dissociate ourselves from the 'Futurist' manifesto which appeared in the pages of THE OBSERVER of Sunday, June 7.

Signed:

RICHARD ALDINGTON. LAWRENCE ATKINSON. DAVID BOMBERG. GAUDIER BRZESKA. FREDERICK ETCHELLS. CUTHBERT HAMILTON. EZRA POUND. W. ROBERTS. EDWARD WADSWORTH. WYNDHAM LEWIS.

P.S. The Direction of the Rebel Art Centre wishes to state that the use of their address by Signor Marinetti and Mr. Nevinson was unauthorized.

REBEL ART CENTRE,
38, GREAT ORMOND-STREET, W.C., *June 8.*

'The Observer' printed, the following Sunday, a plaintive and not very convincing rejoinder, and the honours rested with Lewis.

On Friday 12 June, only two days before the publication of the Vorticists' disclaimer and ignorant that it was impending, Nevinson and Marinetti organized a Futurist demonstration at the Doré Galleries. Nevinson spoke first, reading his speech, which appears to have been an extended version of the English Futurist Manifesto; Marinetti followed. Wyndham Lewis has described his 'counter putsch'.

I assembled [he wrote] a determined band of miscellaneous anti-futurists. Mr. Epstein was there; Gaudier Brzeska, T. E. Hulme, Edward Wadsworth. . . . There were about ten of us. After a hearty meal we shuffled bellicosely round to the Doré Gallery.

Marinetti had entrenched himself upon a high lecture platform, and he put down a tremendous barrage in French as we entered. Gaudier went into action at once. He was very good at the *parlez-vous*, in fact he was a Frenchman. He was sniping him without intermission, standing up in his place in the audience all the while. The remainder of our party maintained a confused uproar.

The Italian intruder was worsted. . . . But it was a matter for astonishment what he could do with his unaided voice. He certainly made an extraordinary amount of noise. . . . My equanimity when first subjected to the sounds of mass-bombardment in Flanders was possibly due to my marinettian preparation–it seemed 'all quiet' to me in fact, by comparison.[1]

Noise, indeed, was Marinetti's element, the necessary accompaniment to all his actions. There was an occasion when he again lectured at the Doré Galleries and declaimed his poems. One of these required to be accompanied by the noise of bombardment, to be 'packed to the muzzle with what he called "la rage balkanique",' so Nevinson 'concealed himself somewhere in the hall, and at a signal from Marinetti belaboured a gigantic drum'.[2] Nevinson himself has described Marinetti's supreme attempt to break the eardrums of Londoners.

It says a great deal for Marinetti [he wrote] that he was able to induce Oswald Stoll to put him on at the Coliseum. Nobody else could have done it. Naturally I went to see the first performance, and I must say it was one of the funniest shows ever put on in London, provided, of course, that one looked at things from the right angle. Marinetti swaggered on to that vast stage looking about the size of a house fly, and bowed. As he spoke no English, there was no time wasted in explanations or in the preparation of his audience. Had they spoken Italian, I do believe Marinetti could have magnetized them as he did everybody else. There was nothing for it however, but to call upon his ten noise tuners to play, so they turned handles like those of a hurdy-gurdy. It must have sounded magnificent to him, for he beamed; but a little way back in the auditorium all one could hear was the faintest of buzzes. At first the audience did not understand that this was the performance offered them in return for their hard-earned cash, but when they did there was one vast, deep, and long-sustained, 'Boo!'

When I went round to the back I found Marinetti in the best of spirits, dismissing the unanimous condemnation of the audience and calmly announcing to the Press, 'C'etait un cabal.'[3]

I have insisted upon some of the boisterous manifestations of the excitement and extremism with which the art world, in London as elsewhere, was so highly charged, because of its effect upon

[1] 'Blasting and Bombardiering', by Wyndham Lewis, 1937, pp. 36, 37.
[2] Ibid., p. 36. Lewis described this occasion as being *before* Nevinson 'declared war on us, especially on me'. According to Nevinson ('Paint and Prejudice', p. 61) it was later, on a subsequent visit of Marinetti's. I think Nevinson's account is more likely to be correct, for Marinetti made his first appearance supported by Nevinson, only five days after the promulgation of the English Futurist Manifesto.
[3] Op. cit., pp. 61, 62.

the art of Nevinson, both immediately and later on by way of reaction.

The last and least ephemeral of these manifestations was the publication, thirteen days after that of the English Futurist Manifesto, and only six after the Vorticist's rejoinder, of 'Blast', No. I, which contained the last of the major manifestos, that of the Great London Vortex. It appeared, too, less than two months before war was declared. 'The months immediately preceding the declaration of war were full of sound and fury,' Lewis wrote, 'and . . . all the artists and men of letters had gone into action before the bank-clerks were clapped into khaki and dispatched to the land of Flanders Poppies to do their bit. Life was one big bloodless brawl, prior to the Great Bloodletting.'[1] Many artists and writers were attuned to war by the time it came, and none more closely than Nevinson.

When the war came the urge which drew Nevinson as strongly as it drew his father towards centres where exciting events were in progress, promptly involved him. His health, never good–and which deteriorated progressively–put enlistment in the armed forces out of the question. 'Still, I was pursued by the urge to do something, to be "in" the war,'[2] he wrote, and it was not long before his urge was satisfied. Hearing from his father of the shortage of ambulance drivers in France, he joined the Red Cross, and he was promptly sent with his unit to Dunkirk. The French medical service, in that area at least, had broken down. A number of French wounded, roughly bandaged, had been packed into cattle-trucks. By the time they had lain there neglected for three weeks, only half of them were alive, and the train being required for purposes more important than taking wounded men to hospital, its contents were dumped into a shed. 'There,' wrote Nevinson, 'we found them. They lay on dirty straw, foul with old bandages and filth, those gaunt, bearded men, some white and still with only a faint movement of the chests to distinguish them from the dead by their side.'[3] This scene, suddenly come upon in darkness, became an unforgettable memory, and the subject of one of the three or four paintings to which, if the reputation of Nevinson survives, it will owe its survival, La Patrie[4] (Plate 44). But for the moment there was no time for painting, for making

[1] 'Blasting and Bombardiering', p. 39.
[2] Op. cit., p. 71.
[3] Ibid., pp. 71–2.
[4] Coll. Mr. L. J. Cadbury.

more than an occasional hasty sketch. There were the wounded—Nevinson served not only as driver but as nurse, stretcher-bearer and interpreter as well—in ever increasing numbers; there were troubles between his unit and the French authorities for attending wounded Germans, for amputating limbs without official permission and thereby entitling those who thus suffered to a higher rate of disablement pension. At Dunkirk he saw the body of a child killed in an air-raid: a memory also retained for translation into a picture. In the meanwhile the French medical service had greatly improved, and Nevinson's health suffered from the strain and the exposure which his duties involved, and he was sent home. After an interlude in London he joined the Royal Army Medical Corps, serving as an orderly at the Third General Hospital in London. In January 1916 he was invalided out of the Army with rheumatic fever.

Such, in brief, was the modest extent of Nevinson's military career, but the nature of his earlier duties as an ambulance driver with the Red Cross in France, involving constant journeys by road, gave him opportunities for studying long sections of the fighting line and the burnt and shattered country, as well as first-aid posts and base hospitals, that were denied to most combatants, for whom the war was often a monotonous alternation of trench and rest camp.

It was not Nevinson's opportunities for observing the Western Front, which though excellent were far from unique, but his particular temperament and the precise point which he had reached in his development as an artist that prepared him so well to represent war.

Until the last years of his life he was usually considered as a 'rebel', and as a young painter he did in fact participate in revolutionary movements. But his instincts, in one essential respect, were those of a popular painter in that he wished his work to be widely and clearly intelligible; he wished its impact to be heavy; he wished, in brief, to share his own strong emotions and impressions with his fellow beings in general, and he delighted in evoking their response. Even a hostile response was more acceptable to him than none. Therefore an event so apocalyptic in the quality of its drama—drama that held every sentient being in its grip—was one to the representation of which he was eager to dedicate himself to the utmost of his powers. In this connexion it is relevant to recall that a number of the artists who worked on the Western Front avoided war as a subject, and confined themselves – sometimes to good purpose – to the kinds of subject which occupied them in times of peace, 'picturesque' buildings. A modern parish church with roof and windows blasted was little different from the mediaeval abbey in like condition from the effects of Reformation and weather. For Nevinson it would have been an irrelevance, almost blasphemous in its frivolity, to have gone to the Western Front to pick out 'picturesque bits'; for him the war was the subject, and from it he never averted his eyes. But such a disposition to address himself to a great public, and a determination to extract all that a theme of overwhelming grandeur would yield up, even supposing considerable artistic powers to have been at their service, might in the event have accomplished little. Nevinson had something besides considerable artistic powers: namely experience that was both recent and intense of two movements which he had the perception to adapt for his purpose. These were Futurism and Cubism. The first had taught not only the glory but the social utility of war, and the glory of machines in general but in particular of those machines essential to the conduct of modern war: guns, aircraft, armoured cars, warships and the supreme glory of these as parts of one great war machine. While other painters brooded in solitude over field or wood, plate of apples or naked girl, arrangements of lines and colours, the Futurists exulted in crowds, in speed, in noise, in conflict, in everything that other painters shunned. That Nevinson was fully aware of this is clear from an interview he gave after the end of the war.

This war did not take the modern artist by surprise [he said] . . . I think it can be said that modern artists have been at war since 1912. Everything in art was a turmoil . . . the whole talk among artists was of war. They were turning their attention to boxing and fighting of various sorts. They were in love with the glory of violence. . . . The intellectuals knew that war was coming before business men . . . and when war came it found the modern artist equipped with a technique perfectly well able to express war.[1]

Futurism awakened them to a charmed acceptance of the beauties of the age of the machines, but it did not equip them with a method of representing mechanized power. For all the talking and writing

[1] 'The New York Times', 25 May 1919.

about the power, the speed and the noise of machines, their most characteristic paintings were not in fact representations of these; they were exuberantly gay, ballroom-bright kaleidoscopes. Their simultaneous representation of the successive stages of movements deprived them of the clarity which is an essential constituent of power. And it was not an objective art. 'It is by abandoning objective reality,' wrote Severini, 'that our Futurist painter arrives at an abstract and subjective expression.'[1] Assuredly a painter who was a Futurist and nothing more would have had an unsuitable instrument to his hand for the representation of the gigantic clash of arms, the sombre bloodletting of the Western Front.

It was Cubism that gave Nevinson's Futurism the weight and the clarity that made it so effective an instrument for this purpose. But it was Cubism with a radical difference.

Few styles or methods in art [Mr. Alfred Barr has truly observed] have provoked more elaborate theories and analogies than has cubism. Cubist works have been likened to structural steel, broken mirrors, Gothic architecture, post-Euclidian geometry, and the drawings of sufferers from dementia praecox and schizophrenia; Cubism has been praised—and used—as an academic discipline and damned for its chaotic licence . . . it has been called both a return to classic traditions and a consequence of reckless revolution.[2]

For Nevinson Cubism was none of these; primarily it was something simpler: a means of communicating, at its most intense, the drama of this most dramatic of all subjects. The Western Front offered to the painter's contemplation a vast yet infinitely complicated panorama, a panorama dominated by the machinery of war. Nevinson was quick to perceive that out of Cubism, with the licence it gave to stark, bold simplifications, to the substitution for curves of jagged angles, to harsh contours, could be formed an instrument in tune with the machines, which could represent modern war with shattering effect. For the Cubist pioneers, according to the foremost among them, 'Cubism is . . . an art dealing primarily with forms.'[3] For Nevinson it was a kind of magnificent shorthand perfectly adapted to convey the simplified essence of a mechanized apocalypse.

[1] Artist's introduction to the Gino Severini exhibition catalogue, London, April 1913.
[2] 'Picasso, Fifty Years of his Art'. Alfred H. Barr, Jr., 1946, p. 74.
[3] 'Picasso Speaks'. 'The Arts' (New York), May 1923.

Nothing could be more different than the subtle apprehension of the complexities of form, the severe remoteness of the early Cubists, and the harsh eloquence of Nevinson. The fact that it was a vulgarization caused Nevinson's Cubism to be discounted by artists and critics, but it was, at its best, that rare thing in modern times, a popular language that could be spoken with dignity.

Nevinson began to make use of his opportunities of observing the Western Front before his discharge from the R.A.M.C. Two of his best pictures, *La Mitrailleuse*[1] and *The Flooded Trench on the Yser*,[2] were painted, he has told us, in two days during the leave granted to him on the occasion of his marriage, in 1915, to Cathleen Knowlman. Directly afterwards he set intensively to work, and by 26 September 1916 he had completed sufficient work to hold a full-scale exhibition.[3] His war pictures shown earlier in the year—*La Mitrailleuse* and two others at the Allied Artists' at the Grafton Galleries in March and *Column on the March*[4] and *The Flooded Trench on the Yser* at the London Group—provoked something of a stir, but his exhibition made a deep impression upon those who saw it; to many it gave their clearest insight into the great events across the Channel—in particular almost all the critics were quick to realize that the deep, harsh note struck by these works was in harmony with the subject.

It made most of the war art they had seen appear false by comparison. Even 'The Nation', principal organ of the 'Bloomsburies', by whom he felt himself treated with a meanness that was a constant subject of his talk to the end of his life, wrote with respect. 'For the first time in recent years, the pioneer seems to be seeking a manner,' its notice concluded, 'which will not be merely the amusement of a coterie, but might, by its directness, its force and its simplicity, appeal to the unsophisticated perception. I can imagine that even Tolstoy might have welcomed this rude, strong style, a reaction against the art of leisure and riches.'[5] 'The Times Literary Supplement' devoted its main article to the elimination of the personal element in modern war, and took the war pictures of Nevinson as its text, as expressing

---

[1] The Tate Gallery, London.   [2] Coll. Mr. Ronald Alley.
[3] The Leicester Galleries, September–October.
[4] The National Gallery of Canada, Ottawa (Massey Coll.).
[5] 30 September 1916.

'his sense that in war man behaves like a machine or part of a machine, that war is a process in which man is not treated as a human being but as an item in a great instrument of destruction, in which he ceases to be a person and becomes lost in a process'.[1] This article is a fair indication of the seriousness with which Nevinson's war pictures were regarded. The painter's treatment of this respectful and fair-minded attempt to place his art in a historical and philosophic context is no less indicative of the melancholy effects of his growing suspicion of intellectuals, which was becoming a disposition to dislike not only certain intellectual coteries in London but the operations of the intellect itself. Even after two decades of reflection he could travesty Clutton-Brock's article into an expression of 'the opinion of a great many people, particularly of the old Army type, that the human element, bravery, the Union Jack, were all that mattered'.[2]

The exhibition was crowded. All the exhibits were sold. Arnold Bennett bought *La Patrie*; Sir Michael Sadler–one of the most influential collectors of contemporary British painting–bought *Column on the March* and three other pictures. Nevinson, conscious of his powers and legitimately proud of the purpose to which he had put them, elated by success, looked forward with confidence to a great career. This confidence was shared by many others, including some whose opinion counted for much. His *La Mitrailleuse* had been described by Sickert as 'the most authoritative and concentrated utterance on the war'.

It is of course too early for final judgments, but looking back it would seem now that in the autumn of 1916 Nevinson was not on the threshold of a career but at its climax. It is difficult to think of anything he made during the thirty years which remained to him that compares in energy or in conviction with what he made during the first two years of the First World War, and difficult to see the course of his life as a painter otherwise than as a slow decline.

How did it come about that this man, industrious, gifted, resourceful, independent and deeply in earnest, should have been unable to advance beyond the point that he reached when he was

[1] 'Process or Person'. Unsigned but written by Arthur Clutton-Brock, art critic of 'The Times'. 5 October 1916.
[2] 'Paint and Prejudice', p. 87.

twenty-seven, and in spite of the possession of these and other qualities should have fallen progressively below it? The answer is to be found, I think, in the spiritual crisis brought upon him by the difference between his conception of what war would be like, and what he saw in the hospitals around Dunkirk. He was a humane man, singularly free from malice, let alone cruelty. Yet he was a faithful follower of Marinetti and deeply imbued with the Futurists' gospel of war and their contempt for the humanitarian sentiments to which war was abhorrent. It would be wrong to suggest that Nevinson, in the depths of his being, fully approved, still less that he hoped for, the coming of any particular war, yet as he himself declared, in the New York interview already quoted, 'Modern artists have been at war since 1912. . . . They were in love with the glory of violence. . . . Some say that artists have lagged behind the war. I should say not! They were miles ahead of it. They were all ready for the great machine that is modern war.' It is significant that these words were spoken after the war, at a time when his own sentiments had changed. Significant also is the date 1912. It was the date of the Balkan War which so enchanted Marinetti; it was the date of Nevinson's own conversion to Futurism, at the Futurist Exhibition held in London in that year.

So when the First World War came Nevinson could not miss the chance to experience war at first hand. He had heard his master imitate the thunder of the guns round Adrianople–at the siege of which he had been present–and Nevinson knew that such a sound was but a whimper compared with the thunder of the guns along the Western Front. He was in love with the Great Machine–scarcely more than tuning up that sunny autumn–and with noise, speed and power.

'It was dark when we arrived,' he wrote. 'There was a strong smell of gangrene, urine and French cigarettes.' That was the deepest, most personal impression he had of the war: incompetence, corruption, callousness, the whimpers of maimed and dying men . . . 'the strong smell of gangrene, urine and French cigarettes'.

In representing with such directness, starkness and force, and with such particular insight, his early experience of the war, Nevinson was, as it were, expending his Futurist and Cubist capital. He was a simple man. The effect of the shock of discovery that war was

not the mechanized Wagner, all thunder and speed, was not 'the
hygienics of the world', was to shatter his faith not only in the
Futurist glorification of war and in Futurism itself, but, by association, in Cubism–in fact in the entire revolutionary spirit in the arts.
So long as he had no time for reflexion, he worked, and worked
brilliantly, in a tradition in which he was losing faith, in a spirit
which was a habit that was being broken. All Nevinson's experience
combined to enable him to represent the war superbly, but the act
of so doing involved the repudiation of that experience.

For many people progress is an inevitable process, operative in
every field of human endeavour, whereby the bad is ameliorated and
the good replaced by the better. This conviction springs from the
belief that human nature seeks and cannot but seek the good and
that but for the malevolent obstruction of a complex of inertia and
vested interest in opposing the beneficent process, of 'reaction' in
fact, it would quickly achieve it.

For such people anything 'advanced' is of necessity better than
what it replaces. So much is self-evident, and to doubt it is a betrayal
of progress. It is as simple as that. When Nevinson was growing up
it seemed simpler still. 'Progress' was accepted as a great self-evident
fact. There had been no blood-lettings on a world-wide scale to dis-
grace the human species; there had been no such complicating factors
as, for instance, the brusquest repudiation by States in certain respects
socially progressive of 'progressive' art. In 1914 a man was either
'of his time', a progressive, or else he formed part of the menacing
shadow that stood between mankind and the sun.

The young Nevinson was a simple man for whom the distinction
between opposing forces was particularly sharp. On the one side was
militant dynamism, 'in love with violence', the Great Machine its
supreme creation; on the other, traitor pioneers 'refusing to resume
the march', decadence, mediocrity, morris-dancing, in two words,
'passeist filth'.

For all his talk of violence Nevinson was a humane man. The sight
of those broken men at Dunkirk lying neglected in the stinking
darkness, and the sound of their cries for their mothers, was a
memory that was always with him.

According to my understanding, this experience began a process
which transformed Nevinson's whole outlook on life. It was plain

that morris-dancing could not have been responsible for the mutilation of these men; it was not long before it occurred to him that they might be victims of his old love 'violence'. If 'violence' could have such degrading consequences–'violence' that was the most glorious mark of 'dynamism'–how could Futurism remain, in his eyes, a glorious movement? He realized that if the Great Machine was to function–and in repose it was without meaning–then it needed victims: victims such as the remains of men who had lain in that dark shed. And if the Great Machine needed victims to fulfil itself, how could he not suspect that not Futurism only but the whole progressive movement had a dark side? A more analytic mind might have disassociated the purely aesthetic elements in Futurism from the bombast and the automobilism, and might have argued that Cubism might be valid simply as a way of painting; but Nevinson was of a simplicity and a wholeheartedness to whom the weighing of pros and cons was repugnant: his was one of those natures in whom the tides run quickly in or out. His humanity, revolted by war which his master had glorified, led him first to doubt and eventually to abhor the validity of the progressive movement in all its manifestations.

As a man who has lost his religious faith may long retain habits of observance, so Nevinson retained much of the air of a progressive. It was not until after his election as an Associate of the Royal Academy in 1939, I fancy, that he altogether ceased to think of himself as a 'rebel'. By then he had long ceased to be anything but a realist of a highly conventional type, and the effects of the change which Dunkirk had set off were to be seen with remarkable promptitude.

In July 1917 he was sent to the Western Front as an Official War Artist, where he spent several months making rapid shorthand sketches, chiefly, he has told us, from memory,[1] but also 'in the front line, behind the lines, above the lines in observation balloons'.[2] In the following March an exhibition of his war pictures in various mediums was held in London. They are various, enterprising and accomplished, but, in comparison with the pictures shown two years

---

[1] Preface to Catalogue of an Exhibition of Pictures of War by C. R. W. Nevincon. The Leicester Galleries, March 1918.
[2] Ibid.

before, they are the works of a man without conviction. The savage feeling of outrage,. the sharp cutting edge, the sombreness, the weight, all survive only in feeble parody. The pictures shown in 1918 might be the works of a disciple of the Nevinson of 1916, so tame is their imagery. The declension may be seen at a glance by comparing one of the best of the later paintings, *Roads of France, Field Artillery and Infantry*,[1] with the earlier *Column on the March*. The themes of the two are closely similar; yet what a difference there is between them! The second is treated with audacious resilience: under a sky of burning blue the column stretches .on for ever. 'The soft thud of the men's feet as they march along the road,' wrote Sir Osbert Sitwell, 'can almost be caught by our ears, and we can almost see the shadows on the cobbles moving as they march.'[2] The soldiers in the first kick up a little dust, but they do not compel us to listen for their footsteps; we are not interested, for they are only toy soldiers.

During his first war exhibition a reporter asked Nevinson whether he was going to repeat his success and paint more war pictures. 'No,' he replied, 'I have painted everything I saw in France, and there will be no more.'[3] At the time he was, of course, unaware of the further opportunities shortly to be offered to him, but the words have a prophetic ring.

For almost thirty years the decline continued. From time to time he painted a picture of merit. The skyscrapers of Manhattan struck in him a spark of the old Cubist fire; an occasional London street or twilight view of the Thames stirred deeply his interest in people and places: indeed for a painter as vivid in feeling and as rich in resource this could hardly have been otherwise. Shocked by his humanity out of the tradition, the way of seeing and the way of painting best suited to foster the gifts of this greatly gifted man, Nevinson, lost and enervated, more often made literal representations of landscape or embarrassing fantasies such as *Pan Triumphant*[4] or *The Twentieth Century*.[5] And as his art declined his suspicion of precise thought

[1] The National Gallery of Canada, Ottawa.
[2] 'C. R. W. Nevinson: Contemporary British Artists'. Text by Osbert Sitwell, 1925, p. 29.
[3] 'The Daily Mirror', 18 October 1916.
[4] Coll. Mr. and Mrs. Barney Seale.
[5] Coll. The Laing Art Gallery, Newcastle-upon-Tyne.

grew more insistent, and his hatred of 'intellectuals' tempted him to speak over their heads to the public at large, and in the role of 'outspoken rebel' he contributed, with increasing frequency, his views to the popular Press. Articles such as 'Do Beautiful Women get away with it?'[1], 'Pretty Women: are there any left?',[2] 'She lived a life of Luxury',[3] 'Making an Age of Faith',[4] appeared at times with a regularity that would have done credit to a full-time journalist. He addressed meetings upon every kind of topic.... 'My last appearance at that time', runs a characteristic sentence in his autobiography, 'was at a luncheon given by the Happy Thought Society. ...'[5]

This continuous spate of vulgar publicity and his pathological touchiness made the older Nevinson an easy target. But a target at which anyone who knew him would be reluctant to aim. To be an oracle can be gratifying and remunerative, but there was something tragic in the spectacle of this man's being forced, by his life-long sense of singularity, his exacerbated sense of ill-usage by intellectuals, to cast his net so indiscriminately in search of admiration and affection. Tragic this would have been in any case, but it was particularly so in the case of Nevinson. He was not only an artist of high gifts but a kindly man and an entertaining companion, and a host of extraordinary charm, to whom Mr. Crawley's description of Mr. Toogood might appropriately be applied, 'a man who conceals a warm heart, and an active spirit, and healthy sympathies, under an affected jocularity of manner, and almost with a touch of vulgarity'. With what eagerness I used to await the parties that he and his wife gave at 1 Steele's Studios, off Haverstock Hill. One entered the big room, crowded with 'celebrities' of stage and screen, of Chelsea and Fleet Street, and made one's way to the centre of the vortex, Nevinson himself, stout, portentous, talking loudly–about himself. I well remember on the first such occasion going up to him to pay my respects, with his booming voice like a fog-horn to guide me through the crowd. 'Poor girls, poor girls,' he was saying, 'sooner or later they all tell me I'm the love of their lives! I give it

[1] 'The Sunday Graphic', 30 November 1930.
[2] 'The Daily Express', 29 October 1930.
[3] 'The Sunday Express', 22 March 1931.
[4] 'The Sunday Referee', 30 August 1931.
[5] 'Paint and Prejudice', p. 201.

up. I can't explain it. I'm fat, ugly, promiscuous and indifferent. What do you make of it?'

⟡   ⟡   ⟡

There was a point at which, in the planning of these studies, I decided to omit Nevinson, so little sympathy was I able to feel with the greater part of his work and so persistent my distaste for writing about that which I cannot admire. The longer I reflected, however, the more clearly was it borne in upon me that even if the later years of his life were productive of little of outstanding merit, the two first years or so of the First World War were years passed in a theatre of action so magnificent, apprehended with such an intensity of feeling and expressed with a power so worthy of the feeling which it conveyed, that they were able to produce as many paintings of outstanding merit as other subjects of these studies produced in their entire lives. I look back with shame at the moment when I considered passing over the painter not only of *La Patrie, La Mitrailleuse, Column on the March*, but of *On the Road to Ypres*,[1] of 1915, *A Dawn, 1914*,[2] of 1916, *After a Push*,[3] of 1916, of *From an Office Window*,[4] of 1917, a group of figures in landscape, which manifest a sense of colour less conspicuous later on, such as *A Thames Regatta*,[5] of two admirable *Self-Portraits*, of 1911[6] and 1915,[7] and a memorable view, *Barges on the Thames*,[8] of about 1916.

[1] Coll. Mr. Clive Morris.
[2] Whereabouts unknown.
[3] The Imperial War Museum, London.
[4] Coll. Sir Osbert Sitwell, Bt.
[5] Coll. Lieut. G. Hoskins.
[6] The Tate Gallery, London,
[7] Coll. Mr. Adolph Lewisohn.
[8] The City Art Gallery, Manchester.

EDWARD WADSWORTH

1889–1949

IN 1914 the name of Wadsworth–a young painter who had left the Slade only two years before–was flung truculently in the face of the public. 'Vital English Art. Futurist Manifesto', signed 'F. T. Marinetti, Italian Futurist Movement (Milan), C. R. W. Nevinson, Art Rebel Centre, London' concluded with the following appeal: 'So we call upon the English public to support, defend and glorify the genius of the great Futurist painters or pioneers and advance-forces of vital English Art.' To it were appended, in bold black type, the names of the nine artists in whom these 'advance forces' were personified. One of these is Wadsworth's.[1]

His membership of the Vorticist Group and his contributions to 'Blast' and to the Vorticist Exhibition[2] confirmed the impression of him as a member of the extreme advance guard in general and a disciple of Wyndham Lewis in particular. His paintings for the most part were essays, competent but undistinguished, in the Cubism that based itself upon the more formal aspects of the work of Cézanne–paintings of a kind and quality common in Paris and among all those groups outside France which looked for leadership to Paris. His drawings, especially the dynamic abstracts which were the most characteristic part of his production, closely resembled those of Wyndham Lewis. These drawings, as is often the case with manifestations of a new movement, are marked by an energy, in spite of his discipleship of the movement's leader, that was lacking in his academic studies in the manner of Cézanne's followers. The close resemblance between the work of Wadsworth and that of Wyndham Lewis did not deceive at least one observer. To Mr. Ezra Pound, friend and advocate of the Vorticists, it was apparent that Wadsworth and Wyndham Lewis were different kinds of men. From a distance of more than forty years and with the knowledge

---

[1] The others are Atkinson, Bomberg, Epstein, Etchells, Hamilton, Nevinson. Roberts and Wyndham Lewis.
[2] Which included four paintings and four drawings by Wadsworth.

of their later work this is clear enough, but it took some wit to perceive it then. In 'Edward Wadsworth, Vorticist' in 'The Egoist' of 15 August 1914 Mr. Pound admirably drew this radical distinction between them.

Mr. Lewis is restless, turbulent, intelligent, bound to make himself felt. If he had not been a vorticist painter he would have been a vorticist something else. He is a man full of sudden, illuminating antipathies . . . a mind always full of thought, subtle, swift-moving.

A man with this kind of intelligence is bound always to be crashing and opposing and breaking. You cannot be as intelligent in that sort of way, without being prey to the furies.

If, on the other hand, Mr. Wadsworth had not been a vorticist painter he would have been some other kind of painter. Being a good painter, born in England in such and such a year of our era, the time, the forces of nature, made him a vorticist. It is as hard to conceive Mr. Wadsworth expressing himself in any other medium save paint as it is to conceive Mr. Lewis remaining unexpressed. . . . Ones differentiation of [their work] arranges itself almost as a series of antitheses. Turbulent energy: repose. Anger: placidity.

It is natural that Mr. Lewis should give us pictures of intelligence gnashing teeth with stupidity . . . and that he should stop design and burst into scathing criticism. . . .

I cannot recall any painting of Mr. Wadsworth's where he seems to be angry. There is a delight in mechanical beauty, a delight in the beauty of ships, or of crocuses, or a delight in pure form. He liked this, that or the other, and so he sat down to paint it.

This prescient appreciation published when Wadsworth was twenty-five, and, for less acute observers, a mute disciple of Wyndham Lewis, insists upon the important fact that Wadsworth was, before everything else, a painter. It suggests that the particular form which his painting assumed was largely a consequence of the intellectual and emotional climate of the time and place in which he was born, and that he chose his subjects because he happened to like them. In the course of his contrasting sketches Mr. Pound has given an indication of the kind of artist Wadsworth was.

⚬   ⚬   ⚬

Edward Alexander Wadsworth was born on 29 October 1889, at Highfield, Cleckheaton, in the West Riding of Yorkshire, the only child of Fred Wadsworth and his first wife Hannah Smith. Fred

Wadsworth was the second son of Elmyas Wadsworth, who, beginning as an overseer, showed such energy and inventiveness as enabled him to establish Broomfield Mills, an important worsted spinning concern which bore his name. A tribute to Fred Wadsworth by the Minister of the Westgate Congregational Church with which he was associated for many years in several capacities, among others as voluntary organist, records that 'his mind was of the critical and analytic type'.[1] It is significant that among the artist's immediate forebears we find energy and inventiveness, love of music and an analytic cast of mind.

Edward Wadsworth was sent to a preparatory school at Ilkley, to Fettes College, Edinburgh, and to Munich to perfect his knowledge of German. In his spare time he attended the Knirr Art School; for the idea that he must become an artist and not a worsted spinner had already taken a firm hold upon him. He had already taken the decision to become a painter. This decision became an issue with his family, who eventually, dourly but without resentment, gave way. Wadsworth spent a few months at the Bradford School of Art where he won a scholarship to the Slade. Here he studied from 1908 until 1912. It was not long before the steady application and the efficiency which marked all his activities justified his decision to be an artist. In 1911 he was awarded the first prize for figure painting at the Slade, and he painted a *Self-portrait*[2] with a turban–an excellently characterized representation of his own sardonic face, with its eyebrows bushy and low-set and its wide mouth habitually compressed. The taut, purposeful, rather ruthless face suggests that he was already a man dedicated to his vocation. The portrait has often been reproduced but I doubt whether it is generally realized that it is a portrait of the artist at twenty-two.

During his last year at the Slade and the following year he painted, besides the conventional post-Cézanne studies mentioned earlier, pictures in the manner of the Camden Town Group, such, for instance, as *Portrait of Mrs. Harold Gilman*,[3] of 1912, and at least one in the manner of the Fauves, a beach-scene[4] made at Havre in 1911.

[1] 'The Cleckheaton Guardian', 7 January 1921.
[2] Coll. Mrs. Edward Wadsworth.
[3] Coll. Mrs. Harold Gilman.
[4] Destroyed in the Second World War.

In 1912 he married Fanny Eveleigh, a violinist. After their marriage Wadsworth and his wife spent six months abroad, going first to Madeira and Las Palmas, where he painted a number of panels, of which none appear to be extant, and later to Paris where he worked daily on landscape subjects on the city's outskirts, completing another series of panels which have likewise disappeared. On their return to London they established themselves over a furniture shop at 2 Gloucester Walk, Campden Hill.

It was probably in 1913 that he made a friend who quickened his imagination and gave him an insight into its nature. Returning home after a day's work at the Omega Workshops (where he was briefly employed, among other tasks, upon the repair of the Mantegna cartoons at Hampton Court) he said to his wife, 'I've met an interesting man; he's coming to see us.' A few days later Wyndham Lewis called. The burning preoccupation of his new friend with art politics (as indeed with politics of every kind) drew Wadsworth into the Vorticist movement, and into participation in its various manifestations. He contributed not only to the Vorticist Exhibition, to 'Blast', but also to Group X which represented a post-war effort to revive it. Their close association continued until 1920; thereafter the intervals between their meetings grew longer.

Wadsworth, in spite of his refusal to become an engineer, had a life-long passion for machinery, and with this passion went a love of hard textures and powerful, streamlined forms. This and a frank enjoyment of the dynamic manifestations of contemporary life evoked in him a sympathy with the Futurist movement. Thus predisposed, it was easy for Wyndham Lewis to persuade him to share his own violent but nevertheless more mature and rational attitude towards the arts, and his contempt for 'the fuss and hysterics of the Futurists'. To his association with Wyndham Lewis he owed the rudiments of a philosophy, which by justifying strengthened his own innate predilections, and a bracing intellectual companionship.

Without this association he might have been tempted to adopt styles and subjects imperfectly suited to his innermost needs. For a time he became a disciple: many of his drawings were tidier but less dynamic versions of his master's. Such drawings, however, were so competent and assured that he came to be regarded, next to Wyndham Lewis, as the representative Vorticist. To Mr. Pound the truth

45. Edward
Wadsworth.
Dunkerque (1924).
Tempera, 25×35 in.
The City Art Gallery,
Manchester.

46. EDWARD WADSWORTH. *Little Western Flower* (1928).
Tempera, 21 × 15 in. Coll. Mr. J. E. Barton.

was plain: he owed his Vorticism to accidents of time and place, but he was quintessentially a painter. In being a painter in this special sense he resembles Steer. Their paintings, of course, could hardly be more different: Steer's atmospheric and suffused with a generous and languid poetry; Wadsworth's metallic and sharply exact. But both men, though in their different ways intelligent men, neither felt nor reasoned deeply about anything but painting. It is a commonplace that however purely aesthetic a work of art may be it expresses the outlook on the world of the man who made it. Sometimes the maker is a man with very positive ideas to communicate, a man such as Leonardo, Michelangelo, David or Delacroix, and in our own time Stanley Spencer or Wyndham Lewis; sometimes he is a man content simply to accept current ideas as motives for his pictures without being greatly concerned about their significance. If such ideas provide sufficient pretexts for the full exercise of his faculties as a painter, they are all he requires. Steer and Wadsworth are both notable contemporary examples of that class—to which indeed the great majority belongs—which simply takes from the repertory of current ideas such as they find to be, as Mr. Berenson would say, 'life enhancing'. Steer added nothing of substance to what Turner, Constable and the Impressionists had already communicated: he selected certain ideas from their repertory to which he gave a slight personal touch when he restated them with a relaxed largeness and dignity and a mastery of his mediums which gives him a foremost place among the English painters of his time. At first glance Wadsworth seems in this respect to belong to a quite different category. The complexity and precision of his compositions, his preference for motives specifically modern, the streamlined, sophisticated look of his work, all suggest the presence of a vigorous, even an adventurous, intellect. But at a first glance only. Closer examination shows that he took from others the ideas and motives he needed to nourish his art, from Chirico, Lurçat, Léger, Pierre Roy and Wyndham Lewis; that like Steer, Wadsworth was a pure painter. I once asked his wife whether he had any interest in religion, philosophy or politics. 'None whatever, and least of all in the politics of art,' she answered; 'painting was his only interest, and with him discussion of other subjects came quickly back to painting.' 'It was the same,' she added, 'with his reading; he read various kinds of books in French and German as

well as English, but the only books that absorbed him, that he returned to, were books on painting, and most of all, books on the
technique of painting. As for Cennino Cennini's treatise,[1] he read it
again and again–he was always reading it.' Wadsworth's disinterest
in everything other than painting extended to people–he was a
steady friend and good company, but human relations played almost
as little part in his scheme of things as figures played in his art.

The development of Vorticism was arrested by the First World
War. Wadsworth's experiences of the war were reflected in his art.
From 1915 until 1917 when he was invalided home, he served as an
Intelligence Officer in the Royal Naval Volunteer Reserve in the
Eastern Mediterranean, and was stationed on the island of Mudros.
On his recovery he was engaged with other painters on the dazzle-
camouflage of ships at various ports. He worked mainly at Liverpool
and Bristol and he superintended the application of camouflage
designs upon over two thousand ships in less than a year, including
the eight hundred foot long 'Aquitania'.

It is reasonable to suppose that these circumstances offered no new
revelation but that they confirmed his innate way of seeing: the
sight of classical civilization and the clear Mediterranean light his
predilection for what was rational and lucid; the designing of
camouflage his predilection for geometrical form; and the whole of
it his passion for the sea.

An exhibition of his woodcuts held in 1919 at the Adelphi Gallery[2]
of a variety of subjects, Greek towns and harbours, ships dazzle-
camouflaged and pure abstractions, was received with serious
attention unqualified by the hostility which might have been
expected, considering how conspicuously Cubist they were. Indeed
he received praise even in the popular Press for the frankness of his
Cubism: 'He has not halted between Cubism and Naturalism',
observed, for instance, 'The Weekly Despatch', 'or backed out of
Cubism like C. R. W. Nevinson.'[3] At no time did Wadsworth's
work provoke the hostility which the work of artists belonging to
extreme and uncompromising movements usually provokes. This
circumstance seems to be worth noting, as it is not due to the chance
disposition of critics but to the character of the work. It is the
original idea which shocks and Wadsworth's art was never the

[1] 'Trattato della Pittura'.   [2] Duke Street, Adelphi.   [3] 23 March 1919.

expression of original ideas: his disposition was to take the ideas he found useful from the common stock and to express them with a workmanlike perfection of finish which won the respect of spectators of varying principles and tastes. Finish of so meticulous a kind suggests a willingness to take an infinity of pains which is apt to disarm the critic. Even the Vorticist *Suggestion for a Building*, which Wadsworth exhibited[1] late the same year, was taken in good part though it could hardly have represented a more extravagant departure from any architectural tradition. His contributions to 'Works of Camoufleur Artists and Examples of Camouflage'[2] were regarded as outstanding.

Wadsworth was recognized, in fact, as one of the most promising artists of his generation. Early in 1920 there occurred an event which caused judges whose opinion counted for much to consider his promise abundantly fulfilled. This was the exhibition of a series of industrial landscape drawings entitled *The Black Country*.[3] Arnold Bennett wrote the preface to the catalogue.

Wadsworth did not discover industry as a subject: earlier artists, Sir Charles Holmes, for instance, and Joseph Pennell, had stressed its general impressiveness and mystery, the picturesqueness of scaffolding and cranes seen through billowing smoke. But it had been represented, as a rule, romantically from afar, and by artists who knew little about it at first hand. Wadsworth was not a romantic and since childhood had been familiar with industry; but for his firmness of purpose he would have been an industrialist himself.

He regarded his subject without illusions but with intimate knowledge; he regarded it as the dramatic and appropriate content for the forms he had evolved under Vorticist discipline. His imagination was stirred by the gloomy grandeur of this wilderness of slag: he came to it with those acute perceptions with which men return to scenes formerly familiar, and he came ideally prepared by his researches in abstract form to see a rhythmic order in smoking chaos. 'He is the fortunate man,' said one critic, 'who first made a map of the country he intended to find and then went out and found it.'[4]

[1] Practical Arts, an exhibition organised by the Arts League of Service at the Twenty-One Gallery, Durham House Street, Adelphi.
[2] Burlington House, October 1919.   [3] The Leicester Galleries, January.
[4] 'The New Age', 29 January 1920.

These were remarkable drawings, remarkable both for the hard logic of their designing and for the immediacy and the sureness with which the vastness and the blighted gloom of the region, the over-whelming energy and scale of the whole industrial process, had been seized: the blast furnaces and the great flames they send upwards, the tides of lava and the endless mountains of slag, the indisposable waste. It was among the blast furnaces, Wyndham Lewis con-sidered, that the true Wadsworth was to be found. It is my own belief, too, that he made nothing finer than *The Black Country*.

It is strange that having occupied himself with a subject to which his earlier experience had ideally attuned him, and made what he must have known were pictures of outstanding quality, he should have failed to continue to work this vein, but instead have faltered and turned away. I can offer only a tentative explanation. *The Black Country* drawings were made in 1919. During 1920 and 1921 he made several paintings of industrial subjects. These showed few of the qualities of *The Black Country*, and were no more than elaborate essays in the conventional cubist manner. Then gradually first rural and then Mediterranean replaced industrial subjects, but not, I think, to the pictures' advantage. My explanation turns upon the death of Wadsworth's father. This took place at the beginning of 1921, before Wadsworth had found the means of perfecting his large industrial subjects. One consequence was that he inherited a considerable fortune, which enabled him to gratify his passion for the sea in general and the Mediterranean in particular. Thenceforward he spent little time in the Midlands and the North of England, and much in Italy and the South of France. It seems to me, then, that in the early nineteen-twenties Wadsworth lost his way. I am fortified in this opinion by the knowledge that the artist himself destroyed a substantial number of these Cubist essays, including industrial, rural and Mediterranean subjects.

It was not long, however, before his passion for the sea gave his development a new impetus and a new direction. Around 1922 he abandoned oil paint for tempera, a medium well suited to those who desire clarity above all else and who are indifferent both to atmo-sphere and to the 'painterly' effects that can be obtained only with pigments mixed with oil. The new medium, more especially when employed to make pictures of his chosen subject, the sea, produced bracing effects. It should be mentioned here that, in spite of his maritime obsession, he was not in the ordinary sense a painter of the sea at all. A painter beside the sea, not of it, was what Zadkine[1] truly called him, and this is just what he was: a painter of harbours, ships, jetties, shells, marine instruments and the like, but of the sea itself only as a background or in a subordinate place, and always dead calm.

Inspired by Turner's *The Harbours of England* he embarked upon a series of paintings of the principal ports of the United Kingdom, but I have been unable to ascertain how far he carried it. During 1923 he painted *Seaport*[2] and some other port subjects in which his efforts to build up compositions complex yet closely knit that should convey an effect of stability are too obvious, and they fail of their effect. But at the end of that year and again in 1924 he visited Dunkirk, where his earlier efforts reaped a rich and sudden reward. The result of these visits was a small group of paintings of sailing ships in port of extraordinary quality. The finest of these, *Dunkerque*,[3] of 1924 (Plate 45), shows him as a composer of exceptional resource and an impeccable craftsman in an academic style of commanding elegance.

On a number of occasions since I have been Director of the Tate, the Gallery has come under criticism on account of alleged preoccupation with 'advanced' art to the exclusion of the academic, and when the first volume of these studies appeared the absence of certain academic painters was noted. The truth is that in this century of perpetual change the larger number of the finest talents tend to be drawn into one or other of the 'advanced' movements, so that worthy examples of academic art are very far from commonly met with. But in these Dunkirk pictures of Wadsworth's the classical tradition lives again in all its limpid harmony.

Yet meditation upon the very success of these attempts at representing the thing before the eyes in terms of a beauty entirely classical, serves, it seems to me, to make one more rather than less conscious of how unfavourable the climate of the twentieth century is to traditional painting, and how positively it seems to foster

---

[1] 'Edward Wadsworth', No. XIII Editions Selection, with tributes by Waldemar George, Michael Sevier and Ossip Zadkine. Antwerp, 1933.

[2] Coll. Mrs. B. C. Windeler.   [3] The City Art Gallery, Manchester.

change. For here in the *Dunkirk* series we have a painter able to combine exact representation of a subject to which he responded with passion, with conformity to the severest canons of traditional design, yet free of the complacent touch which often vitiates so many academic works, and marked, indeed, with an astringent contemporary tang; yet nothing could be plainer than that this particular combination of virtues afforded to the painter himself only the most transient satisfaction. It is difficult to estimate precisely how extensive the series originally was, as one at least, and possibly more, was destroyed by the painter, but it can scarcely have extended to more than half a dozen. There was no question of his taking the series as a basis for a traditional style: as a man very much 'of his time' he was under a compulsion to press forward. It is my belief that until so many of the best artists cease to be subject to such a compulsion and become less liable to suffer, as so many do, from a sense of failure, of guilt even, unless they are for ever on the move, painting cannot recover the perfection that can result only from repeated attempts to attain the same objective. An objective in rapid and continuous movement may evoke an inventive, audacious, exciting art, but not one in any proper sense of the term 'classical'.

From the *Dunkirk* series Wadsworth, then, promptly moved on: first to ships in harbour of a more generalized character, scenes upon which, to their seeming discomfort, a pattern was somewhat arbitrarily imposed.[1] His interest in ships culminated, in 1926, in the publication of a book, 'Sailing Ships and Barges of the Western Mediterranean and Adriatic Seas', for which Wadsworth made engravings on copper afterwards coloured by hand.[2] It is a book of interest and beauty, the aim of which was primarily to serve as a fittingly exquisite record of a disappearing means of transport. The making of these engravings fulfilled his need to represent ships, for after 1926, although his passion for the sea remained, ships entire figure rarely in his work.

About the same time another subject engaged his interest—a very 'period' interest this—the architecture and to a limited extent the life,

---

[1] A characteristic example, of which a photograph survives, was destroyed by the artist: others belong to Mr. Walter Wadsworth and Mrs. Margaret Drew.

[2] With a preface and brief descriptions by Bernard Windeler. Published by Etchells and Macdonald, Frederick Etchells being an associate in the Vorticist Group.

more especially its seamy side, of Southern France. This interest issued in drawings and occasional paintings of streets in Marseilles, Toulon and other ports, narrow streets of ancient fantastically intricate buildings, enlivened with festoons of washing or by flamboyant signs advertising sailors' bordels. A characteristic example is *Marseilles*,[1] of 1925, a lively picture, but neither the subject nor the spirit in which it is represented is particularly Wadsworth's own. The treatment of the architecture is slight and similar to that of others, to that of his friend Richard Wyndham for example, and the evocation of the life of sailors' bistro and bordel lacks altogether the sinister insight of their younger contemporary Edward Burra.

Both formalized shipping-in-harbour (glimpsed sometimes through parted curtains) and narrow street were trivial deviations, for it was about the time when he was engaged upon such themes that he gained a deeper insight into what he wanted to accomplish. That is to say, he began the long series of still-lifes of a highly personal kind upon which he was principally engaged for the rest of his life, and which, in fact, must be regarded as his most characteristic works.

These still-lifes might be taken at first glance for examples of the kind of fantastic painting which the Surrealist movement was inspiring, but closer scrutiny reveals its personal character. Wadsworth's practice of placing together objects which have no congruity with one another he learnt from Surrealism, but the element of fantasy ends with the choice of objects: his representation of them is as precise as a highly skilled craftsman could make it. Not for him watches hanging limply over clothes-lines; his shells, hurricane-lamps, sextants, floats, chains, coils of twine, blueprints, binoculars, propellers and other marine objects, as well as occasional ribbons, masks and flowers, are never placed in positions which, in the world of reality, they would be unable to sustain; all conform to laws of construction, of gravitation and of perspective; all are laid upon foundations which will bear their weight, and all are capable of function. (Even the liberties he seems to take with the scale of objects—with sea-shells, for instance, which sometimes loom enormous in his foregrounds—may be only apparent, for he is known to have made a collection of the largest Mediterranean shells.) For the most part these assemblies of sharply incongruous objects are

[1] The City Art Gallery, Leeds.

law-abiding citizens of a scheme of things which closely corresponds
to the natural. More closely, in one important respect, to Mediterranean than to northern nature, for they are placed in a setting where
the atmosphere has no density or movement and where everything
is without motion and bathed in a merciless white light. These still-
lifes are the culmination of his steady, consistent evolution, the final
expressions of his lucid, logical and supremely unequivocal mind.
One excellent example out of many, *Little Western Flower*,[1] of 1928, is
reproduced on Plate 46.

Law-abiding as they are, they are none the less expressions of a
personality. How definitely was shown by an experiment. Certain
visitors to an exhibition[2] of his paintings in tempera held in 1929
criticized his method as 'excessively photographic'. Doubtful whether
this criticism was well founded, and eager, moreover, to demonstrate the camera's powers, two gifted photographers, Mr. Maurice
Beck and Miss McGregor, set up a number of still-lifes closely
resembling those of Wadsworth, of which they made photographs.
Three of these were reproduced in 'The Graphic'[3] beside three photographs of still-life paintings by Wadsworth. The confrontation
clarifies the contrast between painting and photography, and reveals once again how superior is the power of the painter, by a
hundred delicate touches, to emphasize certain forms and certain
contrasts and affinities, to mute others in a way that is not open to a
photographer, who has the power only to select, even when, as in
the present instance, he also arranged the subject. The painter's
superior power of communication is particularly well illustrated
by this particular confrontation, because Wadsworth's method of
painting in tempera is one that reveals no brushstrokes, which with
most painters are the instrument whereby accents–highlights, for
instance, or contours distinguishing forms that merge in nature and
the like–are emphasized.

Towards the end of the nineteen-twenties Wadsworth's interest
in pure still-life waned: it shows itself thenceforward most often in
the foregrounds of his harbours, beaches or distant prospects of the
sea. This change was followed by another, a change not of vision
but of method. Around 1938 the sharply defined contours and the

[1] Coll. Mr. J. E. Barton.
[2] At Messrs. Arthur Tooth and Son, from 23 May until 8 June.   [3] 30 August.

enamel-like quality of his colour were radically modified by the influence of Seurat: it was as though Wadsworth's paintings of earlier days–for the compositions altered little–were seen through a fine mesh, which at once lightened and broke their surfaces. Pictures painted in dots reflect, it seems to me, the particular character of Wadsworth's mind less immediately than those painted with sharp outlines in surfaces of clear, continuous colour. A few of the pictures painted according to a method close to Seurat's, however, take a high place among his works, notably *Requiescat*,[1] of February 1940. Although the Seurat method was liable to be used by him from time to time for the rest of his life, it was rarely manifest after the early 'forties in quite such forthright terms as in, for instance, *Ouistreham, Caen*,[2] of May 1939, which is nothing more than an accomplished Seurat schoolpiece. I think he had reservations of some kind about this method, and this opinion is strengthened by a note he made beneath a photograph of a painting entitled *Harbour Entrance*,[3] of April 1939, 'Repainted 1944 and spots obliterated.' In a number of works of the 'forties the size of the dots is diminished to restore the primacy of the sharply defined contour, in such pictures, for instance, as the two versions of *Bronze Ballet*,[4] of March and April, and April and May 1940.

My attempt to give an indication of the character and growth of Wadsworth as a painter of still-life has led me to leave behind an important development in his art, of which his still-lifes formed the point of departure during the late 'twenties, namely, his participation in the abstract movement.

There was not, I think, at work in Wadsworth that strong innate tendency towards abstraction of which no student of the work of, say, Mondriaan or Ben Nicholson can be unaware. But there were other reasons which made him sympathetic to its appeal. Like the Futurists who had made so stimulating a din at a time when he was highly susceptible to what was going on around him, sentimentally he was, as already noted, a man very much 'of his time', responsive to the beauty of machinery, in particular to that of the big fast motor-cars he owned, and even had especially built. At the same susceptible

[1] The City Art Gallery, Leeds.   [2] Coll. Mrs. Edward Wadsworth.
[3] Coll. Mrs. Edward Wadsworth.
[4] Coll. Sir Arthur Bliss and The Tate Gallery, London.

age, too, abstract art, in the guise of Vorticism, was demonstrated by Wyndham Lewis to be both a powerful and an intellectually valid means of expression. When the full force of the abstract movement struck England, in the 'thirties, Wadsworth was well prepared to yield to its impact. The impact of abstraction may be seen in the most graphic terms in certain of his still-lifes of 1929 and 1930. Reference was made a few pages back to the strict conformity of Wadsworth's still-lifes to the laws of gravity and perspective. In these still-lifes of 1929 and 1930, however, it is as though the natural laws, especially the law of gravitation, were suspended, and a process of disintegration had set in. A characteristic example of this kind of still-life in which the objects represented, released from the law of gravitation, whirl about in the void, is *Composition*.[1] This anarchic phase was temporary; before long 'objects' tended to disappear, to merge into or be replaced by abstract forms, subject not to the laws of nature but to those of pure design.

Wadsworth's abstracts, an important feature of his work of the early 'thirties, showed the same meticulous workmanship and the same power of making statements that are perfectly lucid and unequivocal as all his paintings. I have never known a painter demand of himself so exacting a standard of technical perfection or any to destroy so many of his works in the belief that they fell below it. Among the many were a number–to judge from photographs and recollection–of the finest of these taut, energetic abstracts of the early 'thirties. One of these, or rather a near abstract, impinged suddenly upon public attention, and became the focus of an incident which had international repercussions. In the autumn of 1938 Wadsworth was commissioned by the London Passenger Transport Board to design a poster for the Lord Mayor's Show. The procession was predominantly a military parade that year, and the artist accordingly incorporated a machine gun and a Lewis gun into his design. Six thousand copies of the poster were displayed when, a few days before the show took place, 'Cassandra', otherwise Mr. William Connor, attacked the poster in 'The Daily Mirror'. 'If we are to show the beauty of engines of war to a peaceful travelling public, why not have the guts,' he asked, 'to show the effects of these instruments? Or would pictures of bullet-riddled bodies be a trifle unseemly?' An

[1] Solomon R. Guggenheim Museum, New York

official of the London Passenger Transport Board explained that they had originally planned to have a design 'embodying a golden coach', and the offending posters were taken down–barely twenty months before an all but disarmed Britain had to fight the gigantic German military machine. The incident appears to have been used widely in the German Press to show that Britain was 'too tired to fight': the Berlin 'Boersen Zeitung', for instance, carried a two-column headline 'England's recruiting need–the Government has to protect itself against Marxist demagogues.'

That year Wadsworth was much before the public. He designed and carried out two paintings for the First and Cabin Class smoke-rooms in the new liner 'Queen Mary', which were so large–they measured about 12 × 8 and 9 × 6 feet respectively–that the parish hall at Maresfield–the Sussex village where he had settled ten years earlier–was the only building in the neighbourhood which would accommodate the panels. Both were completed *in situ*. The one is without interest; the other is a fair example of one of his harbour landscapes with still-life in the foreground. During the same productive year he carried out a decoration–a large still-life of heraldic character–for the new de la Warr Pavilion at Bexhill, designed by Erich Mendelsohn and Serge Chermeyeff.

The last years of Wadsworth's life–he died in a London nursing home after some weeks of illness on 21 June 1949–were marked by no new developments. Although he was able, when occasion required it of him, to expound his aesthetic,[1] this added nothing at all to doctrines current among artists working in the cubist tradition, for he was never deeply concerned with ideas. His art therefore rarely challenged, rarely even disquieted, as art of the most original order almost invariably challenges or disquiets, and he came to be accepted more and more as an advanced painter from contact with whom no harm would be likely to result. His paintings–the verisimilitude of them, in fact–were the subject of jokes in 'Punch' and other journals ('few can deny that to the sextant-lover Mr. Wadsworth's excellent painting is second only to the real thing', and so forth)[2] and in 1944,

---

[1] For example,'The Abstract Painter's own Explanation','The Studio', November 1933, and 'Problems of the Painter, 1935', a discussion between Eric Newton and himself, 'The Listener', 20 March 1935.

[2] 'Punch', 13 April 1938.

without ever having submitted a painting to a Summer Exhibition, he was elected an Associate of the Royal Academy.

My own impression of the later Wadsworth—I neither knew him intimately nor saw him often but it is an impression that persists— is of a man whose earlier interest in ideas, never a particularly lively one, had dwindled almost away, and of a man preoccupied to the exclusion of almost everything else with the technicalities of his art. Of the many works of his hand which he destroyed, I understand that in the great majority of cases the faults he found were not in the conception or the realization of it but in the technique in the narrowest sense. How otherwise account for his destruction of one of the finest of the Dunkirk series, of the abstracts, of *Still Death*, a memorable still-life with a skull, painted between June and August 1937? It seems to me that his horror of being survived by a piece of defective workmanship became at times almost obsessive.

This horror, however, was but one manifestation of this most scrupulous of painter's horror of all imperfection in his own work. His concern at the discovery that the Tate possessed a picture[1] which he considered unworthy is expressed in some correspondence which passed between us in the autumn of 1942.

By the way, [he enquired] what is the *Still Life* by me to which you refer? I believe the Contemporary Art Society presented a painting of mine to the Tate a little time ago and this is no doubt the one. But what is it? I am very much afraid that it is a little picture of a couple of shells and a bit of blue ribbon which turned up at a show at the Leicester Galleries a few years ago—covered with what I can only think was Coach-Milvers' varnish and looking *dreadful*. If it *is* that one it ought not to be in the Tate at all. It was entirely experimental—painted on cardboard (of all poor things). What the experiment was I forget now— possibly something to do with demonstrating Tempera methods to Pierre Roy. In any case it is annoying and humiliating to be represented in our foremost modern National collection by a work that, in my opinion, has no merits at all. If *I* were in your position, in charge of the Tate, I should secretly destroy it—and with great enthusiasm! In these days of fuel economy it is only fit to contribute to the central-heating of the Tate! I suppose it would be out of the question to swap it for another painting.[2]

[1] *Still Life*, bequeathed by Montague Shearman through the Contemporary Art Society in 1940.
[2] 6 September.

It was eventually decided that the Tate should retain the *Still Life*, on the understanding that if deterioration became apparent it should be returned to the artist for treatment, while accepting as a gift *Bronze Ballet*, the picture for which he originally proposed to exchange it. In another letter in which he recognized this arrangement as 'in the long run, fairest to all concerned', he added these illuminating details about *Bronze Ballet*.

It is painted [he wrote] with yolk of egg (and powder colour) on a gessoed panel and was painted in April and May 1940 at Maresfield, Sussex—to the somewhat noisy accompaniment, as far as I remember, of the bombardment of Abbeville, Boulogne and Calais–all mingled with the call of the cuckoo! It is one of a series of many paintings done as a Le Havre series. It is in no sense a topographical view of any particular scene but all the motifs or design elements are to be found in that port and the two jetties 'place' it more or less.[1]

There was a close-knit, all-of-a-piece consistency about Wadsworth: he was efficient, industrious, and, in spite of the readiness with which the thin-lipped smile came to the bronzed saturnine face, and in spite of his powers of enjoyment of things, there was something a little inhuman about him–yet this was, perhaps, a characteristic not unfitting this oddly rare being, a true poet of the age of the machines.

[1] 24 October.

STANLEY SPENCER

b. 1891

I CANNOT at all remember what chance first sent me to Stanley
Spencer's studio, but I well remember the visit. The studio was
at the top of the Vale Hotel, a big public house overlooking the
pond in the Vale of Health in Hampstead. The room was barely
large enough to accommodate the immense canvas, measuring some
eighteen feet long by nine feet high, which leaned against the
longest wall. Up against the canvas stood a small table–which, with
two kitchen chairs and a small tin bath, was the room's only furniture–and upon it a large teapot, half a dozen unwashed plates and
some white marmalade jars, some containing paint brushes and
others marmalade.

Stanley Spencer was a tiny figure with a long fringe of dark hair
hanging low over a face of extraordinary earnestness and animation.
The least observant would have been aware of being in the presence
of a person of unusual energy and originality. After the minimum
of preliminaries he began to speak with the utmost candour of what
most deeply concerned him.

Sometimes the process of getting to know a person is the process,
so minutely described by Proust, of stripping layer after layer of
deceptive appearance and discerning at last the unexpected and
irreducible core of personality.

During the years following that first visit I have had day-long and
night-long talks with Stanley Spencer about aspects of his painting,
but he has never said anything so illuminating of the innermost
springs of his creation as what were almost his first words. At that
time he had held no exhibition, and, so far as I am aware, little or
nothing had been written about him, but I had the good fortune to
know two of his finest paintings *Zacharias and Elizabeth*,[1] of 1912–13
(Plate 47), which I had seen in Sir Muirhead Bone's house near
Oxford, and his *Self-Portrait*,[2] of 1913 (Plate 48), in the flat of

---

[1] Coll. Lady Bone.
[2] The Tate Gallery, London.

Sir Edward Marsh in Gray's Inn. When I spoke of my admiration for these he said:

> Those pictures have something that I have lost. When I left the Slade and went back to Cookham I entered a kind of earthly paradise. Everything seemed fresh and to belong to the morning. My ideas were beginning to unfold in fine order when along comes the war and smashes everything. When I came home the divine sequence had gone. I just opened a shutter in my side and out rushed my pictures anyhow. Nothing was ever the same again.

I spoke of the beauty of the glimpse of the river in the top left corner of the big canvas against the wall – one of a few meticulously finished islets in a wide sea of white priming; 'sometimes,' he said, 'I get a plain glimpse of that earthly paradise, but it's only a fragmentary glimpse'. These words of his were in no sense a personal confidence; they were repeated in one form and another at that time, I suppose, to anybody with whom he engaged in serious conversation; they give a luminous insight into a spiritual predicament that has not ceased to harrow and to drive him. This first great *Resurrection*,[1] he told me, was undertaken in 1923 and, to judge from the fact that it was scarcely begun, this visit of mine took place probably towards the end of that year. When he meets people he is prepared to treat them as friends, and he so treated me from my first visit, on which indeed he gave me the splendid pen drawing of himself which he made in preparation for the Tate *Self-Portrait*.

During the years following I saw him on other occasions. I recall, in particular, a later visit made in the spring of 1926, when *The Resurrection* was almost complete. Shareen, the Spencers' first child, had been born in November 1925. Mrs. Spencer was bathing Shareen, and I had a momentary distraction from her husband's conversation by my impression that the water was too hot. Shareen yelled, but appeared to suffer no harm. I remember, too, that a boiling kettle which stood upon a small iron stove filled the room with steam, which condensed and streamed down the spacious surface of the canvas. A quarter of a century later when certain of the greens showed a tendency to liquefy I invited the artist to come to the Tate to examine the picture. He was as puzzled as I about the cause of this liquefaction until we recalled the baleful perpetually steaming

[1] The Tate Gallery, London.

kettle, which, he became persuaded, was the cause of the instability of areas of the paint.

The great canvas, which I had first seen blank except for a few minutely finished islets, and – at longish intervals – seen fill gradually with figures resurrecting among gravestones and tombs and become suffused with simple, potent, highly personal poetry, moved me so much that I wrote an article on Stanley Spencer. This was accepted by 'Apollo' but remained unpublished. The following year the gift of *The Resurrection* to the Tate Gallery by Sir Joseph, afterwards Lord, Duveen made the picture a focus of widespread controversy. It was violently attacked and warmly praised. Stanley Spencer became a public figure – and my immature pages of eulogy became 'news' and were promptly published.[1]

A friendship had begun to grow up between us when in the spring of 1927 he went to live at Burghclere, near Newbury, to carry out wall paintings in the war memorial chapel specially built to house them by Lionel Pearson. I will speak of these extraordinary paintings in the appropriate place, but I would like to name at once the patrons whose vision and generosity enabled this great project to be realized: Mr. and Mrs. J. L. Behrend. The work occupied four years. In the late summer of the same year I emigrated to America.

It was not until twelve years later that I came to know him well. In the intervening years we met from time to time, and I was responsible for the acquisition, in 1933, of his *Separating Fighting Swans*, of the same year, by the Leeds City Art Gallery, the first example of his work, I fancy, to go into a public art collection outside London. But in the early autumn of 1938 my wife and I gave a party at our house on Primrose Hill to which Stanley Spencer came. There were difficulties about his catching the last train to Cookham. He stayed the night. Next day a toothbrush was bought, and he remained with us all that autumn. In the evenings, returning from the Tate Gallery, I used to find him, in the half-light of the drawing-room, curled up on the floor like a twig. He showed no impulse to draw or paint, but seemed content to live quietly, to meet our friends and above all to talk. On the first evening he was sitting on a small couch between my wife, who spoke of his *Zacharias and Elizabeth*, and Sir Kenneth Clark, to whom he said 'It is astonishing

[1] April 1927.

47. STANLEY SPENCER. *Zacharias and Elizabeth* (1912-13).
Oil, 60 × 60 in. Coll. Lady Bone.

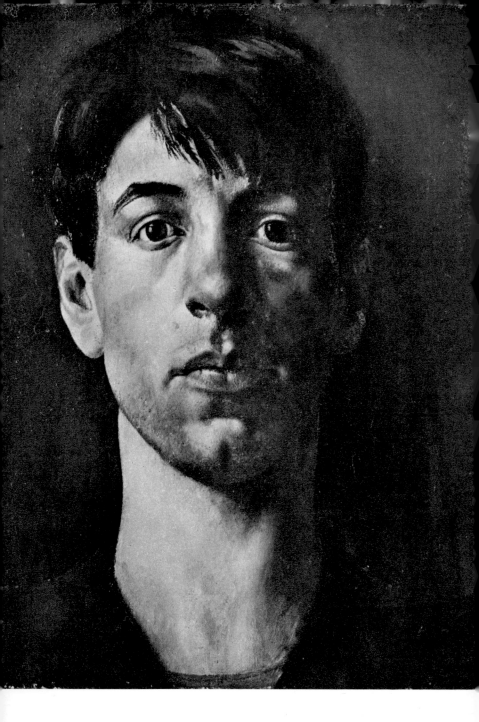

48. STANLEY SPENCER. *Self-Portrait* (1913).
Oil, 23¾ × 20 in. The Tate Gallery, London.

that an American should see most into my mind and painting', and thereafter he used to talk to her with a particular candour. He was prepared to talk, often at prodigious length, upon any topic, but upon the slightest pretext he would revert to two, which are closely interwoven: his early life in Cookham and the subjects of his paintings.

From these conversations we learnt many things about Stanley Spencer, many comic and tragic things, but by far the most important and the most relevant to this study was a deeper insight into what he said to me on my first visit about his earthly paradise and the smashing of it by the war.

In Cookham, the Berkshire village where Stanley Spencer was born,

> he saw Jerusalem in England's green and pleasant land. The church-yard [wrote my wife] would surely be the scene of the final resurrection of man; the river was radiant and serene like the heavenly Jordan, though there was something of the Styx about it too. In the streets when he saw his father, bearded, and venerable, it might have been St. Peter walking there, or one of the Prophets.[1]

He was born on 30 June 1891, the seventh son among the nine children of William Spencer, a music teacher and organist, and Annie, born Slacke, his wife. Earlier, generations of the family had been in the building trade.

Most men and women experience moments of exaltation in the contemplation of a May morning, or the starlit heavens, in performing a heroic act, most often and most intensely in romantic love—but these moments are rarely prolonged. To certain men and women is given the capacity for sustained exaltation—a capacity, I am inclined to think, that is a sign of superior nature, just as the capacity for boredom may be that of inferior. And one of the signs by which the artist of exceptional creative power may sometimes be recognized is the capacity for prolonged exaltation over things that to others are entirely commonplace.

From the time when he grew into a sentient being until the First World War Stanley Spencer experienced exaltation in regard to his native village. To the dispassionate traveller's eye Cookham is a

---

[1] 'Stanley Spencer', by Elizabeth Rothenstein (Phaidon British Artists), 1945, p. 6.

delightful village, but with no more beauty or character than five hundred others scattered up and down the country; but Stanley Spencer's upbringing was one that gave particular opportunity for the growth in him of a deep and enduring sentiment of locality. His father was a man of high character and patriarchal appearance, who if at heart something of an agnostic had a passionate love for the Bible. 'In the evenings, with his children gathered round him,' Stanley Spencer told my wife, 'he read to them from the Old Testament with such conviction that he made it as real to them as Cookham itself, and indeed it seemed as if the story of the Bible had been enacted in their own familiar streets.'[1] A vague sense of the events related in the Bible having been enacted in the region where he was born early took a hold upon Stanley Spencer's imagination and attaches him to the tradition in which Milton, and more militantly Blake, were sharers, according to which the British Isles were the centre of all primitive and patriarchal goodness. 'Jerusalem the Emanation of the Giant Albion! Can it be? Is it a truth that the Learned have explored? Was Britain the Primitive Seat of the Patriarchal Religion?' asked Blake in his 'Jerusalem'. There are no grounds for supposing that in Stanley Spencer's mind there is anything approaching an explicit historical identification of these Islands with the Garden of Eden, but he has been altogether free from the widely current heresy that the Christian religion is something which belongs irrevocably to the past. Indeed it is one of the most pronounced features of Stanley Spencer's mind that past and present, the living and the dead, good and evil all exist together in a vast undifferentiated flux. There is nothing either analytic or sceptical: he is deeply conscious of the continuity of things, and might say that what Blake said of Mr. B. applies equally to Mr. S. 'Mr. B.,' wrote Blake, 'has done as all the ancients did, and as all the moderns who are worthy of fame, given the historical fact in its poetical vigour so as it always happens, and not in the dull way that some Historians pretend who, being weakly organized themselves, cannot see either miracle or prodigy.' Whether because of the benign atmosphere of their churchyard or from some other cause it would seem that to Cookham people the dead who lie there have not gone very far from their homes. My wife recalls Stanley Spencer's delight at

[1] Op. cit., p. 5.

hearing a lady of Cookham call over the fence to her neighbour, 'I'm just going across to the churchyard to give mother a clip round.' He, who has always remained very much of a village boy, shares this sense of the nearness of the dead, and it is apparent in all his *Resurrections*.

Stanley Spencer's exaltation at the beauty of the life surrounding him was heightened by his father's love of music. The three eldest sons were also musicians, and with their father they made up a family quartet. When with his brother Gilbert, afterwards the painter, he was put to bed, they could hear, he told my wife, coming to them from the room below, the strains of music, such music as they would never forget. He told, too, how one Sunday, Will, his eldest brother, took him to the church and played for him on the organ Bach's 'St. Anne Prelude and Fugue', and how, when the last tremendous echoes had died, Will had asked him, 'What did it sound like to you?' 'Like angels shrieking with joy,' Stanley answered, and recalled the pleasure that this answer gave. Both my wife and I have listened for many hours to his talk of his early life in Cookham, walking with him sometimes along its lanes and beside its poetic reach of the Thames, but the essence of what he told us is conveyed in a letter he wrote from Salonika in 1917 for Eric Gill's magazine 'The Game'. Acute homesickness and the limits of space gave this poignant and evocative letter an intensity and a succinctness not paralleled–at any rate in my experience–in either his vivid talk or in his other writings. The following selections, made by my wife, are a microcosm of his early Cookham life, more particularly of the two years between his departure from the Slade in 1912 and the beginning of the First World War.

I remember how happy I felt when one afternoon I went up to Mrs. Shergold's and drew her little girl. After I had finished I went into the kitchen which was just such another as our own (only their kitchen table and chairs are thicker and whiter) with Mrs. Shergold and Cecily. I nearly ran home after that visit. I felt I could paint a picture and that feeling quickened my steps. This visit made me happy because it induced me to produce something which would make me walk with God. 'And Enoch walked with God and was not.' .... To return to the dining room, I remained looking out of the big window at the yew tree, and then turning to Sydney ask him to play some of the Preludes. He does so, though haltingly, yet with true understanding. And now for 2 or 3 hours of meditation. I go upstairs to my room and sit down at the table by the window and think about the resurrection, then I get my big bible out and read the book of Tobit: the gentle evening breeze coming through the open window slightly lifts the heavy pages. I will go out for a walk through Cookham churchyard, I will walk along the path which runs under the hedge. I do so and pause to look at a tombstone which rises out of the midst of a small privet hedge which grows over the grave and is railed around with iron railings. I return to our house and put it down on paper. I go to supper not over satisfied with the evenings thought, but know that tomorrow will see the light, tomorrow 'in my flesh shall I see God' . . . after two or three hours' reading I blow out the candle, and whisper a word to myself 'Tomorrow' I say and fall asleep. . . . I do not remember the exact moment of waking up any more than I know when sleep comes. But although the moment of waking is not known, yet the moment when you become aware that it is morning, when you say 'it's morning', is the most wide awake moment of the day. How everything seems fresh and to belong definitely to the morning. . . . I go and call Gil in the little bedroom. I go downstairs . . . and out into the street and call a friend; we all go down to Odney Weir for a bathe and swim. I feel fresh awake and alive; this is the time for visitations. . . . I swim right in the pathway of sunlight; I go home thinking of the beautiful wholeness of the day. During the morning I am visited and walk about in that visitation. How at this time everything seems more definite and to put on a new meaning and freshness you never noticed. In the afternoon I set out my work and begin the picture. I leave off at dusk feeling delighted with the spiritual work I have done.[1]

Stanley Spencer was connected with the place of his birth by ties more intimate and numerous than is usually the case in a population which ever since its vast uprooting by the Industrial Revolution has, through necessity or disposition, become increasingly inclined to move and increasingly forgetful of local ties. The Spencer family seems to have been long established in Cookham. Stanley's grandfather, he once told me, began as a bricklayer and showed sufficient enterprise to enable him to set up as a builder on his own account, and he built several of the kilns which, many years later, were represented with exceptional sympathy in the paintings of his two grandsons. He had a passion for astronomy, and the little local singing club that he founded long survived him. It was from him that his son William, and two grandsons, inherited their musical talents. The

[1] Op. cit., pp. 9, 10.

two grandsons became musicians of note. Stanley Spencer's maternal grandfather, a man named Slacke, who came from the Isle of Wight, was the foreman in a small boot factory and he owned a grocer's shop. The Spencers conformed to the rites of the Established Church, the Slackes were active Wesleyans, and Stanley is very much aware of the dual nature of his religious inheritance. I have often heard him speak of a projected Resurrection in which the people would ascend the Hill of Zion in two great streams, the Anglican and the Chapel, the last with their red-brick and tin-roofed bethels in the background. As a child he went sometimes to the parish church, at others to the Wesleyan chapel. His early education could not have been more local. In a tiny cottage adjoining the garden of Fernlea, the house where he was born and passed all his early life, was a school in which first a Miss George and later Annie, his eldest sister, taught a small class of local children. There he was able to learn almost nothing. Eventually in despair Annie told him to write his entire life in a notebook and to show it to his father, who glanced at it with resignation, and threw it aside.

The place that epitomized 'the lovely holy feeling' which pervaded all his early life was not Fernlea his home, happy though its associations were, but the churchyard, 'the holy suburb of Heaven', where his grandparents were buried. It was here that he and his brothers played their principal games; it was here that his footsteps turned in times of loneliness and grief, and it was here that his first serious drawings were made.

Even attendance at the Slade School, from 1908 until 1912, did not shift his centre of gravity away from Cookham. Like Constable a little more than a century before, Stanley Spencer went to school in London simply to find technique to express a way of seeing already, in its essential character, in being. The sociable, interested village boy, after a period when he was the victim of bullies, enjoyed the companionship of fellow students and his heightened proficiency; he gained a distant acquaintance, just perceptible in one or two early works, with Cubism, and, more important, he came to know the work of certain Italian primitives. On one ocasion, an exciting one both for himself and his brother Gilbert, he brought home from the Slade a reproduction of a Masaccio—*The Tribute Money*, I think. But these experiences, vivifying as they were, were peripheral. Compared with Cookham, where his heart and mind had their being, London and the Slade were 'like ships that pass in the night'. When his last afternoon class at the Slade was finished, 'Cookham', as Stanley Spencer was called by his fellow students, used to go straight to Paddington, where he sat on the platform waiting for the first train to his Celestial City.

His Celestial City it has remained. On my own most recent visit to him at Cliveden View, the tiny cottage on the fringe of Cookham which he has occupied since 1945, the most recent of many visits, we had some matters of consequence to discuss in connexion with a forthcoming retrospective exhibition of his work at the Tate. We had not talked for more than a few minutes when with an appealing look he said, 'Come on, let's go into the village.' And away we went into the churchyard, deciphered inscriptions on the tombstones, and so into the church, to look at the pew, the fourth back in the left aisle, facing the organ, where he used to sit with his family, and to examine faded photographs of Victorian vicars. In 1954 Stanley Spencer visited China. As the omnibus carried him from London to the airport he pointed with his small brown-paper parcel–his only luggage–along the Great West Road and said to a companion: 'That's the way I go to Cookham.' In China itself Chou En-Lai gave an address on the New China and at its conclusion silence fell on the party. The silence was broken by Stanley Spencer's voice. 'Yes,' he said, 'we ought to know the New China better. And the New China ought to know Cookham better. I feel at home in China, because I feel that Cookham is somewhere near, only just round the corner.'

Those who show themselves friends to artists in their years of need and obscurity are rarer than might be supposed. It should therefore be mentioned that a neighbour, Lady Boston, wife of a generous patron of his father's, not only herself taught Stanley Spencer the elements of drawing, but paid for his first two years at the Slade, after which he won a scholarship which enabled him to remain for two further years.

The time between departure from the Slade in 1912 and his enlistment three years later in the Royal Army Medical Corps was beyond comparison the most intensely creative time of his life. During those three years he made a number of paintings and drawings which, although of varying quality, manifest an exalted spirituality rarely found outside the great periods of religious art.

This extraordinary group of works did not come into being quite unheralded. While still a Slade student he painted *Two Girls and a Beehive*[1] in 1910, *John Donne arriving in Heaven*[2] in 1911–in which, virtually alone in this artist's works, there is a suggestion, in the massive, generalized character of the figures, that he has looked with attention at contemporary continental painting, in this case, that of the Cubists–and *The Nativity*[3] in 1912. As the qualities which make them notable are still more impressively present in the chief works among the later group, I will say no more than that they are astonishing productions for a student.

Not all the pictures in the later group represent explicitly religious subjects, but they do all manifest the vision of a man living in an earthly paradise, in which all things, whether trees, buildings or people, are holy and God's presence is mysteriously manifest. A number, and among these the finest, represent events related or foretold in the Old Testament and the Gospels: the *Apple Gatherers*,[4] of 1912–13, *Swan Upping*,[5] begun the next year, and even *Mending Cowls–Cookham*, of 1914, in which at first glance the human figures, or the people, as the artist prefers to call them, seem to take a subordinate place, are the works of a man to whom his surroundings are sacred. When he represents religious subjects Stanley Spencer is perceived to be a God-centred man, a man for whom God, the Holy Family, the Saints and Prophets are even more real than the streets and fields of Cookham, and the sacredness of Cookham is perceived to derive from his imagining this place to be the theatre of their acts. There was never any question of this artist's having put them into contemporary costume to make them more convincing. He has always represented what he has known. He knew Cookham and its people. The world beyond its fields was a shadowy place and the people strangers. The idea of situating God and his Mother, his Son and his Saints elsewhere or of clothing them in the clothes of strangers is one he would not have entertained. (Not that their clothes are insistently contemporary. In *The Visitation*,[6] of 1913,

[1] Coll. Mrs. Sydney Schiff.   [2] Coll. Mrs. Gwen Raverat.
[3] The Slade School, University College, London.   [4] The Tate Gallery, London.
[5] Coll. Mr. J. L. Behrend.   [6] Coll. Mr. James Wood.

Our Lady, a shy awkward village girl, wears a freshly-laundered dress; in *Joachim among the Shepherds*,[1] of 1912, and *Zacharias and Elizabeth*, of 1912-13, the clothes have a timeless character.)

Besides the three just mentioned, the other principal religious paintings belonging to these years of single-minded creativity are *The Centurion's Servant*,[2] of 1914-15, and *The Resurrection of Good and Bad*,[3] of 1913, the first versions of a theme that has a stronger and more tenacious hold upon his imagination than any other. Of all these beyond comparison the most exalted, in my opinion, is *Zacharias and Elizabeth*. In this picture is expressed in terms that are at the same time local and universal, and with a wonderful radiant gravity, the story of how an angel of the Lord appeared to a certain priest named Zacharias as he was sacrificing in the temple. Zacharias, seeing the Angel standing on the right side of the altar, was troubled, and the Angel said to him, 'Fear not, Zacharias, for thy prayer is heard; and thy wife Elizabeth shall bear thee a son, and thou shalt call his name John.' We cannot see the Angel himself, only the bright light of his presence on the far side of the altar, but we can see the blameless priest, his troubled face as he asks, 'Whereby shall I know this? for I am an old man, and my wife is advanced in years.' And we can see Elizabeth, her face lit by the brightness of the unseen Angel, and the look of intense stillness that it wears.

The story is familiar enough, but Stanley Spencer has not relied upon our knowledge of more than the barest facts. The exalted character of the scene he has constructed compels us to recognize, as though the story were new to us, the momentousness of the announcement that the elderly wife of an elderly clergyman is to give birth to a first child. Each of the figures has a dignity that is inherent and owes nothing to any conventional posture, a serenity remote from relaxation. And the figures are related by a simple, closely knit design, of which the spine, so to speak, is the all but symbolic wall of the temple. Perhaps the noblest feature of this work is the face of Elizabeth, so manifestly alive, so intently waiting, yet so still as to fill the whole picture with its stillness. Certain anonymous critics of the

---

[1] Coll. Mr. J. L. Behrend; there is an elaborately finished pen and wash sketch for the whole composition in the Tate Gallery.

[2] Coll. Mr. Henry Lamb, R.A. This picture is often called *The Bed Picture*.

[3] Colls. the Executors of the late Sir William Rothenstein and Mr. James Wood.

49. STANLEY SPENCER. *Resurrection of Soldiers* (1928–9).
Oil, 21 × 17½ ft. The Oratory of All Souls, Burghclere.

50. STANLEY SPENCER. *Cedar Tree, Cookham* (1934–5).
Oil, 30 × 28 in. Coll. Major E. Beddington Behrens.

first volume of these studies, incensed by my calling in question the commonplace of criticism that an immeasurable gulf still separates the painting of England from that of France, attempted to associate the attitude that prompted this questioning with chauvinism, with parochialism, and with a number of absurd ideas that I have never either defended or presupposed. I will now, however, give these critics an authentic target by offering the opinion that, provided account is taken of the weakness of both the artistic and the religious traditions of the twentieth century compared with the thirteenth, this little picture may be compared without absurdity to a work by Giotto, so astonishingly has Stanley Spencer here (and very occasionally elsewhere) transcended, as a religious painter, the standards of his age. Although smaller and slighter, *Joachim among the Shepherds*, has something of the same character. *The Resurrection of Good and Bad*, a diptych showing in one panel the good who rise serenely from flowers and grass, and in the other the earthbound bad who look despairingly out from jaws of turf from which they struggle with difficulty to free themselves, are grim pictures in which the artist shows himself a highly original painter, but he has envisaged his subject in traditional terms. The paintings were planned with the idea that they might be placed above the chancel arch in Cookham Church.[1] But as the Resurrection motive took hold of his imagination with an almost obsessional intensity his conception of it—without ever losing its traditional meaning—has widened: a few figures have become a host; a graveyard has become an all-embracing panorama; and the distinction between good and bad has disappeared.

When the First World War began and shattered his mood of exaltation he was painting *Swan Upping* and had completed the lower two-thirds of it. In 1915 he joined the Royal Army Medical Corps, and was sent to Salonika the following year. During his two years of service in Macedonia, a country so entirely unlike his own, his capacity for forming deep attachments for places brought him a strange and fruitful experience. When he first went to Macedonia he used to lie awake at nights thinking about Cookham, in particular about his abandoned landscape *Swan Upping* and of his plans for its completion. One day in 1917, when marching, he told my wife,

[1] Note on the picture in the Tate Retrospective Exhibition Catalogue.

they came upon a place in the hills, the mysterious quality of which struck him so forcibly that it, too, came to haunt him at nights so that he found it impossible to sleep. By day he used to look back, longing to return. Apart from going home, to go there was the one thing he desired. Hearing that his own county regiment, the Royal Berkshires, were stationed there, he applied for transfer to this combatant force so that he might go back to this place in the hills. Darkness was falling when he came to the place again, and he hardly dared look at it for fear the strange vision that had haunted him was some trick of memory, but the mystery was indeed there, even stranger and more significant in the dying light. He lay down and slept, he said, as if he had reached a haven. From the emotion stirred in him by this valley in the Macedonian hills—a kind of compensation for his love of home—sprang the most ambitious of Stanley Spencer's works, the work by which his stature may most accurately be measured. Although he stored away in his capacious memory every contour and shadow of it, and its sombre colouring, the time for its translation into a picture, or more strictly a series of pictures, lay some years ahead.

In 1919 in December he returned to England, and went straight to Fernlea, his parents' house, and up the stairs to his bedroom where he found *Swan Upping* leaning against a wall just where he had left it more than three years before. He completed it without hesitation.

The war shocked him to the depths of his being and impaired his imagination, but it did not affect its extraordinary continuity. I know of no artist of any age whose imagination is more consistent. The fruits of it are garnered in a long series of big, cheap notebooks, manufactured for some commercial purpose. These he fills with drawings for innumerable projects, any one of which—even one belonging to his earliest years as an artist—he can take up and carry out unaltered. He is a generous man, without a strong sense of possession, but I have never known him to part otherwise than with grief from any of these projects, however slight. They are simple, almost childish-looking drawings, these studies of the people of his imagination, but they are less simple than they seem, for he is able to adumbrate a large and complicated composition upon a series of small sheets of paper so that when eventually they are put together everything is precisely where he intends and the same scale preserved throughout. Nor is it an easy feat to design with such precision upon a single surface, let alone upon a multitude of small ones, in a painting room so small that they cannot be assembled. The drawings he makes of the people seen by his outward eye, on the other hand, are obviously most accomplished. These he draws fast, with entire sureness, beginning at some arbitrarily chosen point and completing, usually, each feature before passing to the next. I remember seeing shortly after he had begun it a drawing of myself in 1951; and there, quite alone in the middle of an otherwise virgin sheet of paper, was a minutely finished eye. His ability to plan large and complicated compositions upon small sheets of paper and to begin a portrait with a minutely delineated eye springs from his power to envisage the completed work continuously and exactly. He employs the method he considers best suited for a given undertaking and he who has theories about most things has few, I fancy, about technical procedures. His attitude towards these is illustrated by his reply to Cecil Collins, who objected to his use of linseed oil as a medium on the grounds that the paint would come off. 'It won't come off,' he said; 'if you kiss a whore with love you won't get the pox, and if you put on your paint with love it won't come off.'

Nobody who knows Stanley Spencer can be unaware of the effects upon his personality and his art of the First World War. They have been considered by those who have written on him, and I have already quoted his own statement that just as all his ideas were unfolding the war came, and when it ended the divine sequence had gone. (I recall his speaking, in a moment of despair, of suing the War Office for the destruction of his peace of mind and of his talents.)

That his work lost certain of the qualities for which it is most to be valued and that it showed other and unexpected qualities in the years immediately following the end of the First World War is beyond question. But unlike other writers and unlike the artist himself I am inclined to question the conclusion that it was the war which brought about this radical change. Wars are more apt to hasten changes already in process and to reveal developments which might otherwise remain hidden for a time rather than to bring about developments entirely unforeseen. The war carried Stanley Spencer away from his Celestial City; it broke the holy spell; it interrupted the rhythm of inspired and concentrated work; it subjected him to agonizing experiences; but I do not believe that these ordeals, shattering though of course they were, were sufficient to modify a vision of such serene power. It seems to me that by uprooting, shaking and hurting, the finely adjusted creative faculties of the artist they weakened his resistance to inevitable changes. But the change that largely transformed the character of his art would have taken place, I believe, perhaps indeed later, but inevitably none the less. Making the fullest allowance for the effects of the war, his art seems to me to owe its transformation not to them but to a widening of the range of his vital preoccupations, to which no doubt it contributed, but which belonged, quite simply, to the process of growth or of exposure to some current ideas. During his early life, most particularly during the period closed by his involvement in the war, Stanley Spencer was a God-centred boy. He was aware of little beyond his family–which by an easy process of assimilation included the inhabitants of Cookham–and the beloved place in which he had been born. And he was intensely aware of the luminously presiding presence of God, upon whom his deepest thinking and his deepest imaginings were focused. In representing 'the holy suburb of Heaven' he was praising his Creator. Then came the war and its uprooting, and in 1925 marriage, which contributed far more, I think, than war to the transformation of his personality. Marriage, in fact, was a cardinal event in his life as an artist, for this most intimate of human relations had the effect of inspiring in him an absorbed preoccupation not with his wife alone, but through her with the human beings he came to know. There followed preoccupation with evil as well as good, with ugliness as well as beauty, and with sensual love as well as the love of God. The change was radical, and as it took effect the emphasis of his art was no longer upon the Creator but upon the created; there came, in fact, to be less and less emphasis of any kind, as it grew more and more comprehensive. Of the encumbering effects of such baggage Stanley Spencer is very much aware.

> You can't include all that without its taking away from your vision of God; but once you have all that baggage you can't just throw it away. It belongs to you and you've got to bring it with you. After I married Hilda and my work began to include so much besides the divine vision,

I've been incapable of painting a religious picture, religious in the sense of *Zacharias* and some of my early pictures. The fact that many of them are of religious subjects makes no difference. I no longer have a clear vision of God; I'm somehow involved in the created. Sometimes I feel I were showing his creations to God. Take an Edwardian old lady. Five feet high. Bloated. Purple dress. Ridiculous little feet pinched in ridiculous little shoes. I feel that in my painting I'm lifting her up, saying to God 'Look! Isn't she bloody wonderful?'

The change came about gradually. So far as I am aware Stanley Spencer has never had an important experience that has not been reflected in his work, and it was inevitable that the war, with the loneliness, the warm, unsentimental companionship, the unfamiliar scenes and the intermittent threat of extinction that it brought, should demand imperatively to be expressed. As soon as he was back in Cookham he completed *Swan Upping*, and resumed his series of religious subjects with *The Last Supper*,[1] and *Christ Carrying the Cross*,[2] both of 1920, *The Sword of the Lord and of Gideon*,[3] of 1921, and *The Betrayal*,[4] of 1923. Had he not painted *Zacharias and Elizabeth* I would regard these—more particularly *Christ Carrying the Cross* and *The Betrayal*—as among the finest religious pictures of the age. But compared with the passionate, luminously direct response that inspired the earlier pictures the later seem to be the products of artifice.[5] They lack the mysterious power to move us, but we cannot withhold our admiration for the extraordinary dramatic power that the artist has brought to bear in order to bring home to us the momentousness of the events he has represented. These later works have a calculated eloquence that makes them seem almost Baroque beside the primitive simplicity of the earlier. The early Italian and Flemish masters have been, usually in reproduction, his constant companions, but the cloaked Christ of *The Betrayal* suggests

[1] Coll. Mr. J. L. Behrend.   [2] The Tate Gallery, London.
[3] The Tate Gallery, London.   [4] The City Art Gallery, Belfast.
[5] The idea for *Christ Carrying the Cross*, according to information supplied by the artist, was first suggested by a newspaper report of Queen Victoria's funeral—'ladies were weeping openly and strong men broke down in the side streets'. In the foreground is the Virgin. The house is the artist's in Cookham and the ivy-covered cottage is his grandmother's. The onlookers are loafers, some indifferent, some aware of the significance of the event. The window-cleaners are delighted to see someone else 'doing a bit of carrying'. The feeling was one of joy—'and all the common everyday occurrences in the village were re-assuring, comforting occurrences of that joy'.

at least a passing glance at El Greco. I know of no contemporary work in which buildings are used with such effect to enforce our sense of awe as they are in this: the menacing roofs against a lowering sky; the abrupt reminder, in the form of a corrugated iron wall, that what is taking place is not a dream but something that concerns us here and now. At the same time he produced a number of the almost purely retinal landscapes, of Durweston, Petersfield, or wherever he happened to be, that have occupied him intermittently through-out his life. The contrast between the pedestrian efficiency of many of these and the vaulting imagination manifest in his religious pictures has often been remarked with surprise. Religious pictures, in particular very large religious pictures (indeed large pictures of any kind), are extremely expensive undertakings. Stanley Spencer has no source of income except painting and he could not survive, let alone paint huge Resurrections, unless he painted saleable land-scapes. These landscapes vary greatly in quality between such beautiful works as, for instance, *The Harrow, Durweston,*[1] of 1920, *May Tree, Cookham,*[2] of 1932, *Cedar Tree, Cookham,*[3] of 1935, *Gardens in the Pound, Cookham,*[4] and *View from Cookham Bridge,*[5] both of 1936, and some very dry mechanical performances indeed. It is a mistake, however, to dismiss the landscapes, even the more pedestrian, as a manual equivalent of colour photography under-taken with an eye to immediate sale, for they serve at least three other purposes. They give him hours of respite from the fearful effort involved in the production of large pictures, packed with incident and deeply felt; they refresh his vision by constantly renew-ing his intimate contacts with nature; and they charge his fabulous memory.

During the years following his return home from Macedonia the painting of the group of religious pictures, *The Betrayal* and the others of which I spoke just now, and still more the landscapes, were inadequate to express the grand conception that was taking shape in his mind. This was the expression, in a series of related pictures, of his experience of the war, culminating in a Resurrection far larger and more complex than anything he had attempted. This he

[1] Coll. Mr. J. L. Behrend.   [2] Coll. The Earl of Crawford and Balcarres.
[3] Coll. Major E. Beddington Behrens.   [4] The City Art Gallery, Leeds.
[5] Coll. Mr. Victor Gollancz.

conceived as a series of paintings designed to embellish a chapel. As there seemed to be no prospect of its being realized he used to call it 'the chapel in the air'. During a stay in 1922 with his friend Henry Lamb, the painter, at Poole in Dorset, the project assumed, in the course of two weeks, the form of a big cartoon, in pencil and ink, of the two side walls of a chapel, each divided into four panels in turn divided into two and surmounted by continuous friezes. There came to see Henry Lamb two friends of his, Mr. and Mrs. J. L. Behrend, who had already shown an interest in Stanley Spencer by buying *Swan Upping*. Mrs. Behrend's brother had been killed in the war, and they were considering the erection of a memorial of some kind to his memory. The cartoons were standing face to the wall; the visitors looked at them, admired them and afterwards made an offer to commission him to carry them out. 'Not good enough' was his reply. ('Our offer *wasn't* good enough,' Mrs. Behrend said to me years afterwards.) It was revised, renewed and accepted. On my first visit to Vale Studio the following year I saw a number of larger studies for the same project, together with one for the missing end wall. This was a *Resurrection* set in Kalinova, the gloomy Macedonian valley that had so irresistibly drawn him to return there.

Nothing so convincingly illustrates the prodigality of Stanley Spencer's imagination or his unremitting industry as the fact that, having obtained a commission which would enable him to give expression to his most grandiose conceptions, he immediately began the Tate *Resurrection*, by far the biggest picture he had attempted. Few who saw it were aware that this immense picture was a side-show. It occupies in the succession of Stanley Spencer's works rather the position of *The Painter's Studio* in that of Courbet's: an immense repertory of everything that had gone before. There was Cookham churchyard depicted on a great scale yet with a wealth of detail: 'the holy suburb of Heaven' densely populated with figures rising from their tombs, the artist himself among them. A lyrical glimpse of the Thames and its park-like banks summarizes the country round about. There is one innovation: the presence in the shadow of the church porch of the first two Persons of the Trinity. Into this great canvas the artist has poured the abundance of his loving knowledge of this place which means more to him than any other; of this place which he loves not in a general way but inch by inch of stone, plaster, brick, railing, tile, foliage, flower and grass, as though he had made it all himself. With Stanley Spencer it is always the people and the place that are known and loved, never the paint, and he paints them, for all his love, a little severely. Never, like Renoir or Gainsborough, does he caress them into being, and his harsh, brisk treatment of paint often makes his work repellent to other painters. It is as though he sees the people and places of his pictures so completely in his mind's eye, with such sharp, final definition, that all he requires is to transfer them, without modification and without embellishment, to his canvas. It is always *they* rather than their painted images who are the real subjects of his pictures. Although the Tate *Resurrection* is a summing-up of the artist's past achievement, it has one characteristic that marks it as belonging to the later period of his growth when his art had lost its God-centred simplicity and become comprehensive. This picture is full of beauties, full even of splendours. It seems to me to be one of the great pictures of this century. Yet, in comparison with the best of the artist's earlier works, it is over-crowded, loose in composition, imperfectly focused.

In comparing the *Resurrection* which forms part of the memorial commissioned by Mr. and Mrs. Behrend, which was not begun until 1927, with the Tate picture, which was completed early the same year, it should be borne in mind that in certain respects the picture carried out last was the first conceived, and is therefore nearer in spirit to the earlier works. This memorial, which is situated in the Berkshire village of Burghclere, consists of two ranges of almshouses flanking the Oratory of All Souls, the interior of which was designed to meet the requirements of the artist. The buildings were completed in 1927. From that year until his paintings were completed in 1931, the artist lived with his wife and two children at a nearby cottage. He completed the work without assistance.

When he was enabled to begin work in the oratory eight years had passed since he had made his first drawings, and five since the working drawings of the side walls had been completed. His experience of the war was too overwhelming to be expressed in the works he did upon an ordinary scale, admirable as certain of them were, in particular *Travoys arriving with Wounded at a Dressing station, Smol, Macedonia*,[1] of 1919. It began to crystallize about the Kalinova

[1] The Imperial War Museum, London.

valley when he first saw it, and after ten years' meditation it expressed itself in a prolonged outburst of spiritual energy. The side walls of the oratory are scenes of military life: soldiers checking laundry, scrubbing floors; the arrival of wounded in hospital; wounded pointing out their kit-bags to orderlies, and such-like. The artist has made us aware that these scenes are not mere records made by a detached observer, but records of his own intensely felt experience, shared equally by a crowd of other young men of his own age. There is in fact nothing peculiar, still less eccentric, about the experiences recorded; they are the common experience of soldiers. The soldiers are shown doing almost everything that soldiers do except fighting. So positive is his horror of violence that it would be unnatural in him to represent it; but fighting occupies a smaller part of the time of fewer soldiers than civilians suppose. The irregularly shaped friezes above the series of panels are filled by two panoramic scenes, one of them the great tented camp at Kalinova at night. The culmination, not only of the paintings at Burghclere but, I believe, of the artist's life work, is the painting on the end wall of the oratory, behind the altar, *The Resurrection of Soldiers* (Plate 49).

Here [I quote my wife's description of it] he has painted the awakened soldiers holding their crosses. At first they only handle them, exploring them unknowingly. He shows the growth of understanding in all its various stages until at last in the full light of revelation the soldiers know that in suffering and death they have triumphed, and they are shown embracing their crosses in ecstasy.

The design is a great recumbent cross: its base a forest of crosses, and the extremity of the upright shows scattered crosses disappearing into the endless bleakness of the Macedonian hills. The cross-pieces extend from a solid nucleus of alert but recumbent mules, who we are sure will not be excluded from the Resurrection; just above is the figure of Christ, who receives the crosses the soldiers hand him or lay at his feet. I draw attention to the design because this picture, panoramic in its scope, crowded with figures, full of incident, of subtle spiritual observation, forms a design as closely knit and delicately adjusted as it is magnificent. In contrast to many of his later works, which could, it would seem, be extended indefinitely in any direction, the Burghclere *Resurrection* has limits that are clearly defined, and the mass of detail, lovingly observed and meticulously set down, is severely subordinate to the principal theme.

The wall-paintings at Burghclere–inspired by a vast and lofty conception and carried out with mastery to the last detail–are generally regarded with respect, and from time to time they are acclaimed as a major work. But how trifling the stir they make compared, say, with the Chapel of the Rosary designed by Matisse for the Dominican Nuns of Vence. In a letter to the Bishop of Nice the most illustrious French artist of our time wrote, 'This work has taken me four years of exclusive and assiduous work and it represents the result of my entire active life. I consider it, in spite of its imperfections, to be my masterpiece.' It scarcely needs to be said that a building designed (in association with the distinguished architect Auguste Perret) by Matisse and embellished by his wall-paintings– or, more properly, mural drawings on glazed tiles–and with a crucifix, an altar with its furniture, carved-wood confessional door, metal spire and certain vestments all designed by the artist, is a work of very great originality and distinction. Still less need it be said that it stands in brilliant contrast to the shabby and meretricious art so widely patronized by the Catholic Church to-day–an art which tends to substitute conventional pieties for religious truth. But one of the functions of a church is to fill those who worship in it with the sense of being in the house of God. In spite of every beauty that shining talent assiduously employed has been able to lavish upon it the Vence Chapel remains spiritually thin. There is a story according to which the Communist poet Louis Aragon said to Matisse after looking at the working model, 'Very pretty–very gay–in fact, when we take over we'll turn it into a dance hall.' Aragon's words may have been prompted by malice but they were not spoken in folly. Of greater significance is the serious and extended statement published in the 'Chapelle du Rosaire'[1] in which Matisse declared: 'In the chapel my chief aim has been to balance a surface of light and colour against a solid white wall covered with black drawings.' I do not believe that Aragon would propose making the Burghclere Oratory into a dance hall, or that Matisse could describe it as an essay in aesthetics; yet the chapel at Vence was a legend almost as soon as it was begun and the Oratory at Burghclere remains relatively unknown.

[1] A booklet on the chapel published in 1951 at the time of its consecration.

My comparison might draw from an admirer of Matisse the comment that, whatever the artist may have said about the Vence chapel's being his masterpiece, Matisse is not, in any specific sense, a religious artist or one who expresses himself most naturally upon a grand scale. With such a comment I would not disagree. My comparison is not between two artists but between two works of art, and I believe that to-day's critical standards, according to which Matisse is a widely acclaimed master and Stanley Spencer a 'village pre-Raphaelite' with an uncertain reputation in one country only, and that his own, will be regarded by future generations as very odd.

In the preceding volume I commented of Augustus John that he was 'on the way to become "the forgotten man" of English painting'. Since I then wrote he has emerged from the shadows to become the somewhat undependable 'grand old man'. Still more obnoxious to fashionable opinion, cast for John's successor in the part of 'forgotten man', Stanley Spencer has refused to submit, and from time to time has engaged national attention with a canvas too large and too tumultuous and too intensely alive to be ignored. But it would be disingenuous to suggest that the work of this painter is unsympathetic only to fashionable opinion. Instances abound of cruel sayings of illustrious artists about the work of their peers, yet it is true to say that there is apt to be among serious artists something approaching recognition, although this may be grudging or even tacit, of the qualities in one another's work. This may be so even between bitter rivals. Witness the Fourteenth Discourse of Sir Joshua Reynolds and the famous encounter between Delacroix and Ingres. In the case of Stanley Spencer this recognition is minimal. A few artists and a few critics have testified consistently to their belief that he is a major painter, but even these are mostly dead or belong to an older generation. The artists active to-day whose work seems to me most likely to withstand the erosion of time have expressed, in my hearing, their small regard for his work, and, with a few notable exceptions, others, too, whose judgment I most respect are sharers in this disregard. Most of them admit to some respect for his early works; it is the later that provoke their positive aversion. I share their preference for the earlier works, the best of which, however, seem to me to occupy places so outstanding among the paintings of the age that the later, even though they do not rival them, may yet be of extraordinary interest.

The paintings at Burghclere I regard as the last of these earlier paintings, and, even if they lack the radiant purity of spirit that shines out of *Zacharias and Elizabeth*, as the greatest. Once his art ceased to be, in an intimate sense, a religious art, once it ceased to be God-centred, Stanley Spencer's voracious interests ranged without check. Everything became grist to his mill, and his later pictures often give the impression of having been stopped only by the margin of the canvas; that were a strip added he would fill it without premeditation. A comment of my wife's upon his conversation is peculiarly applicable to his later painting. After he and we had engaged in several hours' talk, I said to her that there were few subjects, however remote from his habitual interests, on which he could not shed light. 'The trouble with Stanley,' she replied, 'is that he sheds too much light; and everything is so brightly lit that there isn't either light or shadow.' So in his painting; his passionate love of whatever he happens to see, abetted by an extraordinary skill, robs his painting of emphasis, and there are in consequence pictures which have the monotonous look of a surface covered by some fantastic mechanical process. I once said to him that he'd be happy painting a white sheet, and he replied that this was so, and that a plain brick wall would keep him occupied for weeks. I do not suggest that he has directed his powerful talents to trivial ends. On the contrary he has painted Resurrections and other religious subjects as well as others of deep human significance; but it does seem to me that in so doing he has treated every object represented, every inch of the canvas, with an almost equal intensity, thereby robbing the whole of a great part of the intensity that is one of the greatest qualities of his earlier pictures. (It will not, I hope, be inferred from the foregoing that I regard Tintoretto as a greater painter than Chardin simply because he treated greater subjects. I mean no more, in effect, than that it would have been a misuse of his particular talents had Tintoretto foregathered, in his art, exclusively with loaves of bread.)

After the intense and long-sustained efforts required of him for the completion of the paintings at Burghclere he returned to Cookham, living at Lindworth, a largish house he purchased. For the first year and a half his wife and their two children were with him, but later he was alone. Of all the people he has ever known Hilda Anne Carline, his first wife, whom he married in February 1925, commanded the largest share of his devotion. This did not, however, allay tensions that ultimately brought his marriage to an end, but his devotion to Hilda outlasted his marriage and endured until her death in 1950. The tenderness with which he nursed her during a last illness made the more terrible by mental derangement forms one of several heroic incidents in the life of Stanley Spencer. In May 1937 he married Patricia Preece.

During these years he was mainly occupied with landscapes of Cookham—*Cedar Tree, Cookham*,[1] of 1935 (Plate 50), is a fine example—and the country round about, and occasionally with a religious subject. Although many of them appear to be the products of a hand of extraordinary skill guided by an intensely keen but wholly unreflective eye, commonplace images mechanically transferred to canvas, the landscapes rarely fail to reveal under scrutiny, a quality that makes them less unremarkable. This is his comprehending love of his native place, and by a process of extension of all places. There is a compulsive force about this love: those who look at his paintings of Cookham and who might have been disposed to regard the place as a slightly vulgarized 'up-river' resort, whose pleasant but urbane traditional architecture is being steadily displaced by a species of poor man's 'stockbroker's Tudor', are forced —however reluctantly—to see it as a place very much on its own, the product of special social and historical impulses, and, taken all in all, a very likeable place. We are compelled by Stanley Spencer to look closely at Cookham, just as we are compelled by Mr. John Betjeman to be aware of Victorian churches and villas—previously very generally dismissed as monotonous eyesores, unworthy of serious attention and differing from one another in little except in their degrees of ugliness or absurdity—as *architecture*, subject to the same laws as architecture of any other kind.

For the time being his huge exertions at Burghclere had exhausted, and his widening interests in life had diluted, his religious impulse. But something of it remained and proclaimed itself in his occasional religious pictures, of which *Sarah Tubb and the Angels*,[2] *Villagers and*

---

[1] Coll. Major E. Beddington Behrens.
[2] Coll. Major E. Beddington Behrens.

Saints,[1] both of 1933, and *St. Francis and the Birds*[2] of two years later, are characteristic examples. Indeed in some recent personal comments on his own work[3] Stanley Spencer has recorded that on the completion of the Burghclere paintings he planned in 1933 another chapel 'built also in the air as was first the Burghclere Chapel, that is to say not commissioned'. He planned according to an enormous scheme, in which figure paintings of the last twenty years that one had regarded as independent works all have their place. 'All the figure pictures done after 1932 were part of some scheme, the whole of which scheme when completed would have given the part the meaning I know it had. Having completed a memorial chapel in which I seek to express the joys of peace in spite of being in the midst of war, I then hoped to express the same peace in its more positive state in times of peace.' In this scheme 'the Village Street of Cookham was to be the Nave and the river which runs behind the street was a side aisle. The *Promenade of Women*[4] and the *Sarah Tubb and the Heavenly Visitors* and the *St. Francis and the Birds* and *Villagers and Saints* are fragments of the street scenes, and the quite recent *Listening from Punts* Regatta scheme is a river aisle fragment.' *Sarah Tubb, Villagers and Saints* belong to a cycle that he calls the Pentecost scheme, as also does *Separating Fighting Swans*, of 1933, 'in which saints and angels visit Cookham, making trips round the village and performing various acts of a benevolent kind'.

Dusting Shelves,[5] of 1936, *Workmen in the House*,[6] of 1935, *Love among the Nations*,[7] of 1935–6, are also, according to the artist's account, part of the same scheme; he calls them the 'Cana' cycle–it was begun in 1935–and designs them to stress the value of friendliness and love and the importance of everyday actions. 'He called them the "Cana" scheme because the idea originated while he was working on a picture of *The Marriage at Cana*,[8] in which women handling a trousseau played a major part.'[9]

---

[1] Coll. Mr. Wilfred Evill.   [2] Coll. Dr. Lynda Grier, C.B.E.
[3] In the artist's introduction to the Catalogue of the Retrospective Exhibition of his work held by the Tate Gallery, November–December 1955.
[4] Coll Mr. W. E. Kenrick.   [5] Coll. Mrs. J. M. Image.
[6] Coll. Mr. Wilfred Evill.   [7] Coll. Mr. Wilfred Evill.
[8] Coll. Lord Beaverbrook.
[9] 'Some further notes on his figure painting', Catalogue to the Stanley Spencer Retrospective Exhibition at the Tate Gallery, 1955.

Let it be said at once that these pictures of 1933–5 and others of a like kind express in varying degrees authentic religious feeling and contain passages of unusual beauty and power. But Stanley Spencer had set himself towering standards as a religious painter, and according to them the three pictures just mentioned cannot be accounted as more than minor works. Their minor character, in fact, is manifest throughout, but in nothing so much as the manifestations they exhibit of a desire to shock, even to outrage—a desire nowhere apparent in the earlier works, even though these abound in examples of the most idiosyncratic treatment of the human figure. There is, for instance, something perceptibly clamorous for attention in the figure of St. Francis, bloated, hunch-backed and supported by the atrophied legs of a lazy old man.[1] This turbulent undercurrent no doubt sprang from the painful consciousness that his religious impulse was less vigorous and less elevated than it had been.

Since the time of the Burghclere wall-paintings his imagination would appear to have been dogged by certain obsessions, and in particular by sexual obsessions of an extraordinary character. Unlike the roseate fantasies of the generality of men these obsessions were concerned with relations between the ugly, the infirm, and above all the aged. I do not pretend to be able to cast much light upon this singularity. The mind of Stanley Spencer has always been opposed, in one important respect, to the classical mind, to which there is almost always vividly present the conception of the perfect type of a thing—be it the human face and figure, bird, beast and even tree—towards which it is one of the functions of classical art slowly to evolve. Anything approaching the perfect type of anything, and almost all manifestations of conventional beauty, have always repelled Stanley Spencer; he has shown a preference, which has hardened with the passage of time into a grim determination, for beauty of a very personal sort mined from shafts sunk in unpromising or even forbidding places. It is therefore hardly to be expected

[1] According to the artist, the figure of St. Francis is large and spreading to signify that the teaching of St. Francis spread far and wide. He adds that 'the composition was developed from a drawing made in 1924 of Hilda Carline reading in a hay-stack. The ducks and poultry were taken over almost unchanged, while St. Francis and the roof were fitted into the main lines of what was originally the hay-stack.' I take this information from the note on the picture in the Catalogue to the Retrospective Exhibition at the Tate Gallery, 1955.

that in his erotic imaginings either the classical beauty or her popular equivalent the 'cover girl'–the lowest common denominator of feminine desirability–should play any part; but his preoccupation with the sexual relations of the aged–for such is the focus of these imaginings–is something for which I know no precise parallel. Singular though this preoccupation may be, it accords with certain of his innate predilections. It accords, as I suggested just now, with his rejection of idealization: for the old, whether battered or worn or corrupted or ennobled by their journey through life, are of all humanity the farthest removed from 'perfect types', of all humanity they are most conspicuously personifications of their virtues and their vices, the most vividly revealing of themselves. If at times they may disgust us, these aged lechers, who figure, for example, in *Adoration of Old Men*,[1] of 1937, it would be a serious error to forget the inclusiveness of Stanley Spencer's love, a love which embraces virtually everything he sees–certainly his old lechers–except ideal types of humanity or of anything else. Although he rejects all idealization, I do not believe that he has ever seen a man or woman who is, in the classical sense, ideal; but had he been commissioned to paint a portrait of Adonis himself he would have emphasized a lopsidedness in his face, and a strange look in his eyes which nobody had ever noticed before. Stanley Spencer's predilection was heightened, I think, by his enthralled identification, in those early and radically formative years at home in Cookham, of his parents with sex, which persisted in the form of an identification of sex at its most active with persons older than himself.

Whether this time of absorption in singular manifestations of sex had abated by the Second World War, I am not certain, even though I saw him more continuously on the eve of it than at any previous time. For it was in 1938 that he spent the autumn at our house on Primrose Hill. My impression was that the acute tensions that stimulated his sexual imaginings until they acquired a peculiar domination over his work had begun to relax. It is an almost invariable habit with him to speak about what is uppermost in his mind, and although, in the course of the months he spent with us, his conversation ranged over a vast variety of subjects, the one to which he most often returned was a project for a series of paintings

[1] Coll. Mr. R. Brinsley Ford.

representing Christ in the Wilderness. This series of paintings, each measuring twenty-two inches square, he planned to extend to forty, and he spoke of his wish that each in turn should be shown somewhere on a successive day in Lent, or else all together in the hexagonal or octagonal vault of a church, where the figures in dirty whitish would have the appearance of clouds in a 'mackerel' sky. The series was begun with *Christ in the Wilderness*: '*The Foxes have Holes*'[1] in the second of the rooms, 179 and 188, which my wife found for him in nearby Adelaide Road, and which he occupied from Christmas 1938 until 1940. He often used to speak of the way in which Thoreau's 'Walden' and to a lesser extent the writings of Richard Jefferies gave him a deeper understanding of the relation of men with nature, and in particular of the possibilities of living a passionate life in a wilderness alone.

> Christ may have felt as I have sometimes felt when I have revisited after many years a corner of a field where I had painted a clump of stinging nettles, and have found them there again, hardly altered. I want to show Christ in the Wilderness happy to see His early creations again and to be intimate with them: through Christ God again beholds His creation and this time has a mysterious occasion to associate Himself with it. In this visitation he contemplates the many familiar, humble objects and places: the declivities, holes, pits, banks, boulders, rocks, hills, fields, ditches, and so on. The thought of Christ considering all these seems to me to fulfil and consummate the life of wishes and meaning of all these things.[2]

The second of the series, *Christ praying in the Wilderness*,[3] also constantly occupied his mind. This he intended as a dual revelation of God, a revelation under two aspects, Himself and surrounding nature. The form of the praying Christ would have its complement in the altar-like boulder before which he would kneel, but without having to change its natural form. He stressed at this time, as often before and since, that he never distorts nature wilfully. 'People who are not painters,' he said, 'never see how complicated nature is, a group of moving people, for example. I want to express certain ideas, certain feelings I have about people, or about places. If I could express myself clearly and forcefully without any distortion of nature I would do so, but to do that I would have to draw as well as Michelangelo.

[1] Coll. Mr. Wilfred Evill.
[2] Spencer also wrote down an account of this series for Mr. Dudley Tooth, who has kindly put a copy at my disposal. [3] Coll. Mr. Wilfred Evill.

It's too bad that I don't draw as well as Michelangelo, because it means that in order to say what I want I have sometimes to pull and push nature this way and that.' But in this picture, he said, 'I hope there will be no such strain: Christ's desire to pray and a boulder's roughly assuming the shape of an altar would come inevitably together.' Here and there he intended to introduce features that had a special meaning for himself, such as a place beside a stream where the water had worn away the bank and made a little bay with a shingle beach. Such little bays along the Thames, with steep sides and shingle beaches, were favourite places to play in when he was a child. The idea sometimes troubled him that Christ should be thought of as speaking in a derogatory sense of anything in nature, of a scorpion or a fig-tree for example, and in this series of pictures he wished to show Christ's loving intimacy with all nature, and his being entertained by his creation 'as I sometimes am by my pictures'. If Christ ever referred in such a sense to anything he had created, he would only have meant it not generally but in the sense described in the particular instance. Therefore he had it in mind to show Our Lord's affectionate contemplation of a scorpion. He was more pre-occupied, however, with the theme of Christ's contemplation of a stone, and often spoke of the many references to a stone in the Old and New Testaments and in particular of 'the mysterious words about a stone in "Revelations" which I have long wondered about. "To him that overcometh will I give to eat of the hidden manna, and will give him a white stone, and in the stone a new name written which no man knoweth save he that receiveth it."' These words held a special meaning for him, and he said of them that they revealed to him how he found his own identity in the variety of places and objects he comes to know. It was clear from his frequent talks about this project that it was not part of his aim to draw a distinction between man and the rest of nature, but rather to reveal, by a kind of analogy, Christ's love for mankind by showing 'how He lived in the wildernesses and forests, the fleshy lands of mankind'. Long, however, before *The Forty Days in the Wilderness* was com-pleted he left London to live for a while at Leonards Stanley, a village near Stroud in Gloucestershire, where I saw him from time to time occupied mainly with landscape. By the following year 1940 he was committed to a project far greater in scale than *The Forty*

Days and of infinitely greater complexity, a project that called for the fullest use of all his powers. The War Artists' Advisory Committee—set up in order to organize the making of the most comprehensive possible record of the multifarious exertions of the British people—decided to send Stanley Spencer to Port Glasgow to make paintings of shipbuilding. At first he applied himself dutifully and to some purpose to his subject, and the principal product of this application is the *Shipbuilding Series*,[1] of 1940–5, a series of big pictures lacking in focus, the area of which might have been added to indefinitely without significant addition to their impressiveness. They contain representations of people and things of unusual clarity and energy, but they are the least impressive of his big works. The arid mechanical character that stamps them is due to the gradual reversion of his attraction from the shipyards which he was commissioned to record to the inevitable objects of his uncommissioned interest: people and places. That the shipyards proved sufficient, or almost sufficient for a time, the big composite picture testifies. But

I soon found [he wrote in his notebook] that the shipyard at Port Glasgow is only one aspect of the life there. There were rows of men and women hurrying in the streets, and high sunlit factory walls with men sitting or standing or leaning back against them, and early shoppers going to and fro; one day through the crack of a factory door I glimpsed a cascade of brass taps; in a roadway (a very trafficky one) I saw children lying on the ground using the road as their drawing-board and making drawings in coloured chalk; and there was a long seat on which old men sat removed from the passers-by like statues . . . all this [he continued] seemed to me full of some inward surging meaning, a kind of joy, that I longed to get closer to and understand and in some way fulfil.

And then it came about, as it had come about before, that the recording of all this interest in the life about him, panoramic and minute, impassioned and vivid as it was, was a work that, by itself, failed to bring his highest faculties into play. All this various teeming life had to be drawn together and related by being made subordinate to some large idea. The number of large ideas to which even the most versatile of artists can respond with the whole of their being is very limited. To this rule Stanley Spencer is no exception. It was therefore, as I heard him say:

Back to the Bottle again: I had to paint another Resurrection.

[1] The Imperial War Museum, London.

[More formally in his notebook] I felt that all this life and meaning somehow grouped round and in some way led up to the cemetery on the hill outside the town, an oval saucer-upside-down-shaped hill hedged in by high red brick tenements looking down on it; a sort of green mound in a nest of red. . . . And I began to see the Port Glasgow *Resurrection* that I have drawn and painted in the last five years. As it has worked out this hillside cemetery has become The Hill of Sion.

An identical emotion can affect different people in different ways. Love of his own country, for example, can make one man hostile to foreign countries yet give another a heightened appreciation of them. The love of Stanley Spencer for his native place is not an exclusive one and it stimulates his delight in other places, and on particular occasions it brings him to fall in love with them, and when he loves them he is liable to celebrate the relationship by making them the scene of a Resurrection. There was the particular place among the Macedonian hills, and there was Port Glasgow. At Leonards Stanley in 1940, where he was mostly occupied with landscape of a relatively conventional character, there came a moment when he was moved to imagine a Resurrection in the small nearby town of Stonehouse. The result of this imagining was the triptych *Resurrection: Raising of Jairus's Daughter*,[1] of 1947, of which the two outer panels were drawn in 1940 at Leonards Stanley, although the work was finished at Port Glasgow. In spite of its inspiration by a photograph seen in the house where he lodged at Leonards Stanley and the representation of Stonehouse Church in the left panel, this picture may be placed in the Port Glasgow group, among which indeed it is one of the best. His relationship with Port Glasgow was more passionate and of longer duration than that with the Gloucestershire valley. That Port Glasgow, lived in during the bracing climate of the war, stirred his imagination as no other place since Macedonia, the pictures the place inspired clearly testify; but these pictures–impressive in scale and quality as they are–form only fragments of the gigantic picture he originally conceived, which called for a canvas fifty feet in width. In fact, of all the Port Glasgow pictures, only *The Resurrection: Port Glasgow*,[2] 1947–50, and *The Hill of Sion*,[3] 1946, are on the scale of his original project.

In considering this vast interrelated group that has grown up about

[1] The Southampton Art Gallery.   [2] The Tate Gallery, London.
[3] The Harris Art Gallery, Preston.

The Resurrection: Port Glasgow to which, were the painter given the opportunity, he would doubtless be adding panel by panel still, the mind inevitably turns back to the only two works in the art of modern England with which they can be at all closely compared: their predecessors, the *Resurrections* at Cookham and in Macedonia. From these two the latest group differs in one respect so important as to compel us to assign to it an inferior place among his works. Let it be said at once that the Port Glasgow group are works of an extraordinary character. I know of no painter in England, or indeed Europe, who would express himself, with perfect naturalness, upon so gigantic a scale, who could so easily pack so huge a space with a harvest of such intense and original imaginings and such sustained and minute observation that his constant need is for more space and always more space. Nothing, for instance, could be more unlike the authentic bigness of Stanley Spencer's conceptions than those of Frank Brangwyn, the other English painter who habitually painted large. To Brangwyn belongs big, bold, indeed a somewhat swaggering, handwriting and abundant physical energy, and these have misled him and other persons and corporate bodies into supposing him to be a painter who works naturally upon a heroic scale. But even a superficial examination of a big picture by Brangwyn will show that, at a loss how to fill the space he has claimed, he has introduced exotic heaps of fruit, of bubble-like clouds and other romantic stage properties to garrison, so to speak, areas which he lacks the power to colonize. The power of genuine expression upon a great scale is an indication of exceptional creative power, but it is not a proof of it. And a work, however heroic in scale, however packed with intense, closely related incident, may yet fail, and I believe that the qualities of the Port Glasgow pictures—for all their notable characteristics—do fail according to the standard set by their two great precursors. The chief cause of their comparative failure is that they fail fully to perform their function, the representation of the Resurrection. No matter the variations of emphasis that differing traditions may place upon the event, there is no question of the awfulness of the call, coming like a thunderclap, that will end for ever the daily round of the living and will bring from their graves the countless millions who are now dead, and will be a warning momentous beyond reckoning—the most momentous warning any man has ever heard—that they must shortly face the ultimate ordeal of human existence, the Last Judgement. In order to represent the Resurrection it is necessary to represent the people, called and arising from their graves, but it is also necessary to show that besides emerging from their graves they are entering, in a uniquely intimate yet awful fashion, into the presence of their Creator. In the Cookham and Macedonian *Resurrections*, in spite of the loving and minute way in which the artist has dwelt upon the resurrecting people, he has also charged the atmosphere with momentousness, which compels us to listen, as it were, to hold our breath, to await intently what is to follow. In the Port Glasgow pictures the artist has concerned himself only with the people, with their rich variety, with their distinct personalities and conditions, with touching relations between them; but what he fails to give is any sense of their doing anything beyond emerging from their graves. Of the imminence of the Last Judgement, or even that there is anything momentous—as distinct from extraordinary—about what they are doing, he gives no slightest hint. What he gives us instead is anecdote: anecdote grandly, at points even splendidly, conceived, but anecdote none the less. Conscious always of the presence of the dead, ubiquitously buried underground, what he has painted in the Port Glasgow *Resurrection* is a gigantic Cookham conversation piece; the presence of God and the significance of the Resurrection are alike elbowed out by the surging crowds of the quick and the dead, the throng of Cookham villagers lustily shoving and pushing, meeting and embracing, doing this, that and the other, and endlessly gossiping. Absorbed as Stanley Spencer is in the day-to-day life about him, the holy suburb of heaven has become an uncelestial suburb of London, and he himself much more a village Rowlandson than a village Giotto. The difference between the two earlier works and this one corresponds to the difference between the related scenes from the Old and New Testaments represented by the painters of the twelfth and thirteenth centuries and the episodic popular moralities and fables favoured by those of the later Middle Ages. The light that Stanley Spencer is able to throw upon any great matter here falls too uniformly, illuminating everything well, yet illuminating nothing with the intense brightness that belongs to his most inspired moments.

Like Constable and Wordsworth he received in childhood his most powerful and his most fruitful impressions. The joy of being able to perceive in all the fulness of its meaning the essence of a particular place or situation is the motive power of his art. And this joy really belongs, he wrote, 'to all the happy and benigne [*sic*] religious elements of my early days. . . . In fact nothing has (for me) any meaning of form and shape excepting it is perceived in this religious joy.'[1] It is a melancholy intractable fact that this artist, whose mind is stored with so great an abundance of visual images, and who is so generously responsive to his surroundings, has in the course of more than forty years of painting moved far from the original source of his inspiration, and, inevitably, something has been lost. Two things, however, have not been lost, or even weakened— the prodigality of his imagination and the urgency of his effort to express 'a particular meaningfulness' inherent in a place or situation.

I must add, however, that Stanley Spencer himself, who is the first to confess the fading of a vision in 1922–3, also underlines the adverse effect on his work of his inability to see or to complete the whole of the painting schemes that he has conceived. In connexion with the pictures of 1933–5 and with the more recent *Listening from Punts*, for instance, all conceived, as already noted, as parts of one whole, he has lately written that:

> the whole work was far too big for me to undertake unless I could devote the whole of my time to it and this I was far from being able to do. The not being able to see the *whole* of my way had the same effect on the way I painted as occurred if and when I painted in a state of doubt. I knew if I could spare the time I could do it. But I was doing a lot of landscapes and portraits and this took almost all my time. . . .[2]

In consequence, as he continues,

> as and when I painted them, I never felt the joy I needed to experience in doing this work that I should have felt had I known that I could complete the scheme. The works suffered. They have not the conviction that comes with joy. As I have done them the knowledge that the final meaning may never be done has had a crushing effect.

When *The Resurrection: Port Glasgow* was exhibited in 1950 the artists whose work I most admired and whose opinions I generally

[1] Letter to the writer, 10 October 1952.
[2] In his draft Introduction to the Catalogue of the Retrospective Exhibition at the Tate Gallery, 1955.

respected were among its severest critics. When the canvas proposed for the Tate came under consideration their murmurings against it grew in volume and acerbity. It was acquired, in consequence, only after many difficulties had been overcome. But there were others besides professional painters whose antipathies it provoked. At the Academy Banquet that same year I took an opportunity of inviting the opinion of Sir Winston Churchill upon its merits. In response to a request for mine, I pointed to the back-stretching arm of a figure in the left foreground, saying that if the critics of the picture saw, for instance, such an arm on the murky wall of some church in Italy they would recognize it as masterly. 'But it is incorrectly articulated,' he objected, extending his own left arm in a similar position, 'you must admit that.' 'I don't admit it,' I had to reply, 'and I have the advantage of being able to see both arms.' 'I concede that,' he said sternly, 'but I still don't like the picture; and moreover, if that is the Resurrection, then give me eternal sleep.' Although it does not constitute an excuse for certain of the picture's short-comings, it is relevant to mention that the artist never had the use of a room large enough to accommodate the whole work, and that he never saw it until the pieces were put together at Burlington House. Not long before its exhibition I paid a visit to Cliveden View, his tiny house at Cookham. Disjointed fragments of the picture stood in various rooms, the largest fragment no wall of his little painting room was able to accommodate, and it covered a part of the floor as well. Stanley Spencer, brush in hand, feet in socks, walked with loving circumspection about its surface.

While I was engaged upon these pages, in the summer of 1952, and meditating upon the extraordinary power which continuously emanated from the tiny person of Stanley Spencer, manifest in his painting, his drawing and his conversation, in the endless succession of his ideas, in the energy to give them substance and form, he himself arrived. 'Back at the bottle,' he announced, opening a portfolio. 'This time it's Christ preaching from a boat at Cookham Regatta.' Kneeling on the floor he laid drawing against drawing until it was all but covered with them. He confessed to his jubilation at being able to see, on our own drawing-room floor, all the sketches for this project together, and described the several expedients he had tried unsuccessfully at home to gain this comprehensive view. As he talked he created for us, out of sixty or so slight but careful pencil studies, the compelling image of Christ speaking to multitudes who stood pressing towards Him on the lawn of a Thameside hotel and who sat in innumerable boats; a vast multifarious repertory of the life of Cookham focused on the figure preaching from a boat.

MARK GERTLER

1891–1939

TWO contradictory views prevail about Gertler: the one held by those disposed to favour art that is produced near the centre from which the dominant style of the time radiates; to the other incline those who are disposed to believe that the only way for an art to be universal is to be local and particular. Gertler became a painter with a style of his own, the product of a highly personal character and of an immediate environment that offered the strongest contrast to the rest of the society in which it was set, and narrowly circumscribed. Early in life he emerged from the environment that had so largely formed him, and was drawn within the orbit of Post-Impressionism. To some, therefore, Gertler was a gifted provincial whose art ripened as it moved ever nearer to the Parisian sun; to others he seemed an inspired provincial whose art lost its savour as it became more metropolitan. The despair with which the painter was afflicted at intervals throughout his life sprang from doubts about the road he had taken, as well as the genuineness of his talent.

Both the views I have outlined are extreme ones, and when I visited the discerningly selected memorial exhibition at the Whitechapel Art Gallery in 1949–where it was possible for the first time to see the whole range of the artist's work–it seemed to me that while neither view was fully confirmed by the pictures themselves something of an impressive and even a startling rarity died gradually away as his art conformed more and more closely to the accepted canons of Post-Impressionism, although certain gains, notably in solidity and concentration in design, were also apparent.

The spirit and the form of a work of art are indissolubly interconnected, for the first can find expression only through the second, and yet it is a commonplace that there are works simple, even elementary, in form which touch deeper chords than others more elaborate and accomplished. The impression left by the exhibition was that in the course of his life as a painter his powers of expression grew but that what he had to express diminished: with him, it was, so to speak, youth that knew, and age–middle age at least–that could. If Gertler had been an abstract painter, or even an exponent of the then fashionable doctrine of 'significant form', the increase in his powers of composition, of giving weight and solidity to his forms, might have compensated for the ultimate weakening and coarsening of his sense of actuality, his sense of the dramatic element in life. But Gertler was not solely, not even primarily, concerned with the making of coloured forms which should be their own justification; he was a man whose art was deeply implicated in life. It therefore seems to me that in spite of the indisputable aesthetic qualities of his later work it was the work of his youth that expressed what was finest in him and was most intimately his.

It is for this reason that I propose to give most of my attention to this painter's beginnings.

Gertler was born on 9 December 1891, though he himself always gave 1892 as the year of his birth. (It is an odd coincidence that Stanley Spencer, who was born that year, also supposed 1892 to be the year of his birth, and did not discover his error until he was past fifty.) He was the third son and fifth child of Louis Gertler, master furrier, and his wife Golda,[1] born Berenbaum, of a family of emigrants from Przemysl in Galicia. Shortly before the artist's birth his family decided to 'try their luck' in London, but the foothold they gained there was a precarious one and only a year afterwards they were returned with the help of the Jewish Board of Guardians to their native country 'with only me, as it were', the artist wrote many years later, 'to show for it'. Although he was born in London, at 16 Gun Street, Spitalfields, he lived from 1893 until 1898 in Galicia.

After the artist's death a manuscript was found in his studio. This proved to be an autobiographical fragment he had written covering his earliest years, and of this document I have been permitted to make use.

On account of their obscurity and their poverty, the Gertler family belonged to an order of society the members of which leave behind few records or none at all. There is, therefore, no way of checking the accuracy of these fragments, but they affected me not only as a truthful but as a singularly candid narrative, yet free from any trace of exhibitionism. It is written in a lucid, informal style,

[1] It appears as Kate in the artist's birth certificate.

and it must be a matter for regret that Gertler did not live to complete the annals of his full but troubled life.

This candour is manifest on the first page of the typescript. A constant and affectionate friend, the friend, in fact, who had given him most encouragement for his projected autobiography, gave on a formal occasion a considered judgment upon the character of the subject of this study. 'It would be nonsense to call him a good man,' wrote Sylvia Lynd in her introduction to the catalogue of a posthumous exhibition,[1] '. . . and I doubt if his behaviour was ever consciously influenced by any moral consideration.' Mitigating considerations follow this downright declaration, and these I will take into account later on. But for the present my purpose is to show with what frankness and promptitude Gertler acknowledges the freedom of his family and himself from moral scruples. 'I don't know exactly how old I was and unfortunately I cannot ask my family to help me,' runs the first sentence of his autobiographical fragment, 'because the first incident I remember with clarity contains a certain amount of deception, even slyness on my part.' He is four years old and the family is still in Austria. It is winter and his mother incites an elder brother to steal a warm little coat from the factory where he works so that the little boy may be protected from the cold. The mother promises, if he is successful, that she will pretend that the coat is a present from his father, who is in America. Pretending to sleep the little boy listens to the conversation between his mother and brother. In due course the brother brings back the stolen coat. This is his only clear memory, he tells us, of the five years he spent with his family in Austria.

In relating this incident he does not justify the conduct of his mother and brother on the grounds of their desperate poverty: he treats it as a commonplace occurrence, and the only moral consideration he voices relates not to the incitement to steal and the resulting theft but solely to his own deception in pretending not to hear what in fact he heard. Throughout life Gertler had in fact a hatred of deceit and was particularly straightforward about money: if he needed £5, say, he would ask to be given £5; he would not pretend he was borrowing it. He had a strong sense, too, of human dignity, and this mitigated deficiencies of moral conscience in the

[1] Held at the Leicester Galleries, May–June 1941.

conduct of daily life. Consciously or not, I think that his love of what seemed real to him and his revulsion from what seemed unreal impelled him to proclaim, in this first paragraph of the autobiographical fragment, his detachment from moral considerations.

If his family had been miserably poor in their brief stay in London, in Austria their plight became desperate. Their relations clubbed together to buy them a little inn on the outskirts of Przemysl, frequented mostly by drunken soldiers, but the inn failed and his father tried hawking boots, then buttons . . . 'he actually went out into the market-place with both my brothers–he, a very, very proud man–and in that market-place where he was so well-known –and managed to articulate in a sort of shy undertone, "Buttons, Buttons".' But nobody bought his buttons, and unable to support the misery of his family he determined to try his fortune in the New World. 'Let me have a clean shirt, Golda,' he said, 'for this evening I go to America.' During his absence his family suffered the direst poverty: at one time their mother worked in a restaurant, her only wages scraps of left-over food. But after about four years word came from their father that things had gone well with him–it seems that he had entered the fur trade and learnt some new process–and that they were to meet him in London. Although Gertler's memories of Przemysl remained vague, from the time of the journey to England 'the kernel of each event remains vivid, and the essentials connected and alive'. The arrival is vividly recalled: 'I am standing surrounded by my family all ready with heavy packages straining from their necks, pressing their backs. All available limbs are grasping rebellious packages. My mother strains her eyes and says, "Oh woe is me, but I cannot see your father. He is not there, he is not there. . . ."' Later he caught sight of a bright-coloured shop–Gardiner's of Whitechapel. 'Mother, does the King live here?' he enquired. It was then, he wrote, at the age of six, with Yiddish his only language, that his true life began. This true life was hardly begun when he suffered one of those fits of acute depression which afflicted him throughout his life and at last cut it short. The Gertler family–all seven of them– spent their first night in one of the two tenement rooms in Shoreditch of a friend from Przemysl, and the sight of them lying in a row on a floor covered by sacks brought on a fit of depression that he always remembered as the first which he consciously suffered,

With the friend from Przemysl they lived until their father found work smoothing walking-sticks with sandpaper at 12/6 a week. This enabled them to set up a home of their own. At this point Gertler breaks off his narrative in order to describe an expedition to the scenes of his childhood made with his wife in the middle nineteen-thirties. He notes 'the greater vitality' of the life there, the way in which 'the rich dark-complexioned boys and girls seemed to move and talk with unusual intensity, as if life was fearfully important', and finally he describes their visit to the ancient, dilapidated synagogue he had formerly attended. On first entering, scarcely able any longer to talk Yiddish, he felt extremely uncomfortable, almost a stranger, but by degrees he was drawn momentarily back to the observances of his earlier years. How admirably he describes their visit! The preliminary conversation with the 'shumm', a sort of verger–who, puzzled by their wishing to visit this derelict place, tries to persuade them to go to a smarter synagogue where, he assures them, there are 'well-to-do people'–is related with economy and humour. But the best part of the entire account, to my thinking, is the description of their entry into the building.

Yes, it was impressive, [it runs] the same as ever—scattered here and there, sometimes in groups, sometimes single were these same magnificent old men I used to know. The long silver beards and curls, looking like princes in their rags and praying shawls–swaying, bending, moaning, groaning at their prayer. Passionate, ecstatic, yet casual and mechanical. Lucky old Rembrandt to have lived in a time when such subject matter was still fresh, when it was *right* to paint these men. They look magnificent; but I do not want to paint them. As soon as we entered they noticed our presence, and began slowly but surely to make their gyrations more towards our direction, so that, at last, it seemed almost as if their prayers were directed at us. Meanwhile, one praying man near me pushed a prayer-book into my hand, and looking down at its opened pages, I found that I had even more completely forgotten my Hebrew than my Yiddish. However, I too began to bend a little, moan a little, and sway taking care to do so in the direction of the main group at the far end of the synagogue–whose curiosity had made them turn towards ours. . . .

In part it was, perhaps, a reassertion of old habits, but–for Gertler was always quick at mimicry–in part it was an exercise of his ready and abundant gift of mimicking what struck his imagination.

Before resuming the narrative of his childhood, he made another excursion to the near present: this time to speak of an old cat–a 'visiting' cat of whom he had grown fond. But his wife was away, and the neighbours to whom the cat belonged left, and then the tenants from downstairs, and with them most of the animal's means of subsistence.

How much older, decrepit, shabby and down-at-heel he was looking! [Gertler noted.] Then yesterday–the final blow–an empty house, just he and I. . . . At about 3 o'clock yesterday afternoon I got panicky. How silent the house was. . . . But I have another whole month here. . . . I am suddenly frightened, I don't even know how to get through the next 3 hours, till my teaching. . . . Damn! the cat is getting on my nerves. All right, all right, we'll have tea. Heavens, there's no milk. . . . The cat is still meowing and looking me straight in the eye. I can stand it no longer. I kick him down the stairs! Yes, I kicked him. This morning the man came with the brown basket. Goodbye cat . . .

This small drama of the lonely man and the plaintive cat left by themselves in the empty house sheds as clear a light upon the character of Gertler as the episode of the stolen jacket. There is a touching quality in his sorrow because 'the old cat has been carried off in a basket to be "put to sleep". . . . I shall never see him again,' a sorrow uncomplicated by his own capricious responsibility for the cat's death, and the truthfulness with which it is all related. The power to feel keenly, moral irresponsibility, and innate candour–all are richly manifest.

When he resumes his narrative it is to describe his school days. When he was seven years old he was sent to 'Chaida' or Hebrew class taught by an old rabbi who used to read out the Old Testament in Hebrew, translating into Yiddish 'in a rapid, hardly intelligible, monotone, and we had to drone on after him, repeating the parts we could catch, and filling up the rest with noises that meant nothing whatsoever'.

One day this harmless if unfruitful curriculum was abruptly ended. His parents, who lived in an almost closed society of emigrants from Eastern Europe, rarely moving far from their home and with few contacts with the larger society about them, knew nothing of their obligation to send their children to school. The visit of an angry inspector led to Gertler's enrolment at the nearby Deal Lane School.

He thus describes his entry:

It was a hot day, and as soon as we joined the queue, my mother for some reason lifted me into her arms and held me there in a manner she used when I was younger. I felt uncomfortable but did not protest, and soon I began to notice beads of sweat gathering, like pearls, on her forehead and temples, then join and trickle down her cheeks in thin glistening streams. Then I heard a woman saying, 'Why do you carry such a big boy in your arms, Mrs.? Ain't he old enough to stand?' I felt ashamed and tried to wriggle down, but my mother gathered her arms around me tighter, and held me there, not deigning even to answer the woman.

At last our turn came to approach the desk, at which a man was sitting, very stern and angry, making us feel from the start that we were somehow in the wrong, and that he jolly well meant to 'let us have it'.

'Put that boy down, *at once*. He's not a babe! Name of Gertler, I see. What's his *christian* name?'

Of course my mother could make nothing of it at all, until some women at the back came to the rescue. 'Mux,' she said.

'Mux,' said the man, 'never heard such a name—no such name in *this* country. We'll call him *Mark* Gertler.'

Towards the end of this autobiographical fragment (which covers only thirty-two small typewritten sheets) he mentions various circumstances of his upbringing which afford further insight into his character and situation. In desolation at finding himself at a strange school,

I glanced at the children nearest me, as if to discover whether I dare give way to the tears that were choking me, but realised instantly that here was a new situation; that here, in this atmosphere one must try *not* to cry, and I succeeded in controlling my emotions—perhaps for the first time in my short life.

Both the total absence of any parental training in self-control and the sobering impact of a strange society in which a measure of self-control was the rule clearly emerge from his description of his entry into school. And both these circumstances coloured his relations with the society into which he shortly emerged, a society in which, in spite of much success and many friendships, he felt himself at heart a stranger who continually exposed himself by his inability to control his feelings, and therefore at a perpetual disadvantage among people cooler and more disciplined. Self-control was made

51. MARK GERTLER. *The Artist's Mother* (1911).
Oil, 26×22 in. The Tate Gallery, London.

52. MARK GERTLER. *The Roundabout* (1916).
Oil, 74¾ × 56 in. The Ben Uri Gallery, London.

the more difficult by continual insufficiency of sleep. Golda Gertler, completely self-sacrificing though she was, used him unwisely:

> unfortunately like most people . . . some of the most important things in connection with the upbringing of a child were quite unknown to her, and I consider the most disastrous of these was the fact that we were allowed to go to bed at any old hour. . . . I was a very nervous, highly-strung and emotional child, somewhat undersized, thin and pale, yet I would hardly ever be put to bed before . . . midnight, and at week-ends . . . long past that hour.

This constant lack of sleep in his childhood no doubt played its part in weakening his nervous system, and in particular in darkening and prolonging his fits of depression.

It was while he was at Deal Lane that there occurred what was beyond comparison the most important event of his life. He noticed a poster advertising beef extract. The impression it made was heightened by the sight of some still-lifes by a pavement artist, and he began to draw still-lifes on the pavement beside his parents' house. Encouraged by the oil paints and water-colours that his family gave him and – according to a persistent tradition – by the reading, on long-continued daily visits to a bookshop, of 'My Autobiography and Reminiscences' by W. P. Frith, he determined to be an artist. At the age of fifteen he briefly attended classes at the Regent Street Poly-technic, and in December 1907 he started work for five shillings a week (with the promise of 7/6 after the completion of six months satisfactory service) with Clayton and Bell, glass painters, at 311 Regent Street.

In the October of the following year – on the seventh to be precise – I myself had a glimpse of him. My parents were living at that time at 11 Oakhill Park, Hampstead, and here, on hearing the front-door bell ring, I used occasionally to hurry to the hall and open the door before the maid arrived. Doing so that day I was confronted by a shortish, handsome boy with apricot-coloured skin and a dense mop of dark brown hair so stiff that it stood on end. I took him for a barrow boy, but he said he had been sent to see my father. I was seven years old, but I still remember his nervous, sullen look. Years later I was told that he was accompanied by his elder brother Jack, who used to carry his paintings and slip away upon arrival. I would not, of course, have known the year let alone the date when this unimportant encounter took place had I not seen, quite recently, the letter, dated 8 October, which my father wrote to Gertler's father. 'Your son,' it runs, 'as you know came here yesterday . . . I do sincerely believe that your son has gifts of a high order, and that if he will cultivate them with love and care . . . you will one day have reason to be proud of him. . . .' This letter his parents framed and hung up in their house, and he preserved it after their deaths. The educational society which had sent Gertler to see my father, acting on the advice he gave, sent him to the Slade, where he remained from 1908 until 1912. His precocious abilities won him immediate success: he was awarded the Slade Scholarship for the sessions 1908–9 and 1909–10, a first prize for Head Painting, and a second prize for Painting from the Cast, and in 1909 a certificate for painting: an outstanding record. But besides jumping through all the hoops he became, in the warm yet invigorating air of the Slade, a painter of impressive powers. Some of the pictures he painted while still a student take their place among his finest works; and surely too among the finest painted by a student during the period considered in these pages. Of these to my thinking *The Artist's Mother*,[1] of 1911, (Plate 19), has a place apart. I saw this portrait in 1944, and proposed it for purchase under the terms of the Chantrey Bequest, and this work by an artist not yet twenty years old emerged without discredit from the searching criticism of my Academy colleagues on the Recommending Committee. *The Artist's Mother* possesses, abundantly, the essential quality of a portrait: the power of evoking an entirely convincing presence. In the presence of a self-portrait by Rembrandt we are in the presence not of paint and canvas but, miraculously, of Rembrandt, a silent and immobile Rembrandt, but of Rembrandt himself. So, lower in the scale of creation, does Gertler evoke for us the presence of Golda, his mother, who without the rudiments of education, without having seen a picture, from the first apprehended a mysterious difference between her youngest child and his brothers and sisters, and even the importance of the strange calling to which her son was dedicated. In his mother's reassuring presence, in her little kitchen, he felt a confidence that enabled him to paint. But it is not for the evocation of a personality that this picture is most remarkable, but for the sheer capacity to

[1] The Tate Gallery, London.

paint that it manifests. The patient, devoted face, the sturdy figure, are indeed impressively represented, but the weight and texture of the heavy silk of the voluminous, fusty dress, and above all, the folded hands, solidly realized, modelled with extreme subtlety, and instinct with life, more impressively still. The painting of those hands is masterly by any standards, and in the twentieth century masterly painting is rarer than at other times.

I quoted just now a phrase from the autobiographical fragment about the way in which the East End boys and girls 'seemed to move and talk with unusual intensity, as if life was fearfully important–momentous'. The description fits perfectly Gertler's own way of seeing. And rather as by their long winters spent largely indoors hedged in by familiar faces, the subjects of daily scrutiny, the painters of the Low Countries developed a heightened realism, so was the exuberant yet searching vision of Gertler intensified by its strict confinement within narrow limits. He lived his life in a tiny alien enclave utterly cut off by religious observance, by prejudice, and during these first years by the barrier of language, from the encircling population; and within that alien enclave there was the family circle, if not precisely closed, at any rate exclusive. An eye accustomed to take horizons within its sweep would be less likely to focus so avidly upon small things and to treat them as 'fearfully important–momentous'. Take even The Teapot,[1] painted seven years after the portrait, when his eye had accustomed itself to rather wider prospects: how authoritatively he compels us to recognize the uniqueness of its shape, its colours, its density, in a word its momentousness. Nothing could be more remote from the casual glance ordinarily bestowed upon an ordinary teapot than the absorbed and loving scrutiny in which Gertler held it until it became 'momentous'.

The absorption and love of his scrutiny did not make for pedantry of any kind, for an over-concern with detail, for instance; it gave him, on the contrary, the assurance to represent his subjects largely. The Teapot, indeed, does not stand quite foursquare on the tray, and it has a lid with a knob imperfectly related to it, but neither of these defects disturbs our sense of its 'momentousness'.

At the beginning of this study I mentioned the contradictory

[1] The Tate Gallery, London.

opinions held about Gertler's development, and commented that I myself inclined – with certain reservations – to regard his earlier work as that most likely to survive. For to me the quality, beyond all others, that makes it precious is this power of making the subjects he represented appear 'momentous'. It springs partly from youth, more susceptible than maturity or age to see intensely, but also from the peculiar narrowness of the artist's early surroundings. This narrowness, amounting almost to isolation, imposed upon his emotions a discipline that precluded their dissipation and focused them upon a few loved and familiar things and people. It is in the early works, drawn and painted before his horizon opened out, that this 'momentousness' is most luminous. Something of it appears in *The Apple Woman and Her Husband*,[1] of 1912, which represents his mother and his wistful little father. Although richer, clearer and more varied in colour, and more ambitious as a design, than *The Artist's Mother*, there is about it just a suggestion of self-conscious artistry, and its impact is a little lighter. But in the small group of these early works nowhere is 'momentousness' so poignantly present as it is in *Rabbi and Rabbitzen*,[2] of 1914, an old couple seen with extraordinary insight through eyes at once wise yet innocent, searching yet affectionate. I fall Gertler's work were to perish except this, it would serve as a microcosm of the precisely focused intensity that gives the best of his early work a glowing actuality in the company of which most others seem the lifeless products of indifference.

It was intimate contact with the things that he saw and experienced for himself before he emerged out of the confined existence of a member of a little, isolated group of foreign immigrants that excited all his faculties to their highest pitch. The capital, so to speak, that he accumulated during those early years lasted for some time after he left the Slade, but his sudden exposure as a student to pressures of every kind tried and sometimes compromised the integrity of his way of seeing. The circumstance of his having come from a class in which none of the arts were practised or even thought of made him the more susceptible to such pressures. Emergence from what, for an artist, was penitential bleakness into a world where the arts were practised on all hands and where the evidences of their having been practised for centuries abounded in art gallery,

[1] Coll. Lady Daniel.   [2] Coll. Mr. Jeremy Hutchinson.

church and private house must have been intoxicating; and considering how radically uncertain he always was of the validity of his art, it must be a matter for gratitude that he resisted so strongly and preserved so much. Evidence of pressure from outside is evident from the moment of his emergence. *The Artist's Sister*,[1] the late Deborah Atelson, of 1911, an exuberant figure exuberantly dressed, has energy and largeness of form, but it clearly reveals, particularly in its colour, the influence of Brown and Steer, his teachers at the Slade. This is a handsome painting; but one made the following year, *Portrait of a Girl*,[2] shows how debilitating these pressures could be. In this picture there is no trace of the weight and exuberance, or yet of the close, affectionate scrutiny that marked all the works mentioned above; it is a languid essay in the manner of Augustus John or Henry Lamb: but these artists, so to speak, tidied up, and the girl dressed for the occasion in fashionably 'bohemian' clothes. Ironically, the spotted kerchief on her head is that worn by his mother in *The Apple Woman and her Husband*. This feeblest of the artist's early paintings, in which—fortunately only for the moment—he turned his back upon everything in his past that had made him an artist, was presented to the Tate in 1923 and remained for seventeen years the Gallery's sole representation of the art of Gertler. One of his paintings of the following year reveals susceptibility to influence from another direction, for *The Jewish Family*[3] testifies to his close study of Picasso. In this picture he attempted to represent one of his traditional subjects with the pathos and the attenuated delicacy of a work of this painter's 'blue' or 'pink' period. In spite of his continuing admiration this remained, so far as I am aware, a solitary experiment. His development, in fact, took a different direction. Sometime about the beginning of the First World War a new and fruitful element made its appearance in his painting, an element more easily recognized than described. It was as though life presented itself to this contemplation less as a kind of reality perceptible to the ordinary eye than as a kind of puppet-show at a fair. This is an overstatement, but it indicates something of the impersonal character, the simplified forms, the robust colours, the humour that marked the finest of his paintings after he left the Slade and that

[1] Coll. Mr. Thomas Balston.   [2] The Tate Gallery, London.
[3] The Tate Gallery, London.

gave them something of the character of products of a sophisticated and expressive folk-art. Whether the emergence of this element was due to something he had recently seen, to something innate, or to some childhood or even inherited memory of folk-art in Eastern Europe, I cannot say; but it is perhaps relevant to recall that it was by an example of popular art, a poster advertising a meat extract, that he was first moved to draw.

The first important painting known to me with this folk-art overtone is Mr. Gilbert Cannan at his Mill,[1] of 1914–15, in which the novelist is shown standing with his dog outside the windmill in which he lived at Cholesbury in Hertfordshire, the scene, incidentally, of one of the lamentable occasions of the artist's life. The interest of the scene itself, the odd man beside his strange home, the upright converging Gothic forms, all treated with a robustness, almost, one might say, a heartiness, that makes sinister overtones, naturally contribute to the picture's momentousness. The subject had obvious dramatic possibilities, but it is to the skill with which the highly original composition has been worked out and the intense energy with which every smallest feature of it has been painted, and not the subject itself, to which the picture's impressiveness is due. I am able to state this categorically, for although I have never visited Cholesbury I came upon a photograph, which the artist no doubt used and had preserved among his papers, and this I had an opportunity of comparing with the painting. The photograph bears the same relation to the painting as its score does to the performance of a symphony.

The second of these pictures is The Roundabout,[2] of 1916 (Plate 52). In this extraordinary picture the folk-art figures express, although in a more sophisticated fashion, the brutality that the boisterous jollity of the traditional Punch scarcely masks. The artist sent a photograph of it to D. H. Lawrence, whom it moved to admiration and horror.

My dear Gertler [he wrote, in a letter dated 9 October 1916] Your terrible and beautiful picture has just come. This is the first picture you have ever painted: it is the best *modern* picture I have seen: I think it is great and true. But it is horrible and terrifying. I'm not sure I wouldn't be too frightened to come and look at the original. . . .[3]

[1] Coll. Mr. Thomas Balston.   [2] The Ben Uri Gallery, London.
[3] 'The Letters of D. H. Lawrence', edited with an Introduction by Aldous Huxley, 1932, pp. 368–9.

Never again, as far as I am aware, did his folk-art figures assume so grand or so sinister a form. Indeed the folk-art element in him usually found expression through subjects–Staffordshire figures and the like–already perfectly adapted to it.

Gertler had reached maturity as a painter before he was twenty: the impressive character of his art and his exhilarating personality combined to make him a considerable figure even before he left the Slade. In spite of its palpable hyperbole at certain points a description of him by his friend, the barrister St. John Hutchinson, conveys something of the effect he made. 'There has seldom been a more exciting personality than he was when young ... with amazing gifts of draughtsmanship, amazing vitality and sense of humour and of mimicry unique to himself–a shock of hair, the vivid eyes of genius and consumption. . . .'[1]

On leaving the Slade he quickly took his place among the most gifted of the younger painters. He was immediately elected to membership of the New English Art Club, and of his *Fruit Sorters*,[2] which he showed there two years later, Sickert wrote that '. . . the picture is justified by a sort of intensity and raciness . . . (it) is important also because it is a masterly piece of painting in well-supported and consistent illumination, and the work of a colourist at the same time rich and sober'.[3] He received some commissions for portraits, too, of which one of the best is *Sir George Darwin*.[4] As a draughtsman he had the power of giving weight and dignity and a kind of rugged tragic character, well exemplified in *Head of an Old Man*,[5] of 1912, which, however remote in the order of creation from Leonardo's heads of old men, has something in common with them.

To his precocious talents as painter and draughtsman were joined social qualities of the order–though not, perhaps, to the degree–which St. John Hutchinson claimed for him. It was not long, therefore, before he became a personality in the intellectual and, more conspicuously, the bohemian life of London. D. H. Lawrence and

---

[1] Foreword to the catalogue of the exhibition of the Montague Shearman Collection at the Redfern Gallery, 1940.

[2] Whereabouts unknown.

[3] 'The New English Art Club', 'The New Age', 4 June 1914.

[4] The National Portrait Gallery, London.

[5] The National Gallery of South Australia, Adelaide, from the collection of the late Sir Edward Marsh.

Lytton Strachey were numbered among his friends, and he became a member of the circle which frequented Lady Ottoline Morrell's house at Garsington.

Gertler had little of the snob in his composition, and no ambition to enter fashionable society, although he derived some amusement from the swiftness of his graduation from Whitechapel tenement to Mayfair drawing-room. But it was not the drawing-room but the café-in particular the Café Royal-that provided the setting in which he was most at home. The company of writers gave him more satisfaction than that of painters; he was not deeply interested by ideas and his acquaintance with literature was superficial, but he liked to read books by his friends. For a brief period during the First World War he showed signs of intellectual ambition, but his efforts at learning and at reading Nietzsche yielded insignificant results.

The sense that everything that the great world offered had suddenly been made free to him, a slum boy, by his extraordinary talent he found intoxicating, and he indulged to the full his exorbitant sociability-a sociability so exacting, however, that he could be dull company if alone for long with a single companion. The sudden enrichment of his life afforded him more excitement and gratification than happiness. His success did little to diminish his apprehension that he was and would remain a stranger in this larger world. This apprehension was not entirely unfounded, but the mistrust and dislike which he often discovered in those whom he regarded as friends was due not, as he was inclined to suppose, to social but to personal characteristics. Lack of self-control allowed him to sacrifice even considerations of prudence for the satisfaction of the moment. If he wished, for instance, to shine at some social occasion, the ridiculing and wounding of his closest friends was a price habitually paid without hesitation or regret. The standards generally observed in the society he had entered seemed to him as irrelevant to the actual circumstances of life as the rules of heraldry, and he compared them to their disadvantage with the less artificial, less complicated standards of Whitechapel, especially as regards self-assertion, avarice, lust and the rest. But he never wanted to return to the miserable squalor, the hysterical quarrels, and above all the want of understanding of the art that he cared for above everything else, that marked his early life.

It was not long before he had more than a vague sense of isolation and of insecurity to temper his exuberant enjoyment of his new life: he became involved in situations in which he inflicted and suffered distress.

Hard work and what was once charitably described as 'sociability' before long began to affect his health, and in the summer of 1914 he retired to the windmill home at Cholesbury of his friend Cannan, which at intervals he revisited. One consequence of these visits was the splendid portrait, already mentioned, of the novelist by the painter; the lamentable portrait of the painter by the novelist was another. This was a novel, published in 1916, entitled 'Mendel', in which Gertler is the principal character and his life the theme. D. H. Lawrence wrote of 'Mendel': 'It is a bad book–statement without creation–really journalism. Gertler . . . has told every detail of his life to Gilbert–Gilbert has a lawyer's memory and he has put it all down, and so ridiculously when it comes to the love affair. We never recognized ourselves. . . .'[1] It is scarcely possible to dissent from Lawrence's opinion of it. The novel is indeed a shoddy production, lacking a single spark of creativity; it lacks, too, any value as a record, so closely is fact intertwined with fiction.

It has always been assumed that the responsibility for this novel rested entirely with the author. Gertler certainly claimed that he was unaware that his stories of his life in Whitechapel–which he always delighted to tell–were being memorized and daily set down by Cannan without his knowledge. Mr. Balston accepted this disclaimer. 'Unknown to Gertler,' he wrote, 'Cannan was writing the novel. . . .'[2] An unpublished letter dated 10 May 1916 from Lytton Strachey, however, makes it virtually certain that Gertler knew that a novel was being written. 'I imagine you may be at Cholesbury,' it runs, 'working hard by day, and talking with Cannan by night. Is it true that he's writing a novel about you?' This letter shows that a novel by Cannan based upon Gertler's nightly talks with him was common talk, and had Gertler, by some extraordinary chance, been unaware of what was evidently known to others, it would have appraised him of it. That it reached him may be regarded as certain,

---

[1] 'The Letters of D. H. Lawrence'. Letter to Catherine Carswell, 2 December 1916.
[2] Catalogue of the Memorial Exhibition, 1949.

as it was found among his papers after his death. It is very unlikely, however, that he ever saw Cannan's manuscript.

The description of his visit to my parents' house caused my father to write to him: 'You wrong both of us by giving so sordid and untruthful an account of your feelings and mine.'[1] But although it inflicted a gratuitous wrong upon someone from whom he had received nothing but disinterested kindness at a time when he stood in urgent need of it, this description was a small matter compared with his damaging stories about his own family, stories, however, that he would tell without the slightest doubt cast on his affection or his respect for them. And whatever their shortcomings, his family showed towards him an exemplary loyalty.

The other difficulty in which his temperament involved him was of a less blameworthy but a more harrowing kind. Among his friends at the Slade was a girl of exceptional talent. With her he eventually fell in love, and his relation with her was the most deeply felt one of his life. The girl was fond of Gertler, but hers was a complex and highly independent nature, and she was repelled by his selfishness, which expressed itself in an obsessive desire for complete possession of her and a reluctance entirely to commit himself. That harmony between them was impossible so long as Gertler was obstinately possessive and preoccupied only with himself was apparent to Lawrence. 'If you could only give yourself up in love,' he wrote to Gertler, 'she would be much happier. You always want to dominate her, which is no good. One must learn to relinquish oneself, not to bother about oneself, but to love the other person. You hold too closely to yourself, for her to be free to love you.'[2]

In spite of his periodic fits of despair about his work, he was not self-critical as a man and he could not see the truth of Lawrence's words. The conclusion to which his own feverish and even hysterical reflexions led was that the young woman–herself a highly gifted painter and an acute critic–did not sufficiently respect him as an artist. This conclusion was almost certainly erroneous. If the value of his work and his seriousness of purpose could only be authoritatively impressed upon her, he came to believe, her complicated reserve would be overcome. The proper person to effect this change

[1] Letter found among Gertler's papers.
[2] 'The Letters of D. H. Lawrence', 20 January 1916.

was obviously Lytton Strachey, a man of extraordinary intelligence, of a manner and aspect wholly unfrivolous, of a temperament which made it unlikely that he would wish to replace Gertler in her affections. In August or more probably September 1916 there was a meeting between her and Strachey. It is probable that nobody knows what took place. The result, however, was decisive. The girl fell passionately in love with Strachey, and resolved to devote her life to his interests, and when he left London to live in the country she went with him. She was as conscious of his faults as of Gertler's—in a letter to Gertler written in 1917 she refers to 'Lytton's cynical frigidity'—but she remained devoted until, years later, she ended her own life.

The turn of events reduced Gertler to a frenzy of bitterness.

I am afraid [he wrote to her in September 1916] that I cannot support you over your love for Lytton; because I love *you*, I need not necessarily love what *you* love. I do believe in *you* but nothing on earth will make me believe in Lytton as a fit object for your love—the whole thing in fact is most disappointing to me. . . . I only hope soon that the nausea of this wretched relationship of yours will poison the spirit of my love for you and so diminish the stink of it all. Never would I have contemplated such a nauseous thing. Believe me the whole of these years of struggle have been turned into ridicule for me by this sudden reversal of yours to dead withered (undecipherable). Also he arranges all your life—I must wait with my arrangements for him. Why do you not at least control yourself a bit, must you be so slavish and abject? Surely there is in me also something to study, if only my art, you sicken me with your abject devotion. . . .

The girl's new relationship had an unlooked-for result: instead of separating her from Gertler it brought them for a time to a closer, although not a happier intimacy. 'It is not that I don't love you,' she wrote to him in January 1917. 'It is that I was sad. When one is in sorrow one feels isolated curiously and to be forced into another's animal possessions suddenly makes it almost a nightmare.' And the same month, 'But you must know it is not that I dislike you. It is something between us, that is hateful.'

In 1915 he left Whitechapel for good, and helped by his family, who had prospered, he established himself at Penn Studio, Rudall Crescent, Hampstead, where he remained for fifteen years, lodging latterly at 19 Worsley Road. Though its effect was not immediately apparent, the move corresponded with a change in his art. He moved away from daily experience of the scenes that had made him a painter. The two Post-Impressionist exhibitions had caused him, the least confident of painters, to doubt the validity of his art. A first visit to Paris, made in 1919, satisfied him that his doubt was justified, and his art too dependent upon the interest of his subjects and too little upon purely formal qualities. During the years immediately following he visited the south of France. In his own eyes, his art, round about 1920, ceased to be 'provincial' and began to belong to the tradition forged by Renoir and Cézanne. 'He has naturally chosen work from this latest period since about 1920 to represent him here,' wrote Mr. Hubert Wellington, in his preface to a small volume of reproductions of Gertler's works, published in 1925. 'It shows,' the author noted with approval, 'a determination to realize the form, colour and texture of his subject matter with the greatest possible completeness. Forms are made full and continuous, local colour kept rich and undisturbed, . . .' But he found it necessary to utter a muted warning: '. . . a very personal technique of small accumulated touches yields very handsome surface qualities and renders varied textures with an almost disquieting realism: disquieting because it tends to obscure the interest in pattern and "architectural" design.'[1]

This discerning critic–even though writing rather more subject to the then fashionable doctrine of the over-riding importance of 'significant form' than he would to-day–has divined the two conflicting impulses in Gertler's temperament, the desire, excited by the example of French painting, to excel in purely aesthetic fields, and a fascinated interest in the life around him. Of the fundamental character of the realistic impulse in himself this painter who could scarcely draw a line but in the presence of his subject was inevitably aware. 'I have made up my mind,' he wrote to a friend, 'that if I am to deviate from nature it must be only to add discoveries of my own. . . .'[2] It need hardly be said that these two impulses are not necessarily irreconcilable, or that many artists have found the means to represent the subjects which interest them most deeply in entirely satisfying aesthetic terms. But this, after he left Whitechapel,

[1] 'Mark Gertler' (British Artists of Today.)
[2] From a letter quoted by H. L. Wellington, op. cit.

Gertler was rarely able to accomplish. The people and the things which impressed themselves most deeply upon his imagination were the people and the things that belonged to his early life. He was innately and strongly realistic in his way of seeing: he was, in fact, scarcely capable of envisaging anything that was not before his eyes, and he worked invariably from his subject direct. 'All his later landscapes,' we are told by Mr. Balston, 'were done through windows.'[1] After he left Whitechapel the subjects that had called forth his most intense emotion, being no longer before his eyes, faded from his imagination. They were largely replaced by still-life, the objects of daily use in his studio or ornaments such as Staffordshire figures, but unlike Cézanne Gertler was incapable of responding with his whole mind and his whole heart to a plate of apples. Generally incapable, would be a juster way of putting it, for from time to time he painted a still-life of so splendid a quality as to rank among the finest still-lifes of the century, such, for instance, as the large *Basket of Fruit*,[2] of 1925. Nudes he continued to paint with beauty and conviction until the middle 'twenties. *Young Girlhood*, of 1913[3] and of 1925,[4] are closely observed and taut in handling, but *Sleeping Nude*,[5] of 1928, shows a falling off, and worse were to follow. And all the while, as the memories of his early subjects waned under the influence of Paris, he became more and more preoccupied with the search for such purely aesthetic qualities as 'architecture' and design. The change was not due to a sudden conversion, but to the steady pressure of such concepts as architecture, significant form and the like, and the example, of course, of modern French masters, upon a painter made susceptible to such pressure by the progressive enfeeblement of his own intensely personal and convinced vision of things. For a long time something of its former character remained: he was able, until late in his life, to endow his subjects with a fullness and warmth that was almost haunting. But as the years passed his subjects were too often mere counters chosen to exemplify 'volume' or some other fashionable concept, for its own sake. An example— one, alas, of many—of a subject treated thus is *The Mandolinist*,[6] of 1934, which has neither more nor less merit than scores of other

[1] Catalogue of the Memorial Exhibition. [2] Coll. Mr. Thomas Balston.
[3] Coll. Mr. Edward le Bas. [4] Coll. Mr. Thomas Balston.
[5] Coll. Mr. Thomas Balston. [6] Coll. Mr. Thomas Balston.

similar paintings made in London and Paris that year by imitators of Derain and other leading Post-Impressionists.

Gertler was not an intellectual like Duncan Grant or Paul Nash, still less did he command such powers of thought as Wyndham Lewis wielded, but he was aware of something amiss with his later work, and this awareness brought with it recurrent distress of mind. I do not pretend to know at all precisely how his self-criticism was directed, but in the absence of conclusive evidence I believe that his despair sprang from his consciousness of maladjustment between his failing vision and his growing executive ability. Not that technical problems ceased to absorb him. Like many other painters he made notes for his own guidance. One of these, headed 'Latest system and its advantages' and dated 24 August 1928, tabulates proposed modifications of method and the results expected. 'Contours more varied and lost–working right across and not at any stage defined, advantage–a greater flow and continuation–no stoppage,' reads one such note. Others of the same date prescribe methods for attaining 'more colour in shadows and more air generally', 'freshness and light', and presenting the same surface from whichever angle it is looked at, 'unity and general realizations'. 'Form and design realized by light and shade seems a deep unalterable characteristic–why try and alter it?' he reflects.[1]

As he grew older the fits of depression from which he had suffered since boyhood became more desperate, more frequent and prolonged. To this his recurrent loneliness and the sporadically inharmonious character of his most intimate relationships contributed, but their principal occasion was his work. In times of distress he used to write to friends or set down his thoughts simply for his own relief. For the light it sheds on his processes of thought and feeling, above all upon his lack of confidence in himself as an artist, I here give the whole of what may, perhaps, be the most extensive of his writings of this nature.

> You ask what is the matter with me? Well it is something serious–the greatest crisis of my life–and you know what I have already suffered in the past. In fact–for the time being I see no solution–the trouble is–*my work*–what is my value as an artist? What have I in me after all?

[1] These excerpts have been made from pages of notes found in his studio after his death.

Is there anything there worth while after all? That is the point—I doubt myself—I doubt myself terribly—after all these years of labour and you know how I worked—so so hard—with my blood and I have lived and fed up my work—my work was by faith—my purpose—But—as I find now to my acute discomfort—an essential part of that faith [and] that purpose—was not just to work alone—but the hope that I will—some day—at least produce pictures that will *stand* that will have some place among work that counts—Well have I . . . achieved anything of the sort so far? I doubt it very much. Do I stand a chance of succeeding in the future? *That* is the point! My doubt on this point is what is causing me this acute misery. Oh, I cannot tell you how much I suffer—I hardly dare—My past works keep floating through my mind's eye—awful ghosts that torture me—I cannot bear to go to a house that contain(s) any of my pictures—for at once I am flooded with misery and despair! seeing any good picture or reproduction does the same thing to me—I feel inferior—inferior to all! . . .—of course I contemplate death—over and over again—sometimes it even seeming the logical solution—for you must know—and I frankly confess it—that I cannot live without that *purpose—to create real work*—It seems to me that it is either one of two things—Either I regain sufficient faith for my 'purpose' or I die—. . . sometimes I think of finding something else to do—but what? To kill myself—there is the dreadful selfishness of it—think of my mother—Marjorie and perhaps a few others! . . . I am putting up a strong fight—I feel hopeful at times, that there will be a sort of rebirth—a new sort of adjustment—something I don't know of what nature but I am doing my best—to treat this dreadful period as a sort of pause—interval—giving myself the time to be reborn. . . .

'Dec. 11th 1929

. . . A few days after my last note I went down to Leicester Sq. to buy a revolver—I felt I *ought* to have one—so that I had in my possession an easy means of ending my life—when I got near the shop my tongue went dry with horror—I felt that by getting an 'easy means' I should not be giving myself a chance—anyway I felt cheap and degraded—And I turned away in disgust—

Today set up a new little still life—Pomegranates in a basket with a yellow bow. Yes beautiful—and I saw before me my vision. How *I* see it and I get a fit of depression—How different to the vision of a Matisse a Picasso! Ah! those aristocrats! moving so high above me—what a rough—clumsy peasant they make me feel! What an everyday vision is mine compared with theirs!

Then I went to tea with my mother—why do I feel so down in the company of my relations? Oh! How sorry I feel both for them and myself . . . I feel that we are in the same boat *really*—only I *know* the sort of boat it is – and they don't – and then – How strongly do I feel the Height of men who really *achieve* and my own lowness.'[1]

In his latter years, more particularly after 1920, gay as he generally was in company, and happy often when he had a brush in his hand, he was rarely free for long from the shadows of depression. For in that year he was seriously ill with tuberculosis and was compelled to spend five months in a sanatorium at Banchory; the threat of a renewal of this trouble sent him into the sanatorium at Mundesley in Norfolk in 1925, 1929 and 1936. It is clear that ill-health or the threat of it aggravated his fits of depression. These were eventually accompanied by suicidal gestures or attempts. On his last visit to Mundesley he cut his throat and a vein in his arm – then promptly rang for the nurse.

Gertler's last years provided many occasions for his prevailing melancholy. In 1930 he married Marjorie Greatorex, daughter of George Edmund Hodgkinson, a London solicitor, and a son was born two years later. But the friendship of many had become hostility or indifference. His ill-health gave increasing cause for anxiety and, most painful of all, the relative neglect of his work – though it still held the respect of many painters and lovers of painting – further increased his painful self-mistrust.

Whether he looked within himself or at the world outside he saw – or fancied he saw – causes for distress. Not long after I came to the Tate I remember Sir Edward Marsh's saying to me, in that almost inaudibly high voice of his, 'I saw Mark last night. He was terribly depressed. He thinks you don't like his work. I told him you did, but it was no good.'

During these years he was dependent for pleasure upon social occasions, when he became for an hour the entertaining prodigy he had once been. (On one occasion, meeting Charlie Chaplin at an evening party, the two of them did a comic dance together.) But he led the most regular – the most monotonous it might almost be said – of lives. From ten until midday he painted; then until lunch – which he took alone – he walked. After a rest he painted for a further hour. For the rest of the day he needed amusements, though even in

[1] To whom these pages were addressed is not known to me. They were written in a 1927 diary and the first part is dated 20 November 1929. The pages immediately preceding have been torn out. The diary was found in his studio after his death.

the evenings he preferred a regular routine. On Thursdays and Saturdays he entertained his friends and on Fridays he visited his family. 'His conversation,' a friend told me, 'was trivial, founded upon oddments he had read in "The Daily Mail".' To an old familiar over long periods he had almost nothing to say, but 'one person to tea and his depression lifted and he was soon up to all his social tricks'. The flatness of his life was occasionally broken by an interlude of macabre drama. There was a girl, for instance, who paid him a visit which he described to a friend in a letter dated 3 September 1935: this girl 'who has a passion for me', it runs, 'turned up when I was alone in the house and proved to be quite mad. . . . I lost my nerve and began to beat and kick her, but she kept returning through some window. *Just* like some nightmare . . .'

In June 1939 he was more than usually depressed by Hitler's vilification of Jews and the failure of his exhibition at the Lefevre Gallery the previous month. One night he swallowed a hundred aspirins and turned on the gas, but he had left the window open. On the night of the 22nd he did not forget and the next morning he was found dead. He was buried in Willesden Jewish Cemetery. Because he was Unorthodox, he lay in an unmarked grave, but some prophetic words from a letter written to him by his friend D. H. Lawrence will serve as a sort of epitaph for the talent that for a while shone with so brilliant a light: 'Only take care, or you will burn your flame so fast, it will suddenly go out. It is all spending and no getting of strength.'

GILBERT SPENCER
b. 1892

THE most influential element in the formation of Gilbert Spencer as an artist has been his relationship with his brother Stanley. It was Stanley who first encouraged him to be a painter; it was the heat of Stanley's creative fervour that supplied the motive power to his beginnings; yet it was Stanley who involved him in a predicament that remained unresolved over many years of his life as an artist. Stanley has something of the character of a force of nature. If every night the fairies were to weave a large area of canvas and add it to the picture upon which he were at work, he would cover it with scarcely more awareness of the addition than a feeling of gratitude. Paintings by him do not end, they are brought to an end by some material circumstance. The artist's imagination and his powers of eye and hand do not flag. Likewise his conversation: morning comes or there is a train to be caught, but–except for a brief rest after lunch–neither the originality of his ideas nor the sweep or pungency of their expression is affected by the passage of the hours. Supposing you happen to be the younger brother to such a force, and you follow the same calling, you may be driven to become either a disciple or an eccentric or you may be driven to abandon your calling altogether, but it will be difficult for you to seek, diligently and with an unruffled mind, the corner of the field you are best equipped to cultivate. That without ever losing his reverence for his brother Gilbert Spencer has found his way to such a corner, and that he cultivates it with sobriety and blitheness of spirit, is a measure of his quality as a man, a quality that in happy moments is manifest in his art.

◦   ◦   ◦

Gilbert Spencer was the ninth and youngest of the Spencer children and he was born on 4 August 1892 at Fernlea, Cookham-on-Thames, the house in which all his brothers and sisters were born. The creative urge, so common in his family, with Gilbert first took the form of toy-making. Carts were his favourite models, and he used to go out into the village to study the construction and the colours of all the carts he could find, carts belonging to his family and neighbours or strange carts of passage. Of these toys one example at least, a yellow cart, has been preserved, and it is fine in workmanship and feeling. It is characteristic of the continuity of his interests that similar carts are the central feature of his most ambitious single composition.

While Gilbert briskly hammered and planed, Stanley would bring branches and twigs into the house, tie the branches on to bedheads, plant avenues of twigs along the floorboards, and then, imagining that he had made a forest, would creep and peer among them. Stanley was not content that Gilbert, making toys, should forego the deeper, more various satisfactions that painting affords, and he persuaded him to share his vocation. 'Stanley had become a real painter before I began: he showed me painting, held it up for me to see, then he handed it to me on a plate,' Gilbert told me. 'I was attracted by it, but if it hadn't been for him, I might have gone on simply wondering about it.' The moment of revelation came when Stanley brought back from the Slade a book on Masaccio, in a popular series on the old masters, and showed him *The Tribute Money*. Another moment of revelation followed when he heard Bach's 'St. Mathew Passion' in St. George's Chapel, Windsor Castle. These moments showed him that he could not be content with making toys.

Gilbert Spencer received his general education at the Ruskin School at Maidenhead which he attended from 1909 until 1911. The following year he spent at the art school at Camberwell, and the year after that learning wood-carving at the South Kensington Schools. When it was decided that he should become a painter he went to the Slade, remaining there from the autumn of 1913 until the Spring of 1915. Being able to afford only three days a week at the school, he spent the other four painting on his own at Cookham.

At the Slade he made quick progress. He won a first prize for figure drawing, Professor Brown's prize for the drawing of the head, and he shared the Summer Composition prize in 1914 with T. T. Baxter, a fellow student. The subject, *Summer*,[1] painted at Cookham,

[1] The Slade School, University College, London.

has a clumsy, archaic look, from which something lyrical shines out incongruously. His narrow missing of the Summer Composition prize the previous year led to his first becoming known outside the Slade. The painting submitted, *The Seven Ages of Man*,[1] was a large work also painted at Cookham, which, in spite of the rawness of the handling and the awkwardness of many passages, has intimations of something noble and impressive. The picture was seen and admired by a new friend, Henry Lamb, who, with another painter Darsie Japp, had visited him in Cookham not long before. Lamb asked whether Gilbert Spencer was willing to sell it: the painter was willing and the price asked £20. 'Do you object,' Lamb asked him shortly afterwards, 'to having £100?' The buyer was Lady Ottoline Morrell, a friend and patron of Lamb's, as of the most gifted of a generation of painters and writers. She bought it for the Contemporary Art Society. This triumph was naturally the talk of the Slade. When Tonks next went round the studios, Gilbert Spencer awaited his approach with modest complacency, which, however, the demeanour of his master soon dispelled. Stopping abruptly at a distance, he said, 'So you've sold your picture, have you? Early success invariably leads to ruin,' and turned his back. The incident did not alter Tonks's encouraging disposition towards his successful student. This picture, remarkable to my thinking in spite of its manifold faults and crudities, is still, after more than forty years, without a permanent home. In 1933, when I was its Director, I secured its acceptance by the City Art Gallery at Leeds, but I left soon afterwards, when it was exchanged for *Shepherds Amazed*, of 1920, a maturer work by the same artist, but one which was painted somewhat under the spell of his brother's Biblical pictures.

The Seven Ages of Man, although the most ambitious of the pictures he painted before the First World War, does not stand alone in announcing a new painter of unusual talent. An unfinished *Self Portrait*[2] painted in Cookham in 1914, a bold and assured study, owing little to the work of any other painter, is strongly marked by the quality of genuineness–the word is a vague one but I will try to justify its use in this context presently–that distinguishes the best works of Gilbert Spencer.

[1] The Contemporary Art Society, London.
[2] The City Art Gallery, Stoke-on-Trent.

In May 1915 the artist enlisted in the Royal Army Medical Corps and later transferred to the 2/22 London Regiment, with which he served in the Middle East. On active service he made a number of studies—one of which, representing a ward in the stationary hospital at Mahemdia, Sinai, formed the basis of his large painting, *New Arrivals*,[1] of 1919—but his war experience made no significant addition to his experience as an artist. His mind was fixed upon the country round his home. There exists a Cookham landscape *Sashes Meadow*,[2] which spans the war, for it was begun and largely completed in August 1914, but the large tree on the right was not put in until just after his demobilization in 1919. The contrast that this picture offers between the sombreness of wood and field and the silvery luminosity of rippling water puts one in mind of contrasts of the same kind in the work of Constable. This small picture is a work of dignity and authority and one of the finest of the painter's early landscapes.

The consequence of renewed association with his brother Stanley was that he painted several Biblical subjects, of which the most impressive is *The Sermon on the Mount*,[3] of 1921–2, a large picture showing an assembly of bearded, white-robed figures (the one seated in the right foreground appears to represent Augustus John) of a massive amplitude. It has dignity and purity of feeling and must count among the serious religious paintings made in England between the wars. But religious painting, with the exception of Stanley Spencer's wall-paintings at Burghclere and a very few other works, was not upon a high level. *The Sermon on the Mount* falls short not on account of its archaism (the rocks, for instance, are the rocks of Italian painting), but because the painter is without deep religious insight. The scene conveys no hint of the giving of a momentous message; it represents nothing but an assembly of prophetic-looking elderly men, almost identically wigged and bearded, in vaguely monastic garments. Nothing in the design leads the eye towards the Saviour. As an exercise in religious painting it is worthy of praise, but it is not religious painting; and in any case the painter, never so religious as Stanley, was losing his faith at the time he was engaged upon this picture. Fearful of a cynical conformity, a man as honest

[1] The Imperial War Museum, London.
[2] The Tate Gallery, London.   [3] Coll. the artist.

and as positive as Gilbert Spencer recognizes his loss, when he feels his faith ebbing away, and after about 1923 he confessed himself an agnostic.

> I'm a horizontalist, [he once said to me, discussing this topic] and Stanley's a verticalist. I don't believe I was ever truly religious, but for a time Stanley was able to impart his religious sense to me, partly by his words, partly by paintings like *The Visitation* and *Zacharias and Elizabeth*. But I rarely had much to do with the deeper levels–religion and philosophy–I just loved painting and he was the painter I admired most; so painting was the real link between us.
>
> The Spencers, you know, contrary to what many people think, were *not* a religious family. We went to Chapel–until the old chapel was replaced by a new one, which made bad blood with our family–and then to church. No blasphemy was allowed, but my father used often to say 'Christ was a *man*, like anybody else'. But it was the preachers in the Chapel who inspired so many of Stanley's figures, which are all portraits of a kind, you know. I can recognize their likenesses.

Landscape, not figure painting, has been the principal business of Gilbert Spencer's life, although he has painted a few fine portraits and made a long series of portrait drawings of remarkable beauty. His first one-man exhibition in January 1923 at the Goupil Gallery was received with mild interest by the critics but little more. 'Both (Spencer) brothers,' wrote Frank Rutter, usually responsive to serious new talent, 'in my opinion have done some very good work, and have also painted some foolish, affected pictures; therefore, I have been inclined to sit on the fence.'[1] He slipped off it so cautiously that it is a little difficult to see at this distance upon which side he came down. The landscapes were praised, as also some of the drawings; the figure compositions, more especially *The Seven Ages of Man*, were ridiculed. 'The Times' was amiable but uncommitted; the warmest praise came from 'The Daily Mail'. By painters and collectors, however, the exhibition was warmly welcomed. My father had bought a landscape from the Grosvenor Gallery the year before, and presently Gilbert Spencer himself appeared at our house, an irrepressibly gay and breezy presence: sartorially, compared with his brother Stanley, a dandy; compared with anyone else, a tramp.

Gilbert Spencer's landscapes have been made mostly in the

[1] 'The Sunday Times', 7 January 1923.

Thames valley, in his native Berkshire; in and around the Oxford-shire villages of Garsington and Little Milton where he spent the years 1925 until 1928; but also in Dorset and, during the Second World War, in the Lake District. In 1931 he bought Tree Cottage, at Upper Basildon, Berkshire, to which, in spite of enforced wander-ings, he has constantly returned. These landscapes are of two kinds: pictures of particular places, which are begun and completed in front of the subject, and compositions which are not pure inventions but assemblies of features brought together from particular neighbour-hoods. The first are by far the more numerous. 'Stanley's painting could be judged from a small group of masterpieces,' the artist observed, 'mine is like a chain with a lot of small links.' There is much truth in this modest comparison, especially in so far as it refers to the realistic landscapes. The series is long, the standard high, but while it includes many pictures of great beauty it includes none, I think, which by itself shows the full stature of the artist. Besides *Sashes Meadow, Emmer Green*,[1] and *Garsington Village*,[2] both of 1924, *Home Close, Garsington*,[3] of 1924, *Stour Valley*,[4] of 1927, *Little Milton*,[5] *Burdens*,[6] both of 1933, *From my studio*,[7] of about 1949, all afford intimations of that genuineness referred to a few lines above. By genuineness I mean that nothing, no line, no brushstroke, is set down except as the immediate response to perception or to feeling. This quality is rarer than may be supposed. Some painters, when per-ception or feeling fails them, carry on as though nothing is amiss, and thereby practise a deception; others, impelled by a sense of duty, paint stubbornly on when they neither perceive nor feel, in the hope that the act of painting will restore them. Others again rely on a style that has won approval to disguise their want of anything to com-municate. Gilbert Spencer sets down nothing not fully experienced, so that his series of landscapes is a precious record of the response to landscape of a warm and constant love of the English country. Since he first began to paint, the artist's view of things has undergone few changes and only one that need be mentioned in so brief a study. When he began, his brother, Masaccio and other early Florentines were his masters: his style was linear; his colour, radiant but

---

[1] Coll. Sir Gerald Kelly.   [2] The Contemporary Art Society, London.
[3] Whereabouts unknown.   [4] The Fine Art Society, London.
[5] The City Art Gallery, Belfast.   [6] Whereabouts unknown.   [7] Coll. the Artist.

subdued, ministered to his drawn shapes with dignified subservience. Very slowly, at times scarcely perceptibly, a transforming idea asserted itself: the idea of colour's existing not as subservient to form but as a part of it. The idea came to him from the most obvious source. 'I always loved the French Impressionists,' he said, speaking to me of his debt to them, 'they were a *lovely* crowd, particularly Pissarro, and Cézanne as well. I look at a Michelangelo and I marvel; I look at a Pissarro and I somehow share it. I owe it to them that my aims, as I've gone along, have emerged, more and more definitely, as light and tone and atmosphere.'

Different aims called for different methods. The early landscapes were painted over meticulous drawings, made direct upon the canvas. Summary indications as to form and colour, notes, have gradually taken the place of meticulous drawings, and have enabled him to attain to a greater freedom of handling. All these processes have invariably been carried out in front of the subject. When I questioned him upon this matter, he said, 'I have occasionally put in a bit of extra grass. But I haven't really got any method,' he added. 'I start everything I do from scratch, and I never believe I can do anything until I've done it.' In these landscapes done from nature he never deliberately alters any feature of the scene before him. 'You see *me* moving around, in search of the best viewpoint, but you don't see me moving *trees* around,' he said. 'My imaginary things are entirely imaginary. I couldn't *imagine* something in a real place.'

The landscape compositions, of which a good example is *A Memory of Whithall, Gloucestershire*,[1] of 1948, are less successful than those made directly from nature. The absence of nature tends to weaken his conviction, or rather the partial absence of nature. In the landscape composition he uses drawings made from nature; his imagination shows itself stronger when it has no prop. Of greater merit than his landscape compositions are his figure compositions. Of these, with *The Sermon on the Mount,* far the finest is *A Cotswold Farm*[2] (Plate 53), painted during 1930 and 1931 from studies made in the Cotswolds. It represents no particular place, but many of the studies were made at Andoversford, at a farm belonging to Dr. Austin Lane Poole, President of St. John's College, Oxford. The landscape in works of this kind differs radically from that in the

[1] Coll. the Artist.   [2] The Tate Gallery, London.

landscape compositions, for it is designed, the artist told me 'not so much as an end in itself, as to fit the people'.

Neither his temperament–an essentially *plein aireist* temperament, happiest in the presence of nature–nor his brief professional training equips him for composition on a large scale; in any case it is a rare faculty in these times when there is little demand for monumental public painting. The immense pains he gave himself in working out, in a long series of studies, the composition of *A Cotswold Farm* enabled him to overcome his handicap to a considerable extent, and although at points it falls short of academic perfection it is an impressive picture and one which it is not easy to forget. Although its themes are taken from the Cotswolds rather than the Thames valley, it constitutes almost a repertory of the themes of Gilbert Spencer's art: the farm buildings, the ploughed fields, the labourers, above all the carts, are all there–and even the grove-crowned hill is reminiscent of Berkshire rather than of the Cotswolds. If the composition has had to be struggled for, the innumerable details have been put in with familiar ease: the whole crowded, indeed over-crowded, assembly of facts is knit together not mainly by the composition but by a warm consistency of feeling into a coherent whole in which interest is combined with dignity and transparent candour. The picture enhanced his professional reputation and won a wide popularity as soon as it was shown in February 1932 at an exhibition of his paintings and drawings at the Goupil Gallery. 'The Times' described it as 'a sort of rustic equivalent of Madox Brown's *Work*';[1] Frank Rutter as 'a great painting';[2] 'The Morning Post', whose critic was in general reluctant to see merit in the less conventional artists, as 'a magnificent achievement';[3] while to 'The Scotsman' it was 'one of the liveliest compositions of recent years, and should find a place in the Tate Gallery'[4]–in which it indeed found a place before February was out. *A Cotswold Farm* lives with a greater fullness than *Hebridean Memory*,[5] of 1948–54, an equally ambitious composition based upon studies made on the Island of Canna, which he visited during his residence in Glasgow from 1948 until 1950 as head of the Department of Painting and Drawing at the College of Art.

[1] 6 February.   [2] 'The Sunday Times', 14 February.
[3] 9 February.   [4] 6 February.   [5] Coll. the Artist.

Allied to these two large compositions are the wall-paintings in Holywell Manor, Oxford, an annexe to Balliol, which the painter began in 1934 and completed two years later. These paintings extend in a continuous band of about seven feet in height round the upper part of the four walls of the ante-room to the Junior Common Room, a room about fifteen feet square. They are in oil upon a prepared plaster surface. The foundation of Balliol College is the legend which the paintings illustrate–briefly, that John Balliol, intent upon seizing lands belonging to the Bishop of Durham, ambushed him when he was crossing a ford. For this offence he was arrested, tied to a tree and thrashed. Dervorguilla his wife, considering that he had got off too lightly, gave money to enable sixteen poor students to study at Oxford. A wit said at the time that the painter's treatment of it was Chaucerian rather than Spenserian. There is some truth in this observation, for the drama is played out in a spirit of gentle rustic humour. At first glance the painter's interpretation seems rather too rustic, the actors to have too uniformly the character and the tempo of agricultural labourers, but closer scrutiny discovers subtleties not at once apparent. Of these the most moving is the way in which the scholars' dedication to learning is expressed in their manifest joy in their first distant sight of Oxford, and in the intentness with which, having reached it, they peruse the books in the chained library, and the eagerness with which their upraised hands flutter along the shelves. The landscape background is continuous, the earlier panels showing the craggy character of the Border country–where the painter has had recourse to the Italian primitives–the later the undulating character of Oxfordshire where he has no need to look beyond his own memories. The painter has responded finely to Balliol's imaginative commission.

One further field of his activity remains to be mentioned, namely portraiture, which he has pursued intermittently from his student days down to the present. The best of the portraits in oils known to me are *Portrait of a Man*,[1] *Reading Boy*,[2] both of 1922, *Professor Oliver de Selincourt*,[3] of 1953, *The Artist's Wife*,[4] of 1954. The first is a powerful, archaic-looking full length, in which the painter's delight in homely objects is almost as manifest in his treatment of the black

---

[1] The Southampton Art Gallery. [2] Coll. the Artist.
[3] Coll. Professor Oliver de Selincourt. [4] Coll. the Artist.

iron cottage stove before which his subject is seated as in the cloth-capped, heavily moustached figure itself. The other three are notable for the quality of the insight into character that they show—an insight in which remorseless candour is tempered by the warmest affection—and for the fineness of the heads' construction. But nothing that the artist has done is finer, to my thinking, than the best of his portrait drawings, and these best are numerous. In them line defines form in its plenitude, form perfectly expressive of the character of the subject. To name but a few, almost at random: *French Girl*,[1] of 1920, *Dorset Girl*,[2] of 1921, *Little Girl in Spectacles*,[3] of 1922, and *Mabel Nash*,[4] of 1923, *Mrs. Keep*,[5] of 1930, and *Hebridean*,[6] of 1947. These are drawings that could hang in any company.

When Gilbert Spencer was a young painter the novelty of his work, with its engaging blend of simplicity and skill, won him a place among the leaders of his generation. For some years, without loss of respect, his work has been first taken for granted, and then overlooked. I think that the sober genuineness of which I have written, and the charm which springs from the irrepressible gaiety of the painter, will enable the best of it to survive the coming holocaust of reputations.

[1] Coll. Mr. J. L. Behrend.   [2] Coll. Mr. Henry Lamb.
[3] Coll. Mr. Cyril Mahoney.
[4] The City Art Gallery, Manchester (Rutherston Coll.).
[5] Coll. Sir Geoffrey Hutchinson.   [6] Coll. the Artist.

JOHN NASH

b. 1893

BIOGRAPHIES of landscape painters often convey the impression that nature was their subject's inspiration and that their art was founded upon the study of landscape itself. The art of most landscape painters, like that of most painters in fact, derives principally from the example of other painters.

Landscape, especially landscape undisciplined by man, opposes particular difficulties to painting. Confronted by nature, as it stretches away to the horizon in every direction in infinite complexity, the untaught eye is baffled. Whether it contemplates the scale of nature as it stretches away to the infinitely vast in the one direction or the infinitely minute in the other, it faces the baffling problem of giving order and a finite form to a phenomenon which in its infinite complexity has neither—neither, at all events, discernible to the untaught eye. Most artists, before they can look profitably at landscape, must first learn what to look for by reference, conscious or not, to the work of other artists. Their human experience may offer them some guidance where a human face or body is in question, but guidance of a more specialized kind is necessary if they are not to be altogether lost in the contemplation of the intricate disorder and the immensity of nature. Reason alone would suggest that this could hardly be otherwise; the landscape paintings of the period with which these pages are concerned tend to confirm it. These seem to me to reveal, to a greater degree than portraits or still-lifes, say, reliance upon art rather than nature. All painters, whatever their pretensions to innovation, draw largely upon the experience of their predecessors, but a glance at an assemblage of modern landscape paintings is a particularly forcible reminder of how frankly their makers have taken either Constable, or Turner, or the Barbizon School, or the Impressionists, or Cézanne or his followers, if not invariably as models, then almost invariably as a point of departure. The very intractability of landscape as a subject would seem to demand a rather closer-knit tradition than subjects smaller and less various.

Of the subjects of these essays who have directed their chief efforts towards landscape all have looked harder in the earlier part of their lives as painters at art than they have at nature – with the exception of John Nash, the present subject.

There is nothing spectacular, nothing even strikingly personal, about his landscape because the personality of the painter is quiet, reticent and serene; but it owes little to the example of others, for John Nash seldom looks at a painting and pays no attention to theories: he reads little about painting, and as a subject for reflexion takes no interest in it at all. The example of his friends is certainly discernible in his beginnings; so inevitably is something of the climate of the time in which he grew up, but the real source of his landscape painting, to a degree for which I can think of no parallel among his contemporaries, is landscape itself. John Nash lives in the country; he is an impassioned gardener and botanist and a life-long and single-minded lover of landscape.

⌀   ⌀   ⌀

The principal facts of his uneventful life are soon told. John Northcote Nash was born at Ghuznee Lodge, Earl's Court, on 11 April 1893, the younger of the two sons (Paul being the elder) of William Harry Nash, and educated at Langley Place, Slough, and at Wellington College. He left school without definite ideas about how to spend his life, but was willing to try any kind of work. The possibility of his entering a solicitor's office was considered, but his father found it difficult to provide the necessary premium. Eventually he joined, as an apprentice, the staff of 'The Middlesex & Bucks Advertiser'. Finding that his activities as a reporter were circumscribed by lack of transport, he asked for sufficient money to buy a bicycle. For this importunity he was reprimanded and given notice; his career in journalism was at an end, and he was without occupation or prospects.

Casting about what his brother had best do, Paul urged him to try his hand at painting.

I must have been a very malleable character [John Nash once said to me] for I'd never thought of being a painter, but I at once agreed, and set about making landscapes in water-colour and comic drawings. Paul was not happy at the Slade and he opposed my going there or to any school of art, and he used to tell me how lucky I was to begin free from the disadvantages of conventional training. All the same, [he added] I wish I'd had the advantage of training of some kind.

Paul had sent a packet of John's drawings to his friend Gordon Bottomley, who wrote, on 7 July 1912, that:

he has not only a good sense of decorative disposition of his masses, but his blacks have a beautiful quality, and his pen-touch is crisp and clear and delicate and exquisitely balanced. . . . In facility and lucidity and directness of expression, and in his faculty of keeping his material untroubled, he has advantages over you; but of course it remains to be seen if he can preserve these qualities when he has as much to say as you have.[1]

Paul's informative reply, written about 13 July, shows John as a very tentative beginner both as a draughtsman (the spirited comic drawings with which he had illustrated his letters from Wellington had delighted his family) and as a writer.

Jack is very 'set up for the rest of 'is natural' as the vulgar have it, [runs the letter] upon your high praise–I don't mean he has swollen his head-piece for he ever expresses a mild surprise at any appreciation upon his drawings, which he does at odd times on odd bits of paper when he has nothing else to do. I, from time to time, raid his desk or the waste-paper basket or the corners of the room & collect the odd bits of paper rather like a park-keeper in Kensington Gardens, and after a sorting of chaff from grain tho' to be sure it's all 'chaff' I select the best & cut them into a decent shape & mount them. At first Jack used to be so delighted at the good appearance of his drawings when mounted that he fully believed it was entirely owing to the way I set them up & drew lines round them; gradually it has dawned on him tho' that it must be he has done a good drawing–this is a pity because he now becomes a little too conscious & careful, with the result his designs are not so naive & simple. At present he is working on the staff of a country paper & gaining experience for a journalistic career. All his abilities lie in that direction and he will tell you his ambition is to be 'a man of letters'. These drawings are as yet his only expression of him-self. He is very observant and writes excellent descriptions of things that strike him, always with the same quaint touch you see in these designs. He has so far done very little actual writing save a few articles in the paper & some essays when he was at Wellington. The work for the paper takes all his time & he is riding about & reporting all

[1] 'Poet and Painter, being the correspondence between Gordon Bottomley and Paul Nash, 1910–1946', p. 38.

over the county & at all times of day & night. Unfortunately his time is up in August for this has been experience & work quite unpaid as regards salary, and then I really don't know what happens–a London paper I suppose is the next thing–he likes regular work & routine, unlike me, & works well; at the same time he is not constitutionally robust & v. hard work in London would not be good for him I fear. I myself have no doubt he has a most interesting self to develop, & work to produce, but how & in what direction I really am not certain.[1]

A curious encounter I had, years later, with Paul leads me to think that the doubts he voiced to Bottomley about 'how and in what direction' his brother should express himself still persisted, in spite of the blossoming of John's powers.

Just before the Second World War I was commissioned to write an introductory essay on John Nash for a portfolio of reproductions (which was not published) similar to one that had recently appeared on Paul.[2] When I had completed the essay I told Paul that I would value highly any comments he might care to make on it, and he accordingly invited my wife and myself to lunch. After I had read the essay aloud to him, he said, with deliberation, 'It was I who encouraged Jack to be a painter; and I'm still not sure that I did rightly: I don't know whether he has a painter's imagination.' These words astonished me, and I might have doubted having heard them, although they were several times repeated in slightly differing form, had my wife not heard them also.

Not much more than a year after John Nash began his series of landscapes the brothers held a joint exhibition at the small and long defunct Dorien Leigh Galleries in Pelham Street, South Kensington, and its success confirmed him in his choice of a vocation. The exhibition was a success, not only on account of the number of works sold, but of the favourable impression it made among painters. Among the painters who went to see it were Gilman, Bevan, Sickert, as well as my father, who had known Paul–as a Slade student Paul used occasionally to show him John's satirical drawings of suburban life–since 1910. As a consequence of the success of the exhibition, and of the acceptance, also in 1913, of a water-colour by

[1] Ibid., p. 39.
[2] 'Paul Nash', a portfolio of colour plates, with an introduction by Herbert Read, 1937.

the New English Art Club–a success which resounded far more influentially than it would to-day–John Nash was drawn for a brief period into one of the vortices of London's art world. He accepted in 1914 an invitation to become a member of the newly founded London Group, and the following year, on Gilman's invitation, he joined the Cumberland Market Group, and he became associated with the young painters who used to foregather at 19 Fitzroy Street. It is significant, however, of his essential detachment from the curious, turbulent little world which revolved about these groups that he did not dream, as he told me, 'of visiting the Second Post-Impressionist Exhibition, which was held while I was constantly in London'.

The first visit he paid to 19 Fitzroy Street he recalls with a particular vividness. The spectacle of such an assemblage–seen on arrival through the studio door–Pissarro, Gilman and Gore were present–so overawed him that he had turned to descend the stairs when Gore, watchful and genial, hailed him and drew him inside. This occasion, he thinks, was when he first met Gilman, who began on the spot to impart to him his theories about painting. It was then that Gilman uttered a warning, often repeated, against the mixing of paint with oil: 'There's enough oil in the paint anyhow, without adding more of the treacherous stuff.' John Nash heeded the warning, and like Gilman and his friends Ginner and Bevan he never diluted his paint with oil. There was a further and more important respect in which the teaching of Gilman affected the methods of John Nash; he urged him not to make his paintings from nature but from drawings. This injunction he has mostly followed partly owing to the force of Gilman's argument, but partly because he finds it difficult to carry his landscapes in oils to completion directly from nature. These, with few exceptions, are therefore painted in the studio from drawings made on the spot; his water-colours are carried far towards completion in front of the subject, but worked on afterwards indoors. Gilman's advice carried particular weight with John Nash, as he had been painting in oils for only about a year before his first meeting with him early in 1915. The two previous years he had spent in making landscapes in water-colour round his home in Buckinghamshire and in Berkshire, Norfolk and Dorset. In May 1915 he joined with Gilman and two other members of the Cumberland Market

53. GILBERT
SPENCER.
Cotswold Farm
(1930–1).
Oil, 55 × 72¼ in.
The Tate Gallery,
London.

54. JOHN NASH. *The Moat, Grange Farm, Kimble* (1922).
Oil, 30 × 20 in. The Tate Gallery, London.

Group-Ginner and Bevan-in an exhibition at the Goupil Gallery. A water-colour, *Trees in a Flood*, was presented that same year to the City Art Gallery, Leeds, by Sir Michael Sadler, one of his earliest admirers. It was the first of his works to enter a public collection.

In spite of his fruitful and pleasurable London associations-he enjoyed in particular the weekly meetings 'for tea and picture showing' held by the Cumberland Market Group in Bevan's house overlooking the market-the true centre of his life, then and at all times, was the country. In view of the intimate association between his painting and the places he has lived in, it seems to me that there is little in an account of his life more relevant than the record of these places. From 1901, when his family moved from Kensington into Buckinghamshire, until the First World War, he lived at home at Iver Heath. After serving in the Ministry of Munitions, in the 28th London Regiment, Artists' Rifles, with whom he was on active service in France from November 1916 until January 1918, and in the spring of that year, as an Official War Artist, he lived at Chalfont Common, Buckinghamshire. In the autumn of the following year he settled in Gerrards Cross, but spending that summer at not far distant Whiteleaf, Princes Risborough, and the following at Sapperton, Gloucestershire. In 1921, while looking for a house to buy, he went to Monks Risborough, establishing himself at Meadle, near Princes Risborough, where except for summer painting excursions he remained until the second year of the Second World War. All these places except Sapperton were in Buckinghamshire. In the autumn of 1944 he took Bottengoms Farm, at Wormingford in Essex, where he now lives.

Considering that he was without formal training of any kind and that the First World War disrupted his life and work before he was able to establish himself, John Nash's growth to maturity was extremely rapid. His water-colours were marked by an assurance and a sense of style almost from the start: *Landscape near Sheringham*,[1] for instance, was probably made on a visit to Norfolk in 1912 with an artist friend, when he decided to devote himself to painting. With his oils it was otherwise. For two or three years his understanding of method was so elementary that at first glance his earliest paintings have a look of conscious archaism, an uncandid simplicity;

[1] Private Coll.

only upon close examination is it apparent that they are expressions of a mind with a personal sensibility and inventiveness struggling for clarity and fullness of statement. I have in mind such paintings as *Threshing*,[1] of 1914, in which the painter has been vividly aware of the relations between the ascending member of the machine, the twisting column of smoke, the woods behind and the cloudy sky above, yet been painfully unable to give these relations a logical and fully expressive coherence. Yet these and other paintings of the same unsophisticated character found a warm response among several lovers of painting. 'His railway viaduct[2] also and the wood of slim trees[3] are most beautiful,' wrote Gordon Bottomley to Paul Nash[4] (11 June 1919); the first of these pictures promptly found a place in the collection of Sir Osbert Sitwell, and I recall my father's constant praise of the works of both brothers.

The struggles with his medium of this untaught, untravelled painter were rewarded with a success which came quickly. In 1918 he painted *The Cornfield*, a picture in which strength of construction is united with an exhilarating rhythmic harmony. A Buckinghamshire field and its bounding woods are here realized simply and grandly, all detail merged in a large glowing unity–a vision so direct and solid and so burning that, sharing it in the presence of this picture, it affects one as the work of some humble primitive master. This remarkable painting was bought by Sir Edward Marsh, who early befriended the two brothers, and I remember with what dignity it held its place, year by year, on the walls, ever more densely crowded with the works of young contemporaries, of 5 Raymond Buildings, his chambers in Gray's Inn, and how much it continued to delight him. He made a gift of it to Ivor Novello, his most intimate friend, on condition that he bequeathed it, through the Contemporary Art Society, to the Tate Gallery. It entered the collection in this way after his death in 1952.

Early in 1918 John Nash was commissioned as an Official War Artist to make paintings and drawings of war subjects for the Ministry of Information, with which he was occupied for the larger part of that year and the next. During this time he shared a shed which served as a studio with his brother at Chalfont Common.

---

[1] Coll. Mr. de G. Sieveking.   [2] Whereabouts unknown.
[3] Whereabouts unknown.   [4] Op. cit., p. 108.

Paul wrote a spirited description to Gordon Bottomley of the life which the brothers led there:

> We have taken a large shed, formerly used for drying herbs. It is a roomy place with large windows down both sides, an ample studio–here we work. Jack is lately married–a charming girl whom we all adore. . . . They live in rooms in a little house next the shed & Bunty and I have a room in the old farm–a charming place with a wonderful cherry orchard & fine old barns & sheep and rabbits & all that sort of thing. We all lunch together in the studio where there is a piano so our wives enchant us with music at times thro' the day. A phantastic existence as all lives seem these days but good while it lasts & should produce something worth while I suppose. France and the trenches would be a mere dream if our minds were not perpetually bent upon those scenes.[1]

While he was on active service in France John Nash had made numerous sketches, from which he was able to execute his various commissions. Of these the most ambitious was a large, six feet by seven, painting, *Oppy Wood, Evening, 1917*,[2] completed in 1919. Neither for dramatic intensity nor for insight into the war does this picture compare with the best of the war pictures of Paul Nash. In *Oppy Wood, Evening*, the quiet, modest, peaceful man, the gardener, the botanist, has taken as his theme a moment when war has receded. The earth in front of the trench is shell pitted, the blasted trees have no branches, yet a great quiet has taken possession of the scene, a quiet so potent as to still even the sound of the two shells exploding away on the left, a quiet that is the harbinger of a larger quiet that will eventually still the voices of the guns and in which nations will be reconciled, and sanity come again, and gardening and botany resume their proper places among the pursuits of men. Such, more or less, are the sentiments which have gone to the formation of *Oppy Wood, Evening*. Like many of the best works of the Official War Artists (as of the best artists who have represented war) this is not a war but a peace picture. John Nash also painted some war pictures in the most positive sense. One of the best of these, *Over the Top: The 1st Artists' Rifles at Marcoing*,[3] also painted during 1918–19, shows men of the regiment in which he served climbing out of their

[1] Op. cit., p. 99.   [2] The Imperial War Museum, London.
[3] The Imperial War Museum, London; there is a replica in the Headquarters of the Artists' Rifles.

trench and walking, heads down, into the smoke of the barrage. The slow upward and forward movement is powerfully conveyed; so too the tension between fear and determination in the advancing men. The dramatic moment, and death itself, though represented with a fitting sombreness, are represented without even a hint of melodrama, but in due proportion to the drama as a whole. While he was engaged upon these two important pictures, the War Office having neglected to inform his regiment of his appointment as an Official War Artist, he was posted as a deserter, and an escort sent to apprehend him.

With *The Cornfield* and the war pictures his apprenticeship was ended: the primitive look disappeared from his art and he painted with a modest consciousness of command. I have the impression—which in the absence of a fully representative retrospective exhibition I have not been able to confirm—that in spite of these auspicious beginnings as a mature painter in oils John Nash has succeeded more often in conveying in water-colour his special insights into nature. This may be due to the circumstance that his art is primarily an art of observation and selection, the child of a creative impulse roused to its highest pitch by the presence, rather than by the subsequent contemplation, of the subject. The relative laboriousness of painting in oils, the degree of organization which it demands, offers a hard choice to those who employ it in the representation of landscape. They may complete their pictures in front of the subject and run the risk of being 'put out by nature', of being distracted by the subject from the work of art, of being prevented by changing light, by wind and other difficulties attendant on working outdoors, from giving to the work itself the intense concentration which for most painters is possible only in the studio. Or they may take them away from the subject to complete indoors, and thereby run the risk attendant upon being cut off from the source of their inspiration. As related earlier, John Nash occasionally begins his oils in front of the subject, carries them as far as he can, and takes them indoors for completion, but more usually he paints them entirely in the studio. To a man as immediately dependent as he is in his landscapes upon the heightened feelings he derives from the sight of field and wood, the smell of ploughed earth and corn under a hot sun, the deprivation of such impression accounts, it seems to me, for a listlessness, a fluffy indeterminacy sometimes noticeable in his landscapes in oils but in relatively few of those in water-colour. The lighter medium allows him to complete pictures in the full enjoyment of the impressions that furnish the motive power of his art, so that in his water-colours signs of waning interest, signs of attempts to rely instead upon sense of duty, are rarely to be seen.

But John Nash's occasional proneness to boredom in his oils should not cause us to forget that in every one of the places where he has lived he has interpreted the landscape, and in every season of the year (although it is winter, I think, that most often calls forth his highest faculties), in oils as well as water-colour, with a combination of acute observation and poetic insight that is very rare. His pictures give pleasure not only to lovers of the fine arts, but to lovers of the country as well, especially to informed lovers, such as farmers, gardeners, botanists, and to other painters of landscape.

Once rid of the archaism of the untaught, his work has altered little, and his best works are to be found throughout all his active years. We find the same qualities, for instance, in *The Deserted Sheep Pen*,[1] of 1938, and *Farmyard in the Snow*,[2] of 1947, *Winter Afternoon*,[3] of 1945 (Plate 55), and *Snow at Wormingford*,[4] of 1946, and *Pond at Little Horkesley*[5] of 1953; and *The Moat, Grange Farm, Kimble*,[6] of about 1922 (Plate 54): we find, that is to say, firm, logical structure, deeply informed observation, modest, unaffected candour of statement and poetic insight. They are pictures that one cannot contemplate without a sense of enhanced life. If there has been a change I would say that the broad generalizations, the bold forthright structure of his earlier years, have been enriched by new subtleties of colour and design and a growing inclination towards a 'close-up' view of things. 'Half a haystack interests me now,' I recall his telling me in 1938, 'just as much as a wide stretch of country.' This heightened preoccupation with the intimate and the near–with the foregrounds of landscape–was an expression of his interest in horticulture. This interest was first stirred in 1922 by his possession, with his cottage at Princes Risborough, for the first time, of a garden; it was fostered by the friendship of gardeners, notably

[1] Whereabouts unknown.   [2] Coll. Mr. Simon Nowell-Smith.
[3] The City Art Gallery, Birmingham.   [4] Coll. Mrs. Janet Rath.
[5] Coll. Mrs. Mary Cohen.   [6] The Tate Gallery, London.

Clarence Elliott, and Jason Hill. (He has made a pictorial record of all the best plants he has grown.)

The landscapes of John Nash are uncommon in that they are the work of a countryman. His brother Paul also loved landscape, but he brought to his interpretations of it a town-sharpened and innately literary intelligence and town-forged weapons, but John is a countryman by lifelong residence and in all his interests. Where Paul would write a manifesto or form a group, John transplants some roses; where Paul would cherish the words of Sir Thomas Browne or Blake, John consults a seed catalogue.

If I have so far treated John Nash almost exclusively as a painter of landscape it is because it is upon what he has done in this branch of his art that his reputation will eventually rest, and it is my own conviction that as an interpreter of English landscape he will be accorded a high place among the painters of his time. It would be wrong, however, to suppose landscape to be his exclusive preoccupation, for he is a man whose creative energies have taken many forms, and although his pace of work is unhurried and he is as little responsive to the spur of ambition as any artist I know, he has a body of work to his credit as large as it is various.

For a brief period in 1921 he became 'The London Mercury's' first art critic. He has served from time to time and to good purpose as a teacher, first from 1922 until 1927 at the Ruskin School of Drawing at Oxford, of which his friend Sydney Carline was then Master, and in the Department of Design of the Royal College of Art from 1934 (when my father was Principal) until 1940, and again, at the invitation of the present Principal Mr. Robin Darwin, from 1945. Early in the Second World War he joined the Observer Corps and in 1940 was appointed an Official War Artist to the Admiralty. In November that year, preferring to serve his country more directly, he gave up painting and, being commissioned first as Captain and later as acting Major in the Royal Marines, he held responsible posts under the Commanders-in-Chief, Rosyth and Portsmouth. 'He didn't like being an official artist for the Admiralty—couldn't do anything he said and just went on nagging until he got back into active service. Was there ever such a chap?' wrote his brother to Bottomley.[1] It was not until the end of 1944, after being demobilized,

[1] Op. cit., p. 222.

that he resumed the practice of his art. This act of self-abnegation is characteristic of John Nash, and the measure of the distance between him and the artist for whom the welfare of his art is the sole criterion of conduct.

Apart from landscape painting the two principal activities of his life are drawing and engraving on wood. Drawing, practised since his school-days at Wellington, has been a constant preoccupation, and engraving on wood since before 1920. He has made illustrations for no fewer than twenty-six books, in line, coloured lithograph or wood engraving; the first to be published was 'Dressing Gowns and Glue' by L. de G. Sieveking, in 1919, and the latest 'Parnassian Molehill' by the Earl of Cranbook, in 1953. Until the middle 'twenties his drawings were mainly comic, but from that time onwards, in fact from 1924 when he began to engrave on wood his illustrations for 'Poisonous Plants', published three years later, plants became his chief preoccupation, and his illustrations to Jason Hill's 'The Curious Gardener' (1933), R. Gathorne-Hardy's 'Wild Flowers in Britain' (1938), 'English Garden Flowers' (1948), and White's 'The Natural History of Selborne' (1951) have become classics.

A classic could be written around this artist's life and works, so dedicated and so reticent, its pastoral setting so remote from the envy and competition of the market-place.

ROY DE MAISTRE

b. 1894

THE painting of Roy de Maistre has none of the characteristics which ensure popularity. It is without the dashing rhetoric of John's, the glowing sensuousness of Matthew Smith's, or the comprehensive humanity of Spencer's; it lacks the highly idiosyncratic style which makes it impossible to mistake a Lowry on sight. It is a reticent art, yet not even obviously reticent like Gwen John's. It is difficult to place in a category, which is perhaps one of the reasons why it has been little noticed by the critics. It is an art at first glance deceptively obvious. At first glance a painting by de Maistre might look like another essay in Analytic Cubism. Scrutiny reveals an art, however, not only reticent but extremely complex.

Nearly thirty years ago a thoughtful Australian friend of his described him as a painter as 'essentially . . . a realist'. 'I do not believe,' he added, 'that he is tormented by a desire to express his subconscious in paint . . . that would be opposed to a fundamental reticence in him.'[1] This friend was right to recognize the realist in him, and the reticence too, but the reference to the subconscious, if correct in fact, is, I believe, mistaken in intention. De Maistre is indeed unpreoccupied, so far as I am aware, with his subconscious, but he is so intensely preoccupied with the most delicate perceptions of his conscious self on the spiritual level as to qualify the applicability of the term realist. The content of his paintings is drawn from the depths of his inner experience–experience apprehended and transmuted by a strong and lucid intelligence. 'Why shouldn't intelligence,' asked his friend Burdett, aptly quoting from Maurois's 'Colonel Bramble', 'have an art of its own as sensibility has?'

The springs of Roy de Maistre's art are various and complex. It is an art, moreover, that bears no obvious relation to the artist. The few examples of it that I had earlier come upon appeared to be the products of a personality 'advanced' in opinion and aggressive to the point of harshness. When I visited his studio at 13 Eccleston Street,

[1] 'R. de Mestre', by Basil Burdett. 'Art in Australia', June 1925.

55. JOHN NASH.
Winter Afternoon
(1945).
Water-colour,
14⅞ × 21⅞ in.
The City Art Gallery,
Birmingham.

56. ROY DE MAISTRE. *Crucifixion* (1942–4)
Oil, 48 × 36 in. The City Art Gallery, Leicester.

Victoria, I was surprised to be greeted by a man of neat, somewhat Edwardian appearance and urbane manners; to notice, on the little table in his hall, a collapsible opera-hat reposing beside a Roman Missal. The long painting-room was full of objects miscellaneous yet carefully chosen: a sofa designed by his friend Francis Bacon, a French eighteenth-century chair, shabby in condition but superb in quality. All these objects were overshadowed by the canvasses of de Maistre which face the visitor from wall, floor and easel, from the far end of the room. The paintings of some men look their best in the company of others, but these complemented and reinforced one another. Until I had received the impact of this display I understood nothing of the work of my host. One reason why they gained from one another was the clarity of each. There was no babel, but a number of strong, lucid statements. It is possible for an inferior artist to be lucid and strong if he selects suitably simple subjects, but it takes talent to make lucid, strong statements about complicated matters, and the content of de Maistre's pictures is almost always complicated, whether the still-lifes which stood on the floor or the big *Pietà* and *Crucifixion* on easels above.

Good painters are rare beings and their origins may mostly be regarded as improbable. LeRoy Leveson Laurent Joseph de Maistre came from a place and an environment remote from the painting-room in Eccleston Street and what it stands for. He was born on 27 March 1894, the sixth son among the eleven children of Etienne de Mestre[1] and his wife Clara, daughter of Captain George Taylor Rowe, at a house named Maryvale, a big farm-house, at Bowral in New South Wales, Australia. Etienne de Mestre was distantly related to the illustrious philosopher Count Joseph de Maistre. When Roy was eighteen months old his parents left Maryvale and after renting Ulster Park near Fitzroy Falls for three years they took Mount Valdemar, near the village of Sutton Forest, a colonial-style house formerly the residence of the Governors of New South Wales. Roy's upbringing was unusual: his family life was patriarchal; he attended no school but picked up what he could from the tutors and governesses who ministered to the needs of his large family. The French origin of the de Mestres gave them a sense of detachment,

[1] The family spelt their name thus; from about the middle 'twenties the painter reverted to the earlier form.

slight but distinct, from their neighbours. Racial separateness was a little sharpened by class separateness also. The de Mestres were a great family who formed close associations with successive Governors and their families, who spent the summers at their official country residence near by, and it was in an atmosphere slightly vice-regal, informal yet sophisticated, that he grew up. Until he was nineteen he led a contented life among his numerous brothers and sisters on their father's big farm, a life in which horses played a predominant part, for Etienne de Mestre, in spite of his Tolstoyan appearance, was one of the great racing personalities in Australia, the winner of five Melbourne Cups.

From an early age Roy de Maistre drew and painted 'with a good deal', he told me, 'of preoccupation and passion, but my real interest was in music'. He studied the violin in the State Conservatorium of New South Wales, and the viola as well. Such preoccupations as these, especially in a boy to whom the whole world of sport was open, his father was never able to comprehend. Yet he had no antagonism towards them. His mother, on the other hand, was sympathetic towards his intention to tread what, for a member of their family, were unusual paths. In 1913 he went to Sydney to study music and painting, the last at the Royal Art Society of New South Wales, under Norman Carter and Datillo Rubbo, and later at the Sydney School of Art under Julian Ashton.

Roy de Maistre is in one respect unique within my experience: he is a painter not innately a visual man. The great majority of painters live, from their early years, through their eyes. Not only did the young de Maistre live chiefly through his ears, but his drawings and paintings, so far as I have been able to ascertain, were not expressions of things that he saw or imagined; they were schematic expressions of his active analytical intellect. He must have appeared not only unvisual but altogether uncreative, for even as a musician his aspirations lay in the direction of execution rather than composition.

In the course of his studies he formed a friendship that both quickened and directed his interest in painting. Norah Simpson, a lady of talent and magnetic personality, had not long before returned from England to continue her studies. She had been to the Slade School and was friendly with members of the Camden Town Group, especially with Charles Ginner. The effect of her return upon de Maistre and other students was immediate and fruitful. For more than a quarter of a century the Impressionism of Monet and Pissarro had remained the most modern impulse in Australian painting. It had a long succession of practitioners, a number of them accomplished, and a few, most notably Arthur Streeton, more than accomplished. Little news of subsequent movements had reached Australia. The appearance among them of a persuasive advocate of Post-Impressionism, the friend of men familiar with the work and ideas of Van Gogh, Gauguin and Cézanne, could hardly be otherwise than exciting. But before de Maistre had time to make a serious beginning as a painter the war came, and in 1916 he joinèd the Australian Army, only to be discharged within nine months, a sufferer from tuberculosis. Norah Simpson had made him aware of the ideas which were animating his own contemporaries in England and Europe. The next stage in his development was less direct.

During his convalescence – when he began to paint again – he made several friends in the medical profession. Among these was Dr. Moffat, Director of the Gladesville Mental Hospital, who interested de Maistre in psychology.

Patients in mental hospitals at that time were often placed in wards decorated in colours calculated to ameliorate their condition by virtue of the stimulating or sedative effect of the colours employed.

This feature of their treatment led to his preoccupation with the whole problem of colour in relation to mental health. The current practice seemed to him so crude and elementary that he persuaded the Red Cross authorities to allow him to experiment with colour in one of their hospitals for shell-shock patients. The results were so satisfactory that he raised money to establish the Exeter Convalescent Home – of which Dr. Moffat became the Medical Director – where shell-shocked soldiers were treated in accordance with his own ideas. Here the rooms were painted not in single colours, but in colour-keys, which enabled patients to receive the full benefits of colour treatment without the retinal exhaustion produced by prolonged exposure to single colours. This preoccupation had beneficial results both for shell-shocked soldiers and for the painting of de Maistre. By 1918 his meditations and researches were sufficiently advanced to permit of his delivering, at the Australian Arts

Club, Sydney, a talk entitled 'Colour in Art', in which he outlined his theory for harmonizing colour in accordance with the musical system of harmonizing sound, based upon the analogies between the colours of the spectrum and the notes of the musical scale.

I should like to trace its evolution [he said] from the first scale which I experimented with. It was composed of eight colour notes and was really nothing more than a natural scale based upon the seven principal colours of the spectrum, the eighth note being a repeat of the key note to form an octave musical scale. Having gone this far, it will be easy to understand how the next steps came about. Seeing an obvious similarity between this eight note colour scale and an ordinary well tempered musical scale, and having no colours which would correspond to sharps or flats in music, I decided that it most resembled the scale of C major. I also noticed that two of the most important notes in a musical scale—the 4th and 5th degree—were represented by degrees of colour complementary to the key note, and so, fixing the key note as Yellow, the spectrum band developed into the scale of yellow major—the order of progression being—Yellow, Green, Blue, Indigo, Violet, Red, Orange, Yellow. It then only remained to insert a tone of colour between the 1st and 2nd degree, the 2nd and 3rd degree and between the 4th and 5th, 5th and 6th, 6th and 7th degree and a chromatic colour scale, such as the one we have here, was the result.

The next stage was inevitable. One only had to take the theory of music as it applied to the major and minor scales and transfer its system to the colour keyboard. The key note being decided upon and the intervals between the preceding notes being the same as those of the musical scale, I soon found that the colours representing the various notes bore the correct relation to each other, and that their importance in relation to the colour key note was much the same as the corresponding degrees of the musical scale—the most important feature being the relation of the complementary colour to the key note, this colour invariably representing in a cold and warm degree the dominant and sub-dominant or 5th and 4th degree of a musical scale. In every scale a degree of each of the seven colours of the spectrum is represented, and when these are used in their right proportions, the invariable results are distinct colour harmonies, retaining the general tone quality of the key note, and an intense luminosity. Doubtless, this is due also to the phenomena of simultaneous contrast mentioned before, as each note is being balanced and made more brilliant by the juxtaposition of its complementary on some part of the canvas.

Being an extremely practical man he invented in collaboration with his friend the painter R. S. Wakelin, the disc designed to enable harmonious colour schemes to be selected from a colour scale upon a standard principle.[1]

This disc, which was put on the market in 1926, contained 132 variations of the seven colours of the spectrum, and was fitted with two covering masks, one major and one minor, either on rotation, revealing twelve different colour scales of seven colours each. The invention provided a ready means of determining the relative degrees of harmony and contrast between different colours on a scientific basis.

In later years his interest in colour was matched by his interest in design and form, yet colour continued to preoccupy him in a special fashion. In 1934 he worked, for instance, upon a project for a film-ballet in colour, in which the colour varied in relation to the music. The opening sequences were a direct translation of the music into terms of colour, and in the later, although direct translation ceased, the key, pitch and texture of the colour were determined by the music. Unfortunately the cost of production was beyond the available resources.

During the war years painting gradually supplanted music as de Maistre's chief preoccupation. He exhibited his work for the first time at the Royal Art Society, Sydney, in 1918. His early paintings appear to have been mostly landscapes, schematic both in colour and design. There is little about them to affront the conservative taste of to-day, but their intellectual character, manifest in their precisely calculated patterns and their strong, clear, colour arrangements designed to emphasize harmonies and contrasts, represented so radical a departure from the prevailing Impressionism that they offered a challenge to which established opinion was quick to react. One critic took to task the selection committee which accepted works by de Maistre for exhibition for 'neglecting to throw out some samples of the art the charm of which depends on ignorance, or, at least, negation of drawing and a sense of colour that a house-painter might envy'.[2]

The following year, jointly with Wakelin, a painter rather older

[1] Patented 6 May 1924 (no. 11176): 'Improvements in or relating to colour selecting devices.'
[2] This and the other quotations from Sydney newspapers that follow are taken from Sydney Press clippings which I have been unable precisely to identify.

than himself who shared many of his ideas, in particular those concerning the relationship between music and colour, de Maistre held his first exhibition.[1] This comprised five of his paintings together with exhibits illustrative of the application of his theories of colour to interior decoration, and six works by Wakelin.

The exhibition was intended to be a challenging demonstration of his theories of colour and it was on the occasion of its opening that he delivered the talk from which extracts have been quoted.

All the paintings he showed were of the same highly intellectual and schematic character, expressions of a lucid and analytical mind, a mind so constituted as to be repelled by Impressionism and attracted by subsequent developments of which it had as yet no direct experience. As a consequence of the exhibition de Maistre took a foremost place among those Australian painters possessed by ideas not susceptible of communication in the language of Arthur Streeton and his contemporaries–a language which they were therefore under compulsion to replace. All Sydney was presently talking about the pictures which, if he so wished, the artist could whistle. A friendly critic prophesied that 'the exhibition by these two young and enthusiastic artists will attract interest. These pictures, played in paint . . . are played fortissimo in the treble. . . . No matter how brilliant each seems, it is keyed harmoniously.' To others his works were 'crudities' or 'garish enough to make a sensitive person shudder'.

Most of the works of these early years have remained in Australia (which I have never visited) but the few examples known to me suggest that de Maistre developed very slowly. It is reasonable to suppose that he could evolve no faster for want of direct contact with the sources of the movement by remote intimations of which his own art was formed. It should also be added that he profited little from the formal teaching he received: he was incapable, he told me, of making a realistic drawing much before 1918.

Such contact was not long denied him for, in the spring of 1923, he was awarded the Travelling Scholarship of the Society of Artists of New South Wales, which was a subsidy by the State and tenable for two years. Twenty years had elapsed since this scholarship,

[1] At the Art Salon (of which Gayfield Shaw was manager), 29 Elizabeth Street, Sydney, from 8 August.

worth £250 a year, had last been awarded. The previous recipient
was George W. Lambert, one of the judges in 1923. The works of
the ten competitors were hung in the National Gallery of New South
Wales.

De Maistre's departure for Europe was the cause of general regret.
The novelty of his ideas and his power to express them in words as
well as in paint, and the criticism implicit in them of the ideas upon
which the work of the most revered Australian painters was based,
had made him a controversial figure, but his ability was recognized
(one of his pictures had been bought by the National Gallery of
New South Wales in 1920) and the disinterestedness of his enthusiasms had won general respect. Moreover his abilities as an
interior decorator—uncommon in Australia—were in regular demand.

London was his immediate destination. I did not come to know
him well until just thirty years later, but only just missed meeting
him on his arrival in the summer of 1923. The Governor of New
South Wales, Sir Walter Davidson, gave de Maistre a letter of introduction to my father, who received him not at home—where I was
still living—but at the Royal College of Art, of which he was
Principal. My father, who was the first painter, de Maistre told me,
whom he met in England, received him with encouragement and
kindness, and provided him with letters to painters in Paris. After
six months in London he moved to Paris, taking a studio in Montparnasse. After spending eighteen months there he took a small
party of students for a summer painting holiday to St. Jean de Luz,
a place to which he became greatly attached and to which he
returned in 1930 and remained for three years. In Australia he had
thought of England as 'home', but although he had found satisfaction and even inspiration in London he was not aware, as he immediately was in France, of a kind of preordained harmony between
himself and his surroundings. The terms of his scholarship, however,
required that he should return to Australia and present his best work
to the National Gallery of his native State.

In 1926, the year of his return to Sydney, his first one-man
exhibition, consisting mainly of the work he had done in Europe,
was held at the Macquarie Galleries, in Bligh Street. *Fisherman's
Harbour, St. Jean de Luz*,[1] the painting judged by de Maistre to be

[1] The National Gallery of New South Wales, Sydney.

the most substantial result of his tenure of the scholarship, he presented to the Society which had awarded it. This I know only in monochrome reproduction, from which it would appear to be a sober work, deliberate both in design and execution, and close to, if rather more atmospheric than, the Camden Town paintings of Ginner and his friends. The sobriety of this and the other paintings he brought home–unadventurous expressions of an adventurous mind–is characteristic of his stability and his fastidiousness. Prepared as he was to learn what the formative movements in Europe, especially Cubism, had to teach him, it would not have accorded with the dignity of his character to display any of the superficial marks of conversion. He went to Europe first of all to learn the essentials of painting and only secondly to develop, and without haste, his own ideas and his personal view of nature. The works he brought back suggest that his first three years there helped him towards the realization of both these objectives.

The new pictures he showed at the Macquarie Galleries, which expressed a fuller, warmer view of nature than the schematic works of his earlier years, were received with interest and respect; but also, as a maturer challenge to the entrenched tradition, with an enhanced hostility. One influential critic, Howard Ashton, thus concluded the brief disparaging paragraph–entitled 'Soulful Art'–he accorded to them: 'As a contribution to Australian art, however suggestive they may be to the highbrow, who believes that one should paint soul-striving rather than facts, these pictures are, unhappily, negligible.'

De Maistre's three years abroad had shown him that Europe was the place most favourable to the deepening of his faculties as a painter, and the hostility with which his work was received hastened his decision to leave Australia. In 1928 he accordingly returned to London and two years later to St. Jean de Luz. Until the Second World War he spent about half his time in England and half in France.

Departure from Australia marked the end of a chapter in his life. This was a longer and more important chapter than friends of recent date might suppose. His patronymic and his work, his personality and his experience are so unequivocally European that it is therefore important to recall that in spite of a certain aloofness the de Maistre family were very much a part of New South Wales and that he himself as a young man was fully an Australian and led a free and happy life there. He spoke French no better than average, and his father had abandoned his hereditary religion Not many of those who know him now suspect that there is a sense in which, aristocrat though he is, he is also a self-made man. His establishment in Europe is the consequence of acts of faith and will, as is also his membership of the Catholic Church, even though it was the church of his fathers. Like his art, his religion is not something inherited or supinely accepted, but something won by personal conviction.

France is the country where he is in closest harmony with his surroundings, but the war deprived him of his studio in St. Jean de Luz and he has never been able, for economic reasons, to return there. Three years before the war he transformed a café at 13 Eccleston Street into a studio, and after he settled finally in London this became his home. The sense of isolation that besets him in England contributed fruitfully, however, to the formation of his art.

During the eight years that elapsed between his departure from Australia and his permanent establishment in London he opened out, and he found his place in the abstract tradition which derived, by way of Cubism, from Cézanne and Seurat, an intellectual tradition based upon structure and tending to be geometric and rectilinear. Those who have worked in this tradition are often primarily draughtsmen for whom colour is subordinate to design. The design of de Maistre is always clear and sharp, but his impassioned interest in colour never tempted him to allow it to play a subordinate part. Like Cézanne, his principal master, his consistent aim has been to evolve a way of painting in which design and colour shall become one. This is a high aim, and in much of his early work it was realized self-consciously, by an effort obvious to the spectator; or else it eluded him altogether. It was only gradually that he mastered the art that conceals art, and gained the knowledge and the power to use design and colour so that each completes the other in a unity which, however long struggled for, has the look of inevitability. In his early paintings he ensured a degree of harmony by mixing all his colours with white; the harmony so notable in the later works results from the relation of pure colours—a harmony which gains resonance because it expresses precise and closely-knit form.

When I alluded to de Maistre's having opened out, I intended to convey that his nature as a painter deepened and broadened, and that he became more perceptively aware of himself and of surrounding life. The phrase serves to indicate the development of the man, but not of his work, for this did not broaden out: it became, on the contrary, more sharply focused, more concentrated. The process, no doubt a manifestation of the natural evolution of his mind, was hastened by his English domicile. In the South of France he loved to walk abroad in the strong light, and the social climate fostered in him an expansive disposition. As a painter he habitually makes decisions between clearly defined alternatives, and the prevailing English grey softens the sharp edges of things and blurs distinctions. So in London he stays mostly indoors. The result is that he looks with fascinated intensity at the café transformed into a studio which contains, like Courbet's, a repertory of his past life, and this scrutiny, searching yet affectionate, has made him a kind of *intimiste*. Carafe, fruit-dish, lampshade, electric fan and potted hyacinth, each the object of contemplation, have been combined in lucid, close-knit arrangements expressive of the painter's relation to his surroundings. There are about them none of the cosy overtones that mark the work of most *intimistes*, no attempted creation of a 'little world of Roy de Maistre'. On the contrary there are, even in the gentlest, intimations of energy, of harshness. If the world of de Maistre is not a 'little world', it is governed by a strict sense of proportion which would be offended were the petals of a hyacinth made harsher than the features of Our Lady mourning over her dead Son. *Intimisme* is but one facet—although a large and characteristic one–of the art of de Maistre. Religious subjects are a constant preoccupation with him, but to-day serious religious painting recommends itself even less to religious bodies than it does to the public at large. Of de Maistre's most ambitious and impressive religious paintings, *The Crucifixion*, of 1953, remains unsold in his studio; and *Pietà*, of 1950, was presented to the Tate Gallery in 1955. An earlier version of *The Crucifixion*, of 1942–3 (Plate 56), was acquired by The City Art Gallery, Leicester.

'The painter is always in search of a peg on which to hang his creative urge,' I remember his saying. 'It isn't so much that he is attracted by certain subjects, but simply that he recognizes them as occasions for the exercise of this urge.' This, however, is not the same as maintaining, as a whole school of painters and critics maintains, that, for the painter's purpose, a pumpkin is as good as a human head. De Maistre is moved, not as an eye merely but as a whole man, by the subjects he chooses. He is moved by the images of the Crucifixion and of Mary mourning over the dead Christ not because these are dramatic 'subjects', or dramatic symbols, still less just shapes, but because he believes in what they represent. Even his carafe and fruit-dish are old friends, for whose characteristics he has a keenly analytic affection. Whatever the subject of his choice, his treatment of it–if circumstances permit it to take its full arduous course–is always the same. He begins by making–usually at high speed–a realistic representation, usually in charcoal, from which he proceeds gradually, through a series of further studies, to his final, often more or less abstract, design. *Seated Figure*,[1] of 1954 (Plate 57), neither realistic nor abstract, is a figure caught half-way, so to speak, along this process. In the process he discards everything not relevant to his intention, and adds everything that contemplation of it, including all that his past experience of that particular thing, has taught him. His final representations, however abstract they may seem, are deeply rooted in some total human experience. These series, in which he dwells with an almost obsessive persistence upon a given image, sometimes take years to complete. One of them, for instance, began in 1937 with a realistic half-length portrait of a seated woman. The second version, made eight years later, shows the subject's face (serene in the first) twisted with inner disquietude. In the third, made after two years, the figure is shown less tortured and with a child, symbol, perhaps, of some satisfying work the subject had undertaken. The fourth, made the year following, represents, simply, a room where women had sat, the place where a female drama had been enacted; and in the fifth, of the same year, the empty room had become more agitated and dramatic; and in the sixth and last the figure has again intruded, once again serene and impersonal.[2]

Only rarely, however, is the struggle to make the final statement to which nothing need be added, and from which nothing can be taken away, quite so intricate, various and prolonged.

[1] Coll. the Artist.
[2] All six belong to the painter. The last, completed in 1949, was dated, in absence of mind, 1946.

Roy de Maistre occupies a singular position in England to-day. His work has aroused interest and respect since his first one-man London exhibition, held in November 1929 in the studio of Francis Bacon.[1] The public has had a number of further opportunities of seeing it. The chief of these were exhibitions at the Mayor Gallery, in October–November 1934; of Flower Paintings at the Calmann Gallery in July 1938; at Temple Newsam, Leeds, from June until August 1943, the most representative yet held – fifty-six works illustrative of his development from 1920 until 1937; at the City Art Gallery, Birmingham, 1946; at the Adams Gallery in March 1950, and at the Hanover Gallery in April 1953. Yet his work, held in high respect as it is by a number of painters, chiefly his juniors, and a few critics, remains little noticed by the general public. There are several reasons for his relative obscurity. He is by nature fastidious and reticent; he prefers the cultivation of friendships to social relations that are casual or fortuitous, and for 'public relations' he has neither taste nor aptitude. But most of all his isolation is due to the fact that his art is not an art that lends itself to easy understanding. It is destitute alike of bonhomie and of fashionable cliché. The kind of abstract which aims at being a self-sufficient construction of form and colour, appealing to the eye alone, is to-day fairly widely understood, but abstract painting the source of which is human as distinct from purely visual experience, and often experience that is complicated and obscure, is apt to baffle and to disconcert. 'In contemporary painting, our compositions,' he noted in an unpublished paper, 'being ruled by the laws of order, are in a sense mathematical and geometrical, but far beyond the extent to which we can use geometry and mathematics.' More generally his attitude to art is summed up in a fragment that occurs in another of his unpublished papers: 'The problems of art, like those of life itself, are in the main unsolvable as separate entities – art being a reflection of life – the solution of one problem will be the solution of the other. . . . The forces in art are the forces of life, coordinated and organized.'

De Maistre's is an art which abounds in enchanting by-products – small flowerpieces, still-lifes and the like – but in essence it is the expression of a nature deep, little given to compromise, and harsh. 'In one's life one ought to be gentle and forbearing,' he once said to

[1] At 19 Queensberry Mews West, South Kensington.

me, 'but in one's art one should conduct oneself quite differently. It's often necessary, for instance, to give the spectator an ugly left uppercut.'

This actively benevolent and deeply civilized man inevitably finds much to horrify him in this world of ours in which cruelty and vulgarity play so inordinate a part and which offers so sombre a prospect; yet nothing clouds his confidence in the illumination that awaits the artist with the courage to press forward in search, in his own words, 'of that finality of expression which is the aim of all seekers after truth'.

BEN NICHOLSON
b. 1894

IF the art of painting were nothing more than the creation of forms
and their interrelation and colouring so as to give the greatest
pleasure – as many critics believe it to be – there would be no
particular difficulty in finding a common measure for comparing
representational with abstract works. The common measure would,
of course, be a 'formal' yardstick, to vary the metaphor, a sort of
diviner's rod which would enable the wielder of it to discover and
compare the elements of 'formal beauty' whether in, say, a Rembrandt or a Mondriaan. That forms and their disposition and colour
constitute the essentials of the language of painting I suppose most
critics would regard as self-evident, but a radical difference of opinion
arises as to whether form and colour constitute, by themselves, the
whole of painting or whether they constitute a language which may
legitimately express conceptions from other than the purely aesthetic
fields of human experience. Should the purpose of painting be to
make an appeal exclusively to an aesthetic appetite, as cookery to the
appetite for food? That is the crux of the question. For those whose
conclusions lead them to give one answer a shaggy turnip in a half-
light painted by Rembrandt with the same intensity and skill as one
of his self-portraits as an old man would have a similar value, and
the ceiling of the Sistine might without the slightest loss be regarded
as a noble arabesque. But however severely critics so persuaded may
insist upon the irrelevance of the subject of a work of art, it may be
observed that a supercilious note is apt to creep into their comments
when a modern work with a subject explicitly drawn from the
phenomenal world is under consideration. Critics for whom the
answer to the crucial question is the contrary of this, and who persist
in seeing the distinction – which to their opponents seems unreal if
not perverse – between the head of Rembrandt and a turnip, are apt,
in the presence of an abstract work, to become taciturn, or to take
refuge in reflexions upon abstract art in general. The 'formal'
divining rod, whether the subject of a critic's attentions happens to be

figurative or abstract is a thoroughly useful implement. About this there can be no possible doubt. Yet somehow, even in the most experienced hand, it fails to do more than serve as a very approximate common measure for representational and abstract works of art.

A conspicuous example of the only relative utility of the implement in question is furnished by the subject of the present study. It so happened that I had some part in the selection of two retrospective exhibitions of the work of Ben Nicholson, that sent to the Venice Biennale in the summer of 1954 and the considerably extended and modified version of it held at the Tate the following year. In the course of their organization and showing I heard many opinions about the artist from many different kinds of men. According to some he was a great artist; according to others he was of little significance; but upon one point all seemed to be agreed: that he was the most convinced and consistent exponent of abstract painting at work in Great Britain. It was evident that their estimate of his stature varied with the critic's estimate of the value of abstract art: to those who esteemed it highly he was the leader of an important school, and to those who did not he was an artist of merit exercising his sensibility and skill up a blind alley.

The failure, upon this particularly appropriate occasion for its use, of the aesthetic divining-rod brought finally home to me that, in practice, critics do not judge works exclusively on aesthetic grounds, those who claim to do so being in fact unfavourably prejudiced by a subject drawn from common experience and the others, for whom formal perfection is not the whole of art, by its absence. Abstract painting is not to be judged according to canons applicable to representational painting, and in my own case I fail, beyond a certain point, to respond to the uncommunicative forms and relationships which constitute at the same time the language and the message of abstract art. And the limitations of my pleasure are emphasized rather than removed by the pleadings of its advocates. I think it proper to refer to this disqualification for the full appreciation of what appears to me a highly special province of painting, before I treat particularly of one of its most accomplished denizens.

Ben Nicholson was born on 10 April 1894 in a house made out of two cottages in Denham, Buckinghamshire, the eldest of the four children of William Nicholson, one of the earlier subjects of these studies, and his wife Mabel, born Pryde. His education both general and professional–for it was early assumed that he would be a painter –was sporadic. He was sent to Haddon Court, a preparatory school in Hampstead, and to Gresham's School, Holt, where he overworked and overplayed and whence he was withdrawn exhausted at the end of his first year. If in this brief span he added no artistic lustre to the annals of this ancient school, he made a little cricket history by playing for the First XI. Ben Nicholson is an accomplished player not only of cricket but of all ball games (I had occasion to mention in the previous volume my own first encounter with him, across a ping-pong table). At the Slade–where also he remained only for one year[1]–he spent almost as much time playing billiards at the Gower Hotel as at his studies. 'Although I was not conscious of it at the time,' he once said to me, 'I think that the billiard-balls, so cleanly geometrical in form and so ringingly clear in colour, against the matt-green of the baize, must have appealed to my aesthetic sense, in contrast to the fustiness of the classrooms at the Slade.' But billiards was not incompatible with occasional attendance at the School. Paul Nash, a fellow student and his frequent companion at lunch at Shoolbreds, recalls an occasion when they were painting from the male model in the Life Class. The students, with a single exception, followed the realistic method that was taught. Paul Nash was shocked to notice that Ben Nicholson was not conforming. . . . Upon a large sheet of paper, on a drawing board of Imperial size set upon a painting easel, he had drawn in heavy pencil a small dark figure, a sort of manikin, bearing no resemblance to the model. It was, of course, simply his personal equivalent for the model, characteristically presented, and not the kind of equivalent approved of.[2]

Paul Nash was an acute observer and a lucid writer, and, although a worthy witness, I feel bound to observe that I find this particular item of evidence surprising. For reasons upon which I shall presently

[1] One term is the period for which Ben Nicholson is customarily said to have studied at the Slade, as, for instance, in the Lund Humphries volume p. 22, and the Penguin p. 6. The records of the Slade, however, show him to have been there throughout the first two terms of the session 1910–11 (October 1910 to April 1911) and for half the third term of that session; he then returned to the Slade for the first term only of the session 1911–12 (October to December 1911).

[2] 'Ben Nicholson's Carved Reliefs', by Paul Nash. 'Architectural Review' October 1935.

57. ROY DE MAISTRE. *Seated Figure* (1954)
Oil on board, 36×24 in. Coll. the Artist.

58. BEN NICHOLSON. *Higher Carnstabba Farm* (1944).
Oil, 21½ × 21½ in. Coll. Mrs. Elsie Myers.

enlarge Ben Nicholson felt his way very tentatively, over a period of years, towards an attitude in which he tried, instead of representing some aspect of familiar experience, to find an 'equivalent' for it. I believe that not many works of his early years survive; he was not prolific and I suspect that his sense of perfection leads him to destroy examples when occasion offers. He has spoken to me of his early work as 'Vermeerish' and *The Striped Jug*,[1] of 1911, shows what he meant. Paul Nash refers to a brief early period of portraiture, during which his sitters showed no liking for the 'equivalents' he evolved, of which I have never seen an example, but it would seem that the works described as 'Vermeerish' constitute his effective point of departure.

After leaving the Slade he went to Tours to learn French. Here, after giving much time to tennis and some to painting, he returned with a single oil of a candlestick. Tours was followed by Milan, where he remained for several months, learning Italian and doing a little painting: he brought back two still-lifes, one of a skull. Not long after his visit to Italy his health gave cause for disquiet and he went to Madeira, where he learnt a little Portuguese and brought back one painting. The First World War broke out not long afterwards, and Ben Nicholson, first graded C3, then rejected for military service, went, in 1917, to Pasadena, California, for nine months, coming home on account of his mother's death, in June 1918. In his longish stay in California he made only a single painting: 'a Vermeer-looking thing' was how he described this work to me.

When the war ended Ben Nicholson was twenty-five, and the end of his long and apparently unfruitful apprenticeship was hardly in sight. This would seem an appropriate point to interrupt this summary chronology of his progress by some inquiry into the cause of his failure to find his way, of the inhibition which, indeed, almost prevented him from painting at all. Everything seemed to favour a quick apprenticeship and a flying start. He was naturally dexterous, and able with little effort to master any game or craft; he was ambitious and purposeful, and, far from having parental opposition to contend with, he had for parents painters both of whom favoured his following the family calling and were ready to impart to him the fruit of their experience and able to spare him the necessity of making a livelihood by other means than painting. But appearances were in

[1] Formerly Coll. Sir William Nicholson but untraced after his death.

this respect deceptive: the inhibition was the very consciousness of being heir to an art from which he could not withhold either admiration or affection, yet which, as he vaguely saw, did not offer the means whereby he could express most readily his own apprehension of the world he lived in. To-day the circle into which he was born is regarded as of little consequence. The painting of the members of it is apt to be discounted as a belated, provincial manifestation of the Realist tradition deriving immediately from the Impressionists and Whistler; their lives as unduly self-conscious. But to those who grew up in it the best of their works are not unworthy expressions of the great discontinuous tradition of English painting and their lives a memorable combination of sustained idealism with liveliness and urbanity. They challenged the complacency of the later Victorians and extended a comprehending welcome to the talent of their successors. In ages when the arts are regulated by traditional canons which change imperceptibly, son can follow father with a reassuring sense of inevitability. But in ages like our own, when traditional canons exercise ever diminishing authority and achievement is so preponderantly personal, son can scarcely follow father without some sense of cramping personal subordination, of inviting the risk of doing again what has been done already.

Innately an artist, yet almost overborne by the accomplishment of his father, of his mother and of his uncle James Pryde, the first need of Ben Nicholson's survival as an artist was to make, however modest, a personal beginning, and it was his admiration, affection and sense of indebtedness that made the fulfilment of this need so prolonged and, in the immediate sense, so unproductive a struggle.

Those who have written about Ben Nicholson have underrated his affiliations with the past. Of *The Striped Jug* for instance, Mr. John Summerson, in an excellent appreciation of the artist's work, has written, 'It is easy now to see in its solitariness, its anti-swagger, the painter's horror of . . . becoming a genteel protagonist of Vermeerishness.'[1] Surely in this instance Mr. Summerson has allowed his knowledge of the direction in which the artist was to develop later to colour his judgment of a painting made in 1911. For *The Striped Jug* is by Vermeer out of William Nicholson, and nothing more, and coming upon it stacked among other pictures in

[1] 'Ben Nicholson', The Penguin Modern Painters, 1948, p. 6.

the elder Nicholson's studio, I do not believe that any friend of
father or of son, or Mr. Summerson himself, would have taken it for
anything but the work of the father. Far from being a horrified
protest against the prevailing current, it is an accomplished essay in
his father's manner, a convincing demonstration that he could
vermeer with the best. His father, who liked the picture, asked, 'but
why *one* jug?' 'Well,' responded the son, 'why don't you paint
more?' The result was the father's *Hundred Jugs*.

Little by little, however, forces far removed from the inhibiting
tensions arising from the pervasive influence of his family and his imperative need to escape from it began to exert their influence. On his
return from America he became exhilaratingly aware of Cézanne, and
Vorticism compelled his admiring curiosity, especially as expressed
in the art and advocacy of Wyndham Lewis, and must have made a
forceable appeal to his innate love of clarity. An experience more fruitful than any that he had before came to him in Paris a few years later.

> I remember suddenly coming on a cubist Picasso [he wrote to Mr.
> Summerson] at the end of a small upstairs room at Paul Rosenberg's gal-
> lery. It must have been a 1915 painting–it was what seemed to me then
> completely abstract. And in the centre there was an absolutely miracu-
> lous *green*–very deep, very potent and absolutely real. In fact, none of
> the actual events in one's life have been more real than that, and it still
> remains a standard by which I judge any reality in my own work....[1]

It often happens that the most independent persons are not the
least susceptible to influence. Ben Nicholson is a highly independent
man and his early life was devoted to the search for the means to give
effect to his independence. In the early 'twenties he met and later
married Winifred Roberts, a painter with a way of seeing very
different from his own, who by the discernment of her sympathy
and the example of her instinctive and appealing art was able to help
to unseal the springs of his creativity. In her company the inhibiting
tenseness which for so long had made him virtually incapable of
painting at all finally relaxed.

With her he spent three successive winters at Castagnola, near
Lugano, and the summers at her home in Cumberland with visits to
London in between. Mr. Summerson refers to a scrapbook put
together in 1922 which summarized his loyalties: Giotto, Uccello,

[1] Letter dated 3 January 1944; the paragraphs quoted here were first published
in Summerson, op. cit., p. 7.

Cézanne, the Douanier, Matisse, Derain, Braque, Picasso. The sense of the passing away of the shadows of war, of belonging at last to a tradition to which he could respond without reserve, and the companionship of his wife gave him an exhilarating conviction of having begun his life's work. This least productive of painters began to make three or four pictures a week. Few of them survive, but his energies were released and though he still had far to go to find himself, henceforward he travelled fast.

The intensive search and experiment of these years resulted, from the middle 'twenties until the early 'thirties, in a succession of still-lifes in which features characteristic of his mature work are discernible. These still-lifes conform to those of the contemporary School of Paris alike in their subjects—jugs, bottles, plates and knives reposing upon the scrubbed tops of kitchen tables—and in the degree of abstraction with which they are treated. They also show a delicate sureness of taste and colour which are decidedly his own. But he was still only feeling his way, and there was little evidence of the un-compromising austerity or the precision of design that was to be the most conspicuous mark of his later work. The design of most of his paintings of this time known to me is, in fact, loose and uncertain, and this weakness and his obvious eagerness to discard, in the interests of a franker approach to his themes, the smooth accomplishment of his Vermeerish beginnings give them a tentative air, and on this account I question Mr. Summerson's opinion that their beauty is 'amply appreciated by people who have any liking at all for contemporary painting'. Had the painter died in 1930 I doubt whether such works as *Painting*,[1] of 1923–4, or *Still-Life*,[2] of about 1926–to name two considered sufficiently representative for inclusion in the sumptuous volume 'Ben Nicholson: paintings, reliefs, drawings'[3]–would attract attention to-day. A few, however, notably *Still Life with Fruit*,[4] of 1927, and *Au Chat Botté*,[5] of 1932, merit, chiefly on account of the rare beauty of their colour, places among the artist's finest works.

To the late 'twenties belongs a group of landscapes painted in Cumberland and Cornwall, but with few exceptions these rank below his best work. Landscape evidently failed to evoke in him a response

[1] Coll. the Artist.   [2] Coll. Miss Helen Sutherland.
[3] With an introduction by Sir Herbert Read, 1948.
[4] Coll. Mr. F. L. S. Murray.   [5] The City Art Gallery, Manchester.

sufficiently ardent to enable him to create with conviction, yet, unlike his still-life, it was too complex to be reduced, without doing violence to its character, to the simple, clear-cut terms that his way of seeing demanded. Occasionally, however, in such a picture as *Pill Creek, Cornwall*,[1] of 1928, he was able to maintain an impressive harmony between the requirements of close representation and lucid design.

In the very early 'thirties he relaxed his efforts to reconcile the demands of the effective representation of nature–of nature in her more complex aspects at all events–and those of design, and he turned decisively towards abstraction. Several circumstances favoured this re-orientation. Nicholson described a painting by Miro he saw in 1932 or 1933 as 'the first *free* painting that I saw and it made a deep impression–as I remember it, a lovely rough circular white cloud on a deep blue background, with an electric black line somewhere'.[2] More decisive was his first meeting in Paris with Mondriaan. Nicholson thus described what must have been, I think, the most illuminating experience of his life:

His studio . . . was an astonishing room: very high and narrow . . . with a thin partition between it and a dancing school and with a window on the third floor looking down on to thousands of railway lines emerging from and converging into the Gare Montparnasse. He'd lived there for years and except during the war had scarcely been outside Paris–he'd stuck up on the walls different sized rectangular pieces of board painted a primary red, blue and yellow and white and neutral grey–they'd been built up during those 25 years. The paintings were entirely new to me and I did not understand them on this first visit (and indeed only partially understood them on my second visit a year later). They were merely, for me, a part of the very lovely feeling generated by his thought in the room. I remember after this first visit sitting at a café table on the edge of a pavement almost touching all the traffic going in and out of the Gare Montparnasse, and sitting there for a very long time with an astonishing feeling of quiet and repose!–the thing I remembered most was the feeling of light in his room and the pauses and silences during and after he'd been talking. The feeling in his studio must have been not unlike the feeling in one of those hermits' caves where lions used to go to have thorns taken out of their paws.[3]

And last there was a more intimate circumstance: he met Barbara Hepworth, whom he married after the dissolution of his marriage to Winifred Nicholson. In place of a lyrical and feminine painter at

[1] Coll. Mr. C. S. Reddihough.   [2] Summerson, op. cit., p. 12.   [3] Ibid., pp. 12–13.

work by his side there was an abstract sculptor of the most uncompromising kind. (I have heard him acknowledge in the most generous terms his debt to his wives. 'I learnt a great deal about colour from Winifred Nicholson,' he said, 'and a great deal about form from Barbara Hepworth.')

The decisive cause, however, for change was to be found in the artist himself. In these days many young artists attach themselves to the abstract movement because it is the fashion, a fashion, moreover, which threatens to become a new and stultifying academism, but Ben Nicholson has evidently moved nearer and nearer towards pure abstraction under the impulse of some inner compulsion. Pure abstraction is, in any possible circumstances, the position to which by one road or another he would inevitably have made his way, but the inner compulsion was fostered by the three favourable circumstances enumerated just now.

From time to time Ben Nicholson has painted landscapes with a frank and tasteful felicity, but he is, I believe, one of those for whom the demands of representation are restrictive, and therefore, consciously or not, resented. When he described the Miro he saw in the early 'thirties as 'the first *free* painting I saw', I take his meaning to be that it suggested to him the possibility of creating a work of art which would fulfil his own inner requirements without involving the smallest concession to the, to him, restrictive traffic with phenomenal appearances. And that contact almost certainly inspired such a work as *Painting 1933*[1] with its free-floating red discs.

I take it that the reason for the radical effect of Nicholson's contacts with Mondriaan upon his art was that Mondriaan represented in its extremest and most logical form the abstraction which he felt to be the culmination of his own most intimate promptings. For him as for many others Mondriaan must have been the personification of abstract art. In one important respect the influence of Mondriaan affected his work immediately and for good. 'All art,' Mondriaan declared, 'expresses the rectangular relationship.' Nicholson conformed to this exclusive injunction from the year of this momentous meeting. The further dogma that 'the straight line is a stronger and more profound expression than the curve' also became one of his own articles of faith.

[1] Coll. Edna Nixon.

It is important to draw, at once, a clear distinction between Mondriaan and Nicholson. Mondriaan was an intellectual, a theologian, so to speak, of an artistic faith, who also testified to his faith by painting. Nicholson is an instinctive painter, driven by his inner compulsion to the conclusion reached by Mondriaan primarily through the operations of his intellect: 'I have difficulty in reading Mondriaan because I much prefer the direct impact I get from his painting. I have not read more than a few sentences from Kandinsky.'[1] He paints as he does by instinct, but, although not well read in it, he has picked up a fair working knowledge of the faith which justifies his practice.

It was not only the theory and practice of Mondriaan that affected Nicholson but his personality as well, in particular his solemnity illumined occasionally with a pale flash of humour. On entering for the first time the studio which Barbara Hepworth and Ben Nicholson shared in the 'thirties Mondriaan remarked, 'What a fine studio but' (shading his eyes from looking through the window at a large and very beautiful chestnut tree) 'too much nature.' Such an incident as this – related to me by Nicholson – although he did not miss the element of fantasy which prompted them, appealed none the less to his growing abhorrence of nature as a recognizable theme for art. I have already noted, in this connexion, the influence of Barbara Hepworth, who is as intellectual as her husband is instinctive, which must not be discounted. It was she who kept steadily in his view the end towards which he moved, and who fostered his alignment with the abstract movement. In that she played a more positive part than he, who with Naum Gabo and J. L. Martin was an editor of 'Circle',[2] the journal founded to enable Constructivists to bring their ideas before the public.

Under these strong impulses from within and without Nicholson's art moved quickly towards an abstraction which made, eventually, at its most characteristic, no concession at all to the world of common visual experience. After 1933, when he was occupied largely with paintings in which the design was mostly drawn in white lines with the reverse end of the brush, which gave them the effect of engravings, his work assumed the character which it has since retained. He has continued to make paintings and drawings of landscape, as

[1] I quote his own words to me.
[2] 'Circle: international survey of constructive art', 1937. Only one issue appeared. Contributors included Mondriaan, le Corbusier, Gropius, Lewis Mumford, Moore.

well as still-life, or the two in combination. Absolved from any sense of obligation to represent with any degree of exactitude, and with unrestricted scope for the exercise of his faculties as a designer of pure form, landscapes such, for instance, as *St. Ives*,[1] of 1940, and *Halse Town*,[2] of 1939–41, or *Higher Carnstabba Farm*,[3] of 1944 (Plate 58) express a lyricism absent from the landscapes he made in the late 'twenties. Particularly happy, too, are indications of landscape, sometimes very slight, that appear as backgrounds for still-lifes. *Halse Town*,[4] of 1942, or *Towednarck*,[5] of 1943, are excellent examples. Such landscape indications, moreover, can evoke most convincingly the distinct atmosphere of Cornwall, where the artist has mainly lived since 1932.

Beautiful as many of his pictures are in which so much of a subject is described by a few delicate, precise lines, some of them enclosing sober monochrome washes, others simply areas of virgin paper or canvas, it is, I think, upon his most intransigently abstract works that his reputation will finally depend. For, paradoxically, it is in the narrow world made of a few elementary geometrical forms, of a few simple colours alone, that his spirit moves with that entire freedom to which he has aspired so persistently. In an attempt to define the unusual character of Nicholson's creativity Mr. Summerson alludes to his 'power to deny, discard, eliminate in pursuit of reality'.[6] Or, as the artist himself has written, ' "Realism" has been abandoned in the search for reality: the "principal objective" of abstract art is precisely this reality.'[7]

The fullest definition I have come upon of reality of this order occurs in an essay on the artist by Sir Herbert Read.

Ben Nicholson who, like all the great artists of the past, [it runs] is something of a mystic, believes that there is a reality underlying appearances, and that it is his business, by giving material form to his intuition of it, to express the essential nature of this reality. He does not draw that intuition of reality out of a vacuum, but out of a mind attuned to the specific forms of nature – a mind which has stored within it a full awareness of the proportions and harmonies inherent in all natural phenomena, in the universe itself.[8]

[1] Coll. Mr. C. S. Reddihough.   [2] Coll. E. Q. and Christopher Nicholson.
[3] Coll. Mrs. Elsie Myers.   [4] Coll. Mr. Mortimer Bennitt.
[5] Coll. Mr. Peter Lanyon.   [6] Op. cit., p. 13.   [7] Ibid.
[8] 'A Coat of many Colours, occasional essays', by Herbert Read, 1945 (reprinted from 'The Listener'), RU 1947.

59. Ben Nicholson. *White relief* (1935).
Oil on carved mahogany, 39 × 65 in. The Tate Gallery, London.

60. WILLIAM
ROBERTS.
Masks (1935).
Oil, 40×50 in.
Coll. Count
Vanden Heuvel.

Sir Herbert frequently reminds us that utterances such as these involve philosophical questions. They do indeed, and for quite a few decades philosophers have been suspicious of phrases such as 'a reality underlying appearances': they have been apt to ask for the 'cash value' of these words as used in such contexts and to wonder whether, in most contexts, they have any meaning at all. The antithesis of appearance and reality has, however, a place in the history of philosophy, though it is more than doubtful whether any two classical philosophers have entertained the same notion of it or the same notions of what it is that is being thus contrasted. It is, therefore, problematic whether a phrase so obscure can be currently introduced by any critic to throw light on anything.

It is possible, none the less, that in his use of this contrast Sir Herbert has in mind its great originator, Plato. It is central to Plato's theory of 'Ideas' or 'Forms' that, on the one hand, there are *eide*, ideal 'Forms', on the other, particulars that are not instances but imitations of them. What is it that Plato has in mind? The theory of 'Forms' starts from reflexion about morals and about mathematics, and for the present purpose it is the latter that is relevant. A geometer draws a circle, but this visible circle, though it has its uses as a diagram and a symbol, is not the 'ideal' circle that he has in mind; the circle that he is thinking about and that has all the necessary properties of circle is purely and entirely an object of intelligence alone, not an object of perception or, even, for that matter, of imagination. The circle that the geometer sees or imagines, springboard though it is for his thought, cannot be an instance of the circle that has such and such necessary properties in virtue of circularity, for a little measurement would show up its inaccuracies. It 'imitates' the 'real' circle, that is to say; it is not an example of it.

Now Plato was convinced that 'appearances', that is to say visible and imaginable things, do nothing but imitate 'reality', and he thought it the most important thing in the world to come to some knowledge of 'reality' and that this knowledge was philosophical knowledge. It is in consequence of these convictions that he can see little good in the visual arts. The visual arts, he declares, are concerned with appearances, 'imitations of imitations', not, therefore, with 'reality' at all. And oddly enough, in a passage of the essay from which I have quoted, Sir Herbert Read comes near to echoing Plato's own condemnation of visual art.

> If we consider nature in the objective sense [he writes] as an aggregate of facts, and consider the function of art in relation to such a conception of nature, then we can conceive art only as reproducing in some way the specific facts. That is, indeed, the kind of relation between art and nature which most people seem to want: but they should realize that what they thus get is not the reality, but merely the appearance of nature.

It would seem probable that Sir Herbert's conception of 'appearance and reality', philosophically obscure though it is and not clarified or explained by him, is near to the Platonic model. For after all there have been very many great artists who have thought, with pardonable philosophical heedlessness, if you wish, that behind appearances, partly hidden and partly revealed by them, was a reality that, in their art, they might somehow convey. But they have been representational artists (and in this, as we shall see, they have been better philosophers than Sir Herbert): baffling though appearances might be, they are some clue, they have thought, to 'reality'; in any case they are all the clue there is, and certainly, even were there to be other clues in intelligence itself or in a priori and transcendental reflexion, they are all the clues that painters and sculptors have to do with, seeing that their business (if art has a province of its own, which Plato did not think and perhaps Sir Herbert agrees with him) is of its very nature with the visible and the sensuous.

But Sir Herbert is obstinate in his belief that reality is not revealed by appearance. Or is he? His philosophy of it is perhaps confused. 'Reality underlies appearances' in such a way and is of such a nature (at any rate in the essay on Ben Nicholson) that it can be properly conceived of as being of a 'mathematical and crystalline nature', the object of a special sort of 'intuition' (for it is because he is 'something of a mystic', he claims, that Ben Nicholson has access to this reality), and its apprehension and expression are as abstract as is music. But what is Sir Herbert thinking of here? Is he seriously thinking that the 'reality behind appearances' is circles and squares, which are the proper object of pure intelligence, or is he saying that the structure of the visible world exhibits certain geometrical and mathematical, certain abstract, harmonies, and that it is these that an abstract artist such as Ben Nicholson makes visible to us? In spite of the talk about some species of mystical insight the former is too wild a supposition, and his reference to Nicholson as drawing his intuition of nature not out of a vacuum but out of a mind attuned to the specific forms of nature, by which he appears to mean 'the proportions and harmonies inherent in all natural phenomena', suggests that the second supposition is the correct one.

But if it is, it is comparatively trite, and the argument holds some fallacies. Let us consider it.

It is trite to say that nature has a mathematical structure and that a painter may have some intuition of it. So trite is it, and of so many artists may it be said, that it serves not at all to discriminate one artist against others as being a special sort of artist, namely an abstract painter, nor does it serve to distinguish non-representational from representational artists. To take an obvious example, Piero della Francesca was very much aware of the mathematical structure of the universe, but–and here he displayed a philosophical clarity of mind superior to that possessed by Sir Herbert–he used his knowledge in an art that is not abstract in Sir Herbert's sense (i.e. not non-representational) and in so doing he used language as language is properly used, that is to say, he used it to speak of things other and more interesting than language itself. Let me explain more fully.

Firstly, since, as Plato impressively showed, the visible circle is but an imitation of the 'ideal' circle which is the 'reality', it is not at all clear why, in order to give material form to the intuition of mathematical structure or to express the essential nature of reality, there is an advantage in an art which is 'abstract', i.e. non-representational, over an art which is not; it is not clear what advantage there is in circles and squares, in as abstract a delineation as is humanly possible of sheer formal harmony, over the expression of this same harmony in terms, let us say, of the human figure. The former imitates 'reality' in Sir Herbert's sense no more than does the latter. The latter does it no less accurately, or need not do so–although it must be granted that on Sir Herbert's philosophy of the matter the choice, when we are serious and concerned with 'reality' and not just 'the appearance of nature', is between Ben Nicholson on the one hand and Piero and Alma Tadema indifferently on the other–and it does both what Sir Herbert thinks important and expresses a wide range of experience as well.

Recognition of formal harmonies and hard mathematical structure is a tool, no doubt the major tool, of the painter's craft. But we use tools to make things; it is not self-evident that their proper or their best use is to engrave statements about themselves, about what sorts of tools they are. No doubt at times when artists have lost the standards of their craft and content themselves with anecdotage or emotive illustration of appealing subject-matters, as was the case, both in England and France, for much of the nineteenth century, there is an imperative need for painters to concern themselves, in this way, with the sheer grammar and syntax of painting (although in fact in the nineteenth century the great painters did not choose this road), just as at times when it is realized that considerable linguistic confusion befogs the discussion of philosophical problems it is natural and right that philosophers should talk about language itself. So, too, at such a time, it is natural and perhaps right, cathartically, although otherwise it is absurd, to declare that all poetry, and all art, aspires to the condition of music. But even at times such as these philosophers, delve as deeply as they may into the perplexities of words, use ordinary words to do it, and this they do because there is of course nothing else to use. But so, too, *if* painting and sculpture have a province of their own and are not attempting to do in a peculiar way what philosophers or mathematicians do in their own way, if they are not, that is to say, concerned with objects of pure thought such as the geometer's circle, then this is because they are visual arts; and if they are visual arts, then the proper, and in fact the only, language that they can use to probe 'reality' is the language of the visible and sensuous natural world. There is no other language available to them. 'Reality is appearance,' a distinguished recent artist used to say, and the adage is philosophically sounder than the premise of Sir Herbert's philosophy of abstract art.

The analogy of music cannot be sustained in this connexion. For the language of music is quite a different kind of language from that of painting. Perhaps there are likenesses that may be useful for some purposes, but for Sir Herbert's purpose they are obliterated by the manifest differences. One crucial test brings out one relevant difference clearly enough. On the one hand there is a manifest kinship between the forms of Mantegna and those of the natural world (of appearances); on the other hand, when music endeavours to be representational in the sense of rendering the sounds of farm-yard or of factory, it becomes clearly absurd: we recognize that to render the noises of the farmyard or of the factory is not the musician's proper business.

In fact the philosophy of abstract art, in all the inflation of its currency and the high-flown and tense seriousness of its diction, is unsound from top to bottom. It may be that some day Sir Herbert, to take its most illustrious contemporary advocate, will elucidate his obscurities and cash his words; some day, perhaps, he will tell us why it is that, as a matter of philosophical aesthetics, Alma Tadema is brother to Piero della Francesca and why neither belongs to the family of artists that gives us reality and not appearance. At any rate, although, as I have said Plato's position in this matter is clear, Sir Herbert's is not.

What remains is something so simple and elementary that it hardly deserves the superstructure of turgid theory that has too often been imposed upon it. The mind of Ben Nicholson is a mind 'which has stored within it a full awareness of the proportions and harmonies inherent in all natural phenomena'. As I have already said, so had Piero's and there is no reason to believe that the skeleton is 'more real' than the man. It may be that one is interested in skeletons more than in men, but it is not an interest that has cosmic implications.

If, however, one is concerned with formal harmonies at their most naked (I will not say at their purest), then the artistic activity that will give scope to this narrowly delimited interest is the sort of activity that one engages in when one arranges the furniture of a room and hangs it and fixes the curtains. The analogy of architecture, as Sir Herbert says, is to the point, but, as he rightly comments, 'in this case there is a functional aspect which introduces a certain complication'. The same comment would rightly be made of furni-ture designing. Nearer still, perhaps, because here the functional interference is of the slightest, would be the designing of a front-door, the shape, size, proportions and relations of the panels, in relation to each other and to the knocker and the letter-box. The analogy of hanging and arranging a room, however, is perhaps the closest and purest analogy, and it serves also to emphasize the kind of aesthetic satisfaction that is in question.

It is indeed the satisfaction that comes from the perception of harmonious proportions and relationships. Yet here again it is worth observing that even this satisfaction, although it approaches the satisfactions of elegance and order and economy that a mathematician may find in his theorems, is sharply distinct from the satisfaction that attends the geometer's study of circles and squares and curves. For this study is, to repeat, purely intellectual, and circles and curves are objects of intelligence only. In the ordering of a room we are not at all considering the properties of curves of such and such a curvature; even here we are attentive to what the curves are the curves of, and it makes a difference whether they are the curves of a swag or of a table. For the pure curve is the object of pure intelligence; the curve that satisfies aesthetically is the visual curve, and the visual curve is the curve of something visual, seen or imagined. There is nothing peculiar about this; it cannot be other than what it is.

Of this nature, then, is the satisfaction afforded by good abstract art. Visual satisfaction of this kind is genuine and can be intense, and is its own justification, but as my analogies suggest it is doubtful whether it is a satisfaction from which we can elicit the cosmological or other metaphysical implications that Sir Herbert so persistently claims. The truth is that these implications do not emerge from any analysis; they are unconsciously introduced into the theory of abstract art according to an ideology. 'By *abstraction*,' writes Sir Herbert, 'we mean what is derived or disengaged from nature, the pure or essential form abstracted from the concrete details.'[1] The sentence is proffered as a description of current usage that has 'sufficient scientific validity'. In fact, as the occurrence of the adjectives 'pure' and 'essential' shows, it is nearer a moral judgement; at the very least the dice are already heavily loaded.

Of course, visual satisfactions are not arbitrary. On the whole, were six independent judges asked to grade a dozen of Nicholson's abstracts in order of excellence, their awards would be found approximately to tally. So too is it with food and wine; the connoisseurs tend to agree. Agreement such as this suggests indeed that there are some constants in the constitution of the human palate and guts, as there are in the constitution of the visual apparatus. But of metaphysical implications there are none.

[1] 'Realism and Abstraction in Modern Art', an essay in 'The Philosophy of Modern Art', 1952.

My analogy of the satisfactions of the palate is not a flippant one. Indeed were we to proceed to ask why it is that we experience as much pleasure as we do from the contemplation of balance and proportion in the disposition of masses, of relations of verticals and horizontals, of the curved line and the straight, of colours and of tones, the account of the matter that most commends itself to my own reflexion on the experience is substantially the restricted application of a form of the theory of empathy which, in 1914, Geoffrey Scott outlined in 'The Architecture of Humanism'. Its basis, the underlying mechanism of these pleasures, is physical function and muscular activity. It is not that physical states enter into visual satisfaction, which is primarily a pleasure of mind, but that physical states, or the suggestion of them, are a necessary pre-condition of visual satisfaction of this kind. So, for example, 'any emphasis upon vertical lines immediately awakens in us a sense of upward direction, and lines which are spread–horizontal lines–convey suggestions of rest'.[1] Consciousness of serenity, of restless-ness, of weight, of density–all these are elements of the satisfaction that we have from abstract art, and all of them, I think, ultimately derive from the ordinary physical functions, movement and the ability to stand, and so on, of the human body.

The humanist instinct [to quote Geoffrey Scott once more] looks into the world for physical conditions that are related to our own, for move-ments which are like those we enjoy, for resistances that resemble those that can support us, for a setting where we should be neither lost nor thwarted. It looks, therefore, for certain masses, lines, and spaces, tends to create them and recognise their fitness when created. And, by our instinctive imitation of what we see, their seeming fitness becomes our real delight.

It is not to my purpose to develop this or any theory, still less to demonstrate if it were susceptible of demonstration. It is a reason-able account of the matter which certainly cannot be refuted, and serves well to emphasize what are the springs of the real, although modest, pleasures that abstract art affords: straightforward visual satisfactions, rooted indeed in humanity but with no mystical or cosmic overtones. You will look in vain for metaphysical revela-tions of the structure of reality from Ben Nicholson.

As a way of looking at the world, a 'vision', if this claim is to be

[1] Geoffrey Scott, 'The Architecture of Humanism', Ch.VIII ('Humanist Values').

allowed, abstract art is remarkable for what it overlooks. Any artist's way of looking at the world is inevitably selective. But, as I have commented earlier, all great artists of the past have used knowledge of the hard and mathematical structure of the world to say other things about it; their awareness, in other words, has included the abstract 'vision' and embraced a multitude of other aspects of the world as well. So far indeed is the abstract artist's apprehension from being a 'full' one, as Sir Herbert makes out, that it is (and also by definition) the most narrowly restrictive in history.

There are genuine enjoyments to be had from abstract painting such as that of Nicholson, and they need no ulterior, no non-visual justification; they are their own justification. But to make for them mystical claims that scrutiny explodes is to do the painter a disservice; for it is to falsify and to erode the very satisfaction that he has it in him to give.

Abstract art is even justified, according to some critics, as a fruit of the spiritual life. Concluding a discussion of Ben Nicholson, in which he had declared that 'the only possible re-presentation of an abstract painting in words must be either poetry or metaphysics' and in which he had reasserted the customary theme of the potential hindrance to painting from the side of representation, Mr. Anthony Bertram wrote that when once the point is taken that representation is only a dispensable aid to painting 'Nicholson's work then becomes crystal clear, for its peculiar genius is of a white purity and most tender and sensitive simplicity. It is the simplicity, not of the simpleton, but of the man who has learnt what is unnecessary and has thrown away the clutter: it is the simplicity of the saint.'[1] But simplicity is an essential attribute of sanctity, the perfection and the goal of human life, in an obvious sense in which it is not obvious that representation is as easily dispensed with, in the interest of the perfection and the goal of painting, as clutter. In fact, as I have argued earlier, the 'clutter' of, say, Fra Angelico and Michelangelo is as integral to the forms that they created as it is to our response to them. Nor is it irrelevant to add that to discard clutter, in Mr. Bertram's sense, is not only to discard worlds of experience and the only material an artist has to work with; it is also to sacrifice what would appear to be an essential condition of great art. For such an art is inseparable, in

[1] 'A Century of British Painting, 1851–1951', 1951, p. 99.

its genesis, from mastery of *prima facie* recalcitrant material, 'material', as Mr. Wyndham Lewis wrote in another context, *'in struggle against which* the greatest things in the world have been constructed'.[1] There is no canonizable sacrifice or simplicity for a saint that stops short of coming to grips with a refractory self; nor is there for an artist short of coming to grips with a refractory visible material.

Were abstract artists and their advocates content to allow that abstract art is an expression in the simplest terms of balance and proportion and the other elements I mentioned just now, from the contemplation of which pleasure is to be derived, the incomprehension and the hostility which is so often provoked by this art would be dissipated. But whether from an anti-humanist repugnance for the natural world, or from an unconscious apprehension that if this apparently esoteric art were admitted to be derived from so simple a source it might cause it to be discounted, the fact is that the advocates of abstract art consistently claim for it a metaphysical or mystical basis. 'To treat Nicholson's work as purely decorative, a mere sensuous pleasure to the eye . . . is also an insult to the painter or a confession of failure on the part of the critic.'[2] Kandinsky entitled his book on abstract painting 'The Spiritual in Art'. E. H. Ramsden – on other occasions an illuminating critic – was content to begin, and to end, an article on the subject of this study with the words 'Ben Nicholson is a Constructivist. He comes from both sides of the Tweed.'[3] As the subject was an abstract artist, this was accepted as part of the inevitable accompaniment of mystification. Imagine, however, what her readers would have thought had she begun, and ended, an article on the father with the words 'William Nicholson was a Realist. He came from both sides of the Trent.' Ben Nicholson, it seems to me, lends himself to the process of mystification when he subtitles *Fra Angelico*[4] a still-life of 1945 representing a jug, a bottle, and two wine-glasses.

Were the spectator not mystified or provoked, when abstract art is in question, by cosmic or metaphysical claims, he would have little difficulty in discerning the good qualities in the best, in that of Nicholson in particular. Once his painting is seen as a series of essays

[1] 'The Art of Being Ruled', p. 390.   [2] Anthony Bertram, loc. cit.
[3] 'Ben Nicholson: Constructivist'. 'The Studio', December 1945.
[4] Coll. the Artist. Reproduced plate 145 in 'Ben Nicholson: paintings, reliefs, drawings'.

in the serenely harmonious arrangement of rectangles and circles, calculated with a beautiful precision, exquisite in finish, and coolly elegant in style, and its appeal as not esoteric but addressed to the universal delight in such relations between forms, a delight of which not only painters, sculptors, architects, but craftsmen and designers as well are inevitably aware, there would be no difficulty and no resistance. A visit to an exhibition of abstracts by Nicholson affords something of the same kind of pleasure as a visit to a well-designed yacht: about both there is the same exhilarating sense of things being streamlined, well made, light and fresh.

Very many of his compositions are based upon the simple principle of securing equilibrium by the balancing of a larger, simpler, more lightly coloured rectangle, or complex of rectangles, by a smaller but richer and more complicated unit. This simple principle is employed with much subtlety and variety, but careful scrutiny of the artist's work will reveal the invariable importance of the part it plays. This delicate equilibrium is sometimes achieved by the very simplest means. During the 'thirties and 'forties, renouncing the aid of colour, he constructed his static harmonies by excavating shallow reliefs out of wooden or synthetic boards, which he covered with an even coating of unrelieved white. These Paul Nash hailed as 'the discovery of something like a new world'.[1] But Nicholson's procedure involved, surely, the ultimate step in the renunciation of an old world rather than the discovery of a new. These snow-white harmonies, of which a good example is *White Relief 1935*[2] (Plate 59), calculated to a hair's breadth, represent more completely than any of his other works the ultimate exercise of his 'power to deny, discard and eliminate'. They represent, too, I think, the farthest limits to which Abstraction has effectively been pushed. In these white panels Nicholson has probably extracted the fullest possibilities from an art narrowed to the point of extinction by successive renunciations.

Ben Nicholson has often been derisively contrasted with his father, sometimes as a pioneer who moves in regions undreamed of by his father, sometimes as a cranky prodigal son. But in fact how much there is in common between the work of father and son. Neither belongs in any radical sense to the race of pioneers; each accepted a mode of expression current in his day, and each used his dexterity, his

[1] Op. cit.   [2] The Tate Gallery, London.

pertinacity, but above all an almost impeccable taste, to bring it to a dandyish perfection. Indeed there is one part of the father's work that directly affected the son. The posters which with his brother-in-law James Pryde the father designed under the pseudonym of the Beggar-staffs, with their large yet precisely calculated areas of audaciously empty space, impressed Ben Nicholson at an early age, and may well have implanted in him the idea from which his own art of mono-chrome areas was to grow. Nicholson is fully aware of what he owes to inheritance and early environment. He believes that, as he once put it, something fierce and northern in his mother's temperament counteracted in some degree the effect of his father's sophistication.

I referred earlier, in contrasting the temperament of Nicholson with that of Mondriaan, to its being instinctive rather than intellec-tual. Nothing could be more misleading than to represent Nicholson as doctrinaire, or indeed subject to any rigid principles. On several occasions I have heard him express resentment at the suggestion that he paints in accord with theories. 'It's nonsense,' he says, 'and all dogma, in any case, is harmful.' I am convinced that the delight he takes in the creation of abstract forms arises from an inner necessity. But Nicholson is not a pioneer, but a man of skill and taste who has brought to a peculiar degree of perfection a form of abstract painting already extensively practised before he became a painter. His is not an art based upon a particular theory; it is the product of a tempera-ment stimulated and shaped by the abstract movement widely diffused in Europe and America during his formative years. Ben Nicholson is not an innovator, still less a revolutionary, but the most accomplished living practitioner of a new academism. A movement so shallow in its underlying philosophy is unlikely to have a long life, but the best of Nicholson's works will surely survive the ebb of the abstract tide.

There is a circumstance – largely of abstract artists' making – which opposes an easy relation between abstract art and the public. While they are apt to belittle the 'easel picture' as an obsolete 'bourgeois' conception, they continue to paint 'easel pictures' themselves, and to title, frame and display them in the traditional fashion. They thereby challenge comparison with 'easel pictures' which represent, directly or imaginatively, the world of our actual experience. No system of 'purified constructive elements' setting up 'pure relations' is able, in the long run, to engross and exhilarate as a work of art which represents a profound view of man's experience of the world. To title an arrangement of 'purified constructive elements' *Woman* or *Fra Angelico*, as though they recognizably represented a woman or a painter-priest, cannot but sharpen the detached spectator's sense of the inadequacies in abstract art.

Had abstract painters refrained from challenging the 'easel picture' and directed their efforts towards decoration, their work would have exercised a stronger appeal and would have avoided confusing and alienating comparisons. This is a sphere in which abstract painting is accepted without question, just as the abstract character of the architecture which it embellishes is accepted. The effect of abstract forms, serene or dynamic, painted on walls, on screens, on surfaces which serve as backgrounds rather than as objects for scrutiny, would be to dignify and animate the act of living, just as fine architecture does. Abstract art is not a precise means of communication, and it is the pretence that it is that has perverted and strained a mode of expression which might serve an invaluable purpose. The sharp, singing colour, the precise and subtle sense of relations between forms, and the freshness that mark Ben Nicholson at his happiest–what a serenely exhilarating life they could bring, for instance, to the walls of a room of small or moderate size! The least susceptible would not be insensitive to its radiant influence–and there would be no need for esoteric explanation or defence. For one reason and another it is expected to-day that art should be an expression of an individual, and neither artist nor public is willing that it should take its place as part of the background of living. Once the musician was content that his music, emanating from some hidden source, should enchant without holding all attention; to-day he insists upon applause at brief intervals, which upon the slenderest pretext he must acknowledge with a personal appearance. If the art of painter and sculptor, and in particular the abstract painter and sculptor, were enabled to exercise its influence upon the passer-by, catching him, as it were, off his guard and only half-consciously absorbed, that influence would be deeper and more pervasive than it is in this day of the 'private view' and the 'personal appearance'. Ben Nicholson's painting should be seen as Handel's 'Water Music' was first heard, by a crowd of people pursuing their ordinary avocations.

WILLIAM ROBERTS

b. 1895

PAINTERS differ widely in the degree of their versatility; they differ, too, in the variety of their development. Of great versatility examples abound. There were few activities, creative, speculative or scientific, in which Leonardo da Vinci did not at one time or another engage. In Alfred Stevens we have an English artist able to design a railway train and to paint a miniature, to decorate the walls of a palace, to carry out a huge equestrian sculpture and to design for industry. Among the painters who are the subjects of these studies are those who show a versatility, modest certainly in its range compared with that of Leonardo or Stevens but nevertheless impressive. Wyndham Lewis, for example, who as a satirist and a philosopher has shown qualities that posterity may consider attributes of genius; and Duncan Grant, who has designed costumes and scenery for the theatre and decorated walls, furniture, textiles, pottery and much else.

It is not less easy to point to artists whose work, in the course of their lives, has undergone radical change. It would be difficult for someone ignorant of Turner to recognize one of the elegant, conventional topographical water-colours of his youth, one of the grandiose canvasses painted in his middle years, in rivalry with Claude or some other master, and one of the chromatic fantasies of his last years as works by the same hand. The growth of the art of Corot and of Van Gogh–to name two at random–offer examples of contrasts equally striking.

There exist, however, artists of a different kind, who are not versatile and whose work changes little: artists who early in their lives discover a single, exclusive preoccupation. Constable's painting became looser and more emphatic as the years passed, but the subject and the aim did not change. Chardin's consistency of aim and method is more obvious still. It was noted in the first volume of these studies, that by the middle nineteen-twenties, not long after his delayed beginning as a painter, Matthew Smith had found the essentials of his style, which has altered insignificantly since; that he had found, too, the subjects which have engrossed him for the remainder of his life. Allusion has also been made in the present volume to the extraordinary consistency of the imagination of Stanley Spencer. But there are painters far less versatile and changeful than these two. Ben Nicholson's themes have been few and his treatment of them has varied little. But beside Roberts even the puritanical and rigid figure of Nicholson appears dissipated and capricious. Early in life Roberts discovered the narrow range of subjects he wished to represent, and precisely how he wished to represent them, and to these discoveries he has remained grimly faithful.

William Patrick Roberts was born in Hackney, London, on 5 June 1895, the third child of Edward Roberts, a carpenter, and his wife Emma, born Collins, both Londoners. When William Roberts was about twelve or thirteen years old he wanted to be a painter. His father, whose love of his own craft led him to sympathize with his son's wish to follow another craft, made him an easel and a drawing board. Thus equipped he drew constantly, 'thinking', he once told me, 'of nothing but drawing'. He attended a local school, which he left at the age of fourteen to be apprenticed for seven years to Sir Joseph Cawston, the printers and law stationers. He looked forward to designing posters, but at first he was allowed to assist only in the mixing of colours. Later he had some pleasure in making compositions and designs for poster advertising projects, but he showed no aptitude for lettering. Opportunities to participate in such projects were rare, however, for his principal occupations were preparing the workmen's lunches, buying cakes for their teas and the like. On the advice of the art mistress of a local school he attended classes after working hours at the St. Martin's School of Art in 1909, then in Endell Street, Drury Lane. Here he won a London County Council scholarship that enabled him to go to the Slade, and he was released after serving only one year of his apprenticeship. (It must be noted that this account of his boyhood, which was given to me orally by the artist and written down by me at the time, may need correction in the light of his subsequent disclaiming of it. In a pamphlet entitled 'A Reply to my Biographer Sir John Rothenstein' (1957) he records that his introduction to St. Martins he owed to W. P. Robins, the etcher, who was teaching there, and he repudiates having had anything to do with the workmen's lunches and denies that the artists who worked there were properly called workmen.)

At the Slade–where he remained from 1910 until 1913–his mind opened out and his powerful draughtsmanship was recognized. In the Print Room at the British Museum where he spent much time he met Laurence Binyon, its benevolent and scholarly Keeper, who introduced him to Fry. After the Post-Impressionist exhibitions the curiosity about Fry's ideas and contemporary developments in French painting which prevailed among the students of the Slade was enhanced by the hostility towards them shown by Tonks. Roberts had visited these notorious exhibitions–Cubist works were included in the second of them–and his introduction to Fry led to his working, part-time, at the Omega Workshops, where he designed and decorated boxes, paper-knives and other knick-knacks. It was Fry who drew Roberts in a general way within the orbit of the Post-Impressionist movement, but he affected him in no more specific fashion. After he left the Omega 'I was no longer interested,' he told me, 'in the work of anyone who worked there.' There was one artist, however, who like himself had a brief experience of the Omega and whose work, even before he met him, took a powerful hold upon his imagination. This was Wyndham Lewis. His impact upon Roberts was heavy but beneficial. The effect upon a temperament different from Roberts's of association with the dynamically didactic leader of Vorticism and editor of 'Blast' might have been stultifying, but although its immediate consequence for Roberts was the production of paintings and drawings easily mistaken for those of Lewis, it revealed to Roberts the nature of his talents and set him on the road on which he has travelled to this day. In all essentials his art is identical with the art which he then evolved as soon as he ceased to be a mere imitator of Lewis. On several occasions Lewis claimed, with regard to T. E. Hulme, that 'what he said should be done, I did'. According to Roberts he only once met Hulme, and it is unlikely in any case that Roberts, who has shown little inclination for intellectual discussion and indeed little interest in the operations of the intellect, should have been directly affected by Hulme's theories. Nevertheless Roberts might have claimed, with no less justification than Lewis, that he did what Hulme said should be done. In place of the naturalistic art of the nineteenth century Hulme advocated an art 'where everything tends to be angular, where curves tend to be hard and geometrical, where the presentation of the human body . . . is often entirely non-vital, and distorted to fit into stiff lines and cubical shapes . . .'[1] and which 'exhibits no delight in nature and no striving after vitality. Its forms are always what can be described as stiff and lifeless.'[2] This might serve as a description of the painting of Roberts. To complete it not much need be added except a few words about his subjects.

If theories from the mouth of a philosopher meant little to Roberts, the same theories, reinforced by the capable and aggressive practice of a brother artist, his leader and mentor, were another matter. We may take it that Hulme's theories, developed and illustrated by Lewis, provided both the point of departure and continuing inspiration for the art of Roberts. The effect of the two-fold influence of Hulme and Lewis was constructive and enhancing because it was the seed that fell on good soil. Often an influence is a tyranny which distorts by its power or bemuses by its charm, and its subject cannot become himself until he frees himself from his subservience. But Hulme's and Lewis's influence was not a tyranny but an illumination that revealed to young Roberts, who was temperamentally tough, rigid, unsubtle, sardonic, joyless and unresponsive, precisely how tough, rigid, unsubtle, sardonic and joyless he was and taught him how to make out of a rather charmless combination of qualities a remarkable art. Above all it taught him to disregard the profusion, the growth, the movement, the distorting atmosphere, the deceptive surface, in fact, all that vast variety and changefulness of the world of nature which to a Constable or a Monet was the whole of reality, and to endeavour not to imitate or to interpret nature but to create forms based upon a narrow range of carefully selected natural shapes and to endow them through his art with a clarity and a rhythmic harmony entirely classical, and to make colour neither descriptive nor functional but decorative. Such, in oversimplified terms, was the ideal which Roberts owed to Hulme and to Lewis. No other subject of these studies has been so steadfastly loyal to his original ideals. At times when the air has been full of talk about the New Classicism his work has received favourable attention; at

[1] 'Speculations', p. 82.   [2] Ibid., p. 85.

other times–never more markedly than to-day–it has suffered neglect, but Roberts has not altered his course.

The subject of the greater number of his pictures is cockney life. But his cockneys–bicycling, picnicking and so forth with their racy gestures and grimaces–are the material for an art that is in its essence formal. His compositions derive often from those of the tougher Florentines, and in spirit as well as form he has put more than one critic in mind of Pollaiuolo. These often very elaborate but beautifully lucid compositions are worked out–'engineered' was the apt description applied by one writer to the process–with the utmost deliberation and completeness. Human beings, the subjects of almost all his works, are represented by animated figures of an unmistakable character: studiedly clumsy, tubular-limbed, fish-mouthed, staring-eyed puppets, stuffed with something heavier than sawdust–lead-shot perhaps–which makes their movements ponderous and ineffective. They grin with a mirthless, even on occasion a brutal humour. But their movements are ponderous and ineffective only if we think of them as made in response to the emotions of individual human beings; as soon as we understand them simply as contributions to the harmony of the group as a whole, they become dignified and at moments even noble. These groups of precisely related grimacing tubular-limbed puppets perform their ponderous motions in a space that is without atmosphere and almost a void. Not, however, a space without limits, for there is usually a background, explicit or implicit, which prevents these puppets straying, like a Watteau shepherdess, away from the foreground and keeps them prisoners, pressed, almost, up against the surface of the picture. The contrast between the coarse or even brutal figures and the classical and scholarly way in which they are combined is matched by the contrast between their character and their delicate combination of colouring: the black, petunia-pink, sharp acid green, and pale, chalky-blue are entirely his own.

A person reading these pages who happened to be unacquainted with the work of Roberts might wonder at finding him included in a small company chosen for seeming to the writer 'to have distilled to its finest essence the response of our times to the world which the eye sees–both the outward and the inward eye'. For the artist's work emerges from this study as representations of puppets neither noble nor endearing but rather absurd in their brutality and mirthlessness as they move clumsily within the narrow parallel between a back curtain and the picture surface. It is indeed an art which in the bleakness of its total masculinity cannot be said to fulfil the ultimate Berensonian criterion of enhancing life. Yet to ignore Roberts would leave a gap in the tapestry which, with whatever want of skill, I am attempting to weave. Speaking of Picasso Mr. Berenson once said to me: 'He never remains long enough in one posture for me to form an opinion about him.' Roberts, on the contrary, ever since he freed himself from the imitation of the superficial aspects of the art of Wyndham Lewis, has maintained his posture virtually unaltered. I can sympathize with those who find it an unattractive posture, but for me his faith, at once intense and obstinate, in the particular angle from which he squints at the life about him, has enabled him to create figures which live in the memory with an all but unique persistence. I would instance such paintings as *Jockeys*,[1] of *c*. 1933, *Les Routiers*,[2] of 1933, *Masks*,[3] of 1935 (Plate 60), *He Knew Degas*[4] (an amusing portrait of Sickert), of 1939, *Bicycle Boys*,[5] of 1939. In an age ridden by fashion and enervated by *angst* the creations of Roberts are firm-knit by a conviction which takes no account of critics, public, or even patrons. I can imagine a man once familiar with the London art-world of the middle decades of this century, looking back at it after many years of distant exile, one memory after another having faded away, able to recall at last only three massive figures dressed in pink, bright green and prussian blue, riding their bicycles alone on the sands of Time, the creations of William Roberts.

[1] The Cartwright Memorial Hall, Bradford.
[2] The City Art Gallery, Belfast.   [3] Coll. Count Vanden Heuvel.
[4] Coll. Mr. Ernest Cooper.   [5] Coll. Mr. Ernest Cooper.

DAVID JONES

b. 1895

IT is not often that a chronicler has the good fortune to see something of a painter's beginnings, especially if the painter happens
to be his senior. But by an odd chance I had such an opportunity
in respect of the subject of these lines.

In the summer of 1926 I stayed for a week or two with Eric Gill
at Capel-y-ffin, the house in the Black Mountains of South Wales
where he had settled a few years before to escape the distracting
involvements that had been a consequence of the widespread interest
attracted by the Guild of St. Joseph and St. Dominic and St.
Dominic's Press, which he founded at Ditchling in Sussex. A few
moments after my arrival there came into the sitting-room a small
man who, though I now know that he was thirty-one, looked not
more than twenty-four. 'Well goodbye, Eric,' he said, 'I'm going
now.' In my mind's eye I can still see the two of them shaking hands.
Eric Gill keen-glancing, energetic in gesture, his pedantic aggressiveness softened by a frank and unassuming smile, and wearing his
black biretta, rough black cassock gathered in at the waist, black
stockings cross-gartered and sandals. David Jones: pale face surmounted by a thick ingenuous fringe; languid figure, speaking of a
pervasive quiet. I have said that he looked younger than his years,
and this was so save in one respect: his flesh was of that delicate,
tired texture generally found in old age. The dark eyes, large and
mild, had in their depths a little touch of fanaticism quite absent, for
all his aggressiveness, from Gill's. His clothes were anonymous. The
contrast between the two men was not more apparent than the
friendly understanding between them. David Jones and I were introduced, shook hands (his grip was soft and shyly friendly), and he
went. 'Who was that?' I asked, 'one of your apprentices?' (Gill
usually had several such in his workshops.) 'That was David Jones.
He's been learning carpentry, but he's not much good at it. But he's
a jolly good artist: a lot will be heard of him before long. Look at
this,' he said, pointing to a big water-colour lying on a table

representing two horses on a hillside, 'he's just finished it.' Imperceptive of its qualities I gave it, nevertheless, so long and hard a look as to imprint it on my memory. 'It's done from this window,' Gill explained. I walked up to it and peered out, but I could see nothing except mist lashed by driving rain. The outline of a big hill, when adumbrated by Gill, was just perceptible. It was many years before I saw David Jones or the drawing again, and the drawing must have impressed me more than it seemed to at the time, because I remembered it so clearly. The drawing was *Hill Pastures–Capel-y-ffin*.[1]

         o   *o*   *o*

According to Eric Gill *Hill Pastures–Capel-y-ffin* was the best of a group of mountain landscapes made in 1926 and the previous year. These drawings may be regarded as marking David Jones's point of departure as a mature artist. But they may also be regarded as marking the culmination of an apprenticeship interrupted by war and unduly prolonged. He was backward, he has told us, at any kind of lesson, and, though he had no enthusiasms other than drawing, the few early examples of his work which survive offer no indications of exceptional talent. The active sympathy of his parents, who afforded his inclination every encouragement within their power, led to no early flowering. He possessed, however, the most precious gift of perseverance, which sustained him until he could see his way clear. But that was many years ahead. His mother was able to help him not only by sympathy but by example: as a young woman she had made drawings in the tradition of the Victorian drawing-masters, and one of his earliest recollections is of looking at three of her crayon drawings, one of Tintern Abbey, another of a donkey's head, and a third of a gladiator with curly hair. His father, too, had a positive contribution to make to his formation as an artist, for another of his childhood memories is of his father's singing Welsh songs, 'Mae hen wlad fy nhadau' and 'Ar hyd y nos', and his telling him of the three hills of his birth-place, Foel-y-Crio, Moel Famau, and Moel Ffagnallt, and he has nurtured carefully the sense, first implanted in him by his father, of belonging to the Welsh people. On account of his father's calling he was brought up in a home that took the printed page and its illustration for granted.

[1] Coll. Miss Helen Sutherland.

David Jones was born on 1 November 1895 at Brockley in Kent, the third child of James Jones and his wife Alice Ann, daughter of Ebenezer Bradshaw. James Jones, a printer's manager, was a native of Holywell, North Wales, and a son of John Jones, master-plasterer, who came of farming stock long settled in Ysceifiog below the Clwydian Hills. Resident in London since about 1883, James Jones was on the staff of the Christian Herald Publishing Company, and had worked previously on 'The Flintshire Observer'. David Jones's mother came of an English family of Thames-side ship-builders, and her father was a mast and block maker, of Rother-hithe; she was of Italian extraction on her mother's side. The presence of craftsmen among his immediate forebears on both sides of his family counted for much in the formation of his talent, for, as Mr. Ironside has noted in his discerning appreciation,

> It has been a special object with him that his pictures should be not only the mirror of his imagination or the translation of his sensuous impressions, but should also be things valuable for the very manner of their fashioning.[1]

If it was from his mother's side that he principally inherited the disposition to translate his conceptions naturally into a form both tangible and precious, it was from his father's that he inherited the poetic outlook that has played so predominant a part both in his painting and his writing, above all that peculiarly Welsh time-sense which naturally relates the present with the remote and makes the possessors of it in a special degree the heirs of legend. It is not so much that David Jones has a vivid apprehension of the remote past; of its intimate links with and relevance for the present he has a no less vivid awareness. An illuminating example of the working in him of this special time-sense appears at the beginning of a broadcast talk[2] of autobiographical character that he gave in 1954.

> About eight hundred years ago [he said, as another might say before the First World War] a prince of Aberffraw defeated his Welsh and English enemies at Coleshill between Flint Sands and Halkin Mountain.
> Holywell, where my father, James Jones, was born, is about three miles north-west of the battle-site. The birth of a son to John Jones, plastrwr, Treffynnon, in 1860 would indeed seem a matter having no apparent connection with the battle won by the great Owain Gwynedd

[1] 'David Jones', by Robin Ironside. Penguin Modern Painters, 1949.
[2] 29 October.

in 1149. But however unapparent, the connection is real enough; for that victory symbolised the recovery of a tract of Britain that had been in English possession for well over three centuries. Had that twelfth-century recovery not occurred the area around Holywell would have remained within the Mercian zone of influence. In which case its inhabitants would, centuries since, have become wholly English in tradition, nomenclature and feeling. Had local history taken that course, it follows that I should not now be speaking to you at the invitation of the Welsh B.B.C., as an artist of Welsh affinities. You see by what close shaves some of us are what we are, and you see how accidents of long past history can be of importance to us in the most intimate sense, and can determine integral things about us.

He has chosen to identify himself with one of the smallest of European peoples, yet he exemplifies the truth of the saying that only through being local can something become universal. Through his happy acceptance of his Welsh ancestry and his London ante-cedents and all that these involve of the insular and even the pro-vincial, his imagination reaches out to encompass a vast range of European consciousness But this disposition thus to reach out was roused and continuously nourished by an event which had nothing to do with this pre-history.

David Jones tells us that he was slow in learning to read, 'finding his letters difficult at the age of nine and later, but that he made good this lack on more than one occasion by paying his sister a penny to read to him'.[1] 'In drawing,' the same writer continues, 'he was certainly no laggard.' No laggard in that he applied himself assiduously to his chosen pursuit (chosen largely, he says, 'as a counterweight to my deficiency in all else'),[2] but he remained for years a wanderer unsure what path to follow. A few of his very early drawings survive. One of these—not the earliest, but the first he positively remembers making—of a *Dancing Bear*[3] seen in the street at Brockley was of 1902, when he was seven. Here pity for the great muzzled captive, led to prance for pennies in the gutter, is un-erringly conveyed. Here, too, are clear intimations of his mature

[1] John Petts. Introduction to the catalogue of an exhibition of paintings, drawings and engravings by David Jones, arranged by the Welsh Committee of The Arts Council, 1954. [2] This, and unless otherwise indicated, all other quotations in the text are taken from manuscript autobiographical notes written by the artist at the suggestion of Mr. H. S. Ede, by whom copies have been presented to the Library of the Tate Gallery.   [3] Coll. the Artist.

way of drawing, the modelling with touches which at first glance seem weak and almost irrelevant, but which, on scrutiny, are seen to be so purposeful; there are intimations, too, in the character of the pencil strokes themselves. Yet in quality this beautiful drawing (which with a number of his other early animal drawings was exhibited at the Royal Drawing Society) would not appear to be typical of his early work. This was confined to animals: lions, tigers, wolves, bears, cats, deer, mostly in conflict. 'Only the very earliest of these,' he says, 'show any sensitivity, or have any interest, whatsoever.'

The untempted integrity of childhood quickly gave way to the vulgarizing influence of the illustrations to boys' magazines, old Royal Academy catalogues, and 'the general dead weight of outside opinion'. In imitation of what he found in such publications he made many drawings of mediaeval Welshmen with wolf-hounds on mountains, Russians surrounded by wolves in snow-storms and the like. A photograph of a drawing, *Wolf in The Snow*, of 1900, which may be said to fall within this group, survives. It is without merit.

Many students leave their art schools without learning anything from the instruction provided. What they learn they learn from the example of artists whose work they revere, or from fellow-students. The teaching at the Slade, I fancy, played a negligible part in the formation of Ben Nicholson. Of David Jones the contrary is true. At Camberwell Art School (which he attended from 1909 to 1915) he was promptly rescued from the disintegrating effects of 'the dead weight of outside opinion' manifest in the illustrations which, ignorant of better, he had taken as his models. The effect of the instruction of A. S. Hartrick, Reginald Savage and Herbert Cole was to rekindle the lights of childhood. Through Hartrick, who had known Gauguin and Van Gogh, he was first made aware of the modern movement in French painting, and through Savage of the Pre-Raphaelites and the great Victorian illustrators, Pinwell, Sandys and Beardsley. The sudden widening of horizon that he owed to these enlightened teachers enriched without clarifying his imagination; his sense of vocation was enhanced; yet it remained without particular object. The beginning of the First World War found him vacillating between alternative ambitions to become an illustrator of historical subjects, preferably Welsh, and a painter of animals. It found him, too, he has told us, 'completely muddle-headed as to the function of the arts in general'. On 2 January 1915 he enlisted in London in The Royal Welch Fusiliers, serving with them as a private soldier on the Western Front from December 1915 until March 1918, being demobilized at the end of that year. The terrible ordeal of prolonged trench warfare brought forth no immediate expression. None of the many sketches that he made in trench and billet have any interest as drawings, he says, and little as records, being feeble impressionistic sketches. . . . 'They are without any sense of form and they display no imagination. . . . But the War landscape–the "Wasteland" motif,' he adds, 'has remained with me, I think as a potent influence, to assert itself later.' It was just twenty years later that this and all the imaginative experience that he won from the ordeal asserted itself not, except in a very few instances, in drawings or engravings, but in a work of literature, 'In Paren-thesis', 'certainly a "golden bough",' as Mr. Ironside observes, 'to have cut from such a blasted wood'. This book and the later 'The Anathemata', of 1953, express even more explicitly than anything else he has made his ever pervasive sense of the intimacy between present and past, and between history and legend.

With many-hued threads he weaves all three into a delicately shimmering unity, ennobling the present, though without sup-pression of its meannesses, bringing history near and making legend actual. 'In Parenthesis' comprises a series of descriptions of scenes of regimental life in France, mostly in the trenches. It differs from other 'war books' in that the events and scenes which form its principal subject are enveloped in a diaphanous web of legend: the language of the trenches mingles with the language of many different kinds of legend and of many periods of history. Both the imagery and the language of this most literary of 'war books' are gathered from innumerable sources, from the Welsh heroes of Aneirin's sixth-century epic, from 'The Song of Roland', and from Malory, Milton, Coleridge, Joyce, Hopkins, Welsh Methodist hymn-books, 'The Golden Bough', but most often from 'the frozen regions of the Celtic underworld', from the Arthurian legend and from the Catholic liturgy. Characteristic of David Jones's interweaving of past and present is the closing image, in which the dead lie decorated with flowers, fruit and foliage, picked for them by the presiding spirit of the woods in which they fought their last battle:

The Queen of the Woods has cut bright boughs of various flowering.
    These knew her influential eyes. Her awarding hands can pluck for each their fragile prize.
    She speaks to them according to precedence. She knows what's due to this elect society. She can choose twelve gentle-men. She knows who is most lord between the high trees and on the open down.
    Some she gives white berries
            some she give brown
    Emile has a curious crown it's
            made of golden saxifrage.
    Fatty wears sweet-briar,
he will reign with her for a thousand years.
    For Balder she reaches high to fetch his.
    Ulrich smiles for his myrtle wand.
    That swine Lillywhite has daisies to his chain – you'd hardly credit it.
    She plaits torques of equal splendour for Mr. Jenkins and Billy Crower.
    Hansel with Gronwy share dog-violets for a palm, where they lie in serious embrace beneath the twisted tripod.
    Siôn gets St. John's Wort–that's fair enough.
    Dai Great-coat, she can't find him anywhere–she calls both high and low, she had a very special one for him.

The mass of imagery gathered from so many sources for the construction of 'In Parenthesis', however obscurely it may glimmer on first acquaintance, is in fact presented in the framework of a rational and clearly apprehended world order. Of the existence of such a framework, however, at the time of his experience of the Western Front, David Jones had no faintest intimation.

After demobilization in 1919 he resumed his art studies with the aid of a Government grant, this time at the Westminster School, of which Walter Bayes was the headmaster. The years in the army had sharpened his sense of vocation, and he went to Westminster eager to paint again.

It would have been singular if returning to his apprenticeship ardently but without settled convictions David Jones should not have been attracted by the illustrious figures of the School of Paris and by their transforming achievements. But in spite of all this attraction he has always, then as now, treated this School with a certain reserve

—a reserve in which attentive respect is untouched by submissiveness. Yet its effect on his formation is manifest. Without it he could hardly have evolved the freedom—whether to simplify or to complicate his subject—that is so consistent a feature of his mature style. He began to take an interest, too, in the ideas and the work of the English artists in which were manifest the movements theorized in Paris. Yet it was consistent with his acutely developed sense of the past that his deepest enthusiasms should have been reserved not for contemporaries but for ancestors: for two of the great figures in that mystical tradition in painting towards which he was groping his way: Blake and El Greco. The first appearance, in 1919, on the walls of the National Gallery, of El Greco's *Agony in the Garden* stirred him deeply.

Not less valuable than the quickening and deepening of his ideas about the ends of his art was the enhanced awareness, which he owed also to his years at Westminster, of the importance of ways and means. He is conscious of a particular debt to Walter Bayes for his insistence upon his students' need of acquiring the science of their profession—the same need was taught by Bernard Meninsky, whose life-class he attended.

The principal effect of these influences was vastly to intensify his spiritual and intellectual activity. He had come to Westminster, as he has told us, 'with an open mind', susceptible of influence, respectful of teaching. After a couple of years or so his mind, for so long cramped by the alternation of action and boredom in a soldier's life, had leapt into vigorous exercise, and he was placing himself and all his ends and means in the widest context. It was a mind no longer open, for it had already reached some conclusions about first causes.

Some years earlier, some time, he thinks, in 1917, and in the neighbourhood of Ypres, he found himself wondering about the Catholic tradition. On 7 September 1921 he was received into the Catholic Church. The effect of his religious experience and of the teachings of the Church, clarifying and deepening his thinking, has been to add strength and precision to the arts he practises by giving them the context of a world order of things. The insistence of the Church on the reality and goodness of matter and spirit, wedding form and content, the tradition that declares 'that in each particular the general should shine out and without the particular there can be no general for us men', he has told us, 'has been my sheet anchor in times of bewilderment–that is at all times'. In so saying he has no illusions about the contribution that systems of thought can make to creative art; indeed he is very much alive to the vanity of depending upon them for what they cannot give.

I don't of course mean that any amount of true philosophical or metaphysical definition will aid one whit, necessarily, the painting of a picture. Because the ability to paint a good picture does not come through philosophy or religion in any direct manner at all.

Such definitions could only have indeed a damaging effect on the making of things if thought of as providing some theory to work by– a substitute for imagination and direct creativeness; and would so sadly defeat their own object–which is, to protect the imagination from the slavery of false theory and to give the perfect law of liberty to our creativeness. To protect, in fact, what is natural to man.

I would say [he has written] that as affecting the arts in general, certain ideas implicit or explicit in Catholic Dogma, or anyway, ideas that come to me personally through the channel of the Catholic Church, have had a considerably liberating effect. Others, no doubt, receive them from other channels or discover them for themselves, perhaps; but for me, I must own my indebtedness to Her alone in this.

Of these ideas the most influential with him is, he tells us, one of the basic teachings of the Church.

I learned, I think, at least by analogy, from the doctrinal definition of the substantial Presence in the Sacramental Bread. Thenceforth a tree in a painting or a tree in an embroidery must not be a 're-presenting' only of a tree of sap and thrusting wood–it must really be 'a tree' under the species of paint, or needlework, or whatever. I know this analogy cannot in any way be pressed and is open to every sort of objection, but for me it has its uses and it will loosely serve.

An immediate consequence of his coming habitually to consider his ideas and activities in so wide a context was to diminish his confidence in the value of the instruction which an art school could impart. It was not that he grew critical of his teachers. On the contrary. Even now, more than thirty years after the conclusion of his professional education, he speaks of his teachers with lively gratitude, in particular of Hartrick, with whom he has not worked since 1914. The principal cause of his dissatisfaction with art schools was that the disappearance of the apprentice system involved the disappearance of a thorough art education based upon the continuity of a living tradition, and that the academies which supplanted the Guilds taught a dead tradition or else the idiosyncrasies of the teacher.

One day in 1922 he was taken by a fellow student at Westminster to visit Eric Gill at Ditchling. On their way back to London this fellow student remarked that he was relieved to get away from the shrine of arty-craftiness, to which David Jones answered that he, on the contrary, intended to return there and work with Gill. Not long afterwards he joined the Guild of St. Joseph and St. Dominic at Ditchling. Here he attempted to master the trade of carpentry under George Maxwell, and the use of the engraver's tools under Father Desmond Chute and Eric Gill. As a carpenter he was no use, but as an engraver, though he never reached Gill's precision and finish, he eventually learnt sufficient to enable him to make prints of unusual beauty. Here also he carried out, in 1923, a big wall-painting in oils *Cum Floribus et Palmis*. This is a conventional essay in the early Christian style, but it is lacking neither in tenderness nor in dignity.

The impulse which led David Jones to become Gill's apprentice was a prescient impulse, for what he learnt from Gill exceeded his utmost expectations. At the particular moment of their meeting what Eric Gill had to offer was precisely what David Jones stood most urgently in need of. When he came to Ditchling David Jones was meditating deeply on many things. He was now a Catholic who only vaguely apprehended how his faith could transform his life and his art; he was a student interested in current Parisian theorizing, particularly in the dogma of 'significant form', who was unable to place this theorizing in a setting sufficiently wide to enable him to use it. By his character and his experience Gill was peculiarly fitted to be his guide.

Of anybody I have ever known Eric Gill made the most determined attempt to 'put his religion', as the saying is, 'into practice'. This attempt went far beyond the regulation of his personal life according to the teachings of the Church: it sought to understand these teachings so clearly as to be able to see their bearing upon every problem of life, public no less than private, and, having understood, to act in obedience to them. It must be admitted that his determination to make the teachings of religion, down to the utmost that they implied, the very basis of life led him into some contradictions,

absurdities and even uncharities. David Jones was a man deeply, if
as yet vaguely, stirred by the religious spirit. The intimacy of a man
who attempted, with such singleness of purpose, and such courage,
the application of ancient truths to the refractory fabric of actual life,
was of a value to him beyond calculation. At this critical juncture
Gill was able, in particular, to give to David Jones the benefit of his
own lucid thinking about the arts.

In an article[1] on David Jones which appeared eight years after their
first meeting, Eric Gill writes of the temptation to which contemporary artists were subject of regarding the formal values of painting
– 'significant form' according to the current cliché – as alone possessing merit, and the subject, even in the widest sense, as an irrelevance.

> Such an exclusive insistence on form, [he contends] however useful it
> has been as an eye-opener, is as essentially heretical as a too exclusive
> insistence upon representative veracity, or upon utility, i.e. the value
> of a painting as doing something of service to its owner, for heresy in
> artistic thinking, as in other matters, is little more than a running amok
> after one statement of the truth to the exclusion of others. To David
> Jones [he continues] a painting is neither simply a representation, nor
> simply a painted pattern. . . . What concerns him is the universal thing
> showing through the particular thing, and as a painter it is this
> showing through that he endeavours to capture. . . . Nevertheless, in
> spite of this idealist attitude he never loses sight of the fact that it is a
> painting he is making . . . not merely an essay in Platonic research. My
> object [he says in conclusion] is . . . to make a clear statement of his
> point of view.

The point of view expressed in this article is in fact Gill's own.
It agrees, at all points, with that expressed in his other writings and
in his conversation.

During the years of their close association the older man stamped
the impress of his system of ideas upon the younger. Even this short
article, which is far from being even a summary of Gill's thought,
well expresses a number of the ideas of David Jones mentioned in
these pages. The relation, for instance, between the universal and the
particular. But there is no need to insist upon David Jones's intellectual
indebtedness to Gill, for he himself, always ready in his appreciation
of his teachers, has written that 'the clarifying ideas of Mr. Gill were
at that time, and for me, of very great value. The unity of all made

[1] 'David Jones', 'Artwork', Autumn 1930.

things became clearer.' The mind of David Jones was too original to be confined within another man's ideas; it has developed since his apprenticeship in directions unthought of by his master, but it is true, I think, to say that it has retained the framework derived from Gill. It may sound paradoxical, but I am inclined to think that this framework served David Jones better than it did Gill himself. By temperament Gill was an extremely tidy man, and the several arts and crafts he practised all reflected this extreme tidiness and made one over-conscious of their finish. It was reflected with equal clarity in his somewhat didactic thinking, and it made for rigidity and sometimes for false simplicity. Intellectual issues tended with him to resolve themselves too simply into blacks and whites. An excess of tidiness, material and intellectual, had the effect of giving to the man and his works a self-conscious consistency, in short a touch of smallness and pedantry.

Unlike Gill, David Jones is not naturally tidy: his innate tendency is to be diffuse, vague, delicately expansive. So it is that the same system of ideas that had a restrictive effect upon the innately over-tidy Gill provided for David Jones a firm, logical framework which gave form and direction to an art which, however lovely, wanted for both.

Towards the end of 1924 when Gill, unable any longer to bear the publicity which the Guild of St. Joseph and St. Dominic had attracted, withdrew from Ditchling to Capel-y-ffin, David Jones returned to London, where he continued to make engravings. The next year he followed Gill into the Vale of Ewyas, where he made, in water-colours or chalk, the group of drawings already mentioned of the hills round about. From Capel-y-ffin he paid two visits of some months each to the Benedictines of Caldey Island, off the Pembrokeshire coast, where he made drawings of a similar character of the sea and boats and the rocky coast, and was allowed the use of the scriptorium to work in. 'It was in the Vale of Ewyas and on Caldey Island that I began to have some idea of what I personally would ask a painting to be, and I think from 1926 onwards there has been a fairly recognizable direction in my work.' At this time he was occupied no less with engraving than with drawing.

In 1927 he left Wales and returned to Brockley to live with his parents, staying with them at intervals, too, in a bungalow at

Portslade near Hove, from the balcony of which he made paintings of the sea. It was at Portslade that he wrote down a few sentences that turned out to be the initial sentences of 'In Parenthesis'.

David Jones now entered upon the most prolific period of his life: 'I painted all the time; I never seemed to stop painting in those days. . . . It was during this period that I was most able to concentrate on getting towards what I wanted in painting.' The year of his returning home was chiefly occupied with engraving on wood ten illustrations for 'The Chester Play of the Deluge',[1] of which at least one, *The Dove*, will surely take a high place among the finest book illustrations in an age of finely illustrated books. This engraving proclaims the value to the artist of the faith he had found, and upon which he had meditated so deeply. Many illustrators have taken or been given momentous subjects on account of the pictorial possibilities they offer. Here is no exploitation of pictorial possibilities. For David Jones the compact ark, discovered just before sunrise riding the vast waste of the sea, and the old black tree, projecting above the waves, sending forth fresh shoots, all this proclaiming a world washed clean and a new beginning for mankind, are part of a truth which he accepts as valid. During 1927 he also found time to make drawings at the Zoo and occasional drawings from the life. It was in this year that he joined the Society of Wood-Engravers and held, at the St. George's Gallery,[2] his first exhibition, consisting of water-colours made in Wales and at Brockley and Portslade. The following year, too, was partly occupied with engraving, on copper, ten illustrations for 'The Rime of the Ancient Mariner'.[3] Whether because the subject was one which did not belong to his most intimate spiritual experience or because water-colour rather than engraving had become his chosen medium, it is evident that the later series possesses little of the imaginative force of the earlier. Take for instance no. *V* ('I closed my eyes'): could anything more feebly interpret the great poem than the boat-load of flimsy nudes, with archly-glancing almond eyes, posturing improbably? Yet Gill could write of it that 'Coleridge's poem has for the first time found adequate pictorial accompaniment.'[4] Were it not so widely admired

---

[1] The Golden Cockerell Press, 1927.
[2] In Grosvenor Street, not connected with the existing gallery of the same name.
[3] Published by Douglas Cleverdon, 1929.   [4] Loc. cit.

I would have disregarded this series, considering it as merely one failure in the most richly creative years of his life. It was towards the end of the decade that his water-colours assumed their unique character: they became larger in size, and the slightly naïve manner of their fashioning gave way to the evocative complex of fine, delicate, unemphatic lines and the fluid, opalescent colours from which shines out a light recognizable as that rare thing, something new. This is a time when a high value is set upon originality: indeed for some critics this quality is the measure of greatness. What is certain is that it is a quality a good deal rarer than is generally supposed. I propose to say nothing at this point about the stature of David Jones, but I do suggest that these large water-colours are among the most original creations in modern painting. A sharp eye and a clear view is needed to distinguish between the paintings of Picasso and Braque of the Cubist period, or between those of Matisse, Dufy and Vlaminck, say, of the Fauve period, but nobody in any circumstances could fail to recognize one of these larger water-colours by David Jones.

This fluid and diffusive art owes its intelligibility to its context in a known world order. In spite of the extreme intricacy of the artist's mind and his reticently zestful tendency towards elaboration, it is a comparatively straightforward art–an art far removed from subjectivity. Unlike most of his contemporaries who manufacture their own symbols for themselves, David Jones finds much of his in the public language and the public symbolism of the Catholic Church. Confident as he is in the truth of the Catholic scheme of things, he is equally confident in the validity of the central Christian signs, for example, of the sacramental signs of the Eucharist. Being sure, then, of the absolute validity of this central symbolism, he feels himself free to use it as a key symbolism with which to explore and illuminate human dreams and aspirations, as conveyed in ritual, legend and tradition. In the art of many other contemporaries which seems at first glance far simpler, it is difficult on scrutiny to make out why, except in purely sensuous terms, the artist has chosen to make the particular images he has. Many of David Jones's pictures, on the other hand, are at first sight extremely difficult to grasp in regard both to their form and to their meaning; yet on scrutiny there is to be found nothing arbitrary about the images that make them up.

The gentle, unemphatic style of his utterance springs from confidence in the logic of his symbols.

Much of what he did in the earlier part of this uniquely fruitful period of his life had little symbolic content. Landscape was what chiefly occupied him, 'the rambling, familiar, south-walled, small flower-beddedness of Piggotts' (the house in Buckinghamshire to which Eric Gill had moved); 'the north, serene clear silverness' of Rock, the house of Miss Helen Sutherland, a discerning patron, in Cumberland; back-gardens at Brockley, and the sea seen from window or veranda in Hove and Brighton–these, together with animals, flowers, still-life and an occasional portrait, were his principal subjects. For some obscure reason his rare portraits have not been rated quite as highly as they deserve. The *Eric Gill*,[1] of 1930, is an admirable likeness, and the far more elaborate portrait of Gill's daughter *Petra im Rosenhag*,[2] of 1931, shows her just as I remember her. The least successful of them is *Human Being*,[3] also of 1931, a too summary self-portrait in oils, a medium he seldom uses. In painting landscape he works when possible from a window. 'I like looking out on the world,' he says, 'from a reasonably sheltered position. I can't paint in the wind, and I like the indoors-outdoors contained yet limitless feeling of windows and doors. A man should be in a house; a beast should be in the field, and all that.'

Although less numerous than the landscapes his still-lifes express no less intimately the complex sensibility of the artist's outlook on the world. Like the landscapes, the still-lifes are set in a world in a state of flux, in which one object melts into another, in which, as Mr. Ironside has written,

> the various phenomena embrace one another in a kind of Franciscan sympathy, and the mind, the heart which creates it does so in a mood of Franciscan affection. Franciscan is a term to be applied, with peculiar justice, [the same writer perceptively continues] to the artist's graceful, nervous drawings of animals, to the deer naturally and also to the lynxes and the leopards which are presented to us as God's creatures and not at all as man's possible enemies, and though we see they have a dark side, it is not the darkness of rapacious instincts, but the portentous obscurity of some mythological role. . . .[4]

[1] Coll. the Artist. [2] Coll. Sir Kenneth Clark, K.C.B.
[3] Coll. Miss Helen Sutherland. [4] Op. cit.

The appearance, and in profusion, of manifestations of a sensibility and of an invention so extraordinary led to the growth of a loosely knit circle of fervent supporters of the artist, and to his work's coming to the notice of a considerable public. An exhibition of it was held at the Goupil Gallery, in 1929, consisting largely of water-colours made in the course of a visit to Salies de Béarn and Lourdes the year before; in 1930 at Heal's Mansard Gallery there was an exhibition of animal drawings, mostly made at the London Zoo; and from 1930 until 1933 he exhibited as a member of the Seven and Five Society.[1] From the Goupil exhibition *The Terrace*,[2] a water-colour of 1929, was purchased by the Contemporary Art Society.

This period of happy productivity was brought to a close by the first of a succession of attacks of illness. Whenever his health has permitted, he has continued to make drawings, and although since 1933 his output has been sporadic to this later, less propitious period belong several works in which his rare fusion of imagination and sensibility has found its fullest expression. I am thinking in particular of four water-colour drawings: *Guenever*,[3] of 1940, *The Four Queens*,[4] of 1941 (both illustrations to the Arthurian Legend), *Aphrodite in Aulis*,[5] also of 1941 (Plate 61), and *Vexilla Regis*,[6] of 1947 (Plate 62).

In two important respects these differ from the artist's earlier drawings. With certain exceptions–such, for instance, as *Merlin appears in the form of a young child to Arthur sleeping*,[7] of 1930–David Jones has looked at the now and the near under the inspiration of 'an affection for the intimate creatureliness of things . . . an apprecia-tion of the particular genius of places, men, trees, animals'. In certain of his drawings we are made only vaguely aware of his preoccupa-tion with history and legend, which is explicit, however, only in the title. A water-colour and gouache of the south of France, of 1928, is entitled *The Roman Land*,[8] and a small chapel in a landscape, of 1932, *The Chapel Perilous*.[9] The four later water-colour drawings are the fruits of the perceptions of his inner eye, and their subjects are explicitly legendary. And although the floating forms, as they merge

[1] See note at end of chapter.   [2] The Tate Gallery, London.
[3] The Tate Gallery, London.   [4] The Tate Gallery, London.
[5] Private Collection.   [6] Coll. Mr. H. S. Ede.
[7] Coll. Mr. Michael Richey.   [8] The National Museum of Wales, Cardiff.
[9] Coll. Miss Helen Sutherland.

one into the other in the diaphanous mesh of lines, have an opalescent radiance, the lines themselves play a more crucial part than they do in most of the earlier drawings. *English Window*,[1] of 1931, with its magical evocation of English domestic life, would be almost without meaning in a black and white reproduction, whereas the last four lose much of their beauty but little of their sense. The visitor to the exhibitions of the works of contemporaries may sometimes wonder how most of the pictures ever came to be painted: the impulse behind them is so feeble and their meaning so little worthy of being imparted. Those endless stone outbuildings set in Yorkshire Dales, those endless daffodils standing forlornly in hand-thrown pots from an artshop, or, for that matter, an arrangement of squares and circles of raw and sticky paint, envisaged with a languid regard and not uncommonly with positive boredom: how did it come about that anyone thought it worth while to give permanent form to something that interested him so little? It may be that David Jones made these four drawings when he was troubled about his health, and uncertain how long a period of immunity from affliction could be counted on. I do not know; but what is certain is that he made them as though each represented a last opportunity to make a picture: so instinct are they with experience long pondered, with knowledge of history and legend and of the Catholic liturgy lovingly stored up, besides an undiminished affection for 'the intimate creatureliness of things'.

David Jones's great drawings, unlike most of the pictures in exhibitions of contemporary painting, are, if anything, too rich in content and meaning. They express, and in profuse detail, the religious ponderings of a man for whom, as I noted earlier, the doctrines of Christianity are true and are keys with which other doors may be unlocked; their symbols are paradigms of which legend and the symbolism of other rites are seen as precursors or approximations. For David Jones the incarnation, passion, death and resurrection of Christ are unique historical events, and Christianity is not a continuation of nature-religions; but like some (though not, of course, all) of the early Christian Fathers, David Jones sees Christianity as the fulfilment of the earlier dreams, the reality of which they were intimations. It is only another way of putting this to say that

[1] Coll. Mr. A. H. Wheen.

for him Christianity gives the clue to what legend and myth really were about.

So, for example, *Aphrodite in Aulis* is clearly Aphrodite. Like the Venus of Lucretius 'De Rerum Natura' she is not only *hominum divomque voluptas* but the fosterer of all nature's abundance and activity and turmoil. Soldiers are all about her, and columns and entablatures are broken. But she is also Iphigeneia, shackled by the ankle, a sacrificial victim and voluntary oblation standing on an altar. The altar is an ornate classical pedestal on which is inscribed a ram, whose blood pours into a cup set beneath it. Hand and foot of this victim are pierced, and the British soldier to the left carries a lance; on the right a monk in religious habit swings a thurible of incense. A monk in such a posture is appropriate if, but only if, the symbolism is eucharistic. For David Jones it is the Eucharist that redeems the historical process; accordingly, around Aphrodite are ranged soldiers of those times and places that interest him most, Greek, Etruscan, Roman, Arthurian, British, German; columns and pediments are broken, but around this sign all the orders of architecture retain their validity. Around her neck Aphrodite wears a necklace that carries a cross, and indeed there are stars in her hair with a crescent moon above, as if she were after all the Madonna and the Mother of all the Living (as in Hopkins's 'May Magnificat'), while around her head fly doves, the effulgence of one of which radiates her body. In the eucharistic sign, then, is she seen for what after all she is—even if in aspect she be Phryne or Lesbia.

The same sweep throughout time and the same confidence that the dreams and aspirations and stories and achievements of human kind are to be understood for what they are in the light of the Mass and the Redemption is apparent in the much simpler and deeply moving *Vexilla Regis*. The title of this drawing is taken from the Easter hymn, *Vexilla regis prodeunt, fulget crucis mysterium*. But in the drawing there are no royal standards, and there is no cross. Indeed the only Christian emblems are some of the instruments of the passion and a pelican and doves. But for David Jones the 'mystery of the Cross' is everywhere, in the wolf-helmet of the Roman augur, in the nude goddess on the fountain, in the Doric temple and the pillar surmounted by the Roman eagle, in Stonehenge, all set in a wooded landscape whose atmosphere, like its animals, is Arthurian.

If in what pertains to the content of his art he is one of the most 'traditional' artists alive, his drawing in the manner of its presentation stands somewhat aside from the great tradition. Berenson has defined, in words of high authority, the essential in the art of painting as the power 'to stimulate our consciousness of tactile values, so that the picture shall have at least as much power as the object represented to appeal to our tactile imagination'.

David Jones makes no attempt to appeal to our tactile imagination; he rouses our tactile sense only so far as is necessary to assure us that his symbols are in fact solid and not merely hieroglyphics worked upon a veil. The figure of Aphrodite is shown, by delicate modelling here and there, to be a figure very much of flesh and blood. But if his forms are often floating wraiths, those who have the patience to decipher the intricate tracery of his lines will discover that his art does not ignore the third dimension: that if the spectator has only occasionally the illusion of being able to touch the objects which David Jones represents, he will have the illusion of wandering among them, penetrating so far behind what at first resembles a veil as to lose himself in a diversely populated Lyonesse.

Even for those who have had the privilege of knowing him for many years and have an innate delight in his drawing and his writing, patience is necessary still. But patience is invariably rewarded.

In July 1954 David Jones remarked that I had never visited him at his home in Harrow. I arrived at the house to which he had directed me–a large Victorian boarding-house. No one answering the loud-clanging bell, I went in. A kettle was boiling on the range in the empty kitchen downstairs, but there was nobody there. Floor by floor, room by room I searched the silent house. Upon the overmantel in the dining-room (wherein was a long table set with many places) stood a photograph of a David Jones inscription, evidence that I had come at any rate to the right house. I knocked, knocked again, and, no answer being returned, I looked into one room after another, every one untenanted. Brooding on this Kafka-like predicament, I mounted laboriously from floor to floor, hearing no sound but the wind in the corridors. At last, on an upper floor my knock was answered. The door opened and there was my elusive host, welcoming and reassuring, in his cosy bed-sitting room, with a warm fire and a kettle singing upon it. The narrow bed stood near the window, which gave upon a *hortus inclusus*, and, more distantly, upon a distant prospect of London, and upon the bed was a drawing board and tacked to it a work just begun. At the time a big exhibition of his work was touring Wales, yet some of his best drawings were hanging on his own walls. I twitted him upon his liking for keeping his work beside him, and added that I had long wanted to buy one of his pictures but because of this preference had refrained from trying to do so. 'Don't for a moment think that I haven't appreciated that,' he answered. With the tea and toast he prepared we sat down beside the fire. He had no real knowledge, he told me, of Latin, only what he had picked up from inscriptions and the Liturgy. He also told me that he never worked from studies, but either directly from nature or from imagination; but mostly we talked of our early meetings and of our friendship with Eric Gill. How little changed he was, I thought, since the day when I had first seen him, a young apprentice twenty-eight years before, at Eric Gill's house at Capel-y-ffin in the room darkened by the swirling mist outside. Except as a soldier in France he has always led a cloistered life since. His love for Latin, a language he does not know and yet has an innate feeling for, and Welsh, a language of which his knowledge is smaller still, has given him a singular power of conveying in his own writing their especial beauties. In the same way, from a loving apprehension of things still deeper than language, he has been able, and in the face of persistent ill-health, to reveal, in picture after picture, the Christian fulfilment of myths and images that have immemorially haunted the mind of man.

Note. Although the Seven and Five Society belongs to recent history and numbers among its members artists of contemporary fame, information about it is not easy to come by; its own records appear to be incomplete and no full set of its exhibition catalogues seems to be available. It may be useful, therefore, to append a note about it before it disappears entirely from memory.

The Seven and Five Society (the name signified seven painters and five sculptors) was formed in 1919 and held its last and fourteenth exhibition of work by members and others in 1935 or 1936. It is now defunct but has never been formally disbanded. 'It had a curious and unsuccessful beginning,' wrote Mr. Robin Ironside, 'as an endeavour to co-ordinate any discoverable artistic tendencies that might plant the seeds in this country of Expressionism as it had developed on the continent.'[1] This is possibly too precise a formulation of its aims; but the Society did indeed have as its initial inspiration a conscious reaction from aesthetic views such as those promulgated by Roger Fry and a conscious interest in subject-matter. In the 'thirties, however, largely owing, it would appear, to the energy and influence of Ben Nicholson, a very active member, the Society changed direction in favour of non-representational art.

The rules of the Society allowed for new members and these were elected at every meeting. The list of its members is a remarkable one; it included Ivon Hitchens and P. J. Jowett (both very early members), Ben Nicholson (elected in 1924 or 1925), Evie Hone, Christopher Wood (elected in 1926), Winifred Nicholson, David Jones (elected in 1928), Barbara Hepworth, Frances Hodgkins (elected in 1929, resigned in 1934 – apparently on a disagreement with policy about non-representational art), John Aldridge, Henry Moore, John Piper, Edward Bawden.

Early exhibitions of the Society were held at the now defunct Gieves Gallery and Paterson's Galleries in Old Bond Street and at Walker's Galleries in New Bond Street; at least one was held at the Beaux-Arts Gallery and one at Messrs. Arthur Tooth and Sons; in the early 'thirties the Society exhibited regularly at the Leicester Galleries, and the last exhibition of all took place at the Zwemmer Gallery.

[1] 'Painting since 1939', published for the British Council, 1947.

HENRY MOORE

b. 1898

UNTIL Moore was nearly forty his drawings were regarded as the marginal activity of a sculptor. As an ever growing number of people believed him to be a great sculptor, his drawings compelled interest and respect. Quite apart from their intimate connexion with his sculpture they merited interest and respect as expressions of a mind of unusual originality and power. But had Moore not been a sculptor but a draughtsman only, and had he died before the Second World War, I think it doubtful whether his drawings would have taken an important place in the art of the century. Exhibitions were held respectively at the Zwemmer and Mayor Galleries in 1935 and 1939. In the bibliography appended to the principal work on the artist hitherto published[1] I can find no piece of writing dealing with the drawings separately from the sculpture prior to 1940. There were, of course, numerous notices of the drawings in association with the sculpture, and numerous references to them in articles of more general scope, of which the first appeared in 1933,[2] when Moore was already thirty-five. He himself wrote in 1937, 'My drawings are done mainly as a help towards making sculpture—as a means of generating ideas for sculpture, tapping oneself for the initial idea, and as a way of sorting out ideas and developing them. And I sometimes,' he concedes, 'draw just for enjoyment.'[3] I shall refer later to this illuminating article; for the present I wish merely to suggest that in 1937 Moore regarded his drawing as mainly ancillary to his sculpture. Three years later, in the shelters in which Londoners sought respite from German bombs, he underwent experiences that made him a draughtsman of comparable stature to the sculptor.

ᴼ   ᴼ   ᴼ

[1] 'Henry Moore, Sculpture and Drawings', with an Introduction by Herbert Read, 3rd edition, 1949.
[2] 'On Sculptors' Drawings and Henry Moore in particular' in 'Black on White', by Arnold L. Haskell, 1933.
[3] 'Notes on Sculpture', 'The Listener', 18 August 1937.

61. DAVID JONES. *Aphrodite in Aulis* (1941).
Pen, ink and water-colour, 24⅜ × 19¼ in. Private collection.

62. DAVID JONES. *Vexilla Regis* (1947).
Water-colour, 30×22 in. Coll. Mr. H. S. Ede.

Henry Spencer Moore was born on 30 July 1898 at Castleford, Yorkshire, the seventh child of Raymond Spencer Moore and his wife Mary, born Baker. The elder Moore was an aspiring and industrious man.

> He had begun as a farmer, doing whatever a boy of nine does in becoming a farmer—scaring crows, I suppose, [Henry Moore relates] but had later turned to coal mining. He educated himself: knew the whole of Shakespeare, taught himself engineering to the point where he passed examinations qualifying him to become manager of the mine where he worked. His eyes, however, through an accident down the mine, grew bad enough to interfere with his further advancement.[1]

Moore's paternal great-grandfather came from Ireland, but his father and grandfather were born in Lincolnshire, and for several generations the men on both sides of his family had worked on the land or below it as miners.

At the age of twelve Moore won a scholarship from the elementary school to Castleford Grammar School, but

> I had always wanted to be a sculptor, [Moore has told us] at least since I was about ten. However, my first art teacher at Castleford upset me a great deal; she said I drew figures with feet like tassels! I recall exactly what she referred to: figures with feet in the air, like early Gothic drawings—suspended in the air. . . .[2]

His father strongly opposed Moore's becoming an artist; instead he wished him to follow an elder brother and a sister to York Training College and to become a teacher. The lady who had objected to the feet of his drawn figures was replaced by Miss Alice Gostick, who became a firm ally in the argument with his father, which persisted from his fourteenth to his eighteenth year. Parental authority prevailed and by September 1916 he was a teacher at his old elementary school. From this false start he was delivered by the First World War. In February 1917 he joined the Army, serving as a private in the 15th London Regiment (Civil Service Rifles). He went to France in the early summer, and in November was gassed in the battle of Cambrai, and invalided home. On his recovery, after a course at Aldershot, he was made a corporal and a bayonet instructor. Two

[1] Henry Moore', an interview with James Johnson Sweeney. 'Partisan Review', March-April 1947, with some later qualifications of Moore himself made to the present writer.
[2] Ibid.

years of war had weakened parental authority, and with the help of his friend Miss Gostick he applied for an ex-Serviceman's grant to the Leeds School of Art.

The rigidly academic teaching was little to his purpose, but he won a Royal Exhibition to the Royal College of Art. His two years in Leeds were not wasted years. Visits to nearby Adel, where there are early examples of Romanesque carving, 'opened up,' he said, 'the whole affair for me'.[1] The interest in early sculpture which this aroused was heightened by coming upon Fry's 'Vision and Design' in the Reference Library, from which he first learned of Mexican and Negro sculpture, and which led him to other books on ancient art. His outlook was further broadened by access to the collection of Sir Michael Sadler, Vice-Chancellor of the University from 1911 until 1923, which contained paintings by Gauguin and Van Gogh, as well as by many English independent painters.

In the illuminating interview already quoted Moore gave an account of the struggle which followed his arrival in London.

For the first three months [he said] I was in a daze of excitement. One room after another in the British Museum took my enthusiasm. The Royal College of Art meant nothing in comparison . . . everything was wonderful–a new world at every turn . . . after the first excitement it was the art of ancient Mexico that spoke to me most–except perhaps Romanesque. . . . And I admit clearly and frankly that early Mexican art formed my views of carving. . . .

But my aims as a 'student' were directly at odds with my taste in sculpture. Already, even here a conflict had set in. And for a considerable while after my discovery of the archaic sculpture in the British Museum there was a bitter struggle within me, on the one hand, between the need to follow my course at college in order to get a teacher's diploma and, on the other, the desire to work freely at what appealed most to me in sculpture. At one point I was seriously considering giving up college and working only in the direction that attracted me. But, thank goodness, I somehow came to the realization that academic discipline is valuable. And my need to have a diploma, in order to earn a living, helped.

I now understand the value of an academic grounding: modelling and drawing from life. All sculptors of the great periods of European art could draw from life, just as well as the painters. With me, at one moment, it was just touch and go. But finally I hit on a sort of compromise arrangement: academic work during the semester, and during

[1] Sweeney, loc. cit.

the holidays a free rein to the interests I had developed in the British Museum. Mixing the two things enabled one to continue drawing from life as I have always done. And it also allowed me to win my travelling scholarship to Italy on academic grounds.

My father, who was appointed Principal of the Royal College of Art only the year before Moore's arrival, recognized his outstanding talent, describing him in his memoirs as 'the most intelligent and gifted among the sculptors',[1] and shortly after the Professor of Sculpture, Derwent Wood, retired in 1924 my father entrusted Moore with the temporary charge of the Sculpture School, and the following year appointed him Assistant to Ernest Cole, the new Professor, a post which he held until 1931, teaching regularly for two days a week. Moore told me that he used to enjoy drawing with my father, who in 1931 bought one of his drawings in pen and ink—a massive seated woman—which hung in the hall of our house.

It must have been soon after he came to London that I became acquainted with him, because I met him before becoming aware that he was a sculptor, at one or more of the Sunday evenings when my parents welcomed students to our house. After such an evening, when Moore had been present, I asked who he was, and my younger sister, who was also a student in the School of Sculpture, answered 'He's going to be a great sculptor.'

In the thirty-three years or so since then Henry Moore seems to me to have changed little.

He had the same unassertive assurance, the same kindliness, and the same intense seriousness of purpose half masked by a benevolent sociability and the same never ruffled serenity. In one respect he was different. Only two years before he had been a bayonet instructor threatened by the prospect of having to resume his post as a teacher in an elementary school. The revelation of Mexican and Romanesque and Negro art was very recent: indeed it was in progress; recent, too, was its interpretation in 'Vision and Design'. His philosophy of art was actually being forged, and in consequence his convictions were more rigid than they have since become. In those days his insistence upon 'truth to material', upon, for instance, the error of representing flesh which is soft in terms of stone which is hard, seemed to me a little doctrinaire; so, too, his inclination to discount

[1] 'Since Fifty: Men and Memories, 1922–1938', 1939, p. 236.

the Hellenic element in European art. But I am writing of the time before 1924, when he won a Travelling Scholarship that enabled him to visit Paris, Rome, Florence, Venice and Ravenna. So strongly were Classical and Renaissance art identified in his mind with academism and the mechanical copying of plaster casts that, when the scholarship was awarded to him, he at once pleaded to be allowed to use it for Paris instead of Italy, but no such arrangement was possible. 'I had to go to Italy against my will,' he said, 'but thank goodness now I did go.'[1]

The following letter which he wrote to my father from via Fiesolana, 40, Florence, dated 12 March 1924, gives some account of his journey and of his response to the works of art he saw.

I have until now been moving with the speed of an American tourist-the first week of being out-spent in Paris-has sunk into the very distant past, but the Guimet Museum (the Indian sculptures in the entrance hall, and the room on the ground floor-and the sculptures and paintings from Antinori stands out like-like cypress trees in an Italian landscape-Paris itself I did not like-and after the Louvre and the Guimet Museum the few exhibitions of contemporary work which I saw seemed almost rubbish.

I've made stops at Genoa, Pisa and Rome, before coming on here to Florence. In Italy the early wall paintings-the work of Giotto, Orcagna, Lorenzetti, Taddeo Gaddi, the paintings leading up and including Massacio's are what have so far interested me most. Of great sculpture I've seen very little-Giotto's painting is the finest sculpture I met in Italy-what I know of Indian, Egyptian and Mexican, sculpture completely overshadows Renaissance sculpture-except for the early Italian portrait busts, the very late work of Michael Angelo and the work of Donatello-though in the influence of Donatello I think I see the beginning of the end-Donatello was a modeller, and it seems to me that it is modelling that has sapped the manhood out of Western sculpture, but the two main reasons are, don't you think, the widespread avoidance of thinking and working in stone-and the wilful throwing away of the Gothic tradition-in favour of a pseudo Greek-I believe that even mediocre students at college or anywhere, had they been lucky enough to have entered a sculptor's workshop, later would most probably have been doing work which we should now admire-in Italy of the 14th century, in one small town of 20 or 30 thousand inhabitants there must have been living and working at the same time 50 or 60 painters each of whom were he doing his same work now would be accounted a genius! . . . The only hope I can see for a school

[1] Sweeney, loc. cit.

of sculpture in England, under our present system, is a good artist working carving in the big tradition of sculpture, who can get the sympathy and admiration of students, and propagate good as Dalou and Lanteri spread harm.

I have been seeing rather than doing until now–and I think I have seen examples of most of the Italians–Giotto has made the greatest impression upon me (perhaps partly because he's the most English of the primitives). My present plans are, the Giottos at Assisi, and at Padua, then out of Italy via Ravenna and Venice and on to Munich–from Germany home via Paris so that I can finish up at the Guimet Museum.

I am beginning to get England into perspective–I think I shall return a violent patriot. If this scholarship does nothing else for me–it will have made me realise what treasures we have in England–what a paradise the British Museum is, and how high in quality, representative, how choice is our National Collection–and how inspiring is our English landscape. I do not wonder that the Italians have no landscape school–I have a great desire–almost an ache for the sight of a tree that can be called a tree–for a tree with a trunk.

Yours sincerely,
Henry Moore.

In all his travels the place which made the deepest and most lasting impression upon him was the Brancacci Chapel in Santa Maria del Carmine in Florence. Here Moore came every morning before doing anything else to study the splendid figures painted on its walls by Masaccio. Thither Michelangelo and Raphael had gone before him, and Vasari had written that 'all the most celebrated sculptors and painters since Masaccio's day have become excellent and illustrious by studying their art in this chapel'. The name of none of the masters is so often on Moore's lips as Masaccio's.

The immediate effect of his Italian journey was not illumination but tension which he was scarcely able to bear. 'For about six months after my return I was never more miserable in my life,' he said. 'Six months exposure to the masterworks of European art had stirred up a violent conflict with my previous ideals. I couldn't seem to shake off the new impressions, or make use of them without denying all I had devoutly believed in before. I found myself helpless and unable to work. Then gradually I began to find my way out of my quandary in the direction of my earlier interests. I came back to ancient Mexican art in the British Museum. I came across an illustration of the "Chacmool", discovered at Chichen Itza in a German publication–and its curious reclining posture attracted me–not lying on its side, but on its back with its head twisted around. Still the effects of that trip never really faded.'[1] They did not fade; but neither did they show themselves fully until years afterwards: when they did show themselves they added an element to the art of Moore which made him a great draughtsman.

On his return to London, then, he went back more assiduously than ever to his study of ancient art at the British Museum, especially Mexican art. It was then, too, that he came upon the reproduction of 'Chacmool', the celebrated Toltec-Maya carving in limestone of the reclining figure of the Rain Spirit, which has haunted his imagination. Its effect upon several of his stone carvings–such for instance as *Reclining Figure*,[2] of 1929–is very marked. His untiring research at the British Museum, in Italy, and later on in Greece and Mexico, has made him one of the best educated of sculptors: few scholars–apart from those responsible for the collections–can have so wide a knowledge as he of the sculpture in the British Museum, and his knowledge of European sculpture since the advent of Rodin is no less extensive. The quality of his knowledge is even more impressive than its extent. Moore, who was in Italy in 1948 at the time of a special exhibition of his work at the Venice Biennale, called on Mr. Berenson in Florence. A few days afterwards I took Mr. Berenson round the exhibition of Moore's sculpture in the British Pavilion.

> The two most destructive personalities in European art today [he said] are Picasso and Moore: Picasso consciously destructive, and Moore unconsciously. How strange that it should be so–about Moore I mean, for I've never had a visitor who showed such knowledge and perception about my sculpture–not a piece of which he had ever seen before.

Moore's search for the basic forms and rhythms of nature took him not only to the British Museum, but also and often to the Museum of Natural History, and he has always delighted in the assiduous study of natural forms, bones, shells, pebbles and the like. (On my most recent visit I saw him from a distance bending over, head in the 'boot' of his car, and when I approached I found that he was unpacking a haul of stones worked by the sea, collected on the holiday from which he had just returned.)

[1] Sweeney, loc. cit.   [2] The City Art Gallery, Leeds.

The guiding ideas which were forming in his mind during the 'twenties and which have remained the basis of his art are lucidly outlined by the artist himself in several deeply pondered articles.[1]

Here, and throughout this study, I shall quote extensively from Henry Moore's own writings and statements about his art. It is not rare for artists to write well, but it is rare for contemporary artists to write accurately about their own work. But not only is Henry Moore free from the slightest suspicion of aggrandizing himself and the things that he makes or of inflating their creation into some very privileged exercise of visionary or even mystical power, and not only does he consistently use words in readily ascertainable senses, so that his meaning is always plain, but he is direct and strong as well as lucid. It is true that once or twice in the past he has picked up nonsense from the ambient air, as when he spoke of 'the literary idea that it (an egg) will become a bird,'[2] but such occasions are rare. The expression of a mind thoroughly genuine and robust, his writing is also full of the most incisive common sense, of which his paper on 'The Sculptor in Modern Society' is a good instance.[3] Being, then, so thoroughly informative, I shall have no scruple in using his own writings freely.

I cannot, I think, do better than quote a few key passages from 'The Sculptor's Aims'.

One of Moore's insistent ideas, that of truth to material, I have already mentioned.

Every material [he wrote] has its own individual qualities. It is only when the sculptor works direct, when there is an active relationship with his material, that the material can take its part in the shaping of an idea. Stone, for example, is hard and concentrated and should not be falsified to look like soft flesh—it should not be forced beyond its constructive build to a point of weakness. It should keep its hard tense stoniness.[4]

[1] Of these the chief are 'The Sculptor's Aims', 'Unit One', edited by Herbert Read, 1934, p. 128; 'Notes on Sculpture', 'The Listener', 18 August 1937, reprinted in 'The Painter's Object', edited by Myfanwy Evans, 1937, pp. 21-9, and 'Art in England', edited by R. S. Lambert, 1938, pp. 93-9, and 'Primitive Art', 'The Listener', 24 April 1941. All three are reprinted in 'Henry Moore, Sculpture and Drawings'.
[2] In 'Notes on Sculpture'.
[3] A statement made to UNESCO and reprinted in 'Art News', November 1952.
[4] 'Henry Moore, Sculpture and Drawings', p. xxxix.

Of greater moment, however, for my purpose, is the expression of his ideal of full three-dimensional realization.

Complete sculptural expression is form in its full spatial reality.

Only to make relief shapes on the surface of the block is to forego the full power of expression of sculpture. When the sculptor understands his material, has a knowledge of its possibilities and its constructive build, it is possible to keep within its limitations and yet turn an inert block into a composition which has a full form-existence, with masses of varied size and section conceived in their air-surrounded entirety, stressing and straining, thrusting and opposing each other in spatial relationship–being static, in the sense that the centre of gravity lies within the base (and does not seem to be falling over or moving off its base)–and yet having an alert dynamic tension between its parts.[1]

Closely connected with this ideal is Moore's predilection for asymmetry.

Sculpture fully in the round has no two points of view alike. The desire for form completely realized is connected with asymmetry. For a symmetrical mass being the same from both sides cannot have more than half the number of different points of view possessed by a non-symmetrical mass.

Asymmetry is connected also with the desire for the organic (which I have) rather than the geometric.

Organic forms, though they may be symmetrical in their main disposition, in their reaction to environment, growth and gravity, lose their perfect symmetry.

On Moore's collection and observation of natural objects such as pebbles I have already commented.

The observation of nature [he writes] is part of an artist's life, it enlarges his form-knowledge, keeps him fresh and from working only by formula, and feeds inspiration.

The human figure is what interests me most deeply, but I have found principles of form and rhythm from the study of natural objects such as pebbles, rocks, bones, trees, plants, etc.[2]

Abstract qualities of design [he continues] are essential to the value of a work, but to me of equal importance is the psychological, human element. If both abstract and human elements are welded together in a work, it must have a fuller, deeper meaning.[3]

Finally there is Moore's life-long aversion from every kind of mannerism, every form of art in which primitive vitality and

[1] 'Henry Moore, Sculpture and Drawings,' p. xxxix. [2] Ibid.
[3] Ibid., pp. xxxix-xl.

simplicity, characteristics of an immediate and direct response to life, are 'smothered in trimmings and surface decorations', enfeebled and extinguished by 'technical tricks and intellectual conceits', by academism.

> For me [he wrote, therefore] a work must first have vitality of its own. I do not mean a reflection of the vitality of life, of movement, physical action, frisking, dancing figures and so on, but that a work can have in it a pent-up energy, an intense life of its own, independent of the object it may represent. When work has this powerful vitality we do not connect the word beauty with it.
>
> Beauty, in the later Greek or Renaissance sense, is not the aim in my sculpture.
>
> Between beauty of expression and power of expression there is a difference of function. The first aims at pleasing the senses, the second has a spiritual vitality which for me is more moving and goes deeper than the senses.[1]

Henry Moore has always drawn. 'Drawing keeps one fit,' he said to Sir Herbert Read, 'like physical exercises – perhaps acts like water to a plant – and it lessens the danger of repeating oneself and getting into a formula. It enlarges one's form repertoire, one's form experience.'[2]

Although he regarded his earlier drawings 'mainly as a help towards making sculpture', they early enjoyed a validity in their own right. The earliest known to me, the series representing monumental female figures, generally seated, begun in the middle 'twenties and discontinued about ten years later, are drawings of unusual quality. They are broad in form, serenely aloof in spirit and more personal than some of his admirers seem to allow. Sir Herbert Read, for instance, describes them as if made 'before venturing to express himself in a wholly personal idiom',[3] and he is at considerable pains to suggest that 'it would be a mistake to give the impression that the artist began with a relatively academic style',[4] and he points to earlier and contemporary sculpture of a less academic kind.

As drawings avowedly done from the life they have, naturally enough, something traditional in their character, but even so they are far more personal than the Mexican, African and Egyptian influenced carvings to which Sir Herbert refers. I suggest a simple

[1] Ibid., p. xi.
[2] Ibid., pp. xxi–xxii.
[3] Ibid., p. xxvi.
[4] Ibid.

test. Were *Mask*,[1] of 1924 (one of the works cited), placed with others in a collection of ancient Mexican sculpture, it would take an experienced scholar to pick it out as a modern derivation. Who, on the other hand, who had ever seen one of the early drawings of seated women, could fail to attribute it in any company? Some of the very earliest even, such as *Drawing (from life)*,[2] of 1928, show, in rudimentary form, one of the most personal and permanent characteristics of Moore's drawing, the two-way section, lines, that is to say, indicating the section across the form and along it. (This characteristic is, so to speak, a diagrammatic analysis of form. In contrast to the rendering and definition of form by light and shade, it is an analysis of form by lines that exactly define the shape as it would be in the round, in a longitudinal and a transverse section. For this sculptural and analytical statement Moore has shown an increasing preference over the illusion of chiaroscuro. An example will be found reproduced in Plate 32.) The most obvious target for criticism offered by the drawing I have cited is not its traditional character, but is the intrusion of the borrowed double-focus head. The fact is that Moore, for all his great and manifold natural talents, and for all his formidable industry, grew slowly to full maturity, and much of his early work is closely derived from his favoured models, and some of it marked by a modish chic. And what could be less surprising? Moore did not attain to his deep insights and wide knowledge of sculpture by note-taking, by the way of a scholar that is to say, but by the way of a sculptor actually working in wood and metal and stone.

If his growth to maturity as a sculptor was slow, as a draughtsman it was slower still.

Moore draws from a variety of intentions. As already noted, he draws as an aid to sculpture, either 'as a means of generating ideas', or of 'tapping oneself for the initial idea; and as a way of sorting out ideas and developing them'.[3] Sculpture is too laborious a process to allow of his realizing more than a small fraction of the ideas which form in his mind in prodigious number; drawing is quick and easy and he finds it a pleasurable way of relieving the imaginative pressure. Sometimes he draws simply because he enjoys it, but before

---

[1] Coll. Mr. John Gould Fletcher.   [2] Coll. Mrs. Irina Moore.
[3] 'Notes on Sculpture', op. cit., p. xii.

long the lines he makes provide the nexus of an idea. And finally he draws as a means of study and observation of natural forms. Drawing of this kind is an essential element in his art, because, as he told Sir Herbert Read, 'in my sculpture I do not draw directly upon the memory or observations of a particular object, but rather use whatever comes up from my general fund of knowledge'.[1] The creation of this fund of knowledge is so vital that, as he told the same friend, 'every few months I stop carving for two or three weeks and do life drawing'.[2]

In the late 'thirties he became aware of an error in his method of making drawings for sculpture.

I tried to give them as much the illusion of real sculpture as I could [he wrote]—that is, I drew by the method of illusion, of light falling on a solid object. But I now find that carrying it so far that it becomes a substitute for sculpture either weakens the desire to do the sculpture, or is likely to make the sculpture only a dead realization of the drawing.[3]

He therefore more often drew in line and flat-tone, but the vision behind the drawing was still a three-dimensional vision. The sculptor's meaning is clear when we compare sharply-modelled drawings, all entitled *Ideas for Sculpture*,[4] made in 1938 (Plates 140, 142A, 142B and 143A in 'Henry Moore, Sculpture and Drawings'), with two drawings of the same year in which solidity is subtly suggested, *Ideas for metal sculpture*,[5] and *Drawing for Sculpture*,[6] (Plates 146A and 146C in the same book).

During the 'twenties and 'thirties he made drawings of many kinds, some of them of marked originality, and very few that do not afford some intimation of a mind of singular and increasing power.

But war brought with it, in an improbable fashion, a transforming experience. Until the time of Dunkirk, Moore, living in Kent, continued to work much as usual, but with invasion threatening he wished to help directly and returning to London he applied at the Chelsea Polytechnic for training in the making of precision tools. But the classes in this subject were few and the applicants many. Reluctant to begin sculpture that he might be prevented from

---

[1] Ibid., p. xxii.
[2] Ibid., p. xxi.
[3] 'Notes on Sculpture', ibid., p. xlii.
[4] Private Collections.
[5] Coll. Sir Kenneth Clark, K.C.B.
[6] The Bucholz Gallery, New York.

completing, he spent his time drawing. Months went by without a word from the Chelsea Polytechnic, and he went on drawing.

Then the air-raids began [I quote yet again from his interview with Mr. Sweeney] and the war from being an awful worry became a real experience. Quite against what I expected I found myself strangely excited by the bombed buildings, but more still by the unbelievable scenes and life of the underground shelters. I began filling a notebook with drawings—ideas based on London's shelter life. Naturally I could not draw in the shelter itself. I drew from memory on my return home. But the scenes of the shelter world, static figures (asleep)—'reclining figures'—remained vivid in my mind, I felt somehow drawn to it all. Here was something I couldn't help doing.

The effect of his experience in the shelters was to bring a humanity into Moore's art, above all into his drawing, that it had lacked. I have given above, in summary form, some account of the ideas which underlie his art, and in doing so I have used so far as I could his own formulations of them. But nearly everything he said or wrote about it was concerned with three-dimentional realization, spacial completeness and the like. And not unnaturally, for most artists delight in discussing means, but about the ends which these are intended to serve they are apt to be silent, lest by a process of substitution discussion should lessen their drive to attain them. Moore has never been an abstract artist, and has rarely confused ends and means. He is a man deeply conscious of human values.

It might seem from what I have said of shape and form that I regard them as ends in themselves. Far from it. I am very much aware that associational, psychological factors play a large part in sculpture. . . . I think the humanist element will always be for me of fundamental importance in sculpture, giving sculpture its vitality.[1]

The nights among the 'unbelievable scenes' of the shelter world and the days in the shelters observing the empty spaces in which the nights' dramas were enacted stirred his humanism to a new and grander consciousness. For the expression of the humanistic values the European tradition provides a natural language. Its appropriateness for the expression of the emotions stirred in him by the shelter world became suddenly apparent to Moore. Memories of his Italian

[1] 'Notes on Sculpture', op. cit., p. xlii.

journey leaped into life. The Frescoes in the Carmine had a new relevance for his art.

> It was not until the Blitz in London [he told Mr. Sweeney] that I began to realize how deep-rooted the Italian influence had been. . . . Here, curiously enough, is where, in looking back, my Italian trip [he said] and the Mediterranean tradition came once more to the surface. There was no discarding [he added] of those other interests in archaic art and the art of primitive peoples, but rather a clearer tension between this approach and the humanist emphasis.[1]

It is precisely this tension between those elements in him which respond to the art of primitive peoples and those which respond to the painting of Masaccio which enhanced all his qualities both as sculptor and draughtsman. In the shelter drawings he created a world peopled by figures at once monumental and ghostly. The colours that faintly illuminate this noble yet nightmare world are charged as deeply as the forms with the artist's intense emotion and they both explain and enhance them. In all he filled two sketchbooks and made about a hundred large drawings: standing, seated or reclining figures hieratic and immobile yet subtly expressive of Moore's humanity, encompassed by vast shadowy spaces brought to a vibrant life by the depths and brilliances of his colour. If there exist any works by Moore more impressive than the *Shelter Drawings* they are the sketchbooks in which he set down his recollections of the figures and their settings which he observed on his nightly visits underground, and the original ideas for the finished drawings. These two small books–reservoirs of concentrated imaginative power–have to my thinking a place among Moore's most moving works. Modern works which say more in so small a compass do not come easily to mind: they are worthy of the words which Moore himself applied to massive carvings, the Sumerian sculptures in the British Museum, as being of 'a contained bull-like grandeur and held-in energy'.

It would be useful, I think, to write a few words about how these drawings are made, for the method employed–now widely imitated –was an innovation of Moore's.

Not long before the Second World War, when Moore was living at his cottage near Dover, a niece called and asked him to make a drawing for her; considerately she brought her own materials, a few cheap crayons from Woolworth's and some water-colours. The materials were inadequate, but her uncle set to work. Among them was a white wax crayon, and it was when doing this kindly act that he discovered the method, which since that time he has constantly used, of putting in the main masses in white wax. This has several advantages. Because the water-colour recedes from the white wax, backgrounds can be put in almost instantaneously in broad, rapid strokes, and the white wax may then be worked over with pen and ink, and water-colour applied in small strokes; in case of failure the ink and water-colour applied to it may be readily washed off. The method is productive of accidental effects of colour and texture and it is this that has made it so widely popular. In Moore's hands the effects are in fact so dexterously controlled that the term 'accident' is inappropriate: he creates the conditions in which the happy accident is liable to occur, and promptly avails himself of it when it does. The later water-colours of Moore so abound in exquisiteness, gaiety, and delicate evocations of space and atmospheres that it sometimes happens that his constant and primary concern with powerful monumental form is overlooked. It is the use of white wax which enables him, by putting in the principal forms at the beginning, thereupon to model and refine them. The method, in fact, is directly analogous to his method as a carver. In neither is the process a building up; in both it is a seeking to discover in the original mass of material—be it block of stone or wood or area of wax—the forms of his imagining in the fullness of their energy and strength.

One melancholy fact about modern painters and about English painters perhaps in a special degree is a liability to progressive loss of creative power. In some cases a brilliant studentship is followed by a steady decline into frigidity, an unreflective conformity, disintegration or vulgarity. Millais, for example, was one of the supremely gifted painters of a century wonderfully rich in genius, as a young painter a dedicated being, yet of many of the productions of his later years it could be said without injustice that they would shed no lustre upon a painter of the meanest talents and the most trivial vision. About few categories of men is it so difficult to generalize as it is about painters, who are among the most highly individual of mankind, but there is one which I would hazard, namely that capacity for constant growth is among the surest indications of major creative power. It was most conspicuous in Turner, the greatest visual genius to be born of the English speaking peoples, less conspicuous-for all the splendour and grace of his total achievement-in Gainsborough, while in a little master in his way incomparable, Samuel Palmer, this capacity simply did not exist. Among the greatest masters it is easy to recall at random those whose growth ended only with their lives, Michelangelo, Leonardo, Titian, Rembrandt. Among the reasons for confidence in Moore as a major talent is that he does show a capacity for continuing growth. Indeed the very illustriousness of the position which he has now attained militates against full recognition of his increasing stature. It fosters instead an indiscriminate reverence for everything he has made. It is no part of my intention to criticize, when it does not seem to me necessary, or to disparage the possessions of collectors. If those, however, who had the perception and the foresight to acquire the artist's work in the 'twenties were to compare examples of it with examples of the Mexican and other ancient sculpture which he assiduously studied and which he has always been ready to admit to be the very foundation of his art, it would be plain that many of them were little more than exercises-powerful and perceptive but exercises none the less-in various early styles. Then if, forgetful of who made them, they were to compare them with the later sculpture in stone and wood and metal, with the reclining figures and the family groups of the later 'thirties and the 'forties, and with the shelter drawings and those which followed them, I believe that they could hardly fail to recognize that a great talent, after years of unending stubborn research, had emerged and grown to become fully itself.

I have taken the *Shelter Drawings* as a point of departure. In fact for a year or so before the war the drawing of Moore had assumed a breadth and vivacity which had only rarely marked it hitherto. What an advance upon the series already referred to, of *Ideas for Sculpture*, of 1938, which are small in form, tight and directly imitative of sculpture in treatment, and lacking in sense of space, is represented by such drawings, for instance as *Two Women*,[1] *Figures in a Setting*,[2] *Standing Figures*,[3] *Two Seated Women*,[4] *Two Seated Figures*,[5] and *Two Seated Women*,[6] all made during the ensuing two

[1] Coll. Sir Kenneth Clark, K.C.B.   [2] Coll. Mr. Eric C. Gregory.
[3] Coll. Mrs. Ursula Goldfinger.   [4] Coll. Sir Kenneth Clark, K.C.B.
[5] The Tate Gallery, London.   [6] The Tate Gallery, London.

years, which possess all that the others conspicuously lack. But beautiful as many of them are, these immediate predecessors of the *Shelter Drawings* are surpassed by their successors.

Moore's advance, however, was not resumed immediately after the completion of the *Shelter Drawings*. These number about one hundred in all. From the middle of 1940 until late the following year these drawings absorbed all his interest and he did nothing else. But at that time the air raids became infrequent and the shelters empty. The War Artists' Advisory Committee, which commissioned a number of the *Shelter Drawings*, asked him to make a series of coal-miners at work. This project took him to his native Castleford, where he spent two or three weeks down the mine. Although he had lived the first twenty years of his life in Castleford and came of a family of miners, he had never before been down a coal-mine, and although he welcomed the experience the results did not satisfy him.

> It made clear many things about my own childhood (for my father was a coal miner) and made me know more about miners, [he said] but I didn't find it as fruitful a subject as the shelters. The shelter drawings came about after first being moved by the experience of them, whereas the coal-mine drawings were more like a commission.[1]

Judged by the standard set by the *Shelter Drawings* the coal-miners fall short in dramatic power, having neither the nobility of form, of spacial relation, nor the strangely singing colour. The one scene represented a unique many-sided drama, the other a routine occupation pursued in a narrow space. But the mining theme, prosaic as it must have seemed to an imagination attuned to the courage and the tenderness, the terror and the death-like exhaustion of the shelters, and their eerie vastness, did evoke drawings a few of which, such for instance as *At the Coal Face*,[2, 3] of 1942, must be placed only just below his best. The energetic tautness of the miners' figures as they hacked at the coal face first taught him how to incorporate the male figure into his family of forms, in which it had hitherto played a negligible part. He had never willingly drawn male figures before, having believed in the validity of static forms, forms in repose.

[1] 'Catalogue of the Henry Moore retrospective exhibition at the Museum of Modern Art, New York, 1946'; Introduction by James Johnson Sweeney, p. 71.
[2] The Whitworth Art Gallery, Manchester.
[3] The City Art Galleries, Glasgow.

63. HENRY MOORE.
*Girl reading to a
Woman and Child*
(1946).
Chalk, pen and water-
colour, 18×24 in.
Coll.
Mrs. H. D. Walston.

64. HENRY MOORE. *Family Group* (1948).
Chalk, pen and water-colour, 24¾ × 19¾ in. The Hanover Gallery, London.

Down the coal-mine he discovered the possibilities of the figure in action. His few works at the coal face beneath his native town thus made an essential contribution towards, among others, his most splendid bronzes, *Family Group*,[1] of 1945–9, and *King and Queen*,[2] of 1953–4.

Before long, however, he entered upon the most richly creative years of his life. To attempt to assess his sculpture is outside the scope of this study, but he has made many drawings which surpass even the shelterers, particularly in respect of one of his most obsessive ambitions: to make space.

> Spaces between forms, holes in things, are always an obsession with me. Space is an element as important as what is solid and material. [I quote his words to me.] Turner in his old age made space in its way as positive as a tree trunk, even Matisse, whose painting looks flat, made space in which things can be exactly placed.

In the finest of the later drawings the monumentality of the *Shelter Drawings* is sustained and sometimes even enhanced, the colour is more aerial, but the space has opened out and the relations between the forms have grown more complex. These qualities are exemplified in such drawings as *Group of Figures in a Setting*,[3] of 1942, *Group of draped Standing Figures*,[4] *Crowd looking at a tied-up object*,[5] also of 1942, *Girl reading to Woman and Child*,[6] of 1946 (Plate 63), in which the crowd and the tied-up object are seen through the window of a domestic interior. *Seated Figure*,[7] also of 1946, and *Family Group*,[8] of 1948 (Plate 64).

The year 1946 marks for Moore a further step towards a still fuller humanism. In that year his daughter Mary was born and the effects of this event are immediately reflected in both his choice of subjects and his treatment of them. Domestic scenes, such as *Two Women bathing a Baby*,[9] drawn shortly after Mary's birth, become common, as well as mothers and children, family groups and the like. These

[1] Commissioned for the Barclay School, Stevenage. Casts at the Tate Gallery and elsewhere.
[2] Commissioned by the City of Antwerp for the Open-Air Museum, Middleheim.
[3] Coll. Mr. Paul Magriel.
[4] Coll. Mr. Karl Nathan.
[5] Coll. Sir Kenneth Clark, K.C.B.
[6] Coll. Mrs. H. D. Walston.
[7] The National Gallery of Canada, Ottawa (Massey Collection).
[8] The Hanover Gallery, London.
[9] Coll. Mrs. H. D. Walston.

subjects are suffused with a gentle lyricism rarely manifest in his work before. Moore is able to add new qualities without the sacrifice of the old. Just as he was able to assimilate the humanism of the Mediterranean to his form-system in the *Shelter Drawings* without discarding anything he had learnt from ancient sculpture, so in these latest drawings is he able to imbue his subjects with a lyrical tenderness without loss either of monumentality or of relation to the elemental forces of nature. All these elements are radiantly present in *Girl reading to Woman and Child*: surely one of the finest of Moore's works in any medium.

Speaking of the relation between sculpture and drawing Moore told me that he considered that

> sculpture, involving a life-long struggle to grasp reality in terms of three dimensions, is the most intellectually and imaginatively exacting pursuit I can conceive of. It's an endless pursuit, even Michelangelo, the greatest of the great, pressed on with it until the end of his life.
>
> But drawing enables a sculptor to get atmosphere round his figures—to give them an environment, above all a foreground.

It is too early to try to judge what place Moore will occupy when distorting fashion and current controversy have passed away, but I believe that his creation of a three-dimensional reality in which a remote grandeur is tempered by a large-hearted humanity and encompassed in an atmosphere which intensifies its meaning will not quickly be forgotten.

BIOGRAPHIES

DE MAISTRE, LeRoy Leveson Laurent Joseph, b. 1894

Painter, both abstract and figurative, of religious subjects, portraits and still-life. Born 27 March 1894 in New South Wales, Australia. Educated privately. Studied painting at the Royal Art Society of N.S.W. under Datillo Rubbo and Norman Carter and then at Sydney Art School under Julian Ashton. First one-man show at Sydney 1927. Won Society of Artists travelling scholarship 1923 and went to Paris. Exhibited at Paris Salon 1924. Represented in Australian section of Biennale 1926. First London one-man show 1929 at Beaux-Arts Gallery. Worked in Paris 1923-6, in Australia 1926-9, again in France, particularly in St. Jean de Luz, from 1929 to 1932, in Paris and London between 1932 and 1938 and since then in London. Between 1939 and 1943 in the Foreign Relations Branch of the British Red Cross (French Section), doing no painting between 1939 and the end of 1942. Other exhibitions include Bernheim Jeune, Paris 1931, Mayor Gallery, London 1934, Temple Newsam, Leeds 1943, Birmingham 1946, Adams Gallery, London 1950, and Hanover Gallery, London 1953. His work has also been shown in New York.

GERTLER, Mark, 1891-1939

Painter of figure subjects, portraits and still-life. Born 9 December 1891 in Spitalfields, London, of Polish-Jewish parentage. Went with his family to Austria 1893-8. Spoke only Yiddish up to the age of eight, and was originally called Marks. Educated at the Deal Lane Elementary School. Began attending classes at the Regent Street Polytechnic but in 1907 entered a glass-painting factory. 1908 sent by the Jewish Educational Aid Society to the Slade School. 1909 won a Slade Scholarship and a certificate for painting; 1910 first prize for head-painting and second prize for painting from the cast. 1912 left the Slade and won a British Institute scholarship. Joined the New English Art Club 1912 and the London Group 1915. His *Fruit Sorters* was bought by the Contemporary Art Society in 1914. Worked in London and at Garsington, near Oxford. Visited Paris 1919, and in subsequent years the south of France for the sake of his health. First one-man show at the Goupil Gallery 1921. Married Marjorie Hodgkinson 1930. Began teaching at the Westminster Technical Institute 1932. Died by his own hand 23 June 1939 at Highgate. Memorial exhibitions of his work were held at the Leicester Galleries 1941, the Ben Uri Art Gallery 1944, and the Whitechapel Art Gallery 1949.

GRANT, Duncan James Corrowr, b. 1885

Painter and decorator, designer of textiles, pottery and for the theatre. Born 21 January 1885 at Rothiemurchus, Inverness-shire. Spent his early years in India. Destined for the Army he was educated at St. Paul's but, on the persuasion of his aunt Lady Strachey, was allowed to go to the Westminster School of Art in 1902. Visited Italy and copied Masaccio. Studied under J.-E. Blanche in Paris 1906 and then for six months at the Slade. Travelled in Sicily, Tunisia and Greece. Through his cousin, Lytton Strachey, entered the Bloomsbury circle of Roger Fry, Clive and Vanessa Bell and Virginia Woolf. Was influenced by the works of the Fauves and Cézanne in the First Post-Impressionist Exhibition of 1910 and contributed to its successor in 1912. Worked with Roger Fry in the Omega Workshops, founded in 1913. Member of the Camden Town Group 1911, and of the London Group 1919. First one-man show at the Carfax Gallery 1920. Represented at the Venice Biennale 1926 and 1932. At Cassis, near Marseilles, in 1927 and 1928. Member of the London Artists' Association 1929–31. His decorations for the 'Queen Mary' were rejected in 1935.

INNES, James Dickson, 1887–1914

Painter mainly of mountain landscapes but also occasionally of figure subjects. Born 27 February 1887 at Llanelly, Carmarthenshire, of Catalan descent on his mother's side. Educated at Christ's College, Brecon. Studied painting at Carmarthen, 1904–5, and the Slade, 1905–8. Exhibited at the New English Art Club from 1907; became a member of this and the Camden Town Group in 1911. Visited the Cevennes and the French Pyrenees, 1908; in Paris, winter 1909; again in these places in 1910 and 1912, and also in Spain accompanied by Derwent Lees, and at Marseilles in 1913 with Augustus John. Also worked with John in the spring and summer of 1911 and 1912 in North Wales. Went to Morocco and Teneriffe 1913 for his health but died of consumption at Swanley, Kent, 22 August 1914. Memorial Exhibitions of his work were held at the Tate Gallery 1921–2 and the Chenil Galleries 1923. A retrospective exhibition was held at the Leicester Galleries 1952.

JONES, David Michael, b. 1895

Painter, chiefly in water-colour, of portraits, of animal, landscape and legendary and mythological and religious subjects, wood-engraver and designer of inscriptions; also a writer. Born 1 November 1895 in Brockley, Kent, of Welsh descent on his father's side. As a boy exhibited drawings of animals with the Royal Drawing Society. 1909 entered Camberwell

School of Art and studied under A. S. Hartrick, who had worked with Van Gogh and Gauguin, Reginald Savage and Herbert Cole. Served in France with the Royal Welch Fusiliers 1915–18. 1919 obtained a Government grant to study at the Westminster School of Art under Walter Bayes and Bernard Meninsky. Became a Catholic in 1921; in 1922 joined Eric Gill's Guild of St. Joseph and St. Dominic at Ditchling, Sussex. Returned to London 1924, but rejoined Gill at Capel-y-ffin in 1925. First work as illustrator in 'In Petra' by Eric Gill and Hilary Pepler, 1923; first illustrations for the Golden Cockerel Press 'Gulliver's Travels' 1925. 1927 returned to live with his parents at Brockley and spent some time on the coast at Portslade, near Hove. 1927 exhibited sea pictures and Welsh drawings at the St. George's Gallery. Joined Society of Wood Engravers 1927. 1929 exhibition at the Goupil Gallery included French water-colours painted at Salies de Béarn, Lourdes and Arcachon. Member of Seven and Five Society, 1928–33. Works shown at Chicago in 1933, Venice Biennale 1934, and the World's Fair, New York, in 1939. His chief writings are 'In Parenthesis' 1937, the Hawthornden Prize Novel for 1938, and 'The Anathemata: Fragments of an Attempted Writing' 1952, awarded the Russell Loines Award for Poetry by the National Institute of Arts and Letters, U.S.A., in May 1954. Has held a number of one-man shows at the Redfern Gallery: in 1944 a C.E.M.A. exhibition toured England and Wales, and in 1954 an Arts Council Exhibition visited Aberystwyth, Cardiff, Swansea, Edinburgh and the Tate Gallery, London. Created C.B.E. 1955.

LEWIS, PERCY WYNDHAM, 1882–1957

Painter and draughtsman, novelist, critic, political theorist and pamphleteer. Born 18 November 1882 in Nova Scotia or the U.S.A. according to different accounts; of British parents. Educated at Rugby. 1898–1901 studied at the Slade School where he won a scholarship at the age of sixteen. 1902–8 worked in Paris, Germany, including six months at the Heimann Academy, Munich, Holland and Spain. Returned to England; works occasionally exhibited at the Carfax Gallery. Member of Camden Town Group 1911. Exhibited in the Second Post-Impressionist Exhibition at the Grafton Galleries 1912. Original member of the London Group 1913. Worked briefly with Roger Fry in the Omega Workshops; then in 1914 broke away and formed the Rebel Art Centre with Wadsworth, Etchells, C. F. Hamilton and (later) William Roberts. Founded the Vorticist Group 1914–15 and edited its paper 'Blast'. 1914 issued a folio of twenty drawings of 'Timon of Athens', and wrote his first novel 'Tarr', published serially in 'The Egoist', 1916–17, and as a book 1918. The first (and only) Vorticist Exhibition at the Doré Galleries, 1915. Served with the Artillery 1915–17; 1917–18 Official War Artist to the Canadian Corps Headquarters; exhibition 'Guns' of pictures of war subjects at the Goupil

Gallery 1919. With Louis F. Ferguson published 'Harold Gilman: An Appreciation', 1919. Organized the exhibition of Group X at the Mansard Gallery 1920. His second one-man exhibition, 'Tyros and Portraits', at the Leicester Galleries 1921. Edited the art reviews 'The Tyro', 1921–2, and 'The Enemy', 1927–9. 1922–6 period of semi-retirement, ended by the General Strike. 1928 published the novel 'The Childermass', intended as the first part of a trilogy: in 1951 the B.B.C. commissioned the sequels, 'Monstre Gai' and 'Malign Fiesta'; the complete triology, known as 'The Human Age', broadcast in 1955. 1929 married Anne Hoskyns. 1932 exhibition 'Thirty Personalities' at the Lefevre Galleries; exhibited at the Leicester Galleries 1937 and the Beaux-Arts Gallery 1938. In 1938 the rejection of his portrait of T. S. Eliot by the Royal Academy resulted in the resignation of Augustus John. 1939 reprinted his writings on art together with a survey of his career as a painter in 'Wyndham Lewis the Artist: from Blast to Burlington House'. In Canada and the U.S.A. 1940–8. Retrospective exhibition at the Redfern Gallery 1949. Exhibition of water-colours at Victoria College, Toronto, 1950; Retrospective Exhibition: 'Wyndham Lewis and Vorticism' at the Tate Gallery, 1956. Published autobiographical 'Rude Assignment' 1950: 'The Demon of Progress in the Arts' 1954. Lost his sight in 1951; died 7 March 1957.

LOWRY, Laurence Stephen, b. 1887

Painter chiefly of industrial landscape in Manchester and Salford. Born 1 November 1887 at Old Trafford, Manchester. Studied at the Schools of Art in Manchester 1908–9 and Salford. Lived at Pendlebury 1909–48, since then at the village of Mottram in Longendale. Member of the Royal Society of British Artists 1934, and of the Manchester Group. First one-man exhibition in London at the Lefevre Gallery 1939 and at Manchester in 1948. Hon. M.A. (Manchester) 1945. Member of the London Group 1948. A retrospective exhibition of his work was held at the Salford Art Gallery 1951. A.R.A. 1955.

MOORE, Henry Spencer, b. 1898

Sculptor in stone, wood and later in bronze, and draughtsman. Born 30 July 1898 at Castleford, Yorks., the seventh child of a miner. Educated at Castleford Grammar School; taught in his elementary school 1916. Served 1917–19 in the 15th London Regiment; gassed and invalided home 1917. 1919 resumed teaching, but later the same year went to Leeds School of Art, remaining there until 1921. 1921–4 at the Royal College of Art under Derwent Wood and Sir William Rothenstein, winning a travelling scholarship there in 1924 which took him, in 1924, to France and Italy. 1924–31 taught at the Royal College of Art, 1931–9 at the Chelsea School of Art. First one-man show at the Warren Gallery

1928. His work was shown at exhibitions in Venice and Berlin 1929, Stockholm 1930, Zürich 1931, Hamburg 1932 and New York 1943. Married Irina Radetsky in 1929. A daughter was born in 1946. Member of the London Group 1930-7. Exhibited at the International Surrealist Exhibition at London 1936, and Paris 1938. Visited Spain in 1937, New York in 1946, Greece in 1951, and Paris and Italy on several occasions. 1940 drawings of Underground shelter scenes purchased by the War Artists' Advisory Committee; drawings of coal-miners at work commissioned. Among other public commissions executed *Madonna and Child* for St. Matthew's Church, Northampton, 1943-4. Retrospective exhibitions of sculpture and drawings at Temple Newsam, Leeds, in 1941, New York in 1946, and San Francisco in 1947, Australia in 1947-8, the Venice Biennale (where he was awarded the International Sculpture Prize) and Milan in 1948, Brussels, Paris, Amsterdam, Hamburg, Dusseldorf, Berne and Athens in 1949-51, the Tate Gallery, London 1951, Cape Town and Sweden in 1952, Denmark, Norway, Holland and Germany 1953-4, Sao Paolo Biennale 1953-4 (where he was awarded the International Prize for Sculpture), and Basle and Jugoslavia in 1955. Exhibitions of drawings were shown in Mexico 1950, Berlin and Vienna 1951, and at the Institute of Contemporary Arts, London, in 1953. He was a Trustee of the Tate Gallery 1941-8 and again from 1949, a member of the Art Panel of the Arts Council 1945-51 and since 1948 a member of the Royal Fine Art Commission, London. Made Honorary Doctor of Letters of the University of Leeds 1945, Membre Correspondent of the Belgian Academy and Honorary Associate of the Royal Institute of British Architects, London, in 1948, a foreign member of the Swedish Royal Academy of Fine Arts, in 1951, Honorary Doctor of Letters of the University of London 1953, and Foreign Honorary Member of the American Academy of Arts and Sciences in 1955. Created C.H. 1955.

NASH, JOHN NORTHCOTE, b. 1893

Painter of landscape and still-life, wood-engraver and illustrator, particularly of botanical publications. Born in Kensington, 11 April 1893, brother of Paul Nash. Moved with his family to Iver Heath, Buckinghamshire in 1901. Educated at Langley Place, Slough, and Wellington College. At first thought of becoming a journalist and worked for some months as a reporter on a local paper. Without academic training but encouraged by his brother, started working at water-colour landscapes and imaginary comic drawings. In 1913 held a successful exhibition with his brother at the Dorien Leigh Galleries, South Kensington, as a result of which he was invited to become a member of the London Group and the Friday Club. 1914 began painting in oils. 1915 invited by Harold Gilman to join the Cumberland Market Group; May 1915 exhibited at the Goupil Gallery with three others of the Group, Gilman, Charles Ginner and Robert

Bevan. About this time executed two mural decorations for a restaurant. In 1915 Leeds City Art Gallery accepted a drawing *Trees in a Flood*, his first work to enter a public gallery. Served with Artists' Rifles, November 1916 to January 1918. Official War Artist 1918. May 1918 married Dorothy Christine Kuhlenthal. 1918–21 lived at Gerrards Cross with summer excursions to Whiteleaf in the Chiltern Hills and Gloucestershire. 1921 became first art critic on 'The London Mercury'. 1919 elected member of the New English Art Club; 1921 of Society of Wood Engravers. In the same year involved with seven other artists, Paul Nash, Edward Wadsworth, Jacob Kramer, Albert Rutherston, Stanley Spencer, Gilbert Spencer and P. H. Jowett, in the abortive project for decorating Leeds Town Hall. His first wood-engravings also date from 1921 and were included in his first one-man show at the Goupil Gallery, together with oils and water-colours. 1921 moved to Princes Risborough and began teaching at the Ruskin School of Drawing, Oxford, where he remained until 1927. Became member of the Modern English Water-colour Society 1923. Worked in Dorset 1923, in Bath and Bristol 1924. In Essex and Suffolk 1929 where he bought a summer cottage. One-man shows at the Goupil Gallery October 1930 and at the French Gallery May 1933. Taught at the Royal College of Art 1934–40. Executed large decoration for Paris Exhibition 1937. One-man show of water-colours at the Goupil Gallery 1939. Joined Observer Corps 1939. Official War Artist to the Admiralty 1940; demobilized 1944 and went to live in Essex. Rejoined staff of Royal College 1945. A.R.A. 1940. R.A. 1951. Retrospective exhibition at Leicester Galleries 1954.

NASH, PAUL, 1889–1946

Landscape painter in oils and water-colour, book-illustrator, writer, and designer of applied art. Born 11 May 1889 at Kensington, son of the Recorder of Abingdon and elder brother of John Nash. Moved to Iver Heath, Bucks., in 1901. 1904–6 at St. Paul's School. 1906–9 attended evening classes at Bolt Court, Fleet Street, 1910–12 studied at the Slade School under Brown and Tonks. First one-man exhibition of drawings and water-colours at the Carfax Gallery 1912. Joint exhibitions with John Nash at the Dorien Leigh Gallery, South Kensington, 1913, and at Leeds, 1914, and both invited to exhibit in the Twentieth Century Art Exhibition at Whitechapel 1914. 1914 worked under Roger Fry at the Omega Workshops and on restoring the Mantegna Cartoons at Hampton Court. Member of the Friday Club 1913 and London Group 1914. December 1914 married Margaret Theodosia Odeh. August 1914 enlisted with the Artists' Rifles; invalided home from France 1917 and appointed Official War Artist as a result of his exhibition 'Ypres Salient' at the Goupil Gallery July 1917. Exhibition 'Void of War' at the Leicester Galleries 1918. Member of the New English Art Club 1919, and of the Society of

Wood Engravers 1922. Lived at Dymchurch, Kent 1921–5. First visit to
Paris 1922. Instructor in Design at the Royal College of Art, 1924–5.
Lived in or near Rye 1925–33, again visiting France 1929–30. Represented at the Venice Biennale 1926, 1932 and 1938. September 1931
British Representative on the International Jury for the Carnegie Exhibition, Pittsburgh, U.S.A. Founded Unit One 1933. Visited France, Spain
and North Africa, 1933–4. In Dorset 1934–5, compiling the Shell Guide
to Dorset. Returned to London 1936. Exhibited at the International
Surrealist Exhibitions at London, 1936 and Paris, 1938. Settled in Oxford
1939. Official War Artist to the Air Ministry 1940–5; also commissioned
by the War Artists' Advisory Committee 1941. 1943 exhibition of
applied designs circulated by C.E.M.A.; retrospective exhibitions at
Temple Newsam, Leeds, 1943 and Cheltenham 1945. Died 11 July 1946
at Boscombe, Hants. Memorial exhibitions at the Tate Gallery 1948 and
in Canada 1949–50; an exhibition of his photographs was given by the
Arts Council 1951 and a book of his photographs, 'Fertile Image', was
published the same year; a collection of his water-colours and drawings
was shown at the Leicester Galleries 1953. His illustrations include those
to 'Genesis', 1922, and 'Urne Buriall' and 'The Garden of Cyrus' 1932.
A fragment of autobiography together with some letters and essays were
published posthumously as 'Outline' in 1949; his correspondence with
Gordon Bottomley as 'Poet and Painter' in 1955.

NEVINSON, CHRISTOPHER RICHARD WYNNE, 1889–1946
Figure and landscape painter, etcher and lithographer. Born 13 August
1889 in Hampstead, son of the war correspondent and author H. W.
Nevinson. Educated at Uppingham. Studied painting at St. John's Wood,
the Slade, and in Paris, Julian's and the Circle Russe. In Paris shared a
studio with Modigliani. First exhibited 1910 at the Friday Club and with
the Allied Artists at the Albert Hall. Closely identified with the Futurist
Movement: friendly with Severini and Marinetti; published a joint manifesto 'Vital English Art' with Marinetti, 1914. Lectured on modern art at
the Doré Galleries. The first secretary to the London Group, 1914. Married
Kathleen Mary Knowlman 1915. Served as an ambulance driver in the
Red Cross 1914 and then until 1916 in the Royal Army Medical Corps
until invalided out with rheumatic fever. Exhibited war paintings in 1916,
and was appointed Official War Artist in 1917, exhibiting again in 1918
at the Leicester Galleries. Invited by the Czecho-Slovak Republic to
represent British Art in Prague 1920. Visited U.S.A. in 1919 and 1920 and
exhibited there; represented as an etcher at the Biennale the same year.
Member of the New English Art Club 1929, and of the Royal Society
of British Artists 1932. A.R.A. 1939. Chevalier of the Legion of Honour
1938. Author of autobiography 'Paint and Prejudice', 1937. Died in
London 7 October 1946.

NICHOLSON, BEN, b. 1894

Painter of abstract compositions (sometimes in low relief), landscape and still-life. Born 10 April 1894 in Denham, Bucks., the eldest son of (Sir) William Nicholson and his wife Mabel Pryde, also a painter and the sister of James Pryde. Educated Gresham's School (one year). Studied art at the Slade for one year 1910–11. Studied French at Tours, 1911–12, and Italian at Milan, 1912–13; in Madeira 1913–14. 1914–17 in London and N. Wales; 1917–18 in Pasadena, California. From 1920 to 1931 in Castagnola (Switzerland), Cumberland and London. First one-man show Adelphi Gallery, 1922; exhibited with Winifred Nicholson at the Paterson's Gallery 1923, with Christopher Wood and W. Staite Murray at the Beaux-Arts Gallery 1926, and with Barbara Hepworth at Tooths' 1932. Member of the Seven and Five Society 1925–36; member of London Artists' Association 1932; member of Unit One 1933; member of 'Abstraction–Creation' Paris 1933–4. His works shown at Venice in 1934, Brussels and Lucerne in 1935, Amsterdam and New York in 1936. Co-editor with J. L. Martin and N. Gabo of 'Circle' 1937. Represented in the British section of the International Exhibition, New York, in 1939. Retrospective exhibition at Temple Newsam, Leeds 1944. First prize for painting at the 39th International Exhibition of the Carnegie Institute, Pittsburgh 1952. Retrospective exhibition at the Biennale, Venice 1954, being awarded the 'Ulissi' Prize; this was subsequently shown at Amsterdam, Paris, Brussels, Zürich and Tate Gallery, London 1954–5; since 1940 has lived at St. Ives, Cornwall.

ROBERTS, WILLIAM PATRICK, b. 1895

Painter of groups of figures and of portraits. Born 5 June 1895 in London, the son of a carpenter. Educated at an L.C.C. School. Served one year as apprentice to a firm of commercial designers at the age of fourteen; then studied at St. Martin's School of Art and (1910–13) the Slade. Worked briefly at Omega Workshops under Roger Fry; in 1914 joined Wyndham Lewis in the Vorticist Group and its successor, Group X, 1920. Member of the London Group 1915. Official War Artist 1917–18 and again in the Second World War. Member of the London Artists' Association 1929–32. Represented at the Venice Biennale 1932.

SPENCER, GILBERT, b. 1892

Painter in oil and water-colour of landscapes, portraits, figure-compositions and mural decorations. Born 4 August 1892 at Cookham, Berks., brother of Stanley Spencer. Educated at the Ruskin School, Maidenhead 1909–11. Studied at Camberwell School, the Royal College of Art (wood-carving), and under Brown and Tonks at the Slade School 1913–15 and 1919–20. In his first period at the Slade he won first prize for figure-drawing and Professor Brown's prize for the drawing of the head, and shared the Summer Composition prize in 1914. Served with the Royal Army Medical Corps in Salonika and the Eastern Mediterranean 1915-19. Member of New English Art Club 1919. First one-man show at the Goupil Gallery 1923. Has worked mainly in Berkshire, Oxfordshire, of Dorset and the Lake District. Painted murals of the Foundation Legend Balliol College at Holywell Manor, Oxford, 1934-6. Professor of Painting at Royal College of Art 1932-48. Official War Artist 1940-3. Head of Department of Painting, Glasgow School of Art 1948-50, and Camberwell School 1950. A.R.A. 1950.

SPENCER, Stanley, b. 1891

Painter of landscapes, occasional portraits, and in particular of imaginative and religious subjects. Born 30 June 1891 at Cookham, Berks., son of William Spencer, organist and music teacher. 1907 entered Maidenhead Technical Institute. 1908-12 studied at the Slade School under Tonks; awarded a scholarship 1910, the Melvill Nettleship Prize and the Composition Prize 1912. Exhibited at the Second Post-Impressionist Exhibition 1912. 1915-18 served in the Royal Army Medical Corps and the Royal Berkshire Regiment, mainly in Macedonia; commissioned to paint a war picture. 1919-27 member of the New English Art Club. 1922 visited Jugoslavia with the Carline family, which included the artists Sydney and Richard. 1922-3 at Poole with Henry Lamb and 1923-7 painted *The Resurrection, Cookham* in Henry Lamb's London studio. 1925 married Anne Hilda Carline. 1926-32 wall paintings, The Oratory of All Souls, Burghclere, living there 1927-32. First one-man show at the Goupil Gallery in 1927. Lived at Cookham 1932-8. A.R.A. 1932; resigned 1935; again A.R.A. and R.A. 1950. Represented at Venice Biennale 1932 and 1938. Visited Switzerland 1933 and 1936. Awarded an Honourable Mention at the Carnegie Institute, Pittsburgh, 1933. Visited St. Ives and Southwold 1937. In London 1938-9. Loan exhibition of early works at the Leger Gallery 1939. Moved to Leonard Stanley, Glos., summer 1939. 1940 commissioned by the War Artists' Advisory Committee to paint pictures of shipyards in Glasgow. Moved to Epsom 1941; returned to Cookham 1945. Retrospective exhibition at Temple Newsam, Leeds 1947. Created C.B.E. 1950. Visited China as member of a cultural delegation 1953. A retrospective exhibition of drawings arranged by the Arts Council was on tour 1954-5; a retrospective exhibition of his paintings was held at the Tate Gallery, of his drawings at the Arts Council in 1955.

WADSWORTH, Edward Alexander, 1889-1949

Painter, chiefly in tempera, of views of harbours and coast-lines; of occasional abstract compositions and portraits; and of still-life. Engraver on wood and copper. Born 29 October 1889 at Cleckheaton, Yorkshire.

Educated at the Fettes College, Edinburgh. Went to Munich 1906 to study engineering and while there attended the Knirr Art School; afterwards studied at Bradford School of Art and 1908–12 at the Slade School where he won the first prize for figure painting in 1911. Associated with Wyndham Lewis in the Vorticist and X Groups; an original member of London Group 1913. Served 1914–17 in the R.N.V.R.; engaged on dazzle camouflage for ships 1917–18. Published two books of drawings and copper engravings respectively: 'The Black Country', 1920, and 'The Sailing Ships and Barges of the Western Mediterranean and Adriatic Seas', 1926. Member at various times of the New English Art Club from 1921, Unit One 1934, A.R.A., 1943. Died 21 June 1949 in London. A memorial Exhibition of his work was held at the Tate Gallery in 1951.

INDEX

Page references in bold type refer to the sections of the book dealing with
that particular artist.